Wittgenstein and the Moral Life

Essays in Honor of Cora Diamond

edited by Alice Crary

A Bradford Book
The MIT Press
Cambridge, Massachusetts
London, England

MIT Press books may be purchased at special quantity discounts for business or sales promotional use. For information, please e-mail special_sales@mitpress.mit.edu or write to Special Sales Department, The MIT Press, 55 Hayward Street, Cambridge, MA 02142.

This book was set in Stone sans and Stone serif by SNP Best-set Typesetter Ltd., Hong Kong, and was printed and bound in the United States.

Library of Congress Cataloging-in-Publication Data

Wittgenstein and the moral life: essays in honor of Cora Diamond / by Alice Crary, editor.
    p. cm.—(Representation and mind)
"A Bradford Book."
Includes bibliographical references and index.
ISBN-13: 978-0-262-03359-6 (hardcover: alk. paper)
ISBN-13: 978-0-262-53286-0 (pbk.: alk. paper)
1. Wittgenstein, Ludwig, 1889–1951. 2. Ethics, Modern—20th century. I. Diamond, Cora. II. Crary, Alice, 1967–.
B3376.W564W55548   2007
170.92—dc22
                                                                                    2006033358

10 9 8 7 6 5 4 3 2 1

For Cora

Contents

Introduction

Alice Crary

The essays in this volume celebrate the philosophical writings of Cora Diamond. They focus on two of her central accomplishments: (i) her contribution to the study of Wittgenstein's—early and later—philosophy and (ii) her contribution to moral philosophy. This introduction discusses Diamond's thought with an eye to bringing out the interest of the individual essays' commentary on it. It starts with a basic overview of her work in these two areas (section I), and then turns to a description of how the individual essays take off from and further elaborate these bodies of work (section II).

I

(i) Diamond's Contribution to Wittgenstein Scholarship

Cora Diamond played a pivotal role in the development of an approach to Wittgenstein's writings characterized by unorthodox assumptions about his conception of the aim of philosophy. The approach is one on which Wittgenstein is understood, in both his early and later writings, as trying to get us to distance ourselves from the idea that our linguistic practices depend for their stability on a prior reality and, at the same time, as trying to get us to see that our desire to understand the workings of language is best satisfied, not by metaphysical speculation about what underlies it, but rather by attention to our everyday modes of thought and speech and the world that they serve to reveal. Although the last two decades witnessed a surge in the number of readers concerned to defend versions of this basic exegetical strategy (which is sometimes described as one that attributes to Wittgenstein an *antimetaphyscial* aim), the strategy was poorly represented in philosophical circles until quite recently. When, in the mid-1960s, Diamond began discussing what she saw as the antimetaphysical animus of Wittgenstein's later writings,[1] there were only a handful of philosophers—most prominently, Elizabeth Anscombe, Stanley Cavell, Rush Rhees, and Peter

Winch—defending congenial interpretations. Similarly, when, about ten years later, Diamond began discussing what she saw as the antimetaphysical orientation of various parts of the *Tractatus*,[2] there were only a few philosophers defending congenial claims about aspects of Wittgenstein's early book.[3] Diamond was thus one of the first philosophers to present an antimetaphysical reading of both Wittgenstein's early and later writings. Since she also made a number of original and influential suggestions about how such a reading is best elaborated, she is rightly credited with a pioneering role in its development.

Before discussing what is distinctive about Diamond's contribution to conversations about an antimetaphysical approach to Wittgenstein's writings, I need to mention a sense in which the suggestion that this approach is unorthodox may seem misguided. While it is nonstandard to represent the *Tractatus* as having an antimetaphysical agenda, some of the most prevalent readings of Wittgenstein's later thought characterize his main philosophical ambition as an antimetaphysical one. The interpretative approach just sketched may accordingly seem irregular, not (as I intimated) in representing both the *Tractatus* and Wittgenstein's later writings as characterized by antimetaphysical aims, but only in representing the *Tractatus* in this manner—and in thereby bringing Wittgenstein's early book into an unusually close alignment with his later writings.

It is not incorrect to say that what is most striking about the approach to Wittgenstein's writings that Diamond helped to develop is its suggestion of significant continuity in his philosophical aims, both early and late. The most widely accepted accounts of Wittgenstein's intellectual development center on the idea of a dramatic break in his characteristic philosophical procedures after his return to philosophy in 1929, and there is a straightforward sense in which this approach issues a challenge to these accounts. Nonetheless, we fail to capture what is most interesting about the approach if we limit ourselves to saying that it challenges the familiar idea of such a break. This is because the way in which it challenges this idea is a function of the way in which it departs, in its antimetaphysical understanding of Wittgenstein's conception of the aim of philosophy, not only from traditional interpretations of the *Tractatus*, but also from traditional interpretations of Wittgenstein's later writings.[4]

The account of the development of Wittgenstein's thought that gets presented within traditional interpretations starts with the author of the *Tractatus* presenting a view of the nature of language that centers on the claim that the form of language reflects the form of the world. On this view, the world is composed of simple objects that can combine into facts, and language is composed of names that can combine into propositions. The second of these two kinds of combination mirrors the first, and the fact that it does so is what ensures that propositions have meaning. The meaning of a name is determined by its link to a particular simple object. Simple objects have logical forms, which are their possibilities of combination with other objects, and names have logical forms (or possibilities of combination with other names) derivatively. The meaning of a name fixes what can be said with it in the sense that its logical form mirrors that of the object it denotes.

The traditional account of the development of Wittgenstein's thought goes on to tell us that in his post-*Tractatus* writings Wittgenstein rejects this view of meaning and exchanges it for a view that diverges significantly. Here the meaning of an expression is determined, not by links to a prior reality, but by our public practices with it—by its place in the *language game* or by its *grammar*. Moreover, our public practices with an expression, in addition to determining its meaning, also determine its logical character in the sense of its possibilities of combination with other expressions in particular contexts. It appears to follow that, when we ask whether a given bit of language makes sense, we are asking whether an act of speech is intelligible and, further, that the answer to our question is settled by the character of our linguistic practices.

This account of Wittgenstein's philosophical development is sometimes represented as an account of how he moves from metaphysical theorizing about linkages between language and the world at the time of the *Tractatus* to rejecting such theorizing later on in favor of nonmetaphysical descriptions of the workings of language. It is to the extent that Wittgenstein is thus traditionally taken to be, in his later writings, disavowing any metaphysical ambitions that a description of him as having an antimetaphysical aim—that is, a description of the sort that figures prominently within the antimetaphysical approach to his opus that Diamond favors—may appear to be anything but irregular.

There is, however, a very basic sense in which Diamond and other like-minded advocates of an antimetaphysical approach depart from traditional interpretations of his later writings. Here I have in mind, not only the earliest philosophers to advocate this approach in reference to Wittgenstein's later work,[5] but also a number of well-known philosophers—above all, James Conant, Warren Goldfarb, Hilary Putnam, and John McDowell—who have subsequently followed up on their efforts. These different philosophers' treatments of Wittgenstein's later writings are aptly described as containing a deep criticism of more traditional interpretations. Together they suggest that these interpretations slide into an internally inconsistent representation of Wittgenstein as engaging in the very type of metaphysical theorizing that, according to the interpretations themselves, he is supposed to be eschewing.

The criticism is concerned with the fact that traditional interpretations, in addition to representing Wittgenstein as rejecting the idea of a transcendent perspective on language, for the most part also represent him as construing this gesture of rejection as undermining our claim to certain basic epistemic ideals. Wittgenstein is supposed to be maintaining both that what counts as agreement between the use of a sign and its meaning is fixed (not by a prior, objective reality, but) by grammar and, at the same time, that there can accordingly be no question of fully objective agreement. This portrait of Wittgenstein's philosophical preoccupations is, according to advocates of the less orthodox approach to his later writings that I am considering, deeply problematic. This is because jettisoning the idea of a transcendent perspective only appears to undermine our claim to full-blooded objectivity if we take it for granted that any claim to objectivity we have is a function of features of reality, discernible from such a perspective, that underlie our linguistic practices and ensure their stability, and if we also take it for granted that, in jettisoning the idea of such a perspective, we commit ourselves to concluding that there are no such features. Insofar as Wittgenstein is taken to be lamenting the loss of objectivity, he is accordingly also taken to be clinging to certain metaphysical claims about the nature of a prior reality. He is taken to be assuming that it is possible to adopt a transcendent perspective at least well enough to establish that nothing independent underwrites our practices with words and that something else—for instance, the practices themselves—must supply structure and stability. What thus emerges is that traditional interpretations, despite claiming to represent Wittgenstein as repudiating any metaphysical ambitions, nevertheless depict him as espousing a view of the workings of language that turns for its interest on certain substantive metaphysical claims.

This is the basic criticism of traditional interpretations of Wittgenstein's later writings that gets traced out in the work of advocates of the antimetaphysical approach to his philosophy Diamond helped to articulate.[6] These philosophers maintain that one of Wittgenstein's central ambitions, in both his early and later writings, is to demonstrate that there is something inherently unsatisfactory about the idea of a transcendent perspective on language and that by itself our rejection of this idea therefore has no implications for our claim to basic epistemic ideals like objectivity. They thus present a picture of what it is for Wittgenstein to philosophize about language in a manner free from metaphysical presuppositions that is very different from the picture presented by fans of traditional interpretations. It is insofar as they do so that we are justified in describing their work, when considered together with the work of philosophers who ascribe an antimetaphysical aim to the author of the *Tractatus*, as representing a coherent and unorthodox approach to Wittgenstein's writings.

So, given that we are right to describe Diamond as contributing to the development of a legitimate, unorthodox tradition of thought about Wittgenstein's philosophy, what should we say is distinctive about her work? One of Diamond's distinctive contributions is to have shaped, in the following manner, the terms in which Wittgenstein's philosophy gets discussed. Diamond sometimes glosses her claim that Wittgenstein hopes to get us to relinquish the idea of a transcendent perspective on language by saying that he wants us to reject the idea of such a perspective as no more than *illusion* (or, alternately, *fantasy*). Her point in speaking of illusion here is that Wittgenstein should be understood as saying that, when we envision ourselves occupying a transcendent perspective on language, we do not wind up saying anything coherent about the way things stand. It is not that Wittgenstein wishes us to acknowledge that, when we envision ourselves adopting such a perspective, we are led to come out with sentences that express thoughts the logical structure of language prohibits us from saying—as if he believed our difficulty were that the kinds of thoughts we are attracted to in philosophy are thoughts that, due to the nature of language, are forever out of reach. Rather, he wishes us to see that we do not succeed in articulating any thoughts and that the idea of such a perspective is properly characterized as creating the illusion of understanding words we want to utter in philosophy. This is what Diamond means when she tells us that she is drawing a contrast "between saying that [there] is the illusion of a perspective and saying that it is the correct philosophical perspective only you cannot put into words what is seen from there."[7]

Another of Diamond's distinctive contributions is to have brought out how Wittgenstein's conception of the aim of philosophy gets expressed, in both his early and later writings, in his use of *nonsense* as a term of appraisal. Diamond claims that when Wittgenstein says that a combination of words we are tempted to utter in philosophy is nonsense, he is saying, not that we know what the words attempt to say and that that cannot properly be put into words, but instead that those words do not say anything, that they have not (yet) been given any significant use. She tells us that, in endorsing the modes of philosophical criticism that his use of "nonsense" bespeaks, we accordingly distance ourselves from the idea that we can survey the logical structure of language from a transcendent perspective outside or beyond meaningful uses of language and determine that some nonsensical sentences express impermissible thoughts. And she adds that one consideration that seems to speak for distancing ourselves from this idea—and at the same time for endorsing the pertinent modes of philosophical criticism—is that if we retain the idea, we thereby confusedly retain an image of ourselves as somehow capable of identifying the logical roles played by the parts of nonsensical (and hence logically bankrupt) sentences.[8]

There is, according to Diamond, even more to be learned from reflection on Wittgenstein's use of "nonsense" as a term of philosophical appraisal. Diamond believes that if we see how his use of this term informs his central modes of philosophical criticism, we are well situated to understand central *methods* of both his early and later writings. The point she is making here about Wittgenstein's later writings is—largely as a result of the influence of Cavell's work on the later Wittgenstein's characteristic methods—a relatively familiar one.[9] Diamond is suggesting that the dialectical structure of these writings realizes Wittgenstein's characteristic modes of philosophical criticism. More specifically, her suggestion is that some of what get called the "interlocutory voices" in Wittgenstein's text describe, as if from within the kinds of illusions of sense that seduce us in philosophy, the appeal of metaphysical forms of words and, further, that others aim to show us—by expressing various quite ordinary renderings of the words in question and inviting the recognition that no construal of them satisfies us—that we have competing desires with regard to our own words and that our belief that we understand what we want to say in the midst of philosophizing is illusory. Now Wittgenstein's later writings appear to be designed to—to cite a passage that Diamond herself admires—teach the reader "to pass from a piece of disguised nonsense to something that is patent nonsense" (*Investigations*, §464).

While Diamond thus makes a relatively familiar point about the method of Wittgenstein's later writings in connection with her observations about his use of "nonsense" as a term of philosophical appraisal, she makes a quite radical point when she claims that understanding Wittgenstein's use of the term in the *Tractatus* is essential for understanding the book's method. This brings me to the most groundbreaking aspect of Diamond's work on the *Tractatus*. In the mid-1980s, Diamond outlined a case for thinking that we only properly understand the *Tractatus*'s enigmatic ladder-structure if we understand it as instantiating the modes of philosophical criticism that, for Wittgenstein, talk of "nonsense" bespeak.[10] At about the same time, Diamond began discussing her reading of the *Tractatus* with Conant, who soon became a close collaborator.[11] One result is that the basic reading in question is now sometimes referred to as "the Diamond-Conant reading."

This reading emphasizes Wittgenstein's statements in the preface and at the book's close to the effect that its sentences are nonsense, and, more specifically, it does these things in a manner that draws on Diamond's understanding of Wittgenstein's use of "nonsense" as a term of philosophical appraisal. The idea is that when Wittgenstein describes his sentences as nonsense, he means that they are not logically distinct from gibberish and that we should give up the idea that they are trying to say anything. (Diamond and Conant refer to this as an *austere* view of nonsense.) However, while the *Tractatus* thus excludes logical distinctions among kinds of nonsense as confused, it nonetheless allows for psychological distinctions among nonsensical sentences—that is, distinctions with respect to the tendencies of nonsensical sentences to make us think that we understand them. The book depends for its success on the use of nonsensical words that are psychologically distinguished by the kinds of illusions of sense that they produce. It repudiates as illusory the idea of a transcendent perspective on language from which it is possible to give a metaphysical description of the relationship between language and the world, and it produces nonsense-sentences with an eye toward exploding that illusion from within. These sentences serve as a sort of metaphysical snare—first inviting the reader to imagine herself occupying a transcendent perspective and then, by encouraging her to fully describe the things she imagines doing so allows her to say, positioning her to see that she is herself imposing inconsistent demands on her words and that no rendering of them will satisfy her. Thus the *Tractatus* delivers us from the illusion that we can philosophize in a traditional style through its employment of nonsensical sentences that, insofar as they at first ensnare us, equip us to liberate ourselves from our own state of illusion.

This gives us a rough description of the Diamond-Conant account of the method of the *Tractatus*. It tells us that the book presents us with metaphysical nonsense-sentences that invite the imaginative exercise of articulating the illusion of the idea of a transcendent perspective on language—an imaginative exercise through which we come to recognize that illusion as an illusion.[12]

Insofar as Diamond advocates this account of the method of the *Tractatus* and insofar as she also advocates the account of the method of Wittgenstein's later writings touched on above, she presents us with a picture of Wittgenstein's thought on which it is, to a large extent, unified, not only in its aims and modes of criticism, but also in its method. This suggestion of substantial continuity in Wittgenstein's thought is perhaps Diamond's single most significant contribution to Wittgenstein scholarship, and it has received a great deal of critical scrutiny in recent years. The reading of the *Tractatus* that supports it—the Diamond-Conant reading—has proved especially controversial.

In order to appreciate some of the forms that the controversy has taken, it is helpful to have a slightly more expansive description of the kinds of more traditional, metaphysical readings the Diamond-Conant that reading aims to supplant. These readings typically combine an understanding of the *Tractatus* as imparting metaphysical truths about what gives signs meaning with an account of the book's prefatory and closing remarks about how its sentences are nonsense. The basic idea is that, if we are to appreciate the status of the metaphysical truths that the book is here taken to be trying to convey, we need to consider these remarks together with the book's famous description of a distinction between "saying" and "showing"—so that the remarks are now interpreted as claims to the effect that the relevant truths cannot properly be *said* but can only be *shown*. Traditional metaphysical readings of the *Tractatus* thus often depict the book as containing an ineffable metaphysical doctrine, and, for this reason, they are sometimes described as "ineffability readings."

It was partly with an eye to contrasting the Diamond-Conant reading with ineffability readings that Thomas Ricketts once dubbed it a "resolute" reading. Ricketts's idea was that the author of the *Tractatus*, far from wanting us to combine an understanding of various sentences of the book as unintelligible with an understanding of them as nevertheless imparting significant metaphysical truths, wants us to stick resolutely to the view that various of the book's sentences are simply nonsense—or, rather, to the view that, to the extent that we can find a use on which the relevant sentences do make sense, it will be one on which they do so in a plain manner bereft of metaphysical mystique.

Confronted with the resolute Diamond-Conant reading, advocates of ineffability readings[13]—and others—have responded with a barrage of criticisms. Thus, for instance, this reading is sometimes said to conflict directly with central passages of the *Tractatus* (e.g., the passages on "saying and showing"), and it is sometimes said to contain a deep internal tension; the reading is sometimes said to be inconsistent with things that Wittgenstein, and those close to him, said about the *Tractatus* around the time of its composition, or to be undermined by things Wittgenstein later said about his early book; and it is sometimes said to be incapable of accounting for the extent of the differences between Wittgenstein's early and later thought, or to be incapable of funding a plausible story about why Wittgenstein would have bothered to write the book in the first place.

One of Diamond's projects in recent years has been responding to these and other criticisms, sometimes in concert with Conant. Below I touch on some of her responses in connection with various papers in this volume. Right now I want to say a word about one of Diamond's strategies for rebutting the charge that her reading of the *Tractatus* cannot, in her words, "allow for the depth and significance of the change in Wittgenstein's thought after he returns to philosophy."[14] Diamond has on several occasions argued that it is consistent with an understanding of the *Tractatus* as having an antimetaphysical aim to observe that certain metaphysical doctrines are unwittingly reflected in the way in which it prosecutes that aim. And she has underlined specific respects in which she thinks the view of language that informs the method of the

Tractatus in fact retains various metaphysical commitments that get shed in Wittgenstein's later writings.

For example, Diamond tells us that the Tractarian conception of what it is for an expression to be used in the same way gets spelled out in terms of a metaphysical view of rules that comes under attack in the *Investigations*. The view is one that, as Diamond understands it, represents rules as "determining all their instances in advance."[15] Her thought is that this basic view needs to be understood as at least tacitly taking for granted that rules are underwritten by features of reality that transcend them in the sense of being discernible from a perspective independent of any responses and reactions characteristic of us as participants in rule-governed practices and that accordingly appear to be capable of determining the rules' applications in advance of our reactions in particular cases. Diamond does not claim that the author of the *Tractatus* appeals to this view in order to convey metaphysical insights about the nature of language. Instead, she suggests that, despite his desire to avoid metaphysical theorizing, he nonetheless tacitly draws on a view of rules with significant metaphysical presuppositions.

Diamond occasionally summarizes the philosophical outlook she finds in Wittgenstein's writings by saying that he wants to get us to look at the world in a *realistic* spirit. When she thus speaks of a realistic orientation toward the world, she has in mind a contrast with traditional philosophical realisms, which counsel mistrust of our existing, nonmetaphysical methods of distinguishing between the real and the unreal and stipulate that, if our concept "reality" is in fact legitimate, there must be more to it than such methods reveal. To say that Wittgenstein urges us to adopt a realistic orientation is, for her, to underline his efforts to liberate us from our craving for metaphysical insight and to get us to see that our existing methods, however imperfect and in need of improvement, are nevertheless adequate to the task of expressing or giving content to this concept.[16] To be sure, it follows from the foregoing reflections that, while Diamond represents both Wittgenstein's early and later writings as recommending a realistic posture, there is a sense in which, by her own lights, such a posture needs to be understood as conceived in a more fully adequate manner later on. Nevertheless, given what she takes to be the deep and significant continuity of Wittgenstein's thought, it is, as she sees it, appropriate to describe his philosophizing at both periods as having a substantive realistic strain.

(ii) Diamond's Contribution to Moral Philosophy

While there are important respects in which Diamond's work in ethics bears the imprint of philosophical lessons she derives from Wittgenstein, her central preoccupations depart significantly from those of other influential moral philosophers who undertake to bring Wittgensteinian considerations to bear on questions of ethics. Indeed, in discussing how her work in ethics is inspired by Wittgenstein, she often starts by distancing herself from a line of thought that is central to many conversations about Wittgenstein and ethics.

When Wittgenstein's thought gets discussed in connection with ethics, it is frequently suggested that its main interest lies in making available an *objectivist* account of moral judgments (i.e., an account on which these judgments are treated as essentially a matter of sensitivity to how things objectively are). While an objectivist account is recommended by our ordinary understanding of moral judgments,[17] moral philosophers generally take it to be untenable. The alleged problem has to do with the fact that we ordinarily understand moral judgments, not only as essentially concerned with the objective world, but also as directly relevant to what we have reason to do.[18] This fact seems to create problems for an objectivist account given the philosophically prevalent assumption that no undistorted judgment about the objective world can stand in the sort of immediate relation to affective responses that allows it to be thus intrinsically practical. Now we appear to be obliged to conclude that it is impossible to embrace an objectivist account of moral judgments without thereby taking the unappealing step of relinquishing our ability to take at face value our ordinary understanding of their practical character.

This observation equips us to appreciate the force of a relatively familiar line of thought about the ethical interest of Wittgenstein's writings. According to the line of thought I have in mind—which gets traced out in the work of John McDowell, David Wiggins, and Sabina Lovibond—these writings are of interest insofar as they show that an objectivist account of moral judgments is unproblematically available. That they show this is, it is here claimed, a function of their description of a view of language on which a person's ability to project a concept in an objectively accurate manner is inseparable from her possession of propensities toward affective and other responses that she learned in learning the practice with it. This view is taken to equip us to represent moral judgments as essentially concerned with how things objectively are without at the same time losing our license to represent them as intrinsically practical. The upshot is supposed to be the evanescence of traditional philosophical objections to an objectivist account of such judgments.

What Diamond finds unsatisfactory about this line of thought has to do with the fact that it is exclusively concerned with moral judgments (i.e., judgments that apply specifically moral concepts) and that, as she sees it, it thus reinforces an enormously widespread assumption to the effect that moral thought is the prerogative of such judgments. According to Diamond, no adequate account of the ethical interest of

Wittgenstein's philosophy can fail to mention that his view of language subverts this assumption. To be sure, as indicated by my earlier remarks on Diamond's account of changes in Wittgenstein's view of linguistic regularity between the *Tractatus* and the *Investigations*, Diamond agrees with the moral philosophers mentioned in the last paragraph in taking the author of the *Investigations* to hold that a person's ability to project a concept in an objectively accurate manner is inseparable from her possession of particular sensitivities. Where she disagrees is in thinking that what is ethically most noteworthy about this view is, not that it transforms our image of moral judgments, but rather that it brings within reach an understanding of moral thought that includes more than such judgments.

Diamond in effect invites us to understand the sensitivities that, according to Wittgenstein's view, are internal to all of a person's conceptual capacities as partly constitutive of that person's moral outlook. She suggests that, since, by the lights of this view, a person's efforts to comprehend any stretch of thought may call for her to further develop such propensities, it follows that here there is no obstacle to allowing that any stretch of thought—without regard to whether it deploys moral words or deals with 'moral topics'—may also make the kind of contribution to articulating a person's moral outlook that establishes it as moral. This, very roughly, is what leads her to claim that, on the terms of the view of language that Wittgenstein bequeaths to us, moral judgment making does not have a monopoly on moral thinking. Diamond sometimes formulates this claim by saying that Wittgenstein positions us to recognize that what distinguishes an expression as moral is, not its concern with what we may think of as a 'moral subject-matter,' but rather the way in which it is used on a particular occasion. Wittgenstein is, she writes, rightly understood as teaching that "anything made of the resources of ordinary language may be brought into such a relation to our lives and actions and understanding of the world that we might speak of the thinking involved in that connection as 'moral,'" and that "[i]f a sentence or image or word has this character, it arises not through its content but from its use on a particular occasion."[19]

This description of the larger lesson for ethics that Diamond draws from Wittgenstein is helpful for understanding some of the emphases of her own work in ethics. One significant preoccupation of Diamond's work here is showing that literature is a more significant tool of moral instruction than moral philosophers traditionally assume.[20] This project of Diamond's is helpfully understood as presupposing a view of language of the sort that she inherits from Wittgenstein (i.e., a view on which particular sensitivities are internal to all our rational, linguistic capacities). Diamond typically approaches the project by arguing, in a manner that presupposes the availability of such a view, that literary works are capable of directly contributing to rational understanding—and, more specifically, to rational moral understanding—insofar as they direct our feelings in various ways. Moreover, when she thus describes literary works as, in virtue of their emotional strategies, capable of containing rational forms of moral instruction, she is not merely suggesting that these works may, by engaging us emotionally, equip us to make various rationally respectable moral judgments. She is at the same time suggesting, in a style that presupposes her account of the ethical significance of her preferred, Wittgensteinian view of language, that literary works may thus contribute to our capacities for moral thought, where such thought is now understood as including more than moral judgments.[21]

Let me mention on further area of Diamond's work in ethics. Several of Diamond's essays are devoted to discussing questions of animals and ethics, and Diamond is rightly credited with a decisive contribution to contemporary conversations about this topic. These conversations began thirty years ago when a number of moral philosophers, Diamond among them, took an interest in defending the (intuitively quite plausible assumption) that animals place moral claims on us that are direct in the sense of being more than mere functions of ways in which harming them harms human beings. Where most of the moral philosophers who defend this assumption proceed by rejecting the idea that a (human or nonhuman) creature's species membership is by itself a reason to treat it one way or another, Diamond adopts a very different strategy. She claims that the recognition that a creature is a human, or the recognition that it is an animal, by itself has implications for how we ought to treat it. That is, she claims, in a manner implicitly informed by the basic view of language that she finds in Wittgenstein's writings, that an intellectually respectable understanding of the concepts "human" and "animal" that inform moral reflection necessarily presupposes the (at least imaginative) possession of propensities toward certain responses.[22]

Diamond sometimes draws a connection between this claim and themes of her work on ethics and literature. She sometimes notes that, in advancing the claim, she is suggesting that a good grasp of these concepts may require imaginative activities that further cultivate such propensities and that, as she sees it, may be developed by our engagement with works of literature.[23]

Diamond's work in moral philosophy recommends for ethics the same "realistic" attitude toward the world that she takes Wittgenstein to be enjoining. To be realistic in this sense is to refuse to impugn nonmetaphysical methods of distinguishing the real and the unreal as in principle incapable of legitimating our concept of "reality." When Diamond turns to questions of ethics, she urges us thus be to realistic and at the same time reminds us that our nonmetaphysical methods include reliance on activities that cultivate new sensitivities and shape our imaginations. Her suggestion is that these activities are significant for ethics because, as she sees it, the thinking that composes them may occasion changes in our moral outlooks and may therefore, without regard to whether it takes the form of moral judgment making, establish itself as integral to moral reflection.

II

Part I: Wittgenstein

This brings me to comments on how the essays in this volume engage with the themes in Diamond's writings that I have been discussing. The essays in Part I take as their points of departure Diamond's contribution to Wittgenstein scholarship. Diamond's work on the *Tractatus* represents the most controversial part of her contribution to conversations about Wittgenstein's philosophy, and three of the essays in part I—those by Conant, Michael Kremer, and Juliet Floyd—are devoted to elaborating and defending the basic resolute approach to the book that she advocates.

Conant's essay starts from the observation that any resolute reading will as such be committed to claims about the unity of Wittgenstein's philosophy that appear heterodox from the perspective of more traditional metaphysical readings. Conant argues, not only that it is necessary to court the pertinent charge of heterodoxy in order to do justice to the extent of continuity in Wittgenstein's thought, but also that it is necessary to attenuate the heterodoxy in various respects in order to do justice to the extent of discontinuity in his thought. In developing these two lines of argument, Conant presents himself as defending an account of the continuity of Wittgenstein's thought—or, in his terms, a "mono-Wittgensteinianism"—that, while heterodox, is nevertheless best characterized not as severe or zealous but only as "mild."

One of Conant's central aims in his essay is to demonstrate that resolute readers of the *Tractatus* can account for discontinuity in Wittgenstein's thought without abandoning their distinctive understanding of the early Wittgenstein as aiming to avoid metaphysical theorizing about the relationship between language and the world. Resolute readers can do this if they depict the early Wittgenstein as possessing, in addition to an avowed intention to avoid such metaphysical theorizing, unwitting commitments involving various philosophical conceptions and if they also add that the conceptions in question get scrutinized in Wittgenstein's later writings. Conant's suggestion is that the more of these unwitting philosophical conceptions a given resolute reader attributes to the author of the *Tractatus*, the "milder" the strain of mono-Wittgensteinianism the reader should be said to espouse.

Strikingly, the case Conant outlines for a mildly mono-Wittgensteinian, resolute reading of the *Tractatus* is situated within the framework of commentary by a pseudonymous author, a Johannes Climacus, who claims to have chanced upon Conant's manuscript and who insists on regarding it as blasphemous. Climacus depicts the main tenets of traditional metaphysical readings of the *Tractatus* as items of religious faith and, drawing on this depiction, denigrates the kind of mono-Wittgensteinianism common to all resolute readings as heretical. Part of what is interesting about the portrait we are thus given of Climacus is that, insofar as it encodes the idea that no measure of mildness in a resolute reader's mono-Wittgensteinianism can remove the taint of heresy, it serves as an exaggerated image of those (quite real) commentators who insist that resolute readings of the *Tractatus* are as such disqualified from doing justice to differences between Wittgenstein's early and later writings.

Whereas Conant's essay directly engages the work of such commentators, Climacus's commentary engages it in an indirect and ironic manner. Climacus' polemics in effect ask these commentators to see their unwillingness to seriously consider the possibility that a resolute reading might do justice to discontinuity in Wittgenstein's thought as driven by commitments that are no more rational than a religious fervor. Moreover, there is a sense in which, thus conceived, Climacus' scribblings mimic the method of the *Tractatus* as resolute readers understand it. Where, according to such readers, the *Tractatus* presents us with an image of ourselves as taking an interest in metaphysical theorizing about how language hooks onto the world with an eye to getting us to disown such theorizing, Climacus presents us with an image of ourselves as categorically rejecting any resolute reading of the *Tractatus* as exegetically heretical with an eye to getting us to disown such a gesture of rejection. The upshot is that, like the *Tractatus*, Climacus' writings might aptly be described as embodying a sort of ladder-structure.[24]

Kremer's and Floyd's essays resemble Conant's in mounting defenses of resolute readings of the *Tractatus*, but they adopt quite different strategies. These two papers are organized around discussions of the *Tractatus*'s remarks about a "say/show distinction." Both are concerned to argue that these remarks are best understood as supporting, not some kind of ineffability reading, but rather a resolute reading of the sort that Diamond advocates.

Kremer's essay takes its titular theme from a comment that Wittgenstein makes to Russell in a letter composed just after the completion of the *Tractatus*. In the process of explaining to Russell the larger point of his book, Wittgenstein claims that the theory of "what cannot be expressed by propositions, but only shown" represents "the cardinal problem of philosophy." Why should we take this claim to support a resolute reading of the *Tractatus*? In answering this question, Kremer takes his cue from Wittgenstein's remark in the *Tractatus*'s preface that most philosophical problems depend for their formulations on "the misunderstanding of the logic of our language." Kremer's suggestion is that, in making his epistolary claim to Russell about the theory of "saying and showing," Wittgenstein is signaling both that he takes this theory to represent a philosophical problem of the relevant kind and that he takes it to be one that, as cardinal, is somehow decisive for the dissolution of other philosophical problems. Kremer follows up on this suggestion, arguing that, for Wittgenstein, philosophical problems crop up when particular words are used to signify in different ways and when our tendency to flit unsteadily between their different senses wrongly persuades us that sentences in which they occur express deep philosophical truths. Kremer's larger concern in his essay is demonstrating that this argument has a direct bearing on Wittgenstein's treatment of the problem of "saying and showing."

According to Kremer, the *Tractatus* aims to teach us that we are only inclined to insist that there are deep truths about language that can be shown but not said to the extent that we equivocate between two senses in which we ordinarily speak of "showing." We use this term both in reference to things revealed in a person's practical mastery of an activity and in reference to things propositionally elaborated, and, as Kremer sees it, the "problem" to which the *Tractatus* wants to alert us is that neither of these senses alone facilitates the articulation of a doctrine of deep philosophical truths that can only be shown. For, if we stick consistently to the latter of the senses, our efforts to present such a doctrine involve us in a straightfoward contradiction (viz., one that is a matter of both denying and assserting that certain truths can be propositionally expressed); and, if we stick consistently to the former, our efforts to do so amount to no more than gesturing at a quite commonplace truth about how certain things are shown in our ability to use language. Kremer's thought is that, by confronting us with a dilemma on these lines, the *Tractatus* seeks to get us to adhere "resolutely" to this commonplace truth, thereby putting us in a position in which, in our quest for an understanding of the workings of language, we look for guidance, not in what we may be inclined think of as ineffable metaphysical structures underlying our linguistic practices, but rather in the practices themselves and the humble insights that attention to them reveals. This, very roughly, is how Kremer thinks Wittgenstein applies his general strategy for dealing with philosophical problems to the case of "saying and showing," and one noteworthy feature of the application is that it suggests an image of Wittgenstein's early book, congenial to Diamond and Conant's resolute reading, on which the book has a distinctively antimetaphysical aim.

Although there are significant parallels between Floyd's essay and Kremer's, there are also interesting differences of emphasis. Like Kremer, Floyd sets out to establish that Wittgenstein's treatment of "saying and showing" supports the kind of resolute reading that Diamond champions. At the same time, Floyd is above all concerned with a feature of this reading that Diamond herself emphasizes only in quite recent work. Where, in all of her writings on the *Tractatus*, Diamond represents its author as wanting to get us to abandon the idea that our language is somehow stabilized by metaphysical structures that fix what we can and cannot say, she only recently undertakes explicitly to argue that, in urging us to jettison this idea, Wittgenstein is at the same time urging us, not only to give up the idea that we can give an *a priori*, unified account of the kinds of philosophical problems to which language gives rise, but also to recognize that we are therefore obliged to deal with such problems on a case-by-case or "piecemeal" basis.[25] This recent gesture of Diamond's is striking in that it brings the *Tractatus* into alignment with Wittgenstein's later claim that "[p]roblems are solved . . . not a single problem" (*Investigations*, §133) and a significant portion of Floyd's essay is dedicated to demonstrating that we can see what speaks for the gesture if we first get a clear view of Wittgenstein's treatment of "saying and showing."

One of the opening moves of Floyd's essay—and there is here an obvious parallel to Kremer's essay—is to claim that Wittgenstein takes the question of "saying and showing" to represent a problem of philosophy that depends for its formulation on a "misunderstanding of the logic of our language." Floyd declares that it is important to recognize that Wittgenstein derives the notion of such a misunderstanding from the Austrian poet Paul Ernst. Floyd takes this to be important both because, as she sees it, what Wittgenstein admires in Ernst is a view of language that allows for "complexity and open-ended variety of expression" and because, on her reading, it is insofar as the *Tractatus* is designed to motivate such a view that it is rightly read as recommending a "piecemeal" understanding of philosophical problems. Floyd approaches a discussion of these issues by arguing that the author of the *Tractatus* wants us to adopt an idea of "showing" on which, far from being an (evidently profound) matter of conveying ineffable metaphysical truths about the nature of language, it is a (quite mundane) matter of exhibiting practical abilities encoded in the language we speak and understand. Her suggestion is that, in reconciling ourselves to the thought that this is what showing amounts to, we at the same time make room for a view of linguistic phenomena that is "open-ended and complex" in the sense of being free from any *a priori* metaphysical constraints—and that is accordingly capable of underwriting an understanding of the philosophical problems to which language gives rise as indefinitely various affairs that must be dealt with one at a time.

The next two contributions to this volume—Putnam's and David Finkelstein's—are essays that, while resembling those that I have been discussing in taking off from Diamond's work on Wittgenstein, differ in referring specifically to her work on Wittgenstein's later thought. Both of these essays are concerned, albeit in very different ways, with Diamond's inheritance of Wittgenstein's later remarks about his own philosophical procedures.

Putnam starts from Diamond's interest in Wittgenstein's claim that philosophy as he practices it is characterized by the avoidance of metaphysical theses. Putnam uses this claim as a standard for critically assessing a set of Wittgenstein's own remarks—in particular, a set of remarks on Cantor's diagonal proof that are published as part II of the *Remarks on the Foundations of Mathematics*. Putnam's thought is that in these remarks Wittgenstein not only departs from the very philosophical methods he himself advocates but also, in doing so, commits himself to making a variety of unjustified mathematical assertions. In developing this thought, Putnam is reviving a well-worn complaint (it is, interestingly, one Putnam himself elsewhere challenges in reference to other parts of Wittgenstein's opus) to the effect that Wittgenstein's remarks on mathematical topics are vitiated by an inadequate familiarity with ongoing work in mathematics. What is distinctive about the particular version of the complaint Putnam airs here is that it is framed in terms of Wittgenstein's own conception of appropriate philosophical methods. Where Wittgenstein goes wrong, according to Putnam, is in advancing theses instead of insisting on the kind of attention to actual mathematical practice that, by his own lights, sound philosophical reflections about mathematics require.

The general topic of Finkelstein's essay is the tendency of contemporary philosophers to make claims about the mental capacities of animals that would strike ordinary people as plainly false—for example, claims to the effect that animals are not properly aware of anything and that they cannot properly be said to think, believe, desire, hope, or to have any other "propositional attitudes." One of the skeptics about animal minds whose work Finkelstein discusses is Donald Davidson, and, when Finkelstein turns to Davidson's work, he is particularly concerned with the fact that Davidson represents his skepticism as motivated by a *holistic* view of propositional attitudes.

Davidson claims that a creature cannot have, say, one belief about an object unless it also has a great many other—in part quite sophisticated—beliefs about it, and he argues that it follows from this claim that a nonlinguistic creature therefore cannot rightly be said to have any beliefs at all. This holistic, Davidsonian line of reasoning is one of Finkelstein's main critical targets, and, in attacking it, Finkelstein appeals to Wittgenstein for support. Finkelstein is not unaware that it will seem misguided to some philosophers to enlist Wittgenstein as an ally precisely here. Finkelstein himself points out that, although Wittgenstein does not share Davidson's skepticism about animal minds, he is generally thought of as a championing a kind of conceptual holism. Finkelstein tries to combat the idea that there must therefore be something wrong about appealing to Wittgenstein to challenge Davidson's holistic proclivities by introducing a distinction between two broadly different types of holisms: namely, (i) *metaphysical holisms* that aim to provide metaphysical explanations of what, say, beliefs really are and (ii) *therapeutic holisms* that aim to draw attention to the kinds of circumstances in which we ordinarily speak of people having, say, beliefs. Finkelstein argues that Davidson and Wittgenstein should not be seen as united by their holistic tendencies because, whereas Davidson is properly seen as a metaphysical holist, Wittgenstein is best understood as a therapeutic one. Finkelstein's larger claim—and it is in defending this claim that he turns to Diamond's work on Wittgenstein's later remarks on method—is that we need to understand what speaks for the distinctive type of therapeutic holism that Wittgenstein favors if we are to appreciate how it is possible to acknowledge the genuine insights of a holistic stance without thereby forfeiting our entitlement to represent as philosophically innocuous our ordinary ways of thinking and speaking about animal minds.

Part II: The Moral Life

The essays in part II of this volume are united by concern with Diamond's contribution to moral philosophy. There are, as I mentioned, important respects in which Diamond's work in ethics can be seen as shaped by her reading of Wittgenstein. One of her guiding preoccupations here is bringing out, in a manner that presupposes the view of language that she attributes to the later Wittgenstein, how a person's ability to understand certain aspects of her life may be inseparable from her willingness to refine her modes of response in ways that represent changes in her ethical outlook. Three of the essays in this volume—Cavell's, McDowell's and Sabina Lovibond's—directly address things she says about ethical demands that attending to reality thus imposes.

Cavell is specifically interested in what, in a recent essay,[26] Diamond calls *the difficulty of reality*. Diamond introduces this term in reference to the experience of finding that "something in reality [is] resistant to our thinking about it," and she does so with an eye to doing justice to some of Cavell's remarks about challenges of bringing the world into focus. In his response to Diamond here, Cavell credits her with capturing something he wants to say. He emphasizes that the experience that Diamond is describing is one that, although partly constituted by a response to the world that may separate us from others, need not therefore be impeachable in its cognitive credentials, and he echoes a suggestion she makes to the effect that part of what gives it special significance is that the way in which it separates us from others may mark us out as mad. One thing that particularly interests Cavell is the fact that, in her discussion of these matters, Diamond represents him as raising a question about the possibility of a philosophical practice that, refusing to evade or (in the Cavellian jargon Diamond uses) "deflect" from the experience, takes the threat of madness seriously. Accepting this question back at Diamond's hands, Cavell here undertakes a rich meditation that starts from her central illustration of "the difficulty of reality"—an illustration that is drawn from J. M. Coetzee's lectures *The Lives of Animals* and that concerns the difficulty that the lectures' fictional protagonist Elizabeth Costello, a person nearly unhinged by the thought of the food industry's daily slaughter of animals, has bringing our lives with animals into focus.

Cavell's meditation addresses themes in Diamond's work on animals and ethics. Cavell is particularly interested in the claim Diamond makes to the effect that moral reflections about animals are informed by a nonbiological, moral concept "animal." What Diamond has in mind is a concept of animals as our "fellow creatures,"[27] and Cavell tells us that he agrees with her both that our willingness to develop responses internal to this concept is essential to our ability to understand our lives with animals and that we are therefore right to distance ourselves from the work of moral philosophers who, deflecting from what Diamond sees as demands of understanding, assume that the only tools we have for combatting "the awful and unshakeable callousness and unrelentingness with which we most often confront the non-human world" are philosophical arguments.[28] After observing that Coetzee's Costello adopts the "undeflected" posture that he wants to inherit from Diamond, Cavell asks what follows if, likewise adopting this posture, he accepts an image of animals as fellow creatures.

McDowell's essay consists in a brief rejoinder to Cavell. One of McDowell's main concerns is anticipating a misunderstanding he thinks Cavell may unwittingly encourage. McDowell notes that the topic of the essay of Diamond's to which Cavell is in the first instance responding is "the difficulty of reality" and that, although Cavell discusses this topic only in reference to the case of Coetzee's Costello, Diamond in fact adduces an array of different examples. Among the additional examples of Diamond's McDowell mentions is the case of skepticism about other minds. McDowell points out that Diamond is interested both in how we can be overwhelmed by the thought that we are in some sense profoundly unknowable and in how we can be tempted to deflect from our responses to this thought, treating it as nothing more than a problem to be solved by philosophical arguments.

When McDowell turns to the case of skepticism about other minds, he is giving his response to Cavell a deeply sympathetic "twist." Diamond takes her account of the difficulty of grappling with such skepticism directly from Cavell. So, in moving away from Cavell's nearly exclusive emphasis on Coetzee's Costello and toward a treatment of Diamond's examples of the difficulty of reality that includes the case of skepticism about other minds, McDowell is underlining the extent to which Diamond's project is a philosophical tribute to Cavell. Furthermore, he is providing a demonstration of how it can be fruitful to read parts of Diamond's and Cavell's writings together.

Lovibond's essay resembles those of Cavell and McDowell in taking off from Diamond's discussions of demands of attending to reality. It opens with an allusion to Diamond's hostility to the idea, influential within contemporary moral philosophy, that we are "moral agents" charged with maneuvering in a world whose features are neutrally open to view. Although Lovibond sympathizes with this aspect of Diamond's thought, she develops it in a manner she recognizes Diamond will find uncongenial. She treats Diamond's rejection of a familiar philosophical understanding of moral agency as an occasion to explore an ethical tradition—one that she associates with the work of Aristotle, G. E. Moore, and Aurel Kolnai—that claims that the truly valuable life for a human being is, not a morality-centered one, but rather one of contemplation. Where Lovibond departs most dramatically from Diamond is in arguing that we are obliged to choose between these two kinds of lives, and the argument Lovibond presents turns for its success on the assumption that the life of contemplation may be devoted to the study of (what she thinks of as) "non-moral objects." There is thus an important sense in which Loribond's essay continues a conversation she has been pursuing with Diamond for several years—a conversation about whether (as Lovibond is inclined to think) moral thought is distinguished by a "moral subject-matter" or whether (as Diamond maintains) it is distinguished instead by how the concepts or expressions that compose it are used.[29]

Where the two essays just discussed address Diamond's writings on ethical demands of bringing the world properly into focus, two other essays in part II—Martha Nussbaum's and Stephen Mulhall's—address her closely related writings on ethics and literature. One of the organizing themes of Diamond's work on this topic is, as I noted above, that literary texts can present us with rational moral instruction in virtue of ways in which they engage us emotionally. This is a theme that Diamond sometimes develops in connection with the work of Nussbaum,[30] a philosopher who argues, eloquently and at length, that literary texts may as such present us with rational moral instruction. In her essay for this volume, Nussbaum in turn develops the theme in connection with Diamond's work.

What distinguishes Nussbaum's treatment of the theme here is the peculiar character of the novel it addresses. Whereas in other writings Nussbaum tends to focus on novels with traditional plot structures,[31] now she shifts her focus to a novel—Theodor Fontane's *Der Stechlin*—that, she argues, engages us in the particular way it does in large part because it challenges familiar expectations about such structures. In speaking of familiar plot expectations, Nussbaum has in mind, above all, the way in which the nineteenth-century novel subordinates its characters to its plot, inviting us to become emotionally engaged with them by encouraging us to wonder what they will do next. Further, she has in mind the fact that, as she sees it, the success of the nineteenth-century novel in thus getting us to wonder about the actions of its characters depends on traditional social narratives (such as, e.g., romantic or erotic ones) that we as readers are supposed to recognize and impose on our understanding of the characters. Nussbaum claims that Fontane's *Der Stechlin* is distinctive in that it instructs by frustrating our expectation that these kinds of social narratives will be played out. She argues that this novel self-consciously presents an array of characters whose social circumstances and interests suggest certain of these narratives and that it then surprises us by failing to develop the narratives and by instead asking us to take an independent interest in the characters. The result, she concludes, is that the novel works on us by leading us into relationships with its characters that are marked by openness to them as the particular individuals they are, thereby providing an appropriate model for relationships of our actual lives.

Mulhall's essay takes up Diamond's work on ethics and literature at a different point. Mulhall appeals to her work in the course of a discussion of Bernard Williams's writings that focuses on what Mulhall sees as the development over time of Williams's use of literary examples. Mulhall takes an interest in this development in large part because he takes it to correspond to changes in Williams's view of the ethical importance of character. Early in his career, Mulhall tells us, Williams advocates a relatively rigid view on which it is essential to what it is to be human that some features of our character (say, some of our commitments and attachments) are internal to who we are in the deepest sense, and Williams presents a number of literary cases with an eye to demonstrating that traditional (Kantian and utilitarian) ethical theories fail to accommodate this view. In constructing these cases, Williams aims to make it clear that, when applied to them, traditional ethical theories recommend courses of conduct that are in conflict with our ordinary understanding of the importance of character. The early Williams therefore does not invite us to engage with the cases or suggest that there might be something to learn from an engaged standpoint. In constrast, toward the end of his career, Williams begins to make suggestions along these lines.

This is the development in Williams's thought that Mulhall thinks is helpfully considered together with Diamond's work on ethics and literature. In considering it here, Mulhall is concerned to show that it corresponds to a move on Williams's part toward a less rigid view of character—one on which a character that essentially grounds our selfhood, far from being what makes us human, is something that in propitious social circumstances we humans might each arrive at.

Where, in her work on moral philosophy and literature, Diamond is concerned to illuminate what she sees as the ethical dimension of our efforts to understand how things stand in the world, in her work on animals and ethics, she is primarily concerned with particular features of the world she thinks moral philosophers tend not to bring properly into focus. One of her central preoccupations is arguing that moral philosophers fail to grasp that a certain (nonbiological) concept "animal" can by itself be important for moral thought and underlining how this failure infects a great deal of work on animals and ethics. This area of Diamond's thought is an important reference point for my own essay for this volume. I criticize familiar arguments for the view that animals impose direct moral claims on us, and I make a very different case for this view—one that, unlike its more familiar counterparts, incorporates some of Diamond's insights into how being an animal can by itself be morally significant.

Notes

1. See "Secondary Sense" (1966–1967) and "The Face of Necessity" (1968), in *Realism and the Realistic Spirit*, 225–242 and 243–267.

2. See "What Nonsense Might Be" (1977–1980), in *Realism and the Realistic Spirit*, 95–114, which discusses lines of thought in the *Tractatus* as well as in Wittgenstein's later writings.

3. The philosophers most appropriately mentioned in this connection—Rhees, Winch, Warren Goldfarb, Hidé Ishiguro, and Brian McGuinness—were for the most part primarily concerned with attacking, not the idea that the *Tractatus* has metaphysical ambitions, but rather the idea that it contains a classic statement of realist semantics. Nevertheless, there are important respects in which their writings contribute to an understanding of the book as antimetaphysical in orientation.

4. It is also in part because, although Diamond rejects the *familiar* idea of a radical break in Wittgenstein's mode of philosophizing, it is no part of her project to deny that there are dramatic and philosophically interesting differences between the *Tractatus* and Wittgenstein's later writings. Indeed, one of the preoccupations of her most recent work is describing and discussing the significance of some of these differences. I touch on this aspect of Diamond's work below.

5. I.e., Anscombe, Cavell, Rhees, Winch, and also Diamond.

6. Diamond herself first presents a version of the criticism in connection with a discussion of Michael Dummett's reading of Wittgenstein in her 1968 paper "The Face of Necessity."

7. "Throwing Away the Ladder: How to Read the *Tractatus*," in *Realism and the Realistic Spirit*, 179–204, p. 196.

8. See esp. "What Nonsense Might Be," esp. 104–105. It is appropriate at this juncture to make a gesture toward Diamond's contribution to Frege scholarship. Although I am here focusing on Diamond's work on Wittgenstein to the exclusion of her work on other figures in the history of analytic philosophy, her importance to current Frege scholarship is substantial. One of her contributions is arguing that Frege champions a view of the limits of sense, or of nonsense, fundamentally similar to the view that Wittgenstein later advocates.

9. See esp. Cavell's "The Availability of Wittgenstein's Later Philosophy," in *Must We Mean What We Say? A Book of Essays*, 70–72.

10. See "Throwing Away the Ladder."

11. See Diamond's autobiographical remarks in "On Wittgenstein (III)."

12. See "Throwing Away the Ladder," and "Ethics, Imagination, and the *Tractatus*," in Crary and Read, eds., *The New Wittgenstein*, 149–173.

13. The group of such advocates includes, to list only some of the most influential, Elizabeth Anscombe, Anthony Kenny, Peter Geach, Robert Fogelin, David Pears, Brian McGuinness, and Ray Monk.

14. "Criss-Cross Philosophy," in Ammereller and Fischer, *Wittgenstein at Work*, 201–220.

15. "Does Bismark Have a Beetle in His Box?" in Crary and Read, *The New Wittgenstein*, 262–292, at 283.

16. See esp. "Realism and the Realistic Spirit," in *Realism and the Realistic Spirit*, 39–72.

17. I.e., because it generally strikes us as natural to treat claims to the effect that some action or person is, e.g., "bad" or "selfish" as claims that we assess by attending to what the relevant action or person is like.

18. I.e., because it generally strikes us as perverse to respond to a claim to the effect that some immediately available course of conduct represents, e.g., the "right" or "courageous" thing for us to do by saying "yes, but that doesn't give me any reason at all to do it."

19. "Wittgenstein, Mathematics, and Ethics: Resisting the Attractions of Realism," in Hans Sluga and David Stern, eds., *The Cambridge Companion to Wittgenstein*, 226–260, at 248. In a couple of her papers, Diamond discusses how the expansive view of moral thought in question here is described in the writings of Iris Murdoch. See esp. "We Are Perpetually Moralists: Iris Murdoch, Fact, and Value," in Antonaccio and Schweiker, *Iris Murdoch and the Search for Human Goodness*, 79–109.

20. See especially "Anything But Argument?" and "Missing the Adventure: Reply to Martha Nussbaum," in *Realism and the Realistic Spirit*, 291–308 and 309–318, and "Martha Nussbaum and the Need for Novels."

21. See esp. "Wittgenstein, Mathematics, and Ethics," section 6, in Sluga and Stern, *The Cambridge Companion to Wittgenstein*, 226–260.

22. See "Eating Meat and Eating Animals," 319–334, and "Experimenting on Animals: A Problem in Ethics," 335–366, both in *Realism and the Realistic Spirit*; and "Injustice and Animals," in Elliott, *Slow Cures and Bad Philosophers*, 118–148. A revised version of this paper will appear in Diamond, *Ethics: Shifting Perspectives*.

23. In this connection, see, e.g., her treatment of J. M. Coetzee's *The Lives of Animals* in "The Difficulty of Reality and the Difficulty of Philosophy," in Crary and Shieh, *Reading Cavell*, 98–118.

24. Here it is apposite to observe that "Johannes Climacus" means "John the ladder". Further, it is apposite to note both that Conant borrows this particular pseudonym from various works of Kierkegaard's and that, in a couple of earlier publications, Conant represents Wittgenstein as partly indebted to Kierkegaard for his views of philosophical method. See "Kierkegaard, Wittgenstein, and Nonsense," in Cohen, Guyer, and Putnam, *Pursuits of Reason*, 195–224, and "Putting Two and Two Together: Kierkegaard, Wittgenstein, and the Point of View for Their Work as Authors," in Tessin and von der Ruhr, *Philosophy and the Grammar of Religious Belief*, 248–331.

25. See esp. Diamond, "Criss-Cross Philosophy," and Diamond and Conant, "Reading the *Tractatus* Resolutely," in Kölbel and Weiss, *Wittgenstein's Lasting Significance*.

26. "The Difficulty of Reality and the Difficulty of Philosophy."

27. See "Eating Meat and Eating People," 328–329.

28. The inset phrase, cited in Cavell's essay for this volume, is from "Eating meat and Eating people," 334.

29. For earlier bits of this conversation, see (i) Lovibond, *Reason and Imagination in Ethics*; (ii) Diamond's response to this work in part 2 of "Realism and Resolution"; and (iii) Diamond's further response to it in "Wittgenstein, Mathematics, and Ethics"; and (iv) Lovibond's rejoinder to Diamond in chapter 2 of *Ethical Formation*. For a helpful overview of the conversation, see Mulhall, "Ethics in the Light of Wittgenstein."

30. See especially the second and third of the three papers cited in note 20.

31. See especially the essays in *Love's Knowledge: Essays on Philosophy and Literature*, and *Poetic Justice: The Literary Imagination and Public Life*.

Works Cited

Ammereller, Erich, and Eugen Fischer, eds. *Wittgenstein at Work: Method in the "Philosophical Investigations."* London: Routledge, 2004.

Antonaccio, Maria, and William Schweiker, eds. *Iris Murdoch and the Search for Human Goodness*. Chicago: University of Chicago Press, 1996.

Cavell, Stanley. *Must We Mean What We Say? A Book of Essays*. Oxford: Oxford University Press, 1976.

Coetzee, J. M. *The Lives of Animals*. Ed. Amy Gutmann. Princeton: Princeton University Press, 1999.

Cohen, Ted, Paul Guyer, and Hilary Putnam, eds. *Pursuits of Reason*. Lubbock: Texas Tech University Press, 1992.

Crary, Alice, and Rupert Read, eds. *The New Wittgenstein*. London: Routledge, 2000.

Crary, Alice, and Sanford Shieh, eds. *Reading Cavell*. London: Routledge, 2006.

Diamond, Cora. *Ethics: Shifting Perspectives*. Cambridge, Mass.: Harvard University Press, forthcoming.

Diamond, Cora. "Martha Nussbaum and the Need for Novels." *Philosophical Investigations* 16, no. 2 (1993): 128–153.

Diamond, Cora. "On Wittgenstein (III)." *Philosophical Investigations* 24, no. 2 (2001): 108–115.

Diamond, Cora. "Realism and Resolution." *Journal of Philosophical Research* 22 (1997): 81–86.

Diamond, Cora. *Realism and the Realistic Spirit: Wittgenstein, Philosophy, and the Mind*. Cambridge, Mass.: MIT Press, 1991.

Elliott, Carl, ed. *Slow Cures and Bad Philosophers: Essays on Wittgenstein, Medicine, and Bioethics*. Durham, N.C.: Duke University Press, 2001.

Kölbel, Max, and Bernhard Weiss, eds. *Wittgenstein's Lasting Significance*. London: Routledge, 2004.

Lovibond, Sabina. *Ethical Formation*. Cambridge, Mass.: Harvard University Press, 2002.

Lovibond, Sabina. *Reason and Imagination in Ethics*. Minneapolis: University of Minnesota Press, 1983.

Mulhall, Stephen. "Ethics in the Light of Wittgenstein." *Philosophical Papers* 31 (2002): 293–321.

Nussbaum, Martha. *Love's Knowledge: Essays on Philosophy and Literature*. Oxford: Oxford University Press, 1990.

Nussbaum, Martha. *Poetic Justice: The Literary Imagination and Public Life*. Boston: Beacon Press, 1995.

Sluga, Hans, and David Stern, eds. *The Cambridge Companion to Wittgenstein*. Cambridge: Cambridge University Press, 1996.

Tessin, Timothy, and Mario von der Ruhr, eds. *Philosophy and the Grammar of Religious Belief.* New York: St. Martin's, 1995.

Wittgenstein, Ludwig. *Philosophical Investigations.* Trans. G. E. M. Anscombe. New York: Macmillan, 1958.

Wittgenstein, Ludwig. *Tractatus Logico-Philosophicus.* Trans. C. K. Ogden. London: Routledge and Kegan Paul, 1974.

I Wittgenstein

1 A Recently Discovered Manuscript

Edited by Johannes Climacus

The document before you is by a member of a fanatical sect of heretical Ludwig scholars. Through a twist of fate it has fallen into my hands. I hesitate to make it public, since its circulation may do more harm than good. What speaks against publication is that it has the power to corrupt young minds. I do not take a light view of the dangers it poses in this regard. What speaks in favor of publication is the fact that these people must be stopped. Through their pamphlets and brochures they continue to attract more converts everyday. The importance of this document lies in the fact that it brings to light some of the more esoteric doctrines of the sect, revealing the vulnerable theological underbelly of their creed. It also speaks of quarrelling within the infidel camp. There are even suggestions that the author fears that he himself may be excommunicated by an up-and-coming generation of zealots. He pleads here for a mild interpretation of their creed. (Oblivious to the stench of his own blasphemies, he even imagines entering into dialogue with mainstream Ludwig scholars!) My main aim in making this text generally available is that more learned men than I may make a study of it. A sound theological thrashing of the author's own (according to him, mild!) version of the creed is devoutly to be wished. But my fondest hope is that, in the hands of one of our finer Ludwig scholars, it might become a weapon that can be turned against the infidel camp. I have a Trojan horse maneuver in mind here. A cunningly crafted pseudonymous publication, addressing some of the niceties of their more peculiar doctrines, under the pretence of attempting to heal the looming schism in their sect, ought to be able to bust it wide open.

One particularly confusing feature of the document is that the author occasionally adopts a heavily ironical tone, actually going so far as to refer to himself as an infidel, etc., though without apparently the least appreciation of the fact that the heavier he allows his irony to become, the closer he comes finally to speaking the truth. This makes for some confusing reading. The irony is apparently directed at reputable Ludwig scholars. Alas, the fellow has no sense of the poor impression all this must make on any person of sound theological principles.

I have lightly edited the document and corrected some of its grosser infelicities of grammar and spelling, but have resisted any temptation to improve on the author's barbaric mode of expressing himself. The one great editorial liberty I have taken is to insert a brief abstract of each section of the paper at its beginning, in which I briefly indicate the contents of each of the numbered subsections that follow. The merely curious or theologically squeamish might wish to peruse these first. These abstracts should be of assistance to those who prefer to read selectively in heretical tracts or have weak stomachs for blasphemy. I must confess that I have found it somewhat distasteful to allow my prose thus to mingle so closely with that of the infidel. I have placed my initials in square brackets after each abstract in order to indicate that the preceding words are mine, rather than his, though it is hard to imagine that anyone would ever confuse us. The titles of the sections (which immediately precede my abstracts) and the titles of the subsections (that follow my abstracts) are all his, not mine, and often show a great lack of taste. The quotation from Freud immediately below seems to have been chosen by the author himself to introduce the document. I have no idea what it is doing there. But I have allowed it to stand in case it has a significance that escapes me.

Now comes something strange. After the quotation from Freud, there is a second quotation, also apparently intended to introduce the manuscript. It is attributed to someone who has exactly the same name as I. (Incidentally, no works by this author seem to be listed in the catalogues of any of our libraries or for sale in any of our bookstores.) As you might imagine, I felt a small temptation simply to omit the quotation or at least just the name that follows it, especially since neither sheds any light on anything. But, as I have nothing to hide, I have let the passage stand. If all the rest is nonsense, shouldn't the epigraph be as well?

Johannes Climacus, Assistant Professor, Department of Ludwig Studies, University of Skjolden

Mild Mono-Wittgensteinianism

James Conant

We may now express the issue before us in the shortest possible way by means of the following formula: . . . *two* moments in which a new religious order is founded, the first one overturned by the second and yet reemerging victorious, and *two* founders, who are both called by the same name, . . . and whose personalities we have to separate from each other.
—Sigmund Freud[1]

From the fact that irony is present it does not follow that earnestness is excluded. Only an assistant professor would assume otherwise.
—Johannes Climacus[2]

To Cora

This essay represents an effort to advance the debate between those who advocate resolute readings of Wittgenstein and those who deplore them. It seeks to do so by, on the one hand, attempting to correct certain misunderstandings of such readings (explaining, in effect, why they amount to caricatures) while, on the other, seeking to discourage advocates of such readings from accepting the terms of the debate as defined by the critics (thereby, in effect, embracing the caricature and seeking to defend it). The twin qualifications ("mild" and "mono-") that figure in the title jointly seek to introduce a sort of equilibrium into our reading of Wittgenstein that has hitherto proven elusive to commentary on his work. The difficulty has two sides that must be balanced against each other, without permitting either to assume an undue share of the burden. The first half of the difficulty is to do full justice to the profound discontinuity in Wittgenstein's thinking without neglecting (as those whom I will call "standard readers" do) the extent to which it is folded within a fundamental continuity in his philosophy. The second half of the difficulty is to do full justice to the profound continuity in his thinking without minimizing (as those whom I call "severe mono-Wittgensteinians" do) the extent to which it is folded within a fundamental discontinuity in his philosophy. The aim of this paper will be twofold: (1) to argue that a full acknowledgment of the moment of continuity requires a reasonably heterodox degree of mono-Wittgensteinianism, and (2) that an equally full acknowledgment of the complementary moment of discontinuity requires that the degree of this heterodoxy remain reasonably mild.

I Infidel Wittgensteinianism

[The infidel scholar begins by (1) confessing his membership in the heretical sect, (2) attempting in the most pathetic way to reunite himself with the Church, and (3) discovering that the reconciliation will not hold as long as he persists in his blasphemous practice of defacing copies of the authorized edition of The Life and Works of Saint Ludwig.*—J. C.]*

1   The Heresy

Cora Diamond and I, along with others,[3] have sought to advance and defend an interpretative framework for understanding Wittgenstein's *Tractatus* that has come to be known as "the resolute reading of the *Tractatus*."[4] In this essay, I want to isolate and consider one particular strand of criticism of this reading. The problem with this reading, it is sometimes alleged,[5] is that it commits one to the view that *there is only one Wittgenstein* (whereas every educated person, of course, knows that there are two Wittgensteins).[6] Thus it has come to pass (in the predominantly polytheistic world of contemporary Wittgenstein scholarship) that resolute readers of the *Tractatus* are taken to espouse the heresy of (what one might call) *mono-Wittgensteinianism*. One might lend an Islamic flavor to this credo by summing up its central tenet as follows: "There is no Wittgenstein but Wittgenstein, and his name is Wittgenstein!"

Now, whatever one's attitude toward the corresponding tenet of a genuinely monotheistic creed, one can be forgiven for thinking that this particular sentence (about the man named Wittgenstein) ought to be interpretable as saying something far too innocuous to occasion a scholarly jihad. What alternatives are there to affirming it? What is poly-Wittgensteinianism? Well, presumably, it is the view that there are at least two Wittgensteins: "Early" and "Later" being the names of the two most famous members of the family. Yet, when one is talking about people named Wittgenstein, no one believes Early and Later to bear the sort of relation to one another that William and Henry do (when talking about Jameses) let alone Irving and Isaiah (when talking about Berlins). So what does either side of the squabble (concerning how many Wittgensteins there are) believe that the other would want to deny? How ought one to go about adjudicating disputes between infidel mono-Wittgensteinians and orthodox poly-Wittgensteinians?

2 Premature Ecumenicalism

One might profess to find any dispute of this general form misguided on the ground that the following two sorts of claim regarding the work of a given philosopher are perfectly reconcilable:

(1)   Every important line the philosopher in question ever wrote over the course of his lifetime bears the highly individual marks of his particular philosophical personality: his entire body of work is recognizably the product of a single author and thus marked by numerous points of continuity—in this sense his work forms a unity.

(2)   The philosophical views of the individual in question and the manner in which they are expressed developed very substantially over the course of his lifetime: so substantially, indeed, that it behooves a commentator to distinguish between different significant periods in his thought—in this sense, his work does not form a unity.

(1) and (2) are perfectly compatible because there are two different understandings in play of the sense in which it can be said of a philosopher's work that it "forms a unity." Affirming that his work does so in the first sense does not preclude one from denying that it does so in the second. More to the point, if the dispute at issue concerns Wittgenstein's development in particular, one might well be inclined to affirm each of the following specifications of the foregoing pair:

(1′)   All of the writings currently published under the name of Wittgenstein are the product of a single, highly distinctive philosophical mind, and recognizably so: there are countless discernible points of continuity in philosophical concern, sensibility, aim, style, topic, and mode of authorship across the full range of the corpus.

(2′)   The thought of this philosopher underwent substantial development across the years of his productivity—in particular, at least one such moment of substantial development can be traced to the period beginning sometime not too long after his return to active philosophical work in 1929; and one can quite properly speak of this moment as marking a significant break in his thought.

It should be equally clear that (1′) and (2′) express perfectly compatible thoughts. This opens up the heady prospect that one might go ecumenical and subscribe to *both* (the mono- and poly-) variants of Wittgensteinianism all at once.[7] Or, if that seems too wishy-washy, perhaps go Trinitarian: there is a single being who exists as three indissoluble persons—Early, Later, and Wittgenstein.

3   *The Life and Works of Saint Ludwig*

But let us not be so hasty. When it comes to the very special case of *Wittgenstein*, many are apt to feel that a conjunction of commonsensical observations such as (1′) and (2′) above, if allowed to stand without further qualification, fails in an important respect to do full justice to what they take themselves to know about the intellectual trajectory of this singular figure in the history of philosophy. For the special character of Wittgenstein's achievement is generally thought to lie precisely in the following fact: Wittgenstein's thought did not merely *develop*, as another philosopher's might, rather he accomplished the feat of establishing two *disjoint* schools of philosophic thought in a single human lifetime. Here, for example, is how Wolfgang Stegmüller summarizes the feat in question: "Wittgenstein's position in the history of philosophy is . . . remarkable: first of all, because he developed two distinct philosophies, of which the second cannot in any way be properly characterized as a continuation of the first."[8] Others will want to insist that the relation between these phases in Wittgenstein's thought is not to be characterized merely as one of radical disjunction, but rather as one of radical *contradiction*, his later philosophy being devoted to nothing less than the complete overturning of his early philosophy. Here, for example, is how Anthony Quinton summarizes the point of significant intellectual contact between the early and the later philosophy: "Although Wittgenstein came to reject most of the particular doctrines of the *Tractatus*, the fact that he spent so much of his time in the *Investigations* in refuting them, shows that even if the answers in the earlier book were wrong the questions that they were given to were not."[9]

   Thus, on a streamlined and Promethean telling of it, a rough outline of the tale of Wittgenstein's intellectual trajectory goes like this: Wittgenstein's unique achievement lies in his having, at a remarkably young age, successfully formulated a conception of philosophy sufficiently compelling to transform the entire way in which philosophy was (and, to this very day, still is) conducted by some of its practitioners, and then, after the philosophical equivalent of a decade of wandering in the desert, having seen the light, and in a complete about-face, throughout his later years, tirelessly devoting himself to the task of converting (and, to this very day, from beyond the grave, still converting) practitioners of the subject to the task of undoing that very conception of philosophy. So when the charge is leveled at resolute readers by their critics that they hold the mistaken view that *there is only one Wittgenstein* (whereas every educated person knows that there are at least two), it is not some anodyne mono-Wittgensteinian creed that such readers are taken by their critics to espouse, but rather a genuinely heretical one—heretical precisely because it seeks to challenge even the basic outline of the foregoing canonical version of *The Life and Works of Saint Ludwig* and its account of wherein the uniqueness of his philosophical accomplishment and its pleasingness to all who behold it is supposed to lie.

II   An Alleged Failure to Acknowledge Ludwig's Recantation

[The infidel scholar here undertakes (1) to clarify the grave charge that has been entered against him and all members of his sect by leading authorities of the Church (and he finds a pretext for mentioning Saint Bertrand and Saint Rudolf), (2) to lament that the first phase of the dialogue between the infidels and the Church stalled, thereby causing what he seems to imagine is some great schism, (3) to initiate a second phase of dialogue, and (4) to comment on his fear that finer theological minds than his will be able to show that his doctrine entails an outright denial of the Miracle of the Recantation.—J. C.]

1   The Charge

This essay will not attempt anything like a nailing of *The Ninety-Five Theses of Any Resolute Reading* to the church door, let alone a summary of the ongoing dispute between resolute readers and their critics over how to read the works of Ludwig.[10] I will say a few words about what makes a reading resolute in the next section of the paper. All that matters for this section is the charge against resolute readers already before us: namely, their willful interference in the telling of the canonical tale. The tale presupposes, among other things, that the fundamental aims of Wittgenstein's philosophy suffer little significant misunderstanding in the course of their reception by the unwashed masses, both among those who were converted to his early conception of philosophy and among those converted to his later conception. Whereas resolute readers are obliged to hold, first and foremost, that the aim of Wittgenstein's early philosophy has not been widely understood let alone received. This feature of what is under dispute in exchanges between resolute readers and their critics has remained (in so far as anything ever has in this debate) reasonably clear, accordingly figuring as the central bone of contention.[11] What has not been equally clear (and what I hope to make clearer in what follows) is that it is equally open to resolute readers further to hold, secondly, that it is this very misunderstanding of the aim of Wittgenstein's early philosophy that has helped to bring about a correlative misunderstanding of the aim of his later philosophy. This has an immediate bearing on the original dispute for the following reason: many of their critics look to evidence in Wittgenstein's later writings to bolster their case against the approach that resolute readers take to the early work. This is fair play, of course, if the proper interpretation of the evidence and its bearing on the debate is reasonably clear. If, however, putative refutations of resolute readings proceed in part by looking to passages in Wittgenstein's later writings (that are adduced as evidence against those readings), with the critics in question (in their understanding of the bearing of the relevant passages) simply presupposing their preferred understanding of the later philosophy (reading it in ways that it is open to resolute interpreters to contend rests upon a misunderstanding related to the original one under contention), then such a procedure of refutation runs a serious risk of begging the original question.[12]

It is true that if any version of a resolute approach to reading Wittgenstein were allowed to form a standing part of an introductory philosophical curriculum, then it would interfere with the narration of various episodes in other canonical tales (e.g., from the life of Saint Bertrand or that of Saint Rudolf) as these are typically recounted in the currently popular potted history of the development of early analytic philosophy. But the claim that some piece of potted history might be false is itself hardly a ground for philosophical scandal. Interesting work in the history of philosophy often takes the form of unsettling potted narratives. The charge leveled against resolute readers at issue here (to which this essay seeks to respond) only partly rests on this (comparatively shallow) sort of ground of dissatisfaction. Formulated in the broadest of terms, the charge at issue is therefore most helpfully understood as coming in two separate parts: (i) resolute readings of the *Tractatus* leave us with an account of Wittgenstein's early work that is heretical, in that it flies in the face of what we all already (supposedly) know to be the case about at least the basic outline of Wittgenstein' philosophical development, and moreover (ii) such readers of Wittgenstein's early work leave themselves in the position of having no satisfactory story of their own to tell about the shape of Wittgenstein's overall philosophical development.

It is worth separating out the charges in this way for two reasons. First, resolute readers are more than happy to plead guilty to the first of these charges (the charge of heresy); it is the second of these charges (the charge of being unable to square the *Tractatus* with the *Investigations*) that they ought to deny (and it is to one aspect of this charge that I will primarily seek to respond here). Second, the sense (on the part of at least some of their critics) of there being something scandalously inadequate about the approach to the interpretation of Wittgenstein's work that they take is not merely a function of their refusal to toe a party line. It can be traced at least in part to a prevalent sense that the reading of the *Tractatus* with which they thus saddle themselves is such as to *leave no room* for any plausible alternative story about

Wittgenstein's development—that is, a story in which Wittgenstein's own vehement later criticisms of his earlier thought can be accorded an appropriate gravity.

2 The First Phase

Resolute readers tend, at this point, not to be able to resist going on the offensive, urging that any reader of Wittgenstein ought to be uncomfortable with the following sort of account of the relation between Wittgenstein's early and later thought (to which the quotation from Quinton above gives characteristic expression):

> The *Tractatus* and the *Investigations* are both trying to answer the same philosophical questions, but in each case in which early Wittgenstein aimed to show that the answer to a given philosophical question was *p*, later Wittgenstein aims to refute his earlier self and show instead that the answer to the question is really *not p*.

Let's call this "the doctrinal schema." It is not that resolute and standard readers disagree about which doctrines are to be plugged in for *p* above (in a proper reconstruction of Wittgenstein's own understanding of the character of his philosophical development). It is rather that resolute readers hold that any schema of this form must yield a distorted account of Wittgenstein's philosophical aims early and late.[13] There are in fact many reasons to be uncomfortable with an account of this form, but perhaps the most textually ready-to-hand one, they will urge, lies in the various characterizations that Wittgenstein, early and late, supplies of his own philosophical procedures. To cite just one instance, already in the *Tractatus*, Wittgenstein announces his interest in pursuing an approach to philosophical questions in which the answers to the questions, we are told, are to be seen in the vanishing of the questions themselves.[14] And, in the *Philosophical Investigations*, Wittgenstein says things that are not dissimilar.[15] So resolute readers will want to ask: if the *Tractatus* and the *Investigations* both aspire to bring about a situation in which many of the same philosophical questions are caused to vanish, then in what sense can it be right to say (as not only Quinton does, but many others do): "Although Wittgenstein came to reject most of the particular doctrines of the *Tractatus*, the fact that he spent so much of his time in the *Investigations* in refuting them, shows that even if the answers . . . were wrong the questions . . . were not." One might have thought that, whatever the differences between Early and Later, there is at least this much agreement between them: it is the questions themselves that stand under indictment (and not merely any particular set of answers that we are inclined to give to them). If this is right, then the doctrinal schema would appear to be poorly suited to its purpose.

The critics of resolute readings tend to respond at this point by saying, in effect: ah, yes, but we must distinguish between (Early's conception of) "vanishing" (which is best placed in scare quotes) and (Later's conception of) vanishing. Early only sought to make the questions "vanish" in the limited sense that he wished to show that there could be no stable linguistic formulations of the questions to which we seek answers in philosophy. The really important philosophical questions (about, say, the nature of, and relation between, language, thought, and reality) do not stand under indictment here, but merely the possibility of their successful formulation in language. To say that Early "sought to make the questions vanish" is therefore not to claim that he did not supply answers to them. On the contrary, it is only to claim that he sought to show that the particular answers he favored were (like the questions themselves) such as to be incapable of satisfactory expression in linguistic form, but were, for all that, *qua answers to those questions*, quite correct. Whereas, so this response continues, Later was concerned to show that those very same answers (that Early had sought to impart and defend) had to be made really to *vanish* (now in a much less forgiving sense of the term) because he saw that they were (even qua unsayable answers to the questions) not in the least correct.[16]

3   The Second Phase
In previous exchanges between resolute readers and their critics, the debate has tended to get hung up at just this point—that is, over questions about what ought to count as a satisfactory reading of the overall text of the *Tractatus*, taken on its own terms—with resolute readers, for example, challenging the coherence of the aforementioned distinction between "vanishing" and vanishing, as well as the exegetical adequacy of ascribing the former of these two varieties of "vanishing" to the *Tractatus*.[17] I propose in this essay, to the extent that this is possible, simply to leap over this first stage in the ongoing debate (prior, in the minds of many, no doubt, to any satisfactory clarification of its terms). That is, I propose simply to postpone for the time being any further discussion of the many criticisms to which a resolute approach to the *Tractatus* considered strictly as a reading of the text might appear to be vulnerable, in order to give some indication of what a further possible stage in the dispute between resolute readers and their critics might look like (if it ever were to be reached by less unnatural means)—a stage at which attention could now shift, without prejudging the outcome, to the question of how best to conceive the relation between Wittgenstein's earlier and later thought.

The leap I hope to perform in this essay is, however, not one straight into the midst of this further stage of the dispute, but rather only up to its *threshold*. For, already at this point, the dispute is faced with a source of unproductive gridlock. A central aim of this essay is the limited one of attempting to remove this initial obstacle to this second stage of the dispute. This, in turn, requires, first of all, that we gain a better purchase on the aforementioned reason why it has seemed so evident to some scholars that there is something scandalously inadequate about the sort of approach that resolute readers take to the interpretation of Wittgenstein's work. Why is it that such an approach seems "to leave no room" for a story about Wittgenstein's development that accords his later criticisms of his earlier thought a sufficient weight? In order to pursue this question, we must clarify how we are to understand the second half of the charge stated above.

In the above formulation, it is left unspecified which of the following two possible versions of the charge is at issue: Is it that such heretical readers of Wittgenstein's early work *happen* to leave themselves in the position of being unable to tell a satisfactory alternative story of their own (given, that is, the *specific* character of the textual materials at their disposal in Wittgenstein's later corpus)? Or is it that the very nature of their reading of Wittgenstein's work is such as *necessarily* to leave them in the position of being unable to tell any minimally coherent alternative story (regardless of the specific features of the materials to be found in Wittgenstein's later corpus beyond the single general feature that these materials do contain criticism of his early work)? My aim in this essay is to dispose of this second version of the charge (thus I hope paving the way for more fruitful discussion of the first on other occasions).

4   The Miracle of the Recantation

One way of getting a better handle on this aspect of what is thought to be scandalous about resolute readings is to look at how putative refutations of them formulate the second feature of the charge. Here is how one commentator, Ian Proops, describes the feature of resolute readings that makes them immediately vulnerable to the criticism of espousing an objectionable form of mono-Wittgensteinianism:

[Those who favor the New Reading] tend to be skeptical of the traditional or 'standard' view that the later Wittgenstein came to regard a number of central Tractarian doctrines as seriously mistaken. . . . They question this view because they *have* to. If the *Tractatus* contains no substantive philosophical doctrines, there can be nothing of substance for Wittgenstein to have later repudiated. . . . If the New Reading is correct, there can be no room for an interpretation that involves attributing any substantive philosophical position to the *Tractatus*.[18]

Notice that the charge here is not that New Readers must tell a rather implausible tale about the reasons why Ludwig recanted those of his early views that he came to see were mistaken. The charge is that on the New telling there was nothing in his early work for Ludwig to recant. The startling accusation leveled at New Readers here is that the very nature of their creed debars them from so much as being able to acknowledge the established historical fact of Ludwig's Recantation! If this is right, then it immediately suggests a delightfully straightforward strategy for demonstrating to them, once and for all, the error of their ways—a strategy that permits one to sidestep all of the finer points of Tractarian Hermeneutics. It goes as follows: simply seek out those passages in Ludwig's later work where he evidently is concerned to recant something in his early work. Getting straight exactly which detail of the early work each such passage professes to recant, and exactly why, might be devilishly difficult (partly because it requires that we understand the early work). But the beauty of the situation is that complete clarity on such niceties is not required. If it is evident from the general *tone* of each such passage that it is written in a spirit of recantation, then this is all that is really needed. And it is undeniable that passages characterized by such a tone are legion in the later corpus. So even if the search for a smoking gun inside the text of the *Tractatus* proves inconclusive, the mass of circumstantial evidence (drawn from post-Tractarian writings) against the New Readers becomes overwhelming. If they *have* to hold that Ludwig never changed his mind about anything he believed when he wrote the *Tractatus*, then the sheer quantity of such passages constitutes telling external evidence that their reading cannot be right. (In the context of this dispute, when people speak of "internal evidence," they mean considerations that bear on a reading of the work that can be gathered from a careful reading of the text of the *Tractatus* itself, and by "external evidence," considerations that bear on it but are drawn from sources outside that text.)[19] Instances of such external evidence are easy enough to find, if one operates with a sufficiently permissive conception of how to identify them. You just look for places in the later writings where Ludwig says things such as "I used to think . . . ," "contrary to my earlier view . . . ," "whereas the author of the *Tractatus Logico-Philosophicus* held . . . ," and so on. The evidential value of each such exhibit lies in the fact that it shows Ludwig to have later been concerned to put forward *criticisms* of his earlier self; and this shows that those who favor the New Reading must be mistaken.[20]

Does the bare existence of such putative "evidence" drawn from the later work *suffice* to show that the resolute approach to reading the *Tractatus* must be misguided? Let's call this "the basic initial question." A negative answer to this question ought in itself to be perfectly neutral with respect to assessing the further merits of any particular approach to reading the *Tractatus*. Thus, for example, a critic of the resolute reading might hold that a resolute approach is mistaken and that this can be seen in part from a careful examination of the specific sorts of critical remarks about his early work that Wittgenstein later makes—remarks which, if they reflect a proper understanding on later Wittgenstein's part of his early work, should be taken to cast serious doubt on the viability of a resolute approach to understanding the early work. One could hold this, even while agreeing with resolute readers that any examination of such remarks, however carefully conducted, ought never to serve as a substitute for having an internally motivated, reasonably philosophically coherent, textually grounded account of what the author of the *Tractatus* himself thought he was up to. The interest of such remarks in this context is not that they somehow spare us the labor of having to arrive at such a reading of the early work, but rather that they can furnish us with helpful guidance in trying to arrive at one. Conversely, resolute readers need not deny that such critical remarks in the later corpus can, indeed, serve as a useful additional source of evidence for figuring out what Wittgenstein, when writing the *Tractatus*, thought he was up to in philosophy. The question for them ought, at this stage of the debate, to be the following: Can such remarks figure in a coherent narrative of Wittgenstein's development and yet be read as criticisms of the *Tractatus* on a resolute understanding of its philosophical aim and method? So there may be plenty of room for a dispute between resolute readers and their critics, even if all parties to the dispute answer the basic initial question in the negative. The discussion that would then ensue might be a long and arduous one, but possibly also quite worthwhile. To adjudicate what would here be under contention between resolute readers and their critics would now require a painstaking process of sifting and weighing the evidence, closely examining each of the many rather different things that Wittgenstein says in his later work about his earlier work and assessing in each case its bearing on particular points at issue in the dispute.

This essay will not be a contribution to that dispute, but rather to addressing the primary obstacle that stands in its way, as long as critics of resolute readings hold that a mere framing of the basic initial question (supplemented, of course, with textual exhibits that indicate that later Wittgenstein was concerned to criticize *something* in the *Tractatus*), in effect, clinches the debate. This line of criticism can only have the sort of immediate bearing on the dispute that these critics imagine it does if resolute readers are obliged to hold, not only that the author of the early work *aimed* to prosecute a program of philosophical clarification that rested on no substantive philosophical doctrines, but also that he *succeeded* in that aim.[21] A commitment to the first of these claims evidently does not entail a commitment to the second. Does a commitment to resolution, nonetheless, somehow entail a commitment to all-out mono-Wittgensteinianism?

III What Makes a Reading Resolute?

[Some of the most baffling beliefs of the infidels are to be explained here, such as (1) what they take Ludwig's original aim to have been in writing The Old Testament *and why they think it ends in* The Vision of the Ladder, *(2) how they have the audacity flatly to deny that most sacred tenet of the early Ludwigian creed, namely,* The Dogma of the Paradox, *and why they think* The Paradox *is not even required for an understanding of* The Vision, *and (3) finally, how on their version of* The Vision *the ladder appears to have lots of little rungs that can be seen only in the darkness of night and vanish in broad daylight.—J. C.]*

1 The Avowed Aim

The first phase of the dispute between resolute readers and their critics has tended to center on how to understand the following climactic[22] moment in the *Tractatus*:

My propositions serve as *elucidations* in the following way: anyone who understands me eventually recognizes them as *nonsensical*, when he has used them—as steps—to climb out through them, on them, over them. (He must, so to speak, throw away the ladder after he has climbed up it.)[23]

The next two sections of this essay provide a brief account of what will be meant here by "a resolute reading of the *Tractatus*,"[24] first by saying a bit in this section about what is involved in climbing up and throwing away this ladder on any resolute interpretation of it, and secondly, by saying a bit in the next section about which sentences of the work might make up the rungs of the ladder, thereby indicating ways in which the genus of resolute readings admits of a variety of species. Beyond this, I will have nothing further to say in these pages about the internal commitments of such a reading. In particular, this essay will refrain from rehearsing any of the (exegetically or philosophically motivated) "internal" reasons why an open-minded reader might want to look with sympathy on such an interpretative approach to the *Tractatus*. Its burden will rather be to clarify the "external" commitments of such a reading insofar as they pertain to an understanding of the relation between Wittgenstein's early and later work—and thereby to explore the question whether such an approach to reading Wittgenstein commits one to an intrinsically objectionable form of mono-Wittgensteinianism.

In section 6.54 of the *Tractatus*, the author of the work does not ask us to understand his sentences, but rather to understand *him*. Resolute readers take this particular nicety of formulation to be tied to the way in which we are supposed to come to see, regarding those sentences of the work that are at issue here, that there is nothing that could count as understanding *them*. The primary characteristic that marks out a reading of the *Tractatus* as "resolute," in the sense of the term at issue here, is its *rejection* of the following idea: what the author of that work, in section 6.54, aims to call upon his reader to do (when he says that she will understand him when she reaches the point where she is able to recognize his sentences as nonsensical) is first to grasp, and then to apply to the sentences of the work, a *theory* that has been advanced in the body of the work—a theory that specifies the conditions under which sentences make sense and the conditions under which they do not.[25] In order to be able to give content to the idea that we are able to grasp the commitments of such a theory, a commentator must hold that there is a fairly substantial sense in which we can come to "understand" the sentences that "explain" the theory, despite the fact that we are eventually called upon to recognize these very same sentences as nonsense. Resolute readers hold that to read the *Tractatus* in this way is seriously to underestimate what is involved in the request that we come to recognize these sentences as *nonsense*.

On standard readings of the book, the point of a significant number of the sentences of the work is to achieve the formulation of an adequate set of theoretical *criteria of meaningfulness*. These criteria when applied to the very sentences that adumbrate them yield the verdict that they do not meet their own criteria and thus are to be condemned as nonsensical. Resolute readers are unhappy with any such reading for a variety of reasons. For the present purpose, however, it will suffice to note that they are committed to rejecting any such reading because they are committed to rejecting the idea that the author of the work *aims* to put forward substantive theories or doctrines. Wittgenstein tells us that the kind of philosophy he seeks to practice in this work consists not in putting forward a theory, but rather in the exercise of a certain sort of activity—one of elucidation.[26] The core commitment of a resolute reading for the purpose of this essay lies in its insistence that a proper understanding of the aim of the *Tractatus* depends upon taking Wittgenstein at his word here. A close reading of the text guided by this commitment leads us to the following gloss on his early understanding of the aim of this activity:

> Early Wittgenstein aimed to practice a conception of philosophy in which philosophy is not a matter of putting forward theses, doctrines, or theories, but consists rather in an activity of elucidation; and any apparent theses that are put forward in the course of that activity, if it succeeds in its aim, are to be revealed as either (1) initially philosophically attractive yet in the end only apparently meaningful (*Unsinn*), or (2) either genuinely meaningful (*sinnvoll*) or merely tautologous (*sinnlos*) but only once clarified and hence drained of their initial philosophical eros.[27]

Let's call this "the avowed aim." If one adopts it as a point of departure for reading the text and allows oneself "strictly to think it through,"[28] resolute readers take a proper understanding of the avowed aim to have far-reaching exegetical consequences. It is perhaps not an exaggeration to say that, once this business of strictly thinking it through gets underway, many of the further commitments of resolute readers can be seen to fall into place as corollaries that follow from it. I will confine myself here simply to mentioning three such corollaries.

2   Three Corollaries

The first pertinent corollary (of a resolute rejection of an intended commitment on the part of the author of the work to any theory or doctrine) is the rejection of any intended commitment to an *ineffable* theory or doctrine. This means that resolute readers are bound to reject the widely held view that the relevant "propositions" of the work (namely, those concerning which Wittgenstein said, at §6.54, that they are to be recognized as "nonsensical") are to be "understood" as conveying ineffable insights that the reader is to "grasp" even though the author cannot "express" them. On standard readings of the work, the alleged insights here in question are held to be individuated through an identification of substantive constraints on sense adumbrated through the aforementioned criteria on meaningfulness set forth in the body of the work. It is through the "violation" of these constraints that the sentences in question are revealed as simultaneously meaningless yet able to convey something determinate. The form of their meaninglessness is supposed to highlight, in each case, a particular feature of the general conditions on sense specified by the theory in question. This requires that the meaninglessness of these sentences has, in each case, a logically distinct and specifiable character. It becomes, on standard readings, a central burden of the theory (supposedly adumbrated in the book) to give content to this idea of logically determinate forms of nonsense—where each of these forms of nonsense is alleged to acquire the potential for communication that it specifically possesses in virtue of its violation of a distinct requirement on sense laid down by the theory. This commits standard readers to the idea that the sort of nonsense that is at issue here must come in a variety of logically distinct kinds.

   This brings us to the second pertinent corollary: the rejection of the idea that the *Tractatus* holds that there are logically distinct kinds of nonsense. This is sometimes put by saying that the *Tractatus* aims to show that there is no such thing as substantial nonsense. From the perspective of a resolute reader, it makes little difference whether the candidate criteria for lending substance to nonsense involve considerations of verifiability, bipolarity, logical well-formedness, or some other putative respect in which a "proposition" is held to be intrinsically flawed because of its own internal logical or conceptual structure. Part of what the *Tractatus* seeks to show, according to resolute readers, is that all such "criteria of meaningfulness" cannot do the sort of work to which we want to put them in our philosophical theorizing. Any reading of section 6.54 that takes the recognition on the part of a reader there called for to require a substantive employment of such criteria qualifies as an instance of an irresolute reading, as long as it is committed to ascribing to the *Tractatus* a theory that its author must endorse and rely upon (if he is to be able to prosecute his program of philosophical critique) and yet which he must also regard as nonsense (if he thinks through the commitments of his own theory).[29]

At a minimum, what a resolute reading seeks to avoid here is the mess that commentators get into when they refuse to (allow that they are, at the end of the day, supposed to) throw away the following paradoxical idea:

> The author of the *Tractatus* wants its reader to reject the sentences of the book as nonsense on principled grounds; yet, in the very moment of rejecting them, the reader is to continue to retain a grip on these grounds by continuing to identify, grasp, and believe that which these sentences would say, if they had a sense.[30]

Let's call this "the paradox."[31] To be resolute in one's approach to the *Tractatus* involves taking this paradoxical idea itself to form a *part* of the ladder that we, as readers, are meant to climb up and throw away (rather than taking it to be an account of what it *is* to throw away the ladder). Thus, it involves taking the sort of recognition that readers of the work are called upon to attain in section 6.54 to require a recognition that the intermediate stages which we, as readers, seem to occupy (when we take ourselves to be able to identify, grasp, and believe what these sentences intend to convey) are *aspects of the illusion* that the work as a whole seeks to explode—that they are themselves rungs on the ladder that we are asked to climb up and throw away.

The third corollary has to do with how one ought to conceive the details of the Tractarian procedure of elucidation—and, in particular, the role of the many notational devices (the Sheffer stroke, the truth tables, the special bracket notation for quantification, etc.) that are introduced in the course of the book. It is evident that logical notation is supposed to play some sort of important role in a reader's ascent up the ladder. A standard reader will assume that the notation at issue here is one that is to be constructed so as to reflect the requirements of the theory that are laid down in the book: only those sentences the theory deems permissible will be constructible in the notation; and those sentences the theory deems nonsensical will involve illegitimate constructions forbidden by the syntactical rules governing the employment of the notation. It should by now be evident that it is not open to a resolute reader to construe the role of logical notation in Tractarian philosophical clarification in anything like this way. According to a resolute reader, the forms of logical notation employed by the author of the *Tractatus* (in order to make certain philosophical confusions manifest) must be elucidatory instruments whose employment is not itself supposed to require commitment (on the part of those engaged in an elucidation) to any particular philosophical theses.

We are familiar in ordinary critical discussion with procedures in which confusion in thought can be brought to a person's attention through a procedure of reformulation—in effect, through substituting one expression for another. This is most commonly accomplished by substituting one expression in the speaker's native language for another. But if the speaker is familiar with a foreign language, then that familiarity can be exploited to bring further elucidatory resources to bear on the situation. Thus, an equivocation involving "or" in ordinary English can be brought to a speaker's notice, if he speaks Latin, by asking him whether he wants to translate his English sentence into Latin using "aut" or "vel." No "theory of Latin" is required in order for the speaker to take advantage of this elucidatory tool. All that is required is knowledge of how properly to translate English sentences into Latin ones. By being forced to reflect upon what is involved in the task of having to choose one of these Latin expressions over the other, the speaker can be made to realize that he has been hovering between alternative possibilities for meaning his words without determinately settling on either one.[32] According to resolute readers, this is what philosophical nonsense is for the author of the *Tractatus*: an unwitting wavering in our relation to our words—failing to make genuine determinations of meaning, while believing that we have done so.[33] And the *Tractatus*'s understanding of the character of nonsense, according to resolute readers, is internally related to its understanding of the proper role of logical notation in philosophical clarification.

If our English speaker above did not know Latin, but instead had been taught an appropriately designed logical notation (in which each of these two different possible translations of the English sign "or" corresponds to a different symbol in the notation), then exactly the same clarification could be effected using this notation. No theory of the notation is supposed to be here required, merely a mastery of its proper use. What is needed here—to paraphrase *Tractatus*, §4.112—is not a commitment to some doctrine, but rather a practical understanding of how to engage in a certain sort of activity. The forms of notation to which the *Tractatus* introduces us, of course, involve degrees and dimensions of designed regimentation (in our use of distinct signs to express logically distinct modes of symbolizing) well beyond a simple distinction in the use of signs merely to mark two different ways of using a single particle of speech such as "or." In principle, however, if our aim is restricted to the Tractarian clarification of thought, then the point of the exercise of mastering and applying such notation and the justification of the procedures involved need not differ in any essential way from those involved in the case of asking someone to translate "or" as either "vel" or "aut." The difference here (in the character of the exercise and the procedures it involves) is one of degree not of kind. The forms of notation introduced by the *Tractatus* therefore are not conceived by its author as requiring independent theoretical justification; and, if they did, this would defeat their purpose. They are put forward as *proposals*. If we try this notation, we will see that it allows us to become clear (when there is something we want to say) about what we want to say; and (when there is not) it allows us to become clear about the character of our failure in our having unwittingly failed to say anything. With respect to understanding his purpose in introducing us to these instruments of logical notation, we may be said to understand the author of the *Tractatus* each time we recognize how these alternative forms of expression (which the notation makes available) enable the recognition of nonsense.[34] It is in this way that the notation is meant to serve as a device that facilitates a reader's ascent up the rungs of the ladder.

3 Rumors of a List

Beginning in the next section, I will attempt to furnish a provisional specification of some of these rungs. The extent to which one regards an exercise along these lines as a fairly straightforward matter (rather than one requiring considerable delicacy) will depend largely upon how closely one thinks the body of sentences that make up the rungs of the ladder coincides with the body of sentences that make up the text of the *Tractatus*. To see why an issue of some complexity can open up here, two things need to come into focus. First, one needs to see that there is nothing in the characterization of a resolute reading furnished above that requires resolute readers to agree with one another on this issue. Second, one needs to notice that, in section 6.54 of the *Tractatus*, the author of the work does not ask the reader to recognize *all* of the sentences of the work as nonsense. Rather the reader is told that those of the sentences in the work that are to serve as elucidations are able to serve their purpose only through the reader's eventually (through gradually working her way through the book) coming to recognize them as nonsensical.[35] This leaves it open for a resolute reader to claim that not every sentence in the book forms a part of a stretch of elucidatory discourse. Only those sentences that are thus to be surmounted (or defeated)[36] form rungs of the ladder that is to be thrown away. Which sentences are these?[37] I will attempt to address this question in the next section of the paper, by trying to specify some of the rungs in the form of a list.

Two things should be true of each of the numbered propositions that figure on such a list: first, it should be a sentence that can be associated with a philosophical thesis that readers of the *Tractatus* might be inclined to ascribe to the work, and, second, it should be a sentence that resolute readers take to be an example of Tractarian elucidatory nonsense. If a given standard reader compiles a set of sentences of the first sort and a given resolute reader compiles a set of sentences of the second sort, then the intersection of those two sets will constitute the list of the sentences about whose role within the dialectical strategy of the *Tractatus* they disagree most.[38] If they can come to agreement about the sentences which belong on such a list (i.e., on which sentences form the intersection of their two lists), then they will be in position to specify with a useful degree of further precision how the terms "standard reading" and "resolute reading" are to be understood at the outset of their dispute. Armed with such a list, they can say that what makes something "a standard reading" of the work (for the purpose of their dispute) is its ascription of these theses to the work (as integral elements of the philosophical doctrine that its author seeks to impart and defend), so that in order to understand the work we must understand *them*. What makes something "a resolute reading" (for the purpose of their dispute) is its adherence to the claim that as long as we continue to ascribe to the author (as doctrines that he seeks to uphold) what these sentences (seem to) say, then we have yet to complete the task of reading that he has set us, and as long as we fail to realize this we fail to understand *him*.

According to resolute readers, to take an item on the list to be a *rung of the ladder* is to take it to belong to this aspect of the task that the author of the work has set us. The reader reaches a moment in which she understands the author (and what he is doing with one of his sentences) each time she moves from a state of appearing to herself to be able to understand one of these sentences to a state in which it becomes evident to her that her earlier "state of understanding" was only apparent. This point is reached not through the reader's coming to be convinced by an argument that forces her to believe *that* such-and-such is the case, say, by convincing her that the sentence fails to meet certain necessary conditions on sense. (Why should she ever believe the conclusion of such an argument, if she takes herself still to be able to understand the sentence in question? As long as she is able to do this, doesn't she have good reason to question the premises of the argument?) Rather, the point is reached, in each case, by her experience of the sentence (and the sort of understanding it can seem to support) undergoing a transformation. Each such moment of "understanding the author" involves, in this sense, *a change in the reader*. Her sense of the world as a whole, at each such moment, waxes or wanes, not by her coming to see *that p* (for some effable or ineffable, propositional or quasi-propositional *p*), but rather by her coming to see that there is nothing of the form "*that* _____" (of the sort she originally imagined) to believe. So a point of understanding the author is reached when she arrives at a moment in her relation to a given form of words when she is no longer able to sustain her original experience of "understanding the sentence." The task of thus over-coming each particular appearance of sense (that each such rung on the ladder at first engenders in a reader) is an arduous one. The form of understanding that is at issue here for resolute readers can be attained only piecemeal,[39] sentence by sentence.[40] (That is to say, every reader must begin life qua reader of the *Tractatus* as a standard reader and climb her way up from there to a different way of coming to understand her task as a reader. To attempt to skip this stage in one's evolution qua reader of the *Tractatus* is to undertake to miss the experience of the work altogether.[41] Thus, by the lights of resolute readers, standard readers participate in an essential aspect of the experience that the *Tractatus* seeks to engender in its reader: namely, the production and exhibi-tion of illusory understanding. But, to put the point in psychoanalytic terms, they resist the telos of the exercise by falling in love with their symptom.) Since they hold that the *Tractatus* has no general story about what makes something nonsense, resolute readers are obliged to hold that these moments of recognition that a reader is called upon (in section 6.54) to attain must come one step at a time. This is contrary to the spirit of most standard readings, according to which there can be a possible moment in a reader's assimilation of the doctrines of the book when the theory (once it has been fully digested by the reader) can be brought to bear *wholesale* on all of the (puta-tively nonsensical) propositions that make up the work.[42] According to such a reading of the *Tractatus* (and, starting with the Vienna Circle, many a philosophical project that takes itself to be influenced by the *Tractatus*), once we have equipped ourselves with the right theory of language, we can determine where we have gone right and where we have gone wrong in philosophy simply by applying the theory to each of the things we are drawn to say when speaking philosophically. Here we encounter the first respect in which resolute readers are committed to a significantly heterodox degree of mono-Wittgensteinianism: according to them, Wittgenstein, early and late, rejected such a wholesale conception of how progress in philosophy is to be achieved—philo-sophical clarity must be won piecemeal, one step at a time.

IV   Diagramming the Ladder

[*This section is the longest in the paper, quite muddled, and very hard to summarize. Our author takes to making and seeing lists. (1) An actual list is presented in which each item on it is meant to correspond to one of the rungs as seen by Ludwig himself in* The Vision of the Ladder. *(2) Not content with a merely terres-trial list, the infidel here revives an apocryphal account of a second vision apparently had by some now-for-gotten saint. (Some scholars, I believe, refer to this as* The Vision of the First List.) *This second vision is of a divine list, and our author claims that what is there seen can illuminate the nature of the ladder that Ludwig saw (upon which the faithful are to ascend to Heaven). Things then become very abstruse as new vistas in infidel theology are opened up with respect to a variety of topics. The first of these pertains to (3) the shape of the list that appears to the nameless saint that somehow is supposed to correspond to the shape of the ladder that appears to Ludwig in his Vision. (Mysterious mention is made in this connection of "evil sentences"—possibly a reference to Satanism?) He then (4) offers an explanation of the way that the items on the list seen by the nameless saint are supposed to correspond to the rungs on Ludwig's ladder. (Equally mysterious mention is made here of accepting a proposition and its negation—possibly a reference to Buddhism?) Perhaps dissatisfied with his previous answers, he then begins to go around in circles, and (5) appears to answer for a second time the very same questions previously answered in (3) and (4). Finally, we come to (6) issues in infidel dogmatics concerning the limits of the extent to which infidels are obliged to agree with one another in their answers to any of the foregoing questions (and thus why a variety of factions are now battling for control of their sect). Here, as promised, we get our first glimpses of the vulnerable underbelly of their blasphemous creed that I mentioned in my opening remarks—J. C.]*

1   An Actual List

Notice the indefinite article. There are many possible variations on the actual list below that would have sufficed for our present purpose—though none of them without its troubles. As we shall soon see, a reader constrained by nothing more than a bare commitment to resolution will encounter a variety of sorts of difficulty in trying to offer a specification of the rungs of the ladder in anything that approximates the form of a list. The difficulties that arise here will later prove instructive in clarifying the sorts of philosophical and exegetical difficulty that must beset any attempt to offer anything approaching a resolute account of the relation between the thought of the early and that of the later Wittgenstein.[43]

Rather than specifying the rungs by picking out swatches of text drawn from the *Tractatus* in the form of particular quotations, I do so, on the actual list below, by specifying particular lines of "thought" that either figure centrally in the book or are naturally provoked by those that do and to which commentators (standard and resolute alike) have rightly attached particular importance. This allows us to achieve a higher level of generality in specifying rungs of the ladder than would be possible if we confined ourselves to the letter of particular local formulations of each of these as they surface and resurface over the course of the text.[44] So, in that spirit, I offer the following sample of candidate rungs:

1. A proposition is able to represent a state of affairs because it pictures it.
2. A proposition is a logical picture of a state of affairs when the fundamental elements of the proposition, the simple names, are logically combined in a fashion that parallels the manner of combination of the fundamental elements of the state of affairs, the simple objects.

3. Thought and language are able to represent reality because they mirror the logical form of reality.

4. The logical form that language and reality share cannot be expressed in language.

5. The features of reality that underlie the possibility of sense (or: the features of language that underlie the possibility of representation) are *there* all right, even if they cannot be expressed.

6. These features, though they cannot be expressed, can be conveyed by appropriately structured forms of nonsense.

7. These nonsensical "propositions" are not mere nonsense—they are not utterly devoid of logical structure.

8. Such "propositions" involve determinate violations of logical syntax.

9. Each such violation is coordinate with an (inexpressible) insight into an (ineffable) aspect or feature of reality.

10. Each such insight can be "conveyed" through the employment of the corresponding piece of nonsense.

11. What is brought out into the open in each such case, through its transgression, is a general condition on the meaningfulness of propositions.

12. The totality of such conditions constitutes the limits of (our, my) language.

13. The limits of language are the limits of the (our, my) world.

14. It is the role of a proper theory of language to demarcate these limits.

15. It thereby demarcates the boundary between sense and nonsense.

16. It thereby also demarcates the limits of the (my, our) world.

17. The demarcation of these limits enables one (me) to contemplate from above (outside, sideways on) our (my) language (world) as a bounded totality.

It is important here that each of the items on this list be taken to correspond to a sentence, not a thought. The foregoing is a list of examples of candidates for sentences that ought to be associated with rungs on the ladder. The point of furnishing such a sample of candidates is to attempt to gesture at the sorts of sentence that might be held by a resolute reader to belong on what I shall henceforth call "the first list."

2 The First List

Notice the definite article. The expression "the first list" will not serve its intended purpose in this essay if one takes it to be here defined simply through an enumeration of some actual items in some definite order—say, the items on the actual list above in the order given. As we shall see, the point here applies both to the items themselves and to their order. The items exhibited on the above actual list are meant to furnish a preliminary indication of the character of the first list by specifying some appropriate possible candidate sentences for inclusion on it and by displaying them in a candidate arrangement. Leaving aside constraints on there being world enough and time for the completion of such an exercise, an excessively precise specification of the character of the first list would, at this point, be dialectically premature. It would beg a number of questions that will matter at later points in this essay. So we shall content ourselves here with a less than fully determinate characterization. This necessarily involves a certain degree of idealization. There are three significant dimensions of idealization in play here, each of which serves a particular purpose (and each of which can be seen to be associated with certain peculiarities of the actual list given above). The first of these has to do with the shape of said list, the second with its contents, and the third with the ways in which a bare commitment to resolution underdetermines what one ought to say about either. In what follows, my discussion of each of these dimensions shades into the other two at various points, but in the interests of perspicuity some effort is made to keep them apart.

3   What Is the Shape of the Ladder?

First, there is the question of how and where such a list should *begin*. In the actual list given above, the point at which the sequence starts is chosen fairly arbitrarily. One could, for example, certainly begin further back. But, more importantly, what "further back" means here depends in large part upon what one thinks the order of the items on the list is supposed to correspond to. Let us begin by asking: what might "further back" mean for a standard reader attempting to construct some counterpart to such a list for his own purposes? If we ask a standard reader to compile a collection of Tractarian theses and then instruct him now to arrange them *in the right order*, what order would that be? Well, one way he could interpret this request, in going about creating such a list, would be to have the order of the sentences correspond simply to the order in which the relevant theses figure in the book. For such a reader "further back" here might thus simply mean earlier on in the book. The rungs of the ladder, on such an understanding, would correspond to a structure that is "in the book" on a fairly literal understanding of that phrase. Let us call such a list—in which each sentence on it is associated with a thesis and occurs in the order in which the correlative remark occurs in the book—"a standard reader's list." (We will have more to say about such a list below.) On such a construal, the numbering system of the *Tractatus* may be understood as something like the perspicuous ordering of a set of commitments—in which the most fundamental commitments correspond to the integers and the increasingly secondary commitments correspond to the increasingly lengthy decimal figures that are accordingly subordinated to each of the remarks with numbers of comparatively shorter length that they succeed.

Just as all resolute readers must begin life qua readers of the *Tractatus* as standard readers; so, too, their conception of how the work is ordered must begin as one that participates in a standard reader's conception of what this must entail—and there it will remain as long as the task of reading the book is conceived to be one of (doing anything in the vicinity of) understanding what each of its sentences *say*. This means that all readers of the work must begin by working with something like a standard reader's understanding of the numbering system of the *Tractatus*—taking the apparent significance of that numbering system more or less at face value. If an understanding of the author of the work, however, requires a recognition that there is nothing that can count as understanding what each of these sentences (that are to serve as elucidations) say, then this conception of the ordering of "thought" within the text must eventually yield to another.

What then might "in the right order" mean for a resolute reader? It might at first appear as if she has two rather different ways of going here. Which way she should go about arranging items on her list might seem to depend upon whether she takes the sequence of items to correspond to an order of dialectical steps that is present in the structure of the work itself and that unfolds as one moves sequentially through the sentences of the book (so that the proper shape of the list depends on which sentences figure comparatively earlier in the text and which comparatively later) or whether she takes it to correspond to an order of discovery that unfolds in the course of a reader's coming to terms with the work (so that the proper shape of the list depends upon which sentences are likely to be recognized as nonsense comparatively earlier by a reader in the process of assimilating the work and which comparatively later).[45]

These two different ways of understanding the shape of the list may appear to correspond to two different ways in which a resolute reader might try to unpack the metaphor of a ladder. Each of these, in turn, is differently related to the initial (mis)understanding of the metaphor that she will see a standard reader as prone to go in for—that is, the understanding of the metaphor that any reader will go in for, prior to having achieved an understanding of the author (and the character of the activity in which he is engaged). On a standard reading, the ladder is to be thrown away in a single motion: the rungs of the ladder represent the sentences that set forth the elements of substantial theoretical doctrine that the work seeks to impart, and the reader becomes obliged to throw all of these away at once, when the theory is fully in place and can be applied to the body of sentences that advance it. Whereas, as we have seen, on any resolute reading, the ladder is thrown away bit by bit since the process of recognition required is of necessity an arduous and piecemeal one. But on the first of the two ways that a resolute reader might try to unpack the metaphor (where the order of the rungs of the ladder corresponds to the order in which lines of "thought" occur in the text), it might look as if the standard reader's conception of at least the general shape of the ladder should be allowed to stand, even if his conception of what is involved in throwing away something of this shape needs to be contested. Can it really be allowed to stand? Or to ask a related but comparatively tractable question: might such a resolute reader's list coincide with a standard reader's list? When we return to this issue below, we will see that it cannot. So there is some pressure here for a resolute reader to move to the second way of unpacking the metaphor. On the second way of unpacking the metaphor (in which the order of the rungs of the ladder corresponds to an order of discovery on the part of a reader), neither of these features of the standard reader's way of unpacking the metaphor may be retained. On this second way of unpacking the metaphor, as different readers work through the *Tractatus*, the shapes of the ladders they climb may vary.

The dawning of a realization that the apparent sense of a particular line of "thought" (initially apparently present in the book) is being caused to collapse in on itself (through the character of its development in the work) is the sort of experience that can have drastic implications for one's apparent grasp of other apparently logically related lines of "thought" (also initially apparently present in the work). Thus the shape of the ladder any particular reader climbs, on this way of unpacking the metaphor, depends partly upon which (apparently doctrinal) footholds in the text give way comparatively earlier in the course of her assimilation of the work and which give way comparatively later. As we think this through, we will begin to see that, on this second way of unpacking the metaphor, the idea of the ladder's having a determinate shape starts to require delicate handling.

Both the temporal and the spatial dimensions of the characterization of such an ascent up the ladder require delicate handling. First, let us consider the temporality of the ascent. What (are we to suppose) is realized by such a reader when? The realization that a formerly apparently weight-bearing foothold in the text is starting to vanish into thin air, as soon as it dawns, will be felt by a reader to spell some degree of trouble for other such apparently weight-bearing footholds. But of what sort, and how much? The impending character of the trouble ahead will be apprehended at first only inchoately and thus the severity of its degree will initially not admit of any precise measure. So talk of "what is realized when" here might appear to require some additional parameter that allows for talk of a continuum of *grades* of realization. (The recognition that something you took for sense is nonsense, is in this respect, as in many others, quite different from the recognition that something you took for true is false: sense and nonsense are not two poles of a single bipolar something that has the rough shape of a thought. If something turns out to be false, then inferences can immediately be drawn from it about what else must be false. If something is nonsense, then no inferences can be drawn from it. One is left with unclarity as to where one now stands with respect to much that one previously took to be the case, when one suddenly is no longer able to acquiesce in—not just the truth, but—the very intelligibility of a "thought" that one previously took to be true.)[46] So how are we to unpack the metaphor here? When climbing a real ladder, we need not generally concern ourselves overly with the grades of being of each of the rungs. We might try to supplement the metaphor here with talk about how firmly planted a foot is on a rung. We might try to take comfort in the thought that the temporal dimension of the process (which we might think has more to do with the *ascent* up the ladder) perhaps doesn't matter, inasmuch as the idea of a ladder's having a *shape* is basically a spatial metaphor.

But how is its spatiality to be unpacked, on this second way of unpacking the metaphor? Delicacy is required here for two reasons since (1) it belongs to the nature of the case that the triggering of any such sequence of successively collapsing rungs can only be initiated once a given reader is already quite far along in her effort to orient herself in the text, and (2) such a collapse necessarily exerts an acute dialectical pressure both backward and forward onto other footholds in the text, well beyond the initiating moment itself. Assuming for the purpose of argument that it is clear enough which moment in the text initiates the sequence of falling textual dominoes, questions may arise immediately about which domino can be said to have fallen second and which third, if the dialectical pressure immediately and simultaneously spreads both forward (toward the concluding) and backward (toward the opening) numbered remarks in the text. This may suggest that there are hopelessly severe limits here on the degree of precision that can be placed on the idea of *the* order in which things unfold for such a reader. But what is our picture of "precision" here and in what sense are we unable to attain it?

When thinking about how to unpack the metaphor, there is a tendency only dimly to make out that neither a strictly logical nor a merely psychological account of the shape of the ladder will quite do here. One then responds to this dimly felt difficulty by oscillating in one's construal of the matter between these alternative understandings of what might be at stake, without stably settling on either one.[47] (This oscillation in one's thinking is part and parcel of the sort of confusion that is to be worked through in a successful ascent of the ladder.) If the specification of the moments in the dialectic we pass through in an ascent of the ladder were to be identified with a description of psychological events as they transpire in an individual subject, then it would become mysterious how the items arranged on the actual list above could ever purport to be anything more than a characterization of a sequence of mere psychological contingencies in, say, *my* experience of reading the book (and thus mysterious in what sense *that* order could accurately reflect or fail to reflect anything of possible general interest to us here). If, on the other hand, it is supposed to be a specification of the steps in an argument to a conclusion, then what conclusion is it converging on? (Saying it's a *reductio* doesn't help—if this characterization is to be understood literally rather than merely metaphorically. That would simply mean that the conclusion to be affirmed is the negation of some original assumption. What assumption? The specification of a conclusion or an assumption is only possible where what is to be specified is something that makes sense.) For the author of the *Tractatus*, not only should we not confuse the order of events in a psychological episode of thought with the order of steps in a logical chain of thought, but we should also not identify either of these with the order of clarification in an elucidatory train of "thought." The sort of perspicuity we seek in the ordering of our thought in philosophy for Wittgenstein, both early and late, must always be distinguished both from the sort of descriptive accuracy we seek in empirical psychology and from the sort of inferential validity that we seek in logical argument. For the ultimate aim in the sort of philosophy that Wittgenstein seeks to practice is a sort of *total dissolution* of the problems that neither the mere provision of accurate description nor the mere augmentation of properly justified true belief (however important these may be as secondary means) can ever deliver on their own. Accurate description and valid reasoning each bring with them a certain ideal of clarity, but in neither case of the sort that is Wittgenstein's ultimate quarry—the sort that can make philosophical problems (of the kind that he seeks to address) *completely* disappear. It is to this end that we climb the ladder.

So what does a resolute reader seek to capture in ordering the items on the list? What is to be captured by such a reconstruction is neither merely what happens first and then what happens next and so on in a particular reader's experience while (possibly uncomprehendingly) merely moving through the text, nor a specification of what is to be inferred first and what is to be inferred second and so on if the reader is to become rationally entitled to some (propositional or quasi-propositional) insight. What is to be captured rather is how the illusion of sense that the reader attaches to this sort of sentence is revealed to be an illusion and how this exerts pressure on the illusion of sense that she attaches to this other sort of sentence and so on. Notice I say here: this sort of sentence. It is not that there is some magic handful of seven or eleven or thirty-four sentences that are the evil sentences that confuse us, so that one can confine oneself to that determinate set of culprits and look upon all the other sentences in the vicinity as mere accomplices to the crime. The culprits do not admit of being rounded up in that way. This means that there is an ineliminable degree of choice that enters into the presentation of a train of elucidatory "thought." For one must always work with particular examples of sentences, where the particular examples one chooses will affect the precise details of how the dialectic should be presented. If this is right, then the appropriate sequence of apprehensions on the part of a sensitive reader ought to admit of a variety of equally well-founded alternative reconstructions, each having equal claim to being, in a sense, a perfectly accurate specification of the series of stations through which the reader's train of dialectical "thought" may be said to have passed. The point of a perspicuous arrangement of sentences that occur in the book (and ones like them) is not to capture precisely what actually happened at some point in time to some particular reader, but to arrange things so that something may happen for a general reader. What a perspicuous arrangement of elucidatory remarks seeks to characterize is the order of steps that enables the reader to come to see how the philosophical problems with which she wrestles draw their life from her only apparently conferring on certain sentences a determinate method of symbolizing. It is such sentences and the order in which their elucidation proceeds that we seek to represent through our list. Having said this, the following two points should by now be clear about a proper unpacking of the metaphor: (1) the shape of the resulting ladder, on some reconstruction of it, may correspond at best only loosely to any actual sequence in which the corresponding textual footholds occur in a properly bound copy of the book, and (2) this need in no way be a sign that our reconstruction of the shape of the ladder fails to do justice to the structure of the dialectic that is "in the book" (now on a considerably less literal-minded understanding of that phrase).

4 What Counts as a Rung?

If one fully enters into the spirit in which the items on it are put forward, then it will soon become evident that even in the case of the so-called "actual list" given above a variety of dimensions of reconstruction and idealization are already in play. First of all, one could certainly fill in the list in far greater detail. Each of the lines of "thought" in question is indicated only in a highly schematic fashion, admitting of far greater specification. But, far more importantly, almost every item on the list is meant to indicate a number of other equally pertinent items. Taking the most straightforward case of this first, at many junctures an item on the list could be replaced with something that has the form of its philosophical opposite, without rendering its candidacy for inclusion on the list any less appropriate. Thus, a realist-sounding thesis, such as 3 on our actual list above, could be replaced by its antirealist counterpart:

> 3a. Reality is representable in language because it mirrors the logical form of thought and language.

This, in turn, could be modified to take on a more palpably idealist-sounding edge:

> 3b. Our world is representable because it mirrors the logical form of our language.

Or, if you prefer, you can have a solipsist-sounding variant:

> 3c. My world is representable because it mirrors the logical form of my language.

There are standard interpretations of the *Tractatus* on offer that advocate each of 3, 3a, 3b, and 3c, arguing in favor of the candidate item's role as a central doctrine of the work. Thus, for example, much of the secondary literature on the *Tractatus* has come to assume the form of a debate between those who hold that the direction of explanation should flow from the nature of reality to the nature of language and those who hold that this order of explanation should be reversed (though there are also interpretations which hover unstably between these options without ever settling clearly on either). Resolute readers hold that each of the philosophical positions that results from privileging either of these directions of explanation figures equally as a rung on the ladder that we are invited to climb up and then throw away.[48] For such readers, one has failed to understand the aim of the work as a whole if one takes oneself to be obliged to try to figure out which of such opposed options we are supposed finally to settle upon: the *Tractatus* aims to show that the sense of any of 3, 3a, 3b, and 3c depends on the others and that they all stand or fall together—that, strictly thought through, realism, idealism, and solipsism all collapse into one another.[49]

On a standard reader's list, we can include only one of 3, 3a, 3b, and 3c; whereas there is nothing that debars a resolute reader from placing all four of these items on the same list. So we are now in a position to answer a question that came up before: might a resolute reader's list coincide with a standard reader's list? No. For standard readers, such (putatively) philosophically/logically incompatible "propositions" crowd one another out as candidate rungs on the ladder because such propositions are to be associated with genuine, albeit ineffable, *insights* into the nature of thought, language, and reality, and their negations are to be associated with denials of those insights. For resolute readers, these items need not crowd one another out as candidates for inclusion on the first list since the rungs of the ladder they represent are all equally associated with merely *apparent* insights into the nature of thought, language, and reality—all equally to be overcome. This has implications for how a resolute reader ought to conceive of the *continuation* of the actual list given above. For a resolute reader, at many points, the above list can, and should be, continued in any of several different directions, as it were[50]—each equally pertinent to specifying candidates for inclusion on the first list. Similarly, many of the items that *already* figure on the above list could be unpacked in either of two ways, where each way would be associated with one of two opposed philosophical doctrines. Thus, for example, 2 admits of both a radical atomist and radical holist variant, where, once again, each of the variants in question has frequently been ascribed to the author of the *Tractatus* by standard readers, and where the truth of each has been understood to depend on the falsity (and thus intelligibility) of the other. The two variants at issue here might be specified as follows:

2a. A proposition means what it does (solely) in virtue of the (prior and independent) meaning of the names of which it is composed and the logical relations into which these are (then) combined.

2b. An expression means what it does (solely) in virtue of the logical role that it plays in the totality of propositions in which it can occur.

Here, too, much of the secondary literature on the *Tractatus* has assumed the form of a debate between (i) those who hold that the direction of explanation should flow from the nature of the fundamental elements of the proposition (above all, names and the process by means of which meaning is first somehow independently conferred upon them) to the nature of the proposition (understood as a combination of such antecedently available elements) and (ii) those who hold that this order of explanation should be reversed. And there is a parallel debate about the relation between the nature of simple objects and that of states of affairs. Do the objects first exist and then enter into certain combinations? Or are they what they are only in virtue of their antecedently fixed possibilities of combination? The opposed theses here might be specified as follows:

2a′. A state of affairs is the sort of complex it is (solely) in virtue of the (prior and independent) character of the elementary objects out of which it is composed and the particular sort(s) of logical relation into which these have been combined.

2b′. An object is the sort of element it is (solely) in virtue of the antecedently fixed possibilities of combination into which it can enter and thus can be identified as the object it is only through a specification of the totality of states of affairs in which it occurs.

Here, too, resolute readers will hold that either of the philosophical positions that thus results (from privileging either of these directions of explanation) figures equally centrally as a rung on the ladder that we are invited to climb up and throw away.

At this point, the very idea that there is something that corresponds to placing all of the items on the list "in the right order" can threaten to come apart on us. Even in the rather minimal actual list given above, not all of the propositions that are indicated are sequentially ordered with respect to one another. Starting with item 5 on the list, I have indicated possible (sometimes perhaps apparently minor, sometimes perhaps apparently momentous) variants on the rung in question through a sort of parenthetical shorthand. Each occurrence of this parenthetical notation indicates the possibility of a further (sometimes apparently logically or philosophically opposed) candidate item for the list. This suggests that a proper representation of that which we seek here should not be something of the linear form of a mere list, but rather something with an added dimension that would permit the representation of branching sequences. But we should be careful here not to confuse the retrospective view (of the overall shape of things gradually attained through one's ascent up the ladder) with the prospective view (of someone engaged in an ascent). Even in climbing a tree one can only climb one branch at a time. In any actual movement of "thought" in one's ascent up the ladder, one branch must be explored before another (because it will only be with the benefit of hindsight that certain branching clusters can be seen to have a parallel standing in the larger scheme of things). Nevertheless, certain questions can arise about each further item on the actual list whose possibility is indicated by my parenthetical notation. If each one were spelled out so that it could figure as a separate numbered item on the list, then how should, say, the realist, idealist, and solipsist variants on any one of them be ordered with respect to the others? Is this a good question? As we try to think these two questions through, it is bound to become less and less clear, on a resolute understanding of the metaphor of the ladder, what the expression "to climb a rung of the ladder" is any longer supposed to mean if it is supposed to designate a form of transition between rungs and if each of the items that figure separately on the first list is to be counted as a separate rung.

As we shall see, in response to questions about how things on the first list are to be ordered, an intramural squabble may break out among resolute readers. Though they agree with each other that no preferred order of explanation (from, say, the nature of reality to the nature of language or vice versa) should be ascribed to the author of the work, it is open to a resolute reader to hold that this still leaves room for the idea of a preferred order of elucidation. In their writings about the *Tractatus*, resolute readers certainly tend to construct narratives that (at the very least) strongly suggest that they think that there *is* an order in which things are supposed to unfold in the dialectical strategy of the work.[51] But exactly how such narratives should go is something about which they can disagree. And this, in turn, has bearing on questions concerning how the idea of placing all of the items on the list "in the right order" should be spelled out. The bare commitment to resolution in fact leaves plenty of room for alternative dialectical narratives and lively disagreements about such matters.

Though they may not be able to agree on how to order them, what resolute readers will agree on is that if any member of a set of parenthetically indicated variants on the actual list above belongs on the first list, then all of the other variants (i.e., including the original numbered item of which the parenthetically indicated ones are variants) belong there as well. For what all of the items on the first list are supposed to have in common—that is, what marks them out as sentences belonging on the first list—is that each of them expresses a metaphysical commitment that figures in the *Tractatus* as a philosophical temptation that the author intends to help the reader to overcome. On a resolute understanding of the method of the *Tractatus*, in which these candidate answers to metaphysical questions are to be made to vanish through the vanishing of the questions themselves, at the end of the day, such clusters of answers either have to have been made to vanish all together or not at all—regardless of whether they purport to be about "language," "thought," or "reality," or whether they purport to be about "the," "our," or "my" language (or thought, or reality). You cannot resurrect a piece of nonsense from the grave of semantic emptiness merely by adding or subtracting a "not," or by substituting a "my" or an "our" into a mere sequence of signs. To raise it from the grave, you must confer a determinate method of symbolizing on the propositional sign; and once you have done this, you have thereby also conferred a sense on certain counterparts of it (such as those that can be formed in the appropriate manner by introducing a "not" into the propositional symbol).[52] Conversely, a bringing to light of what turns out to have been a merely apparent success in conferring a method of symbolizing on a string of signs will adversely affect not merely the apparent intelligibility of a single string, but that of numerous other (merely apparently logically related) propositional signs. What this suggests is that if resolute readers (in their attempt to unpack the metaphor of the ladder) are to make useful sense of expressions such as "to climb a rung of the ladder," then each individual rung on such a ladder must be identified (not just with an individual sentence taken in isolation from its dialectical context within the work as a whole, but rather) with a whole cluster of remarks considered in relation to other such clusters.

5   What Counts as a Rung? And What Is the Shape of the Ladder?—Take Two

We saw that for a standard reader the numbering system of the *Tractatus* can be under-stood as something like the perspicuous ordering of a set of commitments—in which the most fundamental commitments correspond to the integers and the less funda-mental ones to the increasingly lengthy decimal figures. If, however, the sentences that figure on the first list are to be recognized as something other than commitments to be ascribed to the author of the work—and, indeed, are eventually to be recognized by a reader as nonsense, so that both they and their (apparent) negations belong equally on the list—then a quite different conception of how the numbering system of the *Tractatus* permits a perspicuous presentation of the dialectical structure of the work ought at some point to come into focus. Consider the following sort of remark that, in writing about the *Tractatus*, a commentator may find himself wanting to make:

The rendition of the metaphysics of facts in the 2.0s is not intended to stand on its own as a piece of metaphysical theorizing. . . .

   The incoherence of the 2.0s is . . . overcome by the say-show distinction elaborated in the 4.12s. We are led to the say-show distinction by the way that the earlier remarks pull themselves apart. At this point, we can throw away the earlier remarks: there is no theory of the constitution of the world, no ontological theory with the generality to which Russell's theory of types aspires. The pursuit of theory, of description, of representation at this level of generality is the pursuit of an illusion.[53]

There are many examples of such prose in the writings of resolute readers—prose in which reference is made to how a comparatively early swatch of sections in the book ought to be understood (at a particular juncture in the unfolding of the dialectic reached at a given point in the narrative of the commentary) in the light of some comparatively later swatch of sections.

   There are two things of interest here. First, if it is right that the incoherence of, say, the 2.0s is fully recognized and overcome only in the light of a proper appreciation of the significance of something elaborated in, say, the 4.12s, then there is a sense in which even a fairly minimal characterization of the dialectic of ascent can require that the same items occur (at least) twice in any perspicuous ordering of the rungs of the ladder through which a reader must pass—on a comparatively earlier pass through these items (say, the 2.0s), it is recognized that they partake of a certain incoherence, but it is only on a comparatively later pass that a full appreciation of the character of this incoherence may dawn. A reader is led to an appreciation of the significance of the later cluster of remarks only given an inchoate recognition that the remarks in the earlier cluster do not quite make sense (that they pull themselves apart), and this later appreciation, in turn, enables a full recognition that there is *no* sense to be made of the remarks in the earlier cluster (that they are simply nonsense). Second, what is also of interest here is how the numbering system continues to furnish a commentator with a way of orienting himself in the structure of the work (by picking out, say, the 4.12s as a significant cluster of successive remarks that bears in a particular way on another such cluster, say, the 2.0s) even as the reader's conception of how "thought" is "ordered" in the book undergoes such radical transformation—as a putative understanding of (what at first comes into view as) a series of logically interlocking theoretical commitments gradually gives way to the recognition of an illusion. In the course of an ascent up the ladder, a sequence of numbered sections may at first take on one aspect (say, a realist aspect), then another, (say, an idealist aspect), and then yet another (in which the two sets of members of such pairs of aspects are seen collectively to collapse into one another). The significance of the numbering system of the work has an important role to play in allowing a reader to track these successive shifts in aspect that (at successive moments in an ascent up the ladder) whole sequences of remarks may undergo at once. A dispute between two resolute readers about the order in which things are supposed to unfold in the dialectical strategy of the work will therefore often be in no small part a dispute about why the sections of the work are numbered just as they are.

The spatial and linear features of a ladder here threaten, once again, to mislead us if the metaphor is construed too literally, especially when combined with too simpleminded an understanding of the point stressed earlier, namely, that the recognition of Tractarian nonsense must proceed piecemeal. What these related forms of literal- and simplemindedness may occlude is the point that has just been emphasized in the previous paragraph: namely, that there be successive episodes of holistic apprehension—of global aspects dawning—that attend an ascent up the ladder. In climbing the Tractrarian ladder, though you can take only one step at a time, nonetheless, at every point in the ascent, you must keep track of (what now appears to be happening in) remarks elsewhere in the book as viewed from the vantage you have just attained in your ascent. From the point of view of a resolute reader, therefore, the expression "to climb a rung of the ladder" is best reserved for cases of apprehension of the sort touched on in the previous paragraph (and it may thereby acquire a far more useful sense than the previously unhelpful one of merely somehow moving from a particular item on the first list to an elusive "next" item on that list). That is, it is best reserved for those moments, in working through the book, when the assimilation of a fruitful set of remarks triggers an episode of significant rethinking, enabling one to re-apprehend—to see in a whole new light—the character of the connection between the fruitful remarks and a whole host of other remarks in the book, so that one now understands the significance of those other remarks (i.e., their role within the dialectical strategy of the work as a whole) in a significantly new way. Even if one restricts the sense of the expression of "to climb a rung of the ladder" in this way, it can still remain quite surprising how many rungs one must climb in order to ascend the ladder of the *Tractatus*. In accordance with this usage, it makes perfect sense, for example, to speak of certain rungs of the ladder as (available to be) climbed only on successive rereadings of the whole book.

Notice: on this new way of talking, not every separately numbered remark in the book (or every separately specifiable sentence on the first list) will any longer count as a rung; rather only a sequence of numbered remarks (or a collection of appropriately arranged items on the first list) will now constitute a rung and then only via a connection that comes into view for a reader between that sequence (or collection) and other remarks elsewhere in the book. On such a way of talking, though it is still the case that the numbered sections of the work can be said to "make up" the rungs of the ladder, it is no longer right to think of each such section as itself constituting an individual rung. Moreover, a given collection of remarks can figure more than once in an ascent of the ladder—in the climbing, as it were, of more than one rung. (And a given remark can figure in more than one such collection.)[54] What recommends this sort of employment of the expression "to climb a rung of the ladder" to a resolute reader is something that itself helps to bring out a profound point of difference between standard and resolute approaches to reading the book. In taking the book, as a standard reader does, to offer something that approximates the presentation of a theory, there is nothing in principle that debars an appropriately brilliant and attentive reader from taking in the point of the book as a whole in a single sequential reading of it. Whereas in taking the book, as a resolute reader does, to involve the aforementioned sort of elucidatory exercise in undoing our attraction to certain confusions (and to the apparently meaningful sentences that we call upon to express them), a full assimilation of the work due to its very design requires successive passes through the same sets of remarks and thus multiple readings of the whole text. A notable feature of any attentive reader's experience of the book, namely, that a seemingly countless number of attempts at assimilating it as a whole appear to be required in order to be able to orient oneself in the book, may now therefore take on a new aspect. This feature of a reader's experience of the book may initially come dimly into view as nothing more than an apparent consequence of some degree of literary or expository failure on the part of the work. (Indeed, on a standard understanding of its aim, there is no reason for this feature of the book ever to cease to appear to be a sign of anything other than poor design.) On a resolute understanding of the aim of the work, this feature of a reader's experience of the work may now come into focus as a constitutive aspect of the method of the work.

6   Further Intramural Dispute

We saw that a dispute between two resolute readers about the order in which things are supposed to unfold in the dialectical strategy of the work will often in no small part be a dispute about why the sections of the work are numbered just as they are. This point can now also be reformulated as follows: a dispute between two resolute readers can assume the form of a disagreement about what constitutes a climbing of a rung of the ladder (in the demanding sense just given to this expression). The third dimension of idealization mentioned above comes with needing to allow for the possibility of yet a further sort of disagreement between resolute readers—one that bears immediately on this one.

The original point of the actual list (of candidate items for inclusion on the first list) was to specify some examples of the sort of thing that one finds in the *Tractatus* that a resolute reader is apt to view as forming part of the target of the work (rather than part of its doctrine), thereby allowing us to put some flesh on the previously rather bare-boned metaphor of a ladder (and the related metaphors of climbing it and throwing it away). But as long as resolute readers disagree about the details of how their general program for interpreting the *Tractatus* is to be implemented—why, as it were, the sections of the work are numbered just as they are—then there is also room for disagreement about what properly belongs on the first list (and thus exactly how the details of the text should enter into a full unpacking of the metaphor). It is important to see that a mere shared commitment to a generically resolute approach to reading the work will not of itself provide sufficient common ground to resolve such a disagreement. The proper demarcation of the first list turns on the proper resolution of all such disputes. The concept of the first list here therefore pertains to this common topic that resolute readers may find themselves in disagreement about (and thus not to any determinate specification of its contents that might be gleaned by reading some supposedly canonical article or book by any particular resolutely minded commentator). What makes someone a resolute reader of the *Tractactus* is that there are many sentences in the book that she will want to earmark for inclusion on the first list for the sorts of reasons touched on above. What a commitment to resolution underdetermines is just which, and how many, such items should be placed on the first list, how they should be clustered, and how the clusters should be arranged.

There are two further issues here—the first having to do with what is already on the actual list and the second with what is not (yet). The first has to do with whether every item there marked out for inclusion belongs on the first list, the second with what it means to continue, as it were, the series here. With regard to the second, resolute readers (even if they agree about all of the items on the actual list) may disagree about *how far* into the text of the *Tractatus* a continuation of the list ought to penetrate. Do all of the sentences which specify features, for example, of the underlying conception of the activity of philosophical elucidation (which the text seeks to practice and into which it seeks to initiate its reader) themselves constitute rungs of the ladder that we are eventually meant to throw way?[55] Any attempt to adjudicate such a question immediately introduces a host of issues pertaining to how one ought to conceive the overall character and scope of the list. The question here at issue might be put as follows: what does it mean to *complete* the list? And how can you tell if you have gone *too far*? A remark of T. S. Eliot's is pertinent here: "[I]t is often true that only by going too far can we find out how far we can go."[56] We will begin to see why in section VIII.

V   An Avowedly Heterodox Degree of Mono-Wittgensteinianism

[Finally, issues concerning the Gospels are broached. The infidel scholar begins to speak openly about his heretical beliefs and practices, as well as about his unabashedly blasphemous account of the relation between The Old Testament *and* The New Testament. *(1) He begins by shamelessly trying to minimize his past sins on the ground that they were always only venal and never cardinal. Then he claims to be able to show that (2) the aims, (3) the methods, and even (4) the devils mentioned in each of the Testaments can somehow aid in the interpretation of the corresponding passages in the other. The latter discussion also alludes to unsavory practices among the infidels pertaining to the exorcism of evil spirits.—J. C.]*

1   Disapproval and Incredulity

Presented with (perhaps a slightly longer version of something like) the actual list above and the news that resolute readers think that the author of the *Tractatus* is no less concerned than the author of the *Investigations* to help us overcome our attraction to sentences such as these, standard readers tend to be left with a version of the following question and an attendant reaction of incredulity: "But what then is the difference between early and later Wittgenstein? There can be no difference! If you allow all of the theses on the first list to count as objectionably metaphysical already by his early lights, then haven't you failed to leave room for anything in his early work that can subsequently count *only* by Wittgenstein's later lights as objectionably metaphysical?"

Let's call this "the incredulous question" and the attitude shared by those who are inclined to pose it "Incredulity." It matters for two reasons. First, it is their supposed vulnerability to the complaint lodged here that sometimes constitutes the heart of the charge directed against resolute readers by their critics that they go in for an unacceptable degree of mono-Wittgensteinianism; and, secondly, it is the supposition that the very idea of resolution itself must entail nothing short of precisely this severe form of mono-Wittgensteinianism that makes resolute readers seem so easily vulnerable to refutation via external evidence drawn from the later writings. It is worth distinguishing the incredulous question from the following one (with which it is often confused): "Aren't resolute readers necessarily committed to some undeniably heterodox degree of mono-Wittgensteinianism?" Let's call this "the disapproving question" and the attitude shared by those who are inclined to pose it "Disapproval." The point of the next few sections of the paper is to help bring out why it matters that we not conflate these questions. A resolute reader *may* plead innocent to the charge leveled by the first question (the one that invites Incredulity), whereas she *must* plead guilty to the charge leveled by the second question (the one that invites Disapproval).

Starting with section VII, we will turn to why a resolute reader need not invite Incredulity. In this section, I will confine myself to touching on why (in their insistence on certain moments of continuity in Wittgenstein's development) resolute readers cannot help but excite Disapproval.[57] So, in this section, we will see why resolute readers are, indeed, committed to a heterodox degree of mono-Wittgensteinianism, and, starting in section VII, why their mono-Wittgensteinianism may remain, nonetheless, in certain respects quite mild.

Since, for the purpose of this paper, all that is required is to show how grounds that warrant Disapproval do not suffice to license Incredulity, the ensuing discussion of moments of continuity in Wittgenstein's philosophy may be brisk and superficial. I will indicate three interrelated moments of continuity in Wittgenstein's conception of philosophy that are emphasized in the work of resolute readers, and which, taken collectively, clearly constitute undeniable evidence of an avowedly heterodox degree of mono-Wittgensteinianism on their part: the first pertains to the aim of the activity, the second to its method, and the third to some of its obstacles. These three examples are hardly meant to exhaust the significant moments of continuity in Wittgenstein's philosophy to which resolute readers have attached importance in their writings. But they suffice to show that their approach to reading Wittgenstein is bound to occasion Disapproval.

2 Continuity in Aim

Consider the following pair of remarks from the *Tractatus* and the *Investigations* respectively, the first of which we have touched on before (in our discussion of the avowed aim of the early work):

The object of philosophy is the logical clarification of thoughts.
Philosophy is not a theory but an activity.
A philosophical work consists essentially of elucidations.
The result of philosophy is not a number of "philosophical propositions," but to make propositions clear.[58]

If one tried to advance theses in philosophy, it would never be possible to debate them, because everyone would agree to them.[59]

The considerable differences in the style and emphasis of these passages notwithstanding, resolute readers will hold that a genuine (if limited) continuity in the conception of the activity pursued in the two books from which they are drawn is registered here—a continuity that the immediate juxtaposition of these two passages may serve to highlight. In the first of these, Wittgenstein gives voice to an aim that the second shows continues to remain central in his later philosophy, namely, the aspiration to practice philosophy in such a way that it does not issue in a doctrine or a theory, but rather in the practice of an activity—an activity that he characterizes, in the first, as one of elucidation or clarification—an activity that he says does not result in *philosophische Sätze*, in propositions of philosophy, but rather in *das Klarwerden von Sätzen*, in our attaining clarity in our relation to the sentences of our language that we call upon to express our thoughts.[60] And the second emphasizes a feature of this aspiration that is already present in his early work, namely, to put forward remarks that can survive clarification yet continue to retain their status as directed at matters philosophical only at the expense of their no longer appearing to admit of disagreement. One can, of course, try to take the remarks put forward in the *Tractatus* as theses (and hence take them as remarks one can disagree with); and indeed, the entire activity of Tractarian elucidation depends upon the reader's willingness to do just this. But, if successfully conducted and fully pursued to its end, the effort will reveal that the remarks in question were unable to bear the weight of a philosophical thesis.[61]

Standard readers may agree that there is an *appearance* of continuity here; but they will also think that the previous paragraph vastly overestimates its significance. When early Wittgenstein says his aim is not to put forward a doctrine, what he really means, according to standard readers, is an *effable* doctrine. For the early Wittgenstein certainly does, on standard readings of him, aim to put forward a number of substantive metaphysical doctrines, only the doctrines in question cannot be expressed, but must rather be conveyed by other means. Standard readers take there to be doctrines that the *Tractatus* fully *aims* to espouse, even if it cannot express them, and it is *just these doctrines* that they take the later Wittgenstein, in his criticisms of his earlier self, to be centrally concerned to criticize. It is clearly not open to resolute readers to understand the relation between early and later Wittgenstein in this way. Since for many standard readers these are the only terms in which they can envision a plausible understanding of the relation between the two, this gives rise to the presumption that resolute readers, in their zeal to be resolute, altogether deprive themselves of the resources required to furnish a coherent account of the relation between early and later Wittgenstein. But, as we shall soon see, their insistence on the moment of continuity touched on here (as well as the two to be touched on below) still leaves resolute readers with ample room to find significant points of discontinuity between Wittgenstein's early and later conceptions of a form of philosophical practice that eschews theses—points of discontinuity both with regard to his conception of the forms of philosophical engagement and criticism that such a practice requires and with regard to his later assessment of the extent to which his earlier conception of such a practice is able to achieve its own ends or live up to its own understanding of the commitments it involves.

3   Continuity in Method

A second way in which resolute readers are committed to a degree of mono-Wittgensteinianism that standard readers are bound to frown upon is in their seeing a moment of continuity in Wittgenstein's conception of the method by means of which philosophical clarification is effectuated. This brings us to another pair of strikingly parallel passages, the first of which we have seen before:

My propositions serve as elucidations in the following way: anyone who understands me eventually recognizes them as nonsensical, when he has used them—as steps—to climb out through them, on them, over them. (He must, so to speak, throw away the ladder after he has climbed up it.)[62]

My aim is: to teach you to pass from a piece of disguised nonsense to something that is undisguised nonsense.[63]

Each of these passages tells a reader of these works about a sort of recognition she must achieve in order to understand the author. In the first of these remarks, we are told that a number of the author's propositions are to serve as elucidations by *our*—that is, the reader's—coming to *recognize* them as nonsensical. In the second of these remarks, we are told the author's aim is to help us pass from something that is a piece of disguised nonsense (so that, at first, we will not recognize it to be the nonsense it is) to something that is shorn of its disguise (so that, at the end of the day, we are no longer able to mistake it for something that has a sense). But how can the recognition that a proposition is *nonsense* ever elucidate—ever shed light on—anything? It is natural to suppose that the only way to answer this question is to suppose that the author of the work must be operating with some highly distinctive conception of nonsense of his own—one that carves out a privileged space for a special class of nonsensical sentences that have the capacity to convey sorts of truth that neither perfectly meaningful nor merely nonsensical sentences are able to express. This supposition, as we have seen, lies at the heart of the standard reading; and we have seen that resolute readers hold such a supposition to be mistaken in connection with Wittgenstein's early work. Now we see that they view this supposition to be no less mistaken when it comes to interpreting his later work.

4 Continuity in Devils

Their view of the mistaken character of this supposition takes us straight to our third and final pair of strikingly parallel remarks:

We cannot give a sign the wrong sense. . . . Every possible proposition is legitimately constructed, and if it has no sense this can only be because we have given no *meaning* to some of its constituent parts. (5.4732–3)

When a sentence is called senseless, it is not as it were its sense that is senseless. (500)

These remarks underscore our third moment of continuity. Many readings of the later work incorporate features of standard readings of the early work in their account of the nature of (what later Wittgenstein calls) "grammar"—a parallel that resolute readers are apt to see as presupposing the very misunderstanding of "the logic of our language" that early Wittgenstein was already centrally concerned to criticize.[64] They will take the above remark from the *Tractatus* to draw attention to the misunderstanding in question, and they will take its counterpart from the *Investigations* to indicate that that criticism remains in force in the later work. But, more importantly, this last pair of quotations touches on a fundamental obstacle that stands in the way of the overcoming of confusion and the achievement of clarity of a sort that Wittgenstein seeks in philosophy, early and late.

The obstacle in question has both a theoretical and a practical aspect. Its practical aspect lies in our capacity to enjoy certain sorts of apparent experiences of meaning—experiences that take the form of our imagining that we are able to understand what a sentence says when, in the relevant sort of case, there actually is no determinate "thought" of the sort that we had imagined. Its theoretical aspect lies in the sorts of accounts we are attracted to in our philosophical theorizing about meaning. These mutually reinforce one another. In our theorizing about those sentences that we take to be meaningful, we are drawn to an account according to which the meanings of the parts of a proposition can be fully identified as the parts they are independently of our understanding of the particular propositional whole in which they figure and apart from the context of use within which that proposition acquires application. This leads us in our theorizing to the idea of there being a special kind of nonsense that arises when there is a failure of fit between the parts of the proposition or between the proposition and its context of use. And this seems to correspond to something we experience in our practical intercourse with certain sorts of sentence: a conflict between the sort of sense we are antecedently inclined to assume the sentence must have and our realization that the sort of sense that we wish to ascribe to it does not really amount to something that we can understand. The theoretical tendency seems to find confirmation in the character of our experience of trying to understand such sentences and our experiences with such sentences draw us to such theories.[65] So we arrive, however inchoately, at the idea of a sign having "a wrong sense" or "a sense-less sort of a sense."

These twin aspects of the obstacle in question can be connected to two related dimensions of continuity in Wittgenstein's philosophy. The overcoming of the obstacle in its practical aspect is a potentially infinite task. There is no set of marks or features that can enable one to tell—from within, as it were—whether one is making sense or not. Posed in the thrall of a possible case of the hallucination of meaning, the question as to whether we are really making sense or not admits of no fast or simple answer. It can only be settled through an arduous process of clarification—over the course of which it becomes clear either what sense there is to be made here or that there was no sense (of the sort that we originally took there to be) to make. Neither on Wittgenstein's earlier nor on his later conception of philosophy can the task of clarification arrive at a definite terminal point—a point at which it is clear that philosophical confusion can no longer arise, so there is no longer any call for the activity to have to continue.[66] Hence the task of clarification is a potentially infinite one. But the task of overcoming the obstacle in its theoretical aspect is a finite (albeit formidable) one. It involves thinking through our attachment to certain very particular sorts of ways of thinking about meaning to the point where they collapse in on themselves. The task of exorcising these particular ways of thinking plays an equally central (albeit very different) role in Wittgenstein's early and later philosophies.

VI The New Way of Thinking against the Background of the Old

[Even a child knows that the true meaning of The Old Testament *is only revealed to those who interpret it in the light of* The New Testament. *In this section we are introduced to the lunatic infidel doctrine that the reverse is somehow equally true. The infidel scholar (1) attempts to derive this bit of blasphemy through*

a Trinitarian gloss on Ludwig's offhand remark that a true believer ought to carry with him at all times a single volume in which both Testaments are bound together. Our author then begins to meander. After (2) a brief excursus on the peculiar dietary practices of his sect, (3) he suddenly takes to whining about the reading habits of the Church Fathers and, in particular, their inability to attend to even minor recitations of who begat whom in The Old Testament *without immediately associating them with glorious* New Testament *passages such as* The Sermon on the Builders *or* The Parable of the Mouse and the Rags. *(4) He claims that this not infrequently causes the Church Fathers to see builders or mice in* The Old Testament *where there are none.—J. C.]*

1   Bound Together

This is a good moment to pause and ask what a remark such as the following is doing in the preface to *Philosophical Investigations*:

Four years ago I had occasion to re-read my first book (the *Tractatus Logico-Philosophicus*) and to explain its ideas to someone. It suddenly seemed to me that I should publish those old thoughts and the new ones together: that the latter could be seen in the right light only by contrast with and against the background of my old way of thinking.[67]

Let's call this "the prefatory remark." Standard readers, on a cursory reading of it, can take it as a bit of textual evidence that the doctrinal schema must be sound. This allows them to have a sort of a story about why he might have wished the *Tractatus* to be bound together in a single volume with the *Philosophical Investigations*. But why does he say that "the latter could be seen in the right light *only* against the background of my old way of thinking"?

Before we take up this question, it is worth noting that, faced with a volume in which these works were bound together to form a single work, we would be presented with a material realization of the problematic with which the first two sections of this paper were concerned.[68] Our question could be reformulated in this way: to what extent should the resulting volume be understood to be a single work by one and the same author, and to what extent should it be understood to encompass two heterogeneous works produced by a pair of authors concerned to pursue very different, and sometimes even opposed, tasks and aims? I take it that the execution of this request (to have the work thus materially bound together) is meant to provoke just such questions in a reader—questions that are meant to stay with us throughout our activity of reading in the resulting volume. The combination of moments of unity and duality in such a mode of presentation are meant to make clear that these halves of the volume are already intellectually bound up in one another, before they come to be physically bound together, in ways that render a consideration of the respective bearing of each on the other mutually illuminating to a degree unlikely to be appreciated if each is read merely successively and separately. An arch way to put this point would be say that there is something right about going Trinitarian here: the author of the resulting twofold volume would be a single being who exists as three indissoluble persons—Early, Later, and Wittgenstein.

Members of a Trinitarian sect of mono-Wittgensteinians will want to place special emphasis on our earlier question: why *"only* against the background of my old way of thinking"? For this suggests that what is in the pages of the *Tractatus* is not simply a recurrence of confusions also to be found in the less difficult writings of lesser philosophers and that it is this difference that recommends those early pages for inclusion in the single volume at issue here. The presence of the "only" suggests that, if we want to see his new way of thinking in the right light, we need first to see it against the background of features of his old way of thinking that he takes to be both peculiar to that way of thinking and peculiarly important to an understanding of the new way of thinking. Otherwise any of a variety of other backgrounds would serve just as well. Which features of his old way of thinking are at issue here? And how do they serve to form the background against which his new way of thinking can be seen in the right light? Are they features of his old way of thinking that he takes to be mistaken to a degree that is peculiar to that way of thinking? Or are they ones that he takes to be essentially correct in a respect that was originally peculiar to the old way of thinking? Is what is at issue here that which he is concerned to repudiate or that which he is concerned to inherit in his old way of thinking?

It is a mistake to think that we need to choose between these options. We can only see what Wittgenstein is most concerned to repudiate in his old way of thinking—and, thereby, what is most original in that way of thinking—against the background of that which he is most concerned to inherit in his earlier way of thinking. Having failed to identify the latter, we are in no position to identify the former. The aim of the previous section of this paper was briefly to highlight some of those aspects of his old way of thinking that resolute readers are apt to think he was most concerned to inherit. The aim of the later sections of this paper will be to indicate some of the aspects of the old way of thinking that he is most concerned to repudiate. The suggestion (of these parts of the paper taken together) is that these jointly constitute the background against which we are asked to see his later philosophy. If we are able to achieve such a view, Wittgenstein thought it would enable us to see his new way of thinking in the right light, enabling us to see what in his old way of thinking he later most seeks to overcome and hence what in his "new" way of thinking is, indeed, *new*.

2 A One-Sided Diet

Wittgenstein is famous for warning against the dangers of nurturing one's philosophical theories on a one-sided diet of examples.[69] Part of the point of broadening the diet is to allow something to become visible that otherwise remains invisible—

namely, how one's assumptions regarding what *must* be the case are in the thrall of a philosophical preconception. The preconception funnels one's attention onto only those aspects of the phenomena that one antecedently expects to find. One takes oneself already to know what one would find if one were to look and see; and the one-sided diet confirms these antecedent expectations. So far, so good. This dimension of Wittgenstein's later thinking has not been neglected. But the character of its reception has itself been subject to a certain partiality—or one-sidedness. The topic that matters here is taken to be the following: how one-sidedness in diet can blind one to certain philosophical temptations, thereby constraining one's appreciation of the sort of thing that a philosophical temptation is and what its overcoming might involve. But an appreciation of this sort cannot be had apart from another; and this complementary dimension of Wittgenstein's later thinking has remained comparatively neglected.

Just as there is, throughout Wittgenstein's later writing, an alternation between a voice of philosophical temptation and a voice of philosophical correction; so, too, there is a concern with a danger of merely exchanging one sort of false conception (fed by a premature temptation to insist) for another (fed by a premature insistence that the temptation be silenced). It is the relation between these twin dangers—and how each can feed on and sustain the other—that the choreography of the alternation of voices in the later writing is in part designed to help bring to a reader's awareness.[70] Commentary on Wittgenstein's later writings has tended to be far less sensitive to his efforts to forestall this second form of partiality in our philosophical thinking in which (nurtured by a false confidence that we have seen to the bottom of the problems) we take ourselves to stand ready to discharge the task of philosophical correction. At the level of reading the text, what goes neglected therefore are the equally numerous warnings in Wittgenstein's later writings issued against the dangers of nurturing one's conception of philosophical correction on the complementary sort of one-sided diet. Part of the point of broadening one's diet in this regard is again to allow something to become visible that might otherwise remain invisible.

Only now what needs to come into view is, first, something about the character of Wittgenstein's later writing, and, second, something about us—his readers—in our approach to the text. What needs to come into view first is the partiality of the many attempts in the text on the part of the voice of correction to silence its interlocutor, and how utterly these efforts to attain philosophical closure are shown (in the subsequent development of the text) to fail to bring the philosophical dialectic to an end. What needs to come into view, second, is how our conception of the activity of correction itself can suffer from no less damaging forms of partiality and blindness than any it seeks to undo. For a false preconception of what is involved in the task of philo-sophical clarification also funnels our attention—now onto only those aspects of Wittgenstein's efforts to avoid false conceptions that we antecedently expect to find in the text. What is needed now is something that might be able to show us that we are self-deluded in our belief that we already stand fully oriented with respect both to what the successful prosecution of philosophical criticism itself requires and to what later Wittgenstein thought it required. This suggests that much might be gained if only we could place Wittgenstein's practice of his later activity of philosophical clar-ification alongside the practice of another—one that closely resembles it in some ways, yet differs from it in just the ways required to help highlight that which is signifi-cantly new in the new way of prosecuting the task. The difference between the two would serve to bring into greater relief aspects of the later activity that we do not notice because we take ourselves already to have the character of that activity prop-erly in view. So what is required here is a very special sort of object of comparison (i.e., an exemplification of a strikingly similar yet profoundly different practice of philosophical clarification)—something that it is not easy to come by.

3   Lop-Sided Reading

It should be evident that we can now bring together our two previous topics: the topic of that which was to be bound together and that of partiality or one-sidedness in one's approach specifically to Wittgenstein's later philosophy. Our discussion of the latter led us to see how a certain tone-deafness in one's parsing of the voices in Wittgen-stein's text can distort one's appreciation of how the clarification of the problems therein is to proceed, thereby constraining one's very conception of wherein that activity consists and what its prosecution might involve. This, of course, suggests a reason for placing the *Tractatus* in the first half of a single volume. But in order for that early practice of philosophical clarification to be "placed" (in the sense of that term at issue) alongside the later, we must avoid the danger of allowing our view of it, too, to be merely refracted through the lens of our false conception of the later work. This, of course, is a danger that attends the employment of any object of com-parison in philosophical elucidation: rather than seeing the old examples from the perspective afforded by the intended object of comparison, we see the latter only through the distorting lens of the picture that has been nurtured through our pro-longed commerce with the former. So, too, with the two halves of the bound volume: if we merely bring our antecedent partial conception of the later work to bear on the early work, eagerly setting about to right it of (what we take to be) its wrongs, we deprive ourselves of an encounter with it (and the tremendous originality of its own conception of philosophical clarification)—thereby depriving it of its intended force as a potentially instructive object of comparison. If this is right, that is, if the overcoming of a certain partiality in our reading of the later work is to be overcome in part through our coming to see wherein the genuine (as opposed to the standardly supposed) partiality of the earlier work lies, then we run the risk of missing both in missing either.

This is a good moment to cast a glance at the form that standard book-length treatments of Wittgenstein often assume.[71] What such a glance, if appropriately directed, can bring to light is a kind of damage that Wittgenstein's teaching has been made to suffer in the course of its ongoing putative dissemination—a kind of damage that is wrought by a lopsided approach to reading Wittgenstein's work. What I have in mind here is a kind of approach in which the old way of thinking is viewed through the lens of the new to such a degree that the reader is no longer able to recover any independent view of the former. It is this approach to reading Wittgenstein (and the conception of the relation between the early and the later work that it engenders) that leaves those who are attached to it with the impression that resolute readers have left themselves with no room for a story that accords his later criticisms of his early work an appropriately severe weight. If we think of the book that Wittgenstein wished to publish (through binding its two halves into the single volume with one set of covers) as a *Bildungsroman*, then the following mostly seems to be true of the literary criticism to which it has been subjected: the beginning of the story is always read by those who have done much more than just peek ahead to the later chapters, thereby running the risk of depriving themselves of an experience of *a first reading* of the novel (and hence of a kind of reading of the later chapters that depends upon a nonretrospective understanding of the earlier chapters). Readings of the early work tend to be controlled by antecedently determined conceptions of how the story is supposed to come out, gleaned from perusing critical remarks about it in the later work prior to properly attempting to encounter it on its own terms.

In the guise of introducing us to the teaching of the *Tractatus*, the aforementioned book-length treatments of his thought typically begin by displaying a set of philosophical views that are simultaneously supposed to represent (1) the central doctrines that the author of the *Tractatus* aims to establish as true and (2) the central doctrines that the author of the *Investigations* aims to overthrow. Many of the views thus displayed are ones that a resolute reader would wish to include on the first list (i.e., a list of targets that early and later Wittgenstein share); whereas in these book-length treatments, the overriding aim is to exhibit substitution-instances of the doctrinal schema ("early Wittgenstein believes p and later Wittgenstein believes *not-p*"), where much more than just the bare outline of the schema has already been decided upon prior to a proper encounter with the early work.[72] For a resolute reader the way in which much that is notably new first emerges on the scene with the advent of Wittgenstein's new way of thinking cannot come into view through such a partial approach to the old way of thinking. Yet if these are the only materials that one has at one's disposal out of which to construct a narrative about how the new way of thinking represents a break from the old, then it is little wonder that one ends up with a story according to which, even if the answers in the earlier book were wrong, the questions were not.

4   A First Sort of Indiscriminateness

From the point of view of a resolute reader, the distortion wrought by these standard book-length treatments of Wittgenstein's thought goes well beyond a mere mistaking of the role that the sort of item that belongs on the first list is intended to play in the dialectical strategy of the *Tractatus*. For these books tend indiscriminately to lump together items of this sort with a whole variety of other sorts. There is a range of different sorts of indiscriminateness in play in these narratives. We will consider two of these—the first here and the second in the next section of this paper. Both sorts are largely due to the determination of commentators to fit most of the philosophical topics present in either of the two (usually separately bound) books into a single nexus of unity—namely, that of the doctrinal schema. What the remainder of this paper will try to show is that this can lead to misunderstandings, not only of the philosophical aspirations of the early work, but equally of those of the later work. For in underestimating the philosophical achievement of the early work, one underestimates the depth at which the investigations in the later work are pitched.

The first sort of indiscriminateness has to do with the first cost of an overeagerness to display eventual targets of the later thought: a failure to distinguish at all carefully between what is central and what is peripheral to the concerns of the *Tractatus*. I will confine myself here to furnishing one sample of the first sort of indiscriminateness. In the early chapters, devoted ostensibly to the *Tractatus*, in the aforementioned book-length treatments of Wittgenstein, there prominently figure (introduced so that they can subsequently serve as targets for the putatively new way of thinking inaugurated by the *Investigations*) mentalistic doctrines of a sort that do not figure prominently in the *Tractatus* itself. Insofar as such doctrines surface at all in that text, they do so *en passant* and always only as objects of criticism. Their relative lack of prominence is tied in part to the ways in which the author of the *Tractatus* took "the great works of Frege"[73] already to have largely disposed of doctrines of this sort (in particular, through his various critiques of psychologism).[74] Although early Wittgenstein's attitude toward such forms of mentalism is not easily reconstructed from a study of the text of the *Tractatus* alone, a proper understanding of his attitude toward them there is not unimportant to the task of properly entering into the spirit of his early thought. But all hope of properly orienting oneself in the text is lost if one's reading of the *Tractatus* is guided by the assumption that the sorts of philosophical doctrine that lie most ready to hand as objects of criticism in the opening sections of the *Investigations*[75] must *therefore* figure among the central doctrines of the early work.[76] Once this sort of distortion is corrected for in one's reading of the early work, the following sort of question can acquire a commendable urgency: why is it that certain doctrines apparently deemed sufficiently confused to warrant a role only on the outer periphery of the target range of the *Tractatus* later come to be positioned so close to the center of the target range of the *Investigations*? To understand this, we must better understand why later Wittgenstein comes to think that philosophical criticism needs to start at a much earlier point than the author of the *Tractatus* ever did. We will return to this topic in section IX.

VII   Unwitting Commitments

[The infidel scholar begins to wax esoteric. He claims to be able to find buried doctrines in The Old Testament. *This apparently requires that we look beyond the mere letter of the text to something like the spirit in which it was written or revealed. The main points of the two sections here seem to be as follows: (1) The Church Fathers are to be castigated for not having detected these hidden doctrines—the fact that they were buried apparently is no excuse for having failed to noticed them. Our author tries to show that the presence of these buried doctrines in* The Old Testament *clears the members of his sect of the most serious charge that the authorities of the Church have brought against them—namely, their failure to acknowledge the Miracle of the Recantation. (2) Finally, it is explained that it is only with the aid of these doctrines that a full interpretation of* The New Testament *may finally now be attempted.—J. C.]*

1   A Second Sort of Indiscriminateness

Moving now to the opposite end of the spectrum, let us turn to a very different sort of indiscriminateness that a resolute reader may be pained to find in standard book-length treatments of Wittgenstein's thought. As we saw in section III, standard readers take there to be substantive doctrines that the *Tractatus* fully aims to espouse, even if it cannot express them (because they are ineffable); and it is just these doctrines that they take the later Wittgenstein, in his criticisms of his earlier self, to be centrally concerned to criticize. And we also saw that resolute readers take there to be *no doctrines* of this sort that the *Tractatus* wittingly *aims to espouse*. The two italicized phrases in this last sentence furnish a pair of clues as to how a resolute reader might wish to understand at least one aspect of the discontinuity between the old and new ways of thinking. If we follow out the suggestion that comes from combining these two clues, we arrive at the following formulation—one that allows us to see how the incredulous question may fail to hit its mark:

Any philosophical commitments that Wittgenstein is later concerned to criticize in his old way of thinking are moments in it of a sort that his old self would have been unable to recognize as sufficiently contentious to require special vindication—let alone vindication through the activity of constructive philosophical theorizing (i.e., the sort of activity that it is the whole point of Tractarian elucidation to supplant).

I will henceforth refer to such moments in the *Tractatus* as "unwitting commitments." To say that they are *unwitting* commitments is to say that the author of the work would not have been prepared, at that time, to see them as open to challenge: they are not in view for him *as* commitments. To say that each of them is an unwitting *commitment* is to say that the author of the work is nonetheless committed to (1) there being something intelligible to think along the lines represented by each, and to (2) affirming in each case the truth of what is thereby thought. As we shall see, the crucial problem arises here, for the author of the *Tractatus*, not so much in his entitlement to (2)—as it might for other authors—but rather already in his entitlement to (1). To make any one of these commitments fully explicit is already to bring our author into conflict with himself.

In the next section of this paper, I will attempt to specify some of these unwitting commitments in the form of a list—as a means of introducing the concept of the second list. Once the possibility of such a list is firmly in view, it should be conceded that a resolute reader is able to accord a central place in his reading of the later work to its criticisms of the early work. This brings us to the second sort of indiscriminateness (on the part of all standard readers and some resolute readers): the failure to distinguish between the items that belong on the first list (merely apparent commitments) and those that belong on the second list (unwitting commitments).

A brief sketch of an example of how on a resolute reading there can be room for unwitting commitments in the *Tractatus* is perhaps in order here.[77] According to most resolute readers, the Tractarian activity of elucidation employs the tools of logical notation in order to clarify propositions. Sentences are to be translated into this notation. The outward appearance of the signs employed by the notation is designed to correlate with the symbolic structure of the proposition. The task of translating our sentences into such a notation requires that we attain clarity about what it is that we want to say with our words.[78] The *Tractatus* holds that, prior to the translation of a meaningful proposition into such a carefully designed notation, the real logical

structure of the proposition is not easy to gather from its appearance—it remains
hidden beneath the outward (surface-syntactical) clothing in which it is wrapped in
ordinary language. If a sentence is successfully transposed into the notation, then the
logical structure of the proposition is brought to the surface, where it can now lie perspicuously open to view. According to resolute readers, if we are to take the avowed
aim of the early work seriously, then it is essential to appreciate that a commitment
to the employment of such notation does not itself constitute part of a doctrine about
anything for the author of the *Tractatus*. He saw the significance of the notation as
resting upon (not some bit of philosophical theory purporting to establish its significance, but rather) its use.[79] Its significance as a tool of clarification was to be demonstrated through its practical application in the context of the activity of making the
philosophical problems completely disappear. The notation would expose the nature
of our confusion and would help to lay bare when we had only apparently conferred
a determinate method of symbolizing on our signs. The proof of its value would lie
in the pudding of its results. Not only was it not to rest upon a philosophical theory,
it was supposed to help wean us from our attachment to such theories.

But it is also open to resolute readers to hold that there were, underlying the author
of the *Tractatus*'s understanding of the efficacy of this elucidatory tool, latent philosophical commitments that he himself failed to uncover and interrogate—commitments of a sort that will figure on the second list—such as that there are essential
features of language, that they can be captured by such a notation, that they otherwise remain hidden, that their mode of presentation in such a notation allows the
true structure of our thought to lie directly open to view, and so forth. So a resolute
reader may, on the one hand, respect the avowed aim of the work, claiming each of
the following three things (regarding the early understanding of the practice of philosophical clarification) and holding that early Wittgenstein himself attached great
importance to each: (1) that the employment of such a notation did not require its
employer ever to *say* anything about the logic of our language, (2) that part of the
point of mastering such a notation was to demonstrate that the sentences to which
we are attracted in philosophy (ones that apparently do say something about the logic
of our language) can be shown not to say anything, precisely by our coming to see
that there is no way to translate them into the notation, and (3) that such a mastery
of the notation itself allows the logic of our language to be shown (without anything
"about" it ever having to be said), thereby enabling us to attain a clear grasp of the
logic of our language through our attaining a clear view of what we do say when we
employ language meaningfully. A resolute reader may also, on the other hand, account
for Wittgenstein's later criticisms of his early self by claiming each of the following

three further things (regarding early Wittgenstein's understanding of the significance of the notation thus employed), while holding that early Wittgenstein himself attached no importance to these things because they were invisible to him: (1) that this understanding itself carried unwitting commitments along with it, (2) that this, in turn, colored his conception of what is revealed by the notation, and (3) that this imported a philosophically nontrivial set of conceptions regarding what logic, language, and clarity themselves are.

A resolute reader therefore need in no way be committed to the idea that Wittgenstein's own self-understanding of what he was doing in the *Tractatus* is unmistaken. Such a reader need only be committed to the view that if we want to understand what the author of the *Tractatus* thought he was up to (at the time of writing the book), then we need to be clear about the terms of that original self-understanding. But claiming this is perfectly consistent with maintaining that that self-understanding proved to be, in various respects, deluded. If resolute readers are perfectly free to ascribe misconceptions to early Wittgenstein, then this means that the following is far too coarse-grained a question to allow for a division of readers into those who are resolute and those who are not: Are there important differences between early and later Wittgenstein? As is this question: Did later Wittgenstein regard the author of the *Tractatus* as committed to problematic metaphysical theses?[80] What question will effect a proper division? We already know that this question divides them: Did the author of the *Tractatus* understand himself (rightly or wrongly) to have found a way to do philosophy that eschews any commitment to a metaphysical thesis? But merely having this question in view does not permit a formulation of the significant differences that separate commentators when what is at issue is a proper understanding of the relation between the author of the *Tractatus* and that of the *Philosophical Investigations*.[81]

2   Reading the New in the Light of the Old

The unwitting commitments matter here. What can be hard to understand is how the author of the *Tractatus* could have been able to view everything in his philosophical work through them and yet have been unable to see these commitments themselves as being in the slightest degree weighty—let alone see them, as he later did, as coming heavily laden with philosophical freight. This *is* difficult to understand. But not to be able to understand this is not only to fail fully to understand the *Tractatus*; it is to fail fully to understand the *Investigations* (and, above all, those sections of the *Philosophical Investigations* centrally concerned with the criticism of the author of the *Tractatus Logico-Philosophicus*). For the difficulty of understanding this feature of how things looked to the author of the *Tractatus Logico-Philosophicus* is internally related to the difficulty of understanding a central aspect of the teaching of the *Philosophical Investigations*. The prefatory remark asks us to view the *Investigations* against the uniquely illuminating background afforded by the *Tractatus*. This requires that we be able to view the later work through the lens of the earlier (and not just the other way around).[82] As we have seen above, most contemporary Wittgenstein scholars are drawn to read the pair of works together in, as it were, a single direction, taking their point of departure in Wittgenstein's work from the new way of thinking and working their way back to the old. Because they are thus drawn to view the *Tractatus* through the lens of the *Investigations*, it has become singularly difficult for them to imagine their way back into anything like early Wittgenstein's original position.[83] This requires, above all, coming to appreciate what would have struck him as philosophically contentious and what would have struck him as merely obvious—the kind of thing to which (if one were to happen upon the peculiar idea of attempting to advance it in the guise of a thesis) everyone ought to agree.

If there are weighty philosophical commitments that later Wittgenstein is concerned to criticize in his old way of thinking that his earlier self would have been unable to recognize as such at the time of writing the *Tractatus*, then these will be the ones that readers comparatively better versed in Wittgenstein's later work will be least competent to separate out and properly assess (namely, as ones that possessed the peculiar sort of weightlessness that they did for the author of the *Tractatus*). As connoisseurs of the *Investigations*, it may, of course, be all too easy for them to pick out just these commitments as ones that are deemed by later Wittgenstein to be of great portent and thus evidently somehow important to a proper philosophical treatment of the *Tractatus*. But if they are always readers of the *Investigations* first and only readers of the *Tractatus* second, then they will be unable to appreciate the surreptitious role that these commitments play in holding up the edifice of the early philosophy. On the contrary, as disciples of the *Investigations*, they may be all too eager to regard these commitments as necessarily portentous and thereby fall into the error of assuming that they must have seemed no less portentous to the author of the *Tractatus*. They will therefore see these not just as commitments present in the *Tractatus* but as ones *undertaken*. This is primarily what occasions the second form of indiscriminateness: these readers will be happy to include sentences giving voice to such commitments on a single list together with the many other sorts of sentence they are inclined to lump together under the single broad heading: Doctrines the Author of the *Tractatus* Aims to Establish and the Author of the *Investigations* Aims to Overthrow. From the point of view of some resolute readers (including this one), such readers of Wittgenstein not only thereby conflate the varieties of role that different kinds of moment of philosophical reflection play in the *Tractatus* but they show themselves therein to be unable to exercise a form of discrimination essential to an appreciation of how Wittgenstein's old way of thinking bears on his new and vice versa.

We earlier touched on the topic of a lop-sided approach to reading Wittgenstein. This approach can be seen to exact an additional cost here. For the achievement of any degree of appreciation of some of the central lessons of the later work involves nothing if not a cultivation of an exquisite degree of sensitivity to just how philosophically momentous and altogether noninnocuous precisely these unwitting commitments are.[84] Yet much of the point of these later lessons will be missed, if one tries to assimilate them without having acquired some antecedent sense of how someone as hell-bent on avoiding philosophical theses as the author of the *Tractatus* could have persisted in viewing commitments such as these as philosophically innocuous. Indeed, some of the sorts of misunderstanding that we have just touched upon (that flow from the aforementioned one-sided approach to reading the *Investigations*) are arguably part of what Wittgenstein hoped to forestall through the prefatory remark.

We are now in a position to bring a number of points together. The criticisms of the very idea of a resolute reading that have hitherto concerned us in this paper (from the basic initial question to the complaint of the incredulous inquirer) rest upon a failure to get any of the following five things a resolute reader may hold into focus: (1) that a commitment to resolution does not preclude a reader of the *Tractatus* from distinguishing between items that belong on the first list (i.e., apparently substantive commitments that are to be discharged as merely illusory) and those that belong on the second list (i.e., undischarged commitments that are unwittingly retained as such), (2) that a proper reading of the *Tractatus* requires an appreciation of how the unwitting commitments can persist in the face of the avowed aim, (3) that such an appreciation is something that the *Philosophical Investigation* aims to impart, (4) that therefore a proper appreciation of both the unwitting commitments of the *Tractatus* and the correlative teachings of the *Philosophical Investigation* requires that each of these works be read in the light of the other, and thus (5) that in the absence of a resolute reading of the early work something central to the teaching of the later work must go missing in our reading of it.

VIII   Another List

[Our author returns to making and seeing lists. (1) An actual list is presented in which each item on it is meant to correspond to one of the buried doctrines that the young Ludwig himself inexplicably failed to see at the time of his Vision of the Ladder. (2) Again, not content with a merely terrestrial list, the infidel

revives yet another apocryphal account of a vision, apparently also had by some nameless saint (possibly the same one as before, though there is also a suggestion that perhaps this vision was enjoyed by Ludwig himself after he returned from his wanderings in the desert). Some scholars, I believe, refer to this as The Vision of the Second List. *In any case, this second vision is, again, of a divine list. (3) Our author then becomes preoccupied with comparing these four lists, two actual and two spiritual. It turns out that each is quite different from the others. (4) We then return to issues in infidel dogmatics concerning the limits of the extent to which infidels are obliged to agree with one another, how their discussions ought to be conducted, and what to do about the zealots in the sect. Our author gives some hints as to why he himself favors a mild form of heterodoxy and finds zealotry distasteful. The larger point of the whole section seems to be that what is seen in* The Vision of the Second List *illuminates both why the Miracle of the Recantation transpired and why* The New Testament *had to be written.—J. C.]*

1 Another Actual List

Again, there are many possible variations on the actual list below that would have sufficed for our present purpose—though none of them is without its troubles. As we shall soon see, a reader constrained by nothing more than a bare commitment to resolution will encounter a variety of sorts of difficulty in trying to offer a specification of the unwitting commitments in anything that approximates the form of a list. Once again, the difficulties that arise here will be instructive in clarifying the sorts of philosophical and exegetical difficulty that must beset any attempt to offer anything approaching a resolute account of the relation between the thought of the early and that of the later Wittgenstein.[85]

Before we turn to the actual list below, it might help briefly to remind ourselves what sorts of moment in his early work are singled out for attention in Wittgenstein's later criticisms of it. Here is a representative passage that, I take it, attempts to summarize an aspect of how things looked to his early self at the time of writing the *Tractatus*:

But now it may come to look as if there were something like a final analysis of our forms of language, and so a *single* completely resolved form of expression. That is, as if our usual forms of expression were, essentially, unanalysed; as if there were something hidden in them that had to be brought to light. When this is done the expression is completely clarified and our problem solved.

It can also be put like this: we eliminate misunderstandings by making our expressions more exact; but now it may look as if we were moving towards a particular state, a state of complete exactness; and as if this were the real goal of our investigation.[86]

This is a characterization of how things came to look to the author of the *Tractatus* at the time of writing that book. It is a characterization of some of the implicit philosophical preconceptions that came with his earlier practice of eliminating misunderstandings by subjecting the sentences that occasioned them to his earlier procedures of interrogation—preconceptions regarding what must be involved in the prosecution of such an activity for eliminating philosophical perplexities (that it must involve, e.g., a transition from a state of comparative inexactness in our mastery of language to a state of complete exactness in which our relation to our words and their essential possibilities of meaning can be laid completely bare and open to direct view). The target in this passage therefore is not the set of items that figure on the first list—the philosophical doctrines that (resolute readers must hold) already figured as candidates for dissolution through the activity of clarification in the *Tractatus*. Rather the target here (resolute readers may hold) is the undissolved metaphysical residue that came with his early understanding of what such an activity must itself involve (an uncovering of hidden structure) and the (exact and essential) character of that which is thus brought to light.

Again, rather than specifying the commitments here at issue by picking out swatches of text drawn from the *Tractatus* in the form of particular quotations, I do so again, on the actual list below, by specifying particular preconceptions about how things must be that figure centrally in the book and to which any sensitive reader of the *Investigations* cannot help but attach importance—only now what are at issue are philosophical conceptions from which the author of the *Tractatus* failed to wean himself (rather than, as before, ones from which he attempts to wean his reader). Again, this procedure will allow us to achieve a higher degree of clarity and generality in specifying the relevant sorts of commitment than would be possible if we confined ourselves to the letter of their manifestations in the text. The need for such a procedure, with respect to the items on this list, is even greater than with the previous list because (though some figure fairly explicitly in the text) many of the relevant commitments are incurred in a relatively oblique, peripheral, implicit, or otherwise indirect fashion, and several are, as it were, textually off-stage. So, with these provisos in mind, I offer the following candidate formulations of some of the unwitting commitments:

1. The logical relations of our thoughts to each other can be *completely* shown in an analysis of our propositions.
2. These relations can be displayed through the employment of a logically *absolutely* perspicuous notation.
3. Through the employment of such a notation, it is possible for propositions to be rewritten in such a way that the logical relations are *all* clearly visible.
4. A proposition *must* be complex.[87]
5. *Every* proposition can be analyzed.[88]
6. Logical analysis will reveal *every* proposition to be either an elementary proposition or the result of truth-operations on elementary propositions.

7. *All* inference is truth-functional.

8. There is *only one* logical space and everything that can be said or thought forms a part of that space.

9. There is such a thing as *the* logical order of our language.

10. Antecedent to logical analysis, there must be this logical order—one that is *already there* awaiting discovery—and it is the role of logical analysis to uncover it.

11. By rewriting them in such a notation, *what* propositions our propositions are will become clear.[89]

12. By rewriting them in this way, it will also become clear what *all* propositions have in common.

13. There is a general form of proposition and *all* propositions have this form.

14. In its thus becoming clear what propositions are, it will also become clear how misleading their appearances are—how much the outward form *disguises* the real *hidden* logical structure.

15. A logically perspicuous notation is *the* essential tool of philosophical clarification.

16. Through our inability to translate them into *the* notation, despite their resemblance in outward form to genuine propositions, certain strings of signs can be unmasked as nonsense, that is, as strings of signs to which no determinate meaning has been given.

17. *All* philosophical confusions can be clarified in this way.

18. By demonstrating the significance of this tool and its application in the activity of clarification, the problems of philosophy have *in essentials* been finally solved.

Each item above is associated with something that a resolute reader may hold that the author of the *Tractatus* (1) was committed to (given his conception of how philosophical elucidation proceeds and the role that a perspicuous logical notion must play in it), (2) would not have taken to be in any way inconsistent with his aspiration to eliminate metaphysics (by means of an activity in which no philosophical theses are propounded), and (3) would not have taken to be a contentious theoretical commitment (let alone one that was somehow peculiarly his).

2 The Second List

As with "the first list," the expression "the second list" will not serve its intended purpose here if defined through an enumeration of some actual items in some definite order—say, the items on the actual list above in the order given. The actual list above is of examples of candidate formulations of philosophical commitments that underlay the conception advanced in the *Tractatus* of how the activity of philosophical clarification ought to proceed. The point of furnishing such a sample of candidates is to attempt to gesture at the sorts of thing that might be held by a resolute reader to belong on the second list. To say that an item belongs on the second list is to say that it is the sort of thing that a resolute reader ought to hold is to be counted among the unwitting commitments retained by the author of the *Tractatus*. As we shall see, there is plenty of room for disagreement about what ought thus to be counted.

3 Comparing Lists

The point of the first actual list was to bring out how the doctrinal schema distorts our understanding both of the avowed aim and the avowed method of early Wittgenstein's philosophy, thereby occluding important moments of continuity between his old and his new ways of thinking. The moment of continuity in aim is to find a way to do philosophy that does not consist in putting forward philosophical theses. The moment of continuity in method is to specify a series of steps that a reader can take that will allow her to pass from a state of philosophical perplexity to one of clarity in which the philosophical problems completely disappear. A proper arrangement of the items on the first list would be a specification of how the early method is to achieve the aim. The point of the second actual list is to bring out how, within an acknowledgement of these overarching moments of continuity, due weight can be given to the incessant effort on Wittgenstein's part in his later writing to purge himself of (what he evidently took to be) the deeply rooted philosophical misconceptions of his earlier self. The second actual list thereby attempts to illustrate the extent to which, from the standpoint of his later thinking, there was an entire metaphysics of language tacitly embodied in his earlier method of clarification.

It is instructive to notice how many of the questions that were of concern in connection with the first list have no application in regard to the second. Let's first consider questions regarding the shape of the list. We saw before that questions about how properly to understand the philosophical dialectic in the *Tractatus* were related to questions about how to arrange items on the first list. One's understanding of the book could be sharpened through reflection on which items should come comparatively earlier and which comparatively later on the first list. Such reflection can no longer pay the same dividend when it comes to the second list. *We* can give it a shape. But there is nothing which is *the* shape it had for the author or was *meant* to have for a reader of the *Tractatus*. The philosophical preconceptions which figure as separate numbered items on the actual list above certainly do form a kind of unity—to hold any one is naturally to begin to slide into holding many of the others. But, as long as all of the items on it properly belong on that list, not much sense is to be made of the following question: which ones did the author of the *Tractatus* take to be comparatively primitive and which comparatively derived? In this respect, the linearly ordered structure of a list is no longer really apposite here, and some other arrangement (a circle?) would serve better.

The whole point of the second list is that all the items on it figure as equally primitive in his thinking. And this means: once one goes about making such a list and begins to see how long it can become, one begins to see how much hidden dogmatism there is in the book. To see some of these items as requiring derivation from the others would be to allow at least some of them to come into view as the sort of thing (1) to which one may not yet be entitled since a nontrivial commitment is incurred, (2) to which one can then labor to vindicate one's entitlement, and (3) to which one can then have acquired entitlement (having successfully discharged that labor). Wittgenstein's later criticism of his early self (insofar as it pertains to those aspects of his old way of thinking that correspond to items on the second list) is not directed at instances of step (2) or step (3) in this thinking, but at his inability even to get to step (1). This is not to say that there is no point in arranging things on the second list.[90] It is only to say that there is no point in asking the following: which arrangement, from the point of view of the author of the *Tractatus*, is a placing of items in the right order? To allow the items in question to come into view on an understanding of each that coherently admits of such a question regarding its relation to the others is to have them in view for oneself in a way that they were never in view for him.

Now let's consider the sort of issues that invited the employment of a parenthetical notation in the representation of the first of our two actual lists. No parentheses occur in the second actual list. But, more to the point, parentheses cannot play the role here that they did formerly. (Instead we now find a different form of notation for which no need was felt formerly: the italics.) What is at issue in the first actual list are commitments that for the author of the work are merely apparently substantive (though for the reader they can only gradually come clearly into view as such); whereas what is at issue now in the second actual list are commitments that are neither merely apparent nor philosophically innocuous (though for the author they cannot come clearly into view as simultaneously neither). With the first actual list, at many junctures, an item on it could have been replaced with something that had the form of its logical opposite, without threatening its candidacy for inclusion. Recall the main respect in which the first actual list differed from a standard reader's list. For standard readers, logically incompatible propositions crowded one another out as candidate items because they were to be associated with genuine (albeit ineffable) *insights* into the nature of thought, language, and reality, and their negations were to be associated with denials of those insights. For resolute readers, (apparently) opposed items did not crowd one another out as candidates for inclusion on the first list since they were all equally to be associated with merely *apparent* insights into the nature of thought, language, and reality— all equally to be overcome. In this respect the items on a resolute reader's version of the second list resemble those on a standard reader's version of the first list: in both cases, the negations of the items on the list do not belong.[91] Any alternative understanding of the items on the actual second list above (that would admit of their negations also being placed on the list) would threaten the underlying conception of *the* logic of our language (that underwrites the logically perspicuous forms of notation upon which the activity of Tractarian elucidation relies). This conception requires that there be a significant asymmetry for the author of the *Tractatus* between the items on the second list and their negations (and hence between the items on the second list and those on the first)—an asymmetry that his understanding of the activity of philosophical clarification both requires and to which it cannot be entitled.

Tremendously delicate questions attach to the issue of where one should draw the line between the first and second lists. The line cannot be a bright one. These questions become particularly evident if one considers any of items 5, 6, 12, 13, or 17— items in which the surface form of the proposition already strongly suggests that what must be at issue is an attempt to quantify over *all* (possible) propositions—a fairly reliable (though not surefire)[92] telltale surface-syntactical sign, by the lights of the author of the *Tractatus*, that no determinate method of symbolizing has been conferred on a propositional sign. And many of the other items have surface-syntactical forms that bespeak a corresponding aspiration to attain such an apparently maximal degree of quantificational generality—an appearance characteristic of many of the merely apparently meaningful sentences that constitute rungs on the ladder. So, once explicitly formulated (as a self-standing set of mutually self-supporting commitments) and collectively exhibited (as a list of commitments expressed in propositional form), it is difficult to see how the resulting sentences could escape a sustained encounter with Tractarian elucidatory procedures with their pretensions to intelligibility unscathed.[93] Having achieved a full appreciation of the unsustainably fragile character of the items on the second list, there are two options open to a resolute reader at this point. The first is for her to take this as evidence that these items do not belong on the second list at all, but rather on the first list (and hence that there is no second list). The second is for her to take this as evidence that the author of the *Tractatus* was remarkably able to blind himself to the character of the apparent commitments here incurred. As we shall see in the next section of this paper, there is good reason to think she will only be able to make sense of the author of the *Investigations* (and his criticisms of the author of the *Tractatus*) if she takes the second option.

4 Mild, Severe, and Zealous Mono-Wittgensteinians

The differences between the first and second lists explored immediately above relate to clarifying how resolute readers may attach a kind of significance to the items that occur on the second list that standard readers cannot. The differences between the first and second lists explored immediately below relate to clarifying how resolute readers may thus differ from one another—differences that the mere shared commitment to resolution does not suffice to resolve. As with the first list, the proper demarcation of the second list turns on the proper resolution of these differences, and the concept of it relates to the topic over which these readers differ.

So we are now in a position to return to the matter that was left hanging at the end of our discussion of the first list: namely, why it is that, even if resolute readers agree about the items now on the first actual list, they are likely to differ over how it ought to be continued? For any quarrel about what properly belongs on the second list (and, as it were, how short it is) is, at one and the same time, a quarrel about the first list (and, as it were, how long it is) and vice versa. For, in this intramural contest between resolute readers, moving something off the second list usually means moving it onto the first. This internal connection between the topics of the two quarrels notwithstanding, the one over the second list is in some respects of a very different sort than the previous one, as we shall now see.

Their shared commitment to resolution requires of resolute readers that they agree on the following point: there are things that belong on the first list, including most of what is ascribed to the *Tractatus* by standard readers. Their shared commitment to resolution does not, however, oblige them to agree on this point: there are things that belong on the second list. Some resolute readers may wish to place (perhaps along with many others) *all* of the items on the actual list immediately above on to the second list; some may wish to place only a *few* of these on to it (perhaps along with a few others, moving the rest to the first list); and some may wish to place *none* there, holding that a proper understanding of the *Tractatus* requires that all apparent candidates for the second list are only merely apparent candidates and, before the end of the day is reached, are to be sucked back onto the first list.[94] These possible differences in how a resolute reading is to be filled out correspond to positions along a spectrum of degrees of mono-Wittgensteinianism. The longer the second list: the milder the mono-Wittgensteinianism. The shorter: the more severe. If the second list shrinks to the point of vanishing into thin air, the degree of mono-Wittgensteinianism threatens to become toxic, inasmuch as it would appear to leave the resolute reader in question vulnerable to the basic initial question and thereby open not only to Disapproval (as any resolute reader must be) but also to Incredulity (as no resolute reader as such need be).[95]

Let us call a resolute reader who holds that there are no unwitting commitments in the *Tractatus* a "zealous" (as opposed to a merely "mild" or a comparatively "severe") mono-Wittgensteinian.[96] We need to be clear about what the mild, severe, and zealous interpreters are in disagreement about. The question that distributes them across a spectrum of comparative degrees of severity is one that we encountered at the end of our discussion of the first list: how many of the aspects of the underlying conception of the activity of philosophical elucidation (which the *Tractatus* seeks to practice and into which it seeks to initiate its reader) themselves constitute rungs of the ladder that we are eventually meant to throw away? A zealous interpreter maintains that the entire underlying conception of the activity is brought to implode on itself: everything on the second actual list is not only the product of a succumbing to philosophical temptation but also self-consciously put forward by the author as something that is to be recognized as such by his reader. It is only with this last clause that the moment of difference between the zealous and mild interpreters is broached, as their disagreement is not about the *de re* standing of the commitments of the author of the *Tractatus*. On the contrary, a main part of the point of mild mono-Wittgensteinianism is to be able to make sense of later Wittgenstein's efforts to dissolve the philosophical preconceptions that give rise to the unwitting commitments.[97]

Now how can the mild and zealous interpreters make progress in their conversation with one another? A bare commitment to resolution does not represent a principle to which any party in such an intramural squabble can appeal. But it does introduce an important constraint on how the squabble is to be adjudicated. Here is the basis of the constraint: if resolution requires a piecemeal understanding of how elucidation proceeds (as I have argued it must), then there ought not to be any *wholesale* way to dispose of the second list by collapsing into the first. For such a wholesale determination would require the reintroduction of a set of substantive criteria for determining what is (and what is not) nonsense. The constraint on adjudication therefore is the following: the mild and zealous interpreters' differences over how to implement their shared program for reading the *Tractatus* can be resolved only by turning it into a reading of the book that is no longer in the slightest degree programmatic.[98] A resolute *program* for reading the book must be transformed into (i.e., completely spelled out as) a detailed reading of the book before it is in a position to demonstrate which

apparent commitments are actually discharged and which (if any) are not. Her demurral from this constraint does not license a zealous interpreter to wrap herself in a
mantle of purity and declare herself to be the more faithful adherent of a formerly
shared resolute conception of how to read the *Tractatus*. Correlatively, it is not a
demurral that can entitle her to view the mild mono-Wittgensteinian as somehow
backsliding on the original ground of their agreement.[99] On the contrary, denying the
constraint is itself a form of backsliding—in particular, one of falling back into the
basic mistake of the standard reading: namely, imagining that there is some criterion
through which, or Archimedean point from which, the collective nonsensicality of
the sentences in the book can, in advance of our interrogating them individually,
simultaneously be ascertained. The only way the zealous mono-Wittgensteinian can
be entitled to declare herself the victor in this squabble is by furnishing a detailed
reconstruction of the entire dialectic of the *Tractatus*—demonstrating, step by step,
how and where in an ascent up the ladder each of the (putatively merely apparently)
"unwitting" commitments comes to be dissolved. A declaration of victory in this
dispute in the absence of the provision of such a full reading would simply be a gesture
of dogmatism.

This has a bearing on the terminology that I am seeking to introduce here. The
terms "mild," "severe," and "zealous" can only be taken to distinguish degrees of
resoluteness if one is fundamentally confused about what a commitment to resolution as such involves. The bare idea of resolution requires the following: if there are
undischarged philosophical commitments in the book, then they are unwitting. There
is nothing in the bare idea of resolution, however, that either requires or precludes
that we accept or deny the antecedent of that conditional.[100] So the threefold distinction introduced here between mild, severe, and zealous is a distinction along a
spectrum of degrees not of resoluteness but of mono-Wittgensteinianism.[101]

We saw above that it is only on a misunderstanding of what resolution requires that
a critic can take the bare existence of unsifted "external" evidence to be probative in
a case against resolute readings as such. But (regardless of what one thinks its standing is in a dispute between standard and resolute readers) such evidence, once sifted,
does threaten to become quite probative in the dispute between mild and zealous
interpreters of Wittgenstein. More to the point, the zealous alternative robs a resolute
reading of what strikes me as potentially its most significant contribution to an understanding of Wittgenstein's philosophy: namely, its capacity to illuminate why and how
the new way of thinking is best understood against the old and what sort of criticism
of the old way this is meant to involve.[102] This point, taken in isolation, is not dis-
positive.[103] Pending, however, the full implementation of a resolute program for inter-

preting the *Tractatus*, it seems to me that, at least with regard to this particular intramural dispute, the present balance of available evidence ("internal" and "external" taken together) tips more than mildly in favor of a mild mono-Wittgensteinianism.

IX   The Old Way of Thinking against the Background of the New

[We learn (1) about a kind of magic annotation of the text that can cause the buried doctrines in The Old Testament *to rise to the surface for all to behold, (2) how, according to the infidel reading of* The New Testament, *philosophical demons are to be exorcised, especially those that are released by the satanic ink employed to reveal the hidden doctrines of the Mosaic Law, (3) how the two Testaments are to be placed with respect to each other if one is so unfortunate as to have separately bound copies of each, and finally (4) about the infidel teachings regarding Moses himself, including a blasphemous suggestion that he perhaps did not exist. (An illusion here to the mysterious epigraph from Freud?)—J. C.]*

1   Why Italics (Instead of Parentheses)?

We saw above that there was no room (in specifying candidates for the second list) for the sort of parenthetical notation employed on the first actual list. The time has come to explain its successor: the notation of italics deployed on the second actual list. The inapplicability of the one sort of notation is internally related to the need for the other. The first sort of notation has no place because the commitments in question on the second list cannot be discarded as merely apparent. They must surreptitiously play a genuinely weight-bearing role in the elaboration of the early philosophy; and this means, for example, as we just saw, that their (putative) negations cannot join or replace them on the list. This raises the need for a form of notation in the specification of candidate items for the second list that highlights the logical or modal force of the commitment that would go missing in a complementary candidate item that sought to modify the modal dimension of the commitment—for example, by placing the relevant aspect of the commitment within the scope of a negation.

In the actual list above, the italicized expressions in each of the above sentences indicate the occurrence of a moment of (what would count by later Wittgenstein's lights as) *metaphysical insistence*—a moment in which a requirement is laid down. The feature of the items on this actual list that marks them out as the sort of thing that properly belongs on the second list is the way in which their insinuation of such a requirement escaped the notice of the author of the *Tractatus*. In some of these cases, the note of metaphysical insistence comes with an emphatic accenting of the italicized expression (such as "completely," "absolutely"); in others, the metaphysically emphatic note is already present (prior to any emphasis introduced by italicization) in the apparent modal force of the expressions themselves ("all," "every," "must"). So, in some cases, the role of the italics is to raise the note of insistence to a metaphysical register; in others, merely to highlight the presence of such a note. Thus, for example, if the italics were simply omitted from items 1 and 2 on the list and the adverbial expressions (formerly italicized) are construed as having their point relative to an elucidatory purpose, then the resulting sentences could easily be construed as saying something that would be perfectly innocuous by Wittgenstein's later lights.[104] With items 3 through 7, 12, 13, and 17, the moment of metaphysical insistence comes with the modality of expressions such as "all," "every," and "must"—one that insinuates a requirement on how things must be. In items 9, 15, and 16, if the definite article were replaced by an indefinite one, the note of metaphysical insistence would vanish. And so on. This is not to say, however, that the metaphysical moment in each of these remarks is confined to the italicized portion of each. On the contrary, on the one hand, the italicized expression in each case may be understood to induce a moment of philosophical subliming that laterally affects many of the other expressions that occur in each numbered remark above—"proposition," "language," "analysis," "logical," "complex," "elementary," "notation," "thought," "relation," "meaning," "possible," "order," "in common," "general," "form," "clarity," "clarify," "perspicuous," "visible," "problems," "philosophy," "solved"—a moment of subliming to which the author of the *Tractatus* was himself oblivious. On the other hand, it is perhaps more accurate to put things the other way around: it is the author's tendency to sublime what proposition, language, logic, order, clarity, and so on, are—it is his prior conception of how and what these *must* be—that induces the requirements that the italicized expressions ("all," "every," "the") above each in its own way reflects.[105]

Each of the items on the list is to be associated with an example of what later Wittgenstein refers to as the dogmatism into which we so easily fall when doing philosophy.[106] The author of the *Tractatus* would not have viewed himself as proceeding dogmatically—putting forward theses (that are to be associated with each of the items above) that might be taken by a reader to seem to call for vindication. Rather, he would have regarded each of the above as pertaining to matters that become clear through the process of clarifying propositions, and, in particular, through the adoption and employment of a perspicuous notation—a notation that enables one to avoid "the fundamental confusions" ("of which the whole of philosophy is full")[107] by furnishing an *absolutely* clear way of expressing thoughts.[108] The italicized expression in this last sentence again highlights one such undetected moment of dogmatism. But the freedom from such moments to which the later work aspires will seem easier to attain than it is if one fails to register how much of the ambition of the early program of philosophical clarification is to be retained in the later work, both in its peculiarity of method (providing the reader with a *perspicuous* representation of the possibilities available for making sense) and its peculiarity of aim (making the problems *completely* disappear).[109] The task of the later philosophy lies in seeking a way to retain these early original aspirations to perspicuity and completeness while purging them of the metaphysical spirit with which they are unwittingly imbued in the early work.[110] The point of each of the italicized expressions (in the candidate items for inclusion on the second list) is to underscore a particular moment within his early conception of clarification that must be purged in order that features of its general outline may continue to be of service in his later conception of philosophical clarification if it is to eschew any moment of dogmatism.[111]

2 A Form of Expression That Strikes Us as Obvious

Each of the italicized expressions on the above list furnishes an example of how, as later Wittgenstein puts it, the most crucial moments in the philosophical conjuring trick are the ones that are apt to strike one as most innocent.[112] This directly bears on the evolution of his later philosophy in two ways. First, it is tied to his later apprehension that it is much more difficult to avoid laying down requirements in philosophy than his earlier self had ever imagined—where this is tied in the later work, in turn, to the need to develop a form of philosophical practice that can diagnose, identify, and clarify the precise moments in which such requirements on thinking are first unwittingly laid down, well prior to their manifesting themselves to the thinker as commitments of any consequence.[113] Second, it required a set of procedures for the conduct of the new activity of diagnosis, identification, and subsequent clarification that would not themselves prove to carry further unwitting commitments in their train (introducing yet a further metaphysics, now newly built into the successor conception of clarification). Hence the need to develop a nondogmatic mode of philosophical correction (an, as it were, further layer of correction directed at each of the moments of correction themselves, and a further layer upon that, and so forth). An elucidatory procedure whose steps are arranged in the form of a ladder is no longer up to this task: the procedure must be able to crisscross in such a way as to allow each step in the investigation devoted to exorcising a philosophical demon to itself be pondered, reassessed, and purged, in turn, of the possible latent forms of overstepping or overstatement that may unwittingly have insinuated themselves in the course of the elucidation of the original misconception.[114] It is in this context (of cultivating such a nondogmatic mode of philosophizing) that a method of writing characterized by an alternation of voices (including ones of overly insistent temptation and ones of overly zealous correction) proves its value and comes to transform the face of Wittgenstein's authorship.

This raises many questions (regarding the aims and methods of Wittgenstein's later philosophy) well beyond the scope of this paper. It will suffice to confine our attention here briefly to the ever-recurring first step in this crisscrossing procedure—a step that has no role and can have no role to play in his earlier ladder-climbing mode of philosophical elucidation: namely, the step in which one seeks to uncover that crucial sleight of hand in the philosophical conjuring trick that is apt to strike one as most innocent. Attention to this step alone (without attending to much else that is also new and no less important in the later work) suffices for our present purpose inasmuch as an appreciation of it suffices to allow us to see: (1) why it is precisely the moments in the early work that correspond to items on the second list that come under repeated fire in the *Investigations* (while items that belong on the first list essentially never do)[115] qua criticisms of the author of the *Tractatus*, and (2) why the moment of discontinuity in question here must become invisible if one imposes the doctrinal schema (thereby permitting moments of discontinuity to come into view only if they correspond to explicit doctrines that early Wittgenstein self-consciously sought to advance and defend and that later Wittgenstein rejected).[116]

Wittgenstein's original aim, in writing the *Tractatus*, was to bring metaphysics to an end; and the method of clarification he thereby sought to practice, to achieve that end, was to be one that was itself free of all metaphysical commitments. The following remark brings out how his later writing (unlike most of the commentary on it) continues to keep this feature of his earlier thought firmly in perspective while seeking to focus attention on its problematic commitments:

We now have a theory, a "dynamic theory" of the proposition; of language, but it does not present itself to us as a theory. For it is the characteristic thing about such a theory that it looks at a special clearly intuitive case and says: "*That* shews how things are in every case; this case is the exemplar of *all* cases."—"Of course! It has to be like that," we say, and are satisfied. We have arrived at a form of expression that *strikes us as obvious*. But it is as if we had now seen something lying *beneath* the surface.[117]

This passage brings out nicely why things must go wrong if one's reading of Wittgenstein is organized around the following question: "Which parts of the theory that the *Tractatus* aimed to put forward did later Wittgenstein think was wrong?" If one reads Wittgenstein in this way, then one is apt to skip over the following seven aspects of later Wittgenstein's interest in (what one thereby calls) "the theory of the *Tractatus*": (1) that what we are able to see (often with the benefit of later Wittgenstein's help) as heavily freighted philosophical commitments in the early work did not present themselves to the author of the *Tractatus* as such, (2) that it is the characteristic thing about such "theories" that, at the deepest level, they garner their conviction, not from a conscious intention to put forward an ambitious philosophical claim, but rather from an apparently innocent attention to what presents itself as a special clearly intuitive case, (3) that an unprejudiced view of such a case already appears to permit one (without any additional theoretical underpinning) to exclaim: "*That* shews how things are in every case; this case is the exemplar of *all* cases," (4) that it is therefore particularly helpful to look at examples of philosophers who are already in the grip of such apparent forms of clarity in those moments in their thinking that occur prior to any in which they take themselves yet to have begun philosophizing, (5) that it is even better, if one can find one, to look at the example of a philosopher who, in the teeth of an avowed aim to eschew any such commitments, nonetheless falls into them, (6) that the author of the *Tractatus* is later Wittgenstein's prime example of such a philosopher, and therefore, at least in this respect, his favorite target of philosophical criticism, (7) that the ultimate quarry of philosophical criticism here for later Wittgenstein is never this or that philosophical thesis or theoretical commitment, but rather a characteristic form of expression—one that holds us captive and strikes us as so very obvious that we imagine that it allows us to be able to penetrate the appearance of language and see what *must* lie beneath the surface.

3 Aligning the Old and New Ways of Thinking

"So this is what you are saying: Later Wittgenstein disagrees with early Wittgenstein because he thinks everything on the second list belongs on the first list!" No. First of all, early Wittgenstein does not himself *have* (in the sense required here: as an available topic for reflection) a second list. Second, later Wittgenstein does not have a first *list* (in the sense required here: as something that has the form of a linear sequence of steps). What is right in this exclamation is that, from the vantage point of later Wittgenstein, the unwitting commitments could be said in a sense to belong on something like a first list in that they, too, like the items that were to have been placed on the first list, stand in need of philosophical interrogation. But the "in a sense" and "something like" matter here. The first list was supposed to represent the rungs of a ladder; and there is no ladder, in this sense, in *Philosophical Investigations*: not only because the topic of "the right order" no longer has evident application, but also (mild mono-Wittgensteinians may maintain) because the envisioned task now requires the composition of a very different kind of a book informed by a very different conception of philosophical clarification—one that no longer can take the form of a ladder made up out of philosophical temptations, but must now be made up instead out of a crisscrossing series of investigations punctuated by voices other than merely that of philosophical temptation. (That voice must now be joined by other voices: a voice of correction, a voice of reminding, a voice that asks us a question that we must answer for ourselves, a voice that invites us now to imagine the following, a voice that asks us if we can do what the previous voice asks us to do, a voice that asks what we would say if . . . , a voice that teaches us a new way of speaking, and so on.) A linear metaphor of an ascent (a ladder) here gives way to a nonlinear metaphor of a movement that stays close to the ground—of peripeteia (a crisscross). It is open to a mild mono-Wittgensteinian to take this to be the sign of a severe degree of change in Wittgenstein's thinking.[118] What makes her a mono-Wittgensteinian is only her insistence on the forms of continuity that invite Disapproval. What makes her a mild one is that nothing in her mono-Wittgensteinianism precludes her from understanding the forms of evolution Wittgenstein's thinking undergoes as being anything less than quite extreme, providing they are consistent with those forms of continuity.

If such a reader wishes to align the old and new ways of thinking so as properly to be able to identify those moments in Wittgenstein's early thought that provide the focal points for critical attention in his later writing, then she most go about the task rather gingerly. As we have seen, what she is seeking to identify are those commitments in the *Tractatus* that must have appeared to the author of the *Tractatus* as *obvious*—to be the sort of thing that anyone who was thinking clearly about the matter in question would have to agree to. But this also has implications for her understanding of the character of the criticism that is directed at the unwitting commitments in the later work. In his later writing, when he draws our attention to such moments in his early thought, later Wittgenstein is seeking to show not only (1) that the crucial moments in the philosophical conjuring trick performed by the author of the *Tractatus* are always ones that strike him as philosophically uncontroversial, but especially also (2) how these moments in his early thought constitute singularly illustrative exhibits of the sort of philosophical entanglement that the later work as a whole is concerned to display and dispel. Thus without a proper understanding of (1), we must fail also to understand (2), and hence an important dimension of the later work as a whole.

Throughout his later work, Wittgenstein is pervasively concerned to practice a method of philosophical investigation that enables us to locate those moments in the progress of a thinker's reflections in which, unbeknownst to himself, he first broaches philosophical ground—those moments in which, though nothing beyond the obvious seems yet to have been asserted, a note of metaphysical insistence has already crept in and an unwarranted requirement has been laid down. The items on the second list help us to see how and why the author of the *Tractatus* provides the author of the *Investigations* with his favorite example of such a thinker. Since the crucial moments take place at a stage prior to any at which the author of the *Tractatus* imagines the activity of propounding substantive philosophical doctrine to have begun, it must also remain unclear in Wittgenstein's later attempted reformulations of his early ideas at *which* moment he can be said to have successfully pinpointed a transition from the philosophically innocuous to the philosophically momentous. This requires that he circle around such remarks, essaying a variety of formulations, assessing the extent to which a moment of unearned insistence has crept into a wording of one of his early ideas. It is worth noticing how unlike the actual method of the *Tractatus* such a practice of circling is.[119] Early Wittgenstein is eager to drive his reader up the ladder, so that he can surprise her at the top.[120] Whereas later Wittgenstein is concerned, first and foremost, to try to slow his reader down and keep her close to the ground, so that he can spot the precise moment at which she first touches so much as a toe to the bottommost rung of any ladder of words that might appear to enable her to ascend up into philosophical space.[121]

A resolute approach to reading the *Tractatus* is of especial benefit in helping to bring more sharply into relief this aspect of Wittgenstein's later philosophical practice—the one that is concerned with identifying our moments of transition into philosophy. As long as the assumption remains in place, however, that the aim of the *Tractatus* is one of propounding a set of substantive metaphysical doctrines, then the importance of the moments in his old way of thinking that correspond to items on the second list must remain invisible. If a reader fails to appreciate the extent to which (what Wittgenstein later regards and criticizes as) the central philosophical commitments of the *Tractatus* were of such a sort that they were able to appear to its author, at the time of writing, not to be "philosophical doctrines," then that reader will also fail to appreciate wherein the later task of criticism lies—and therefore also how this task applies to the reader himself and his own thinking. He will take the point to be to derail a train of thought that is already far under way and has fully come into view for the thinker as a philosophical theory with a determinate set of commitments. He will thus fail to see that an important dimension of the aim of the investigation is to heighten the reader's awareness of his tendency to stray unwittingly into a moment of metaphysical insistence, while occupying what he takes to be the solid ground of merely affirming things (that anyone thinking clearly ought to view as) innocent of such commitment.

We can now return to the question we left hanging at the end of our discussion of the first sort of indiscriminateness, at the end of section VI. We saw that, once the sort of distortion it introduces is corrected for, the following question can arise: why is it that certain doctrines apparently deemed sufficiently confused to warrant a role only on the outer periphery of the target range of the *Tractatus* later come to be positioned so close to the center of the target range of the *Investigations*? It is precisely these comparatively offstage moments in the *Tractatus* that later Wittgenstein wants to show are where the most fateful conjuring tricks—the ones performed by the author of that early work on himself—take place. So, with respect to its bearing on his early thought, the point of reopening questions about how a word can come to be correlated with a meaning, whether a mental act can effect such a correlation, and so on is, not to charge his earlier self (or, say, Frege) with the (e.g., mentalistic) philosophical "theories" that are apt to present themselves as the most immediate temptations in reflecting upon these questions, but rather to bring out how philosophically fateful the character must be of the very first steps taken in any attempted rejection or correction of just such temptations. For it is here, precisely in the vehemence of its rejection of these temptations—especially in its immediate recoil from (a certain picture of) the psychological—that the initial subliming of the logical takes place, mostly offstage, in the text of the *Tractatus*.[122]

If we fail to appreciate the depth of the antimetaphysical aim of the *Tractatus*—if we fail to understand the radically antidoctrinal character of the author's undertaking in that book—and look instead for explicit doctrines of the sort we would look for in other books, then most of what we will end up identifying as expressions of its central doctrines are items that figure on the first list—"propositions" that serve as the central targets of the early (and continue to remain targets in the later) work. If equipped with such an understanding of how the old way of thinking aligns with the new, we then set about the task of writing a commentary on the opening sections of the *Investigations* in which, each time such a philosophical temptation manifests itself, we provide a helpful scholarly indication of which Tractarian doctrine the temptation in question is supposedly to be associated with, we have not only misled the reader of our commentary about the character of the philosophical undertaking of the *Tractatus*, but we have severely harmed her chances of understanding the character of the investigation before her in the opening pages of the *Investigations*—and how it bears on the comparatively direct criticism of the early work that first begins several dozen sections further on in the text. In their eagerness to mark the discontinuity between Wittgenstein's early and later philosophies, such commentaries simultaneously obstruct the reader's access to both what is newly distinctive in the later conception of philosophical clarification and what is specifically at issue in its very particular criticisms of what was already comparatively distinctive in his earlier conception of philosophical clarification.

An insistence on this point in no way commits a resolute reader to having to hold that the discontinuity between Wittgenstein's early and later philosophy is somehow of a lesser magnitude of philosophical momentousness than is supposed by the authors of these (standard) commentaries. It only commits her to having to hold that it must be of a very different sort than commonly supposed—that we need to look at the later writing in an altogether new way in order to comprehend the full enormity of its break with his old way of thinking. Indeed, we are now in a position to see why the degree of continuity in aim and method must be severely limited—and thus why it does not follow that resolute readers as such are committed to holding that Wittgenstein in no way altered his conception of the aim of his philosophizing, its method, or what is involved in liberating oneself or others from philosophical confusions or illusions. Their insistence upon a heterodox degree of continuity notwithstanding, mild mono-Wittgensteinians will be no less insistent in emphasizing a strong contrast between Wittgenstein's early and later understandings of the aim and nature of the activity of philosophical clarification. This, in turn, will be tied to their insistence that we come to appreciate the difference between the sorts of items that belong on the first list and those that belong on the second list. Indeed, the difference between these two sorts of item may take on a further relevance in this connection. For an important respect in which they differ can now be seen to be tied to an important distinction in Wittgenstein's later thinking (one that can have only a very attenuated parallel in his early thinking): namely, the distinction between criticism of a full-blown theory (a form of philosophical commitment some of whose overt assumptions and implications lie open to view to proponent and critic alike) and criticism of a picture[123] (i.e., a way of looking at things that is like a pair of glasses on our nose through which we see whatever we look at, but which it never occurs to us can be removed).[124] What the reader of the aforementioned commentary on the *Investigations* will be deflected from getting into focus is the degree to which later Wittgenstein regards his earlier self as in this sense held captive by a picture of language—that is to say, already standing on metaphysical ground *without his having then realized it*.

We can now see better why it is precisely its lack of overt commitment to philosophical theory that renders the *Tractatus* such an ideal object of comparison for the *Investigations*. It is just this feature of the work that enables philosophical criticism of it to proceed in the absence of the usual distractions presented by the products of full-blown theorizing. This allows for a desirable form of focus in an investigation that seeks to excavate and characterize the role that a picture can play in the funneling of philosophical thought. Early Wittgenstein's targets of criticism were philosophical theories of thought, language, and reality, and the primary aim was to achieve freedom from such theory; whereas later Wittgenstein's primary objects of criticism are the forms of philosophical fixation and insistence that come with being held captive by our pictures of thinking (as, e.g., a kind of inner process), language (as, e.g., a game to be played according to rules), and reality (as, e.g., that which is coordinate with description).[125] And this is correlated with a fundamental difference in aim: to achieve freedom from the forms of philosophical fixation and insistence attendant upon being held captive by a picture—a dimension in aim that is both *necessarily absent* from his early work (given its subservience to various forms of fixation and insistence—such as in its conception of the role of a *Begriffsschrift* in philosophical elucidation and what is revealed through its application) and *necessary to* (so he later thought) the successful completion of the task that he already sets himself in that early work (of making the problems completely disappear). Not only are resolute readers as such therefore in no way precluded from taking there to be profound discontinuities between Wittgenstein's early and later thought, but, on the contrary (if later Wittgenstein viewed his early work as an exemplary illustration of how, in philosophy, one can take oneself to have resolutely eschewed all metaphysical commitments while still remaining knee-deep in them), then a resolute reading may help us to attain a better understanding of why later Wittgenstein took his early work to be the expression of the metaphysical spirit in philosophy par excellence.

4   Moses and Mono-Wittgensteinianism

This raises the question: how does one go about telling which moments (in a work such as *Philosophical Investigations*) are ones in which later Wittgenstein is concerned to advance criticisms of the *Tractatus*? The tendency here is tacitly to assume something like the following: if a passage does advance a criticism of his early work, then it, of course, is not concerned thereby, at one and the same time, also to mark a point of continuity with that work; and vice versa. This assumption is seldom made explicit, but it implicitly structures a good deal of commentary on Wittgenstein's later work. Mild mono-Wittgensteinians will hold not only that this assumption is not generally sound, but that it is only a mild exaggeration to say that roughly the opposite is true: some moment of commonality in philosophical target and/or aim can be seen to obtain between almost any passage in the *Investigations* (starting with its opening paragraphs and working forwards) and any number of moments in the *Tractatus* (starting with its closing paragraphs and working backwards). And it is even less of an exaggeration to say that one can usually perceive a further moment of fundamental opposition within each such moment of continuity—sometimes due to the presence of an unwitting commitment (that plays a weight-bearing role in the architecture of the

Tractatus and figures later as a target of criticism) and sometimes because of the manner in which the criticism of the target is prosecuted (especially where the target is a form of philosophical theorizing that the early and later work are equally concerned to exorcize, but in very different ways).

If one chooses a passage from the *Investigations* more or less at random, it will often exhibit the aforementioned sort of complexity in its relation to Wittgenstein's early work. If one looks at, say, section 79, here are some of the topics that come to the surface already in just the brief compass of an excerpt from it: "names," "reference," "existence," "propositions," "truth" and "falsity," "descriptions," "definitions," "identity" "statements," "use," "meaning," the relation between "meaning" and "use," "fixity" of meaning, "deciding" or "determining" what one means, the "independence" (or "dependence") of the truth of one proposition from (or on) that of another.[126] With respect to these topics, later Wittgenstein certainly has a bone, in each case, he wants to pick with early Wittgenstein. But with respect to each, in the process of conducting this quarrel, there are also numerous moments at which, not only are aspects of the target under criticism in part ones that were already in his sights at the time of writing the *Tractatus*, but, in fact, he is often at pains to preserve crucial aspects of his earlier criticism of them. This dual movement of inheriting and elaborating his most valuable early insights in the very process of prosecuting his most vehement criticisms of his earlier self renders his later treatment of the ideas of his early work exceedingly delicate and dialectical.

We must be able to see Wittgenstein in this passage (i.e., section 79) trying to show his earlier self, not merely that a sentence such as "Moses did not exist" might be able to mean any of various things depending upon the context of use (because early Wittgenstein could not possibly have been more committed to that point[127]), but rather that the sorts of difference in what this form of words ("Moses did not exist") might be taken to mean in the examples adduced (in the subsequent portion of the passage) cannot be captured in terms of (even) a (resolute) Tractarian understanding of what ought to count (and what not ought to count) as a genuine difference in symbol.[128] The mere slogan "meaning depends upon use" cannot mark a moment of discontinuity in philosophical conception between the *Tractatus* and the *Investigations*; but a full appreciation of the kinds of difference that differences in use here make to differences in meaning can. The point here is not just that the *Tractatus*'s method of clarification would be powerless to elucidate the sorts of differences of meaning here at issue (neglect of which leads to philosophical confusion), but rather that the earlier method of clarification and its attendant reliance on certain tools of logical notation brings with it a substantively impoverished conception, not just of how to go about individuating such differences in meaning, but of *what* it is that one thereby individuates.

"Are you saying that later Wittgenstein would not permit the employment of logical notation in conducting a philosophical clarification of what someone means by his words?" No. First, there is no call in the later work for such a ban on logical notation.[129] (A novel form of notation can often be very useful in identifying and clearing up confusions.)[130] Second, the main point is here missed: it is not the mere fact of an employment of such notation that is the culprit but rather the misconceptions that may accompany its employment. The object of the critical task here is to bring into focus the extent of early Wittgenstein's captivity to a certain picture of what is shown through the use of such notation and the forms of insistence that this gives rise to (some examples of which are detailed on the second list). One cannot exorcise these misconceptions by simply banning the notation (though once they are exorcised, the notation will be drained of a significant portion of its original philosophical eros). When the old and new ways of thinking are properly aligned, later Wittgenstein, in a passage such as this and those that follow, can be seen as indicating (1) how the earlier (mis)conception of what is shown in clarification is implicitly shaped by unwitting commitments to certain (mis)conceptions of what is involved in the analysis of propositions,[131] (2) how this insinuates a particular understanding of the character of (the supposed chasm between) surface and depth grammar, and finally (3) how (this conception of) what is thus revealed through the employment of the notation, in turn, gives rise to a (further shaping of the) conception of what is *really* of interest to us in philosophy, namely, the underlying form of the thought, which is necessarily *hidden* from view and can only be brought to the surface with the aid of a logical notation—a notation that captures all and only that which is essential to *the* logical form of the thought. That is to say, on a proper alignment of early and later Wittgenstein, it can begin to come into view how the targets here are the items on the second list.

X   A Final List

[Sadly, our author's mania for making and seeing lists recurs. (1) An actual list is presented in which each item on it is to correspond simultaneously to one of the buried doctrines that the young Ludwig inexplicably failed to see at the time of his Vision of the Ladder *and to something that he did see at that time. Each item on this list is held also to correspond to something that the mature Ludwig was concerned to criticize in* The Old Testament *and at the same time something he was not concerned to criticize but rather to promulgate in* The New Testament! *Alas, the madness of the infidel doctrine here speaks for itself. Passing mention is even made here of a fourth list, but fortunately the suggestion is not pursued. (2) Again, not content with a merely terrestrial list, the infidel revives yet a third apocryphal account of a vision of a*

divine list (though no reputable scholar has ever alluded to a Vision of the Third List*). (3) Our author then begins to muse over what is seen in the vision of the third list. (4) He becomes engrossed in the most pitiable fashion in contemplating these many lists, three actual and three spiritual, abruptly concluding with final reflections on infidel dogmatics and injunctions to the members of his creed to go in for a mild form of their heterodoxy. A lost soul if there ever was one!—J. C.]*

1   A Final Actual List

Each of the items on the list below corresponds to a moment in Wittgenstein's work, early and late, that a mild mono-Wittgensteinian may take to mark either a moment of continuity or one of discontinuity, or (alternating between variant understandings of the sentences that figure on the list) both. It would be a gross understatement, with regard to the list below, merely to say that there are many possible variations on it that would have sufficed for our present purpose. What is still true is that a reader constrained by nothing more than a bare commitment to resolution will encounter a variety of sorts of difficulty in trying to offer a specification of what belongs on this list—partly, though not merely, because of the difficulties that must attend any attempt to specify the items that belong on each of the previous two lists. Nevertheless, once again, the difficulties that arise here are immensely instructive in clarifying the sorts of philosophical and exegetical difficulty that must beset any attempt to offer anything approaching a resolute account of the relation between the thought of the early and that of later Wittgenstein.

Now, with respect to the third list, it becomes well-nigh impossible to specify the relevant items in a useful way without remaining fairly close to the wording of swatches of Wittgenstein's own text. But some delicate degree of abstraction is still required inasmuch as the items in question must also be able to mark moments of continuity. For this requires that they can be closely correlated to sentences in both the *Tractatus* and the *Investigations*. In this spirit, I offer the following small sample of candidate formulations of such moments of continuity/discontinuity in Wittgenstein's thought:

1. Every sentence in our everyday language is in order as it is.

2. There must be perfect order even in the vaguest sentence.

3. A sentence of ordinary language must have *a* definite sense.[132]

4. An indefinite sense would not really be a sense at all.

5. In philosophy, we are driven to seek elsewhere, in the abstract features of an ideal language, what is already to be found in the most concrete features of our everyday language.

6. Philosophical misunderstandings are often caused by superficial analogies between forms of expression drawn from different regions of language.

7. Such misunderstandings can be removed by substituting one form of expression for another.

8. What does not get expressed in the signs (words) themselves comes out in their application (use): what the signs (words) fail to express their application (use) declares.

9. In order to gather the logic (grammar) of what is said, we must consult the context of significant use.

10. In philosophy the question, "Why do we actually use this word or this proposition?" repeatedly leads to valuable insights.

11. The object of philosophy is the logical (grammatical) clarification of thought(s).

12. Philosophy is not a theory but an activity.

13. The result of philosophy is not a number of "philosophical propositions," but to make propositions clear.

14. Anyone who understands me eventually recognizes certain of my sentences as nonsensical.

15. We cannot give a sign the wrong sense.

16. Every possible proposition is legitimately constructed.

17. If a sentence has no sense, this can only be because we have given no meaning to it.

18. Logic (grammar) must take care of itself.

19. We cannot draw a limit to thought. That would require that we could think both what can be thought and what cannot be thought.

20. Strictly thought through, idealism can be seen to collapse into pure realism.

21. Doubt can exist only where there is a question; a question only where there is an answer; and this only where something *can* be *said*.

22. The solution of the problem lies in the vanishing of the problem.

This list has been rather haphazardly created. Part of my point below will be that such a list is not all that hard to create, once one has developed the forms of sensitivity required to make one at all. And, once one has created such a list, it will not be at all clear how it should be ordered. Each of the items on this list are to be associated (on one understanding of it) with (1) a particular unwitting preconception about how things must be and how philosophy must proceed that falls out of the early conception of clarification (and therefore is to be included on the second list), and (on another understanding of it) with (2) something that may be ascribed to both the author of the *Tractatus* and the author of the *Investigations* without obviously misrepresenting either (i.e., something that might therefore be included on a possible fourth list devoted merely to detailing moments of continuity in Wittgenstein's thought). It is in this latter connection that the parenthetical notation plays its role here (serving a very different purpose than before): namely, helping to bring into sharper relief such moments of continuity by allowing for the reformulation of his earlier ideas into his preferred later idiom.

2   The Third List

As with its predecessors, the expression "the third list" will not serve its intended purpose here if defined through an enumeration of some actual items—say, the items on the actual list above. The actual list above is of examples of candidate formulations of sentences that may equally well be taken by a resolute reader alternately in either of the two relevant ways: first, as candidate specifications of requirements that are laid down in (because not separable from) the course of the *Tractatus*'s development of its own parochial (and, by Wittgenstein's later lights, problematic) conception of how the activity of philosophical clarification ought to proceed, and, second, as candidate specifications of those comparatively global aspects of his understanding of the activity of philosophical clarification that are shared by both the author of the *Tractatus* and the author of the *Investigations*. The point of furnishing such a sample of candidates is to attempt to gesture at the sorts of thing that might be held by a given resolute reader to belong on the third list. As long as intramural disputes between resolute readers of the sorts canvassed above continue, questions regarding the candidacy of particular sentences for the third list must also remain in dispute.

3   What Belongs on the Third List?

I have drawn the first five items on the actual list above from what is essentially a commentary on certain sections of the *Tractatus*—one that is initiated in §97 and continues through the following sections of the *Investigations*.[133] This is an autobiographical fact about me and where I first went to look for items to place on the third list. I take it that something like these items might have arrived on the list by a very different route, inasmuch as they each represent the sort of thing that an attentive reader of the *Tractatus* might find herself with occasion to say in writing about the teaching of that work. Taken out of context, some readers of Wittgenstein might take any of the first four items to suggest metaphysical elements present in the old way of thinking that the new seeks to undo. On the other hand, read within their dialectical context (i.e., §§97ff. of the *Investigations*), they do not obviously represent exclamations on the part of a voice in the grip of a wayward philosophical temptation.[134] Part of my point in placing some items with this particular provenance on the actual list above is to bring into sharpest possible relief the degree to which moments of breathtaking continuity surface even in those later passages whose concern is focally one of criticizing the *Tractatus*.[135] This means that even in those stretches of the later writing where criticism of the *Tractatus* reaches its highest pitch, candidates for the third list are still not in short supply. Conversely, as a matter of the mere letter of their formulation, the majority of the remaining items, starting with the eighth, on the actual list above are most easily recognized as corresponding to sentences from the *Tractatus*. Yet I take it that they each represent the sort of thing that an attentive reader of the *Investigations* might find herself having occasion to say in writing about the teaching of that work. One point of the exercise of attentively trying to construct a candidate third list of one's own is to discover the (possibly surprising) extent to which the following is true: you don't have to look far or wide in Wittgenstein's writings to find items that belong on it.

It is important here, again, that each of the items on the third list corresponds to sentences, not thoughts. Each sentence on it admits of alternative understandings of how much its affirmation commits us to, and thus of what it says. Would the author of the *Investigations* want to agree with that which his earlier self here would, in each case, want to affirm in affirming the item in question? When we come to the items on the third list, if we try to locate the differences between early and later Wittgenstein in this area by sorting them into the items early and later Wittgenstein agree on and those they do not, then (qua narrators of the story of Wittgenstein's development) we are lost. The only accurate thing to say here, at this hopelessly unhelpful level of generality, is perhaps the following: later Wittgenstein agrees with early Wittgenstein about each of these items (in wanting to affirm a sentence that the other would affirm), and he disagrees with him about each of them (in not wanting to affirm precisely what the other would thereby affirm). For there are significant aspects of the *Tractatus*'s unwitting commitments that substantially color its early understanding of each of the philosophical issues associated with the items on the above list. For example, his early understanding of what is at stake in each of the following expressions (at least some one of which figures in each of the items on the list above) is implicated in the surreptitious metaphysics of the early work: "order," "perfection," "form," "vagueness," "definiteness," "sense," "logic," "language," "application," "use," "context," "say," "show," "philosophy," "abstract," "concrete," "ideal," "language," "everyday," "clarity," "clarification," "theory," "sign," "proposition," "thought," "strictly thought through," "solution," "problem," "vanishing."

This collection of expressions, considered as a set, nicely epitomizes both the extent of the continuity and the discontinuity in Wittgenstein's philosophy.[136] A significant moment of continuity can be uncovered by reflecting on the parallels in Wittgenstein's early and later philosophies that can be associated with how these expressions occur in the *Tractatus* and the *Investigations* respectively. Yet a significant moment of discontinuity in Wittgenstein's philosophy can also be uncovered by reflecting on the points at which these parallels begin to give out (with respect to the manner in which each of these expressions occurs in the *Tractatus* and the *Investigations* respectively). What marks a sentence out as belonging on the third list is that it simultaneously invites alternate construals of terms such as these—on a first construal, the sentence in which it figures says something that early Wittgenstein has it at heart to say; on a second construal, it says something that later Wittgenstein equally has it at heart to say—where what each would mean would in part be importantly the same and in part importantly different.

4   Putting the Three Lists Together

In reflecting upon what to make of the items on the third list, in the context of trying to understand the relation between early and later Wittgenstein, one way of going extremely wrong is to take the possibility of constructing such a list itself to constitute a proof of the truth of some very severe variant of mono-Wittgensteinianism. But there is also an opposite way of going extremely wrong here. It takes its departure from the following (in itself perfectly sound) thought: any sort of understanding that the author of the *Tractatus* is able to have of any of the items on the third list must be shaped through and through, at every point, by his (metaphysically emphatic) understanding of the items on the second list. This is true as far as it goes: any attempt to construe the third list as a list of things that early and later Wittgenstein "simply agree about" may run the risk of attributing to later Wittgenstein an allegiance to items on the second list—that is, to the very commitments of the *Tractatus* that he is later most concerned to single out for criticism. What this shows is the following: one must be careful about taking items on the third list to represent unproblematic formulations of points of common ground between the early and later philosophy. But it would be equally point-missing to go to the other extreme and to construe the items on the third list as merely a set of ambiguous sentences that coincidentally each admit of the relevant pair of alternative understandings. It would be the ultimate in perverse poly-Wittgensteinianism to conclude that early and later Wittgenstein, while agreeing about nothing of importance, are for some reason happy each to call upon almost precisely the same forms of words to express their respective utterly incommensurable philosophical aspirations. Clearly the truth must be somewhere in the middle, between these two unhappy extremes (of overly zealous mono-Wittgensteinianism and overly intractable poly-Wittgensteinianism); and the telling of it is nothing if not a delicate matter, requiring exquisite care.

By reflecting upon what belongs on each of our three lists, the true complexity of the relation between early and later Wittgenstein can come into view. All three lists involve sentences that figure (or appear to be implied by sentences that figure) in the *Tractatus*. Commentators (such as standard readers) who wish sharply to emphasize the discontinuities in Wittgenstein's development tend to move, when identifying the early doctrines that are criticized in the later work, indiscriminately between items drawn from the first and those from the second list (as if the mere existence of items of the second sort sufficed to show that what resolute readers say about items of the first sort must be mistaken). Commentators (such as zealous mono-Wittgensteinians) who wish sharply to emphasize the continuities in Wittgenstein's development tend often to distinguish items belonging on the third list from those that belong on either of the other two, but fail not only to distinguish those that belong on the second list from those that belong on the first (as if they were all figured in the *Tractatus* as rungs of the ladder to be thrown away), but, in so failing, thereby also fail to appreciate the extent to which later Wittgenstein, in his criticism of items on the second list, is at one and the same time concerned to criticize his earlier self's understanding of the supposedly "shared" items on the third list. When the first (standard) note of sharpness is introduced into a narrative of the story of Wittgenstein's development, the most interesting moments of continuity are obliterated. When the second (zealous) note of sharpness is introduced, the already devilishly difficult task of balancing these moments against those of equally profound discontinuity becomes impossible.

XI Conclusion

I have tried to show in this essay that part of an appeal of a resolute reading may be that it permits the *Tractatus* to come into focus in a manner that brings distinctions between different sorts of commitment in the early work into relief. It thereby allows one to make good sense of why Wittgenstein is concerned to focus on precisely those commitments that are singled out for criticism in the passages in his later work where he is occupied with the task of criticizing the *Tractatus* (and thus also of why he is not drawn to mention the *Tractatus* when singling out for criticism in his later work items that figure on the first list—items that resolute readers do not ascribe to the early work). I have also tried to show that if we have the possibility of a mildly mono-Wittgensteinian approach to understanding Wittgenstein's work as a whole firmly in view, it should be evident that a resolute approach to reading the *Tractatus* should not be identified with any comparatively severe variant of mono-Wittgensteinianism. One can be simultaneously maximally resolute and mildly mono-Wittgensteinian in one's approach to reading Wittgenstein. Finally, I have tried to show, not only that it is not built into the very idea of a resolute reading as such that it involve an apologia for a severely mono-Wittgensteinian creed, but rather that its central motivation *can* be to improve upon existing accounts of the discontinuity in Wittgenstein's philosophy.[137]

Notes

1. Sigmund Freud, *Der Mann Moses und die monotheistische Religion* (Frankfurt: Fischer, 1975), p. 63 (my translation).

2. Johannes Climacus, *Concluding Unscientific Postscript*, ed. S. Kierkegaard, trans. David Swenson and Walter Lowrie (Princeton, N.J.: Princeton University Press, 1941), p. 246n (I have amended the translation).

3. To mention only some of the other notable resolute readers: Kevin Cahill, Alice Crary, Edmund Dain, Rob Deans, Piergiorgio Donatelli, Burton Dreben, Juliet Floyd, Warren Goldfarb, Logi Gunnarsson, Martin Gustafsson, Michael Kremer, Oskari Kuusela, Thomas Ricketts, Rupert Read, Matt Ostrow, and Ed Witherspoon.

4. I have allowed myself to speak here, in the first sentence of this paper, of "*the* resolute reading" because these are the terms in which our critics define their target. From now on, however, I will speak rather of resolute reading*s*. For, as some of my remarks below will help to make clear, there is no reason why there should not be a variety of such readings. A resolute reading is better thought of as a *program* for reading the book than as itself comprising a *reading* (in any very demanding sense of the term "reading"). To be a resolute reader is to be committed at most to a certain programmatic conception of the lines along which interpretative questions pertaining to the text are to be worked out. The approach to reading Wittgenstein here at issue is also sometimes called "the austere reading." This seems to me an unfortunate label, as it suggests that the commitment to austerity (i.e., the claim that there is no such thing as substantial nonsense) drives the commitment to resolution rather than the other way around. It is also sometimes called "The New Reading"—another label I am not prepared to use. It is for others to judge how new it is. But it seems to me that various strands of extant resolute readings are anticipated in the writings of all of the following earlier commentators: Hide Ishiguro, Brian McGuinness, Rush Rhees, and Peter Winch. Though neither Peter Geach nor Elizabeth Anscombe could possibly be counted as resolute readers, their writings contain accounts of certain lines of "thought" (along with understandings of why the scare quotes might be in order here) that anticipate themes that

later become central in the writings of resolute readers; see especially Geach's "Saying and Showing in Frege and Wittgenstein," in *Essays in Honor of G. H. von Wright*, ed. Jaakko Hintikka, in *Acta Philosophica Fennica* 28 (1976), pp. 54–70; and Anscombe's "The Reality of the Past," collected in Volume 2 of her *Collected Philosophical Papers*—the volume titled *Metaphysics and the Philosophy of Mind* (Minneapolis: University of Minnesota Press, 1981).

5. Meredith Williams, for example, accuses resolute readers of holding (what she calls) the strong continuity thesis; see her "Nonsense and Cosmic Exile: The Austere Reading of the *Tractatus*," in *Wittgenstein's Lasting Significance*, ed. Max Kölbel and Bernhard Weiss (London: Routledge, 2004), pp. 6–31.

6. The point here could also be put by saying: *at least* two Wittgensteins. With the exception of my remarks in the penultimate note, in this essay I will not have occasion to enter into the niceties that make it appropriate to insist that, once one begins distinguishing Wittgensteins, there is no particular reason to stop counting at two. Some hold that an understanding of Wittgenstein's development depends crucially upon the postulation of a further discrete "middle-period Wittgenstein," fully distinct from either of the other two. Yet others are equally enthusiastic about the idea of a "third Wittgenstein," but wish to reserve this label for yet another, supposedly equally importantly distinctive, thinker who penned *On Certainty* (and perhaps also Wittgenstein's late writings on the philosophy of psychology and on color). I think there is something to be said on behalf of these claims, but the further issues they raise (in favor of identifying yet further Wittgensteins) go well beyond the scope of this essay. But the general terms of the solution this essay seeks to propose (for avoiding the impasse of mono- vs. poly-Wittgensteinianism) ought to be perfectly neutral with respect to the topic of the wisdom of multiplying Wittgensteins on grounds other than those addressed here.

7. David Stern actually seems to think there is something heady about this thought. He is dishearteningly representative in his willingness to assume that the standing situation in Wittgenstein scholarship can be summarized as follows: "[I]t is nearly always presupposed that either there was one Wittgenstein, that in essentials Wittgenstein's philosophy never really changed, or that there were two Wittgensteins, that there was a fundamental change between the early and the later philosophy." There are two things that are disheartening here: first, the idea that most commentators fall into one of these two camps (and therefore that resolute readers, since they supposedly do not fall into the latter camp, must fall into the former), and, second, that this could even seem to constitute a sensible principle for classifying commentators. There is perhaps more truth in the claim that the work of many commentators can be so classified than I would like to believe. Nonetheless, "nearly always presupposed" is a grotesque overstatement. Already starting with early work by Elizabeth Anscombe, Rush Rhees, and Peter Winch, there has been concerted resistance to the standard "two-Wittgenstein" view without any hint of an intention of seeking to exchange it for a monolithic one-Wittgenstein view. See especially Rhees's "The Philosophy of Wittgenstein," *Ratio* 8 (1966): 180–193; Winch's "The Unity of Wittgenstein's Philosophy," in *Studies in the Philosophy of Wittgenstein*, ed. Peter Winch (London: Routledge, 1969); and my remarks about Anscombe in note 134. But very few commentators, and certainly none of these three, have denied that there are significant discontinuities. Stern continues: "Very

few interpreters seem prepared to even consider the possibility that these are restrictive and constricting alternatives, or that the best interpretation might well be one that recognizes both continuities and discontinuities in Wittgenstein's philosophical development" ("How Many Wittgensteins?" in *Wittgenstein: The Philosopher and his Works*, ed. Alois Pichler and Simo Säätelä, *Working Papers from the Wittgenstein Archives at the University of Bergen*, no. 17 [2005], p. 170). What Stern says here ("very few interpreters seem prepared to even consider") ought to strike one as a bit of a stretch, given that the revelation ("the best interpretation might well be one that recognizes both continuities and discontinuities") is a truism—true about pretty much any interesting philosopher. Plato, Kant, Russell, Heidegger, and Putnam all come immediately to mind as particularly pertinent examples about whom this is obviously true, although it is not at all easy to say how it is true. As it is especially difficult in the case of Wittgenstein to see precisely how properly to balance the continuities against the discontinuities in a full narrative of the character of his philosophical development, an emphatic pronunciation of such truisms can strike one as an empty gesture. The devil lies in the details here. It has been a central motivation of mine in developing a resolute reading of the early work—as well as of Cora Diamond's—to begin to fill in some of the requisite details here. This makes it all the more ironic that Stern claims (as do many others) that Conant, Diamond, and various other resolute readers (must?) hold "the one-Wittgenstein view." I would be happy if this essay were able to put an end to any simpleminded (or severe) ascription of such a claim to a commentator simply on the grounds that she advocates a resolute reading. As will become clear, I personally would not in the least mind the ascription of a nonsimpleminded (i.e., mild) version of the claim.

8. Wolfgang Stegmüller, *Hauptströmungen der Gegenwartsphilosophie*, vol. 1 (Stuttgart: Alfred Kröner Verlag, 1978), p. 524.

9. Anthony Quinton, "Contemporary British Philosophy," in *Wittgenstein: The Philosophical Investigations*, ed. George Pitcher (South Bend, Ind.: University of Notre Dame Press, 1968), p. 9.

10. It would take an additional note of several pages, at this point in the dispute, to detail all of the relevant literature, pro and con, on resolute readings. But certainly a good place to begin to get a sense of what such a reading involves are the essays collected in the first half of Cora Diamond's *The Realistic Spirit* (Cambridge, Mass.: MIT Press, 1991). Peter Sullivan offers a particularly trenchant critique of such readings in "On Trying to Be Resolute: A Response to Kremer on the *Tractatus*," *European Journal of Philosophy* 10 (2002): 43–78. It is, in the first instance, a reply to Michael Kremer's "The Purpose of Tractarian Nonsense," *Noûs* 35 (2001): 39–73. To mention just one collection of material on each side of the fence: see the essays collected in *The New Wittgenstein*, ed. Alice Crary and Rupert Read (London: Routledge, 2000), which mostly contains essays sympathetic to resolute readings, and those in the July 2003 issue of the journal *Philosophical Investigations*, which mostly contains articles critical of them. For an interesting attempt to sit on both sides of the fence, see Marie McGinn's "Between Metaphysics and Nonsense: The Role of Elucidation in Wittgenstein's *Tractatus*," *Philosophical Quarterly* (October 1999): 491–513. Many further pertinent articles are cited in the notes that follow.

11. The one point on which standard readers and resolute readers are generally able to agree is that they deeply disagree about how to read the *Tractatus*—and, in particular, how to understand

its conception of nonsense. Meredith Williams's piece, cited above, does a nice job of laying out some of the basic points of disagreement here. For two particularly vehement statements from standard readers of their agreement with resolute readers on this point (i.e., that there really is deep disagreement here) and on no others, see Hans-Johann Glock's "All Kinds of Nonsense," in *Wittgenstein at Work*, ed. Erich Ammereller and Eugen Fischer (London: Routledge, 2004), 221–245, and Peter Hacker's "Wittgenstein, Carnap, and the New American Wittgensteinians," *Philosophical Quarterly* 53, no. 210 (January 2003): 1–23. See also Cora Diamond's reply to the latter, "Logical Syntax in the *Tractatus*," *Philosophical Quarterly* 55, no. 218 (January 2005): 178–189. But even about this supposed point of agreement there is controversy. Adrian Moore and Peter Sullivan seem to agree with each other that the differences between standard and resolute readers on even this issue are not as great as either side seems to think, thereby eradicating this one prior fixed point in the dispute. See their contributions to the symposium on "Ineffability and Nonsense," *Proceedings of the Aristotelian Society* (2003). Moore suggests that "there are ways of construing the two readings whereby . . . suddenly what seems to make the difference between them has the width of a knife-edge" (p. 180), and Sullivan doubts whether it "has *even* the width of a knife-edge" (p. 204). There is a way in which I am inclined to agree with Sullivan here; inasmuch as I am inclined to think that the standard reading strictly thought through must, at the end of the day, collapse into a variant of a resolute reading. This is connected to a point to which I will return below: all readers of the *Tractatus* must begin life as standard readers. But I doubt most standard readers would look upon this as a friendly suggestion for how to achieve rapprochement. The possibility of rapprochement seems to be envisioned by Moore and Sullivan by assuming that a resolute rejection of substantial nonsense could, if appropriately packaged, be agreeable to a standard reader. But Glock and Hacker (in their articles mentioned above), to cite just two examples, seem determined to rule out any form of détente negotiated along these lines. For an excellent discussion of Glock's treatment of this issue, see Edmund Dain's "Contextualism and Nonsense in Wittgenstein's *Tractatus*," *South African Journal of Philosophy* 25, no. 2 (2006): 91–101.

12. There are at this point a number of articles devoted in small or large part to a series of attempts to embarrass resolute readers with passages thus drawn from the later philosophy. Two of the rhetorically more refined and polemically more piquant examples of the genre are Peter Hacker's article "Was He Trying to Whistle It?" in *The New Wittgenstein*, ed. Crary and Read, 353–388 and Ian Proops's "The New Wittgenstein: A Critique," *European Journal of Philosophy* 9, no. 3 (2001): 375–404.

13. It is therefore a consequence of a resolute reading that one must reject certain fairly standard sorts of account of how Wittgenstein's thought changed. For example, as we shall see, a resolute reading must reject the idea that Wittgenstein changed his views by giving up, in his later thought, a theory of meaning (or of anything else) that he aimed to put forward in the *Tractatus*. If, as resolute readings have it, he did not aim to put forward a theory of meaning (or anything else) in the *Tractatus*, that account of the change in his thought must be rejected. But if one assumes that the *only* way to account for the profound changes in Wittgenstein's thought is in terms of his having put forward a metaphysical theory or a theory of meaning or both in his earlier thought, and his having given up the theory or theories later, then one will take resolute readers to have no choice but to be committed to "a strong continuity thesis." It is this supposed lack of choice that is at issue here.

14. For further discussion of this topic, see my "On What Ethics in the *Tractatus* is *Not*," in *Religion and Wittgenstein's Legacy*, ed. D. Z. Phillips and Mario von der Ruhr (Aldershot: Ashgate, 2005), 39–88.

15. "For the clarity we are aiming at it is indeed *complete* clarity. But this simply means that the philosophical problems should *completely* disappear" (*Philosophical Investigations*, trans. G. E. M. Anscombe [Oxford: Blackwell, 1953], §133). The point figures no less prominently in Wittgenstein's Middle Period writings:

> As I do philosophy, its entire task is to shape expression in such a way that certain worries disappear.
> If I am right, then philosophical problems really must be solvable without remainder, in contrast to all others.
> When I say: Here we are at the limits of language, that always sounds as if resignation were necessary at this point, whereas on the contrary complete satisfaction comes about since *no* question remains.
> The problems are solved in the literal sense of the word—dissolved like a lump of sugar in water. (*The Big Typescript*, ed. and trans. C. Grant Luckhardt and Maximilian A. E. Aue [Oxford: Blackwell, 2005], p. 316)

16. This then leaves the critics of resolute readings with three broad generic options for how to understand the relation between Wittgenstein's early and later thought: (1) they can contend that later Wittgenstein sought to give the correct answers to the questions that he earlier answered incorrectly, (2) they can contend that later Wittgenstein criticized earlier Wittgenstein above all on the ground that he thought that such questions could be answered, or (3) a combination of (1) and (2) in which his earlier answers to certain questions are refuted while his answers to yet other questions are made to vanish along with the questions themselves. It doesn't much matter for the purpose of this essay whether the critic in question prefers option (1), (2), or (3).

17. For a discussion of these issues, see the response to Meredith Williams's criticisms of resolute readings in James Conant and Cora Diamond, "On Reading the *Tractatus* Resolutely," in *Wittgenstein's Lasting Significance*, ed. Kölbel and Weiss, 46–99.

18. Ian Proops, "The New Wittgenstein," pp. 375–376.

19. There are in fact typically many types of passage that are brought into play when such "external evidence" is adduced by critics of resolute readings, including both of the following types: passages from the later work criticizing doctrines held by the *very* early Wittgenstein before he writes the *Tractatus*, and passages in the later work in which Wittgenstein criticizes what he "earlier" thought subsequent to his return to philosophy in 1929. Not every sort of criticism by a comparatively later Wittgenstein of a comparatively earlier one is therefore relevant to our present purpose. And, in fact, passages in the later work often need to be scrutinized carefully in order correctly to ascertain which Wittgenstein is the intended target of the criticism. The only kinds of passage that are relevant to the topic of the present essay are ones in which the criticisms are directed at misconceptions to which later Wittgenstein took the author of the *Tractatus* to be committed. From now on in this essay, when I speak of "external evidence," this is what I will mean. This restriction is justified inasmuch as the aim of this essay is to respond to the criticism that resolute readers are unable to account for Wittgenstein's later criticisms of the *Tractatus*. The introduction of such a restriction, however, threatens to introduce serious

distortions into our understanding of later Wittgenstein if it is taken to license the assumption that all criticisms of "earlier work" are criticisms of the author of the *Tractatus*. I will return to this topic briefly, at the end of this paper, in the penultimate note.

20. In practice, what seems to qualify each item on the list as germane is often little more than the fact that the quotation in question contains in it expressions such as "I used to think . . . ," "contrary to my earlier view . . . ," etc. This, of course, can raise problems of the sort mentioned in the previous note.

21. The existence of such putatively damning external evidence is bound to be comparatively more awkward for a resolute reader who is willing to go so far as to hold that later Wittgenstein thought that his earlier project of philosophical clarification did not involve any commitments (and thus none that he was later concerned to criticize). I will return to this topic below.

22. Pun intended.

23. *Tractatus Logico-Philosophicus*, §6.54 (my emphases). Quotations from the *Tractatus* will be drawn from either the David Pears and Brian McGuinness translation (London: Routledge, 1963) or the reprint of the C. K. Ogden translation (London: Routledge, 1981), or some emendation or combination thereof.

24. The characterization of such readings as "resolute" is first due to Thomas Ricketts and first used in print by Warren Goldfarb in his "Metaphysics and Nonsense: On Cora Diamond's *The Realistic Spirit*," *Journal of Philosophical Research* 22 (1997): 57–73, at p. 64; cf. also p. 73, note 10. Goldfarb's article lays out some of the issues here in dispute very well. See also Diamond's "Realism and Resolution" (which replies to Goldfarb), 75–86 in the same issue.

25. Notice: this feature of a resolute reading—as, too, with regard to each of the other features to be mentioned below—merely says something about how the book ought *not* to be read, thereby still leaving much undetermined about how the book ought to be read.

26. For more discussion of this topic, see my "The Method of the *Tractatus*," in *From Frege to Wittgenstein: Perspectives in Early Analytic Philosophy*, ed. Erich H. Reck (Oxford: Oxford University Press, 2002), 374–470.

27. It would be a mistake to read this paragraph as saying (as the writings of standard readers sometimes seem to suggest) that we can just go about inspecting sentences and (apart from consulting their context of use) sorting them into categories such as the *sinnlos* and the *sinnvoll*. For discussion of this topic, see Cora Diamond, "Crisscross Philosophy," in *Wittgenstein at Work*, ed. Ammereller and Fischer, 201–220. In the interest of keeping things as simple as possible, I will have nothing further to say about the topic of that which is *sinnlos* in this paper. For a discussion of some of the points that arise in connection with this topic and how to accommodate them within a resolute reading, see Michael Kremer, "Mathematics and Meaning in the *Tractatus*," *Philosophical Investigations* 25 (2002): 272–303.

28. I am alluding here to a formulation of Wittgenstein's regarding what is involved in philosophical elucidation that surfaces in passages such as the following: "[I]dealism, strictly thought

out [*streng durchgedacht*], leads to realism."—and: "[S]olipsism, strictly followed through [*streng durchgeführt*], collapses into pure realism." The first is from *Notebooks: 1914–1916*; ed. G. H. von Wright and G .E. M. Anscombe, trans. G. E. M. Anscombe (Chicago: University of Chicago Press, 1979), p. 85. (I have emended the translation.) The second is from the *Tractatus*, 5.64. (I have emended the translation.) For further discussion of the importance in Wittgenstein's work of such a conception of thinking things through, see my "On Going the Bloody Hard Way in Philosophy," in *The Possibilities of Sense*, ed. John Whittaker (New York: Macmillan, 2003).

29. Many critics of resolute readings notice that resolute readers are committed to one or another of these corollaries without ever managing to get the guiding commitment of such a reading clearly into view. Such critics, for example, may notice that resolute readers are committed to rejecting some particular putatively Tractarian account of what makes some sentences nonsensical (say, an account based on illegitimate syntactical combination), while assuming that a resolute reader must share with the proponent of a standard sort of reading the idea that the charge of nonsense leveled at the end of the *Tractatus* is to be underwritten by *some* theory—be it one that is advanced within the body of the work or one that is imported into the work from the outside. These critics thereby assume that these readers must want to substitute some alternative theoretical account of the grounds of sense for the particular one under criticism. These critics then become understandably very puzzled about how such a reading can possibly be thought to be sustainable. For they assume that the discovery that there are no logically distinct kinds of nonsense is itself arrived at through the elaboration and application of a theory of sense that these readers are now committed to viewing as having somehow been successfully articulated by the author of the *Tractatus*, even though the propositions by means of which it is to have been articulated have been relegated to the status of mere nonsense. This then leads to the criticism that the resulting reading renders the propositions of the book too semantically impoverished to be able to articulate the theoretical resources required to fund the conception of the nature of nonsense that the readers in question are committed to ascribing to the work. I enthusiastically endorse this line of argument as a criticism of a possible (misguided) reading of the *Tractatus*. But it is a species of irresolute reading that is here criticized. (For further discussion of this point see Conant and Diamond, "On Reading the *Tractatus* Resolutely.")

30. This idea that we can grasp what certain sentences would say if they had a sense is sometimes called *chickening out*. See Diamond, *The Realistic Spirit*, chapter 6, especially pp. 181–182, 194–195.

31. I am indebted, in rather different ways, for this suggestion to Johannes Climacus, *Concluding Scientific Postscript*, and to Meredith Williams, "Nonsense and Cosmic Exile." For a less abbreviated version of the repudiation of the claim that Ludwig adhered to anything like *The Dogma of the Paradox*, see part 2 of Conant and Diamond, "On Reading the *Tractatus* Resolutely." For discussion of the connection between Climacus's and Wittgenstein's respective ladders, see my "Must We Show What We Cannot Say?" in *The Senses of Stanley Cavell*, ed. R. Fleming and M. Payne (Lewisburg, Pa.: Bucknell University Press, 1989), "Kierkegaard, Wittgenstein, and Nonsense," in *Pursuits of Reason*, ed. Ted Cohen, Paul Guyer, and Hilary Putnam (Lubbock: Texas Tech University Press, 1992), and "Putting Two and Two Together: Kierkegaard, Wittgenstein, and the

Point of View for Their Work as Authors," in *The Grammar of Religious Belief,* ed. D. Z. Phillips (N.Y.: St. Martins Press, 1996).

32. For further discussion of this example, see Conant and Diamond, "On Reading the *Tractatus* Resolutely," pp. 61–62.

33. See *Tractatus*, §5.4733.

34. A story about this can count as a version of a resolute reading only to the extent that an understanding of the author here rests upon nothing more than a cultivation of the reader's logical capacities—capacities that she exercises whenever she thinks or speaks. These capacities are honed in the context of philosophical elucidation through our learning such things as how properly to parse sentences whose surface grammar confuses us, how properly to employ the fragments of logical notion to which the author of the *Tractatus* introduces us, and so on. But the point of exercising such comparatively more determinate logical capacities is to refine the antecedently available general capacity that the reader brings with her to an encounter with the text: namely, her ability to discern sense, recognize nonsense, and distinguish the one from the other. It is a mistake to assume (as many standard readers do) that possession of this general capacity is something that the author of the *Tractatus* aims to confer on his reader through an encounter with the text.

35. For more discussion of this topic, see my "The Method of the *Tractatus*."

36. The German word in the text of §6.54 to which I mean to allude here is *überwinden*.

37. This question has been pressed by critics of the resolute reading, most notably Peter Sullivan, and it *should* be pressed. I think it is fair to say that the plausibility of a resolute approach to reading the book will depend partly upon how satisfying an answer this question can be given.

38. Any two standard readers may disagree about which sentences belong in the first set; and any two resolute readers may disagree about which sentences belong in the second set. Thus any talk about such a list in the context of a more general discussion of debates between standard and resolute readers, such as the one that follows, will involve a certain degree of idealization. I will return to this topic in the next section.

39. The term "piecemeal" was, as far as I know, first employed by Warren Goldfarb in "Metaphysics and Nonsense" in connection with this issue. It is important to be clear about what, according to a resolute reading, must be piecemeal here. A remark such as the following introduces the possibility of confusing this issue with another:

Don't get involved in partial problems, but always take flight to where there is a free view over the whole *single* great problem, even if this view is still not a clear one. (*Notebooks, 1914–1916,* (2nd edition, trans. G. E. M. Anscombe [Oxford: Blackwell, 1979], p. 23)

Marie McGinn glosses this remark as follows: Wittgenstein "instructs himself not to try to treat each of the problems piecemeal" ("Wittgenstein's Early Philosophy and the Idea of 'The Single Great Problem'," in *Wittgenstein: The Philosopher and His Works,* ed. Pichler and Säätelä, p. 100). What McGinn takes early Wittgenstein to be here instructing himself not to do (in her use of the expression "treat each of the problems piecemeal") and what resolute readers take early

Wittgenstein to be committed to doing (in their use of the expression "treat each of the problems piecemeal") is not the same thing. I take it that the ambition touched on in the remark from the *Notebooks* (the ambition to attain a view of the problems of philosophy that allows them all simultaneously to come into view as aspects of "a whole *single* great problem") is an ambition that Wittgenstein takes himself to have realized by the time of completing the *Tractatus*. It is tied to the remark in the preface of the *Tractatus* that "the problems have in essentials finally been solved." The problems have in essentials been solved because *the* method of their (dis)solution has been found. The application of this method to the problems of philosophy (that require treatment by the method) is for early Wittgenstein, nonetheless, a piecemeal process— that is why the problems have been solved only in essentials, and not in their details. It is the latter distinction (between solving the problems in essentials vs. in their details) that mandates the early procedure of piecemeal interrogation of sentences that resolute readers insist upon. This opposition (between the piecemeal procedure common to the *Tractatus* and the *Investigations* and the wholesale procedure of philosophical criticism commonly ascribed to the former) is not to be confused with a more fundamental distinction in philosophical conception between the methodological monism of the early Wittgenstein (who seeks to present *the* method of clarification) and the methodological pluralism of the later Wittgenstein (who seeks to present an open-ended series of examples of method*s*—a series that can be continued in both unforeseen and unforeseeable ways). A resolute reader who insists upon things being piecemeal in the former sense need not hold that they are piecemeal in the latter sense (and therefore need not deny that there is this enormous difference in methodological conception between early and later Wittgenstein). The definite article in the title of my paper "The Method of the *Tractatus*" (a paper which, incidentally, insists upon the piecemeal character of any application of *the* method) is supposed to mark an important point of difference between early and later Wittgenstein. A resolute reader who fails carefully to distinguish these senses in which something about the early method can be said to be "piecemeal" runs the risk of falling into thinking that a bare commitment to resolution itself entails a needlessly severe form of mono-Wittgensteinianism.

40. The successive publications of a number of commentators bear witness to how considerable a span of time and effort can intervene between a first resolute recognition of the collapse of a particular sequence of rungs and a subsequent resolute recognition of the collapse of a further sequence of rungs. (For instance certain readers—who are now resolute readers—seem to have first noticed that the apparently realist doctrines in the work collapsed well before they realized that their idealist counterparts must fall, too.) That this sort of time and effort can be required to climb the ladder is one of the features of the phenomenology of seriously working with the book to which a resolute reading aims to do justice. One complaint that such readers are apt to have about standard readings is that they make the process of assimilating the teaching of the work look much *easier* than it is. A slightly arch way to put this point would be as follows: according to resolute readers, the *Tractatus* is much longer than it looks—a quarter of a century of intensive engagement with the text (judging from my own case) may well not be enough time for a reader to be able to claim to have completed a single ascent of the ladder. This seemingly bottomless character to the task of simply working through the text is one of the respects in which resolute readers are apt to think there is an important affinity between the *Tractatus* and the *Investigations*.

41. Some critics of "the resolute reading" seem to think that resolute readers wish to convince us that there is some general philosophical claim (about, say, the nature of nonsense) that one is supposed to take on board right at the outset and which constitutes the proper *starting point* for a process of reading through the work. (See John Koethe, "On the 'Resolute' Reading of the *Tractatus*," *Philosophical Investigations* 26, no. 3 (2003): 187–204, for an example of this line of criticism.) Such critics have understandably declared themselves to be utterly perplexed about how such a process of reading is supposed to get off the ground if one is supposed to begin by taking on board a commitment to the effect that each sentence one comes across in the course of reading through the book is to be regarded as never anything more than a piece of plain nonsense. There are three basic misunderstandings here. First, it mistakes what resolute readers take to be the *termini ad quem* (of the activity of reading of the book) for the *terminus a quo*. Second, it takes resolute readers to share a standard reader's conception of wherein the recognition of nonsense (on the part of a reader) consists: namely, in the application of a set of independently available criteria (for distinguishing sense from nonsense) to the sentences of the book. Third, it takes the discovery that many of the sentences in the book are nonsense to be something that can take place wholesale rather than only piecemeal.

42. At the cost of discouraging some overly zealous professed converts, it should be pointed out here that this also means that there is no such thing as a well-founded moment of *wholesale conversion* to the program shared by resolute readers. Such an approach to reading the book must prove its interpretative mettle piecemeal, by illuminating how a dialectical ascent up the ladder unfolds rung by rung. This fact has been obscured by the fact that, in many of the early publications of those of us sympathetic to a resolute approach, we were initially concerned simply with highlighting the very possibility of such a program for reading the book. Such programmatic statements, however, are often read by critics (and even by some overly enthusiastic advocates) as if they purported to settle all the relevant basic questions regarding how to interpret the book rather than—as was intended—to unsettle them all, so that they can be settled again one by one. (This is not to deny the presence of infelicities of formulation and thought in these early writings. I would certainly like to omit or reword the occasional sentence or two from here or there in my earlier writings on this topic. I know that Cora Diamond feels the same.)

43. I take the difficulties at issue here not to be ones that are mere artifacts of a resolute account of this relation, but rather to be ones that themselves belong to Wittgenstein's conception of the task of philosophical criticism and, in particular, to his conception of the *difficulty* of that task.

44. This exercise would be pointless, however, if it were not possible to associate particular passages in the text with *some* of the entries on this list. I take it to be relatively easy to locate moments in the text that correspond to the following two clusters of items 1–5, 13–17. Items 6–12 on the actual list given here, however, play a rather different role in filling in the structure of the ladder. If one were set (say, as an examination question) the task of finding a passage in the text to associate with each of items 6–12, one might be surprised to discover how hard it is to find textual correlates for any of these items on the list, though it would be quite easy to associate them with things that one finds in standard commentaries on the work. (In fact, it is easier

to find passages in the text that take issue with these items—especially item 8; see e.g., §§5.473–5.4733.) These items therefore do no represent explicit moments of apparent doctrine in the text as much as implicit lines of "thought" into which a reader is naturally drawn: lines of "thought" that appear to provide a way of filling in the missing links that would enable one to pass from the first cluster of items to the second—a way of filling things in that most commentators on the *Tractatus* have found irresistible. Any specification of the rungs of the ladder in the form of a list will probably require both these sorts of item—both those that figure explicitly in the text as candidate doctrines of the work and those (to which a reader is strongly attracted in making sense of those doctrines) that figure explicitly in the text at most only as targets of criticism.

45. The actual list, given above, is in essence a pastiche, hovering somewhere between these two ways of understanding what the shape of the list ought to be. As a reconstruction of the sequence in which things occur in the text (aside from the fact that it starts things off too late, contains things that are not in the text, breaks off too early, and moves too swiftly), this list allows itself to cheat in all kinds of further ways. Yet the sequence given is even less plausible if it is meant simply to sketch a possible order according to which apparently weight-bearing moments in the text are successively discovered to collapse by some actual reader. The list is purposely constructed so as equally to invite these alternative understandings of how to understand the shape of the ladder. This means that it does not constitute a serious attempt to reconstruct the elucidatory dialectic as it unfolds in the work.

46. This asymmetry in the relations between sense/nonsense and true/false is a source of many of the confusions that the *Tractatus* seeks to address. Propositions do not have sense-nonsense poles in the way that they have true-false poles, so that there can still be a determinate something that we may take "the" proposition to (be striving to) say when we recognize "it" to be nonsense (as there can still be when we recognize a proposition to be false). Our reluctance to come to terms with how little we are left with if we have failed to make sense yields the peculiar phenomenology of our imagining (in our ascent up the ladder) that we are able to recognize what a piece of nonsense is trying to say even as we recognize that it is nonsense.

47. It is such an oscillation that I have briefly sought to enact in my preceding presentation of the two ways of unpacking the metaphor.

48. Peter Sullivan points out, in "On Trying to Be Resolute," pp. 46–49, that certain resolute readers seem to evince a disproportionate hostility to explanations of features of language via an appeal to features of reality and seem to evince a corresponding tolerance toward the reverse order of explanation. This can make it seem as if resolution had something "particularly to do with repudiating a certain sort of realism" (p. 47). I think it is true that certain resolute readers have written things that appear to contain such a lack of equilibrium in attitude (toward realism and idealism respectively) and that Sullivan is right that, insofar as they endorse the appropriateness of this imbalance, they thereby compromise their commitment to resolution. A full explanation of why one finds this tendency in this body of tertiary literature would require a story about how certain strains of an incipiently resolute reading evolved, early on, out of a rejection of certain realist readings. A no-longer merely incipiently resolute reading, however, should be

equally committed to rejecting an order of explanation in either direction here, and therefore should not accord realism any privileged status as the target of criticism.

49. See the quotations given in note 28.

50. If there figures on the list at some point both a certain form of words and its (apparent) negation, then the list can be continued in two different directions. If there figures on the list a triad of (apparently) mutually divergent philosophical options (such a realism, idealism, and solipsism), then it can be continued in three different directions. And so on.

51. With respect to questions about the relation between realism and idealism, a nice example of such a dialectical reconstruction (that offers cogent reasons for privileging a particular narrative about how things are supposed to unfold) is to be found in Thomas Ricketts's article, "Pictures, Logic, and the Limits of Sense in Wittgenstein's *Tractatus*," in *The Cambridge Companion to Wittgenstein*, ed. Hans Sluga and David G. Stern (Cambridge: Cambridge University Press, 1996), pp. 59–99; see especially pp. 88–94. With respect to the relation of both of these to solipsism, a further pertinent example of this genre of philosophical exegetical narrative (its author's public lashings of the resolute heresy in his other writings notwithstanding) is to be found in Peter Sullivan's "The 'Truth' in Solipsism, and Wittgenstein's Rejection of the A Priori," *European Journal of Philosophy* 4, no. 2 (1996): 195–219.

52. For discussion of the distinction between propositional sign and propositional symbol in the *Tractatus*, see my "The Method of the *Tractatus*," pp. 398–405.

53. Thomas Ricketts, "Pictures, Logic, and the Limits of Sense in Wittgenstein's *Tractatus*," pp. 90, 93.

54. This, in turn, means that a remark that on one construal does make sense—and, so construed, can be taken to contain an intelligible proposal (concerning, say, the employment of a certain sort of notation) or a coherent instruction to the reader (concerning, say, how the reader is to relate herself to the sentences in the book)—on another construal (if taken to form a part of one of the aforementioned collections of remarks) may involve an illusion of sense. As long as there are terms such as "proposition," "nonsense," "sign," "symbol," etc., that figure centrally in sentences that a reader is able to take as forming a part of one of the aforementioned collections of remarks, then her "understanding" of those sentences is likely, in turn, to color that reader's "understanding" of all the other sentences in the book in which those terms figure. Whether a given sentence (such as, e.g., §6.54) is nonsense or not depends on how one takes it to be related to the other sentences in the book. The following challenge, commonly leveled at (nonzealous) mono-Wittgensteinians by standard readers, is ill posed: what are the marks or features that single out the sentences of the work, as they stand on the page, as being the ones that make sense from the ones that do not? The apparent inability of resolute readers to answer this question has been taken to constitute an argument against them. What a (nonzealous) resolute reader needs to hold is only that there are certain sentences of the book that a reader can (on a certain construal of them) come to understand—*not*: that there are certain sentences of the book that the reader is supposed to be able somehow (based on the application of some supposed criteria of meaningfulness) first to separate out from the others as those that are to be understood,

prior to and independently of struggling with the task of working her way through the task that the author of the work has set us. A propositional sign has a perceptible sense, according to the author of the *Tractatus*, only given a method of employment; and it belongs to the task that the author sets the reader to discover for herself when, in assimilating the sentences of the book, she has genuinely conferred such a method of employment on her signs and when she has only apparently done so. Apart from a reader exhibiting the sort of use to which she takes the sentences she finds in the book to have been put (apart, that is, from attempting to make out a method of symbolizing that has been conferred upon them), there is no question to be asked regarding the sentences in the book (taken as mere propositional signs) as to which ones make sense and which ones do not. This is why the challenge mentioned above is ill-posed. As the author of the *Tractatus* might have said, where there is no question there is no answer either.

55. This is related to a question that came up earlier: namely, to what degree a given resolute reader thinks the body of sentences that make up the rungs of the ladder coincides with the body of sentences that make up the text of the *Tractatus*.

56. T. S. Eliot, "The Music of Poetry," in *On Poetry and Poets* (London: Faber and Faber, 1969), p. 36.

57. A full discussion of this topic would take us well beyond the scope of this essay. But the three moments of continuity hinted at in this section of the essay should suffice to focus the questions to be explored here. For a brief discussion of further significant moments of continuity, see notes 133 and 134 below.

58. *Tractatus*, §4.112.

59. *Philosophical Investigations*, §128.

60. After some correspondence on the topic, Ogden stays with "to make propositions clear" as a translation of *das Klarwerden von Sätzen*; Pears and McGuinness render it as "the clarification of propositions." Neither of these renderings is ideal; each has something to be said in its favor. Wittgenstein objects to Ogden's translation as follows:

This seems to me wrong now. I think it cannot be the RESULT of philosophy "to make propositions clear": this can only be its TASK. The *result* must be that the propositions *now have become clear* that they ARE clear." (*Letters to C. K. Ogden* [Oxford: Blackwell, 1973], p. 50)

One can see why Ogden might have found this unhelpful.

61. This similarity between the early and the later work, however, is already connected to an important difference. The early work is full of apparent theses that the reader is supposed to come to recognize as merely apparent theses; whereas, in the later work, part of the struggle is to find a way to speak philosophically while systematically eschewing *even the appearance* of philosophical assertion. I discuss this difference in modes of authorship in my "Putting Two and Two Together: Kierkegaard, Wittgenstein, and the Point of View for Their Work as Authors," pp. 293–303.

62. *Tractatus*, §6.54.

63. *Philosophical Investigations*, §464.

64. For further discussion of this topic, see my "Why Worry about the *Tractatus*?" in *Post-Analytic Tractatus*, ed. Barry Stocker (Aldershot, U.K.: Ashgate, 2004).

65. For further discussion of this topic, see my "Wittgenstein on Meaning and Use," *Philosophical Investigations* 21, no. 3 (1998): 222–250.

66. This topic should be distinguished from the topic briefly touched on in note 39: is it possible to attain a perspicuous overview of all of the possible forms of philosophical confusion—so that, even if the task of philosophical treatment never comes to an end, at least the scope and shape of all the possible forms of confusion can be grasped as aspects of a single unity—a single big problem? If this were possible, then, even if there remained, in one sense, an infinite amount of work still to be done, in another, it would be right to say that the really *hard* part of the task will have been completed and, in this sense, the problems will have, in essentials, all been solved. This is a point on which early and later Wittgenstein sharply diverge; and this, in turn, is connected to the topic of the second list, to which we will turn below.

67. *Philosophical Investigations*, p. x.

68. There is a German edition of the two books bound together that is published by Suhrkamp Verlag (Frankfurt am Main, 1984). In this respect it comes close to respecting this wish of Wittgenstein's (and, to my knowledge, is the only volume published in any language that does so to any degree). This may have come about largely by accident: these are Wittgenstein's only two authorized book-length publications and the Suhrkamp volume in question is *Band I* of their *Wittgenstein Werkausgabe*. Those who are inclined to doubt that Suhrkamp was motivated by any desire to honor Wittgenstein's wishes here will find various grounds for their skepticism—including the following: the volume also includes the *1914–1916 Notebooks* (the inclusion of which would not have struck Wittgenstein as a merely minor variation on his plan; see e.g., *Letters to C. K. Ogden*, p. 46), and the volume bears the following title on its cover and spine: *Tractatus Logico-Philosophicus*. So there is a sense in which Wittgenstein's book still remains unpublished!

69. "A main cause of philosophical disease—a one-sided diet: one nourishes one's thinking with only one kind of example" (*Philosophical Investigations*, §593 [I have amended the translation]).

70. This point is first developed by Stanley Cavell in "The Availability of Wittgenstein's Later Philosophy," collected in *Must We Mean What We Say? and Other Essays* (Cambridge: Cambridge University Press, 1976), 44–72, and is central to the reading of Wittgenstein he offers in *The Claim of Reason* (Oxford: Oxford University Press, 1979).

71. Arguably part of the way that standard readings of the *Tractatus* first developed was through commentators attributing to the early work as substantive theoretical commitments a great many of the doctrines that later Wittgenstein is concerned to criticize, so that they could provide themselves with a tidy target at which those criticisms could be directed. Perhaps the now three most classic instances of this genre are Norman Malcolm's *Nothing is Hidden* (Oxford: Blackwell, 1986), Peter Hacker's *Insight and Illusion*, rev. ed. (Oxford: Oxford University Press, 1986), and David Pears's *The False Prison* (Oxford: Oxford University Press, 1987). Malcolm developed his version

of such a narrative much earlier than the others. Malcolm's 1967 article on Wittgenstein in the *The Encyclopedia of Philosophy*, ed. Paul Edwards (London: Macmillan, 1967) is a fascinatingly vehement statement of the standard reading, adamant in its rejection of the possibility of an even mildly mono-Wittgensteinian view (probably directed, above all, at Erik Stenius's somewhat idiosyncratic and not at all resolute proposal for such a reading, as put forward in his *Wittgenstein's Tractatus* [Oxford: Blackwell, 1960]). I say at the beginning of this note that this is only *part* of the way (that standard readings of the *Tractatus* first developed) because a full story would also have to take into account the paths of reception encouraged by the work of Russell, Ramsey, Schlick, Carnap, Waismann, Black, Anscombe, Stenius, and many others. A good *Rezeptionsgeschichte* of the *Tractatus* has yet to be written.

72. This tendency is reinforced by an academic environment in which commentators spend much of their time studying each other's work and in which most of the commentary there is to study is written by authors whose interest in wrestling with the letter of the text of the *Tractatus* has mostly been whetted through reading the later work—and through expectations that have been thus formed regarding what sort of philosophy there must be in the early work, as well as what it is they are supposed to do with it once they find it. This generally leads to their getting down to the business of criticizing the *Tractatus* prematurely.

73. *Tractatus*, sixth paragraph of the preface.

74. This point acquires special pertinence if one thinks, as some resolute readers do, that the criticism of Frege represents a central task for the *Tractatus*. This is itself a topic of some controversy now—one that cuts interestingly across the standard/resolute divide. Elizabeth Anscombe, Cora Diamond, Peter Geach, Michael Kremer, Marie McGinn, Erich Reck, Thomas Ricketts, and I have all argued for the importance of the Fregean background to an understanding of the *Tractatus*. This approach to reading the book has been challenged; see especially Warren Goldfarb's "Wittgenstein's Understanding of Frege: The Pre-Tractarian Evidence," in *From Frege to Wittgenstein*, ed. Reck; and Ian Proops's "Early Wittgenstein on Logical Assertion," *Philosophical Topics* 25, no. 2 (1997): 121–144.

75. There are countless relevant examples here, but to mention only one: the doctrine that the meaning of a primitive term is conferred by a mental act of concentration or through a sufficiently emphatic gesture of ostensive definition. One need not enter at all into the commitments of a resolute reading in order to think it is a serious mistake to ascribe a doctrine of this sort to the *Tractatus*. Without yet having taken a step on the path toward resolution, one can easily begin to worry about the fairly standard ascriptions of such doctrines to the *Tractatus* in many of the book-length treatments. One consequence of this is that the relation of some of the comparatively early disputes—between commentators (such as Ishiguro, McGuinness, and Winch) who deny the presence of *these* doctrines in the *Tractatus* and commentators (such as Malcolm, Hacker, and Pears) who insist upon the presence of one of these doctrines there—to the comparatively later disputes (between resolute readers and their critics) is by no means a straightforward one. One the one hand, the denial of these doctrines need not push a commentator toward accepting any part of a resolute view of the items that ought to figure on the first list. Yet it is surely no accident that commentators such as Ishiguro, McGuinness, and Winch have proved comparatively receptive to the writings of resolute readers and

vice versa. For a relevant article by each of the latter three authors, see Hide Ishiguro, "Use and Reference of Names," in *Studies in the Philosophy of Wittgenstein*, ed. Winch, 20–50; Brian McGuinness, "On the So-Called Realism of the *Tractatus*," in *Perspectives on the Philosophy of Wittgenstein*, ed. Irving Block (Cambridge, Mass.: MIT Press, 1981), 60–73; and Peter Winch, "Language, Thought, and World in Wittgenstein's *Tractatus*," collected in his *Trying to Make Sense* (Oxford: Basil Blackwell, 1987), 3–17. For a discussion of the bearing of such articles on resolute readings, see the controversy between Peter Hacker, especially his "Naming, Thinking, and Meaning in the *Tractatus*," *Philosophical Investigations* 22 (1999): 119–135, reprinted in *Wittgenstein: Connections and Controversies* (Oxford: Oxford University Press, 2001), 170–183; and his "Postscript" (also in the same volume), 184–190, and Cora Diamond, see especially her "Peter Winch on the *Tractatus* and the Unity of Wittgenstein's Philosophy," in *Wittgenstein: The Philosopher and his Works*, ed. Pichler and Säätelä, 133–143.

76. And, indeed, one often comes across a commentator who can strike one as, in this sense, lost—adrift, as it were, in the text of the *Tractatus*. The three most telling symptoms of such disorientation on the part of a reader are: (1) that his reading seems to be guided, above all, by a desire to find certain doctrines (such as naïve mentalism) *somewhere* in the book, (2) that this leads him to cast about for hooks onto which to hang such doctrines, regardless of how little weight the candidates for hooks can bear, and (3) that this impetus to suppose that the doctrines in question are in the text seems to flow (not from an encounter with the text itself, but rather) from firmly entrenched antecedent assumptions about what *must* be there.

77. Considerations of space regrettably preclude more than intermittent brief discussion of this topic in the pages that follow.

78. For more on this topic, see my "The Method of the *Tractatus*," 411–418.

79. Indeed, early Wittgenstein went to some trouble (1) to redesign his logical notation so that it could best serve the exclusive ends of philosophical elucidation (as opposed to, say, those of formalizing mathematical proof, eliminating a reliance upon intuition, etc.), and (2) to drain it of the sort of potential doctrinal philosophical significance with which Frege and Russell wished to invest a *Begriffsschrift* in the context of (their respective understandings of) a logicist demonstration of the true metaphysical character of the truths of mathematics.

80. The assumption that these questions can effect such a division informs much of the relevant body of critical tertiary literature on resolute readings.

81. Some further questions that may do the trick are the following: How important is *that* question (i.e., the question about how to read the *Tractatus* that divides them) to an understanding of later Wittgenstein? How important is it to arrive at an accurate account of Wittgenstein's original self-understanding as author of his early work, in order to achieve an accurate appreciation of what he later thought was confused and self-deluded in his earlier self-understanding of what he had achieved in philosophy? And how important is an appreciation of *that* to an understanding of much else in his later philosophy?

82. What Wittgenstein perhaps did not anticipate is the extent to which this might become an extraordinarily difficult thing for a later generation of students of his work to undertake to do— in part because of the extraordinary success that his later work would come to enjoy.

83. I do not mean in the least to suggest here that reading the *Tractatus* through the lens of the *Investigations* is simply irrelevant to the task of viewing the old and new ways of thinking together, but only that what will thus come into view for us when we read in that direction will inevitably suffer some distortion if we are not equally adept at the complementary task of reading in the opposite direction—if we are not able to see clearly what stands out as genuinely new and what does not in the new way of thinking when it is contrasted with the old way of thinking. But to see this we need some independent appreciation of how tremendously radical (even if, by his later lights, very insufficiently radical) his old way of thinking already was.

84. The validity of the point made here is not restricted to an appreciation of the momentous yet unwitting character of the specific commitments of the author of the *Tractatus*. Throughout his later work, Wittgenstein seeks to instill in us an appreciation of how we can become philosophically ensnared without being aware of it. The specific form of sensitivity that he wishes to impart here (which a properly attentive critical reading of the *Tractatus* calls for) acquires its primary significance in relation to these more general aims of the *Philosophical Investigations*. For what is required of us in such a mode of reading the *Tractatus* is meant to offer a particularly vivid illustration of a sort of sensitivity that later Wittgenstein wants us to learn to exercise more generally—in our relation, not only to the philosophical utterances of others, but especially in relation to those moments in our own philosophizing with respect to which we ourselves feel on most secure ground. This means that we will have understood the object-lesson here (i.e., the example that his later interrogation of his own earlier philosophy is meant to provide) only when we have learnt to direct the same exquisite degree of sensitivity to discovering just how philosophically momentous and altogether noninnocuous many of the forms of expression that presently strike us as obvious and innocent actually are.

85. Again, I take the difficulties at issue here not to be ones that are mere artifacts of a resolute account of this relation, but rather to be ones that themselves belong to Wittgenstein's conception of the task of philosophical criticism and, in particular, to his later conception of the difficulty of that task.

86. *Philosophical Investigations*, §91.

87. It was, above all, in connection with this presupposition that Piero Sraffa's Neapolitan gesture of disdain (along with his query "What is the logical form of *this*?") was able to do its fixation-shattering work.

88. This commitment involves a great many subsidiary commitments about the character of the process of analysis, about such a process presupposing a point at which the analysis terminates, about when such a point is reached, about what is thereby disclosed, etc. A great many items could be added to the list in this connection.

89. There are a great many subsidiary commitments that come into play here through the commitment to the idea of an absolutely perspicuous notation. That any entailment can be set out as a truth-table tautology is perhaps the most famous such commitment. Additional commitments come into play through his attachment to the Sheffer-stroke notation and the topic of the nature of logical constants, through the operator N and the topic of the general form of the proposition, and through the *Klammerausdruck* notation and the topic of the nature of

quantification. It would go well beyond the scope of this essay to show why Wittgenstein did not, at the time of writing the book, take his attachments to any of these to reflect a substantial doctrine and why he later changed his view about each. The point that matters for our present purpose is simply that a great many additional items, tied to more determinate commitments regarding *the* logic of our language, could be added to the list in this connection.

90. I have attempted to arrange the items on the actual list above so as to give some sense of how one of these commitments quickly begins to bleed into another and so on.

91. A standard reader might be happy to include all of the items on the second list on his (standard reader's) list. This might suggest the following conclusion: standard and resolute readers are at least in full agreement about the status of the set of sentences that belong to the intersection of the standard reader's list and the second list. One can think this only if one overlooks many of the points established previously, including the differences between standard and resolute readers with respect to the following topics: (1) the role of the doctrinal schema, (2) the role of the paradox, (3) how to understand the prefatory remark, and, above all, (4) the second sort of indiscriminateness.

92. See part 4 of "On Reading the *Tractatus* Resolutely" for discussion of this point, in which Conant and Diamond reply to Peter Sullivan's article "What Is the *Tractatus* About?"; the latter is also in *Wittgenstein's Lasting Significance*, ed. Kölbel and Weiss, 32–45.

93. Such sentences themselves could not even apparently be expressed in anything that would count, by the author of the *Tractatus*'s lights, as a proper logical grammar—i.e., a perspicuous logical notation with the sorts of properties that these sentences aspire to claim such a notation must have.

94. This latter option requires an understanding of the early procedure of elucidation in which it can be brought to a kind of completion in which its commitments to its own canons of analysis (which underwrite its employment of logical notation) are themselves dissolved. The threat of reinstating a variant of the paradox looms here. Later Wittgenstein has a ground to stand on here (in espousing such a nondogmatic ideal of clarification) that early Wittgenstein lacks: the ground of the ordinary. The availability of such a ground requires taking seriously the thought that in ordinary language *nothing* is hidden. Each of the commitments on the second list is tied to early Wittgenstein's picture that what is of real interest—the logical structure of the proposition— *is* hidden, disguised by its surface appearance in language, and must be brought to light.

95. To show that a zealous interpreter must invite Incredulity does not, of course, suffice to show that he is wrong. It is open to the zealous to maintain that, at the end of the day, standard readers and mild mono-Wittgensteinians alike ought to learn to embrace that which presently excites their incredulity.

96. There seem to be a number of these. Burton Dreben is sometimes rumored to be the founder of this denomination of resolute readers. Rupert Read and Rob Deans are clearly zealous. (Rupert Read claims in print that Warren Goldfarb is, but I don't see the evidence for this claim.) Some things Matthew Ostrow says suggest an inclination to lean this way (see his *Wittgenstein's*

Tractatus: A Dialectical Interpretation [Cambridge: Cambridge University Press, 2002]), but he also says "it is unquestionable that the notion of a canonical *Begriffsschrift* plays an important (if extremely unclear) role in the *Tractatus*" (p. 9). There seems to be a variety of ways to flesh out a zealous approach. Warner Goldfarb, Rupert Read, and others have found the most provocative elaboration of this variant of mono-Wittgensteinianism in several of Juliet Floyd's recent articles. She has seemed to such readers to be concerned to advance (what Goldfarb, in his unpublished article *Das Überwinden*, without endorsing the reading in question, calls) a *Jacobin reading*—a reading that denies that the *Tractatus* is committed to any canons of analysis, and *a fortiori* to the metaphysical commitments that figure on the actual second list above. (In "On Reading the *Tractatus* Resolutely," Diamond and I also read Floyd in this way.) See, for example, Floyd's "Number and Ascriptions of Number in Wittgenstein's *Tractatus*," in *From Frege to Wittgenstein*, ed. Reck, 308–352). She appears to claim there that "the best answer that can be given to those critics of Diamond (and other anti-metaphysical readers of the *Tractatus*)" is to allow that early Wittgenstein "does not think any notation can depict *the* grammar of language . . . *the* logical order" (p. 340). It is perhaps helpful to note in this connection that Floyd's phrase "anti-metaphysical readers of the *Tractatus*" is ambiguous. On one understanding of it (i.e., as denoting those who read the *Tractatus* as aiming to avoid metaphysics), it is well suited to sort comparatively resolute readers from others; on another understanding of it (i.e., as denoting those who read the *Tractatus* as having largely avoided metaphysics), it is better suited to sort the (much narrower class of) comparatively zealous resolute interpreters from all others. On the second understanding of the phrase, what Floyd appears to say here (about what such readers should hold) is arguably correct, but then Diamond is not, in fact, such a reader. On the first understanding of the phrase, Diamond is such a reader, but what is here said (about what such readers should hold) is arguably no longer correct. Perhaps the intention of the remark is to claim that those who wish to join Diamond in being "anti-metaphysical readers" in the first sense will be able best to answer her critics if they join Floyd in taking the further step here mentioned in the direction of becoming "anti-metaphysical readers" in the second sense. This seems to be the invitation that Rupert Read and his coauthors find in Floyd's work and enthusiastically take up. (I fear, however, that rather than answering the critics of resolute readings, this plays directly into their hands.) I am told that Floyd takes such readings of her work to be misreadings and that she seeks to redress them in her contribution to the present volume.

97. This means that mild and zealous mono-Wittgensteinians alike will insist, though with rather different motives, that it is no less important to a proper understanding of the items on the second actual list (than it was to those on the first) that they be taken to be associated with sentences, not thoughts.

98. And this means that the dispute is not likely to be resolved, at least by appeal only to "internal" textual evidence, any time soon.

99. Some of what Rupert Read has written in a number of his recent writings suggests that he takes something of this sort to be true. He seems to take resolution to define a certain direction one can go in one's reading of the *Tractatus*, but then sees Conant and Diamond as wanting to jump off the train while it is still en route, whereas he (along with other zealous mono-

Wittgensteinians) "resolutely" remains on board until the last stop. (See, for example, his "A No-Theory? Against Hutto on Wittgenstein," *Philosophical Investigations* 29, no. 1 [January 2006], where on p. 81 it is suggested that Conant and Diamond are enacting "something of a retreat" from the program of reading that they once shared with him.) Conant and Diamond take resolute readers to be committed to trying to make as much sense of the *Tractatus* as is possible in the light of a certain approach to understanding Wittgenstein's *aim* in that book. Resolution thus understood is an interpretive strategy for *making sense of a book* not a self-standing *measure of the book's philosophical success*. To read the *Tractatus* resolutely is to try to make out what the author of that book took himself to be up to in the light of this particular understanding of his aim. Someone who tries to read the book in this way need not claim that the author was completely successful in realizing that aim. It might be that the only way to make full sense of the book requires sensitivity to where it falls short of its aspirations. To claim that early Wittgenstein had a resolute conception of his project in the *Tractatus*, on this understanding of what it is to be "resolute," does not commit one to claiming that the project, conceived in its original terms, was free of misconception, any more than claiming that Kant was a transcendental idealist commits one to the claim that transcendental idealism is true. If one saddles oneself qua interpreter with an additional commitment to the effect that Kant (not only never intended to be, but actually) never was wrong about anything, then it may be very hard to make sense of everything he says. Similarly, if resolution is a strategy for making sense of a text, one ought not to saddle oneself with any further commitment of this sort up front. One ought to have an understanding of what Wittgenstein was trying to do that is able to tolerate the possibility that he may not have succeeded in doing it. It seems desirable therefore to employ the term "resolution" (as a label for a program of reading the text) in such a way as to leave room for debate about the further question of the success of the project thus understood. This is not to deny that early Wittgenstein's aspiration in the book was to think the problems through in such a way that one cleanses oneself of all apparently weighty philosophical commitments, rids oneself of all confusion, and makes the problems completely disappear. One can easily slide, for this reason, into using the term "resolute" as a term for a measure of a philosopher's success in living up to these aspirations. Using the term in this second way, one can now say that Wittgenstein turns out to have been more resolute on Read's assessment of his early project than he turns out to have been on the Conant-Diamond reading. It seems to me that Read falls into using the term "resolute" in this second way on occasion and that doing so runs the risk of begging important interpretative questions both about the early work and about its relation to the later work. This possible slide in the usage of the term "resolute" contains two dangers: (1) it can lead one into thinking that one needs to claim that early Wittgenstein is fully "resolute" in the second sense in order to be entitled to claim that one's reading of him is fully "resolute" in the first sense, (2) it can thereby lead one (in a zealousness to be resolute in the second sense) to lose track of the original interpretative task: namely, to make the best possible sense of the text as it stands on the page.

100. Unless, as indicated in the previous note, one wants to build the following extra premise into the very idea of resolute reading: ". . . and, moreover, the author of the *Tractatus* was in no way mistaken about anything." First, for reasons indicated in the previous note, this must be an additional premise. It cannot be a consequence of a mere commitment to resolution (understood

as a program for reading the book). A pithy (and slightly misleading) way of putting the point is to say: the latter is a *de dicto* ascription of certain philosophical aims to the early Wittgenstein; whereas the former is a *de re* claim about the successful prosecution of those aims. Second, it is hard to see how the *de re* claim in question, without further backing, can constitute anything more than a dogmatic assertion. Third, the premise, if added, would entirely rob a resolute reading of its greatest feature of interest to its original progenitors—the feature of it that will pre-occupy us, beginning with the next paragraph, for the remainder of this essay.

101. Rupert Read and Rob Deans, in their article "Nothing Is Shown," *Philosophical Investigations* 26 no. 3 (2003): 239–268, distinguish between (what they call) "weak resolutism" and "strong resolutism" in ways that worry me partly for the reason raised here. In fact, their distinction between two purported kinds of resolute reader tries to tie so many (potentially independent) issues together that only some of what they say about it is evidently pertinent to the topic of mono-Wittgensteinianism per se. But at least some of the criteria (see, e.g., pp. 251–252) they wish to employ to effect their division seem to be intended to sort readers into those who are, by my lights, mildly and those who are zealously mono-Wittgensteinian. Their classification does not appear to admit of degrees of severity, however, partly because of extraneous considerations that are introduced. At points, Read and Deans, for example, try to distinguish the "strong" from the "weak" (versions of "resolutism") by further stipulating that members of the strong camp hold that the *Tractatus* (further?) seeks to show that no language or logical system is able to express perfectly general truths about which "possible configurations of signs" as such can or cannot make sense (while members of the weak camp are said not to hold this). But *any* con-figuration of *signs* can be given a sense, according to the *Tractatus*. If this is changed to a claim about permissible configurations of *symbols*, it still cannot serve as a principle for classifying such readers. Any (unconfused) resolute reader is obliged to hold that such sentences about what can and cannot be expressed are no better off than sentences about the (supposed) inexpressibility of "There are objects" (see, e.g., *Tractatus*, §4.1272)—which is not to say that there is a determi-nately intelligible something in view here in either case that it turns out that one *cannot* express. (Read and Deans further muddy the water here by sometimes suggesting that this disagreement has something to do with a claim about no system being "powerful enough" to "express" such "truths"—a claim that the strong camp is said to affirm and the weak to deny; see, e.g., p. 250.) If members of the strong camp take there to be something in this vicinity for the *Tractatus* to "establish" (and over which they and the members of the weak camp can then disagree as to whether the book is further seeking to establish *that*), then it is hard to see why they are not chickening out. If they do not, it is hard to see how at least this one of their criteria for classi-fying resolute readers is supposed to do any work. This example is representative of the manner in which Read and Deans tend to conflate issues on which all resolute readers as such ought to be able to agree (at least if the issues come to be expressed more carefully) with ones that may genuinely divide them (such as whether early Wittgenstein's conception of the activity of eluci-dating such sentences—i.e., ones that purport to express such "truths" as, e.g., that "no language [or logical system] can express truths about what can be expressed in any language [or logical system]"—itself implicitly rests on certain philosophical preconceptions regarding what language [or logic] is). In a later article, Phil Hutchinson and Rupert Read appear to wish to draw a far less

complicated but related distinction between what they call (borrowing the terminology of Floyd and Goldfarb) "Girondin" and "Jacobin" versions of a resolute reading. See their "Whose Wittgenstein?" *Philosophy* 80 (2005), see p. 444n. These articles certainly testify to how resolute readers can find themselves in disagreement with one another!

102. A central interest of mine from the beginning in developing such a reading of the *Tractatus* has been to try to understand why later Wittgenstein singles out for criticism only (what are, from a standard reader's point of view, *very*) particular aspects of the *Tractatus*. It is clear from Cora Diamond's writings—and, in particular, from the way she draws the contrast between the metaphysical spirit and the realistic spirit—that this has also been true of her. (See her *The Realistic Spirit*, especially pp. 20–22.)

103. It is open to a zealous interpreter to claim either (1) that such (mildly mono-Wittgensteinian) readings of the relevant passages in the later work involve a complete misconstrual of their critical intention, or (2) that later Wittgenstein misrepresented (perhaps because he came no longer to understand) his own early work. Neither option strikes me as overly promising. An attempt to assess the merits of either is well beyond the scope of this essay. A brief remark about how each option might go is, however, perhaps in order. One way a zealous interpreter could go about trying to pursue option (2) is to point out that there does seem to be a certain bias in later Wittgenstein's discussions of the *Tractatus*. I think there is something to this point. (See note 110.) One way a zealous interpreter could go about trying to pursue option (1) is to urge that most of the criticisms of "earlier work" in later writings are criticisms of some other Wittgenstein than the author of the *Tractatus*. Though I do not see how to make this strategy work for a great many passages, this is not because I think criticism of "earlier work" is, for the most part, exclusively focused on the *Tractatus*. Many of the passages I discuss below drawn from later writings (that I contend contain criticisms of the *Tractatus*'s unwitting commitments) equally involve, for example, criticisms of Middle Wittgenstein. I will return to this issue briefly in the penultimate note.

104. Though, as a mere matter of nomenclature, the author of the *Investigations* might have been slightly inclined to prefer the term "grammatical" (over "logical") in his formulation of each of the resulting remarks.

105. In my subsequent remarks in this section, I occasionally borrow and elaborate points made in the final pages of Conant and Diamond, "On Reading the *Tractatus* Resolutely."

106. "The only way namely for us to avoid prejudice—or vacuity in our claims, is to *posit* the ideals as what it is, *namely* as an object of comparison—a measuring rod as it were—within *our way of looking at things*, & not as a preconception to which everything *must* conform. This namely is the dogmatism into which philosophy can so easily degenerate" (Wittgenstein, *Culture and Value*, 2nd ed., ed. G. H. von Wright, trans. Peter Winch [Oxford: Blackwell, 1998], p. 30). See also *Philosophical Investigations*, §131: "For we can avoid ineptness or emptiness in our assertions only by presenting the model as what it is, as an object of comparison—as, so to speak, a measuring-rod; not as a preconceived idea to which reality *must* correspond. (The dogmatism into which we fall so easily in doing philosophy.)" The differences that come out through

Winch's and Anscombe's respective translations of (these two slightly different versions of) this passage are helpfully suggestive and pertinent to our present topic. I take it that there is a connection between the topic of this passage and that of the following famous passage that is more focally concerned with the preconceptions of the author of the *Tractatus*:

We see that what we call "sentence" and "language" has not the formal unity that I imagined, but is a family of structures more or less related to one another. . . . The *preconceived idea* of crystalline purity can only be removed by turning our whole examination round. (One might say: the axis of reference of our examination must be rotated, but about the fixed point of our real need.) (Philosophical Investigations, §108 [I have modified the translation.])

The first of these passages connects the topic of dogmatism (of a sort into which we easily fall in doing philosophy) with that of an object of comparison (and what its proper role in philosophy should be). Later Wittgenstein sees his earlier self as employing helpful objects of comparison (comparing a proposition with a picture, a natural language mode of expression with its translation into a particular logical notation, etc.) for the purpose of overcoming certain philosophical confusions, but in the process in each case mistaking the role that the object of comparison plays in the demonstration, taking it to be something more than a mere object of comparison, and thereby subliming that which he takes the comparison to reveal. The second of these passages touches on some of the notions that thus come to be sublimed in his early thought—"sentence," "language," "unity," "structure." This suggests that, by Wittgenstein's later lights, a way to eliminate the italicized expressions (and the corresponding moments of insistence) from some of the items on the second list would be to attain clarity regarding the role that objects of comparison (e.g., forms of notation) ought to play in the activity of philosophical elucidation. This dimension of his later engagement with aspects of his early philosophy is a central theme in Oskari Kuusela's work. See his "From Metaphysics and Philosophical Theses to Grammar: Wittgenstein's Turn," *Philosophical Investigations* 28, no. 2 (April 2005), as well as his forthcoming book *Wittgenstein and the Concept of Philosophy*.

107. *Tractatus*, §3.324.

108. That is, early Wittgenstein fails to realize that the very idea of "an absolutely clear way of expressing thoughts" itself represents a substantial metaphysical commitment. For an illuminating discussion of this idea, see Martin Gustafsson, "Travis, the *Tractatus*, and Truth-Conditions," in *A Philosophical Smorgasbord*, ed. Krister Segerberg and Rysiek Sliwinski, Uppsala Philosophical Studies 52 (Uppsala: Uppsala University, 2003), pp. 169–182.

109. The later Wittgenstein differs from the early even here, however, inasmuch as there is no longer room on his later conception for anything that could be correctly described as *the* method or *the* aim of his philosophy. Not only the realization of "the aim" and the application of "the method" must unfold piecemeal over time (as was already the case in his early philosophy), but now a new dimension of pluralism is introduced into the heart of his very conception of each. The aims and methods of the later philosophy no longer have the unity of the aspects of a single great problem, but rather that of a family, deriving their unity from the interrelated family of problems of which they treat—a form of unity that admits of the possibility that hitherto unanticipated members of the family may constantly continue to burst onto the scene, newly

demanding a degree of genuine innovation in both aim and method. This difference in the early and later philosophies is, in turn, tied to a profound difference in their respective conceptions of *essence*—e.g., of language—and the forms of novelty, surveyability, and surprise that these can tolerate.

110. The difficulty of attaining a clear view of this is compounded by the fact that in his later writings Wittgenstein is primarily concerned to highlight what is *wrong* in his earlier way of thinking; he is not primarily concerned to highlight continuities in his philosophy. His overt aim, generally, when later reflecting on one or another aspect of his earlier way of thinking, is to try to pinpoint its philosophical Achilles heel. One therefore needs to handle such retrospective comments in his later writings with some care if one wishes to tease out of them a portrayal of what his earlier way of thinking might have been, such that it would have had the power to captivate a philosopher with his high standards of rigor and clarity, with his determination to think things through to the bloody end, and with his desire not only to avoid but to put an end to metaphysics.

111. Do the "must" and the "any" in this sentence reintroduce moments of dogmatism into Wittgenstein's later philosophy? This question takes us beyond the scope of this essay. But it is the right sort of question to ask, if one wants to begin to locate the fundamental differences between the early and the later work.

112. *Philosophical Investigations*, §308.

113. One way of summing up this immense difference between early and later Wittgenstein would be to say that the following question assumes a pivotal importance in later Wittgenstein's investigations that it never (could have) had in early Wittgenstein's procedures: How does philosophy begin? On this, see Stanley Cavell's "Notes and Afterthoughts on the Opening of Wittgenstein's *Investigations*," in *The Cambridge Companion to Wittgenstein*, ed. Sluga and Stern, 261–295.

114. "[M]y thoughts were soon crippled if I tried to force them on in any single direction against their natural inclination—And this was, of course, connected with the very nature of the investigation. For this compels us to travel over a wide field of thought crisscross in every direction" (*Philosophical Investigations*, p. ix).

115. This parenthetical remark involves some overstatement in part for the following reason: any condidate for a first step on the ladder must be one whose character is equivocal as to whether it represents an unobjectionable aspect of the elucidatory process or part of the beginning of an ascent up the ladder. This therefore allows a different sort of consideration to acquire importance in reflection upon the shape of the first list—one that puts a new pressure on the question: how should the list begin? The first item on the actual first list above, if shorn of its insinuation of an explanatory order, might be turned into a formulation about which it would no longer be clear as to which list it belonged on. As long as the so-called "picture theory" of the *Tractatus* is formulated so that its theoretical pretensions are unmistakable (which requires slanting "the theory" so as to privilege a direction of explanatory order), the resulting formulation corresponds to a rung on the ladder. As long as formulations of observations about picturing take on the

aspect of (what for the author of the *Tractatus* might be) remarks internally related to those on the second list, it must become less clear as to how we should answer questions as to which list these particular formulations themselves belong on. (These are questions for *us*. There are no such questions for the author of the *Tractatus*—there is no second list made up of items of this sort for him.) Resolute readers are committed to the idea that any version of something properly called "the picture *theory*" is, at the end of the day, to be thrown away. But this does not entail that the idea that comparing a proposition with a picture might be helpful (for dispelling certain philosophical confusions) needs to be thrown away. (Incidentally, and for internally related reasons, a similar point holds about the notion of *showing* that the *Tractatus* opposes to saying—as long as a formulation of that notion turns it into a form of "quasi-saying," resolute readers are obliged to see it as comprising a rung of the ladder; as long as it does not, they are not obliged thus to regard it. [See Conant and Diamond, "On Reading the Tractatus Resolutely," for further discussion of this point, especially pp. 65–67; and Michael Kremer's "The Cardinal Problem of Philosophy," in the present volume].) So a mere commitment to resolution cannot suffice to decide the question as to whether any given remark about picturing in the *Tractatus* is best regarded as a candidate for inclusion on the first or on the second list. For it depends on the point at which one thinks the second list begins to bleed into the first. (Again, it must be an interpretive error to suppose that this point could have itself been a clearly marked one for the author of the *Tractatus*.) These are matters about which resolute readers can disagree and whose adjudication can be settled only through closer attention to the details of the text.

116. It is interesting in this connection to note how many of the doctrines of the sort that standard readers ascribe to the *Tractatus* and that resolute readers are committed to rejecting—such as the commitment to the existence of ineffable truths, various optional subsidiary doctrines (such as realism, mentalism, solipsism, etc.) and optional subsidiary commitments (such as the distinction between understanding propositions and "understanding" nonsense, between saying and "conveying" truths, etc.)—never figure in any of the passages in Wittgenstein's later writing where he is explicitly concerned to criticize something he identifies as a questionable philosophical commitment actually held by the author of the *Tractatus*. What figure in such passages instead are the sorts of metaphysical commitments that belong on the second list.

117. *Zettel*, trans. G. E. M. Anscombe (Oxford: Blackwell, 1967), §444.

118. The questions that exercised us in section IV regarding how to specify the shape and rungs of the ladder no longer have straightforward application to the crisscross. What counts as a *step* along such a philosophical path? Or if you prefer: What counts as a *philosophical* step along such a path? And what counts as a step *forward* in the direction of progress and clarity in one's thinking? These become questions that acquire in Wittgenstein's later philosophy new degrees of difficulty.

119. This difference in early and later Wittgenstein's respective conceptions of philosophical procedure is tied to a further difference in their conceptions of what it is to exhibit forms of order—or systematicity—in language. As we have seen above, a resolute reader may hold, for example, that Wittgenstein's having taken himself to have dissolved the "Big Question" of the nature of language (and thus to have solved the problems of philosophy "in essentials" by having

demonstrated a method through which *all* confusions could be clarified) itself reflected a kind of philosophical confusion that colored also his ideas about philosophical method. Such a reader may take a remark in the later writing such as the following to be concerned to mark a further aspect of this difference between the early and later philosophies: "We want to establish an order in our knowledge of the use of language: an order with a particular end in view; one out of many possible orders; not *the* order" (*Philosophical Investigations*, §132).

120. It is partly this quest to identify the moment at which philosophy begins that makes what Wittgenstein later engages in (properly termed) *Untersuchungen*. There are no *Untersuchungen*, in this sense, in the *Tractatus*, only *Erläuterungen*.

121. What I here present as a contrast between the procedure of the *Tractatus* and that of the *Investigations* might be more happily reformulated as a contrast between sorts of procedure both of which are present in the *Investigations*. That would allow us to see the *Investigations* as inheriting and reshaping a feature of the early procedure while supplementing it with procedures that were originally foreign to it. I briefly attempt such an alignment in my "Varieties of Skepticism," in *Wittgenstein and Skepticism*, ed. Denis McManus (London: Routledge, 2004), see especially pp. 124–128.

122. The following remark of Stanley Cavell's is to the point here: "[T]he shortest way I might describe such a book as the *Philosophical Investigations* is to say that it attempts to undo the psychologizing of psychology" (*Must We Mean What We Say?* p. 91). Part of what is so nice about this remark is how it simultaneously marks a moment of significant continuity in Wittgenstein's philosophy (the quest to preserve the gains of his early attempts to undo the psychologizing of logic) while drawing attention to an equally significant discontinuity (the quest to recover the logical/grammatical aspects of so much that had been tossed into the early garbage can of the "merely psychological"). Many of the specific investigations undertaken in the later work— into the grammar of pain-talk, the intentionality of sensation, the epistemic standing of avowals, first-person authority, the first-person pronoun, our apparent immunity to errors of self-identification, our picture of the inner, the expressive dimension of language, etc.—are contributions to this task (of undoing the psychologizing of psychology).

123. "A picture held us captive. And we could not get outside it, for it lay in our language and language seemed to repeat it to us inexorably" (*Philosophical Investigations*, §115). I take this passage, among other things, to be an autobiographical statement by the author of the *Investigations* looking back on the author of the *Tractatus*.

124. *Philosophical Investigations*, §103.

125. It is not the *pictures* themselves that are to be criticized, but the forms of fixation and insistence to which they give rise if we are, in our philosophizing, held captive by them. One way we can go wrong, in seeking to liberate ourselves from such captivity, is to place the blame on the pictures themselves rather than on ourselves and our miscontruals of their application. For discussion of this point, see my "Introduction" to Hilary Putnam's *Words and Life* (Cambridge, Mass.: Harvard University Press, 1994), pp. xlvi–lviii. See also John McDowell, "Intentionality and Interiority in Wittgenstein," collected in *Mind, Value, and Reality* (Cambridge, Mass.: Harvard University Press, 1998), 297–324.

126. Such as, e.g., the following excerpt:

If one says "Moses did not exist," this may mean various things. It may mean: The Israelites did not have a *single* leader when they withdrew from Egypt—or: their leader was not called Moses—or: there cannot have been anyone who accomplished all that the Bible relates of Moses—or: etc., etc.—We may say, following Russell: the name "Moses" can be defined by means of various descriptions. For example, as "the man who led the Israelites through the wilderness," "the man who lived at that time and place and was then called 'Moses'," "the man who as a child was taken out of the Nile by Pharaoh's daughter" and so on. And according as we assume one definition or another the proposition "Moses did exist" acquires a different sense, and so does every other proposition about Moses.—And if we are told "N did not exist," we do ask: "What do you mean? Do you want to say, ... or . . . . . etc.?

But when I make a statement about Moses,—am I always ready to substitute some *one* of these descriptions for "Moses"? I shall perhaps say: By "Moses" I understand the man who did what the Bible relates of Moses, or at any rate a good deal of it. But how much? Have I decided how much must be proved false for me to give up my proposition as false? Has the name "Moses" got a fixed and unequivocal use for me in all possible cases?—Is it not the case that I have, so to speak, a whole series of props in readiness, and am ready to lean on one if another should be taken from under me, and vice versa? (*Investigations*, §79)

127. See *Tractatus*, §3.326.

128. This passage and those that follow it in the *Investigations* seek to bring out not just how "Moses did not exist" might mean various things, but how, on some of the nontrivially different understandings of what it would thus mean, the resulting differences in meaning would not be a function of differences of a sort that could be reflected through symbolically distinct *Begriffsschrift* expressions corresponding to each. Thus they would not be the sorts of difference in meaning that could be made perspicuous by the *Tractatus*'s method of clarification. The attempt to understand each of the possible differences in meaning here as possible ways of conferring alternative Tractarian methods of symbolizing on one and the same propositional sign leads to a representation of the differences we are concerned with here in which the difference between any two such cases comes out being either too small (for, *qua* propositions, they end up occupying the same position in logical space) or too large (for, *qua* propositions, they end up being utterly distinct—having nothing more than their mere signs in common—each expressed in a proper logical notation by a distinct propositional symbol).

129. This can be seen, for example, simply by noting the degree of continuity in conception to be found between many passages in the *Tractatus* and a passage such as §664 of the *Investigations*:

In the use of words one might distinguish "surface grammar" from "depth grammar." What immediately impresses itself upon us about the use of a word is the way it is used in the construction of the sentence, the part of its use—one might say—that can be taken in by the ear.—And now compare the depth grammar, say of the word "to mean," with what its surface would lead us to suspect. No wonder we find it difficult to know our way about.

A modified version of a central Tractarian idea—that one cannot immediately gather from the language of everyday life what sort of logical (or grammatical) role a sign is playing merely from those outward features of it such as how it appears to the eye or is taken in by the ear—is still very much alive here; along with a continuing commitment to the complementary thought: "Thus there easily arise the most fundamental confusions (of which the whole of philosophy is full)" (*Tractatus*, §3.324). An important difference here, however, is that in the later thought this idea (that we can be misled by superficial similarities between sentences) is no longer taken to underwrite a conception of there being something hidden—*the* structure of the proposition. The virtue of a good notation, for later Wittgenstein, is simply that it helps us overcome confusion. It no longer is taken to supply a logical X-ray of hidden structure.

130. Consider, e.g., §90 of *Philosophical Investigations*. Although the passage occurs in the midst of a series of remarks critical of the *Tractatus*, it also seeks to make clear that there is still an important place in the later conception for the following three ideas—all of which play a central role in the early conception: (1) that *some* misunderstandings concerning the use of words are caused by analogies between the forms of expression in different regions of language, (2) that these *can* be removed by substituting one form of expression for another, and (3) that this process *may* be called "analysis" because it is like taking a thing apart. All of this shows that in the later conception there is still plenty of room for the idea that a misunderstanding may be removed by substituting a logically regimented form of expression for its natural language counterpart. I have, however, here used italics to mark the way in which the modal force that attaches to each of these ideas has been weakened. Each of the italicized expressions in (1)–(3) above now corresponds to a nondogmatic moment (of noninsistence, as it were). This is typical of the manner in which even those of the earlier ideas that are most fully preserved in the later writings still undergo significant reformulation.

131. More focally at issue in §79, in particular, is the role that Russell's theory of descriptions played for the author of the *Tractatus* as a paradigm of analysis—as an exemplary demonstration of how depth structure in a proposition can be shown to differ from surface structure. (See, e.g., §4.0031.) The three ideas mentioned in the previous note (all of which figure in §90 of *Philosophical Investigations*) fit very nicely together with the sort of use to which the author of the *Tractatus* wished to put the theory of descriptions. The "misunderstandings" here at issue lead to the idea that something *must* exist (in some way or to some degree) in order to be spoken about. This means, I take it, that (if we can keep ourselves from being seduced into certain misconceptions by various features of the tool that we are employing) the theory of descriptions, even by his later lights, can serve as a helpful tool in philosophical clarification in bringing out how *some* misunderstandings concerning the use of words are caused (by analogies between the forms of expression in different regions of language), that these *can* be removed by substituting the Russellian form of expression for its natural language counterpart, and that this process *may* be called "analysis". So while §§79ff. in part seek to show that the author of the *Tractatus* was seduced into certain misconceptions by the Russellian tools that he employs for elucidatory purposes, at the same time, §90 in part seeks to recover and modify aspects of this very moment in the early philosophy that is subjected to such severe criticism in §§79ff.

132. The italics in items 3 and 21 on this list are Wittgenstein's.

133. The commentary is, above all, on §5.5563 of the *Tractatus*. It brings out how the achievement of a proper alignment of the old and new ways of thinking requires sensitivity to yet a further moment of discontinuity folded with an overarching continuity in Wittgenstein's thought. The text that is the immediate object of this commentary runs as follows:

All propositions of our everyday language are actually, just as they are, logically completely in order. That simple thing which we ought to give here is not a model of the truth but the complete truth itself.

(Our problems are not abstract but perhaps the most concrete that there are.)

The *Tractatus* is here concerned to effect a break with Frege's and especially Russell's disparagement of ordinary language. What for Frege can only be the structure of an ideal language is for early Wittgenstein the structure of all language. This thought itself contains a moment that is inherited and one that is repudiated by later Wittgenstein. The overly neglected moment of continuity here constitutes another instance of how some of what is standardly put forward by commentators as a criticism that later Wittgenstein directs against his earlier work is in fact already partially developed in the *Tractatus* as a criticism of Frege and Russell. In his remarks clarifying his emendations of Ogden's initial attempt to translate §5.5563, Wittgenstein says:

By this [i.e., §5.5563] I meant to say that the propositions of our ordinary language are not in any way logically *less correct* or less exact or *more confused* than propositions written down, say, in Russell's symbolism or any other *Begriffsschrift*. (Only it is easier for us to gather their logical form when they are expressed in an appropriate symbolism.) (*Letters to C. K. Ogden*, p. 50 [emphases in the original])

On the one hand, we see here that, already in the *Tractatus*, Wittgenstein's interest in a logical symbolism is not that of someone who seeks to overcome an imprecision in ordinary thought through recourse to a more precise medium for the expression of thought. On the other, this early rescue of ordinary language from false philosophical conceptions of it is, in turn, shaped by the Tractarian conception (toward which we have just seen, in the previous section of this essay, later Wittgenstein directs critical attention) regarding how the logic of our language can be gathered from a transposition of sentences into a suitably constructed symbolism, modeled on Frege's *Begriffsschrift* (though designed now solely to further the clarificatory ends of the *Tractatus*, without ostensible further constructive or theoretical aspirations constraining or deforming its design). So what we have here is a moment in the early thought which is a *defense of ordinary language* on the part of the author of the *Tractatus* (against what he takes to be Frege's and Russell's failures to appreciate its perfection within concreteness) and yet also a central example for the *Investigations* of his earlier impulse to *sublime ordinary language* (mistaking its concreteness for a kind of crystalline purity)—again, a moment of subliming in his thinking to which he himself was, at the time of writing the *Tractatus*, oblivious. It is to the final parenthetical sentence of §5.5563 that the following remark is directed: "[T]his crystal does not appear as an abstraction; but as something concrete, indeed, as the most concrete, as it were the *hardest* thing there is" (*Philosophical Investigations*, §97).

134. This is a feature of the text that was already well understood and emphasized by Elizabeth Anscombe in a number of writings, including her book *An Introduction to Wittgenstein's "Tractatus"* (London: Hutchinson, 1959). Thus, for example, in connection with the topic of the previous note, she is quite sensitive to how the moments of continuity and discontinuity intertwine here. She goes to a slightly earlier moment in the text (than I do in the previous note) to illustrate the complexity of the relation, connecting the discussion of ordinary language being "all right" in *Investigations*, §95 with *Tractatus*, §5.5563: "It is a mistake to suppose that the dictum 'Ordinary language is all right' is an expression only of Wittgenstein's later views" (p. 91). She explores this connection to show how Wittgenstein is "dialectically expounding, not opposing"

(pp. 91–92) his earlier view. (I would prefer to say: "not merely opposing." I am sure Anscombe would agree.) Her discussion of ordinary language being all right comes after her discussion of an equally central Tractarian point—one that, at first blush, constitutes another such moment of significant continuity: "What does not get expressed in the signs, comes out in their application: What the signs fail to express their application declares" (*Tractatus*, §3.262). Anscombe takes the continuity here to be obvious, but she also rightly worries that it might lead one to overestimate the extent of the continuity. So she seeks to bring out (albeit very briefly) the moment of discontinuity here as well, by focusing on what can be meant by "application" in the philosophies of early and later Wittgenstein respectively. This discussion of Anscombe's shows, on the one hand, how you do not need to be a resolute reader in order to be sensitive to the complexity of the relation between the philosophies of early and later Wittgenstein, and, on the other hand, how such a sensitivity does require a willingness to forgo conceiving that relation in the terms dictated by the doctrinal schema. The impressive depth of Anscombe's sensitivity to the intricacy of the relation raises an interesting question about *how far* one can go here (in recognizing the complexity of continuities that enfold discontinuities) within the constraints of a nonresolute reading. This question lies outside the brief of this essay (which is merely to show that a resolute reading *can* go quite far here). As mentioned in note 7, alongside Anscombe, Rhees and Winch are the two other commentators who are particularly sensitive to this dimension of complexity in Wittgenstein's development. An exploration of this question (concerning how far one can go here within the constraints of a nonresolute reading) would need to take account of the work of at least these three commentators.

135. Of particular interest in this connection is the entire stretch in *Philosophical Investigations* that runs from §89 to §133. In almost every remark, we have some effort on Wittgenstein's part to bring his later methods of philosophy into relief by contrasting them with his earlier conception of *the* method (cf. §133) of philosophy, and yet numerous local moments of continuity surface within this overarching contrast. This contrast—between *the* (early) method and the (later) *methods*—draws many of the other points of difference between the early and later philosophies together and, in particular, the difference between the *Tractatus*'s point of view on the problems of philosophy (according to which they have in essentials been solved) and the refusal of such a point of view in the *Investigations* (in which the essentials can no longer be separated in such a manner from the details). The confidence expressed in the claim (in the preface to the *Tractatus*) that the problems of philosophy have in essentials been solved is tied to a confidence that, at least in its essentials, the basic outline of the method for dissolving *all* such problems has been put in place. (This, in turn, is tied to a confidence that there is something which is *the* logic of our language—the structure of which can be displayed in a perspicuous notation—and hence to the items on the second list.) The *Tractatus* is to furnish this basic outline and demonstrate its worth. Once it has successfully done so, it is now to become clear, in retrospect, that the prior absence of a serviceable method had been the big problem for the early philosophy—for the solution to all other problems had depended on the solution to this one—and now that *it* has been resolved, they, are in principle (if not yet in practice) also resolved. This central (apparent) achievement of the early philosophy, in turn, becomes a central target of the later philosophy. The entire stretch in *Philosophical Investigations* that runs from §89 to §133 can be read as

seeking to expose the latent preconceptions that allowed early Wittgenstein to imagine that he had done this—that he had been able to survey *the* structure of the problems *as such* and attain a perspective on them from which there could appear to be one big problem that could admit of an overarching form of solution (at least in its essentials). Yet, at the same time, there is much of local value in his early conception of clarification that is to be recovered within this fundamental break with the early conception. Hence, even in the course of this markedly critical sequence of reflections on the relation between the early and later conceptions of philosophical method, a crisscrossing method of investigation is required—one that denies nothing of value and recoups each of the gains of the early philosophy, while laboring to identify each of the moments in which it oversteps or overreaches.

136. The question of "the extent of the continuity and the discontinuity in Wittgenstein's philosophy" here at issue has to do with the relation between the author of the *Tractatus* and the author of the *Investigations*. This, however, is by no means the only question worth addressing regarding the extent of continuity and/or discontinuity in Wittgenstein's philosophy. The narrow focus here is a function of the aim of this essay (i.e., to show that a resolute reader can make sense of the relation between the *Tractatus* and the *Investigations*). This limitation, however, can introduce its own sort of distortion into a narrative of the development of Wittgenstein's philosophy. And this is especially the case in connection with the last sentence of §133. The contrast emphasized in my remarks in the previous note is between the Tractarian methodological conception (the conception of *the* method) and that of §133 (the conception that there is not *one* philosophical method, though there are indeed method*s*). But there is also criticism by Later Wittgenstein of *Middle Wittgenstein* here. For this idea of "the method" did not immediately die with Wittgenstein's return to full-time philosophizing in 1929. §133 is arguably equally concerned to draw a contrast between the later methodological conception and the very emphatic views of Middle Wittgenstein. Despite the far-reaching differences in their respective methodological conceptions, there remains the following important similarity between Early and Middle Wittgenstein: each believes he has hit upon *the* method. One of Middle Wittgenstein's favorite ways of putting this, in the context of discussing his "new" method, is to emphasize how philosophy can now become a matter of *skillful* practice. There can be skillful philosophers as there are skillful chemists because "a new method" had been *discovered*, as happened when chemistry was developed out of alchemy: "The nimbus of philosophy has been lost. For we now have a method of doing philosophy . . . Compare the difference between alchemy and chemistry; chemistry has a method" (*Wittgenstein's Lectures: Cambridge, 1930–1932*, ed. Desmond Lee [Ottawa, N. J.: Rowman and Littlefield, 1980], p. 21). What matters now is not the truth or falsity of any specific philosophical results but rather this all-important fact: "a method had been found" (ibid.). (Joachim Schulte explores this topic of the relation between middle and later Wittgenstein on method in his article "Wittgenstein's 'Method'," in *Wittgenstein and the Future of Philosophy*, ed. Rudolf Haller and Klaus Puhl [Vienna: ÖBV & HPT, 2002], 399–410, emphasizing the contrast between there being *a* philosophical method [according to Middle] and there being philosophical method*s* [according to Later].) This suggests that it would be no less a mistake (than any of the ones this essay seeks to correct) to insist that §133 (in its denial that there is "*a* philosophical method") must be concerned to draw a contrast solely with the "early" view (where

early = *Tractatus*). It is worth noting in this connection that the predecessor version of §133 in *The Big Typescript* (p. 316) is missing the last sentence (about there not being *a* philosophical method, but rather different methods). Yet most of §133 is in *The Big Typescript*, and is clearly concerned with drawing contrasts between the author (i.e., Middle Wittgenstein) and Early Wittgenstein. This nicely brings out one aspect of the way in which the break with the *Tractatus* was a graduated one. Here we see two crucial steps coming one after the other. Middle Wittgenstein (who still thought there was one method) thought that Early Wittgenstein had been confused (in thinking that it was possible to solve *all* the problems *at once* by solving them *in essentials*). Yet Later Wittgenstein (who thinks there can only be methods) thinks Middle Wittgenstein is still confused in his criticisms of Early (i.e., he has unwittingly preserved an essential feature of the metaphysics of the *Tractatus*). This shows how, as a matter of historical fact, the process of purging *himself* of the unwitting commitments is one that unfolded for Wittgenstein, over the course of his own philosophical development, piecemeal. A proper treatment of this topic would require another essay at least as long as this one.

137. This essay is indebted to several decades of lengthy and lively long-distance telephone conversations with Cora Diamond (including some very helpful recent ones), to several years of less lengthy but equally lively short-distance conversations with Michael Kremer, and to several of Peter Sullivan's recent writings and several short but stimulating conversations with him about them. It is indebted to Martin Gustafsson and to Martin Stone for comments on a previous draft, to Alois Pichler for several corrections, to Judy Feldmann at MIT Press, and to Alice Crary for enormous forbearance and assistance in her capacity as editor. Finally, it would not exist but for the encouragement and patience of my wife, Lisa Van Alstyne, who had to live in uncomfortably close proximity to the conditions of its gestation and birth.

2 The Cardinal Problem of Philosophy

Michael Kremer

One of Cora Diamond's most significant and lasting achievements is a reorientation of the study of Wittgenstein. In particular, her seminal paper, "Throwing Away the Ladder," has done much both to revive interest in Wittgenstein's early work and to reshape our way of reading and thinking about that work. Sparked in large measure by Diamond's writings, a scholarly debate has arisen over the proper interpretation of the *Tractatus*. This essay makes a small contribution to that ongoing debate—entering on the side of Diamond, as is, perhaps, appropriate in a *Festschrift*.[1]

Prior to the publication of "Throwing Away the Ladder," the dominant interpretation of the *Tractatus* was some variant of what is sometimes called the "ineffability" reading. This reading is enshrined in numerous textbooks, encyclopedia articles, and other secondary sources.[2] For example, in the *Concise Routledge Encyclopedia of Philosophy*, we are told that the *Tractatus* "presents a logical atomist picture of language and reality." It teaches "deep truths about [the] nature of reality and representation." But, these truths "cannot properly be *said* but can only be *shown*. Indeed Wittgenstein claimed that pointing to this distinction was central to his book. And he embraced the paradoxical conclusion that most of the *Tractatus* itself is, strictly, nonsense. He also held that other important things can also be shown but not said, for example, about there being a certain truth in solipsism and about the nature of value."[3]

Diamond rejects this picture, and especially the use made in it of the idea of ineffable truths, which cannot be expressed in language, but can be "shown," and which the *Tractatus* in some way conveys. This view, she says, is "chickening out."[4] It refuses to take at face value Wittgenstein's claim that "philosophy is not a theory but an activity" and that "the result of philosophy is not a number of 'philosophical propositions,' but to make propositions clear."[5] It does not take seriously Wittgenstein's demand that we recognize his propositions as nonsense, and so throw them away, as a ladder that we have climbed up and no longer need. The view itself "dissolves into incoherence when pushed slightly,"[6] since to say such things as "that language and reality share a common logical form, cannot be said but can only be shown" is to say the very thing that one claims to be unsayable.

For Diamond: "What counts as not chickening out is then this, roughly: to throw the ladder away is, among other things, to throw away in the end the attempt to take seriously the language of 'features of reality.' To read Wittgenstein himself as not chickening out is to say that it is not, not really, his view that there are features of reality that cannot be put into words but show themselves."[7] As Diamond's philosophical ally James Conant puts it: "the idea that nonsensical sentences can embody a content comes apart on us. And it is meant to. The doctrine of ineffable content represents one of the rungs of the ladder the reader of the *Tractatus* must ascend and surmount— and (along with the rest of the ladder of which it forms an integral part), in the end, throw away. . . . to genuinely throw away the whole of the ladder means completely relinquishing the idea of an 'it' that cannot be put into words but can still show itself. This idea also turns out to be nonsense."[8]

Conant and Diamond have developed an alternative approach to reading the *Tractatus*, one which avoids "chickening out" and throws away "the whole of the ladder." This reading emphasizes Wittgenstein's adherence to the context principle, that words have meaning only in the context of a sentence,[9] and the corresponding idea of nonsense as arising only because some words have not been given a meaning in the context in which they occur.[10] On this reading, the propositions of the *Tractatus* are recognized as nonsense. But this is *not* the result of the application of some theory or criterion of meaningfulness presented in the book to the book itself—a paradoxical view that seems to require that the theory, while nonsensical, remains in some sense true, and hence leads to the postulation of ineffable but graspable truths that can be shown but not said. Rather, the process of working through the ostensible theory of the book is simply a process in which the illusion of sense possessed by that theory dissolves. The resulting disillusionment is all the insight the *Tractatus* hopes to convey. And, for both Diamond and Conant, one of the main illusions that the *Tractatus* means to dispel is the idea of "ineffable content," of truths that can be shown but not said.

In their early papers, as exemplified by the quotations above, Diamond and Conant make use of strong rhetoric in their effort to dethrone the ineffability reading of the *Tractatus*. This has sometimes misled critics into thinking (1) that on their view every proposition of the *Tractatus* is consigned irredeemably to the category of "nonsense" and (2) that in particular there is no room on their view for any distinction between saying and showing. Critics then seize on the apparent conflict with (1') their apparent reliance on certain passages of the *Tractatus* in arguing for their interpretation and

(2′) their willingness to talk of what the *Tractatus* "shows." However, it is clear from much of their later work that (1″) on their view at least some propositions of the *Tractatus* can be redeemed as making sense, once we have learned the lessons of the *Tractatus*, and in particular (2″) there is an innocent version of the saying/showing distinction that can be applied to make sense of at least some uses of that distinction in the *Tractatus*. (1″) is actually a necessary consequence of the account of philosophical confusion and the resulting philosophical nonsense, an account inspired by Diamond and Conant, which I develop below. On this account, philosophical nonsense derives from a kind of equivocation in which we try to make one word conform to two uses at once. Once we become aware of this confusion, we can decide to use the word in one of these two senses. Our propositions, so understood, will then make sense and may even be true—but they will be incapable of doing the philosophical work that we earlier confusedly wanted them to do. I will argue below that (2″) is merely an instance of this general point; but it is important to be clear to begin with that the idea rejected by the resolute reading is that of an "it" which can be shown but cannot be said, but which nonetheless has *something like* the structure of a *proposition*, a *truth*. Rejecting this idea need not mean rejecting all talk of "showing" as contrasted with "saying."

Diamond and Conant's interpretation of the *Tractatus* has been dubbed "resolute" by Thomas Ricketts.[11] This label reflects the idea that to "chicken out" is to unstably waffle between two views—the view that the *Tractatus* presents true metaphysical doctrines, and the view that the propositions of the *Tractatus* are nonsense. In contrast, the "resolute" reading of Conant and Diamond holds firmly to the view that the propositions of the *Tractatus* are simple nonsense and refuses to countenance the idea of inexpressibly true theories or doctrines. Proponents of the resolute reading (myself included) have also taken to labeling the ineffability reading "irresolute," to mark the waffling, oscillating character they attribute to the view. In this essay, however, I will speak in terms of "ineffability" and "resolute" readings, in the hope that this will be acceptable to both the so-labeled camps.[12]

In earlier work, I have made an attempt to contribute to the resolute reading of the *Tractatus*.[13] In "The Purpose of *Tractarian* Nonsense," I sketched an answer to one outstanding question facing the resolute reading: why, if the *Tractatus* consists entirely of nonsense, would Wittgenstein bother to write such a book at all? My response built on Wittgenstein's well-known remark that the point of the book was ethical.[14] I argued that the *Tractatus* aims to relieve us of a felt need for justification of our thoughts, our words, and our lives "by revealing that all such justificatory talk is in the end meaningless nonsense," made up of sentences that "cannot serve the purpose for which they are intended," since "any system of ethical or logical propositions will itself stand in need of justification." I suggested that the idea of an ineffable proposition-like content that can nonetheless be "shown" if not "said" tempts us as a way in which we may "have our justificatory cake and eat it too." Seeking a source of justification that cannot itself be put into question, we hit on the idea of an "internal" justification, which is "present unspeakably in what I do and what I say." Thus we seek "something sufficiently like a proposition to serve as a justification, an answer to a question, yet sufficiently different from a proposition to need no further justification, to raise no further questions in turn." It is this that the doctrine of "truths" that can be "shown" but not said seems to provide. But, by unmasking the idea of such ineffable content as itself nonsensical, I argued, the *Tractatus* "reveal[s] to us in the end that this temptation is founded on illusion, confusion, and nonsense. Only by rejecting the demand for justification, and thus the temptation to satisfy that demand in the realm of the 'shown,' can we resolve our difficulties."[15]

My interpretation of the ethical point of the *Tractatus* turns on the "irresolute" character of the ineffability reading. The central idea of the ineffability reading, that there are truths that are "shown" but cannot be said, involves an unstable combination of two notions: the notion of a truth, something with the structure of a proposition, and the notion of an insight that is beyond expressing in propositions. Ineffability readers sometimes recognize the incoherence of this idea, but nonetheless do not hesitate to saddle the *Tractatus* with it—after all, they say, the book was later recognized by Wittgenstein as defective. Resolute readers, on the other hand, see this idea as a temptation that the *Tractatus* presents to its readers only to show them in the end its incoherence. Resolute readers, therefore, must look elsewhere for the difficulties that Wittgenstein eventually came to see in his early work.[16]

The resolute reading of the *Tractatus* has not gone unanswered. Defenders of the ineffability reading, and others, have been quick to respond with detailed critiques of the resolute interpretation.[17] Their criticisms have taken a number of different forms, often combined in a single article. The resolute reading is argued to be internally incoherent, inconsistent with the text of the *Tractatus*, out of line with the descriptions of the *Tractatus* given by those who knew Wittgenstein best, refuted by what Wittgenstein wrote about the book in his pre-*Tractatus* journals, looking forward, or in his later work, looking back. Each such argument deserves its own response—with the result that a list of criticisms contained in a single article might require a whole list of articles in reply. This essay will take up only one of these many criticisms—but one that is especially significant because it is based on what Wittgenstein said about the *Tractatus* shortly after its completion.

Wittgenstein completed the *Tractatus* in the summer of 1918, while on leave from his service in the Austrian army.[18] By early 1919, he found himself in an Italian prisoner of war camp, and from there he was able to send a copy of his manuscript to Bertrand Russell, who apparently received the book sometime in late June or early July, 1919.[19] By mid-August, Russell had read the manuscript and concluded that it was "of first-class importance." He wrote to Wittgenstein on August 13, commenting: "I have now read your book twice carefully.—There are still points I don't understand—some of them important ones—I send you some queries on separate sheets. I am convinced you are right in your main contention, that logical prop[osition]s are tautologies, which are not true in the sense that substantial prop[osition]s are true."[20] Wittgenstein replied on August 19—roughly one year after completing work on the *Tractatus*: "I'm afraid you haven't really got hold of my main contention, to which the whole business of logical prop[osition]s is only a corollary. The main point is the theory of what can be expressed [*gesagt*] by prop[osition]s—i.e. by language—(and, which comes to the same, what can be *thought*) and what can not be expressed by prop[osition]s, but only shown [*gezeigt*]; which, I believe, is the cardinal problem of philosophy."[21] Wittgenstein went on to address some of Russell's queries, in two cases apparently applying the "theory of what can be expressed . . . by propositions . . . and what cannot be expressed by propositions, but only shown" in constructing his replies.[22]

Wittgenstein's insistence that this "theory" is the "main point" of his book is repeatedly cited by ineffabilist readers in support of their interpretation.[23] Critics of the resolute reading have also seized on this passage as proving that the ineffability reading accurately captures Wittgenstein's own understanding of the book. P. M. S. Hacker, noting both Wittgenstein's insistence on the importance of the "theory" of saying and showing and Wittgenstein's apparent use of this theory in responding to Russell's queries, writes that "It is implausible to suppose that he was pulling Russell's leg and that the *real* point of the book is that there is nothing at all to be shown."[24] Ian Proops further argues that Wittgenstein's talk of a "theory" of the expressible and the inexpressible gives "reason to doubt that 4.112 ['philosophy is not a theory but an activity'] could be intended to refer to philosophy as embodied in the *Tractatus*."[25] And John Koethe sees the letter as providing "straightforward" and "decisive" evidence against the resolute reading.[26]

Nonetheless, I will argue, the evidence of the Russell letter, not only does not conflict with the resolute reading, it actually supports it. In "The Purpose of *Tractarian* Nonsense," I already sketched such a response,[27] albeit one that has not proved convincing (except to the already converted). While admitting that Wittgenstein calls the "theory" of what can be said and what can only be shown his "main contention," I focused on the fact that he also describes this theory as the "cardinal *problem* of philosophy." I linked this description to the *Tractatus*'s claim to have solved the "problems of philosophy" by showing that "the method of formulating these problems rests on the misunderstanding of the logic of our language,"[28] and argued that "if the showing/saying distinction is a 'problem of philosophy,' the *Tractatus* must have 'solved' it by showing how it 'rests on the misunderstanding of the logic of our language,'" and that "if it is the 'cardinal' problem of philosophy, then we will find the key to the resolution of all the problems of philosophy in its dissolution."[29]

This response has not met with universal approbation, to say the least. In fact, both responses to it that I am aware of have been dismissive. John Koethe considers it "quite strained," arguing that "the problems of philosophy alluded to in the Preface are most naturally taken to be those the *Tractatus* actually discusses, including realism, solipsism, epistemology, causality, induction, synthetic a priori knowledge, and ethics. These are to be dissolved by a proper understanding of 'the logic of our language' (which includes the showing/saying distinction) the book is meant to instill in us."[30] Peter Sullivan finds my suggestion more mysterious than strained: "I cannot explain what attracts Kremer to this wholly unpersuasive juxtaposition of unconnected texts, and I think it better simply to discount the argument."[31] In light of this reception, perhaps a more fully spelled-out defense of my suggestion is in order; such is the task I have set myself in this essay. I will try to show, contra Sullivan, that the texts I have juxtaposed are not simply unconnected, and contra Koethe that the showing/saying distinction as a "problem of philosophy" belongs among the "problems of philosophy" alluded to in the preface and actually discussed in the *Tractatus*.

My reading of Wittgenstein's letter to Russell puts great emphasis on his description of the showing/saying distinction as a "problem of philosophy." Sullivan thinks that linking this to Wittgenstein's claim in the preface to have solved the "problems of philosophy" is unmotivated and unpersuasive. Yet it must be admitted that there is something curious in the description of a philosophical "theory" as a "problem." Moreover, Wittgenstein uses the phrase "the cardinal problem of philosophy" in a letter to *Russell*, the author of *The Problems of Philosophy*, a work that, as Russell knew, Wittgenstein hated.[32] Wittgenstein surely would have expected Russell to take note of his claim to have solved "the problems of philosophy," and would therefore have expected the phrase "cardinal problem of philosophy" to have some resonance for Russell, especially after his reading of the *Tractatus*. Yet most authors who cite this passage do not mention Wittgenstein's use of "problem" at all. But some ineffabilist readers do try to account for it. The best attempt I know of is that of David Stern:

The 'cardinal problem of philosophy' is the question of the limits and nature of language, the question of what, in general, can be said, and what can only be shown. In the Preface to the *Tractatus*, Wittgenstein expressed his belief that he had arrived at the definitive 'final solution' to the problems of philosophy. That confidence was based on his conviction that the book makes clear the limits of language by sharply demarcating what can be said—namely, factual assertion— and placing all philosophical theses about such matters as the nature of self and world, aesthetics, morality, or religion on the other side of the limit. The demarcation depends on a conception of language and logic that was not so much defended as presented in the text of the *Tractatus*, where Wittgenstein aims at an insight that lies beyond assertion, argument, or theory formation. For that reason, my exposition of the *Tractatus* began with a discussion of the crucial role of insight in the picture theory. As the very use of the term "picture *theory*" suggests, however, Wittgenstein's insistence that all philosophical theories are nonsense was subverted by his own dependence on a distinction between plain nonsense, which can be dismissed, and important nonsense, which points to philosophical insights that cannot be put into words. The concept of showing is supposed to bridge the gap: while any attempt to state the picture theory as though it were an empirical fact must lead to nonsense, the truth of the theory can be shown by drawing the reader's attention to the structure of certain sentences.[33]

Stern here treats the "cardinal problem" as a straightforward philosophical question; the problem is to demarcate the limits of what can be said. The solution to this is to be given in the "picture theory" and the accompanying "concept of showing." The difficulty here is that Stern's response seems to make "the theory of what can be expressed . . . by propositions . . . and what can not be expressed by propositions, but only shown" into the *solution* of the cardinal problem of philosophy rather than explaining its status *as* the cardinal problem of philosophy.[34]

Can we do better? In order to answer this question, I want to spend some time unpacking the phrase "the cardinal problem of philosophy." I begin with "philosophy." In the *Tractatus*, Wittgenstein uses "philosophy" in two senses—on the one hand, positively, to refer to the activity that the *Tractatus* itself inculcates, and on the other hand, negatively, to refer to the activities of philosophers in general, which are something like an illness for which the philosophy of the *Tractatus* is something like a cure. Of the former, Wittgenstein says that it "is not one of the natural sciences,"[35] that it is "not a theory but an activity," whose object is "the logical clarification of thoughts" and whose result is "not a number of 'philosophical propositions,' but to make propositions clear."[36] Philosophy in this sense is to "limit the unthinkable from within through the thinkable" by saying clearly all that can be said clearly.[37] In doing so, however, philosophy in this sense will unmask the pretensions of philosophy in the second, negative, sense, with its multifarious "problems."[38]

Traditional philosophy, with its problems and questions, consists for the most part of simple *nonsense*, according to the *Tractatus*. Wittgenstein states in the preface that "the method of formulating these problems rests on the misunderstanding of the logic of our language."[39] He reiterates this claim at 4.003, connecting it to the nonsensicality of traditional philosophy:

Most propositions and questions, that have been written about philosophical matters, are not false, but nonsense. We cannot, therefore, answer questions of this kind at all, but only state their nonsensicality. Most questions and propositions of the philosophers result from the fact that we do not understand the logic of our language. . . .

   And so it is not to be wondered at that the deepest problems are really *no* problems.[40]

But in what way do philosophers fail to "understand the logic of our language," and how does this result in nonsense? To answer this we need to turn to Wittgenstein's distinction between sign and symbol.

   Wittgenstein tells us that "the sign is the part of the symbol perceptible by the senses."[41] Conversely, the symbol is the linguistic sign that has been put to use in propositions with sense, and so endowed with a meaning. "An expression [symbol] has meaning only in the context of a proposition."[42] "In order to recognize the symbol in the sign we must consider the significant use [*sinnvollen Gebrauch*, use with sense]."[43] Nonsense, then, is the result of concatenating signs that do not have a determinate meaning: "Every possible proposition is legitimately constructed, and if it has no sense this can only be because we have given no *meaning* to some of its constituent parts."[44] To put in another way, in nonsense we have signs in which we cannot recognize any symbol. How does this come about?

   Wittgenstein's answer is, on the surface, surprising: often, we fail to recognize the symbol in the sign because there are *too many* ways in which we might do so. Since the symbol is simply the sign put to some use, "Two different symbols can . . . have the sign . . . in common—they then signify in different ways."[45] James Conant has dubbed the resulting confusion "cross-category equivocation." Wittgenstein traces the problems of philosophy to this root:

In the language of ordinary life it very often happens that the same word signifies in two different ways—and therefore belongs to two different symbols—or that two words, which signify in different ways, are apparently applied in the same way in the proposition.

   Thus the word "is" appears as the copula, as the sign of equality, and as the expression of existence; "to exist" as an intransitive verb like "to go"; "identical" as an adjective; we speak of *something* but also of the fact of *something* happening. . . .

   Thus there easily arise the most fundamental confusions (of which the whole of philosophy is full).

   In order to avoid these errors, we must employ a symbolism which excludes them, by not applying the same sign in different symbols and by not applying signs in the same way which signify in different ways.[46]

Thus philosophical nonsense, according to Wittgenstein, typically involves an equivocal sign, which is part of two symbols. The philosopher generates problems by using the sign simultaneously in two incompatible ways. The solution of the philosopher's puzzlement consists in distinguishing among the meanings his words might have. This can be accomplished by introducing a notation within which the distinct symbols involved are associated with distinct signs. Once such distinctions have been made and such symbols introduced, the philosopher can be asked to choose which meaning he intends his signs to have. Confronting this choice, he will see that he actually confusedly intended his signs to have both meanings at once and that it was this confused intention that resulted in his philosophical puzzlement.[47]

Wittgenstein embraced this conception of the source, and resolution, of the problems of philosophy throughout his career.[48] In his lectures at Cambridge in 1930, he is recorded as saying: "When a philosophical problem is elucidated, some confusion of expression is always exposed. For example 2×2 *is* four, the door *is* brown. (Remember the trouble the word 'is' has given to philosophers.) The confusion is resolved by writing = for the first phrase and ε for the second."[49] One of Wittgenstein's characteristic examples of a problem of philosophy is Augustine's puzzlement about time in the *Confessions*. In the *Blue Book* (1933–34) he offers this analysis:

Consider as an example the question "What is time?" as Saint Augustine and others have asked it. . . . it is the grammar of the word "time" which puzzles us. . . . Now the puzzlement about the grammar of the word "time" arises from what one might call apparent contradictions in that grammar.

It was such a "contradiction" which puzzled Saint Augustine when he argued: How is it possible that one should measure time? For the past can't be measured, as it is gone by; and the future can't be measured because it has not yet come. And the present can't be measured for it has no extension.

The contradiction which here seems to arise could be called a conflict between two different usages of a word, in this case the word "measure." Augustine, we might say, thinks of the process of measuring a *length*: say, the distance between two marks on a travelling band which passes us, and of which we can only see a tiny bit (the present) in front of us. Solving this puzzle will consist in comparing what we mean by "measurement" (the grammar of the word "measurement") when applied to a distance on a travelling band with the grammar of that word when applied to time. The problem may seem simple, but its extreme difficulty is due to the fascination which the analogy between two similar structures in our language can exert on us. (It is helpful here to remember that it is sometimes almost impossible for a child to believe that one word can have two meanings.)[50]

Here a philosophical problem arises from the fact that the word "measurement" is used in two senses—the same sign is part of two distinct symbols. We are thus led to think of the "measurement" of time as somehow like the measurement of a length, a process which itself takes place in time. To remove the problem, we need to compare the two uses of "measure." We may be helped in this by the introduction of distinct signs for the distinct symbols.

In the *Tractatus*, Wittgenstein appends to his remark that "most propositions and questions, that have been written about philosophical matters, are not false, but nonsensical"[51] the comment: "All philosophy is 'Critique of language' (but not at all in Mauthner's sense).[52] Russell's merit is to have shown that the apparent logical form of the proposition need not be its real form." Wittgenstein's reference here appears to be to Russell's theory of descriptions. In light of 4.002, which emphasizes that "language disguises the thought; so that from the external form of the clothes one cannot infer the form of the thought they clothe," one might take Wittgenstein's compliment to Russell to refer simply to the idea that the true, more complex, logical form of an apparent subject-predicate sentence with a definite description in the subject place can be revealed in Russell's logical notation. However, if we reflect on Russell's argument in "On Denoting," we can see a direct link to Wittgenstein's conception of philosophical problems as arising from "the fact that we do not understand the logic of our language"[53] because "in the language of everyday life it very often happens that the same word . . . belongs to two different symbols."[54]

Russell proposes in "On Denoting" that "a logical theory may be tested by its capacity for dealing with puzzles" and presents three such puzzles that his theory of descriptions is supposed to solve: a puzzle about informative identity, a puzzle about the law of the excluded middle, and a puzzle about nonexistence.[55] What is most significant for our purposes is that Russell's solutions to the first two of these puzzles turn not just on revealing a hidden logical form in the sentences of ordinary language, but on revealing a hidden structural equivocation therein. Thus consider the second puzzle, concerning the law of the excluded middle. Starting from consideration of the sentence

(A) Either the King of France is bald or the King of France is not bald

we seem to be driven into a contradiction. For on the one hand, (A) is an instance of the law of excluded middle, and so must be true. On the other hand, if (A) is true, then either

(B) The King of France is bald

or

(C) The King of France is not bald

must be true. Searching through the bald men, we fail to find the King of France. So we conclude that (B) is false. This implies that (C) is true. On the other hand, searching through the nonbald men, we also fail to find the King of France. This leads us to conclude that (C) is false, and so (B) is true. Hence our contradiction.

As is well known, Russell solves this puzzle by pointing to an ambiguity in (C), and so also in (A). (C) can be read as either

(C1)   The King of France is (not bald),

or

(C2)   It is not the case that (the King of France is bald).

The difference between (C1) and (C2) is made explicit using Russell's logical notation: (C1) comes out as

(C1′) $(\exists x)(y)((Ky \equiv x = y) \bullet {\sim}By)$ (There is exactly one King of France, and he isn't bald),

while (C2) comes out as

(C2′) ${\sim}(\exists x)(y)((Ky \equiv x = y) \bullet By)$ (It is not the case that there is exactly one King of France, and he's bald).

Here (C2) is the negation of (B), which is represented formally as

(B′) $(\exists x)(y)((Ky \equiv x = y) \bullet By)$ (There is exactly one King of France, and he's bald).

Given this disambiguation of (C), we can see that (A) is ambiguous as well, between

(A1)   (B) or (C1),

and

(A2)   (B) or (C2) (that is (B) or not-(B)).

(A1) does imply that there is a present king of France, and that he is both bald and nonbald; so (A1) is contradictory. But there is no need to assert (A1) as it is *not* an instance of the law of the excluded middle. On the other hand, (A2) *is* an instance of the law of the excluded middle, but there is no difficulty in asserting it as true, since it implies neither that the King of France exists, nor that he is either bald or nonbald.

From Wittgenstein's point of view, what Russell has pointed out is that in both (A) and (C) we have cases in which the same (propositional) sign belongs to two different symbols (different propositions). When properly analyzed, the two readings of (C) (and so of [A]) have different logical form. Russell suggests, in introducing the puzzle, that "Hegelians, who love a synthesis, will probably conclude that he [the King of France] wears a wig."[56] This conclusion is dispelled by logical analysis, which reveals the equivocation on which it turns. Anyone who holds onto the problem and continues to remain puzzled by it must be intending (A), incoherently, as *both* (A1) and (A2), slipping between the two meanings at different stages of his argument, thereby failing to mean *anything* determinate by his words. Thus, (A), when seen as philosophically puzzling, is in fact not false, but nonsensical—it has no fixed sense.

Here we have a model of Wittgenstein's account of philosophical problems as nonsense arising from the "misunderstanding of the logic of our language." I believe that this model can be applied to many of Wittgenstein's discussions of more serious philosophical problems in the *Tractatus*. For example, an interesting case can be made concerning Wittgenstein's treatment of identity in the *Tractatus* and his accompanying dissolution of the problems concerned with Russell's Axiom of Infinity.[57] The claim that this case can be seen as the application of the model we have been discussing for the resolution of philosophical problems may be surprising. Nonetheless, I believe that it is correct. I plan to address this in detail in further work. But the basic idea can be spelled out briefly.[58]

The key point is that in the *Tractatus* Wittgenstein recognizes *two* uses of the identity sign, one to mark the intersubstitutability of expressions with the same meaning, as in the giving of definitions in *Principia Mathematica*,[59] the other, in combination with quantifiers, to express counting, number, and the like, as in the use of "$(x)(fx \supset x = a)$" to say that only a is an f.[60] A *confusion* of these two uses of "=" can lead to the idea of identity as a relation between things. On the one hand, the use of identity in stating a "rule of substitution" allows us to place the identity sign between *names*, outside the scope of any quantifier. On the other hand, the use of identity in combination with quantified variables requires that the variables range over nonlinguistic objects, not signs. If we allow these two uses to slide together, we will come to think that "$x = x$" and "$x = y$" respectively express a property of x and a relation between x and y. This confused thought results in the formation of such things as "$(x)x = x$" and "$(\exists x)x = a$," which Wittgenstein dismisses as pseudo-propositions at 5.534; it is also at the heart of *Principia Mathematica*'s formulation of the Axiom of Infinity. For the Axiom of Infinity states that the result of adding one repeatedly to zero is always a nonempty class. Zero, in turn, is defined as the class whose only member is the empty class, and the empty class is defined as the class of all x such that $x \neq x$. Similarly, one is defined to be the class of all unit classes, where a unit class is the class of all y such that $y = x$, for some fixed x. The first definition requires that $x \neq x$, and so also $x = x$, express genuine properties of x, and the second requires that $x = y$ expresses a genuine relation between x and y.[61] This is why clarification of the different meanings of identity can lead to the resolution of the problems surrounding the Axiom of Infinity—

the very formulation of the axiom, for Wittgenstein, trades on the way that the sign "=" is part of more than one symbol.[62]

In response to these confusions, Wittgenstein offers a new notation. He dispenses with the second use of "=," instead expressing "identity of the object by identity of the sign," and "difference of the objects by difference of the signs."[63] Thus, for example, "$((\exists x)fx \supset fa) \bullet \sim(\exists x)(\exists y)(fx \bullet fy)$" says that only a is f.[64] In this new notation, there is no longer a temptation to view "=" as expressing a relation between things; indeed supposed propositions like "$(x)x = x$" and "$(\exists x)x = a$" have no counterparts in this notation.[65] For in moving from the old notation to the new, uses of identity within the scope of quantifiers are best seen as indications for how to identify or distinguish the quantified variables. But this requires propositional functions other than identity within which the identified or distinguished variables can occur. For example, "$(x)(y)(x = y \supset Rxy)$" would be replaced by "$(x)Rxx$" (identifying the variables), whereas "$(\exists x)(\exists y)(x \neq y \bullet Rxy)$" would be replaced by "$(\exists x)(\exists y)Rxy$" (distinguishing the variables). But this pattern would have us replace "$(x)x = x$" by something like "(x)," and "$(\exists x)x = a$" perhaps by something like "$(\exists a)a$"—in both cases the result is not something for which we have fixed any meaning at all. Thus, if we accept this new notation, the puzzlement we may have felt over self-identity simply disappears along with the puzzling sign $x = x$.

Thus we see how Wittgenstein in the *Tractatus* understood the problems of philosophy as resting on the misunderstanding of the logic of our language, and how he saw in this the key to their resolution. In the letter to Russell, however, Wittgenstein speaks of the *cardinal* problem of philosophy. Here we encounter an idea which was central in Wittgenstein's early thinking, but which he gave up in his later philosophy. As Matthew Ostrow puts it, Wittgenstein's early thought is dominated by the "governing idea of an essential confusion from which we can be essentially liberated."[66] In his pre-*Tractatus* journals,[67] this theme recurs repeatedly. Wittgenstein speaks of "the whole philosophical problem,"[68] the "main problem,"[69] "the whole *single* great problem,"[70] his "whole task,"[71] "the great problem round which everything I write turns."[72] He seeks a "correct overview"[73] that will allow him to see "that every problem is the main problem,"[74] and so find an "*extremely* simple" "solution to all my questions."[75] He hopes to find the key to all his difficulties through discovering a single "liberating thought" or "liberating word" (*erlösende Gedamke, erlösende Wort*).[76]

Over the course of these journals, Wittgenstein offers a variety of formulations of his "single great problem": "the logical identity of sign and thing signified,"[77] "the general concept of a proposition,"[78] "the principles of representing *as such*,"[79] "explaining the nature of the proposition . . . giving the nature of all facts . . . giving the nature of all being,"[80] and finally "is there an order in the world *a priori*, and if so what does it consist in?"[81]

In my view, these are so many different ways of formulating the same problem: to give the general concept of a proposition would be at the same time to give the principles of representation as such, the form of logic and the world that provides the identity of sign and thing signified, the a priori structure of the world. It would be to fix the limits of that which can be said. The "one single great problem" is none other than that which Wittgenstein identifies as the task of the *Tractatus*: to "draw a limit to thinking, or rather—not to thinking, but to the expression of thoughts."[82] Seen in this light, the "cardinal problem of philosophy" that Wittgenstein describes to Russell is yet another variation on the same theme: to distinguish that which can be expressed in propositions from that which cannot be so expressed, but only shown, is yet another way of trying to establish the limits of the expression of thought in language.[83]

Wittgenstein was convinced at the time of writing the *Tractatus* that through solving this one great problem, all the problems of philosophy would disappear. We must be brought to see that "every problem is the main problem," so that one "extremely simple" solution will suffice for them all.[84] As Matthew Ostrow has emphasized, this idea, unlike the general conception of the problems of philosophy and of their resolution discussed above, is one that Wittgenstein rejected in his later philosophy. Ostrow cites *Philosophical Investigations* §133: "Problems are solved (difficulties eliminated), not a *single* problem."[85] Ostrow sees here a rejection of Wittgenstein's "Tractarian views," a "deepening" of "his original insight." But, I will argue, it is really a consequence of the *Tractatus*'s solution to the "cardinal problem of philosophy." In dissolving this problem, we do *not* thereby solve all other problems. Rather, in revealing the "cardinal problem" to be an illusion, we at the same time show that the thought that all problems are solved in solving it is a part of that very illusion. Thus, if my argument is right, Ostrow has not identified here the real discontinuity between the thought of the *Tractatus* and that of the *Investigations*.[86] Yet, as we shall see, the discontinuity *is* spelled out in the very remark Ostrow cites, *Investigations* §133.

Toward the end of his wartime journals, with his mind turning more and more to matters of religion, ethics, and the mystical, Wittgenstein expresses frustration at his inability to bring unity to his thinking. In a passage noted by both his biographers, he writes: "Colossal exertions in the last months. Have thought a great deal on every possible subject. But curiously I cannot establish the connection with my mathematical modes of thought."[87] The next day, however, he exclaims: "But the connection will be established! What can't be said, *can't* be said!"[88] Neither Ray Monk nor Brian McGuinness mention this remark, but Monk tells us that: "the connection between

Wittgenstein's thought on logic and his reflections on the meaning of life was to be found in the distinction he had made earlier between *saying* and *showing*. Logical form, he had said, cannot be expressed *within* language, for it is the form of language itself; it makes itself manifest in language—it has to be *shown*. Similarly, ethical and religious truths, though inexpressible, manifest themselves in life."[89] Certainly, in the apparent tautology "what can't be said, can't be said," Wittgenstein sees a way to unite his diverse thoughts on ethics and logic, mathematics and the mystical. The preface to the *Tractatus* tells us that the "whole meaning" of the book "could be summed up somewhat as follows: What can be said at all can be said clearly; and whereof one cannot speak, thereof one must be silent."[90] Doesn't this require some positive way to delimit "what can be said" from that "whereof one cannot speak"? Don't we then need a "straight solution" of the "cardinal problem" rather than its dissolution? Aren't Monk and the other ineffabilist readers right after all?

I will argue, to the contrary, that the connection Wittgenstein needs is made not through the distinction between saying and showing, in the form Monk appeals to here, but through its dissolution. This thought itself is part of the illusion that the *Tractatus* aims to dispel. To see this is to see in what way the "cardinal problem" is a *problem* of philosophy in precisely Wittgenstein's sense. But if this is so, then there must be some sort of cross-categorial equivocation involved in "the theory of what can be expressed . . . by propositions . . . and what can not be expressed by propositions, but only shown." Some sign used therein must be part of two distinct symbols, and the theory itself must require us to waffle between these two uses of the one sign. What might this equivocal sign be?

In a largely unsympathetic presentation of the *Tractatus* in general and the saying/showing distinction in particular, Graham Priest remarks: "the word 'show' in English has both a propositional use and a non-propositional use. In its propositional use, 'show' is followed by a that-clause (she showed that she could play cricket); in its non-propositional use it is followed by 'what,' 'how,' etc., or even a simple noun-phrase (she showed him the bat/how to use it/where he could put it, etc.).[91] Priest clearly thinks that Wittgenstein himself is guilty of equivocation here, claiming that "Structures in the world and language show in both these senses." But, alert to the importance of such equivocation in the formulation of the problems of philosophy, we can turn his observation to more sympathetic uses.[92]

Of particular importance to us is the contrast between propositional "show" followed by a that-clause ("He showed me that the door was locked") and nonpropositional "show" followed by "how" ("He showed me how to pick the lock"). A number of readers of the *Tractatus*, myself among them,[93] have been drawn to the idea that the *Tractatus*'s talk of "showing" can be redeemed through an association with *practical* knowledge, knowledge-how rather than knowledge-that.[94] In "The Purpose of *Tractarian* Nonsense," I spoke of the *Tractatus* as "showing" us "a way of life." I argued that this use of "showing" need not be thrown away with the ladder of the *Tractatus*. What we have to discard is the thought that what is shown is "something like a proposition." But, I argued, if what is shown is practical knowledge, this "is not even the sort of thing we could be tempted to take for a proposition."[95] In "To What Extent Is Solipsism A Truth?" I suggested further that "uses of 'showing' in the *Tractatus* may be two-sided. On the one hand, talk of showing can tempt us into the nonsensical illusion that we grasp a realm of super-facts beyond the reach of language. On the other hand, talk of showing can, innocently enough, direct us to the practical abilities and masteries that are part of our ongoing talking, thinking and living."[96] But if talk of showing is "two-sided," given our account of the roots of philosophical problems, we should expect this two-sidedness itself to be part of what tempts us into philosophical difficulties and nonsensical illusions. Any awareness of "a sense that can be given to some of . . . uses of 'showing' [in the *Tractatus*] which does not degenerate into the incoherence of envisaging in the form of a fact that which we declare not to be a fact,"[97] can only be something that we arrive at after working through the *Tractatus*. It is only after we have seen through the difficulties, and the equivocation that is their source, that we can choose one of the two symbols expressed using the sign "show" and decide to use that sign as one symbol rather than the other.

How, though, might the fact that "showing" can have both a propositional and a practical use contribute to philosophical illusions and difficulties? Recall my suggestion in "The Purpose of *Tractarian* Nonsense" that the doctrine of truths that cannot be said, but only shown, seems to fulfill a certain purpose: it provides an "internal" justification for our language, our thoughts, our lives. For this purpose, I argued, we "need something sufficiently like a proposition to serve as a justification, an answer to a question, yet sufficiently different from a proposition to need no further justification, to raise no further questions in turn"—an insight that can be shown, but not said—but an insight into a truth nonetheless.[98] If we allow ourselves to use the word "show" in a way that trades on the fact that this one sign is part of two different symbols—"practical" showing and "propositional" showing—we may come to think we have a grip on just such an insight. For what is shown can't be said, we think, running in the grooves laid down by the use of "shows how," yet it is certainly something like a fact, we convince ourselves, running in the grooves laid down by the use of "shows that." And so we seem to have what we want.

This little story may seem hopelessly far-fetched, however. Has any philosopher really thought like *that*? I want to make this more plausible by considering one of the most subtle and persuasive presentations of the ineffabilist reading, Peter Geach's "Saying and Showing in Frege and Wittgenstein."[99] Peter Sullivan rightly remarks that Geach's essay "is at once an inspiration and a stalking horse" of Diamond's and points out that it is an early source of the idea of "connecting showing with practical knowledge."[100] Geach argues that the saying/showing distinction has roots in Frege's philosophy of logic. He posits four theses, the first of which is: "Frege already held . . . that there are logical category-distinctions which will clearly show themselves in a well-constructed formalized language, but which cannot be properly asserted in language: the sentences in which we seek to convey them in the vernacular language are logically improper and admit of no transformation into well-formed formulas of symbolic logic. All the same, there is a test for these sentences' having conveyed the intended distinctions—namely, that by their aid mastery of the formalized language is attainable."[101] Geach's second thesis adds that "the category-distinctions in question are features both of verbal expressions and also of the reality our language is describing."[102] Geach thinks this "notion of what comes out but cannot be asserted is almost irresistible, in spite of its paradoxical nature, when we reflect upon logic."[103]

Geach here *seems* to commit himself to the view that there are inexpressible truths, truths about reality, language, and the features that they share. Peter Sullivan, however, has argued that it is unfair to impose this conclusion on Geach. Sullivan makes much of Geach's use of the term "features" here: "Wittgenstein, and those of his interpreters Kremer condemns as irresolute, typically talk of what is shown as certain *features*—features of a proposition, of state of affairs, of language, of reality, the world."[104] Sullivan's claim is demonstrably false of some of the "interpreters Kremer condemns as irresolute"—it is at least as true that Hacker, Hans-Johann Glock, Monk and others *typically* talk of what is shown by producing apparent propositions—and is only partially true of Wittgenstein, who often does the same.[105] What is correct, however, is that *Geach* speaks of what is shown as "features of reality;" and in "Throwing Away the Ladder," Diamond *does* accuse Geach of thereby "chickening out." Sullivan, however, denies that by countenancing talk of inexpressible "features of reality" one necessarily countenances "the idea of a quasi-truth or inexpressible state of affairs." He bases his argument on the claim that "that is not true of ordinary talk of features—of a landscape, for instance, or a face."[106]

Of course, ordinary talk of features does not bring with it the idea of a "quasi-truth or inexpressible state of affairs." But this does not suffice for Sullivan's point. For ordinary talk of features, even of facial features, often *does* bring with it the idea of an *ordinary* truth or an *ordinary* state of affairs. Thus, a diagnosis of fetal alcohol syndrome is made "based on the history of maternal alcohol use, and detailed physical examination for the characteristic major and minor birth defects and *characteristic facial* features."[107] These features include "small eye openings (measured from inner corner to outer corner), epicanthal folds (folds of tissue at the inner corner of the eye), small or short nose, low or flat nasal bridge, smooth or poorly developed philtrum (the area of the upper lip above the colored part of the lip and below the nose), thin upper lip, and small chin." A doctor making such a diagnosis on the basis of such "facial features" will surely include in her report *propositions* stating such *truths* as that the patient has a short nose, a thin upper lip, and so on.

But if ordinary talk of features can thus bring with it talk of truths and states of affairs, by the same token might not talk of inexpressible features bring with it talk of inexpressible truths and states of affairs? Certainly, this transition is a natural one for the ineffabilist Peter Hacker, who is happy to move from the claim that "categorial features of things" are inexpressible to the claim that "one cannot say of a thing that it belongs to a given category, for example that red is a colour or that *a* is an object."[108]

Hacker's move from talk of features to talk of categorization, and so of seeming propositions like "that red is a colour," is encouraged by Wittgenstein's own talk of "features" (*Züge*) in the *Tractatus*. Two of the three propositions in which the word "feature" occurs lie in the stretch of the *Tractatus* from 4.12 to 4.127 in which Wittgenstein officially introduces the saying/showing distinction (*Tractatus* 4.1212) and develops the related idea of "formal properties of objects and atomic facts," the "holding" of which "cannot . . . be asserted by propositions but . . . shows itself."[109] At 4.1221, Wittgenstein introduces the phrase "feature of a fact" as an alternative expression for "internal property [*Eigenschaft*] of a fact," writing that the phrase is used "in the sense in which we speak of facial features." At 4.126, he writes that "in the sense in which we speak of formal properties we can now speak of formal concepts [*Begriffe*]," and adds that "the expression of a formal property is a feature of certain symbols." Thus for Wittgenstein the three notions: "feature," "formal property," "formal concept," are closely intertwined, if not identified. Over the course of this stretch of remarks, he gives as examples of things that can only be shown, not said, that the object *a* occurs in the sense of the proposition *fa*; that two propositions *fa* and *ga* are about the same object; that two propositions contradict one another; that one proposition follows from another (all in *Tractatus* 4.1211); that internal properties and relations hold of objects (*Tractatus* 4.122, 4.124); that one blue color is brighter or darker than another (*Tractatus* 4.123); and that an object falls under a formal concept (*Tractatus* 4.126)— only to go on to declare such seeming propositions nonsensical (*Tractatus* 4.124, 4.1241, 4.1272). Given all this, Geach's insistence on the "paradoxical" nature of the "Frege-Wittgenstein notion of what comes out but cannot be asserted"[110] is easy to understand, whereas it would be hard to fathom if talk of "features" were as innocent as Sullivan maintains.

So far, however, I have left out a crucial aspect of Geach's story, the connection that he draws between practical knowledge and the idea of showing, when he writes that "mastery of the formalized language" provides a test for having grasped the distinctions and features that certain nonsense sentences are meant to convey. Geach emphasizes that "the insight we gain . . . into the workings of logical notation can be definitely tested—even by University examiners."[111] Sullivan thinks that this idea can be used to defend Geach against the charge that he assigns to "nonsensical elucidations" the "additional positive role of conveying a kind of inexpressible insight."[112] Sullivan makes two claims here: "First, and somewhat trivially, Geach nowhere in his article actually describes an elucidation as imparting an 'inexpressible insight.' But secondly, and much more importantly, it is absolutely plain from Geach's discussion that, had he described an elucidation in this way, this would not be to ascribe to it an *additional* role, but only to redescribe its 'didactic' role in instilling the mastery of the symbolism."

The first claim is literally true—the phrase "inexpressible insights" does not occur in Geach's paper. But the *concept* appears to be present—Geach does speak of the "insights" "conveyed through ethical, aesthetic, and religious utterances," and by "the elucidatory sentences that introduce us to the use of logical notation," and clearly Geach thinks these insights *are* inexpressible.[113] Thus the only question is whether these insights amount to anything *over and above* "mastery of the symbolism." But here a return to the claim that "the category-distinctions in question are features . . . of the reality our language is describing" does *seem* to yield this conclusion (*pace* Sullivan's remarks about the innocence of talk of "features").

Let us consider this situation a little more closely. Geach holds that the nonsensical elucidatory sentences used to introduce us to a logical notation convey to us "category-distinctions" that are "features" of both the symbolism we are mastering and the "reality" it describes; and he holds that our mastery of the symbolism is evidence of our having grasped these distinctions. From this it follows that mastery of a notation is sufficient for grasping "features" of reality. But why should this be? The fate of Frege's own logical work should give us pause here. For Russell's paradox convinced him in the end that his logical notation was defective, and in fact *described no reality*— yet Frege was able to reach this conclusion only because of his mastery of his own symbolism.[114]

One might argue that since "the formal articulation of a proposition precisely reflects—i.e. simply *is*—the formal articulation of the situation it presents,"[115] to master a symbolism is to grasp the structure of propositions, and so of the reality corresponding to them. This argument presupposes, however, that the symbolism we are mastering *does* present situations, *does* consist of meaningful propositions. Here the question of justification raises its head: how do we know our symbolism is not, like that of Frege's *Grundgesetze*, radically defective? And we seem to be tempted by an answer: in mastering the symbolism we achieve an insight into the "formal articulation" of the reality that our language depicts. With this thought, however, we seem to be moving close to the transcendental idealism that Sullivan himself sees as the target of the *Tractatus*.

In my view, Geach's understanding of "showing" involves precisely the confusion of practical and propositional showing that I have argued is at the heart of the ineffability reading of the *Tractatus*. It may be that the use of the word "feature," far from being innocent, helps to compound this confusion. For, as we have seen, talk of features, even facial features, *can* simply point us to the facts about a face—facts that might form the basis for a medical diagnosis. Yet not all talk of features is of this sort. When I recognize my daughter by her facial features, I may not be able to articulate a set of concepts to describe precisely what it is that allows me to pick her out of a crowd. Hence, Sullivan is right after all to say that not all talk of features necessarily brings with it talk of propositions and facts. Talk of "facial features" may call on abilities of recognition and of comparison involved in the understanding and use of "family resemblance" terms without requiring the articulation of a concept.

In fact, the very word "feature" has the same equivocal nature we have found in "show." When a doctor speaks of the characteristic facial features of a patient with fetal alcohol syndrome, she is, I suppose, saying something about how the patient's face *is*. In contrast, when we speak of the features of language, we are saying something about how the language is *used*. But if we speak of "reality" as having "features" that we can grasp *in* mastering a symbolism, and go on to illustrate this through examples such as one proposition's following from another, or one color of blue being lighter than another, we are confusedly thinking of these features both as having to do with how reality *is*, *and* as having to do with how language is to be *used*.[116]

It is this confusion that is at the root of the "cardinal problem of philosophy." The notion of a "showing" of inexpressible truths, while sorely tempting to us, is also the source of great philosophical puzzlement. For the desire to express the truths we think we grasp is constantly competing with the thought that these truths must not—and so cannot—be expressed. But the *Tractatus*, in bringing us to recognize its propositions as nonsense, brings us to see that no meaning is attached to the ineffabilist use of the word "showing," which had seemed to be the key to understanding the book. And once we see that there is no clear notion here at all, the perplexities that it brought in its train disappear.[117]

But if this is how the "cardinal problem of philosophy" is resolved, does its resolution then lead, as Wittgenstein had hoped, to the solution of all the problems of philosophy at one stroke? The answer to this question must be negative—the hope for one solution to all problems is itself part of the problematic illusion that the *Tractatus* aims to dispel. The solution to the "cardinal problem of philosophy" is *not* to be found in a "theory" of that which can be said and that which can only be shown, or a *criterion* of sense and nonsense. The desire for such a theory is itself part of the problem and involves the same philosophical fantasy. Once this fantasy loses its grip on us, we are left with simply an awareness of that which does, in an entirely innocent sense, show itself—our ability to use the language that we speak and understand, and with it our ability to recognize when the use of language makes sense and when it does not. Relying on this awareness, we can get down to the difficult work involved in tackling philosophical problems, revealing the confusions involved in them, showing in what ways they degenerate into nonsense. But, as Diamond and Conant put it, this work most proceed "piecemeal," case by case.[118]

Hence, the real conclusion of the *Tractatus* is already in harmony with Wittgenstein's insistence in *Investigations* §133 that "problems are solved . . . not a *single* problem." Nonetheless, to use Diamond and Conant's lovely phrase, there is here a "profound discontinuity in thinking that is folded within a fundamental continuity in Wittgenstein's philosophy."[119] For, according to the *Tractatus*, there remains a single "correct method in philosophy": "to say nothing except what can be said, . . . and then always, when someone else wished to say something metaphysical, to demonstrate to him that he had given no meaning to certain signs in his propositions."[120] The method of which Wittgenstein speaks is that of the "logical clarification of thoughts"[121] and its fundamental tool is the construction of "a symbolism . . . which obeys the rules of *logical* grammar"—a *Begriffsschrift*, a language in which, as in the model from Russell discussed above, every philosophical equivocation can be laid bare and every philosophical problem thus put to rest.[122] As Diamond and Conant argue, it is the *Tractatus*'s implicit commitment to the idea that *this* method can be used to dissolve every philosophical problem that Wittgenstein later came to reject as the metaphysical dogmatism of his early work—and indeed this commitment came under pressure as soon as it was made explicit in Wittgenstein's first attempt at serious philosophy after his return to Cambridge, "Some Remarks on Logical Form."[123] At *Investigations* §133, Wittgenstein tells us not only that there is no *single* problem, but also that "there is not *a* philosophical method, though there are indeed methods, like different therapies." If the argument of this essay is correct, it is the second of these claims, not the first, which marks the real discontinuity between Wittgenstein's early and late works.[124]

Notes

1. Versions of this essay were presented to the University of Chicago Wittgenstein Workshop, to the philosophy department of the Universitá di Roma, La Sapienza, and to the philosophy department of the University of Illinois at Chicago. Thanks are due to all three audiences for helpful comments and discussion. Special thanks go to Jim Conant for invaluable comments on an earlier draft.

2. The view stems from G. E. M. Anscombe, *An Introduction to Wittgenstein's Tractatus* and is adopted by P. M. S. Hacker, *Insight and Illusion*; Anthony Kenny, *Wittgenstein*; Peter Geach, "Saying and Showing in Frege and Wittgenstein"; Robert J. Fogelin, *Wittgenstein*; David Pears, *The False Prison*; Brian McGuinness, *Wittgenstein: A Life*, and *Young Ludwig 1889–1921*; Ray Monk, *Ludwig Wittgenstein: The Duty of Genius*; David G. Stern, *Wittgenstein on Mind and Language*; Hans-Johann Glock, *A Wittgenstein Dictionary*; Martin Stokhof, *World and Life as One*; and Ray Monk, *How to Read Wittgenstein*, among others.

3. Jane Heal, "Wittgenstein, Ludwig Josef Johann (1889–1951)."

4. Cora Diamond, "Throwing Away the Ladder," 181.

5. Ludwig Wittgenstein, *Tractatus Logico-Philosophicus*, *Tractatus* 4.112. Quotations from the *Tractatus* will be by numbered proposition and will be from the Ogden translation, unless otherwise noted.

6. Diamond, "Throwing Away the Ladder," 195.

7. Ibid., 182.

8. James Conant, "Throwing Away the Top of the Ladder," 340.

9. *Tractatus* 3.3.

10. *Tractatus* 5.4733.

11. The terminology of "resolute" and "irresolute" interpretations is introduced in Warren Goldfarb, "Metaphysics and Nonsense: On Cora Diamond's *The Realistic Spirit*," where it is attributed to an unpublished manuscript of Thomas Ricketts.

12. In the debate, inspired by Diamond's work, over the proper way to read the *Tractatus*, some interpreters have tried to stake out a third position, intermediate between the ineffability and resolute readings—for example, Marie McGinn, "Between Metaphysics and Nonsense: Elucidation in Wittgenstein's *Tractatus*"; Roy Brand, "Making Sense Speaking Nonsense." A. W. Moore's *Points of View* and "Ineffability and Nonsense" may also belong in this category; but his project

sometimes appears to aim rather at a reconciliation of resolute and ineffabilist readings. At times, he argues, as does Peter Sullivan, that the difference between resolute readers and the best ineffabilist readers does not really amount to anything—see Peter Sullivan's articles: "On Trying to Be Resolute"; "Ineffability and Nonsense," 198. See also Moore, "Ineffability and Nonsense," 180. Presumably none of these interpreters would be happy with a simple dichotomy between "resolute" and "ineffability" readings. My hope is only that the labels "resolute" and "ineffability" will be acceptable to those interpreters to whom they are here applied.

13. In the essays mentioned in the bibliography.

14. Ludwig Wittgenstein, "Letters to Ficker," 94.

15. Michael Kremer, "The Purpose of Tractarian Nonsense," 51–52.

16. For illuminating discussions of this issue see James Conant and Cora Diamond, "On Reading the *Tractatus* Resolutely"; and Oskari Kuusela, "From Metaphysics and Philosophical Theses to Grammar: Wittgenstein's Turn."

17. P. M. S. Hacker, John Koethe, and H. O. Mounce criticize the resolute reading in order to defend the ineffability reading—see P. M. S. Hacker, "Was He Trying to Whistle It?" and "When the Whistling Had to Stop"; John Koethe, "On the 'Resolute' Reading of the *Tractatus*"; and H. O. Mounce, "Critical Notice: The New Wittgenstein." Ian Proops seems more concerned to argue that the textual basis for the resolute reading is no better than that for the ineffability reading; See Proops, "The New Wittgenstein: A Critique." Peter Sullivan, while sympathetic to some of the main themes of the resolute reading, thinks that what is clearly right in the resolute reading is also present in the best versions of the ineffability reading. See Sullivan, "On Trying to be Resolute," and "Ineffability and Nonsense."

18. McGuinness, *Young Ludwig*, 264; Monk, *The Duty of Genius*, 155.

19. Ludwig Wittgenstein, *Ludwig Wittgenstein: Cambridge Letters: Correspondence with Russell, Keynes, Moore, Ramsey and Sraffa*, 120. Copies had already been sent to his friend Paul Engelmann and to Gottlob Frege. Monk, *The Duty of Genius*, 157.

20. Wittgenstein, *Cambridge Letters*, 121.

21. Ibid., 124.

22. I have addressed Wittgenstein's appeals to "showing" in replying to Russell in Kremer, "The Purpose of Tractarian Nonsense," 64–65, and will not repeat here what I have said there.

23. For example in Pears, *The False Prison*, 142; Hacker, *Insight and Illusion*, 19; Glock, *A Wittgenstein Dictionary*, 330; Stern, *Wittgenstein on Mind and Language*, 69; Anscombe, *An Introduction to Wittgenstein's Tractatus*, 161; McGuinness, *Young Ludwig*, 277; and Monk, *How to Read Wittgenstein*, 19.

24. Hacker, "Was He Trying to Whistle It?" 129.

25. Proops, "The New Wittgenstein," 377.

26. Koethe, "On the 'Resolute' Reading," 202.

27. Kremer, "The Purpose of Tractarian Nonsense," 64.

28. *Tractatus*, preface, 27.

29. Kremer, "The Purpose of Tractarian Nonsense," 64.

30. Koethe, "On the 'Resolute' Reading," 202, n. 33.

31. Sullivan, "On Trying to Be Resolute," 74, n. 15.

32. McGuinness, *Young Ludwig*, 173.

33. Stern, *Wittgenstein on Mind and Language*, 70.

34. Similarly Monk writes that the *Tractatus*'s "main point is to answer 'the cardinal problem of philosophy,' i.e. the question of where the limits of expressibility lie" (Monk, *How to Read Wittgenstein*, 23).

35. *Tractatus* 4.111.

36. Ibid., 4.112.

37. Ibid., 4.114–16.

38. For much of what I think about Wittgenstein's account of the "problems of philosophy," I am indebted to Conant's "The Method of the *Tractatus*."

39. *Tractatus*, preface, 27.

40. Following Pears and McGuinness in translating *"unsinnig"* and *"Unsinnigkeit"* as "nonsense" and "nonsensicality."

41. *Tractatus* 3.32.

42. Ibid., 3.314.

43. Ibid., 3.326.

44. Ibid., 5.4733.

45. Ibid., 3.321.

46. Ibid., 3.323–3.325.

47. Sullivan memorably calls this kind of philosophical confusion "double-think." Sullivan recognizes that the Tractatus holds such "double-think" to be "characteristic of philosophical discourse." Peter Sullivan, "What Is the *Tractatus* About?," 35. But, I will argue, he fails to see how deeply the ineffabilist notion of showing involves such double-think.

48. Wittgenstein often mentions Hertz's treatment of the concept of force in *The Principles of Mechanics* as a model here; but arguably Russell's application of the theory of descriptions to solve philosophical puzzles is another source, as I argue below.

49. Ludwig Wittgenstein, *Wittgenstein's Lectures: Cambridge, 1930–1932*, 4. Similar thoughts are recorded in notes from Wittgenstein's conversations taken in 1939 and 1946, both times with explicit mention of Hertz. In the first case, after expounding Hertz on force, Wittgenstein is reported to have said that "he must confess that this passage seemed to him to sum up philosophy." Ludwig Wittgenstein, *Public and Private Occasions*, 378–380, 398–399.

50. Ludwig Wittgenstein, *The Blue and Brown Books*, 26–27. See also Wittgenstein, *Public and Private Occasions*, 379. In the full passage from the *Blue Book* which I am excerpting here, Hertz's *Principles of Mechanics* is again mentioned.

51. *Tractatus* 4.003.

52. Ibid., 4.0031.

53. Ibid., 4.003.

54. Ibid., 4.003.

55. Bertrand Russell, "On Denoting," 485.

56. Ibid., 485.

57. *Tractatus* 5.53ff.

58. The story is made more complicated than the sketch I give here by the fact that "=" is a defined sign in *Principia Mathematica*, whereas Wittgenstein seems to proceed as if it were primitive. This objection can be met, but only at the cost of introducing a third layer of ambiguity—distinguishing the use of "=" to refer to the defined relation of sharing all predicates, the use of "=" to express intersubstitutability, and the use of "=" to express counting and the like—as in the theory of descriptions. I thank Peter Hylton for bringing to my attention the significance here of the defined status of the identity predicate in *Principia*.

59. *Tractatus* 4.241–3.

60. Ibid., 5.53ff. These two uses of the identity sign and the potential for confusion they bring with them were discussed at length by Wittgenstein in his lectures at Cambridge in 1932–1935. Ludwig Wittgenstein, *Wittgenstein's Lectures: Cambridge 1932–1935*, 146ff., 207ff.

61. The Axiom of Infinity is defined at *120.03 in Alfred North Whitehead and Bertrand Russell, *Principia Mathematica*, vol. 2, 203:

*120.03   Infin ax . = : $\alpha \in$ NC induct . $\supset_\alpha$. $\exists! \alpha$ Df.

"NC induct" refers to the class of all inductive cardinal numbers, that is, the cardinals resulting from 0 by repeated addition of 1 (*120.01, 2:203). Working through the definitions of 1 (*52.01, 1:347) and of 0 (*54.01, 1:360) yields:

$0 = \hat{\alpha} (\alpha = \hat{x}(x \neq x))$

$1 = \hat{\alpha} \{(\exists x) . \alpha = \hat{y}(y = x)\}$.

62. In his pre-*Tractatus* wartime journals, Wittgenstein stated that "all the problems that go with the Axiom of Infinity have already to be solved in the proposition '$(\exists x)x = x$'" (Wittgenstein, *Notebooks*, 10, entry for 9.10.14) and worried that the "Russellian definition of nought" might be "nonsensical" since it is doubtful that either $x = x$ or $x \neq x$ is "a function of x." (*Notebooks*, 16, entry for 21.10.14). He found satisfaction in the realization that the identity sign could be dispensed with, so that "'$x = y$' is not a propositional form" (*Notebooks*, 19, entry for 27.10.14) and "the pseudo-proposition $(x)x = a$ or the like would lose all appearance of justification." Ludwig Wittgenstein, *Notebooks: 1914–1916*, 2nd. ed., 34, entry for 29.11.14.

63. *Tractatus* 5.53.

64. Ibid., 5.5321.

65. Jaakko Hintikka's logical regimentation of Wittgenstein's method of dispensing with the identity sign fails to capture Wittgenstein's thought here, since on Hintikka's account, $(x)x = x$ is translated into a tautology in the new notation, while $(\exists x)x \neq x$ is translated into a contradiction. Jaakko Hintikka, "Identity, Variables, and Impredicative Definitions," 231–234. But for Wittgenstein, neither of these pseudo-propositions corresponds to anything that can be said—not even to something *sinnlos* such as a tautology or a contradiction. *Tractatus* 5.534.

66. Matthew Ostrow, *Wittgenstein's "Tractatus": A Dialectical Interpretation*, 134.

67. Wittgenstein's journal entries were written partly in (a very simple) code. The uncoded parts have been translated by Anscombe in *Notebooks*. The coded parts have been published in German as *Geheime Tagebücher*, but have not been translated into English. Except where noted, translations from these entries are my own.

68. Wittgenstein, *Notebooks*, 3, entry for September 3, 1914.

69. Ludwig Wittgenstein, *Geheime Tagebücher: 1914–1916*, 25, 38, entries for September 29, 1914; November 1, 1914.

70. *Notebooks*, 23, entry for November 1, 1914.

71. *Notebooks*, 39, entry for January 22, 1915.

72. *Notebooks*, 53, entry for June 1, 1915.

73. *Geheime Tagebücher*, 24, 25, 30, entries for September 21, 1914; September 29, 1914; October 14, 1914; *Notebooks*, 23, entry for November 1, 1914.

74. *Geheime Tagebücher*, 25, entry for September 29, 1914.

75. *Notebooks*, 7, entry for September 29, 1914.

76. *Geheime Tagebücher*, 32, 44, entries for October 17, 1914; November 21, 1914; *Notebooks*, 39, 54, entries for January 1, 1915; June 3, 1915. Baker and Hacker note the "frequent" occurrence of the idea of the "liberating word" in the wartime notebooks. They also point out that in a letter

of about the same time (July 24, 1915), Wittgenstein tells Ludwig von Ficker "You are living, as it were, in the dark, and have not found the saving word [*erlösende Wort*]." Wittgenstein goes on to recommend to Ficker Tolstoy's *The Gospel in Brief*. Gordon Baker and P. M. S. Hacker, *Wittgenstein: Understanding and Meaning*, part 2, 284; Wittgenstein, "Letters to Ficker," 91. Matthew Ostrow builds his interpretation of the *Tractatus* around this notion of the "liberating word." He begins with remarks taken from the early 1930s in which Wittgenstein says that the philosopher's task is to find "the liberating word," and then asks "could such claims be applied to Wittgenstein's early work as well?" arguing for a positive answer (Ostrow, *Wittgenstein's "Tractatus"*, 1). He fails to note that Wittgenstein uses the very phrase four times in his pre-*Tractatus* journals—perhaps because the coded entries (*Geheime Tagebücher*) are not available in English translation, while in the translation of the uncoded entries in *Notebooks*, Anscombe renders the phrase "erlösende Wort" as "key word," not "liberating word."

77. *Notebooks*, 3, entry for September 3, 1914.

78. *Notebooks*, 7, entry for September 29, 1914.

79. *Notebooks*, 23, entry for November 11, 1914.

80. *Notebooks*, 39, entry for January 22, 1915.

81. *Notebooks*, 53, entry for 1.6.15.

82. *Tractatus*, preface, 27.

83. Peter Sullivan has argued that it is illuminating to see the target of the *Tractatus* as transcendental idealism (Sullivan, "What Is the Tractatus About?" 42–43). This strikes me as also right—the problem of an a priori order in the world is one of the forms of the cardinal problem. But I think this is entirely compatible with seeing the book as exposing the ineffabilist form of the showing/saying distinction as itself problematic.

84. This point is recognized by Monk, *How to Read Wittgenstein*, 23, as well as by Baker and Hacker, *Understanding and Meaning*, part 2, 284, and Garth Hallett, *A Companion to Wittgenstein's "Philosophical Investigations,"* 232. But none of them understands the way in which the "cardinal problem" is resolved in the *Tractatus*.

85. Ostrow, *Wittgenstein's "Tractatus,"* 134. This passage dates at least to the "Big Typescript" of 1933. Ludwig Wittgenstein, *The Big Typescript: TS 213*, 316.

86. Hallett, and Baker and Hacker, both see Wittgenstein as rejecting what he "previously" thought (Hallett, *Companion*, 232), "the spirit of [his] early work" (Baker and Hacker, *Understanding and Meaning*, part 2, 284) in asserting that "problems are solved, . . . not a single problem." If "previous" and "early" refer to Wittgenstein's thought at some time before he completed the *Tractatus*, I would agree with these assessments. But on my view, the *Tractatus* itself has already rejected its author's "previous" conception that the solution of one great problem will solve all other problems in its wake.

87. Wittgenstein, *Geheime Tagebücher*, 72, entry for July 6, 1916; McGuinness, *Young Ludwig*, 245; Monk, *The Duty of Genius*, 142. Monk misdates the entry as July 7, 1916. The translation here is from Monk.

88. "Was sich nicht sagen läßt, läßt sich nicht sagen!" *Geheime Tagebücher*, 73, entry for July 7, 1916.

89. Monk, *The Duty of Genius*, 142.

90. *Tractatus*, preface, 27.

91. Graham Priest, *Beyond the Limits of Thought*, 2nd ed., 186.

92. I focus on the distinction between propositional and practical showing below; as Priest points out, there is also a sense in which what is shown can be an object. This usage is also relevant to some occurrences of "show" in the *Tractatus*. Eli Friedlander's reading of the *Tractatus* makes the "showing" of objects fundamental. Eli Friedlander, *Signs of Sense: Reading Wittgenstein's "Tractatus."* I will not discuss issues of the relative priority of practical showing and the showing of objects here. (For brief discussion see my review of Friedlander's book.)

93. Others include Peter Geach, Marie McGinn, Roy Brand, and A. W. Moore. While McGinn and Brand, and perhaps also Moore, try to use this idea in service of constructing readings of the *Tractatus* alternative to both ineffabilist and resolute readings, the idea itself is, I think, implicit in much of Conant and Diamond's work, and explicit in their "On Reading the *Tractatus* Resolutely," 65–67.

94. The distinction between knowledge-how and knowledge-that is famously drawn in Gilbert Ryle, *The Concept of Mind*. Recently, however, the distinction has been questioned, in Jason Stanley and Timothy Williamson, "Knowing How," 411–444; Paul Snowdon, "Knowing How and Knowing That," 1–29; and A. W. Moore, *Points of View*, 166–173. Stanley and Williamson's arguments in particular have met with many replies, notably: Stephen Schiffer, "Amazing Knowledge," 200–202; John Koethe, "Stanley and Williamson on Knowing How," 325–328; Ian Rumfitt, "Savoir-Faire," 158–166; Tobias Rosefeldt, "Is Knowing-How Simply a Case of Knowing-That?," 370–379; and Alva Noë, "Against Intellectualism," 278–290. As Moore himself points out, however, the important question for our purposes is not whether every instance of "knowing how" is irreducible to "knowing that." All that matters are that there are some instances of practical knowledge that can't be equated with propositional knowledge. I am not going to enter this debate here, but will only record my agreement with Moore against Stanley and Williamson that not all practical knowledge can be reduced to propositional knowledge, though much practical knowledge certainly involves propositional knowledge. However, in my view Moore comes too close to treating "knowledge" as a genus of which "propositional knowledge" and "practical knowledge" are species, when he gives "marks" of knowledge that both are supposed to share (Moore, *Points of View*, 173–180). I think these "marks" are more like the "family resemblances" of *Philosophical Investigations* §67—so that the table of types of knowledge provided by Moore (*Points of View*, 192) is somewhat like a table of games with headings "board games," "ball games," and so on.

95. Kremer, "The Purpose of Tractarian Nonsense," 62.

96. Ibid., 63.

97. Michael Kremer, "To What Extent Is Solipsism a Truth?," 59–84.

98. Kremer, "The Purpose of Tractarian Nonsense," 52.

99. I hope to show, contra Sullivan, that one can get considerably more than a cigarette paper between Geach's interpretation and that of Diamond and Conant. Sullivan, "Ineffability and Nonsense," 204, n. 19.

100. Ibid., 203–204.

101. Geach, "Saying and Showing," 55.

102. Ibid.

103. Ibid., 56.

104. Sullivan, "On Trying to Be Resolute," 50.

105. Instances in Hacker's writings abound; a compendium of things that can be shown but not said, many of which have the form of propositions, is provided in Hacker, "Was He Trying to Whistle It?" 98–100; see also Glock, *A Wittgenstein Dictionary*, 330–331. For a recent example, see Monk, *How to Read Wittgenstein*, 29. After discussing the merits of the resolute reading, Monk insists that Wittgenstein "does indeed, for example, believe that: 'ethics has nothing to do with punishment and reward in the ordinary sense', but he also believes that, strictly speaking, this ethical truth cannot be stated but has to be shown." Monk's use of quotation marks here does not diminish the incoherence of the "beliefs" he attributes to Wittgenstein.

106. Sullivan, "On Trying to Be Resolute," 50.

107. Laurie H. Seaver, "Fetal Alcohol Syndrome," *Gale Encyclopedia of Medicine*, Gale Group, http://www.healthatoz.com/healthatoz/Atoz/ency/fetal_alcohol_syndrome.jsp (accessed September 29, 2005) (my emphasis).

108. Hacker, "Was He Trying to Whistle It?," 99; "When the Whistling Had to Stop," 148.

109. *Tractatus* 4.122.

110. Geach, "Saying and Showing," 56, 68.

111. Ibid., 70.

112. Sullivan "On Trying to Be Resolute," 73, n. 7.

113. Geach, "Saying and Showing," 69.

114. In 1924 or 1925, Frege wrote that the "formation of a proper name after the pattern of 'the extension of the concept a' . . . appears to designate an object; but there is no such object for which this phrase could be a linguistically appropriate designation. . . . I myself was under this

illusion when, in attempting to provide a logical foundation for numbers, I tried to construe numbers as sets." Gottlob Frege, *Posthumous Writings*, 270.

115. Sullivan, "On Trying to Be Resolute," 47.

116. Jim Conant helped me to achieve clarity on the issues discussed in the last few paragraphs.

117. In the final paragraphs I am again indebted to Jim Conant for clarification of my conclusion.

118. Conant and Diamond, "On Reading the *Tractatus* Resolutely," 79–80.

119. Ibid., 84.

120. *Tractatus* 6.53.

121. Ibid., 4.112.

122. Ibid., 3.325.

123. Conant and Diamond, "On Reading the *Tractatus* Resolutely," 80–87; 96, n. 78.

124. I believe, nonetheless, that the abandonment of the fantasy of a single method is ultimately required by the abandonment of the fantasy of the single great problem, the solution of which will solve all other problems. It is this that Wittgenstein began to come to see once he tried to apply his single method in "Some Remarks on Logical Form."

Bibliography

Anscombe, G. E. M. *An Introduction to Wittgenstein's "Tractatus"* (1957). Philadelphia: University of Pennsylvania Press, 1971.

Baker, Gordon, and P. M. S. Hacker. *Wittgenstein: Understanding and Meaning. Part I–Essays.* 2nd ed. Oxford: Blackwell, 2005.

Baker, Gordon, and P. M. S. Hacker. *Wittgenstein: Understanding and Meaning. Part II–Exegesis §§1–184.* 2nd ed. Oxford: Blackwell, 2005.

Brand, Roy. "Making Sense Speaking Nonsense." *Philosophical Forum* 35 (2004): 311–339.

Conant, James. "The Method of the *Tractatus*." In *From Frege to Wittgenstein: Perspectives on Early Analytic Philosophy*, 374–462. Ed. E. Reck. Oxford: Oxford University Press, 2002.

Conant, James. "Throwing Away the Top of the Ladder." *Yale Review* 79 (1991): 328–364.

Conant, James, and Cora Diamond. "On Reading the *Tractatus* Resolutely: Reply to Meredith Williams and Peter Sullivan." In *Wittgenstein's Lasting Significance*, 46–99. Ed. M. Kölbel and B. Weiss. London and New York: Routledge, 2004.

Diamond, Cora. "Throwing Away the Ladder: How to Read the *Tractatus*" (1984–1985). In *The Realistic Spirit: Wittgenstein, Philosophy, and the Mind*, 179–204. Cambridge, Mass.: MIT Press, 1995.

Fogelin, Robert J. *Wittgenstein* (1987). 2nd ed. London: Routledge, 1995.

Frege, Gottlob. *Posthumous Writings*. Ed. H. Hermes, F. Kambartel, and F. Kaulbach. Trans. P. Long and R. White. Chicago: University of Chicago Press, 1979.

Friedlander, Eli. *Signs of Sense: Reading Wittgenstein's "Tractatus."* Cambridge, Mass.: Harvard University Press, 2001.

Geach, Peter. "Saying and Showing in Frege and Wittgenstein." In *Essays on Wittgenstein in Honour of G. H. von Wright*. Ed. J. Hintikka. *Acta Philosophica Fennica* 28 (1976): 54–70.

Glock, Hans-Johann. *A Wittgenstein Dictionary*. Oxford: Blackwell, 1996.

Goldfarb, Warren. "Metaphysics and Nonsense: On Cora Diamond's *The Realistic Spirit*." *Journal of Philosophical Research* 22 (1997): 57–73.

Hacker, P. M. S. *Insight and Illusion: Themes in the Philosophy of Wittgenstein*. 2nd ed. Oxford: Clarendon Press, 1986.

Hacker, P. M. S. "Was He Trying to Whistle It?" In *Wittgenstein: Connections and Controversies*, 98–140. Oxford: Clarendon Press, 2001.

Hacker, P. M. S. "When the Whistling Had to Stop." In *Wittgenstein: Connections and Controversies*, 141–169. Oxford: Clarendon Press, 2001.

Hallett, Garth. *A Companion to Wittgenstein's "Philosophical Investigations."* Ithaca, N.Y.: Cornell University Press, 1977.

Heal, Jane. "Wittgenstein, Ludwig Josef Johann (1889–1951)." In *Concise Routledge Encyclopedia of Philosophy*, 933–934. London and New York: Routledge, 2000.

Hintikka, Jaakko. "Identity, Variables, and Impredicative Definitions." *Journal of Symbolic Logic* 21 (1956): 225–245.

Kenny, Anthony. *Wittgenstein* (1973). Cambridge, Mass.: Harvard University Press, 1981.

Koethe, John. "On the 'Resolute' Reading of the *Tractatus*." *Philosophical Investigations* 26 (2003): 187–204.

Koethe, John. "Stanley and Williamson on Knowing How." *Journal of Philosophy* 99 (2002): 325–328.

Kremer, Michael. "Mathematics and Meaning in the *Tractatus*." *Philosophical Investigations* 25 (2002): 272–303.

Kremer, Michael. "Review of Eli Friedlander, *Signs of Sense*." *Philosophical Quarterly* 209 (2002): 652–654.

Kremer, Michael. "The Purpose of Tractarian Nonsense." *Noûs* 35 (2001): 39–73.

Kremer, Michael. "To What Extent Is Solipsism a Truth?" In *Post-Analytic Tractatus*, 59–84. Ed. B. Stocker. Aldershot: Ashgate, 2004.

Kuusela, Oskari. "From Metaphysics and Philosophical Theses to Grammar: Wittgenstein's Turn." *Philosophical Investigations* 28 (2005): 95–133.

McGinn, Marie. "Between Metaphysics and Nonsense: Elucidation in Wittgenstein's *Tractatus*." *Philosophical Quarterly* 49 (1999): 491–513.

McGuinness, Brian. *Wittgenstein: A Life; Young Ludwig 1889–1921*. Berkeley: University of California Press, 1988.

Monk, Ray. *How to Read Wittgenstein*. New York: W. W. Norton, 2005.

Monk, Ray. *Ludwig Wittgenstein: The Duty of Genius*. New York: The Free Press, 1990.

Moore, A. W. "Ineffability and Nonsense." *Proceedings of the Aristotelian Society*, supp. vol. 77 (2003): 169–193.

Moore, A. W. *Points of View* (1997). Oxford: Oxford University Press, 2002.

Mounce, H. O. "Critical Notice: The New Wittgenstein." *Philosophical Investigations* 24 (2001): 185–192.

Noë, Alva. "Against Intellectualism." *Analysis* 65 (2005): 278–290.

Ostrow, Matthew. *Wittgenstein's "Tractatus": A Dialectical Interpretation*. Cambridge: Cambridge University Press, 2002.

Pears, David. *The False Prison: A Study of the Development of Wittgenstein's Philosophy* (1987). 2 vols. Oxford: Clarendon Press, 1997.

Priest, Graham. *Beyond the Limits of Thought*. 2nd ed. Oxford: Oxford University Press, 2002.

Proops, Ian. "The New Wittgenstein: A Critique." *European Journal of Philosophy* 9 (2001): 375–404.

Rosefeldt, Tobias. "Is Knowing-How Simply a Case of Knowing-That?" *Philosophical Investigations* 27 (2004): 370–379.

Rumfitt, Ian. "Savoir Faire." *Journal of Philosophy* 100 (2003): 158–166.

Russell, Bertrand. "On Denoting." *Mind* 14 (1905): 479–493.

Ryle, Gilbert. *The Concept of Mind* (1949). New York: Barnes and Noble, 1960.

Schiffer, Stephen. "Amazing Knowledge." *Journal of Philosophy* 99 (2002): 200–202.

Seaver, Laurie H. "Fetal Alcohol Syndrome," *Gale Encyclopedia of Medicine*. 2002. Gale Group. Available at http://www.healthatoz.com/healthatoz/Atoz/ency/fetal_alcohol_syndrome.jsp/. (Accessed September 29, 2005.)

Snowdon, Paul. "Knowing How and Knowing That: A Distinction Reconsidered." *Proceedings of the Aristotelian Society* 104 (2003): 1–29.

Stanley, Jason, and Timothy Williamson. "Knowing How." *Journal of Philosophy* 98 (2001): 411–444.

Stern, David G. *Wittgenstein on Mind and Language*. Oxford: Oxford University Press, 1995.

Stokhof, Martin. *World and Life as One: Ethics and Ontology in Wittgenstein's Early Thought*. Stanford: Stanford University Press, 2002.

Sullivan, Peter. "Ineffability and Nonsense." *Proceedings of the Aristotelian Society*, supp. vol. 77 (2003): 195–223.

Sullivan, Peter. "On Trying to Be Resolute: A Response to Kremer on the *Tractatus*." *European Journal of Philosophy* 10 (2002): 43–78.

Sullivan, Peter. "What Is the *Tractatus* About?" In *Wittgenstein's Lasting Significance*, 32–45. Ed. M. Kölbel and B. Weiss. London and New York: Routledge, 2004.

Whitehead, Alfred North, and Bertrand Russell. *Principia Mathematica*. 3 vols. 2nd ed. Cambridge: Cambridge University Press, 1927.

Wittgenstein, Ludwig. *Culture and Value*. Ed. G. H. von Wright. Revised 2nd ed. (1998). Oxford: Blackwell, 2004.

Wittgenstein, Ludwig. *Geheime Tagebücher: 1914–1916*. Ed. W. Baum. Vienna: Turia and Kant, 1992.

Wittgenstein, Ludwig. "Letters to Ludwig Ficker." In *Wittgenstein: Sources and Perspectives*, 82–98. Ed. C. G. Luckhardt. Ithaca, N.Y.: Cornell University Press, 1979.

Wittgenstein, Ludwig. *Ludwig Wittgenstein: Cambridge Letters. Correspondence with Russell, Keynes, Moore, Ramsey, and Sraffa* (1995). Ed. B. McGuinness and G. H. von Wright. Oxford: Blackwell, 1998.

Wittgenstein, Ludwig. *Notebooks: 1914–1916*, 2nd ed. Ed. G.H. von Wright and G. E. M. Anscombe. Trans. G. E. M. Anscombe. Chicago: University of Chicago Press, 1984.

Wittgenstein, Ludwig. *Philosophical Investigations*, 3rd ed. Trans. G. E. M. Anscombe. Oxford: Blackwell, 2001.

Wittgenstein, Ludwig. *Public and Private Occasions*. Ed. J. C. Klagge and A. Nordmann. London: Rowan and Littlefield, 2003.

Wittgenstein, Ludwig. "Some Remarks on Logical Form." In *Philosophical Occasions, 1912–1951*. Ed. James Klagge and Alfred Nordmann. Indianapolis: Hackett, 1993.

Wittgenstein, Ludwig. *The Big Typescript: TS 213*. Ed. and trans. C. G. Luckhardt and M. A. E. Aue. Oxford: Blackwell, 2005.

Wittgenstein, Ludwig. *The Blue and Brown Books* (1960). 2nd ed. New York: Harper and Row, 1965.

Wittgenstein, Ludwig. *Tractatus Logico-Philosophicus*. Trans. C. K. Ogden (1922). Reprinted with corrections 1933. London: Routledge and Kegan Paul, 1985.

Wittgenstein, Ludwig. *Tractatus Logico-Philosophicus*. Trans. D. Pears and B. McGuinness (1961). London: Routledge and Kegan Paul, 1981.

Wittgenstein, Ludwig. *Wittgenstein's Lectures: Cambridge, 1932–1935*. Ed. A. Ambrose. Totowa, N.J.: Rowan and Littlefield, 1979.

Wittgenstein, Ludwig. *Wittgenstein's Lectures: Cambridge, 1930–1932*. Ed. D. Lee. Chicago: University of Chicago Press, 1982.

3   Wittgenstein and the Inexpressible

Juliet Floyd

The greatest clarity [*Deutlichkeit*] was to me always the greatest beauty.
—G. H. Lessing, *Das Testament Johannis*

Lessing once said, "Language can express everything we think clearly."
—M. Heidegger, *Holzwege*[1]

The most fundamental divide among interpreters of Wittgenstein lies, for me, between those who detect in Wittgenstein's writings some form of semantic or epistemic resource argument, an argument ultimately appealing to the finitude or expressive limitations of language—whether it be truth-functional, constructivist, social-constructivist, antirealist, assertion-conditionalist, formalist, conventionalist, finitist, empiricist, or what have you—and those who instead stress Wittgenstein's criticisms of the assumptions lying behind the desire for such resource arguments, criticisms that in the end turn upon stressing the open-ended evolution, the variety, and the irreducible complexity of human powers of expression. The former kind of reader sees the inexpressible as a limitation, a reflection of what is illegitimate in grammar or fails to be epistemically justifiable; the latter sees the inexpressible as a fiction, an illusion produced by an overly simplified conception of human expression.[2]

While there are several important readers of Wittgenstein who have insisted on the fundamental character of this divide in relation to Wittgenstein's later thinking (I am thinking here especially of my teachers Stanley Cavell, Burton Dreben, and Warren Goldfarb), it is to Cora Diamond that we owe the most wide-ranging and pointed articulation of what is at stake in this contrast of interpretive approaches for Wittgenstein's thought as a whole. Her work has forcefully and very originally pressed the latter approach forward, deepening and broadening it to include topics of central concern to contemporary philosophy—among them the nature of truth, fiction, realism, ethics, logic, mathematics, language, and experience.

An especially important feature of Diamond's work is her insistence that Wittgenstein's thought does not divide itself up neatly into isolated topics on the philosophy of x or y or z. The unity to be found in his thinking (both evolutionarily, within Wittgenstein's own historical development, and thematically, within his writings as a whole) is on this view not doctrinal or a function of subject matter or domain of concern, but instead a distinctive way of thinking about philosophical topics and problems, and, in particular, about the limits of empiricism (traditional and Viennese logical) as a reductive theory of knowledge, meaning, and human experience. This is for me the most fundamental insight to be found in Diamond's writings about Wittgenstein, one that has risked becoming obscured by recent debates, however influential and interesting they have been, about how to understand the topics of nonsense, irony, realism, and the *Tractatus*'s framing remarks.

I want in this essay to make a few suggestions about how we might come to see Diamond's idea of a "resolute" reading of the *Tractatus* (as Ricketts dubbed it[3]) in the light of wider themes in her writings, themes that were first broached in writings not explicitly devoted to reading the *Tractatus*. I believe Diamond's total corpus of work on Wittgenstein, and not merely her works explicitly advocating "resolution," are what allow us to see that this theme of the complexity and open-ended variety of expression is already present, in significant ways, in the *Tractatus*. Thanks to her corpus one can come to see the *Tractatus* as already containing within itself recognizable seeds of Wittgenstein's later philosophy, even if they occur in nascent form.

First, however, I give a brief account of how I personally have been most centrally influenced by Diamond, in order to make my own orientation on her writings clearer.

From Stanley Cavell I learned that Wittgenstein's modes of writing are internal to his thought rather than mere literary embellishments, and that these features of his thought, with their particular idiosyncratic manifestations, require us to read him as a thinker opposed to tendencies within analytic philosophy that aim to divide content from style, expression's content from its form. From Burton Dreben and Warren Goldfarb, I learned that one cannot have any genuine appreciation of analytic philosophy in general, and Wittgenstein's philosophy in particular, without understanding how their roots lie, to a significant extent, in the development of logic as a branch of mathematics, inaugurated in the 1870s (when Frege developed the *Begriffsschrift* and Cantor's work began to have its effects) and firmly in place by 1936 or so (when Gödel's, Tarski's and Turing's work began to be appreciated and exploited by philosophers).

What Diamond's work did for me was to show, not merely the possibility of usefully combining these approaches with one another, but how much each of them is, in fact, very much in need of the other.

Broadly put, there is the Cavellian tradition, importantly furthered by Diamond, that makes ethics, self-understanding, and the complexity of human expressiveness central concerns for Wittgenstein in all his writings.[4] But there is simultaneously the mathematically oriented tradition that insists on understanding the detailed interplay between mathematics and philosophy in the early decades of the twentieth century as crucial for our view, not only of Wittgenstein, but of the history of the very notions of analysis, content, and expressibility. For over a decade my own work on Wittgenstein has been focused on bringing the former, figurative tradition to bear on Wittgenstein's remarks on mathematics and ethics while simultaneously taking advantage, in interpreting him, of an increasingly precise and sophisticated literature relating to the history of mathematical logic and the philosophy of math-ematics.[5] Each of these two traditions, as I understand them, are driven by a concern to explore the temptation toward, and then overcoming of, a quest for "some general conception of meaning," to use a phrase from Diamond's most recent work (Diamond 2004, 217).[6] My work would not have been possible without Diamond's writings, which insist that Wittgenstein's remarks on mathematics are best taken to form an indispensable element of his philosophy as a whole, rather than an articulation of one position within the philosophy of mathematics, and which also insist on seeing Wittgenstein's philosophy as part of a wider tradition in early analytic philosophy.[7] Conversely, however, the power of Diamond's work on Wittgenstein is not comprehensible, at least to me, without a firm understanding of how central her writing on Wittgenstein's remarks on mathematics and logic have been to her philosophical thinking, including her writing about the *Tractatus*.

In the first section, I touch on the question of whether there is a unified conception of "showing" at work in the *Tractatus*. In the second, I consider the idea of exploring the *Fragestellungen* of philosophical questions, inspired by the text of the *Tractatus* and by Diamond's 1975–1976 essay "Riddles and Anselm's Riddle" (Diamond 1991a, Chap. 10). In the third, fourth, and fifth sections, I turn to the conception of the *Tractatus* as a work expressing a commitment to a metaphysics of "logical atomism," a conception that seems to me to stand in need of further investigation and that may be conceived differently if we place it against the backdrop of the idea of "completeness" as it exercised logicians in the generation that followed Wittgenstein. In closing I make a few suggestions about how to look at Wittgenstein's own view of his philosophical evolution (pre- and post-*Tractatus*).

1 Showing versus Saying

In the context of attempting to work out what Diamond's idea of a "resolute" reading of the *Tractatus* entails, Peter Sullivan and Warren Goldfarb have recently raised the interesting question whether there is one or at least one primary distinction involved in the contrasts Wittgenstein nominally draws in the *Tractatus* between "saying" and "showing." Goldfarb has gone some distance in arguing that the answer is No.[8]

Traditional commentary on the *Tractatus* has often assumed that this is so. And in inaugurating the idea of a "resolute" reading of the *Tractatus* by offering criticisms of readings that take "what is shown" in the *Tractatus* to point toward an ineffable truth or content or special inexpressible domain of metaphysics, Diamond herself, at least initially, left this question open. This is understandable because she was attempting a large-scale revision of attitudes toward the *Tractatus* contrast(s) between showing and saying as they had been interpreted in the past. In her wake, Thomas Ricketts, James Conant, and Michael Kremer went on to suggest that the idea of a show/say distinction must itself be seen to be nonsensical for a resolute reader; as Peter Sullivan put it, there was a "spreading" of that to which Diamond's idea of resolution was held to apply. Sullivan, for one, found it difficult to see why or how that spreading could have been necessitated by the idea of a resolute reading alone.[9]

For those interpreters who have taken the *Tractatus* to commit itself to an ineffable domain of necessities, contents, or things—that is, a number of claims that, though they cannot be said, may be shown or articulated in nonfactual or nonsayable discourse—such a view of a unitary or primary distinction has seemed, by contrast, to form part and parcel of a proper articulation of the book's aims and scope. A natural picture suggested by the assumption of a unified distinction between showing and saying is that of a line marking out a division between the sayable and the not-sayable.[10] Yet even if one accepted Diamond's view (articulated in concert with James Conant, as time went on) that traditional commentators failed to establish that the relevant remarks in the *Tractatus* give us (in Goldfarb's good phrase [2005]) "a ticket to the inexpressible" conceived as a domain of necessities, quasi-facts, or unsayable insights, one might still ask a question about the status of Wittgenstein's repeated contrasts between showing and saying and what our proper attitude toward them should be.

As I have conceived them since the mid-1990s, Wittgenstein's uses of the terms "formal," "nonsense," and "show" are like punctuation marks: they are question markers, not categorizations, flagging *particular* points at which misunderstandings of the logic of our language (our *Sprachlogik*) emerge, and they neither invoke nor presuppose a *general* frame of meaning, much less a doctrine about which concepts *must* have formal uses and which may not.[11] I find this obviously the most charitable reading of the book, if one could secure it: as Quine (1981, 87) said of Austin, praising him for operating with no general theory of meaning, but only investigating particular cases of usage, "there is a certain immunity in the concrete case." When possible, I prefer *not* to saddle a philosopher with a view for which I see no need. Moreover, for me there was always an important difference to be borne in mind between Carnap's notion of the *formal* or the *analytic* and Wittgenstein's in the *Tractatus*. For Carnap the enterprise of labeling a truth "analytic" was itself empty of content, but not nonsensical—as, I assumed (following Diamond), the labeling of a usage as "analytic" or "purely logical" or as one involving a formal concept might well, by the *Tractatus*'s lights, end up being. If the *Tractatus*'s labelings with these notions were not taken to be nonsensical, but only remarks calling our attention to contrasting uses of words in sentences, they would not be conceived of in Carnap's way, it seemed to me, if only because I did not see in the *Tractatus* anything like a Carnapian interest in the engineering of formalized languages to unearth meaning- or logical-consequence relations (cf. Floyd 1997). (For more on the idea of the *Tractatus* on logical syntax and on Wittgenstein's way of excluding a theory of meaning-relations from logic, see sections 3–4 below.)

For these reasons—and *not* because I thought there was any argument that could flow from the very idea of an "austere" conception of nonsense to such an understanding & Wittgenstein's distinctions as a conclusion—I have always been uncomfortable beginning with locutions such as *the* show/say distinction, or of *the* notion of the *formal*, or *the* logic of language, or nonsense as a general term of criticism or category. The "spreading" of resolution (to use Sullivan's phrase) worried me. Global talk about Wittgenstein's use of the term "nonsense," or the show/say distinction—talk I am afraid has been, unfortunately, encouraged by Diamond's joint work with Conant—positively encourages a tendency to talk about content-in-general globally or in terms of a method of analysis. This goes against certain tendencies that seem to me, not only documentable within the *Tractatus*, but crucial to its aims. It thus became important to me, beginning in the early 1990s, to try to articulate a refinement of the "resolute" reading that appeals to better angels I saw at work in Diamond's writings on Wittgenstein. Some of my suggestions for refinement have earned me the name of a "radical" or "Jacobin" or "strongly" resolute reader,[12] but accounts of my views in the literature—including accounts in work of P. M. S. Hacker (2001), I. Proops (2001), and recent joint work of Conant and Diamond (2004)—have misconstrued them. Part of what I shall be doing in what follows, therefore, is to clarify my own views.

When looking at the text of the *Tractatus* (as opposed to meditating on the concept of nonsense), it has never been clear to me, prima facie, that all of Wittgenstein's remarks concerning showing or nonsense fit together in one way, or, perhaps, even at all. It has never been clear that each individual remark involving a contrast between showing and saying has a univocal purpose or unique path of application. Nor have I ever been inclined to think that Wittgenstein's uses of the contrast between showing and saying are best conceived as primarily concerned with straddling and/or exploring the limits of the expressible. On the contrary, it seemed plausible to suppose that Wittgenstein was sometimes working with a contrast drawn *within* the domain of expression, and thereby resisting talk about content-as-such, generality-as-such, sentences-as-such. So much I surmised by thinking through Wittgenstein's criticisms of Russell's multiple-relation analysis of judgment (aided especially by Diamond 2002, Pears 1979, and Ricketts 1996), by pondering his resistance to Frege's essay "Der Gedanke" (Floyd 1998; Frege forthcoming), and by scrutinizing Wittgenstein's treatment of number words as they figure in arithmetic and in mixed statements (Floyd 2001a). Each of these represents an overcoming, on Wittgenstein's part, of the picture of thought as a relation between a judger's mind and a fact or proposition. Of course Russell too had resisted Frege's conception of the *Sinn* of a declarative sentence as a thought (*Gedanke*) even before he met Wittgenstein: the aim of his multiple relation theory of judgment was to avoid earlier theories according to which judgment is understood to involve a relation between a mind and a proposition. So Wittgenstein's resistance to a picture of thought as relational was, from one point of view, only a sophisticated extension of his teacher's.[13] As I shall be suggesting below, however, Wittgenstein's extension may be taken to radicalize an already skeptical point of view in ways that outstrip Russell's conception of analysis in important respects. The complexity needed to analyze forms of judgment just blows up in the *Tractatus*. (*Tractatus* 5.54–5.542, offering "'p' says p" as a form of "A judges that p," admits as much.)[14]

Most readers, resolute and nonresolute, can make out that in the *Tractatus* showing has to do with that which does not admit of the question, "is it true or is it false?" something that is connected somehow with logical form, with specific features of our modes of expression of thought in language. But this leaves an awful lot of different examples swimming in the same stream.

Textually speaking, there is on the surface a quite daunting variety of cases of showing, both within the *Tractatus* and in Wittgenstein's post-*Tractatus* writings. In the *Tractatus* itself, we have remarks about a proposition showing its sense, showing how things stand if it is true (4.022), we have an analysis of statements of propositional attitudes that shows that there is no soul or subject (5.5421), we have a sign for an elementary proposition showing that in its sense an object appears (4.1211), the remark that a proposition shows a logical form of reality (4.121), a remark that the falling under a formal concept by an object shows itself in the symbol for the object itself, so that the name shows that it signifies an object, the numerical sign that it signifies a number, and so on (4.126), the remark that generality is shown through the fact that one can infer by universal instantiation (5.1311), the idea that Frege's and Russell's employment of the logically meaningless assertion sign shows only that what they mark in this way they take to be true (4.442), the remark that tautologies show the formal—logical—properties of language, of the world (6.12), the famous self-reflexive, at first blush destabilizing "what *can* be shown *cannot* be said" (4.1212) (destabilizing, that is, if one insists that this remark *says* something about that-which-cannot-be-said and construes the latter as a something that we can gesture at in a quasi-propositional way), a remark in which operations are said to "show themselves" (5.24), another in which tautologies themselves "show" that they are tautologies (6.126, 6.127) and, last but not least, Wittgenstein's remarks about the inexpressible, which is said to "show itself" in connection with the solution to the riddle of the meaning of life (6.522). There are also, within the *Tractatus* itself, both explicit uses of the verb "to show" and also cases where Wittgenstein uses the slightly different locutions of "recognizing [*erkennen*] the symbol in the sign" (6.113, 6.1203), or just "seeing" or "being seen" (as in mathematical equations; see 6.232).[15] The connections among, and potential applications of, the various cases are not obvious, and are not to be promised at the outset by a general theory of meaning or of nonsense, or by a general theory of how to read the *Tractatus*. They are to be earned, as both Goldfarb (1997, 70–71) and I (Floyd 1997) put it to Diamond, case by case.[16]

This point about showing and saying (or "formality") not involving a single, over-arching doctrine of meaning does not imply there is no interest in looking for some unity, some lines or paths of thought that help us see connections among apparently disparate remarks in the text.[17] In particular, by offering a bold and novel way of seeing how Frege's context principle might be brought to bear on the kinds of reflections on realism she discerns in the *Tractatus*, Diamond has helped us to see how many cases in the *Tractatus* may be seen to express an effort to think through and past the tendency to reify or missummarize or oversimplify our means of expression in particular cases—just the kind of error Frege suggested we fall into when we ask for the meaning of a word outside the context of the propositions in which it figures.[18]

But this point about the importance of Frege's context principle to Wittgenstein, though nearly impossible to overstate, cannot secure a reading of every remark of the *Tractatus* on its own, even when coupled with Diamond's use of the context principle to support resolution. For one thing, it cannot help us directly with reading passages in the 6s that concern *Scheinsätze*.[19] For another, Wittgenstein's distinctive effort to resist miscasting of our modes of expression is more far-reaching than Frege's, applying both to Frege's and to Russell's ways of analyzing many parts of discourse.

I admit that in the face of the *Tractatus*'s daunting variety of showings, it is only natural, and is in fact desirable, to try to gain an overarching point of view. Goldfarb has, in particular, developed the beginnings of a sorting of passages on showing into at least three kinds that seems to me illuminating (see note 8). Other attempts to unify showing under a single banner are less persuasive. Thus it is sometimes held that there is a doctrine about showing in the *Tractatus* that derives from Wittgenstein's picture theory of the proposition. Although this may do as a first pass, to orient us with respect to the text, we need to refine our understanding of it. Showing is not always linked to the notion of picture or model: indeed, it was introduced in the pre-*Tractatus* "Notes on Logic" before Wittgenstein hit on the analogy between propositions and models of reality. There it is linked, as in the *Tractatus*, with the notion of expressive structures that "show themselves" (such as tautologies) in contrast to propositions that exhibit bipolarity, are true or are false. But it strikes me as important that the notion of picture or model, when it did enter his thought in the *Notebooks*, is not a fixed point for an analogy between sentences and pictures. To briefly illustrate this theme with but one example, we may consider the *Tractatus*'s transformation of the notion of generality as Frege and Russell analyzed it with the quantifier.

In the *Tractatus* the use of concepts as so-called formal or pseudoconcepts are not genuine or "material" uses of concepts, but, at best, only apparently material: these uses do not classify or sort, despite their surface appearance. Their proper expression is tied, not to concept words, but to *Satzvariablen*. But Wittgenstein's notion of *Satzvariable* is not our (i.e., Frege's) notion of a "variable," that is, he does not conceive a variable as a letter of *Begriffsschrift* that ranges over objects. Instead, a *Tractarian Satzvariable* displays a fixed collection of genuine propositions whose meaningfulness it presupposes. Its values *are* the propositions (3.316, 3.317, 5.501). Thus no *Satzvariable* can be used to state something about a general notion—say, the notion of *being a proposition* or *being a concept* or *being an object* or *being a number* (cf. 5.5351).[20] There simply is no gap between such purportedly general notions and what they may be seen to classify, no room for what we tend to think of as instantiation according to a general rule.

This is because Wittgenstein rejects, along with Frege's notion of a variable, Frege's and Russell's quantificational analysis of generality. First, he resists the idea that there is one notion of generality to be analyzed by bifurcating "material" from "formal" generality and then divvying up the latter into various kinds ("formal" sometimes is related to the recursive presentation of a formal series, sometimes not). Then he denies that in any of its forms generality belongs to the content of what is said.[21] Differently put, the logical content and force of generality is for Wittgenstein something shown in our language through our ways of expressing instances, but is not a separable element of what is said; and its ways of being evinced are various. The logical or formal character of generality comes in, ready-made, with our manner of expressing and/or operating with particular instances. But this is very far from Frege's and Russell's quantificational conception of generality as a functional part of a sentence contributing a distinctive element to its sense. Wittgenstein is conceiving generality to be expressed in something like the way a genre painting expresses an archetypical feature or scene. Such a picture is applicable to an aspect of each concrete situation exemplifying the relevant features. That is what its being a genre painting is, and that is what makes any exemplar an exemplar of *it*. Its own way of representing is, of course, not reducible to the depiction of any *one* such example, but each such example exemplifies the characteristic on its own, without an intermediary principle. This is reflected in the fact that the very *same* picture could be used to depict a *particular* scene and also a genre scene; there is nothing in its internal structure that *says* how it should be interpreted. This comes out in our applications of it.

Such is but one example, briefly sketched, of how complicated Wittgenstein's transposition of the notions of picture and generality becomes within the *Tractatus*. (Similar complexity may be seen in the way he attempts to revitalize and transpose the notion of logical necessity, necessity having been traded away by both Frege and Russell in favor of universality.)[22] And if we pursue the fate of Wittgenstein's various analogies turning on the notion of picture after the *Tractatus*, we see that far from surrendering these metaphors he explores, extends, and elaborates them. He applies the notion of *Bild* constructively, to all sorts of cases: the generality of recursive proofs, proofs by diagram, number words, ordinary pictorial representations, illusory models of grammar, world-pictures, and so on. Further transposition of the notion goes on through his last writings (e.g., the notion of a world-picture in *On Certainty*).

Taken together these transpositions seem to me to give the lie to the notion that Wittgenstein's evolution can be fully understood by holding that there was a picture theory of language in the *Tractatus* that carried with it a commitment to a single show/say distinction, and that this commitment to an overarching show/say distinction fell when Wittgenstein surrendered his ways of thinking about logic in the late 1920s.[23]

Wittgenstein is a thinker who explores and fashions new analogies and models of his own: he rips phrases and ideas out of one context (sometimes from his own earlier writings, sometimes from the writings of others) and throws them into another, often shifting metaphors over time into a number of different directions. This densely rich allusiveness, this transformation and self-transformation of language, this ramification and retransformation of words, formulations, problems, metaphors, and questions is an important feature of his writing throughout his life, constituting a kind of unity of approach that is not merely literary, but part and parcel of his ambition to transpose, revitalize, and recast our relation to philosophical questions. As Wittgenstein said to Waismann in a conversation about philosophical method in the early 1930s, "to make the unclarities and vagueness of our words perspicuous, one might exhaust oneself in devising pictures and similes" (Baker 2003, 277).[24] I shall return to this theme of transformations of problem formulations in a moment because it is this theme that lies at the heart of what I find deepest in Diamond's writing about Wittgenstein. But in making a transition to this idea, I would like to make one final remark about the attitude I have toward *Tractatus*'s ways of contrasting showing with saying.

It seems to me important to allow for a certain looseness in the ways we invoke the contrast between showing and saying in explicating Wittgenstein's writing, and especially in the case of the *Tractatus*, where the literary form of its remarks is more or less obviously self-allusive and poetic. Consider the word structure of his terminology as it is laid out in the opening lines of the book. At the risk of sounding too Heideggerian, Burton Dreben used to emphasize that the structure of the opening lines (untranslatable into English) sought, among other things, with a kind of word-play, or movable word-structure on the page, to display the internal relatedness—if you like, the non-genuineness or formal uses—of the notions in play in phrases like *Sache*, *Tatsache*, *Sachverhalt*, *Sachlage*, *sich verhalten*, *Fall*, *zerfallen*, *Zufall*, and so on. By this he took Wittgenstein to be suggesting that the apparently substantive metaphysics formulated in the opening lines allows itself, in its very formulation, to be seen as a kind of verbal rearrangement or restructuring of words. Whether or not this is the right way to state the intent behind the construction of these opening lines, on Dreben's account the important point is that the lines may themselves be taken to show the reader the need to reflect on the character of the concepts themselves, rather than, as it appears at first blush, to apply them in statements true or false.[25]

This, if there is anything to it, would count for me as one kind of exemplification of a Tractarian contrast between showing and saying, even though the word "show" does not occur there in the text. In this sort of case, "show" would not, perhaps, best be understood as "proves that," or "gives us reason to believe"—each of these are part of the idea of showing *that* something is the case—but, rather, as showing us *how* to do something, perhaps by example, in virtue of what the author's words *do*.

Among other things, these words apply to, as they conjure up and transpose, the language of previous philosophers. Wittgenstein's accepting the translation into English of Russell's language of "atomic facts" makes it clear that he wanted to connect his remarks with Russell's philosophy, in particular. But the idea that he simply agreed with Russell about the existence of such facts, or had a direct concern with discovering a basic ontology, has struck many readers (H. Ishiguro, R. Rhees, B. McGuinness, Goldfarb, Ricketts, and Diamond among them) as not the only possible, or even the best reading of this allusion. It has been felt that Wittgenstein is trying to put these terms themselves into question.

Now for many such readers, what is happening is best viewed as a kind of pretence talk. McGuinness ([1981] 2002, 85) called the opening remarks of the *Tractatus* "a kind of ontological myth," one of whose chief results would be "the rejection of all such myths," when its status as "a transferred and illegitimate use of words (like *bestehen*)" is shown. Wittgenstein is, on this view, setting us up for an unmasking of the emptiness of such ontological talk; he will encourage us to think through the talk to the point where it "falls apart" on us (Goldfarb 2000), where his rhetoric "cancels itself out" (Ricketts 1996b), where we "throw it away" or "transition" beyond what is a "masquerade" (Diamond 1991a,b). Perhaps, it has been suggested, the whole book might be viewed as a grand reductio, or an effort to "liberate" us via a certain kind of "therapy," or a form of "deconstruction".

Though each of these summary terms have been pursued by interpreters—and, let it be said, interpreters from whom I have learned a great deal—I myself have never felt comfortable employing them. For the record, let me stress that I have never jumped to the closing lines of the book to understand its opening.[26] Nor have I ever thought of the progress of the *Tractatus* as having the familiar form of a reductio.[27] And although I do think the ideas of therapy and liberation have their perfectly legitimate uses, I have always resisted relying on them as clarifying notions with respect to Wittgenstein's philosophical methods.[28]

My approach, indebted above all to Diamond's writing on riddle-talk (see her 1991a, chap. 10, 2000b, 2004), has attempted to distill something more constructive from Wittgenstein's words. Without sounding Polyannish, I think the *Tractatus* offers a great (if evidently flawed) defense of philosophical activity itself—understood, of course, as a distinctive sort of activity. I prefer the idea of "overcoming" to that of "transcending" for the *Überwinden* recommended at the close of the book, but that is because I do not see that overcoming connotes the idea that we are to be left in just one kind of space or place when we achieve it, and I see it as a positive construction or creation, not merely a negative turning away or letting go.[29] To repeat: I prefer not to look at Wittgenstein's idea of philosophical clarification in terms of any one overarching aim or end or goal, but instead, in terms of a mode of thinking that is, if not "transitional" somewhere, then is at least reflective and transformative in a distinctive way.[30] Following out Diamond's idea of philosophical clarification as analogous, in certain respects, to the solving of riddles, I incline toward seeing some of the opening of the book posing and/or confronting what may helpfully be thought of as opening questions, some of which are riddles like the riddles of myth, some of which may be conceived of as conceptual problems that Wittgenstein was hoping to solve, or resolve, in the course of the book.[31] On this view, the opening passages aim at refining the reader's understanding of what its own talk might come to by inaugurating reflection on the *Fragestellungen* within which discussions of logic, the world, objects, facts, and philosophy might proceed. The next three sections elaborate this suggestion.

2 Fragestellungen

The German word *Fragestellung* (setting of a question, question-context, question formulation) occurs in the very first place where Wittgenstein uses the word "show" in the *Tractatus*, in the preface:

The book deals with philosophical problems and shows [*zeigt*], as I believe, that the formulation of these questions [*Fragestellung*] rests on misunderstanding the logic of our language [*Logik unserer Sprache*]. Its whole meaning could be summed up somewhat as follows: What can be said at all can be said clearly; and whereof one cannot speak thereof one must be silent.

The notion of a "misunderstanding of the logic of our language" was not drawn by Wittgenstein from Frege or Russell, but from an afterward to an edition of *Grimm's Fairy Tales* by the Austrian poet Paul Ernst.[32] Wittgenstein (1993, 3: 266, item 110, p. 184) later wrote that he was sorry he had not acknowledged this in the *Tractatus*; we may conjecture that that is because he felt that the Nietzschean literary tradition lying behind his idea had been underplayed by those (such as the members of the Vienna Circle) who appropriated the book without taking this tradition seriously. Brian McGuinness (1988, 251–252) has suggested that Wittgenstein drew from Ernst the idea of "graphic modes of expression and metaphors" being mistakenly taken "literally." I do not disagree, but I would add that a closer look at Ernst's *Nachwort* suggests a view of the evolution of language more complicated than one that can be understood through the distinction between literal and nonliteral (poetic or metaphorical) language, the critique of myth by reality, or reality by myth, alone. (For a translated excerpt from this *Nachwort*, see the appendix to this essay.)

Ernst's idea seems to have been that there are specific forms of language belonging to different eras, hence a variety of *Fragestellungen*, and therefore a variety of different misunderstandings of *Sprachlogik* (cf. *Tractatus* 4.002). In particular, he stresses the tendency of later eras of thought to try to solve the "insoluble" problems of earlier eras by means of descriptive "inventions," inventions that inevitably encounter problems "insoluble through the experience of reality"—riddles about God, the soul, the world, and so on. In the end, Ernst imagines a point at which the aim of solving such problems by the fashioning of new modes of description or accurate depiction will end, leaving one to drop the whole process of descriptive correction of myth as "insignificant or foolish." Intellectual, poetic, and spiritual progress, on this view, require us to get past the need to critique our means of expression when they do not stand up to a comparison with reality and to appreciate how modern science itself (Ernst mentions Darwin's theory of evolution) may play a mythological role as well (compare and contrast *Tractatus* 4.1122 on Darwin). Hence the importance of fairy tales, which, Ernst agrees with the brothers Grimm, contain within them our "ethics" and perhaps what is ethical for all humankind (cf. Diamond 1991b on Wittgenstein and fairy tales). Hence too the character of modern poetry, according to Ernst: this is poetry in which the search for new materials or subject matter (a more detailed comparison with reality) has exhausted or transformed itself.

If we trace the history of Wittgenstein's ideas about *Fragestellungen* and the evolution of language, I think we see a similar picture of language in play in the *Tractatus*, at the very least in regard to a fascination with the idea of shifting the *Fragestellungen* of questions. I am suggesting here that at least some of the showing at work in the *Tractatus*, some of its images of philosophical clarification, may be understood by reflecting on how it serves this end of transforming philosophical questions. If this idea has any merit, it suggests that the *Tractatus* contains within it the seeds of Wittgenstein's later idea of a philosophical investigation, the form of which, as we read in the *Philosophical Investigations*, is in the first person: "I don't know my way about" (*ich kenne mich nicht aus*: "I'm stumped," "I'm at a loss," "I don't know what's what") (*Investigations* §123).

An "investigation" in the relevant sense always involves a kind of search that is not purely empirical, but partly conceptual, a problem whose very formulation contains terms that require interrogation, or reconception, in order to be solved. Over and over again, throughout his life, Wittgenstein drew a sharp contrast between searching when you haven't any idea in advance what will serve you as a satisfactory answer and searching when you do have some such idea; searching when you have a framework within which to ask and to answer questions and searching when you do not. What goes on in a philosophical investigation is always searching without a method of inquiry, outside a system, as he would say in the middle period. In such an investigation, we face a problem of expression, not of discovery, a need for clarification of a question, not unearthing of an ontology. We work, in part, on ourselves (in the first person) because we work on coming to an understanding of our own words.

Wittgenstein always contrasts this sort of unsystematic searching with empirical inquiries, the sort of inquiry that might be settled by observation or comparison with reality. He also always contrasts it with searching in contexts where rules may be followed in an automatic, mechanical, unreflective way, as in calculations. Philosophy is not the only activity that relies on this sort of nonsystematic searching, such conceptual or symbolical or expressive investigations: Wittgenstein gives many such examples, many of them from the history of mathematics, often likening them to the search for a new means of expression, a new symbolism, or new concept. He gives the example of a word puzzle or riddle, recounting the story in which the king told the princess to come to him neither naked nor dressed: she answered him by arriving wearing fishnet. Wittgenstein constructs his own examples of mathematical problems whose solutions demand that we develop a whole new conception of what a solution must be (the trisection of the angle, classical impossibility proofs in geometry, the semantical paradoxes). He likens these in turn to cases where one understands the verbal form of what one is supposed to do, but has no idea what it would be to do it: being ordered to try to wiggle one's ears without hands or to will an object to fly across the room when one doesn't have any idea what it would be like to do it. (This latter is a favorite of mine because I *can* wiggle my ears without hands.)[33] In his later remarks on psychology, he brings in under this rubric certain first-person investigations. To ask what my own thoughts or beliefs are involves, not an empirical inquiry, but some kind of movement in language or self-expression, perhaps the invention of a new symbolism, a symbolism that might at least in certain cases come (in words of Whitehead that were known to Wittgenstein) "to do the thinking for us." (The solution may lie then in what thinking can make visible to the eye or the ear through the hand, allowing us not to *have* to think when we use it.)[34]

Commenting on Wittgenstein's early views on ethics and religion, G. E. M. Anscombe (1971, 171) writes:

The most important remark he makes [in the *Tractatus* about ethics] is: "The facts all belong to the task set, and not to the solution" (6.4321). "*Aufgabe*," which I translate "task set," is the German for a child's school exercise, or piece of homework. Life is like a boy doing sums. (At the end of his life he used the analogy still.)

As I read it, this analogy is not meant to make ethics look like an intrinsically inso-luble, hopeless task, much less like an algorithm or a machine.[35] Instead, life itself is a task like a child learning to do elementary mathematics: as soon as you solve one life problem, you are faced with another that you haven't any idea how to solve. In such cases, you need to rearrange your own conception of what a solution would be. You adapt your means of expression to particular applications and come to measure the facts in a new way. There is no guarantee or necessity or theory that can make clear in advance what success will look like to you since success comes through a reconception of the *Fragestellung* itself. It may not be clear, before you do so, whether or not you have failed to give a *Bedeutung* to a given expression, and so spoken non-sense. In such cases a context remains to be constructed, has not yet been seen. The job of philosophical clarification consists in investigating the contexts in which an expression might appear to be apt.

I shall call this sort of problem or question a conceptual problem, so long as we remember that what is at stake in the answer is not the application of a previously given framework of concepts to a new case, but the forming and structuring of con-cepts, a new way of thinking about a question for a new occasion, a distinctive process of clarification. Such conceptual inquiries have the peculiar feature that once an answer has been found, one can't wonder about whether or not the question is really settled. For part of what it is to give an answer is to settle on a proper understanding of what the original question was. To doubt the answer would then be to doubt one's understanding of the question. Where there was a riddle, there remains none—not because of a general theory of the meaningfulness or meaninglessness of riddles. Instead, a question one had no idea how to solve is no longer asked. In the words of Ernst and the *Tractatus*, it vanishes as a problem. The dynamic of this is not directed first and foremost at a fixed Yes or No—a sense, in the *Tractatus*'s understanding of this—even if the result is in the end something to which we do incline with a Yes or a No.

Under the influence of Diamond's powerful essay "Riddles and Anselm's Riddle," I have often emphasized this idea of transformation as reformulation in connection with philosophical questions in Wittgenstein's writing: the transition, if one wants to use that phrase, is from not really understanding what one wants to say to under-standing how to say it better (see Floyd 1995, 2000 and Diamond's borrowing back from this idea in her 2002). This idea of philosophical clarification as expressive trans-position Diamond has called, in her most recent writing on Wittgenstein, the "trans-formation" or "reconception" of a problem or question, and she has become more and more explicit, as time has gone on, that she takes this idea to be one that we can see at work, however imperfectly, in the *Tractatus* (this is a major theme of Diamond

2004; cf. especially p. 215 and also Diamond 2005). She has also come to emphasize, as I had long ago urged that she should, that resolution in reading the *Tractatus* does *not* require one to subscribe to a "general" or "wholesale," but only a "piecemeal" or "retail" kind of investigation of purported sentences and their senses.[36] The two ideas: the transformation of questions and the rejection of a general theory of meaning, go hand in hand. So the "resolute" reading has matured into something much more subtle than its original formulation in the context of resisting certain forms of realism and metaphysics as proper interpretations of the *Tractatus*.

3 Logical Syntax and "Logical Atomism" in the Tractatus: Some Questions for Resolute Readers

I once wrote (Floyd 1998, 85) that it is "a great myth of twentieth century philosophy that Wittgenstein was a logical atomist." I intended "great myth" in something akin to an Ernstean sense. What I had in mind is that readers of the *Tractatus* would do well to take with a large grain of salt Russell's vision of logical atomism in the *Tractatus* as a research program to which he and Wittgenstein had contributed as part of a common scientific enterprise. This "great myth" struck me as a profoundly influential idea of Russell's for which he deserves philosophical credit rather than a primary constraint on how to read the *Tractatus* and Wittgenstein's evolution beyond it. I simply do not believe that at the time of writing the *Tractatus* Wittgenstein conceived himself as signing on as an underlaborer to an intellectual program that would discover, like chemistry, an analysis of ultimate substance or simples in anything like the way that Russell conceived of it.[37] That he later felt he had conceded too much to the structure of Russell's epistemologically saturated idea is undeniable. But the concession, whatever else we want to say about it, was complicated. At the very least its ultimate motivations, applications, and structure within the *Tractatus* remain worthy of further conceptual scrutiny, especially in relation to sections of the *Tractatus* that have remained less scrutinized in detail than they should be. In particular, I believe that we should not assume that because the later Wittgenstein came to reject the *Tractatus*'s notion of a "final" or "complete" analysis as dogmatic and mistaken, we already have to hand a full or even primary account of his philosophical evolution away from the *Tractatus*, much less a sufficient guide to interpretation of the *Tractatus* itself. Something more Ernstean, something more akin to a philosophical transformation of the idea of analysis itself, is going on within the *Tractatus*.

   This is not to deny important connections between Wittgenstein and Russell, but to insist that interpreters of the *Tractatus* think through the nature of these relations in light of their complexity. Of course Russell assented, at one time or another, to many remarks made in the *Tractatus*, remarks we would not be wrong to see Russell as having in some way begotten through his impact on Wittgenstein. Among them are the claim that the theory of classes is superfluous in mathematics; that the transition from one term to another in the series of natural numbers doesn't require intuition, but in some way comes built-in with the logical structure of our language; that surface grammatical form must be separated from analyzed form, as in the theory of descriptions; that it is a mistake to take judgment to consist in a relation between a mind and a proposition. But, while important to emphasize, this nominal agreement is misleading if left to stand on its own, as a marker of full-throated "doctrinal" agreement. The trouble lies with interpretations that list various commitments associated with the "ism" without sufficiently investigating the conceptual problem contexts within which Wittgenstein's philosophy was formulated. Better, as an approach, is to see how Wittgenstein is transforming that which Russell really should have wanted to say, using an "inchoate" understanding of, for example, *truth* (cf. Diamond 2002 on "inchoate" understandings).

I suggest, more generally, that we should beware of insisting that the best way to do history of philosophy is to look for labels that join these philosophers together in a tradition by way of commonly held doctrine or method. Instead, we should look toward how the *Tractatus* is transforming the *Fragestellungen*, the problem-contexts and concepts that it inherits from Frege, Russell, and others. This implies that we may sometimes need to look outside the *Tractatus*, to its wider intellectual context, in order to gauge its language's purposes, effects, debts, successes, and failures. It also implies that we need to be willing at times to question the idea that the most interesting way to account for Wittgenstein's philosophical evolution, and the evolution of early analytic philosophy as a whole, is in terms of the mistaken-thesis, correction-of-the-mistaken-thesis model. The situation is more complex. The evolution might be better conceived as an evolving expressive tradition within philosophy, a way in which the formulation of various kinds of conceptual questions and problems is constructed rather than foreseen, in which certain questions and problems come to be solved in their very formulation and certain others are, in Ernst's vivid phrase, simply allowed to fall away as silly or insignificant.

My worries about pinning the phrase "logical atomism" on the *Tractatus* were several. First, an insistence that logical atomism is the primary, overriding story about the *Tractatus* had led to the neglect, historically, of study of parts of the book that fail to fit easily into the mould of Russell's program. (The *Tractatus's* passages on ethics and on arithmetic are but two clusters that spring to mind here.)[38] Second, an insistence on assimilating Wittgenstein's overall aims to the ontological orientation of Russell—however sophisticated an analysis of Russell that might be forwarded in this context—had misled some readers about Wittgenstein's commitments in the *Tractatus* (see n. 66 below). Finally—and most important relative to my aims in this essay—Diamond's own articulation of a "resolute" reading of the *Tractatus* had left underdetermined, at least for the first decade of its reception, precisely what we are to say about the *Tractatus*'s atomism and Wittgenstein's *Tractatus* conception, both of the outcome of logical analysis and of the formalization of language in a logically perspicuous notation such as Frege's or Russell's.

Longstanding tradition, from Russell's introduction onward, holds that Wittgenstein *did* think an analysis of language could be carried through, that he did take himself to be laying down conditions on a logically adequate notation. This, as F. P. Ramsey (1923) already remarked in his review, is not at all obvious; the *Tractatus* sees the sentences of our language as, logically speaking, already in perfect logical order. But a natural question then arises about how Wittgenstein viewed the activity of formalization or translation of our ordinary language into logical notation when he wrote the *Tractatus*. For the Russellian tradition of reading the *Tractatus* as a work of ideal-language philosophy encourages the idea that there is some characteristic, logical form that our language reflects and that, as a kind of underlying grammatical framework, may be used to characterize *the* logical structure of language.

Although Diamond was the first and most influential critic of the idea that Wittgenstein was committed in the *Tractatus* to a domain of ineffable necessities or contents or truths, it was clear in the mid-1990s that she intended, if not to join, then at least not to question this part of the longstanding Russellian tradition of reading the *Tractatus*.[39] On her view, as initially articulated (see Diamond 1991a), the nonsensical quality of the apparent propositions of the *Tractatus* may be conceived of in quite Fregean, ideal-language terms: they are elucidations (*Erläuterungen*) of basic notions, transitional and often metaphorical remarks designed to exhort us to adopt the use of a good notation. She took the *Tractatus* to generalize Frege's stance vis à vis Kerry: we can only attain the right logical conception by seeing how to work within an adequate or correct *Begriffsschrift*. Elucidations, in not being expressible in the notation, may not make sense by its lights. But we neither need nor are able to account for basic logical notions and categorical contrasts in prior or independent terms. We simply accept and grasp them in the use of language. Logical analysis, reflected in the activity of translating our thoughts into the formalized language of a Russell-or-Frege type reveals what our uses of logical notions—such as *object, number, concept,* and *proposition*—come to, even if it does not reflect certain real categories comprehensible independently of that activity.

Yet, as Warren Goldfarb pointed out in 1995 (cf. his 1997), Diamond's initial Fregean picture of the *Tractatus* runs the risk of chickening out precisely in accounting for the notion of *analysis*. Logical distinctions would be ineffable yet in some way genuine if they could be shown in the workings of what could be conceived of as a correct or adequate concept-script—what would be, one supposes, an outcome, however idealized, of successful analysis. For Frege, logical distinctions expressed in the *Begriffsschrift* reflect something deep in the nature of logic itself. But, one wondered, how could that be so for Wittgenstein in the *Tractatus* if, as Diamond was emphasizing, the whole idea of a *something* deep in the nature of logic (or of language) is part of the idea under attack in that book? As Peter Sullivan (2002, 47) would put the point later on, "Why can a notation be designed to make logical similarities and differences clear *unless there are* logical similarities and differences?"[40]

My reaction by 1996 to this cluster of issues—partly under the influence of conversations with Burton Dreben, Eli Friedlander, and Matthew Ostrow—was to deny that Wittgenstein's attitude toward logical notation, analysis, and the elucidatory activity of philosophy ought to be conceived of as a smooth or undifferentiated extension of Frege's and Russell's. And I pressed Diamond explicitly to say so (Floyd 1997). I proposed an alternative interpretive approach, an approach on which the very idea of a canonical, *correct* concept-script reflective of *the* logical order of thinking would be seen to be an idea Wittgenstein was trying to overcome in the *Tractatus*.[41]

The way toward such a revision of Diamond's earliest writings seemed open if only because, as Goldfarb, (1997, 72) noted, the *Tractatus* faces us with "a silence on what guides analysis." It seemed desirable in light of the obviously programmatic state of resolute readings of the *Tractatus*: one wanted detailed interpretive work on specific passages within the *Tractatus*, not just slogans and disputes about how to read the preface.[42] And when one did look at the inner details of the *Tractatus*, it seemed clear that Wittgenstein's remarks on notation are so vague and scattered that the idea that the development of a smooth-running formalized language was his aim requires, at the very least, some working out.[43] More generally, present in Wittgenstein's writing is something absent in Frege, namely, repeatedly expressed worries about uncritical idolatry of *Begriffsschrift* notation (for example: confusing the structure of an equation with the holding of a relation, confusing the sign for generality with a functional element of a sentence contributing separately to its sense or content, confusing two distinct uses of the same sign though they express different symbols, as in Russell's paradox). As the contradiction emerging within Frege's own

Grundgesetze system illustrated, "just because a *Satzzeichen* may be logically parsed and operated upon in a formal system is no guarantee that there is thinking going on" (Floyd 1998, 85).

Russell and Ramsey were—I would say in contrast to Wittgenstein—out to advance a positive program of research in analysis: the proving of theorems, causal accounts of belief, and so on. Their implementation of these programs was, after they read it, unquestionably shaped in part by their respective understandings of the *Tractatus*. Wittgenstein himself clearly wanted to leave open the possibility that further clarification might take place in mathematics, psychology, and physics; he hung out with the crowd, so to speak, and it is natural to assume that he shared something of their attitudes. And yet, beyond the use of the truth-operational structures and the discussion of simples and objects, the most striking applications that he makes of the various analyses he proposes in the *Tractatus* are negative: to cut off certain paths and routes into certain philosophical questions and problems, to show that the *Fragestellungen* of certain purported a priori analyses are illusory, in some way not genuine.[44] This suggests that what Sullivan (2004a) has called Conant and Diamond's idea of "the replacement strategy"—that is, the idea that Wittgenstein had primarily in mind, in cases where formal uses of concept words confuse us, to replace our philosophical talk with the activity of fashioning or translating it into the setting of a formalized language that is logically perspicuous—has its limits in relation to our understanding of the *Tractatus*'s conception of philosophical clarification.

Back in 1997 I began to try to work out a different picture of Wittgenstein's Tractarian conception of logical syntax and of analysis by means of a logically perspicuous language. I came to the conclusion that the various notational proposals that were made in the *Tractatus* were, in fact, critical of the ways in which Frege and Russell had conceived their uses of formalized languages. As I (Floyd 1997) wrote, "Wittgenstein's [*Tractatus*] remarks concerning notation can, on reflection, be shown to undercut the whole attempt to construct a correct *Begriffsschrift*. *That*, I wish to claim, is precisely their purpose." Again, in my 2001a I wrote that

by examining the details of what Wittgenstein actually *did* with the *Begriffsschriften* of Frege and Russell in the *Tractatus*, we can see that he is rejecting [their] ideal of clarity of expression. According to this ideal—vividly set out by Diamond—we imagine ourselves to be depicting *the* inferential order among thoughts (or sentences of our language) when we work with a logical notation. But on my reading, one aim of the *Tractatus* is to depict such notions as "*the* inferential order," "*the* logical grammar of language," and "*the* logical form of a proposition" as chimeras. In this sense the Frege (Russell) ideal stands as a primary philosophical target of the *Tractatus*, and not just an ideal Wittgenstein inherited from them. For Frege and Russell write as if, at least ideally, there is a single context of expression within which we may discern the structure of thought, a systematically presented *Begriffsschrift* within which we can use logical notation to make perspicuous *the* logical order. In contrast, I have emphasized Wittgenstein's insistence in the *Tractatus* that no single imposition of a logico-syntactic order on what we say is or can be the final word, the final way of expressing or depicting a thought. On the *Tractatus* view (as I interpret it) there is thinking, but thinking without thoughts, thinking without an inferential order. For Wittgenstein—even in the *Tractatus*—however useful the formalized languages of Frege and Russell may be for warding off certain grammatical and metaphysical confusions, these languages must simultaneously be seen as sources of new forms of philosophical illusion—indeed the deepest kind of illusion of all, the illusion of having found ultimate clarity.[45]

In beginning to work out this idea I was egged on, not only by an interest in how Diamond's interpretation of the *Tractatus* might be made to answer the worries about analysis that had been raised, but also by reading Frege's reaction to the *Tractatus*, as revealed in his correspondence with Wittgenstein (see Frege forthcoming). These letters strike me as of some genuine philosophical importance. For Frege did to the opening lines of the *Tractatus* exactly what Carnap would later do to Heidegger's remarks in *What Is a Metaphysics?*: he held up the language of the opening lines of the *Tractatus* against the standards of clarity appropriate to his *Begriffsschrift* and found them intrinsically wanting. Just as Heidegger's language failed miserably to find plausible translation into such a logically perspicuous language, so did Wittgenstein's. Since Wittgenstein did not, in the face of these requests for clarification, rework the opening lines of the *Tractatus*, we know that he was aware of the anomalous character of his remarks. They are anomalous, moreover, in a way that goes beyond the kind of anomalousness that made the Kerry paradox a challenge to Frege.[46] The "totality of facts" would be expressed, in a notation, by a collection of elementary propositions. But whose? What would they be? How would their totality be expressed or given to us? And why could Wittgenstein write (5.5571) that to try to specify them in any other way but a priori would be nonsense?

For me it is of great philosophical interest, quite apart from questions about how to read Wittgenstein, that the language of the world, of facts, things, and states of affairs, fails to be illuminable by such an exercise in *Begriffsschrift* translation. (Quine [1980, 1] admitted as much in the opening lines of his famous "On What There Is" when he answered the ontological question with a joke, namely, "Everything.")[47] But the important point for my purposes here is that Frege's effort to come to grips with the logic of the opening lines of the *Tractatus* (those that I have suggested, following Dreben, are intended, at least in part, to put their own status and logical structure into question) led to his transforming his understanding of the kind goal of for which the author of the *Tractatus* was striving. As Frege (forthcoming), wrote to Wittgenstein

What you write me about the purpose of your book strikes me as strange. According to you, that purpose can only be achieved if others have already thought the thoughts expressed in it. The pleasure of reading your book can therefore no longer arise through the already known content, but, rather, only through the form, in which is revealed something of the individuality of the author. Thereby the book becomes an artistic rather than a scientific achievement; that which is said therein steps back behind how it is said. I had supposed in my remarks that you wanted to communicate a new content. And then the greatest clarity [*Deutlichkeit*] would indeed be the greatest beauty.

Frege, if I am right, was an acute, though unsympathetic reader of the *Tractatus*. His allusion to Lessing (probably conscious) invokes an aesthetic appropriate to his own conception of logic, and it was intended to show Wittgenstein that he understood at least some of the author's distinctive philosophical aspirations. Not a "new content," but a new way of conceiving an old way of talking about content: this is what the *Tractatus* seems to be after.

Because I have always felt philosophical fascination with what gets called radical opinion, I do not mind being called a "Jacobin" (after all, look what happened to the Girondistes!!!). But I am not chopping off philosophy's head. My interpretive position is not to be understood as embracing anything like an "end of philosophy" thesis— unless one believes, with Frege, that "the greatest clarity" *must* involve what we do recognize as communicating a new content (say, a new ontological insight). I say this because some of my suggestions as to why and how we should differentiate Wittgenstein's *Tractatus* aims from the kinds of attitude toward logical notation found in Frege and Russell have, unfortunately, been misconstrued. Some (Goldfarb [2000]) understood me to be claiming that the *Tractatus* is one grand reductio designed to show the illusoriness of the content of any notion of clarity, an "all-pervasive under-mining" of the notion of analysis itself. Some (Conant and Diamond [2004]) took me to be denying that there are any canons of analysis at work in the *Tractatus*, and even that the *Tractatus* is committed to the idea of a "completely adequate" analysis of the proposition (ibid., 97 n. 82).[48] Some (Hacker and Proops) found it preposterous that I was calling for investigation of the notion of *logical syntax* in the *Tractatus* and questioning whether the evolution from Russell to Wittgenstein was as yet well understood. Hacker (2001, 119 n. 32) thought that my remarks could only be understood to be "deconstruction with a vengeance." Proops (2001), wrongly assuming that I agreed with Conant's emphasis on resolution wholesale, took me to be denying that Wittgenstein could have been right when he said that he had been mistaken in the *Tractatus* about the whole idea of a complete analysis.

For the record, I have never said or believed that there is an absence of significant or interesting evolution in Wittgenstein's philosophy. Nor have I ever denied that by the later 1920s he would have rejected significant portions of the *Tractatus*. Nor have I ever said or believed that all the remarks about showing and pictures in the *Tractatus* are nonsensical. Nor have I ever said or believed that there are no canons of analysis at work in the *Tractatus*, or that the whole has the simple form of a reductio. On the contrary, where many have seen doctrine or general strategies or methods, or a theory of meaning, or—even absent each of these—the dream of a single, overarching, perspicuous formalized language at work in the *Tractatus*, I have seen unclarity and complexity, the kind that begins to make sense of at least some of the complexity we see, both in Wittgenstein's early writings about a "complete" analysis and in his post-*Tractatus* remarks in which the in-principle "completeness" of analysis is transposed into the in-principle "completeness" of a grammatical system. So, rather than being willing to latch on to metaphysical doctrines or attitudes that might be listed as clear "metaphysical" commitments of the early Wittgenstein (as even Conant and Diamond now do [2004, 82–83]), I have tried to begin documenting some of the idiosyncracies and complexities of Wittgenstein's *Tractatus* talk about analysis, both from his point of view as it evolved and against the background of the historical evolution of logic that he lived through and which we today have imbibed. This is not to deny that some of what Diamond (for one) now formulates as the "metaphysical" commitments of the *Tractatus* might indeed be pinned upon it. But it is to call for a complicated investigation of the significance of such "commitments" by investigating the very terms in which they are phrased ("all" propositions, "complete" analysis, "one logical order," and so on).

Peter Hacker and David Pears were perfectly in order, it seems to me, to ask for concrete interpretations of passages and to ask of Diamond and New Readers, "What will you say about Wittgenstein's evolution, and specifically about the remarks he made in the 'middle' period about his 'mistakes' in the Tractatus?" But for all the breadth and range of scholarship they have applied to this question in their own works, neither one of them has looked in detail at the logico-mathematical problem context in which the *Tractatus* inserted itself. This has led to oversimplifications of the *Tractatus*'s notion of logical syntax.

For Wittgenstein in the *Tractatus* it is not, of course, that we have a notion of expression wholly independent of what is subject to the logical. But, as I have just said, it seems hardly obvious that the *Tractatus* must be taken to have insisted that all expression is beholden to the logical, to the structure of the proposition, in the same kind of expressible-in-the-one-ideal-formalized-logical-language way. As I see it Wittgenstein never insisted on, but instead resisted the idea that thoughts must be imagined to be expressible, in principle, in a single universally applicable, logically fully perspicuous "ideal" language. As I put it, "the *Tractatus* was written to wean its readers from Fregean and from Russellian accounts of the definiteness of sense, from all accounts intended to explain or justify the application of mathematical logic to everyday language and from all accounts attempting to use mathematical logic to explain or justify the application of language in general" (Floyd 1998, 86). Part of the point is the case-by-case nature of philosophical reflection: Wittgenstein is stalking and criticizing particular analyses of notions that Frege and Russell had actually offered (e.g., "One is a number"). But part of the point is a shift in the very idea of what goes on in the translation of sentences into a logically perspicuous notation.

One measure of the kind of conceptual difficulties that faced Wittgenstein's attempt to recast and readapt Russell's picture of analysis as a classification of forms is that there are fluctuations in his own writings, both before and within the *Tractatus* (and especially in his *Notebooks 1914–1916*, in June 1915) about what definiteness of sense presupposes and requires—what he imagines is entailed by the specific demands on clarity and explicitness in grammar involved in thinking through the nature of the proposition.[49] This is one index of the problem-situation within which his thoughts about the nature of, and constraints on, analysis, were being formulated.

Peter Sullivan has recently pressed to the fore a connection between these June 1915 passages and the idea of logical atomism, offering a novel account of the latter that will serve as a stepping stone into a suggestion I shall be making later on, about what differentiated Wittgenstein's *Fragestellung* from Frege's and from Russell's. Writes Sullivan (2003, 72):

Wittgenstein seems to be committed to a project of analysing everyday propositions as truth-functional compounds of elementary propositions, in which reference is made only to what is ultimately, intrinsically simple. At the same time, he admits complete ignorance of how, in any particular case, this analysis would work out. So we are led to ask, first, and specifically,

1) How can he know in advance that analysis would vindicate a particular inference?

2) Just what does Wittgenstein suppose is going on when logical principles are applied to ordinary propositions *as if* the expressions occurring in them were simple?

Yet another question is why—assuming it makes some sense to regard the image of an ultimately articulated language as a limit that may not be reachable—Wittgenstein held onto the demand that elementary propositions should be logically independent; but Sullivan separates the latter question off from the former two and goes on to suggest that a certain form of "atomism" may be motivated by way of the business (more or less explicitly grappled with in the June 1915 *Notebook* passages) of taking logical notions to apply to surface patterns of our language in connection with the deductive validity and invalidity of arguments. His discussion has the virtue of locating Wittgenstein's ideas about atomism and the idea of an ultimate analysis within a broader context than the usual one that interprets Wittgenstein's talk of "simples" in terms of the practice of straightening out existential import in connection with singular terms and/or talking about modal properties of objects at the ground level.[50] Whether or not atomism has to do with these as projects, on Sullivan's account each of these practices may be seen to find a place within a more immediate, intuitively accessible kind of activity, namely, the process of depicting, massaging, and altering our linguistic means of expression to a point at which we can *see* logical patterns (e.g., tautologousness) exemplified within them. This engages with the issue of how we are to view the *Tractatus*'s attitude toward logical syntax and the role of a logically perspicuous notation.

Sullivan (2003, 73) begins with a remark about our uses of logic:

There is in general nothing very puzzling about how we show or explain the invalidity of a given invalid argument. Nor is it in itself puzzling that such explanations should sometimes be available: as Frege said, we do not speak a language designed to meet the special needs of an exact science; in particular, we do not speak a language over which any purely grammatical criterion of correct inference could ever be sound. But what *is* puzzling, I think, is that we can sometimes be certain, without any obviously adequate grounds, that such an invalidating explanation is *not* available.

Unless we could, on occasion, be certain of this, deductive inference would be a less impressive epistemic instrument than it is. To know that one may be as certain of the conclusion of an inference of a given form as one is of its premises would be of relatively little use if *whether* an inference *is* of that form were always a matter of doubtful speculation.

Sullivan regards this concern about what he calls "covert complexity" as an "epistemic" question facing Wittgenstein, and possibly ourselves. What it naturally yields, if we think of our ordinary practices with logic, is a "maxim of minimum mutilation" that Sullivan (2003, 74–75) associates explicitly with Quine:

In applying logical principles to actual arguments we make a virtue of not pushing analysis too far. In recommending that as a maxim we presume that, in another sense, one cannot push analysis too far: that is, we presume that, by delving deeper into the structure of an argument than is necessary to establish its validity, one wouldn't undercut the results of the relatively superficial analysis. . . . the commitment carried by our mundane explanations is this: if an argument *really* has a certain form, then *the real form* of the argument is a substitution instance of that form.

That commitment might well be described as a form of atomism.

Now it would take me too far afield to try to assess the merits of Sullivan's characterization, both of our ordinary maxims in formalizing arguments and of the *Tractatus*'s talk of simples (much less of Quine). All I have space to do here is to concur that for

Wittgenstein, analysis does indeed have to do with the identification of validity, but add that the phenomena to which Sullivan calls our attention (covert complexity, contingent presuppositions, and so on) do not have to be viewed either in clearly epistemic or in clearly ontological terms, much less in terms of a notion of logical *truth*.

I would like to emphasize this idea for a number of reasons that will, I hope, become clear in what follows. Proops (2000, 86) has, like Sullivan, explicitly maintained that "Wittgenstein's true target is an attempt to answer . . . the question what kind of fact it is about a particular argument that makes it a valid argument." But Michael Kremer has explicitly denied that Wittgenstein was in any way directly concerned with the concept of validity. He (Kremer 2002b, 327) writes that Wittgenstein "is not concerned with theoretical characterizations of validity, but with the justification of particular inferences," because "no rule can justify inference." Kremer (2002c, 654) prefers to say that on Wittgenstein's *Tractatus* view, "*logic* itself is beyond justification, neither a source of justification nor something to be justified, neither a theory nor a principle, but an ability which pervades all our thinking, even our thinking of objects." In the spirit of Kremer's view, Conant and Diamond (2004) criticize Sullivan's discussion of the *Tractatus* on "p entails q" (set out explicitly in Sullivan 2004b) by suggesting that in that phrase "entails" can be "replaced" by the rewriting of a particular sentence as a tautology.

Now I am sympathetic enough with Kremer's idea of logic as an ability pervading our thinking that I (1998, 83) have myself written that "Neither logic nor ethics are 'theories' or 'points of view' which may be attacked or defended by philosophy." But I feel that Kremer (and Diamond and Conant) have been too quick to dismiss the very notion of validity from the purview of their concerns. In the following section of the essay, I want to say why.

In exploring the extent to which Wittgenstein's attitude toward the development of a *Begriffsschrift* differed in spirit, commitment, and aim from attitudes to be found in Frege and in Russell, I place great weight on the book's notion(s) of the *formal*: indeed, the formality of the notion of the *analysis* itself is one of the *Tractatus*'s most important hallmarks. But my picture of the formal is (to repeat) not exhausted by the kind of clarification that the translation of sentences into *Begriffsschrift*- or *Principia*-style notation accomplishes (say, by replacing a formal-use concept with a variable, or writing out an equation between a tautology and a sentence).[51] Instead, the emphasis I would place on Wittgenstein's idea of a formal use of notions ties the *Tractatus* in, historically and conceptually, with certain important strands in the philosophy of logic that pushed, *via* Carnap, to the center of more recent philosophical attention in the work of Quine. These strands are deeply critical of the epistemic and meaning-theoretic strands of thinking about analysis (and formalization) that we see at work in Russell. They are also deeply critical of (at least one way of reading) Frege's idea that each declarative sentence may be taken to express a thought, that style and content may be severed from one another, that different sentences in different languages *must* reflect a common store of thought-contents. That the Quinean strands find a kind of distant lineage in the *Tractatus* is, I think, historically and philosophically important to bear in mind.

4   Some Difficulties with Logical Atomism Enumerated

I am glad that since I bothered to question how useful a label "logical atomism" is for the *Tractatus*, readers of the book have striven to make it stick through further articulation of its attendant themes and ideas.[52] What is interesting is that commentators have tended to differ with one another about precisely what this "ism" of "logical atomism" involves. Is it the ontology of Tractarian objects and facts? The idea that there is one and only one analysis of the proposition? Is it the claim that in analyzing we must reach the point where we have atomic propositions because of the determinacy of sense? Does it include the independence thesis about the elementary propositions? Wittgenstein's evident commitment to classical negation or two-valued logic? The content of the supposed doctrine(s) is and remains under discussion.

Now in the pre-Diamond period of reading Wittgenstein, this unclarity encouraged interpreters to lay down certain kinds of constraints on interpretation of the book that have, after Diamond, come to seem questionable to many readers. Some supposed that a proper interpretation must tell us whether Wittgenstein was a realist or antirealist or a mystic or an antimystic or an empiricist or a modal realist. Others have held that a restrictive answer to the question, "What kind of objects were the ones Wittgenstein had in mind in the *Tractatus*?" is required to specify the content of his atomism (that is, a specification of the objects as phenomenological, as phenomenalistic, as space-time points, as physicalist, or what not). None of these interpretations has held sway for very long, though many of them help to situate and apply the *Tractatus*, bringing it to life against a larger and very complicated history of philosophy.[53]

I think that an interpretation of the *Tractatus* need not bother with such ways of specifying the atomism, the particular character of the simple objects. The first thing to note is that Wittgenstein himself fails to do so. Why? Is it that he was merely uninterested in the practical business of analysis (or perhaps not smart or decisive enough)? Is it because he thought it a purely empirical matter? I would say that it cannot be just this. Wittgenstein was not a lazy programmatic thinker. Nor was he ever an empiricist about matters of logic. Instead, I suggest, he was trying to recast the conceptual framework, the very *Fragestellungen*, within which Russell's talk of analysis could proceed. Analysis was not just an empirical or logical problem for a rainy day. It was a problem needing reformulation, reconception of its very *Fragestellung*. Wittgenstein's attempted recasting of the idea misfired, but in a variety of ways not best reduced to a matter of an overarching doctrine. These ways are better understood as unclarities arising from some of the very *Fragestellungen* he himself constructed for himself in the *Tractatus*.

Wittgenstein's Tractarian connection between the notions of *analysis* and *internal relation* is neither equivalent to, nor obviously dependent upon, having a "method" of analysis, or a "methodical procedure" for analysis, or even a recognizably ontological "doctrine" of simples.[54] First, the theory of descriptions is not a method, but a contextual device. Second, it may best be viewed, as Sullivan (2002, 80ff.) suggests, as a device whose usefulness, if construed generally across all terms of a speaker's language, is relative to a particular speaker's language at a particular time (recall the difficulties about "Moses" in *Investigations* §79: these are connected with the *Tractatus*'s effort to leave what is empirical out of logic, and yet nevertheless have something to say about the logical as such, names as such). Third, Wittgenstein's way of treating the quantifiers as nothing more than a way of presenting elementary propositions, along with his elimination of identity, does not allow him to view the implementation of the theory of descriptions in a Russellian way—not only because that way essentially involves reliance upon identity, but also because the elimination of apparently referring phrases is regarded by Wittgenstein as a rearrangement in expression of form of the original sentence. Wittgenstein's own notational proposals amount to the denial that there are such things as identity *conditions* for objects or senses, and this positively rules out debates about the correctness or incorrectness of given applications of the theory of descriptions based upon the vagaries of our empirical assessments or the meanings of our complex referring expressions. It is worth adding that although Wittgenstein clearly has the theory of descriptions in mind in various passages, he in no way limits analysis, when it eliminates an individual sign as unnecessary or misleading to clear expression of a thought, to the application of this technique.

Finally, it is important that Wittgenstein's requirement of simple signs—which the *Tractatus* holds is equivalent to the definiteness of sense—seems at times to amount to no more than the idea that analysis is analysis of propositions, and insofar as it is, it must begin and end in expressions that are determinately true or false—expressions subject, that is, to logic. This is the innocent-sounding, pleonastic face of his talk of analysis—perhaps, as he seems later to have thought, its most seductive and dangerous face. Analysis will stop where it stops, "will reveal what it reveals" (Moore 1932–1933, 3b, 2/6/1933, p. 88; quoted in Proops 2001, 392). What could be wrong in this? It will terminate, either in there being no proposition to be analyzed—the speaker acknowledging unclarity, an indeterminateness in what he or she was saying— or in the production of an expression to which the truth-operations determinately apply in such a way as to capture the original sentence's logical place.

Appeal to notions of *formality* is intrinsic to Wittgenstein's conception of analysis, but such appeals are foreign both to Russell and to Frege, and not simply because they are intended to be antimetaphysical. For analysis in the *Tractatus* is expressive (re)construction at the level of the sentence, ideally adequate for assessing the totality of its logical role within language. Analysis is *not* aimed at discovery of forms adequate to derive other forms we already have in view as deducible, as in Frege's and Russell's respective systems.[55]

There is no distinction within the parameters of the pleonastic strand of the discussion between bottom and top, surface and depth, apparent and real logical form. We can think of it, in fact, as a kind of extensionalized, Quinean view, however nascent and unclearly articulated. When we formalize language, we paraphrase, for purposes local to whatever context we are in. Paraphrase is context- and purpose-relative. Paraphrase has no commitment to meaning- or content-preservation, and there is probably no general method or systematic routine for achieving it. This is partly because paraphrase involves an exercise in the home language as much as in the object of assessment. For Quine, there is in this sense nothing to be correct or incorrect about in formalizing (applying logic to) our language. "Paraphrase" is his phrase for avoiding space for the kind of worries about meaning he saw Russell and Carnap generating. We apply logic and formulate its structure. We need no general (kind of) justification to do so.

From this perspective, questions such as: What strategies and techniques do we need to employ in order to stop? Does analysis depend upon accepting certain empirical truths? Certain meaning-theoretic principles? How will we recognize when we have made a complete catalog of the complexity in an expression? What is our right to the "*must*" in the idea that analysis "must" end at the elementary propositions? How can we be sure, for any given analysis of an argument, that an invalidating explanation of its deeper logical structure will not be found?—Each of these is a question asking for something we cannot have and do not need. So long as truth-functional orientation (*sense* in the sense of the *Tractatus*) is preserved through the entire context relevant for reasoning, replacement (i.e., expressive rearrangement) can proceed as it proceeds. And that is all.

This is not even to begin to give a full reading of the role of the remarks on objects and simples in the book, much less of the kind of activities that would characterize philosophy in contexts where we are not involved in working on developing a logically perspicuous language.[56] But it is to suggest that there were materials within the *Tractatus* leading Wittgenstein to suppose that the requirement of determinacy of sense was innocent sounding enough to have accomplished what he wanted without having committed him either to ruling out or ruling in any particular analysis of phenomena involving subsentential complexity. And it is to suggest that we can take the *Tractatus* to be recasting our understanding of the formal use of the notion of analysis itself, away from an image of a quest for *the* logically correct notation (logical syntax conceived as *a* correct syntax) and toward a more complicated, piecemeal conception of the role that translation into formalized languages may play in the activity of philosophical clarification. With this comes a more complicated conception of the relationship between ordinary language, with its variety of expressive powers, and the kinds of translations ordinary language may or may not be capable of receiving in a formalized language designed to make logical form perspicuous.

5   The Universalist Conception of Logic Transformed: The "Tractatus" and the Idea of the "Completeness" of Logic

That it is essential to take into account the problem context within which Wittgenstein was writing about logic is something long emphasized by those whom I would count as part of the wider logical tradition of reading the *Tractatus*, among them not only J. van Heijenoort, Dreben, and Goldfarb, but also Thomas Ricketts, and Jaakko and Merrill Hintikka. Wittgenstein's conception of logic, his very concept of an object, swims in the wake of the universalist conception of logic forwarded by Frege and Russell. Frege's and Russell's mark of the logical had been the explicit formulability and universal applicability of its truths: they conceived of logic as a maximally general science of the most general features of reality, framing the content of all other special sciences. Their quantificational analysis of generality was what they had on offer to make this conception explicit. But as is well known, there were internal tensions within this universalist view. Since the content and applicability of logic is assumed by the universalist to come built-in with the maximally general force of its laws, it is difficult to see how to make sense of its application as *application*, for from what standpoint will the application of logic be understood, given that the application of logic is what frames the possibility of having a standpoint? Frege's and Russell's views led them to resist the idea of reinterpreting their quantifiers according to varying universes of discourse, for they conceived their formalized languages as languages whose general truths concern laws governing all objects, concepts, and propositions whatsoever, full stop; there was no clear conception of ascending to a metalanguage. Hence there is, both in Frege's *Grundgesetze* and in Whitehead and Russell's *Principia Mathematica*, ample precedent for the drawing of a contrast between what must be shown and what can be said, ample precedent for a perspective that squeezes out any room for general questions about how language hooks on to the world (cf. Floyd 2001a). Moreover, this perspective formed a tradition in thinking about logic. Wittgenstein was not the only philosopher to get interested in the inexpressible by thinking about Frege and Russell: in 1908 Harry Sheffer submitted a dissertation on the subject of logic at Harvard that grappled with just these issues.

Such considerations illustrate how misleading the phrase "logical atomism" is as an umbrella phrase for a supposed common doctrine or philosophical method that Russell and Wittgenstein are often alleged to have shared. If there is a shared problem context, then it is the universalist conception of logic and the problems that this conception generated according to its own lights. But, I would emphasize, this is a background problem-context to the *Tractatus*, not a doctrine advocated in the book. Here I differ with Jaakko and Merrill Hintikka, who believe Wittgenstein belonged, like Frege and Russell, to a doctrinal tradition, "the universalist tradition," in which logic and language are conceived of as the universal medium within which all thought takes place. A corollary to this conception, according to the Hintikkas, is that semantics is ineffable. As J. Hintikka (2003, 12) has put it,

It would have been virtually predictable that a thinker in Wittgenstein's historical situation should have thought that semantics is ineffable. . . . In different ways, and for different reasons, Wittgenstein's two main background figures, Frege and Russell, both entertained a variant of the ineffability view. It should therefore come as no surprise that Wittgenstein, too, should have done so. What makes the difference between him and his predecessors and what makes his statements so striking is the boldness of his thinking and of his ways of expressing himself. . . . Frege and Russell had noted some of the particular problems into which the ineffability view leads in special cases. But neither of these two earlier thinkers had the temerity to raise the question of the expressibility of the entire enterprise that would later be called logical semantics. What distinguishes Wittgenstein's attitude toward the ineffability of semantics from that of his predecessors is thus not his mysticism, but his *chutzpa*.

Now what I want to do is to shift Hintikka's interpretive framework, precisely by emphasizing that the *Tractatus* was trying to transform the universalist *Fragestellung*, not simply elaborate it. This angle is important for indicating the legacy of the idea of a show/say contrast within early analytic philosophy, including within Wittgenstein's own development, which emerged partly in reaction to the reception of the *Tractatus*.

For Hintikka's story has a distinguished lineage. In his introduction to the *Tractatus*, Russell held that a hierarchy of languages might defeat what he called the *Tractatus*'s "precise sense" of the inexpressible—this is perhaps the first place in print where the idea of a hierarchy of languages and metalanguages was aired. Later Carnap held in *The Logical Syntax of Language* that Gödel's technique of the arithmetization of syntax refuted Wittgenstein's contrast between showing and saying. Carnap, like Russell, took the showing/saying contrast to amount to the thesis that you cannot make claims about a language from within that language itself, that is, he took Wittgenstein to have denied the possibility of meaningful ascension to a metalanguage. Many readers of Wittgenstein's later remarks on Gödel would argue that Wittgenstein could never have accepted model theory, on a priori grounds, because he remained mired in the *Tractatus*'s ineffabilist view.

But I think the *Tractatus*'s uses of showing and saying are not refutable in the way that Carnap, Russell, and others believed, and I think Wittgenstein thought so as well—not because he had no theses in the *Tractatus*, and so could make no mistakes; not because he thought there was something wrong in principle with Gödel's rigorization; and certainly not because of verificationism. Instead, what Wittgenstein wrote in the *Tractatus* does not rule out as meaningless the notion of a metalanguage (or self-reference of a certain sort) a priori.[57] I think Carnap, like Hintikka, failed to see that certain kinds of "self-referential" uses of language were not being ruled out by Wittgenstein. But unlike Hintikka, I am skeptical that a general thesis about the so-called "ineffability of semantics" can fully account for the issues.

The *Tractatus* suggests, following the *Principia* itself, that we operationalize (treat as formal) the idea of ascent at work in the theory of types, in the sense that we view the generality of that process of iteration as recursive in nature, and as such fully acceptable. Wittgenstein takes the ellipsis, the "...," the "and so on ..." to be basic to our formulation of logical notions as logical (cf. Floyd 2001a). Indeed, as I would emphasize, this suggestion formed part of Wittgenstein's rejection of Frege's and Russell's respective extensions of the notion of *function* across the logical operations, and, in particular, their functional, quantificational analysis of generality. That Wittgenstein's use of his notion of an *operation* did not carry within it the solution to all kinds of problems we now recognize as requiring an adjustment of stance at the metalevel is clear. But that is a different matter from claiming that he ruled out an adjustment of stance altogether from within a single language. The *Tractatus* does paint an image of *the* language that I speak. But, to repeat, it also paints an image of that language having a great variety of open-ended, evolving expressive complexity—complexity I believe Wittgenstein took Frege and Russell to have masked in their analyses of the basic logical notions.

The most striking difference in problem context involves Wittgenstein's bringing to the fore a question that Frege and Russell had not addressed, namely, What is the nature of the logical? This is a conceptual question requiring the formation of new concepts, not a problem that can be couched in terms that Frege and Russell already had clearly to hand. Given that it had been shown how formally to derive basic arithmetical truths and principles from basic logical principles, in what sense may these principles themselves be held to be "purely logical"? Frege's basic laws seem, it is true, to involve no obvious appeal to intuition or empirical knowledge, and his formal proofs (*Aufbauen*) appear to be fully explicit, gap-free logical deductions. On the surface, his basic principles express laws concerning fundamental notions (such as *concept*, *proposition*, *extension*) that had long been acknowledged to be logical in nature. Yet neither Frege, nor after him Whitehead and Russell, provided a satisfactory account of why their systematized applications of the traditionally mathematical notion of *function* to the logico-grammatical structure of sentences should compel us to regard their analyses as purely logical in anything more than a verbal sense.

The universalist conception seemed to leave no room for any model-theoretical approach to logic. This left insufficient room for the kind of rigorization of the notion of *logical consequence* with which we are now familiar.[58] Neither Frege nor Russell had any means of formally establishing that one truth *fails* to follow from another because they had no rigorous systematization of what in general it *is* for one truth to follow by logic from another. All they had conceptual space for were explicit formulations of the logical laws and rules of inference that they regarded as universally applicable and the display of (positive) proofs in their systems. The *completeness* of the system with respect to logically valid inference could not be assessed except inductively and in general philosophical terms, by pronouncing on the maximal generality of logic in its role of framing the content of all thought.

Enter Wittgenstein, who was operating, as Frege and Russell were not, at a generalized level: he was attempting to depict the logical as such.[59] The unity of the logic demanded no less than that he be able to display the logicality of the notion of *logical consequence* on its face. Yet Wittgenstein was also interested in exploring the variety of possible forms of expression; the unity of language in its diversity (a Romantic, Ernstean idea). Strangely, this led him to emphasize against Frege and Russell the expressive complexity of our language and also, at the same time, to try to surmount the limitations of any particular syntactic formulations of logic that might be developed in the future. Wittgenstein was striving after a perspective that would be free of any idolatry of a particular notation or *Begriffsschrift*, any particular syntactic analysis, but would set the whole idea of a logical notation into proper conceptual place. The aim was to set forth the logical as such without resting on any particular logical forms or notation at all (compare 5.553–5.5541, echoed in Moore 1932–1933).

Now I think it is worth noting that this is, in a certain sense, precisely what Gödel's completeness theorem of 1930 does for us (see Gödel 1986). This theorem lies in the background of the incompleteness theorem of 1931, and to my mind it is perhaps even more important for our understanding of Wittgenstein's development than his later remarks about the incompleteness of arithmetic. Why is this?

As Dreben and van Heijenoort insisted (1986), it took nearly fifty years after Frege's 1879 *Begriffsschrift* for the (essentially model-theoretic) question of completeness with respect to the notion of *logical validity* to be properly formulated, in part because of the universalist conception that informed their formalization of logic. In his early work, even before he wrote the *Tractatus*, while responding to the internal conceptual tensions within the universalist view, Wittgenstein began to zero in on the project of isolating a notion of *logical consequence*.[60] This is somewhat ironic in light of the fact that Wittgenstein's own later remarks about the notion of *following a rule* appear, at least at first blush, to sit uncomfortably with the idea that we *have* a clear intuitive idea of *one sentence's following with necessity from another*.[61] Nevertheless, oddly enough, the seeds for his appreciation of how difficult and complicated it can be to extensionalize and/or rigorize certain concepts were planted in what he came to see, thanks in good part to Ramsey, were the overly schematic, nebulous gestures he made in the *Tractatus*. The later rule-following remarks may in fact be seen as a meditation on, or reaction to, this failure.[62]

What I want to suggest is that part of the reason for the garbling in the *Tractatus* was that Wittgenstein tried (wrongly and unsuccessfully) to do with the work with simples and objects what must be done, by our present lights, at the metalevel in making sense of the notion of *validity*. What the completeness theorem does is to capture, not merely at the metalevel, but systematically, via a recursively enumerable (i.e., mechanically effective) scheme, the interplay between the quantifiers through their negations in our talk about validity: either *all* instances follow consistently or *there exists* a counterexample. As we now know, there is an intrinsic barrier to forming a decision procedure to determine a general solution to the question of whether a sentential form is logically valid: here is one sense in which we are, if we demand a systematic resolution, faced with potential inscrutability of a sort.[63] But one reason Quine, for one, thinks that the systematic rigorization of the notion of *following from* that we do have *is* important is that so many philosophers have been misled both by the image of *necessity* as an inevitable companion of our talk about *validity*, and by an overly naive conception of logical truth as a basic datum or distinctive sort of truth (compare Quine 1989, chap. 4; Goldfarb 2001). The completeness theorem extensionalizes the notion of *following from*, if you like, through the production of a search procedure, a procedure rigorizable in a mechanical way. And it is the fact of the procedure, rather than any *one* notation, that rigorizes it.

To allow that theorem to kick in, of course, one must do away with all intensional notions having to do with *relevance*: we assume a rigorization of first-order logic is in place before the terms of the theorem begin to apply—which is to say, we assume that we can treat our logic as itself a mathematical object about which we may reason.[64]

To speak very broadly, I see a kind of tension within the *Tractatus*'s approach to logical analysis between its intensional and its extensional strands. The objects of the *Tractatus* try to ride an intensional and an extensional approach all at once. They express a hope that the rigorization of logic would, at least ideally, keep pace with some sense of relevance in the application of logic to our language, namely, its engagement with our willingness to ascribe truth or falsity (exclusively and universally) to declarative sentential forms. The truth table is an imagined diagram of the constaints that would lay into conceptual place a notion of *logical consequence*. What we may be left with saying is that Wittgenstein vastly underestimated how complicated the idealization and rigorization of the notion of *logical consequence* would turn out to be. He had the idea of, or instinct for, the completeness of logic, but without any of the techniques—in contrast to Skolem, who might be said to have had the techniques without the idea (Wang 1970, esp. 22–23; and Dreben and van Heijenoort 1986). What Wittgenstein never was to underestimate after 1929 was how complicated would be the application of any such rigorization to various kinds of philosophical questions. And so he, unlike Quine, came to emphasize that dispelling philosophical worries about necessity via grammar was an enterprise fraught with the potential to create new forms of confusion and was in a basic way highly relative to context (cf. Floyd 2001b).

Of course, I am fully aware that my remarks are highly anachronistic: there are second-order quantifiers used in the *Tractatus* explicitly (at 5.5261), and we know that second-order logic, in contrast to first-order logic, is not complete. The first-order/second-order distinction was in any case not well understood until some years after the publication of the *Tractatus*. But Wittgenstein cannot be expected to have been omniscient about the need to distinguish second- from first-order logic.[65]

After 1929 Wittgenstein could not go along with Ramsey's effort to generalize his "extensionalism" to the foundations of mathematics by working with propositions in extension: for one thing it pulled too harshly away from the *Tractatus* idea of a proposition as model, which incorporated within it his rejection of identity as a primitive notion and his treatment of generality in arithmetic via formal series (cf. Sullivan 1995, for an account). But what Ramsey picked up on—the aim of *operationalizing* notions like *Sinn* and *Bedeutung*—is part and parcel of what the other, extensionalizing strand of the *Tractatus* is about. To the question, "Did Wittgenstein propound in the *Tractatus* a 'contrast' theory of meaning or sense?" one might reply "No, he was trying to eliminate an appeal to notions of *sentence meaning* and *sense* altogether from his account of logic by extensionalizing and if possible operationalizing them." I suggest that one trouble Wittgenstein came to see with the *Tractatus* was that he had, unwittingly—and as he came to see it, wrongly—half-way tangled himself up in mathematical questions to which the book provides no clear answer. He had been too schematic, and thereby not only failed to provide a way out of philosophical problems connected with characterizing the nature of logic, but also appeared to hold his views hostage to the outcomes of particular solutions to certain mathematical problems. When he writes in the *Investigations* that there are no leading problems of mathematical logic, he is of course explicitly alluding to Ramsey and to Ramsey's paper solving a part of the decision problem (Ramsey 1928), but we must consider that there is a side of the remark that is self-directed. For it was Ramsey who had made Wittgenstein see, in 1929–1930, just why it was important to emphasize that his conception of logic, of grammar, should not allow itself to be held hostage to any particular answer to any particular mathematical problem. This is part of why two of the most important themes in Wittgenstein's subsequent writings on the philosophy of logic and mathematics are (1) the nature of infinity, and (2) the nature and limits of rigorization, mathematization, and extensionalization of everyday notions.

6 Wittgenstein's Evolution

Of course Wittgenstein evolved, came to see mistakes in the *Tractatus*. He did come to think, and rightly, that he had been myopic, vague, and naive—if you like, metaphysical—about the image of a "final" or "complete" analysis that would display the logical as logical and prevent misunderstandings for all possible contexts. In trying to set Russell and Frege straight about logical constants by showing that they had been far too uncritical about applying their logical advances to the basic logical notions themselves, he had granted too much sense to the fiction of analysis as a quest for logical simples and indefinables. In some way he thought he had a general scheme or model (I would *not* call it a method or a substantive independent requirement or an a priori condition or a semantics) that would be able to accommodate future developments and show at one blow how to carry this self-criticism through, once and for all.

What altered over time, with much help from the pressure of others' work, was his understanding of how misleading and partial that general scheme was: how little it allowed in the way of coming to an understanding of the essence of the logical. What was in error by his later lights were his nebulous gestures involving the notion of *analysis*, coupled with the insistence that it *must* terminate somewhere, even if the termination point lies infinitely in the complex distance, and his sketch of the sort of expressive structures it would terminate in. He did not simply say, "analysis ends in that which is not defined, and we don't know its precise form yet, nor do we need to." He treated it as ending in that which is intrinsically somehow indefinable, if properly viewed or seen. And the indefinability was to be understood partly in virtue of the idea that the path from sentence to sentence in the process of analysis is itself formal, that is, sense-preserving in *his* sense of this notion.

That the *Tractatus* created new forms of confusion of its own, precisely in the effort to unmask older ones, is perhaps in the end not surprising. Progress always looks greater than it is. The author of the *Tractatus* came to see that philosophical problems do not have as unified a source, or as unified a means of escape, as he had once suggested—indeed his suggestion of this had generated yet more problems and difficulties. But one of his major philosophical contributions, at least for me, is incipient in the *Tractatus* and survives some of its more glaring problems—in fact, it is an insight whose importance was brought home to Wittgenstein precisely because of what he saw had happened with some of the *Tractatus*'s most glaring errors—and that prescient insight is that the successes and glories of Frege and Russell in logical analysis would give rise to new forms of philosophical confusion, deeper and more difficult to extricate ourselves from than that of earlier philosophies, precisely because in their hands genuine scientific advance masquerades as metaphysics rather than the other way around. After Frege and Russell, we have to struggle with more subtlety to free ourselves from mythological ideas about what formalized languages can show us.

In closing, let me remark that I have only made a pass at one way we might look at Wittgenstein's development through the Ernstean perspective of evolving *Fragestellungen* or *Sprachlogike*. There were other sins of the *Tractatus* besides those it committed in connection with the notion of logical analysis that I have mentioned. Other sins of "nebulousness," were connected to Wittgenstein's treatment of number and its connection with the general form of a proposition (Cf. Wittgenstein 1975, 127ff.). As Russell and Ramsey helped Wittgenstein to see, problems about the cardinality of all objects made a mess of his Tractarian effort to integrate numbers directly into the form of elementary propositions while at the same time leaving open whether the resulting complexity in their forms would be infinite or finite in nature. Here again, the trouble was vagueness, not definiteness of doctrine.[66]

In many of the passages in which he talks about his errors and mistakes in the *Tractatus*, he makes it clear that the book contains tensions within itself that he had not faced or thought through sufficiently, ways of sinning against its own better strands and lines of thoughts (one of which is the idea that "in philosophy you cannot discover anything").[67] But some of those sins were a matter of tone and style rather than positive metaphysical commitment—sins that concerned the form and literary structure of the text. In certain stylistic respects, the *Tractatus* was a poor first draft. The articulated numbering of propositions has a far too aprioristic, "arrogant," and "dogmatic" tone, by his later lights, inviting an image of *the* way of getting to clarity about logic and the structure of the proposition as such, for all contexts and purposes (Wittgenstein 1973a, 182–183). Philosophy, as he remarked in his Cambridge lectures of 1930, is like an organism, it has neither beginning nor end—and the *Tractatus* style has a clear endpoint, literarily speaking. Moreover, as he also remarked, though philosophy was traditionally viewed as eternal and necessary, it was supposed to have results that could help one in life, without waiting years to see what the endpoint might be of a particular scientific program (Moore 1932–1933, 2a, Mich. Term 1930, p. 10).

We can contrast the *Tractatus*'s form with the numbering of remarks in the *Investigations*, and Wittgenstein's explicit emphasis in the later work upon the idea of an album of pictures that cross a landscape from multiple points of view. Anscombe (1969) suggests at one point, reflecting on a comment of Wittgenstein's, that the *Tractatus* might have been a superior work of art to the *Investigations*. This suggests that perhaps its literary ambitions, its interest in giving "pleasure" (among other things) to a reader, may have stood partly in its philosophical way. The important point is that the contrast we then draw between early and later Wittgenstein is not best reduced to one of assertion and negation, mistake and correction.

Wittgenstein's summoning up of traditional, medieval, theological terminology in the opening lines of the *Tractatus* was a brilliant way of getting the reader to cast the scope of the discussion broadly, across a larger philosophical tradition, to wonder what it signifies to lump Russell's discussion of "atomic facts" in with such a tradition of "the old logic," and to indicate that, as it were, the reader is not in Kansas anymore with any of the notions at work on the page. This summoning is ironic in the best and most serious sense—which does not mean that we exclude here its airing substantial intellectual aims, commitments, and ambitions, any more than we do with irony in other contexts. It is a kind of strategy of beginning, one he would pursue (though differently) in the *Investigations* by quoting from a particular, admired source, Augustine. Again, in his diary from the mid-1930s we read:

My book the Log.Phil. Abhandlung contains alongside good and genuine also Kitsch, that is, passages with which I filled up holes and so to speak in my own style. How much of the book consists of such passages I do not know and it is difficult now rightly to evaluate. (Wittgenstein 2003, 39; my translation)

I am sure we will never be able to say precisely wherein the Kitsch begins and ends. But we ought to be open to the idea that there are such holes to be wary of.

In a manuscript of 1943, drafting what was to become the preface to the *Philosophical Investigations*, Wittgenstein (2000, Item 128, pp. 46ff. at p. 51) wrote

Philosophische Untersuchungen,
der Logisch-philosophischen Abhandlung contrasted

—a conception of the juxtaposition of the two titles suggesting that his own relation to the evolution of his thought was a matter to be *investigated* rather than something either settled in his own mind or understandable in terms of concepts, doctrines, or principles that could be made clear in advance.[68] We might set beside this Wittgenstein's remark to Drury that every sentence of the *Tractatus* is "syncopated" and must really be read as the title of a whole chapter (Rhees 1984, 159). If that is so, we ought not to expect that individual propositions of the *Tractatus* can simply be negated, giving us truth about Wittgenstein's later position and falsity about his earlier one. Although we cannot ignore his subsequent attempts to summarize the evolution of his thought, we cannot ignore the fact that he had not thought through certain issues, that he was himself in a position of great unclarity when he wrote the *Tractatus*, and for more than one reason.

Appendix

Excerpt from "Nachwort," Ernst 1900

Page 272:

The fairy tales, sayings and short stories of all peoples display a quality of conspicuousness. This can explain itself either through the borrowing and alteration of motives, or, if one considers a spontaneous coming into being in the hands of a single people, through a self-development of the motives according to general laws of logic and of association with intuitions, which are found generally in any grounds or reasons.

Probably both explanations are right.

The first exhibits throughout especially many existences [*Bestehendes*], because in it certain scientific gatherings are made possible, in which one can trace the wanderings of stories up to a certain degree through translations and works on books, which lie before us. Now most remarkable is that by following such traces one always comes to India, to the first Buddhist centuries. . . .

One can however discover by one or another path that which will be comprehensible to us. And in any event it is for the final ground of the being of stories equal, whether they find themselves said in one place or everywhere in the whole world. The two origins, which will be set forth in what follows, find themselves in any event everywhere possible: whether from them something comes into being everywhere, that is a question of the second kind.

Pages 307–308:

Whoever compares, without prior fixed opinions, modern poesy with that of the middle ages will find, among many distinctions, one that is especially remarkable: the nearer we come to the present the smaller becomes the number of subjects and motives—we shall say: materials.—Indeed, it seems as if recent materials will not be found, and only an ever more narrow, shrinking circle of old materials can be newly treated.

At least one must reflect for a very long time before one finds material in a new poet that wholly belongs to our time. Perhaps one could say: the finding or invention of new materials was always something that happened seldom; in the course of four thousand years, however, the material has amassed itself, and what can the approximately four hundred years of modernity mean against this long time before? But with this objection the narrowing of the circle of materials is not explained. An artist of today no longer risks himself with a collection of materials, because one generally assumes that it will not stand up to the critique of reality. One can observe real deposits of the objection against certain kinds of materials.

Periodically literary strivings come to power, which represent themselves as a turning back to nature; each such period among other things clears away determinate kinds of material which one then in the subsequent time of the so-called artistic style are not ventured upon again.

By far the predominant part of the motives and styles applicable up to today in no way originate from reality. It is often very old qualities [*Gute*] of the peoples, in mysterious and always as yet unexplained ways occurring through the progress and differentiation of the peoples, accruing, beyond the detailed representations of these two ways, through the alterations of language, in which a later time fails any longer to understand the logic of language [*Sprachlogik*] of the past and interprets it through inventions; through changes of the intuitions of the inner connectedness of the world, of death, the soul, eternity, God, and so on, in which one interprets the misunderstood remains of earlier faith rationalistically; through the wandering of the materials to other peoples, through further recounting in altered circumstances of the people and, inappropriately, to modernity. The process is in essence always this: something which is through the experience of reality an insoluble problem is solved through an invented rationalizing history. In the progress of time are set forth in this history once again insoluble problems, and a new invention comes closer again to reality. In the subsequent age the critique of reality will be still sharper and a new rationalization will arrive, until one at last lets the whole fall as insignificant or foolish.

Notes

1. Thanks to Wolfgang Kienzler for supplying me with this pair of quotations, a pair that reminds us of Frege's words to Wittgenstein (in Frege's letter of September 16, 1919, quoted below). Thanks also to Kenneth Haynes, who had pointed me toward the Heidegger quote some years ago, in mind of Wittgenstein (a translation of this quote by Haynes [with J. Young] may be found in Heidegger 2002, 255). Heidegger is said to have copied the Lessing quote into the copy of *Sein und Zeit* that he gave to Edmund Husserl in 1927; thanks to Daniel Dahlstrom for the reference, which is in Husserl 1997, 21ff., and for the suggestion that Heidegger might have learned of the Lessing source from Lorentz 1909, 98.

2. Versions of this talk were read at the Wittgenstein Workshop at the University of Stirling, Scotland, the Boston Colloquium for the Philosophy and History of Science, Macalaster College, and the University of Chicago Wittgenstein Workshop and the university of Perugia. I am grateful to my audiences for their helpful feedback, especially to Janet Folina and Thomas Ricketts. To Enzo De Pellegrin I owe thanks for very useful discussion of my translations, and for comments as the final draft thanks are also due to Laurence Goldstein, Nadine Cipa, Andrew Lugg, and Edgar C. Boedeker, Jr.

3. Goldfarb (1997, 73 n. 10; 2000) notes that Ricketts first concocted the label of "resolute" for Diamond's idea that we should not "chicken out" in reading the *Tractatus* by attributing to it an ineffable metaphysics or contentful form of nonsense; Diamond picked the term up, favorably impressed with its moral connotations. (Sullivan 2002a, 46 erroneously credits Goldfarb with introducing the term.)

4. As I have put it in Floyd 2002, philosophy was for Wittgenstein "a way to expose the places where vanity, received authority, unclarity and lack of resolve blunted his powers of expression, making him dishonest with others and himself. His difficulties were thus the kind of difficulties we all face one by one as we inherit a language, and it is one of his great intellectual contributions to have made this struggle worthy of the name of philosophy." Compare Floyd 1998, 102ff., on what I call the "private" side of solipsism for the early Wittgenstein. My remarks in no way are intended to reduce interpretation of the *Tractatus* on ethics, in principle, to biography or psychology as opposed to philosophy. For a relevant discussion, see Friedlander 2001, especially at pp. 195ff. Sullivan 2002, 63 says that the first person "I" "doesn't figure much in 'the resolute reading,'" but it did figure centrally, alongside solipsism, in Floyd 1998.

5. See Floyd 1995, 1997, 1998, 2001a, 2001b; Floyd and Putnam 2000; Floyd 2005b; Floyd and Putnam 2006.

6. Diamond criticizes the idea of such a "general account" here in relation to Wittgenstein (early and later); compare to Floyd 1997 and 1998, p. 100. That a preoccupation with overcoming the need for general accounts of meaning also may be said to characterize the philosophies of others in the analytic tradition after Frege (among them Austin, Quine, and Putnam) is emphasized in Floyd 2003 and 2005a; the latter contrasts this image of the development of early analytic philosophy with one offered by Dummett, according to which the theory of meaning is central to the analytic tradition. Much of Diamond 1991a is devoted to questioning Dummett's perspective on early analytic philosophy, and on Frege and Wittgenstein in particular.

7. Diamond 1991a (especially chap. 9, "The Face of Necessity") offers telling criticisms of Dummett's influential idea that for Wittgenstein mathematics and philosophy have "nothing to say to one another" because language divides itself up into isolated islands of language-games with no possible communication between them (see Dummett 1978, 167–168). What Diamond's work has shown is that the interplay between mathematics and philosophy in Wittgenstein's hands is extraordinarily subtle and open ended, forming a crucial part of his larger investigation of human claims to self-evidence, clarity, intuitiveness, and truth. Compare Diamond 1996 on connections between Wittgenstein's remarks on mathematics and on ethics and see also Floyd 2000.

8. Goldfarb (2005) distinguishes at least three different ways Wittgenstein invokes showing in the *Tractatus* (leaving aside what he calls the "informal" uses of "show" that are more or less equivalent, as he understands them, to "x gives us reason to believe y," or "x proves y"): those drawing categorical distinctions, those that maintain that the logical form of sentences is not represented in sentences, but may be read off from them, and those having to do with limits of language. As Goldfarb sees it, none of the passages seems likely to be able to support a metaphysical reading of the *Tractatus* that countenances a domain or realm of necessary, yet ineffable things, properties, or truths.

9. See Sullivan 2002a, especially 49–52. He mentions Conant 2000 and Kremer 2001; a similar "spread" may be seen in Ricketts 1996, 94.

10. The image of this line is criticized in Diamond 1991b.

11. This was the view laid out in Floyd 1997; it was influenced by conversations with Dreben and Goldfarb (cf. Goldfarb 1979, 1997, 70–71 and, later, 2002). I have thus always advocated what Diamond now calls, with Conant (following Goldfarb 1997), a "piecemeal" approach to examples of meaningfulness in the *Tractatus* (Conant and Diamond 2004, 71). What, for example, Diamond says in her 2004 and 2005 about the notion of a formal use of a concept (such as "number") not serving as a touchstone of legitimacy for all possible uses of number words in the *Tractatus* is an idea I explicitly stressed both in Floyd 1997 and in Floyd 2001a (especially at p. 174, n. 50.) Diamond says (2004, 219) that she did not appreciate the importance of this "piecemeal" approach until after 1995. My guess is that she was then still too much in the grip of the idea that "resolution's" primary task was to get clear about how to resist interpretations of nonsense of the ineffabilist variety.

12. Floyd 1997 contains the basic interpretive proposal, which I shall discuss below in sections 3–5. This manuscript was never published, though it was circulated and read at the first conference at which resolute and nonresolute readers confronted one another, a meeting of the Boston Colloquium for the Philosophy and History of Science, April 17, 1997. (Present were Diamond, Hacker, Pears, Goldfarb, Ricketts, Hintikka, Hylton, and myself, urged on by our immoderate moderator, Burton Dreben.) At the conference Thomas Ricketts dubbed my proposals for interpreting the *Tractatus* "Jacobin," an epithet I accepted (in partial homage to Dreben 1992, which sees Quine-to-Putnam as Jacobin-to-Girondiste, especially on the topic of meaning). I was arguing that Diamond's reading ought to be developed in a direction beyond where it had been articulated at that point, especially on the issue of the role of logical notation—what Goldfarb (1997, 72) called "the deep difficulty facing the resolute reading." (cf. Diamond 1997). My view was that if Diamond held back from confronting this difficulty, she would fail to carry through her program in relation to the *ancien regime* of Pears, Hacker, and Hintikka. For an account of the conference, see Hofman 1998 and Biletzki 2003, 10.

13. On the background to Russell's struggles overcoming the original theory of judgment to which he had subscribed, see Pears 1977; Hylton 1990, 2005; Ricketts 1996b; and Carey 1999.

14. While I do not have a reading of these passages that satisfies me, it seems to me eminently desirable that we have one, if only because such various suggestions about reading these passages have been made over the years. I have profited here from a talk by Sullivan at Cambridge University in the summer of 2003.

15. The perceptual locutions Wittgenstein always associated with mathematical practice are discussed in Narboux 2005 and Narboux forthcoming, as well as in Floyd forthcoming.

16. Compare note 11.

17. Sullivan 1996, 2000, 2002a, 2004a, 2004b express particular concern with developing a unified, overarching view of the *Tractatus* , as does Potter 2000, chap. 6. Unifying threads have also been discerned in more explicitly "resolute" readers, for example, Ricketts 1996b, Floyd 1997, Kremer 2001, and, in book-length form, Friedlander 2001, Diamond 1991a and Ostrow 2002.

18. The importance of the context principle of Frege as background to the *Tractatus* is stressed throughout Diamond 1991a. Compare Kremer 1997 for a further articulation of this theme of a kind of holism in the *Tractatus*.

19. Here Floyd 2001a and Kremer 2002a go beyond appeals to resolution and Frege's context principle (Conant and Diamond 2004 adapt some of Kremer's ideas at pp. 73ff.).

20. This is so even if one takes it that the general form of the proposition is—as Wittgenstein explicitly writes that it is (4.53)—a variable. Remark 6 of the *Tractatus*, where Wittgenstein sets forth the general form of proposition with a piece of bracket notation, is notoriously vexed to interpret, and it remains unclear to me how to read it as a variable. (Some doubt might be garnered from 4.5 that says that it *"appears to be possible* to give the general form of proposition" [my emphasis].) For some doubts about whether it can be read as anything more than an operational schema, as opposed to an object-language piece figuring in a unified formalized language, see Floyd 2000, 2001a; Sullivan 2004a; and Ricketts 2005.

21. See, for discussions of generality, Kremer 1992; Floyd 2001a, 2005b; and Ricketts 2004. Diamond (2000a) uses Wittgenstein's conception of generality against Russell's idea of private acquaintance with sensations.

22. For more on the historical evolution and transposition of the notion of logical necessity, see Dreben and Floyd 1991 and Floyd 2005b, especially 84ff.

23. Detailed consideration of why the analogy between pictures and propositions need not be viewed as a theory of representation may be found in Ricketts 1996b, Friedlander 2001, McGinn 2001, and Ostrow 2002.

24. I discuss this passage in relation to Feyerabend's appropriation of Wittgenstein in Floyd 2006b.

25. Friedlander 2001 launches from this idea of a confrontation with language in the *Tractatus's* opening lines into a larger discussion of the themes of finitude and meaning as they are raised in the *Tractatus* as a whole. He notes (22n) that we find no draft of the opening lines of the *Tractatus* in the pre-*Tractatus* writings, suggesting a calculated ambition for these lines in tone, allusion, and style.

26. As Friedlander 2001, 23n notes, he and I have a more "circular" view of the progress of the *Tractatus*. As he (ibid., 22) puts it well,

The relation between beginning and end [of the *Tractatus*] must indeed be conceived in the context of the ontological tone of the opening, but not necessarily in order to reject the ontological perspective. . . . In a circular structure, the book starts with the world as such, a world as if beyond language, only to return to it at the end through an understanding of the limits of language. Overemphasis on the figure of the ladder as the key to understanding the structure of the [*Tractatus*] distracts attention from this circle.

27. As Goldfarb (2000) stated. This kind of reading has been pursued by Nordmann 2005.

28. This is in contrast to what Read and Deans (2003, 264ff.) characterize as a "strong" version of resolution. They speak (as I did not) of "the say/show distinction" having "a purpose" (ibid.,

264, 266). Incidentally, though I am named in this essay (267), and several passages (264, 266) appear to lift phrases directly from Floyd 1998, that essay is not cited—an oversight, as Read has said to me in conversation. The question, raised by Read and Deans, of whether my form of "resolution" is or is not "stronger" than that of Conant and Diamond must await further discussion. I haven't a clear concept of the scale on which we are to measure strength (though see in this connection Biletzki 2003, 101).

29. As Goldfarb once pointed out, Pears and McGuinness had been tendentious, at least in my view, in translating *Tractatus* 6.54 using the verb "transcend."

30. On "transitional," see Diamond 1991b. The term can invite the idea of transitioning *somewhere*, which is why I prefer her idea, broached in the same essay, of "imaginative" activity, though I think this idea requires embedding within the context of what she had already written about riddle talk and conceptual investigation in her "Riddles and Anselm's Riddle" (in 1991a).

31. Example: the motto of the *Tractatus* from Kürnberger poses a riddle that is nominally answered at 4.5: the three words for "all that one knows" are, roughly translated, "so it goes," or "thus matters stand," or "that's the way it is." It takes a very long time to get to the point where one understands how to take the general propositional form as a solution to this riddle. Moreover, it is a constraint for me in understanding the *Tractatus* that this solution, like the solution to Anselm's riddle, will have an ethical, as well as a logical significance. I hope in future work to explain how this might be connected with issues discussed in Wiggins 2004 and in Floyd 2006a.

32. For more on Ernst and Wittgenstein, see McGuinness 1988, Baker and Hacker 1980, 535–537, Hübscher 1985, and Majetschak 2005. For Wittgenstien's own references, see Wittgenstein 1993, 3:266 (item 110, p. 184), Wittgenstein 2000, items 115, 155 (p. 30v), 183 (p. 182), 212 (p. 1203), 213 (p. 433, translated in Wittgenstein 2005), and Wittgenstein 2004, Hermine to Wittgenstein (1920er) and Wittgenstein to Jean Rhees, 8.4.1945.

33. Incidentally, I wasn't born knowing how to do this. My father could do it. I asked him how. He said that he learned from watching his dog as a boy. I watched my horse.

34. According to Michael Potter (correspondence), Wittgenstein asked to be sent a copy of Whitehead 1911 during the war. In the book we find this:

by the aid of symbolism, we can make transitions in reasoning almost mechanically by the eye, which otherwise would call into play the higher faculties of the brain.

It is a profoundly erroneous truism, repeated by all copy-books and by eminent people when they are making speeches, that we should cultivate the habit of thinking of what we are doing. The precise opposite is the case. Civilization advances by extending the number of important operations which we can perform without thinking about them.

For more on the *Tractatus* and Whitehead, see Floyd 2001a, 2005b, and forthcoming b.

35. Compare Wittgenstein to Engelmann, 16.1.1918 (in Wittgenstein 2004, 1967, p. 11):

If you tell me now that I have no faith, you are *perfectly right*, only I did not have it before either. It is plain, isn't it, that when a man wants, as it were, to invent a machine for becoming decent, such a man has no faith.

36. See Conant and Diamond 2004, 71, as well as Diamond 2004 and 2005. The terms "whole-sale" and "retail" are used in a parallel way by Ricketts 1996b, 62. See note 11 above.

37. I thus agree with the statement of P. Simons (2003, 383) that "logical atomism is a complex doctrine . . . *associated with* Russell and Wittgenstein" (my italics) and that "there are significant differences between [Russell's and Wittgenstein's] versions" of it; compare Proops 2004.

38. Floyd 1998, 2001a; Ostrow 2002; Friedlander 2001; and Kremer 2002a are all relevant as anti-dotes to this tendency.

39. Diamond (forthcoming) explicitly holds that in the *Tractatus* Wittgenstein develops and gen-eralizes Frege's notion that "differences in logical kind can be made clear in a good notation." It is only later, as she puts it, that Wittgenstein came to see that "differences in logical kind cannot in general be made perspicuous by a conceptual notation" (ibid.) These views, though only in draft form, express a reading of the *Tractatus* that periodically surfaces in Diamond's other work (cf. especially 1991a).

40. See Conant and Diamond 2004, 93 n. 45 for an acknowledgment of the difficulty. They don't recognize Sullivan's worry as a version of Goldfarb's and my earlier expressed concern, but it seems to me that it is.

41. So in Floyd 1997:

[Given what he writes at 3.325], is Wittgenstein aiming to devise a *Begriffsschrift* to preclude all such gram-matical errors? I think not. In particular circumstances a concept-script *can* be used to show that certain signs haven't been given meaning. But a concept-script can *equally well* serve as a source of superstition and illu-sion. This happens if and when—as in Frege and in Russell—it is taken to yield a complete or correct analy-sis of the logical structure of thought, an uncovering of logical objects and genuine logical distinctions. One aim of the *Tractatus* is to fully think through the idea that there could be such a notation, fully think through a conception of objects and facts perfectly mirrored in the structure of such a canonical notation, in order to unmask Frege's and Russell's philosophical claims. Nevertheless, I take every remark in the *Tractatus* about a *correct logical notation* (*eine richtige Begriffsschrift*) to be an attack on the very notion.

42. Calls for more specific textual analysis were put out in Goldfarb 1997 and Floyd 1997, as well as in Sullivan 2002, 43–44. That "resolution" is really a program and not a "key" to reading the whole of the *Tractatus* was quite explicit in Conant and Diamond 2004, 78.

43. As I wrote in Floyd 1998, 85, following Goldfarb 1997, in the *Tractatus*, unlike in Frege's and Russell's writings, no appeal is ever made to the fully explicit or definite rules of a formalized language (such as Frege's *Begriffsschrift* or the system of *Principia*), if only because no such lan-guage is written down. Hacker (2001, 118 n. 32) finds it "surprising" that I hold this, but it seemed (and still seems) obvious to me that this is so. As I discuss in Floyd 2001a, Hintikka (1956), R. Fogelin (1982), P. T. Geach (1981), S. Soames (1983), G. Sundholm (1990), and K. F. Wehmeier have raised and addressed fundamental questions about the expressive adequacy of Wittgenstein's notational proposals, questions which leave interpreters a lot of leeway in writing down a "*Tractatus* formalism" (see also Weihmeier 2004).

44. Like Marie McGinn (1999) and Matthew Ostrow (2002), I include in this the discussion of the proposition as a logical picture in the 2s.

45. As I put it in Floyd 2001a, his remarks "undercut the possibility of his formulating a formal system in either Russell's or Frege's sense," indicating that he "did not share either Frege's or Russell's (or for that matter the logical positivists') conception(s) of what an ideal or formalized language could do for us in philosophy. Unlike these philosophers, he does not think any notation can depict *the* grammar of language, or make clear *the* limits of sense, *the* logical order."

46. For a discussion of this Kerry anomalousness for Frege, see Diamond 1991a and also Weiner 1990, 2004. For a discussion of the anomalousness of the *Tractatus*'s opening lines, see Floyd 1998 and Sullivan 2000.

47. "Everything" is not an answer, for it is not a sentence. So Quine (1980):

A curious thing about the ontological problem is its simplicity. It can be put in three Anglo-Saxon monosyllables: 'What is there?' It can be answered, moreover, in a word—'Everything'—and everyone will accept this answer as true. However, this is merely to say that there is what there is. There remains room for disagreement over cases; and so the issue has stayed alive down the centuries.

48. For the record, I tried to notify them of their mischaracterization of my views by e-mail, suggesting a rewording of this footnote. The rewording, whether by design of the authors or the printer, did not make it in. So I'll reiterate my note to Diamond here:

I do think there is a notion of "complete analysis" at work in the *Tractatus*; I just think it is a kind of expressive ideal that isn't the same as Frege's and/or Russell's *even* under the most sophisticated readings of them we might, after Wittgenstein, try to offer.

49. For discussion of these passages, see Floyd 1998 and Sullivan 2002. Compare Ostrow 2002.

50. For an account of these more usual ways of treating Wittgenstein's atomism, see Proops 2004.

51. The limits of the proposal Conant and Diamond (2004) make, following Kremer, for replacing "p entails q" with an equation conceived as a "record of a calculation" are obvious if the number of names in the language is infinite. The completeness theorem of Gödel may be seen as a way of overcoming this limitation while keeping the idea of fashioning a mechanical procedure. On Wittgenstein's having underestimated the complexity of fashioning a formal system for the infinite case, see note 66 below.

52. Proops 2004, Sullivan 2002, and (though they don't use the phrase "logical atomism") Conant and Diamond 2004.

53. J. P. Griffin (1997) holds the objects are space-time points; Hintikka and Hintikka (1986) that they are phenomenological objects. The Vienna Circle, of course, tended to think of the constituents of facts as elementary experiences.

54. Proops (2001, 396) speaks of doctrine and of "methodical procedures" in connection with analysis.

55. Although Proops does not disagree with what I say positively here about the formality of Wittgenstein's conception of analysis, he seems to think that it does not contrast with the latter idea of the project of deducing given forms, an idea I see at work in Frege and Russell, but not in the *Tractatus*. For Proops (2002) assimilates Wittgenstein's attitude toward logical entailment

to a "proof-theoretic" conception he takes to be implicit in Frege (*via* the deduction theorem). My suggestion below about the relevance of the concept of completeness in the sense of Gödel 1930 to the *Fragestellung* sets out a very different point of view on the conceptual pressures that faced, not only Wittgenstein, but Frege and Russell as well. There is some textual justification for this in the texts from Moore 1932–1933, where Wittgenstein is clearly concerned to explore (e.g., 11/25/1932, pp. 33ff.) the difference between "p entails q" or "p therefore q" and "p ⊃ q."

56. Conant and Diamond 2004, as well as Diamond 2004 and especially 2005 broach the idea that Wittgenstein may have had room to distinguish between clarification by means of a logically perspicuous language and that by means of ordinary language. That would be to admit just the kind of distinction between Frege's and Russell's attitudes toward notation and Wittgenstein's that I have been trying to articulate.

57. Indeed, in 1932 (as Hintikka has himself emphasized), Wittgenstein invited the assimilation of at least some of his views to Carnap's when he alleged in his outraged letter to Schlick that "Carnap is not taking any step beyond me when he is in favor of the formal and against the "material mode of speech" [*inhaltliche* Redeweise]".

58. For an account of Frege's conception of logic that is highly relevant to this point, see Goldfarb 2001.

59. Schlick took this to be the "turning point" in philosophy to which the *Tractatus* had contributed. Later on Wittgenstein gently tried, in a letter, to wean Schlick from the idea that this was as much of an advance or kind of advance that would further the aims of the Vienna Circle. See Wittgenstein 2004.

60. Kang 2004 analyzes the "class theory" of inference in Wittgenstein's wartime notebooks; the evolution of Wittgenstein's thoughts on logic from the *Prototractatus* to the *Tractatus* is discussed in Dreben and Floyd 1991, Kremer 1997, and Kang 2005.

61. It is not certain that Wittgenstein ever read Gödel's completeness theorem (of 1930; in Gödel 1986), and quite certain that he did not appreciate its mathematical significance, given that he died in 1951, before which time the theorem's significance and fertility were not yet well understood. No explicit discussions of the theorem are so far known in Wittgenstein's works, though it is not impossible they might be found in the future. It would be nice if they were, for it is the completeness theorem, much more than Gödel's incompleteness theorems, that would seem to be most difficult for Wittgenstein to interpret philosophically, given his later rule-following discussions. For further discussion, see Floyd 2005b.

62. This suggestion would fit with the reading I give (Floyd 1991) of the passages forming *Investigations* 186ff. as they occur in the opening of *Remarks on the Foundations of Mathematics* 1.

63. If, that is, a schema is *not* first-order valid (if there is an invalidating interpretation of premise and conclusion), then the search (proof) procedure may *run forever*.

64. Compare the very important passages in Wittgenstein 1973a, 37 on Weyl on the decision problem: Wittgenstein here insists that the word "relevant" ought to be eliminated from Weyl's

presentation of the mathematical decision problem (Weyl, according to Wittgenstein, stated the problem as whether every "relevant" sentence can be decided according to a single rule.) Much later Wittgenstein states explicitly that "the notions of *consequent* and *inconsequent* are not mathematically analyzable" (Wittgenstein 2000, 162b, p. 68r, 8/14/1940).

65. Besides, one may reasonably doubt that the *Tractatus* is committed to anything beyond a restricted predicative fragment of full second-order logic that would be formulatable in a complete theory.

66. Unlike Proops (2002, 391) I do not think these problems, or the associated difficulty of Wittgenstein's having confused dots of laziness with infinite conjunctions and disjunctions of truth functions in his treatment of quantification, resulted from an "unfounded bet" (much less an "unwitting" one) on Wittgenstein's part about the finitude of the universe, but instead resulted from an underestimation of how complicated and misleading it was to speak about all possible cardinalities and kinds of complexity at once while granting the idea of a final analysis. (This is one reason he so emphasizes the distinction among the grammars of different cardinalities in the early 1930s, and the analogy with limit notations in the calculus [in Moore 1932–1933.] The *Tractatus* explicitly remarks that its discussion of atomic facts and elementary propositions applies even if every atomic fact is composed of an infinite number of objects (4.2211). According to M. Marion (1998, 34), Wittgenstein later told Kreisel that in the *Tractatus* he had used the finite as his primary field for thinking about examples and assumed that the basic scheme would apply, without significant alteration, to the infinite case. This is not the same as embracing finitism, and it is (to quote Wittgenstein in Moore 1932–1933 3b:34–35), "not as absurd as it looks." On confusing dots of laziness with infinite sums, compare the criticisms brought to Wittgenstein's attention by Ramsey (1960, 7) in "The Foundations of Mathematics." Note also that one way to look at the completeness theorem is its showing us how to reduce consequence from an infinite system of sentences to consequence from a finite subcollection of those sentences (cf. Gödel [1930] in his 1986, especially p. 119).

67. Compare Wittgenstein 1973a, 182–183. Proops (2001, 387) takes himself to disagree with me on how to read the passage, but I do not see a fundamental difference between our readings on this point.

68. In the handwritten image of this remark one can see that Wittgenstein substituted the softer "contrast" ("*entgegengestellt*": contrast, set beside, compare) for the initially written "in opposition to" (*entgegengesetz*), which he crossed out (thanks to Enzo de Pellegrin for pointing me toward this fact). For more on what is known about the history of the title, see von Wright's "The Origin and Composition of the *Philosophical Investigations*" (in his 1983), Baker and Hacker 1983, Malcolm 1984, 58, and Monk 1990, 457. In Item 128 the remark follows discussion of the individuality of human suffering and incompleteness—the private side, so to speak, of the *Tractatus*. Recall too Ramsey's remark to his mother in writing from Puchberg: "Some of his sentences [in the *Tractatus*] are intentionally ambiguous having an ordinary meaning and a more difficult meaning which he also believes" (Wittgenstein 1973b, 78, 9/20/1923).

Works Cited

Anscombe, G. E. M. 1969. "On the Form of Wittgenstein's Writing." *La Philosophie Contemporaine* 3: 373–378.

Anscombe, G. E. M. 1971. *An Introduction to Wittgenstein's "Tractatus."* Philadelphia: University of Pennsylvania Press.

Baker, G. P., ed. 2003. *The Voices of Wittgenstein: The Vienna Circle.* New York: Routledge.

Baker, G. P., and P. M. S. Hacker. 1980. *Wittgenstein: Understanding and Meaning: An Analytical Commentary on the "Philosophical Investigations,"* vol. 1. Oxford: Basil Blackwell/University of Chicago Press.

Baker, G. P., and P. M. S. Hacker. 1983. *An Analytical Commentary on Wittgenstein's "Philosophical Investigations."* Chicago: University of Chicago Press.

Baldwin, T. E., ed. 2003. *The Cambridge History of Philosophy 1870–1945.* New York: Cambridge University Press.

Biletzki, A. 2003. *(Overinterpreting) Wittgenstein.* Boston: Kluwer Academic.

Block, I., ed. 1981. *Perspectives on the Philosophy of Wittgenstein.* Cambridge, Mass.: MIT Press.

Carey, R. 1999. "Bertrand Russell on Perception and Belief: His Development from 1913–1918." Ph.D. diss. Boston University.

Conant, J. 2000. "Elucidation and Nonsense in Frege and Early Wittgenstein." In Crary and Read 2000.

Conant, J., and C. Diamond. 2004. "On Reading the *Tractatus* Resolutely: Reply to Meredith Williams and Peter Sulliven." In Kölbel and Weiss 2004, 46–99.

Copi, I. M., and R. W. Beard, eds. 1966. *Essays on Wittgenstein's "Tractatus."* New York: Macmillan.

Crary, A., and R. Read, eds. 2000. *The New Wittgenstein.* New York: Routledge.

Diamond, C. 1989. "Rules: Looking in the Right Place." In D. Z. Phillips and P. Winch, eds., *Wittgenstein, Attention to Particulars: Essays in Honour of Rush Rhees*, 12–34. London: Macmillan.

Diamond, C. 1991a. *The Realistic Spirit: Wittgenstein, Philosophy, and the Mind.* Cambridge, Mass.: MIT Press.

Diamond, C. 1991b. "Ethics, Imagination, and the Method of Wittgenstein's *Tractatus*." In R. Heinrich and H. Vetter, eds., *Wiener Reihe: Themen der Philosophie*, 55–90. Vienna and Munich: Oldenbourt. Reprinted in Crary and Read 2000, 149–173.

Diamond, C. 1996. "Wittgenstein, Mathematics, and Ethics: Resisting the Attractions of Realism." In Sluga and Stern 1996, 226–260 (references are to the reprint).

Diamond, C. 1997. "Realism and Resolution." *Journal of Philosophical Research* 22: 75–86.

Diamond, C. 1999. "How Old Are These Bones? Putnam, Wittgenstein, and Verification." *Proceedings of the Aristotelian Society*, suppl. vol. 73: 99–134.

Diamond, C. 2000a. "Does Bismarck Have a Beetle in His Box? The Private Language Argument in the *Tractatus*." In Crary and Read 2000, 262–292.

Diamond, C. 2000b. "Interview: Cora Diamond, 'What Time Is It on the Sun?'" *Harvard Review of Philosophy* 8: 69–81.

Diamond, C. 2002. "Truth before Tarski: After Sluga, after Ricketts, after Geach, after Goldfarb, Hylton, Floyd, and Van Heijenoort." In Reck 2002, 252–283.

Diamond, C. 2004. "Criss-Cross Philosophy." In E. Ammereller and E. Fisher, eds., *Wittgenstein at Work: Method in the "Philosophical Investigations,"* 201–220. New York: Routledge.

Diamond, C. 2005. "Logical Syntax in Wittgenstein's *Tractatus*." *Philosophical Quarterly* 55: 78–88.

Diamond, C. Forthcoming. "Inheriting from Frege: The Work of Reception, as Wittgenstein Did It." In T. Ricketts et al., eds., *The Cambridge Companion to Frege*.

Dreben, B. 1992. "Putnam, Quine—and the Facts." *Philosophical Topics* 20: 293–315.

Dreben, B., and J. Floyd. 1991. "Tautology: How Not to Use a Word." *Synthese* 87: 23–50.

Dreben, B., and J. van Heijenoort. 1986. "Introductory Note to 1929, 1930, and 1930a." In Gödel 1986, 44–59.

Dummett, M. 1959. "Wittgenstein's Philosophy of Mathematics." *Philosophical Review* 63: 324–348. Reprinted in Dummett 1978, 166–185.

Dummett, M. 1978. *Truth and Other Enigmas*. Cambridge, Mass.: Harvard University Press.

Ernst, P. 1900. *Die Grimmschen Märchen,* 3 vols. Munich und Leipzig: Georg Müller.

Fann, K. T., ed. 1969. *Symposium on J. L. Austin*. London: Routledge.

Floyd, J. 1991. "Wittgenstein on 2, 2, 2 . . . On the Opening of *Remarks on the Foundations of Mathematics*." *Synthese* 87: 143–180.

Floyd, J. 1995. "On Saying What You Really Want to Say: Wittgenstein, Gödel, and the Trisection of the Angle." In Hintikka 1995, 373–426.

Floyd, J. 1997. "From Frege to Wittgenstein." Talk delivered at the Boston Colloquium for the Philosophy and History of Science, April 1997.

Floyd, J. 1998. "The Uncaptive Eye: Solipsism in Wittgenstein's *Tractatus*." In Leroy S. Rouner, ed., *Loneliness*, 79–108. Notre Dame, Ind.: University of Notre Dame Press.

Floyd, J. 2000. "Wittgenstein, Mathematics, Philosophy." In Crary and Read 2000, 232–261.

Floyd, J. 2001a. "Number and Ascriptions of Number in Wittgenstein's *Tractatus*." In Floyd and Shieh 2001, 145–191.

Floyd, J. 2001b. "Prose versus Proof: Wittgenstein on Gödel, Tarski, and Truth." *Philosophia Mathematica* 3, vol. 9: 901–928.

Floyd, J. 2002. "Review of J. Klagge, ed., *Wittgenstein: Biography and Philosophy*." *Notre Dame Philosophical Reviews* (June 4, 2002). Http://ndpr.icaap.org/content/current/floyd-klagge.html.

Floyd, J. 2003. "The Fact of Judgment: The Kantian Response to the Humean Condition." In J. Malpas, ed., *From Kant to Davidson: Philosophy and the Idea of the Transcendental*, 22–47. London: Routledge.

Floyd, J. 2005a. "Putnam's 'The Meaning of "Meaning"': Externalism in Historical Context." In Y. Ben Menachem, ed., *Contemporary Philosophy in Focus: Hilary Putnam*, 17–52. Cambridge: Cambridge University Press.

Floyd, J. 2005b. "Wittgenstein on Philosophy of Logic and Mathematics." In S. Shapiro, ed., *Oxford Handbook to the Philosophy of Logic and Mathematics*, 75–128. Oxford: Oxford University Press.

Floyd, J. 2006a. "On the Use and Abuse of Logic in Philosophy: Kant, Frege, and Hintikka on the Verb 'To Be.'" In E. Auxier, ed., *The Philosophy of Jaakko Hintikka*, 137–188. Library of Living Philosophers Series. Chicago: Open Court.

Floyd, J. 2006b. "Homage to Vienna: Feyerabend on Wittgenstein (and Austin and Quine)." In K. R. Fischer and F. Stadler, eds., *Paul Feyerabend (1924–1994): Ein Philosoph aus Wien*, vol. 14, 99–152. Institut Wiener Kreis Publications. New Yord: Springer Verlag.

Floyd, J. Forthcoming. "On Being Surprised: Remarks on the Concept of Surprise in Wittgenstein." In V. Krebs and W. Day, eds., *Seeing Wittgenstein Anew: New Essays on Aspect Seeing*. Cambridge: Cambridge University Press.

Floyd, J., and H. Putnam. 2000. "A Note on Wittgenstein's 'Notorious Paragraph' about the Gödel Theorem." *Journal of Philosophy* 45: 624–632.

Floyd, J., and H. Putnam. 2006. "Bays, Steiner, and Wittgenstein's 'Notorious' Paragraph about the Gödel Theorem." *Journal of Philosophy* 103, 2: 101–110.

Floyd, J., and S. Shieh, eds. 2001. *Future Pasts: The Analytic Tradition in Twentieth-Century Philosophy*. New York: Oxford University Press.

Fogelin, R. 1982. "Wittgenstein's Operator *N*." *Analysis* 42: 124–128.

Frege, G. Forthcoming. "Translation into English of 'Gottlob Frege, Letters to Ludwig Wittgenstein.'" Trans. J. Floyd and B. Dreben. In E. De Pellegrin, ed., *Successor and Friend: Georg Henrik von Wright and Ludwig Wittgenstein*. New York: Springer Verlag. (German version of the letters may be found in Wittgenstein 2004.)

Friedlander, E. 2001. *Signs of Sense: Reading Wittgenstein's "Tractatus."* Cambridge, Mass.: Harvard University Press.

Geach, P. T. 1981. "Wittgenstein's Operator *N*." *Analysis* 41: 168–171.

Gödel, K. 1986. Vol. 1 of *Publications 1929–1936. Kurt Gödel: Collected Works,* ed. S. Feferman et al. New York: Oxford University Press.

Goldfarb, W. 1979. "Logic in the Twenties: The Nature of the Quantifier." *Journal of Symbolic Logic* 44: 351–368.

Goldfarb, W. 1997. "Metaphysics and Nonsense: On Cora Diamond's *The Realistic Spirit.*" *Journal of Philosophical Research* 22: 57–73.

Goldfarb, W. 2000. "Das Überwinden: Anti-Metaphysical Readings of the *Tractatus.*" Unpublished manuscript.

Goldfarb, W. 2001. "Frege's Conception of Logic." In Floyd and Shieh 2001, 25–42.

Goldfarb, W. 2002. "Wittgenstein's Understanding of Frege: The Pre-Tractarian Evidence." In Reck 2002, 185–200.

Goldfarb, W. 2005. "Showing." Unpublished manuscript.

Griffin, J. P. 1997. *Wittgenstein's Logical Atomism.* Bristol: Thoemmes Press.

Hacker, P. M. S. 2001. *Wittgenstein: Connections and Controversies.* New York: Oxford University Press.

Heidegger, M. 1950. *Holzwege.* Frankfurt am Main: V. Klostermann.

Heidegger, M. 2002. *Off the Beaten Track.* Trans. and ed. J. Young and K. Haynes. New York: Cambridge University Press.

Hintikka, J. 1956. "Identity, Variables, and Impredicative Definitions." *Journal of Symbolic Logic* 21: 225–245.

Hintikka, J., ed. 1995. *From Dedekind to Gödel: Essays on the Foundations of Mathematics.* Boston: Kluwer Academic.

Hintikka, J. 2003. "What Does the Wittgensteinian Inexpressible Express?" *Harvard Review of Philosophy* 11: 9–17.

Hintikka, J., and M. B. Hintikka. 1986. *Investigating Wittgenstein.* New York: Blackwell.

Hofman, V. 1998. "Ein Bostoner Streitgespräch über Wittgensteins *Tractatus.*" *Frankfurter Allgemeine Zeitung.* June 10.

Hübscher, P. 1985. *Der Einfluss von Johann Wolfgang Goethe und Paul Ernst auf Ludwig Wittgenstein.* Bern: Peter Lang.

Husserl, E. 1997. *Psychological and Transcendental Phenomenology and the Confrontation with Heidegger.* Ed. T. Sheehan and R. E. Palmer. Dordrecht: Kluwer.

Hylton, P. 1990. *Russell, Idealism, and the Emergence of Analytic Philosophy.* New York: Clarendon Press.

Hylton, P. 2005. *Propositions, Functions, and Analysis: Selected Essays on Russell's Philosophy.* New York: Oxford University Press.

Ishiguro, H. 1969. "Use and Reference of Names." In Winch 1969, 20–50.

Ishiguro, H. 1981. "Wittgenstein and the Theory of Types." In Block 1981, 43–59.

Kang, J. H. 2004. "The Road to the *Tractatus*: A Study of the Development of Wittgenstein's Early Philosophy." Ph.D. diss., Harvard University.

Kang, J. H. 2005. "On the Composition of the *Prototractatus*." *Philosophical Quarterly* 55: 1–20.

Kölbel, M., and B. Weiss, eds. 2004. *Wittgenstein's Lasting Significance.* New York: Routledge.

Kremer, M. 1992. "The Multiplicity of General Propositions." *Noûs* 26: 409–426.

Kremer, M. 1997. "Contextualism and Holism in the Early Wittgenstein: From *Prototractatus* to *Tractatus.*" *Philosophical Topics* 25: 87–120.

Kremer, M. 2001. "The Purpose of Tractarian Nonsense." *Noûs* 35: 39–73.

Kremer, M. 2002a. "Mathematics and Meaning in the *Tractatus*." *Philosophical Investigations* 25: 272–303.

Kremer, M. 2002b. "Review of Ian Proops, *Logic and Language in Wittgenstein's "Tractatus.*" *Philosophical Review* 111: 327–329.

Kremer, M. 2002c. "Review of Eli Friedlander, *Signs of Sense: Reading Wittgenstein's "Tractatus.*" *Philosophical Quarterly* 209: 652–655.

Kremer, M. 2004. "To What Extent Is Solipsism a Truth?" In B. Stocker 2000, 59–84.

Lorentz, P., ed. 1909. *Lessings Philosophie: Denkmäler aus der Zeit des Kampfes zwischen Aufklärung und Humanität in der deutschen Geistesbildung.* Leipzig: Meiner.

Luckhardt, C. G., ed. 1979. *Wittgenstein: Sources and Perspectives.* Ithaca: Cornell University Press.

Majetschak, S. 2005. "Philosophie als Arbeit an sich selbst." Unpublished manuscript.

Malcolm, N. 1983. *Ludwig Wittgenstein: A Memoir.* 2nd ed. New York: Oxford University Press.

Marion, M. 1998. *Wittgenstein, Finitism, and the Foundations of Mathematics.* Oxford: Clarendon Press.

McGinn, M. 1999. "Between Metaphysics and Nonsense: Elucidation in Wittgenstein's *Tractatus*." *Philosophical Quarterly* 49: 491–513.

McGinn, M. 2001. "Saying and Showing and the Continuity of Wittgenstein's Thought." *Harvard Review of Philosophy* 9: 24–36.

McGuinness, B. 1981. "The So-Called Realism of the *Tractatus*." In Block 1981. Reprinted as "The Supposed Realism of the *Tractatus*" in McGuinness 2002, 82–94 (references are to the reprint).

McGuinness, B. 1985. "Language and Reality." *Teoria* 5. Reprinted in McGuinness 2002, 95–102 (references are to the reprint).

McGuinness, B. 1988. *Wittgenstein, A Life: Young Ludwig 1889–1921.* Berkeley: University of California Press.

McGuinness, B. 2002. *Approaches to Wittgenstein: Collected Papers.* New York: Routledge.

Monk, Ray. 1990. *Ludwig Wittgenstein: The Duty of Genius.* New York: Free Press.

Moore, G. E. 1932–1933. Notes of Wittgenstein's Cambridge Lectures. Manuscripts, Cambridge University Archives ADD 8875.

Narboux, J. P. 2005. "Diagramme, Dimensions et Synopsis." In *Théorie-Littérature-Enseignement* 22, *Penser par le diagramme de Gilles Deleuze à Gilles Châtelet*, 115–141. Saint-Denis: Press Universitaires de Vincennes.

Narboux, J. P. Forthcoming. *Dimensions et Paradigms, Wittgenstein et le problème de l'abstraction.* Paris: Vrin Mathesis.

Nordmann, A. 2005. *Wittgenstein's "Tractatus": An Introduction.* New York: Cambridge University Press.

Ostrow, M. B. 2002. *Wittgenstein's "Tractatus": A Dialectical Interpretation.* New York: Cambridge University Press.

Pears, David. 1979. "The Relation between Wittgenstein's Picture Theory of Propositions and Russell's Theories of Judgment." In *Wittgenstein: Sources and Perspectives*, ed. C. G. Luckhardt, 190–212. Ithaca: Cornell University Press.

Pears, D. 1987. *The False Prison.* Vol. 1. Oxford: Clarendon Press.

Pears, D. 1988. *The False Prison.* Vol. 2. Oxford: Clarendon Press.

Potter, M. 2000. *Reason's Nearest Kin: Philosophies of Arithmetic from Kant to Carnap.* New York: Oxford University Press.

Proops, I. 2000. *Logic and Language in Wittgenstein's "Tractatus."* New York: Garland Press.

Proops, I. 2001. "The New Wittgenstein: A Critique." *European Journal of Philosophy* 9: 375–404.

Proops, I. 2002. "The *Tractatus* on Inference and Entailment." In Reck 2002, 283–307.

Proops, I. 2004. "Wittgenstein's Logical Atomism." In *The Stanford Encyclopedia of Philosophy.* Http://plato.stanford.edu/entries/wittgenstein-atomism/.

Quine, W. V. O. 1969. "On Austin's Method." In Fann 1969. Reprinted in Quine 1981, 86–91 (references are to the reprint).

Quine, W. V. O. 1980. *From a Logical Point of View.* 2nd rev. ed. Cambridge, Mass.: Harvard University Press.

Quine, W. V. O. 1981. *Theories and Things.* Cambridge, Mass.: Harvard University Press.

Quine, W. V. O. 1989. *Philosophy of Logic*. 2nd ed. Cambridge, Mass.: Harvard University Press.

Ramsey, F. P. 1923. "Review of *Tractatus*." *Mind* 1923: 32, 128 465–478. Reprinted in Copi and Beard 1966, 9–30.

Ramsey, F. P. 1928. "A Problem of Formal Logic." *Proceedings of the London Mathematical Society*, 2nd ser. 4: 338–384. Reprinted in Ramsey 1960, 82–111.

Ramsey, F. P. 1960. *The Foundations of Mathematics*. Ed. R. B. Braithwaite. Paterson, N.J.: Littlefield, Adams.

Read, R., and R. Deans. 2003. "'Nothing Is Shown': A 'Resolute' Response to Mounce, Emiliani, Koethe, and Vilhauer." *Philosophical Investigations* 26: 239–268.

Reck, E. H., ed. 2002. *From Frege to Wittgenstein: Perspectives on Early Analytic Philosophy*. New York: Oxford University Press.

Rhees, R. 1970a. "'Ontology' and Identity in the *Tractatus* à propos of Black's *Companion*." In Rhees 1970b, 23–36.

Rhees, R., ed. 1970b. *Discussions of Wittgenstein*. New York: Schocken Books.

Rhees, R. 1984. *Recollections of Wittgenstein*. New York: Oxford University Press.

Ricketts, T. 1996. "Pictures, Logic, and the Limits of Sense in Wittgenstein's *Tractatus*." In Sluga and Stern 1996, 55–99.

Ricketts, T. 2002. "Wittgenstein against Frege and Russell." In Reck 2002, 227–252.

Ricketts, T. 2005. "Some Remarks on Logical Segmentation and Higher-Order Quantification in the *Tractatus*." Unpublished manuscript.

Shanker, S. G., ed. 1986. *Ludwig Wittgenstein: Critical Assessments*, vol. 3: *From the "Tractatus" to "Remarks on the Foundations of Mathematics": Wittgenstein on the Philosophy of Mathematics*. London: Croom Helm.

Simons, P. 2003. "Logical Atomism." In Baldwin 2003, 383–390.

Skolem, T. 1970. *Selected Works in Logic*. Ed. J. E. Fenstad. Oslo: Universitetsforlaget.

Sluga, H., and D. G. Stern, eds. 1996. *The Cambridge Companion to Wittgenstein*. Cambridge: Cambridge University Press.

Soames, S. 1983. "Generality, Truth Functions, and Expressive Capacity in the *"Tractatus."* *Philosophical Review* 92: 573–587.

Stocker, B., ed. 2004. *Post-Analytic Tractatus*. Aldershot: Ashgate Publishing.

Sullivan, P. M. 1995. "Wittgenstein on 'The Foundations of Mathematics,' June 1927." *Theoria* 61: 105–142.

Sullivan, P. M. 1996. "The 'Truth' in Solipsism, and Wittgenstein's Rejection of the A Priori." *European Journal of Philosophy* 4: 195–219.

Sullivan, P. M. 2000. "The Totality of Facts." *Proceedings of the Aristotelian Society* 100: 175–192.

Sullivan, P. M. 2002. "On Trying to Be Resolute: A Response to Kremer on the *Tractatus*." *European Journal of Philosophy* 10, 1: 43–78.

Sullivan, P. M. 2003. "Simplicity and Analysis in Early Wittgenstein." *European Journal of Philosophy*: 72–88.

Sullivan, P. M. 2004a. " 'The General Propositional Form Is a Variable' (*Tractatus* 4.53)." *Mind* 113: 43–55.

Sullivan, P. M. 2004b. "What Is the *Tractatus* About?" In Kölbel and Weiss 2004, 32–45.

Sundholm, G. 1990 "The General Form of the Operation in Wittgenstein's *Tractatus*." *Grazer Philosophische Studien* 42: 57–76.

von Wright, G. H. 1983. *Wittgenstein*. Minneapolis: University of Minnesota Press.

Wang, H. 1970. "A Survey of Skolem's Work in Logic." In Skolem 1970, 17–52.

Wehmeier, K. F. 2004. "Wittgensteinian Predicate Logic." *Notre Dame Journal of Formal Logic* 45: 1–11.

Weiner, J. 1990. *Frege in Perspective*. Ithaca, N.Y.: Cornell University Press.

Weiner, J. 2004. *Frege Explained: From Arithmetic to Analytic Philosophy*. Chicago: Open Court.

Whitehead, A. N. 1911. *An Introduction to Mathematics*. New York: H. Holt.

Wiggins, D. 2004. "Wittgenstein on Ethics and the Riddle of Life." *Philosophy* 79: 363–391.

Winch, P. ed. 1969. *Studies in the Philosophy of Wittgenstein*. London: Routledge and Kegan Paul.

Wittgenstein, L. 1922. *Tractatus Logico-Philosophicus*. Trans. C. K. Ogden. New York: Routledge and Kegan Paul. Originally published as "Logische-Philosophische Abhandlung," final chapter. In Ostwald's *Annalen der Naturphilosophie*. A critical edition in German containing the *Prototractatus* is Wittgenstein 1989a.

Wittgenstein, L. 1973a. *Ludwig Wittgenstein and the Vienna Circle*. Shorthand notes recorded by F. Waismann. Ed. B. McGuinness and J. Schulte. Trans. B. McGuiness. Oxford: Blackwell.

Wittgenstein, L. 1973b. *Letters to C. K. Ogden*. Boston, Mass.: Routledge and Kegan Paul.

Wittgenstein, L. 1975. *Philosophical Remarks*. Ed. R. Rhees and R. Hargreaves. Trans. R. White. Chicago: University of Chicago Press.

Wittgenstein, L. 1979. *Notebooks 1914–1916,* 2nd ed. Ed. G. H. von Wright and G. E. M. Anscombe. Trans. G. E. M. Anscombe. Oxford: Blackwell.

Wittgenstein, L. 1989a. *Logische-Philosophische Abhandlung-Tractatus Logico-Philosophicus, Kritische Edition*. Ed. F. McGuinness and J. Schulte. Frankfurt: Suhrkamp Verlag.

Wittgenstein, L. 1993–. *Wiener Ausgabe*. Vols. 1–5. Ed. Michael Nedo. Wien: Springer-Verlag.

Wittgenstein, L. 2000. *The Collected Manuscripts of Ludwig Wittgenstein on Facsimile CD-ROM*. Oxford: Oxford University Press.

Wittgenstein, L. 2001a. *Philosophical Investigations*. 3rd ed. Ed. G. E. M. Anscombe and R. Rhees. Trans. G. E. M. Anscombe. Oxford: Blackwell.

Wittgenstein, L. 2001b. *Philosophische Untersuchungen, Kritisch-genetische Edition*. J. Schulte et al. eds. Frankfurt am Main: Suhrkamp.

Wittgenstein, L. 2003. *Ludwig Wittgenstein: Public and Private Occasions*. Ed. J. C. Klagge and A. Nordmann. New York: Rowman and Littlefield.

Wittgenstein, L. 2004. *Ludwig Wittgenstein: Briefwechsel*. Ed. Monika Seekircher, Brian McGuinness, Anton Unterkircher, Allan Janik, and Walter Methlagl. CD-ROM. Innsbrucker elektronische Ausgabe.

Wittgenstein, L. 2005. *The Big Typescript: TS 213, German-English Scholars' Edition*. Ed. and trans. C. G. Luckhardt and M. A. E. Aue. Malden, Mass.: Blackwell.

4   Wittgenstein and the Real Numbers

Hilary Putnam

Introduction

A number of people have remarked that Wittgenstein has had a significant influence on my own philosophical work. If that is right (and I believe that it is), a lot of the credit (or blame, if you happen to be one of the unfortunate philosophers who "hates" Wittgenstein) should go to Cora Diamond. At Harvard, for many years the most vocal (in every sense of "vocal") advocate of Wittgenstein was my dear friend and long-time debating partner Burton Dreben, and Dreben was a firm advocate of what he called a "Jacobin" (and what the rest of us called an "end of philosophy") reading of *Philosophical Investigations.* I always resisted this view, although I had no doubts about Wittgenstein's genius. In early 1987, Cora Diamond sent me a copy of her "The Face of Necessity," a paper which I still regard as a masterpiece, and one which enabled me to see both what was right and what was wrong in the "Jacobin" interpretation.[1] More significantly, it enabled me to appreciate Wittgenstein's importance as a philosopher.

However, I do not describe myself as a "Wittgensteinian." In part this is because I do not like sects in philosophy, and I do not like treating mere mortals as divinities.[2] But it is also because there are elements in Wittgenstein's writings that I cannot defend. In this essay, I shall talk about some of those latter elements, but it should be kept in mind that if this essay emphasizes what I see as the negative in some of Wittgenstein's thoughts, first, I still regard Wittgenstein's work as some of the most important philosophical work done in the twentieth century, and, second, the thoughts I shall be criticizing are *unpublished* thoughts. *The Remarks on the Foundations of Mathematics*, in particular, are a selection made by others from notebooks Wittgenstein kept for his own use. None of them made their way into *Philosophical Investigations.*[3] I find it appropriate to discuss them here because they clearly relate to both my own and Cora Diamond's philosophical work and interests.

A Troublesome Part of Wittgenstein's *Remarks on the Foundations of Mathematics*

If there is a part of Wittgenstein's oeuvre that I find deeply troublesome, it is the brief part 2 of the revised edition of *Remarks on the Foundations of Mathematics*,[4] henceforth cited simply as "*Part 2.*" As I interpret Wittgenstein's later philosophy, and as the interpreters I most admire, including Cora Diamond, interpret it, a central feature of that philosophy is meant to be the avoidance of "philosophical theses." The marvelous exchanges between the different "voices" in *Philosophical Investigations* bring out the different ways in which one may be led into confusion in thinking about philosophical problems. When this way of dealing with a problem is most successful, one comes to see that the "thesis" that created the problem (if, indeed, it began with someone's enunciating a thesis) is one that does not require a "yes" or "no" answer, but instead requires to be picked apart, disentangled. Yet in *Part 2* one finds Wittgenstein himself enunciating what sound like a number of philosophical theses—in fact, I think they *are* philosophical theses, and, moreover, ones that I strongly reject. In order to explain what I mean by this claim, however, I need to say something about the terminology Wittgenstein uses in *Part 2*.

Part 2 deals with Cantor's diagonal proof, a proof that Wittgenstein regards as containing a confusion, and represents an attempt to remove this supposed confusion. Although elsewhere in *Remarks on the Foundations of Mathematics*, he talks about the "real numbers" and "the number line," in *Part 2* Wittgenstein often finds it convenient (as indeed it is for expository purposes) to consider the diagonal argument, not as applied to infinite series of real numbers, but rather as applied to series of "expansions," by which term he means decimal representations of real numbers, for example, the representation of π as 3.141592. . . . (The relevant difference is not that expansions are infinite series of digits with one decimal point somewhere and real numbers are, according to most philosophers, "abstract entities,"[5] but that some real numbers correspond to two different expansions and not one: for example, the real number three corresponds both to the expansion 3.0000 . . . , with infinitely many zeroes, and to the expansion 2.9999 . . . , with infinitely many nines. Wittgenstein does not take note of this, however.) Applied to expansions, what Cantor's diagonal argument would be taken by mathematicians to show is that the set of all expansions is nondenumerably infinite. What does Wittgenstein say about this?

He tells us, amazingly, that it *means nothing* to say of any class X of numbers that it is nondenumerable! I quote the amazing paragraph in full: "10. It means nothing to say [after one has shown that any given infinite series of expansions can be diagonalized]: '*Therefore* the X numbers are not denumerable.' One might say something like this: I call number concept X nondenumerable if it has been stipulated that, whatever numbers falling under this concept you arrange in a series, the diagonal number is also to fall under that concept."

The argument that comes with §10, and that indeed runs through all of *Part 2*, goes like this: (according to Wittgenstein) the very notion of an *expansion*, that is, of an infinite sequence of digits (with a decimal point somewhere) is an indeterminate notion. We have, indeed, decided that certain "developments" are expansions, for instance the decimal expansion of π, and we can even produce infinite sequences of expansions. And Wittgenstein concedes that, when we produce such a sequence, Cantor's diagonal argument does indeed give us a way of producing something different from all the expansions in the particular sequence (or to use Wittgenstein's terminology, the particular "system") of expansions. But as §10 makes clear, Wittgenstein thinks that it already involves a *stipulation*—it is not fixed in advance—to say that what we get by the diagonal proof is itself an "expansion" in the original sense. For Wittgenstein, the expansions are an *indeterminate class*—we have not fully specified what it would mean to speak of "all expansions."

This does not mean, however, that Wittgenstein wants us to simply *reject* the whole of Cantor's argument. Rather, he wants to separate what he sees as the genuine mathematical content of that argument from what he sees as the confused add-on (the add-on that led Cantor and others into what he saw as the pseudo-Paradise of set theory). The problem is that in deciding what is confused, he imports some rather strange convictions of his own, convictions I want to describe.

In the case of Cantor's proof, it is fairly easy to see what Wittgenstein is saying. What Cantor proved, according to Wittgenstein, is that if you are given a denumerable "system" of real numbers (or, alternatively, expansions), then you can exhibit (assuming we have made the "stipulation" mentioned in §10) a real number or an expansion that is not in the system. But what is misleading, and what should be avoided, is expressing this by saying "*The* real numbers are nondenumerable," or "There are *too many* real numbers to enumerate."

That this is, in fact, what Wittgenstein means is not conjecture on my part. He tells us as much in so many words. In §16, for example, Wittgenstein writes,

That, however, is not to say that the question "Can the set R [the real numbers] be ordered in a series [i.e., enumerated]?" has a clear sense. For this question means e.g. Can one do something with these formations corresponding to the ordering of the cardinal numbers [Wittgenstein means the natural numbers] in a series? Asked, "Can the real numbers be ordered in a series?" the conscientious answer might be "For the time being I can't form any precise idea of that."—"But you can order the roots and the algebraic numbers for example in a series; so you surely understand the expression!"—To put it better, I *have got* certain analogous formations which I call by the common name 'series'. But so far I haven't any certain bridge from these cases to that of 'all real numbers'. Nor have I any general method of trying whether such-and-such a set 'can be ordered in a series'.

Now I am shown the diagonal procedure and told: "Now here you have the proof that this ordering can't be done here." But I can reply: "I don't know—to repeat—what it is that *can't be done* here."

And again:

19. The dangerous, deceptive thing about the idea: "The real numbers cannot be arranged in a series," or again "the . . . set is not denumerable" resides in its making what is a determination, formation, of a concept look like a fact of nature.

Wittgenstein continues:

20. The following sentence sounds sober: "If something is called a series of real numbers, then the expansion given by the diagonal procedure is also called a 'real number', and is moreover said to be different from all members of the series."

And again:

28. Why should we say: the irrational numbers cannot be ordered?—We have a method of upsetting any order.

(In §29):

Cantor's diagonal procedure does not show us an irrational number different from all in the system, but it gives sense to the mathematical proposition that the number so-and-so is different from all those in the system.

(And again):

31. Cantor gives a sense to the expression 'expansion which is different from all the expansions in a system', by *proposing* [my emphasis] that an expansion should be so called when it can be proved that it is diagonally different from the expansions in a system.

32. Thus can be set as a question: find a number whose expansion is different from all those in the system.

It is not just my "interpretation" that in these remarks Wittgenstein is giving a very weak constructive interpretation to the Cantor proof, namely, that it provides a method whereby, for any given "system" of expansions,[6] it is possible to exhibit an expansion—provided we are willing to *stipulate* that the term "expansion" applies to this new object—different from all the expansions in the system; but he is not willing to agree that Cantor showed anything that should be formulated as "the set of all real numbers is nondenumerable." Here is my proof text:

33. It might be said, besides the rational points there are *diverse systems* of irrational points to be found in the number line.

There is no system of irrational numbers—but also no super-system, no 'set of irrational numbers' of higher-order infinity.[7]

There is no system of irrational numbers—but also no super-system, no "set of irrational numbers" of higher-order infinity. This from a philosopher who doesn't put forward philosophical "theses"?!

Stop and think about this remark. Here Wittgenstein has taken one of the central theorems, not just of set theory but of all modern mathematics, namely, that there is a set of all irrational numbers, and that set is nondenumerable, and arrogantly asserted its negation!

Nor is it merely my conjecture that Wittgenstein's reason for saying "there is no set of irrational numbers" (and, a fortiori no set of real numbers[8]) is that the notion of an "expansion" (which he treats as interchangeable with "real number" in *Part 2*) is not "determined." On the contrary, here too the work of the interpreter is done by Wittgenstein himself: "30. Cantor shows that if we have a system of expansions it makes sense to speak of an expansion that is different from them all—but that is not enough to determine the grammar of the word 'expansion.' "[9]

Thus in *Part 2* we have a clear and unmistakable rejection of Cantorian set theory and everything that presupposes it on the part of Wittgenstein—and we have a partial explanation of this attitude, namely, his belief that although the notion of an "expansion" does have meaning in certain contexts (we have many "developments" that we are willing to count as expansions), nevertheless the grammar of the notion "all expansions" (all infinite series of digits) has not been "determined" (and presumably can't be determined in a way that would suit Cantor's purposes). In order to understand *why* Wittgenstein thinks this, however, it is necessary to inquire into Wittgenstein's attitude toward the mathematical notion of infinity. Fortunately, that too is the subject of many of the remarks in *Part 2*.

Wittgenstein's Account of Infinity

What Wittgenstein criticizes, not only in *Part 2*, but throughout the material we have as *Remarks on the Foundations of Mathematics*, is thinking of statements of the form "There are infinitely many _____" as meaning that there is a vast number of _____. His alternative is expressed very simply:

45. To say that a technique is unlimited does *not* mean that it goes on forever without stopping—that it increases immeasurably: but that it lacks the institution of the end, that it is not finished off. As one may say of a sentence that it is not finished off if it has no period. Or of a playing field that it is unlimited when the rules of the game do not prescribe any boundaries—say by means of a line.

It is also interesting to look at §26 and §27 of *Part 2*:

26. We say of a *permission* that it has no end.
27. And it can be said that the permission to play language games with cardinal numbers [integers] has no end. This would be said e.g. to someone to whom we were teaching our language and our language games. So it would again be a grammatical proposition, but of an *entirely* different kind from "25 × 25 = 625." It would however be of great importance if the pupil were, say, inclined to expect a definitive end to this series of language game (perhaps because he had been brought up in a different culture).

That he means these rather strange analogies perfectly seriously is shown by §47 and §48:

47. What is the function of such a proposition as "A fraction has not a next biggest fraction, but a cardinal number has a next biggest cardinal number"? Well, it is as it were a proposition that compares two games. (Like: in draughts pieces jump over one another, but not in chess.)
48. We call something "constructing the next biggest cardinal number" but nothing "constructing the next biggest fraction."

This picture of what it means to talk of infinity in mathematics is utterly inadequate even if we confine our attention to elementary number theory. It is not, after all, just that number theory fails to "stipulate" that we are to say of any number that it is the last number, or that we are to say after counting to any number "We are not allowed to go on." We make the positive assertion—even in intuitionist mathematics—that it is *always possible* to go on. And this is not merely a misleading statement in words,[10] a misleading metastatement that we are accustomed to make, it is an axiom of arithmetic that every number has a successor.

Perhaps Wittgenstein would have taken the same scornful attitude toward Peano's axiomatization of arithmetic that he took toward *Principia Mathematica* and toward set theory; but if so, his position was a radically "eliminationist" one, indeed!

A Brief Summary Up to This Point

To sum up what we have found so far in *Part 2*: Wittgenstein unquestionably makes three flat (and in my view unbelievable) assertions:

1. The notion of an expansion (an infinite series of digits) is indeterminate and requires new stipulations as new techniques for developing such expansions are invented.

2. Because of this indeterminacy, "it means nothing to say '*Therefore* the X numbers are not denumerable.'"

3. To say that a mathematical technique produces an infinite series does not mean that it goes on without stopping. It means simply that "that it lacks the institution of the end, that it is not finished off."

But before attempting to draw any moral from all this, we should look at the closing sections of *Part 2* in which Wittgenstein himself considers saying "there is nothing infinite" in mathematics, and, I think, draws back from saying it:[11]

59. This way of talking: "But when one examines the calculus, there is nothing infinite there" is of course clumsy—but it means; is it really necessary here to conjure up the picture of the infinite (of the enormously big)? And how is this picture connected to the *calculus*? For its connection is not that of the picture | | | | with 4.

60. To act as if one were disappointed to have found nothing infinite in the calculus is of course funny; but not to ask, what is the everyday employment of the word "infinite," which gives it its meaning for us; and what is its connection with these mathematical calculi?

61. Finitism and behaviorism are similar trends. Both say, but surely all we have here is . . . Both deny the existence of something, both with a view to escaping from a confusion.

62. What I am doing is, not to show that calculations are wrong, but to subject the *interest* of calculations to a test. I test e.g. the justification for using the word . . . here. Or really, I keep on urging such an investigation. I show that there is such an investigation, and what it is like to investigate there. Thus I must say, not: "We must not express ourselves like this," or "That is absurd," or "That is uninteresting," but: "Test the justification of this expression in this way." You cannot survey the justification of an expression unless you survey its employment, which you cannot do by looking at some facets of its employment, say a picture attaching to it.

§62 seems to me completely unobjectionable—and when we remember that these are remarks in Wittgenstein's personal notebooks, it is natural to take "Thus I must say, not: 'We must not express ourselves like this,' or 'That is absurd, or 'That is uninteresting,' but: 'Test the justification of this expression in this way.'" as a warning by Wittgenstein *to himself*. Nevertheless, I do not find in the remainder of *Remarks on the Foundations of Mathematics* any indication that Wittgenstein ever gave up his utterly negative attitude toward set theory or his rather simplistic interpretation of such statements as "There are infinitely many natural numbers."

The Continuum in Physics

What Wittgenstein wanted was, not to *change* our use of the word "infinite" in what he was prepared to count as mathematics (or at least as "chapter headings" in mathematics[12]), but rather to understand that use; but as we have just seen his *way* of understanding it is decidedly "minimalist," guided by the analogy he sees between the infinite and the playing field to which no limit has been stipulated. But there is also another line of criticism of set theory running through much of *Remarks on the Foundations of Mathematics*, based on Wittgenstein's conviction that set theory is *useless* in the sense of lacking application. For example, about the proposition that $2_0^\aleph > \aleph_0$, he writes (in §35): "In what practice is this proposition anchored? It is for the time being a piece of mathematical architecture which hangs in the air, and looks as if it were, let us say, an architrave, but not supported by anything and supporting nothing." And he follows this with: "36. Certain considerations may lead us to say that 10^{10} souls fit into a cubic centimeter. But why do we nevertheless not say it? Because it is of no use. Because, while it does conjure up a picture, the picture is one with which we cannot go on to do anything."

A similar attitude seems to underlie his well-known pooh-poohing of the concern of logicians like Frege and Russell with achieving a formalization of mathematics that is free of contradictions. Wittgenstein expresses the attitude that, as long as contradictions didn't keep cropping up all over the place, mathematics could go on perfectly well even if some arguments did lead to contradictions. We could, so to speak, just avoid those arguments.[13] The search for rigorous and consistent foundations for mathematics is, thus, also seen by Wittgenstein as useless.

But this is simply ignorance on Wittgenstein's part. The fact is that the confusions about the correct formulation of the notion of a set in nineteenth-century mathematics exactly parallel, and are intimately related to, confusions about the correct formulation of the notion of a function, and those confusions did not only effect pure mathematics, they interfered with the resolutions of difficulties having to do with the understanding of certain physical systems. Documenting this in detail, however, goes beyond the scope of the present essay.[14]

It is even easier to show that the full importance of the investigations Wittgenstein pooh-poohed has become even clearer since his death. For example, in appendix 3 to part 1, just before the *Part 2* that we have been discussing, Wittgenstein writes: "19. You say: '. . . so P [the Gödelian proposition] is true and unprovable.' That presumably means: 'Therefore P.' That is all right with me—but for what purpose do you write down this 'assertion'? (It is as if someone has extracted from certain principles about natural forms and architectural style the idea that on Mount Everest, where no one can live, there belongs a châlet in the Baroque style. And how could you make the truth of your assertion plausible to me, since you can make no use of it except to do these bits of legerdemain."

This looks like an argument against taking Gödel's work seriously on the ground that it has no use except to do bits of "legerdemain." In fact, *precisely* the argument that Gödel used to prove his theorems immediately generalizes to yield the major Fixed Point Theorems of recursion, theorems that have numerous applications in the whole domain of today's computer science. Moreover, Church's Theorem[15] is easy to prove once one has appreciated the techniques Gödel invented; and my own work in logic and number theory (with Martin Davis, Julia Robinson, and Yuri Matyasevich[16]) involved—as is well known—showing that the same technique can be extended to show that there is no decision method for Diophantine equations (Hilbert's Tenth Problem). The very arguments in which Wittgenstein saw only useless "legerdemain" are in fact the foundation of a whole new science.

In the rest of this essay, however, I shall just focus on one question: "Is the assertion that there is a set of all real numbers" simply a useless and misleading picture?" For this claim is, after all, one that Wittgenstein clearly makes in *Part 2* (more precisely, he asserts that there is no set of all irrational numbers, and he also puts "real number" in inverted commas in almost all the passages I quoted above). To put it another way, is the idea that there is a set of all real numbers just a piece of useless "legerdemain"?

In the present section, I shall move away from Wittgenstein's text and try to explain from my own "scientific realist" point of view[17] why it would be very wrong to say this.

So far I have said that Wittgenstein clearly rejects set theory, including the idea that there is such a thing as a set of all real numbers and the theory of infinite cardinals. I could have added that in part 5 of *Remarks on the Foundations of Mathematics*, he reinterprets the theory of Dedekind cuts (the heart of the theory of functions of a real variable!) in the same way: he says that "The idea of a 'cut' . . . is a dangerous illustration," and the idea that we understand the idea of an arbitrary Dedekind cut (i.e., an arbitrary real number) is called "a frightfully confusing picture." He treats it with the same scorn that he treated the notion of a "set of all irrational numbers": "37. The misleading thing about Dedekind's conception is the idea that the numbers are there spread out on the number line. They may be known or not; that does not matter. And in this way all that one needs to do is cut or divide into classes and one has dealt with them all."

Now, it is a fact about mathematical physics, and one of which Wittgenstein was surely aware, that ever since Descartes's invention of analytic geometry, which is the beginning of mathematical physics as we now know it, the notion of a spatial point—and today the notion of a space-time point—is dependent on the notion of a real number. In physics we fix, that is, the logic of talk about points precisely by making the Cartesian assumption that every point in space can be associated with a triple of real numbers. Thus the consequences for our understanding of physics of the view that we do not have a determinate notion of a real number are immediate and large. If Wittgenstein was right, then we lack a determinate notion of a point in space, as that notion is used in mathematical physics. In addition to saying, "[T]here is not a 'set of irrational numbers,'" Wittgenstein might as well have said, "There is no 'set of all points in space.'" To understand physics as a scientific realist does—that is, to understand it *without philosophical "reinterpretation"*—is dangerous naïveté, on such a view.

In contemporary physics, the notion of a particle has lost the fundamental role that it had in atomistic physics. That role has been taken over by the notion of a field (or, in quantum mechanics, by the notion of a quantized field). But a field—for example, the electromagnetic field, or the gravitational field—is something that has a magnitude that can be measured by a real number (or by an n-tuple of real numbers) *at each point in space* (or each point in a certain region of space). If the notion of "any point in space" is indeterminate and the notion of a real number is indeterminate,[18] then the notion of a field must suffer a corresponding indeterminacy.

Here it might be argued that the idea that there are infinitely many points in space is "only an idealization." "Given that we use just the theory of the real numbers that Wittgenstein is criticizing to do mathematical physics," it might be said, "it is not surprising that we use just that idealization. But we must not be misled by what is only a picture."

To this I would reply that, while it may of course *turn out*, as a matter of physical fact, that space is discrete, or that space-time is discrete, or that quantum mechanics can be done with discrete mathematics—perhaps because there are minimal volumes of space-time that can carry information, as postulated by some (speculative) theories of quantum gravity—these are clearly questions to be decided by *empirical science*. The best physical theories we have today, and the best physical theories we have had ever since the time of Newton and Descartes, are ones that postulate that space and time are continua in precisely the sense Wittgenstein finds unclear. If that view has to be abandoned, it should be for physical, not for "Wittgensteinian," reasons. The choice is a choice among *meaningful* physical pictures, at least by any ordinary scientific standard of meaningfulness. The fact that Wittgenstein questions continuum mathe-matics (which is to say, virtually *everything* that mathematicians know as twentieth—and now twenty-first—century mathematics) on *philosophical* grounds, as he does in these parts of *Remarks on the Foundations of Mathematics*, shows, to my mind, that Wittgenstein was led fundamentally astray. (Indeed, I suspect that if Wittgenstein had written something called *Remarks on the Foundations of Physics*, it would, like the *Remarks on the Foundations of Mathematics*, contain much that is fascinating, but that it would also, in the end, amount to an attack on much that is essential to the science.)

Why Wittgenstein Went Astray

In the appendix to my "Was Wittgenstein *Really* an Antirealist about Mathematics?"[19] I wrote:

In the preceding essay, I said that I do not believe that Wittgenstein's *Remarks on the Foundations of Mathematics* spring from an antirealist philosophy. That doesn't mean that there are no prob-lems with Wittgenstein's remarks, and I understand perfectly well why some of them would seem to invite an antirealist reading. In particular, it does seem that Wittgenstein thought, when he wrote the material that the editors have collected under this title, that a mathematical proposi-tion cannot be true unless we can decide that it is true on the basis of a proof or calculation of some kind.[20] Not only is this quite explicit in his 1937 remarks about the Gödel theorem,[21] but the view appears as late as the 1944 remark that even God's *omniscience* cannot decide whether people would have reached "777" in the decimal expansion of π "after the end of the world."[22] How can such a view *not* spring from antirealism?

—And I answered my own question thus:

What I want to say, in brief, is that the inadequacies that I find in *some* (by no means all) of Wittgenstein's *Remarks on the Foundations of Mathematics* represent a peculiar combination of genuine insight with an inadequate knowledge of actual mathematical practice and of sciences which depend on mathematical practice, in particular mathematical physics.

This is still my diagnosis today. But there is something more we can learn about Wittgenstein as a philosopher if we look, in addition, at the "Lectures on Aesthetics."[23] What I have in mind is this. Very often both the critics and the admirers of the later Wittgenstein share the view that Wittgenstein is only concerned to clear up confusions (or better: to begin to show us how to clear up confusions, or to show us how to begin to clear up confusions) in *philosophy*. But in the "Lectures on Aesthetics" as well as in the material I have discussed, Wittgenstein makes it quite clear that he is interested—passionately interested—in clearing up confusions in science—or in what we are inclined to think about science. Unfortunately, as the preceding discussion illustrates, much of what Wittgenstein mistakenly regards as just misleading pictures is actually good and important science. Nevertheless, the fact that Wittgenstein had these larger ambitions for his philosophy should lay to rest the idea that he is just "an end of philosophy" philosopher. The philosophical investigation of conceptual problems connected to science (and not only to science![24]) is enormously important. But I believe that Wittgenstein failed to see that it requires a much better knowledge of science, and much more *respect* for science, than he possessed.[25] Here, for once, the philosopher who famously said "Take your time" failed to take his time.

Notes

1. "The Face of Necessity" is collected as chapter 9 of Diamond's *The Realistic Spirit*. I discuss the importance of the insights in this paper in my third Dewey Lecture, collected in *The Threefold Cord: Mind, Body, and World*.

2. For similar reasons, although I am often described as a "pragmatist" by other philosophers, I do not (not often, anyway) describe myself as one.

3. The "Editors' Preface to the Revised Edition" of *Ludwig Wittgenstein, Remarks on the Foundations of Mathematics* tells us (p. 30) that "It must have been Wittgenstein's intention to attach appendices on Cantor's theory of infinity and on Russell's logic, as well as the appendix on Gödel's theorem ... to *Philosophical Investigations*." However, it also tells us (p. 29) that "Wittgenstein did not return to this subject matter in the last years of his life."

4. In the 1956 edition, this material was in (what was then) appendix 2 of part 1. The present part 2 includes a few remarks that were left out of the 1956 edition, and, in addition, "the arrangement of sentences and paragraphs into numbered Remarks corresponds to the original text (which was not wholly the case in the 1956 edition)." (The "Editors' Preface to the Revised Edition," p. 31). The numbers of the remarks are, therefore, different from those in the 1956 edition, as is the order of some of the remarks.

5. For a criticism of this "ontological" way of talking about numbers as "entities," see part 1 of my *Ethics without Ontology*. Here, I expect, Wittgenstein and I are in agreement, but my reasons are not his.

6. By a "system" Wittgenstein seems to mean, roughly, any recursive series of expansions—however, if that is what he meant, Wittgenstein's idea that we have to keep extending the notion of what counts as an "expansion" or as a "development" would seem to indicate that he was unaware of Church's Thesis.

7. In §14, Wittgenstein seems to identify irrational numbers with certain methods of calculation, and the assertion that the irrational numbers are nondenumerable, with the assertion that "these methods of calculation" cannot be ordered in a series. And he adds in a footnote: "And here the meaning of 'these' just gets vague."

8. In any case, the denial of the existence of a set of all real numbers and the denial of a set of all irrational numbers, along with his criticism of the notion of a Dedekind cut (discussed below), are equally rejections of the heart of what is today considered the theory of functions of real and complex variables.

9. See also §14 (quoted in note 7); §20 "If something is called a series of real numbers. . . ."; §22 "One pretends to compare the 'set' of real numbers. . . . ; §31 "Cantor gives a sense to the expression 'expansion which is different from all the expansions in a system. . . .'"

10. In §55, Wittgenstein writes "If someone says I have proved the proposition that we can order pairs of numbers [positive integers] in a series, it should be answered that this is not a mathematical proposition, since one doesn't calculate with the words 'we', 'can', 'the', 'pairs of numbers', etc. The proposition 'one can . . .' is rather a mere approximate description of the technique one is teaching, say a not unsuitable title, a heading to this chapter, But a title with which it is not possible to calculate." Wittgenstein does not realize—or does not care—that mathematics is not simply calculation, and that what he calls "not a mathematical proposition" is, on the contrary, a paradigmatic mathematical proposition.

11. That talk of the infinite in mathematics does not have to be taken to mean that mathematics literally deals with a Platonic realm of "abstract objects" that is enormously big is something with which I agree. See chapter 3 of my *Ethics Without Ontology*. But §45, that I quoted earlier, disappoints us by making it seem as if comparison of the idea that there are infinitely many numbers with the fact that no boundary has been prescribed for the playing field were sufficient to show this.

12. Recall (see n. 10) that the theorem that the ordered pairs of integers are denumerable is not "mathematics" in Wittgenstein's view (but only a "chapter heading"), although the particular recursion by which we enumerate them (Wittgenstein gives one) is a "calculation," and hence counts as mathematics.

13. See, for example, §11 and §12 of appendix 3 to part 1; and §78 and §80 of part 3.

14. I am indebted to Mark Wilson for the following examples. One of the great crises in physical theory arose because Riemann and Kelvin (in a physical context) assumed that a set of decreasing solutions for, for example, how soap would attach to a wire rim would assume a lower bound position of least energy with suitable regularity (Riemann called this assumption the Dirichlet Principle), but Weierstrass showed some counterexamples, provoking a famous crisis in the mathematics of the time. And Cantor's work arose directly out of studying the accumulation points of sequences like this. The notion of accumulation points of sequences itself is clearly set-theoretic in character, and the existence conditions for differential equations are entangled with set-theoretic questions (and also with the general question of measure). Wittgenstein may have been misled by Hardy and Littlewood's view that the questions of pure mathematics they worked on are "useless" (and they prided themselves on this uselessness). But they turned out to be very wrong!

15. Church's Theorem is that there is no decision method for quantification theory.

16. Martin Davis, Hilary Putnam, and Julia Robinson, "The Decision Problem for Exponential Diophantine Equations"; Yuri Matyasevich, "Enumerable Sets Are Diophantine."

17. By "scientific realism" I mean just what I meant in "Introduction: Science as Approximation to Truth," pp. vii–xiv of my *Mathematics, Matter, and Method, Philosophical Papers*, vol. 1. In particular, a scientific realist (in my sense) counts mathematics as a central part of science, and she or he rejects the idea that any significant part of science needs justification from philosophy.

18. It is true that Wittgenstein does not use the word "indeterminate." But he does say (§30) that we have not "determined" whether the result of Cantor's diagonalization is an "expansion." And his denial that there is a "set of irrational numbers" is based on the idea (§10) that we have to "stipulate" whether an expansion arrived at by the diagonal process applied to a series ("system") of real numbers is also a "real number." It is clear that he doesn't think that just this one "stipulation" is needed, and then we can speak of a "set of irrational numbers"; what he thinks is that there is no surveyable totality of "developments," and hence the notion of a real number may need an indefinite number of future "stipulations." (His view that the intentional notion of a development is prior to the extensional notion of a cut also plays a role here, as do his discussions with Ramsey over whether logic is to be understood intensionally or extensionally, but these matters must be left for another occasion.)

19. In Timothy G. McCarthy and Sean C. Stidd, *Wittgenstein in America*.

20. But see n. 1 of "Was Wittgenstein *Really* an Antirealist about Mathematics," in which I contrast what Wittgenstein published on this question—§516 of the *Investigations*—with the unpublished material collected as *Remarks on the Foundations of Mathematics*.

21. What I had in mind here was §§6–8 of appendix 3 to part 1 of *Remarks on the Foundations of Mathematics*. However, now I am no longer convinced that these remarks should be read in this way. The equation of truth in Russell's system with provability in Russell's system does not tell us much about Wittgenstein's attitude toward truth in mathematics; Russell's system is full of set theory, which Wittgenstein did not think was mathematics.

22. *Remarks on the Foundations of Mathematics*, part 5, §34.

23. These are collected in Ludwig Wittgenstein, *Lectures and Conversations on Aesthetics, Psychology, and Religious Belief*.

24. Wittgenstein's famous remark to Norman Malcolm, criticizing the latter for talking about "national character," indicates that our everyday life, and the way we talk about it, is something he wanted to teach us to criticize as well. In *Ludwig Wittgenstein: A Memoir*, 39, Malcolm quotes a letter from Wittgenstein in which Wittgenstein writes, "You & I were walking along the river towards the railway bridge and we had a heated discussion in which you made a remark about 'national character' that shocked me by its primitiveness. I then thought: what is the use of studying philosophy if all that it does for you is enable you to talk with some plausibility about some abstruse questions of logic, etc., & if it does not improve your thinking about the important questions of everyday life."

25. In *Lectures and Conversations on Aesthetics, Psychology, and Religious Belief*, §36 (p. 27), Wittgenstein's auditors record him as saying: "Jeans has written a book called *The Mysterious Universe* and I loathe it and call it misleading. Take the title. This alone I would call misleading. . . . I might say the title The Mysterious Universe includes a kind of idol worship, the idol being Science and the Scientist." Apparently Wittgenstein so feared Science Worship—which I agree is a bad thing—that he felt he had to debunk the idea that the universe is mysterious. But it is! Immediately after this remark he adverts again to Cantor's proofs, which he had discussed with Ursell, and he says "it has no charm for me. I loathe it," (the same verb he used in connection with The Mysterious Universe), and goes on to say: "38. Cf. Cantor wrote how marvelous it was that the mathematician could in his imagination transcend all limits. 39. I would do my utmost to show it is this charm that makes one do it. Being Mathematics or Physics it looks incontrovertible and this gives it a still greater charm. If we explain the surroundings of the expression we see that the thing could have been expressed in an entirely different way. I can put it in a way in which it will lose its charm for a great number of people and certainly will lose its charm for me." These lectures are from the same period as *Part 2*, and these remarks illustrate how important attacking Cantorian set theory was for Wittgenstein at that time (and later, apparently, if he really planned to add the material in *Part 2* as an appendix to *Philosophical Investigations*).

Works Cited

Davis, Martin, Hilary Putnam, and Julia Robinson. "The Decision Problem for Exponential Diophantine Equations." *Annals of Mathematics* 74, no. 3 (1961): 425–436.

Diamond, Cora. *The Realistic Spirit*. Cambridge, Mass.: MIT Press, 1991.

Malcolm, Norman. *Ludwig Wittgenstein: A Memoir*. Oxford: Oxford University Press, 1958.

Matyasevich, Yuri. "Enumerable Sets Are Diophantine." *Soviet Mathematics Doklady* 11, no. 2 (1970).

McCarthy, Timothy, and Sean C. Stidd, eds. *Wittgenstein in America*. Oxford: Clarendon Press, 2001.

Putnam, Hilary. *Philosophical Papers*, vol. 1: *Mathematics, Matter, and, Method*. Cambridge: Cambridge University Press, 1975.

Putnam, Hilary. *The Threefold Cord: Mind, Body, and World*. New York: Columbia University Press, 2000.

Putnam, Hilary. *Ethics without Ontology*. Cambridge, Mass.: Harvard University Press, 2004.

von Wright, G. H., R. Rhees, and G. E. M. Anscombe. "Editors' Preface to the Revised Edition." In *Ludwig Wittgenstein: Remarks on the Foundations of Mathematics*. Ed. G. H. von Wright, R. Rhees, and G. E. M. Anscombe. Cambridge, Mass.: MIT Press, 1991.

Wittgenstein, Ludwig. *Lectures and Conversations on Aesthetics, Psychology, and Religious Belief.* Ed. Cyril Barrett. Berkeley and Los Angeles: University of California Press, 1966.

Wittgenstein, Ludwig. *Remarks on the Foundations of Mathematics,* revised edition. Ed. G. H. von Wright, R. Rhees, and G. E. M. Anscombe. Trans. G. E. M. Anscombe. Cambridge, Mass.: MIT Press, 1978.

Wittgenstein, Ludwig. *Philosophical Investigations*, 3rd ed. Trans. G. E. M. Anscombe. Oxford: Blackwell, 2001.

5　Holism and Animal Minds

David H. Finkelstein

1

It's not unusual for influential philosophers to make statements about the minds of nonlinguistic creatures that to a nonphilosopher would seem not merely implausible, but plainly and obviously false. For example, in his *Philosophy and the Mirror of Nature*, Richard Rorty (1979, 187) defends the claim "that knowledge, awareness, concepts, . . . all descend on the shoulders of the bright child somewhere around the age of four, without having existed in even the most primitive form hitherto." According to Rorty, a creature without language—whether human or nonhuman—is not aware of *anything*, and, contrary to what you might imagine when he climbs into bed with you each night, your dog has never once even noticed you.

In arguing for this thesis, Rorty takes himself to be following the lead of Wilfrid Sellars. He quotes approvingly a passage from "Empiricism and the Philosophy of Mind" in which Sellars (1997, 63) describes his own position as one "according to which *all* awareness of *sorts, resemblances, facts*, etc., in short all awareness of abstract entities—indeed, all awareness even of particulars—is a linguistic affair." According to Rorty, Sellars finds an innocent way to allow that brutes may be said to enjoy a *kind* of awareness. As Rorty (1979, 182) reads him, Sellars distinguishes "between aware-ness-as-discriminative behavior and awareness as . . . being 'in the logical space of reasons, of justifying what one says.'" He goes on: "Awareness in the first sense is manifested by rats and amoebas and computers; it is simply reliable signaling. Aware-ness in the second sense is manifested only by beings whose behavior we construe as the utterance of sentences with the intention of justifying the utterance of other sentences" (ibid., 182). According to Rorty's Sellars—and Rorty himself—we can, if we like, speak of your dog's becoming "aware" of you. But this kind of "awareness" (it positively cries out for scare quotes) comes to nothing more than the "awareness" that a thermostat has of the ambient temperature.[1] Thus, while we may choose to use the

word "aware" where all that's at issue is reliable signaling, we should not imagine anything like a continuum of kinds of awareness, with the awareness enjoyed by a dog
or a young child lying substantially closer to our sort of awareness than that exhibited by thermostats and waffle irons. We adult humans are conceptually cognizant of
objects and states of affairs; dogs and two-year-old children merely respond differentially to stimuli in their environments.

  Like Rorty, Donald Davidson holds strikingly skeptical views about the minds of
brutes. In his "Rational Animals," he quotes the following from a paper by Norman
Malcolm:

Suppose our dog is chasing the neighbor's cat. The latter runs full tilt toward the oak tree, but
suddenly swerves at the last moment and disappears up a nearby maple. The dog doesn't see this
maneuver and on arriving at the oak tree he rears up on his hind feet, paws at the trunk as if
trying to scale it, and barks excitely into the branches above. We who observe this whole episode
from a window say, "He thinks the cat went up that oak tree." (Malcolm 1977, 49; quoted on
p. 97 of Davidson 2001a)

Davidson argues that we who say that our dog "thinks the cat went up that oak tree"
are mistaken, for a creature without language can have no beliefs; it thinks nothing.
His commitment to this claim should be understood as connected to his holism concerning propositional attitudes. Throughout his career, Davidson argues that any belief
owes its content to its location in a rich, open-ended network of (among other things)
beliefs. Now, why can't your dog share your opinion that a cat has run up an oak tree?
Davidson has much to say in reply to this question, some of which we'll examine
later, but the following short quotation suggests why it is that, for him, holism about
beliefs leads to skepticism about attributing any to brutes:

[C]an the dog believe of an object that it is a tree? This would seem impossible unless we suppose
the dog has many general beliefs about trees: that they are growing things, that they have leaves
or needles, that they burn. There is no fixed list of things someone with the concept of a tree
must believe, but without many general beliefs, there would be no reason to identify a belief as
a belief about a tree, much less an oak tree. Similar considerations apply to the dog's supposed
thinking about the cat. (Davidson 2001a, 98)

In order to believe that something is a tree, a creature must know what a tree *is*; it
must have the *concept* of a tree. And in order to have the concept of a tree, it must
believe quite a number of things about trees, which in turn entails that it have quite
a number of other concepts (perhaps *leaf, needle, burning, growth, plant, ground*, and
wood) whose acquisition requires still *more* beliefs and *more* concepts. In this vein,
Sellars argues that the concept of something's *looking green* presupposes not only the

concept of something's *being green*, but also concepts as sophisticated as *standard lighting conditions*, and he goes on to remark that "there is an important sense in which one has *no* concept pertaining to the observable properties of physical objects in Space and Time unless one has all of them" (Sellars 1997, 44–45).[2]

Thus, a commitment to holism about beliefs and concepts might lead one to conclude that in order for an ascription that takes the form, "He thinks the cat went up that oak tree," to be true of some creature, the creature in question would need to have a conceptual repertoire about as rich as yours and mine. Given this conclusion, if I were to say of Malcolm's dog, "He thinks the cat went up that oak tree," I would be guilty of an anthropomorphic mistake.

* * *

Wittgenstein would appear to be *some* kind of holist about quite a range of things. In his late writings, he seems always to be pointing out how one thing or another—an expectation, a meaningful word, a coronation, an ostensive definition—is what it is only thanks to the "pattern of life" of which it is a part. I have in mind remarks such as the following:

Could someone have a feeling of ardent love or hope for the space of one second—*no matter what* preceded or followed this second?——What is happening now has significance—in these surroundings. The surroundings give it its importance. (Wittgenstein 1953, §583)

"Grief" describes a pattern which recurs, with different variations, in the weave of our life. If a man's bodily expression of sorrow and of joy alternated, say with the ticking of a clock, here we should not have the characteristic formation of the pattern of sorrow or of the pattern of joy. (Ibid., p. 174)

When would we say of a child, for instance, that it is pretending? What all must it be able to do for us to say that?

Only when there is a relatively complicated pattern of life do we speak of pretence. (Wittgenstein 1992, p. 40)

I can't see that Davidson or Rorty would find anything in these passages to complain about. Indeed, it's hard not to view *their* commitments to holism as essentially post-Wittgensteinian. Yet Part II of the *Investigations* begins as follows:

One can imagine an animal angry, frightened, unhappy, happy, startled. But hopeful? And why not?

A dog believes his master is at the door. But can he also believe his master will come the day after tomorrow? (Wittgenstein 1953, p. 174)

Notice what we *don't* find here. We don't find Wittgenstein saying anything like this: "Since beliefs are intelligible only as situated in the weave of *our* life, it's a mistake to think of dogs as having any." Or like this: "While it's not *wrong* to describe a dog as 'believing' that his master is at the door, this way of speaking involves a sort of courtesy that we extend to some selective responders and not others—to dogs and horses but not to thermostats and burglar alarms."[3] Wittgenstein's holism doesn't lead him to the jarring conclusions about animals that we find in Rorty's and Davidson's writings. To understand why this is, we need to come to grips with (what turn out to be) profound differences between Wittgenstein's holism and the sorts of holism that tend to be defended (or attacked) by more contemporary philosophers such as Davidson and Rorty. One of my aims in this essay is to help bring these differences into view.

2

Let's bracket Wittgenstein's holism for the moment; we'll return to it soon enough. Before Wittgenstein was introduced into the discussion, we saw the beginnings of an argument that leads from a commitment to holism about beliefs to what we might regard as a skeptical conclusion—that brutes don't have any beliefs. Such arguments might be, and sometimes are, understood as giving us a reason to *reject* holism about beliefs. Thus, someone might say: "What these arguments really show, or start to show, is *not* that brutes lack beliefs, but that mental holism has absurd consequences. Not only is the holist unable to understand how my dog and I can share a belief (e.g., that some cat is up some tree); the holist can't make sense even of my sharing a belief with *you* unless you share *all* of my beliefs." This complaint about mental holism—that it renders the very notion of agreement between believers problematic—has been articulated by quite a number of philosophers. The most sophisticated version of the argument of which I'm aware is due to Jerry Fodor and Ernest Lepore.

At the start of their *Holism: A Shopper's Guide*, Fodor and Lepore (1992, 2) define a holistic property as one such that if one thing has it, then many things must.[4] In their opening chapter, they present an argument that, in one form or another, seems to show that a variety of properties cannot be holistic. Fodor and Lepore set out several versions of the argument. The version most relevant for our purposes goes as follows. They define T* as the property "a belief has iff it expresses a proposition that is the content of some belief of mine" (ibid., 13). Let the word "mine" in this definition index me (not you); then, a token belief of yours may be said have the property T* if and only if it has the same content as some token belief of mine. In other words, if you and I may rightly be said to *share* a belief, then some belief of *yours* has the property T*. Now Fodor and Lepore (1992, 14) ask us to suppose that this property is holistic:

Then, since you and I surely have widely different belief systems (think of all the things you know that I don't) and since, by definition, a property is holistic only if nothing has it unless many other things do, it may well turn out that none of your thoughts has the property [T*]. It would follow that not more than one of us ever has thoughts about color or thoughts about red.

The point could be put as follows: According to, say, the kind of holism that Sellars or Davidson defends, you cannot share only one belief with me; in order to share one, you must share many. But, obviously, you and I don't share *all* our beliefs; we have "widely different belief systems." So, given the truth of this sort of holism, what ensures that we share *enough* beliefs for us to share even one?

It is important that we appreciate just what kind of worry is being expressed here. This requires that we not be puzzled by the fact that, in the first sentence of the block quotation above, Fodor and Lepore use the expression "it may well turn out." Their point is not that we should reject holism about belief content because it *entails* that you and I cannot share any beliefs. (It doesn't—or, anyway, it needn't—entail any such thing.)[5] Nor is the point that the truth of this sort of holism would make it too *difficult* for you and me to share a belief:

The problem isn't, notice, that if holism is true, then the conditions for belief identity [i.e., the conditions that would have to be met in order for some belief of yours and some belief of mine to be of the same semantic type—to have the same content] are hard to meet; it's that, if holism is true, then the notion of "tokens of the same type of belief" is defined *only* for the case in which *every* belief is shared. Holism provides no notion of belief-type identity that is defined for any other case and no hint of how to construct one. (Ibid., 19)

A holist about belief content will likely maintain that in order for you to share my belief that, say, cardinals are red, you must share my concept *red*, which in turn entails that you share many beliefs with me having to do with, among other things, colors. But precisely *which* beliefs must you and I share in order for us to share the concept *red*? Fodor and Lepore (1992, 21) ask, "[D]oes believing that Mars is red count more or less for having the concept *red* than believing that tomatoes are?"[6] They complain that holism offers no "principled answer" (ibid., 21) to such a question. Holism yields no definition of belief-type identity, so no real account of what it takes for two people to share a belief (except in the event that two people share *all* their beliefs). Thus, for all that the holist says, it *could* be—"it may well turn out"—that you and I don't (can't) share a single belief because our networks of beliefs are insufficiently alike. As I am reading Fodor and Lepore, they think that holism about belief content should be rejected because it ought to rule this out as a possibility, and it fails to.

Notice that this objection to holism presupposes a particular picture of what an account of belief content ought to accomplish.[7] If one wanted to foreground this picture more than Fodor and Lepore do, one might say something like the following: "Except perhaps when we are doing philosophy, we take it for granted that people often agree about things—that you and I, for example, can, and do, share some beliefs. To say that we take this for granted is not to deny that on some occasion when you and I appear to agree, reasonable doubts may arise about whether we do in fact agree. But we take ourselves to have procedures for determining—in many cases, at least— whether people agree or disagree, and we simply don't question the truism that people do often manage to share beliefs. Now, a satisfactory philosophical account of belief content would, as it were, underwrite or vindicate this truism by specifying—or, anyway, putting us in a position to specify—just what's involved in two people's having the same belief. ('[T]he notion of "tokens of the same type of belief"' should be 'defined' [ibid., 19].) In other words, a satisfactory account of belief content would be, or would yield, an account of *shared* belief. As such, it would enable us to see that the conditions that must be met in order for two people to share a belief are, in fact, often met."

3

We might extract from the discussion thus far two claims about mental holism that merit further consideration. Davidson and Rorty would endorse the first claim. Fodor and Lepore assume the second:

(1)   Holism about beliefs commits one to—or, anyway, suggests compelling reasons for—rejecting the idea that nonlinguistic animals have beliefs.

(2)   A satisfactory philosophical account of belief content would yield an account of shared belief. Thus a satisfactory mental holism would underwrite or vindicate a pair of truisms—that we often agree in our beliefs, and that we are, by and large, correct in our assessments of when we agree.

Either of these claims could be embraced by either a mental holist or an opponent of holism. Someone might accept (1) and count it as a reason for rejecting mental holism. And a holist might grant (2) to Fodor and Lepore, while maintaining (against them) that a satisfactory mental holism has been, or could be, set out.[8]

Here's where I mean to go in the remainder of this essay. In what immediately follows, I'll discuss a lesson that Cora Diamond draws from Wittgenstein. We'll see that if we accept this lesson, then we cannot, with Fodor and Lepore, assume claim (2). Indeed, I'll argue, in §4, that Wittgenstein's continual calls to think about things (e.g., mental states) holistically are meant to help us get over the attraction we feel to assumptions of this sort. In §5, I'll return to claim (1), that is, to the idea that mental holism gives us reason to be skeptical about animal minds. I'll discus an argument of Davidson's, one of whose conclusions is that brutes have no propositional attitudes, and I'll try to elucidate the differences between Davidson's sort of mental holism and Wittgenstein's. Finally, in §6, I'll say how I think we should answer a question like "Do dogs really have beliefs and desires?"

Now, let us turn to Cora Diamond and the lives of the saints.

*   *   *

In her paper "Realism and the Realistic Spirit," Diamond points out that according to the norms that governed medieval hagiography, one can write of a saint, that for example, he tried to hide his stigmata, even if he (the hagiographer) adduces no evidence in support of this conclusion—indeed even if the story he tells suggests that the saint in question *wasn't* trying to hide his stigmata. Following Hippolyte Delehaye, Diamond compares hagiography with painting. Just as one may paint a picture of the Baptism of Jesus that shows "besides one man pouring water on the head of another, a dove above their heads, and above that the head of an old man" (Diamond 1991a, 53) without worrying about whether there were, in fact, doves on hand at the original event, just so, "such sentences as 'St. N hid signs of divine favor' may be put into N's *vita* simply because that is how one describes saints" (ibid., 53). Diamond notes that a writer of today who wants to write an accurate biography of a medieval saint might try to address the question of what is true, and not merely conventional, in the old *vitae*. This question makes sense; we distinguish between what it is proper for a medieval hagiographer to write about a saint, on the one hand, and what is true of said saint, on the other. Our acknowledgement of this distinction expresses a commitment to what Diamond (ibid., 54–55) calls "elementary realism":

[W]hat is conventionally put into a saint's *vita* may by no means be true, and we recognize this when we make use, in judging the truth of what is said, of our techniques for weighing and sifting evidence. The fact that these techniques would not have been of interest to the author of the *vita*, who was not attempting to produce an accurate life, nor to his audience, does not mean that our judgments about what is said in the *vita* are in any way out of order or conceptually confused. In dealing with the material in the *vita*, we may perfectly properly adopt a sort of realism: the existence of rules or conventions concerning what may be *said* and indeed *thought* about a certain matter, here saints' lives, leaves open the question what is *true* about those matters. . . . Our elementary realism (as we may call it) has at its heart that contrast between what is said, adhering to the practices, the conventions, governing the writing of saints' lives, and what the facts are.

As I said, my focus in the present section will be a lesson that Diamond takes from Wittgenstein. The lesson could be put as follows: A way in which we often go wrong when we are doing philosophy is by misguidedly taking ourselves to be asking the sort of question that the contemporary biographer of saints asks when he examines old *vitae*. So a philosopher might say, "I know that there are conventions according to which it's perfectly correct for me sometimes to describe myself or someone else as 'following a rule.' What I'd like to determine is whether we really *do* follow rules—whether what is said in these instances is ever really *true*." Diamond (ibid., 55) writes:

I want to suggest that the philosophical realist attempts to take up a position analogous to that of elementary realism—but confusedly. The philosophical realist's conception of *room for* a position analogous to that of elementary realism: *that* is a fantasy.

What's at issue here has as much to do with justification as with truth. Part of Diamond's point—part of what she's getting at when she suggests that the philosophical realist imagines that there is room to take up a position where there is not—is that in doing philosophy, we sometimes describe ourselves as asking whether some assertion is justified, when we have, as it were, so removed ourselves from the familiar terrain on which we know how to give and ask for reasons in support of such assertions that we don't have any real idea what we are asking.

Toward the end of "Realism and the Realistic Spirit," Diamond (ibid., 66) quotes the following from Wittgenstein's *Remarks on the Foundations of Mathematics*:

I can train someone in a uniform activity. E.g. in drawing a line like this with a pencil on paper:

— ·· — ·· — ·· — ·· — ·· — ··

Now I ask myself, what is it that I want him to do, then? The answer is: He is always to go on as I have shewn him. And what do I really mean by: he is always to go on in that way? The best answer to this that I can give myself, is an example like the one I have just given.

   I would use this example in order to shew him, and also to shew myself, what I mean by uniform.

   We talk and act. That is already presupposed in everything that I am saying. (Wittgenstein 1978, 320–321)

Imagine that I draw a line of dots and dashes and ask someone—a child, let's say—to extend the line, going on in the same way. I watch him, and he seems to have no trouble with the task. Now, in a philosophical mood, I wonder: "Has he really done what I asked him to do—gone on 'in the same way'? What justifies me in judging that he has?" Perhaps at first, I'm not sure what to do with these questions; it's not clear to me what their answers should look like. At this point, I might seek a philosophical account of what going on in the same way consists in; or of what the words, "going on in the same way," really mean (or, anyway, of what they mean *here*). Such an account would, I suppose, provide me with a kind of test with which I could assess as true, or as justified, my judgment that the child has gone on in the same way. So I ask myself: "What did I really mean when I told him to go on in the same way? What, exactly, was I asking him to do?"

Wittgenstein suggests that the best answer I can give here is "an example like the one I have just given," that is, an answer that I might enact by looking again at the pattern of marks I drew and saying to myself, "I meant for him to go on doing *that*." Of course, this isn't the *kind* of answer that I take myself to want. Commenting on this passage from *Remarks on the Foundations of Mathematics*, Diamond (1991a, 68) writes, "I want to explain it—and I do not want, do not think I want, something that would in fact, *does* in fact, *do* to explain to someone how to go on." I seek an explanation of what I mean by "go on in the same way." I'm not interested, however, in how I instruct another human being—in what I actually say and do—when I want him to go on in that way. I imagine myself to be asking a question whose answer cannot lie in such mundane instructions and examples. The sort of account I want, or think I want,[9] is one that would reach *past* what I actually do with, or say to, another person. After all, my instructions and examples succeed, if they do, only because I share sensibilities with the person whom I'm instructing. But a philosophical account of going on in the same way cannot take shared sensibilities for granted; it should provide a standard to which our sensibilities—our intuitive assessments of things—can *measure up*. Diamond (ibid., 68–69) writes: "[T]he idea of a philosophical account of what I really mean by 'he is always to go on in that way' is of an account addressed to someone on whose uptake, on whose response, we are not at all depending." I seek an account, an explanation, of that in virtue of which I'm getting it right when I tell the child that *he's* got it right, that is, when I tell him that he has succeeded in extending the pattern that I began. And I won't be satisfied with an account that sounds like this: "I'm right when I tell him that he's got it right by virtue of my recognizing that he has, in fact, continued the pattern I started." For this "recognizing" must be explained too. How do I do it, and by virtue of what is it genuine recognition, rather than misrecognition, or something altogether noncognitive?

As Diamond reads the passage from *Remarks on the Foundations of Mathematics*, it is aimed at getting us to see that this seeming desire for an explanation or an account is not innocent; we can't just take it for granted that when we ask for a philosophical account or explanation of going on in the same way (or following a rule or being afraid), we are in fact asking for anything.

The demands we make for philosophical explanations come, seem to come, from a position in which we are as it were looking down onto the relation between ourselves and reality, some kind of fact or real possibility. We think we mean something by our questions about it. Our questions are formed from notions of ordinary life, but the ways we usually ask and answer questions, our practices, our interests, the forms our reasoning and inquiries take, look from such a position to be the "rags"[10] [i.e., details that don't matter]. Our own linguistic constructions, cut free from the constraints of their ordinary functioning, take us in. . . . (Ibid., 69–70)

How can we tell if we are being "taken in" in this way? There is no quick, surefire test. Whether or not we have convinced ourselves that there's something, a kind of "account" or "explanation" that we want, when in fact we have no coherent idea of anything we want—this needs to be examined on a case-by-case basis. Still, there is much in Wittgenstein's writings to suggest that we should be especially on guard, that we are especially liable to lapse into this sort of illusion, when what we take ourselves to want is a philosophical account of something belonging to the family of phe-nomena that comprises: following a rule, continuing a series, meaning or intending one thing rather than another, sharing an intention or a belief, and so on.

4

Toward the end of §1, I noted that Wittgenstein seems to be some kind of holist, and I indicated that one of my goals in the present essay would be to help make clearer just what kind he is. As a step toward this goal, I want to repeat a sentence from §3: "Part of Diamond's point . . . is that in doing philosophy, we sometimes describe our-selves as asking whether some assertion is justified, when we have, as it were, so removed ourselves from the familiar terrain on which we know how to give and ask for reasons in support of such assertions that we don't have any real idea what we are asking." I suggest that Wittgenstein urges us to think about, for example, mental and semantic phenomena holistically—in terms of the "weave" of life and of human sen-sibility—primarily in order to bring us *back* to the familiar terrain on which we know (among other things) how to give and ask for reasons. The aim is *not* to show us where to find raw materials for an account of, say, rule-following that will finally enable us to underwrite our ordinary assessments of when a person may rightly or justifiably be said to be following a rule. It is, rather, to dissolve the illusion that we want anything, when we tell ourselves we want *that*.

Here, it might be helpful to think about two different ways in which holistic-sounding remarks in the *Investigations* might be understood. Consider, for example, the following remarks:

We ask "What does 'I am frightened' really mean, what am I referring to when I say it?" And of course we find no answer, or one that is inadequate.

The question is: "In what sort of context does it occur?" (Wittgenstein 1953, p. 188)

"Then can whatever I do be brought into accord with the rule?"—Let me ask this: what has the expression of a rule—say a sign-post—got to do with my actions? What sort of connexion is there here?—Well, perhaps this one: I have been trained to react to this sign in a particular way, and now I do so react to it.

But that is only to give a causal connexion; to tell how it has come about that we now go by the sign-post; not what this going-by-the-sign really consists in. On the contrary; I have further indicated that a person goes by a sign-post only in so far as there exists a regular use of sign-posts, a custom. (Ibid., §198)

One reading of these passages might be stated as follows: "In the first passage, the one about fear, Wittgenstein is saying that we tend to go wrong philosophically by looking in the wrong place for an account of fear. The only way to arrive at a satisfactory explanation of what fear is—of what 'I am frightened' really means—is to look to the ways in which what we call 'fear' is situated in people's lives, that is, to fear's surroundings. The point of *Investigations* §198 is similar: if we want to know what going by a rule or a signpost really consists in, we must look to the contexts in which people can and do go by rules and signposts, and this means recognizing that any example of someone's going by a rule or a signpost should be understood as part of something larger, a custom. In both passages, Wittgenstein is suggesting that we can arrive at an adequate account of one thing or another only by viewing it as part of a larger whole."

Here, Wittgenstein is read as what we might call a "metaphysical holist"—someone who thinks that questions like "What does going by a signpost really consist in?" or "What does 'I am frightened' really mean?" may be answered by reference to the contexts in which mental and semantic phenomena occur. But Wittgenstein's holism isn't metaphysical. It could be described as "therapeutic." And the felt need for an account—even a holistic account—of fear or rule-following that will underwrite (or vindicate or justify) our ordinary practices of assessing when someone has managed to follow a rule is a symptom of the neurosis that it is meant to treat. Thus, in the first quotation above, when Wittgenstein says, "And of course we find no answer, or one that is inadequate," he's not suggesting that we look somewhere else (to context or custom) for a satisfactory explanation of what "I am frightened" really means. The suggestion is, rather, that when we find ourselves asking, "What does 'I am frightened' really mean?" it is likely that we don't understand our own question—likely that we haven't managed to mean anything by it. Wittgenstein's appeals to context, custom, "the weave of our life," and so forth are meant to facilitate an awareness of this point by reminding us of what it looks like for a real person—someone with a life—to be, for example, afraid and of what questions we might sensibly ask about (or of) such a person.[11]

5

Let's review. In §1, I sketched an argument that leads from holism about beliefs to skepticism about a nonlinguistic animal's having any. In §2, we saw an objection to holism about beliefs: that it renders mysterious not only a *dog's* agreeing with me that some cat is in some tree, but *your* agreeing with me as well. I pointed out that Fodor and Lepore's version of this objection assumes that a holist about beliefs owes us an account of mental content that would underwrite our ordinary judgments concerning both *when* people agree and (even) *whether* people ever do. One moral of §§3 and 4 is that a holist need not accept this assumption about what he owes—needn't accept that the assumption even makes sense. To say that we can see a creature as believing something (anything) only if we view it as having *many* beliefs (and perhaps much else besides) is not to admit that we have any grip on what it would mean to provide an account of mental content that would yield a standard to which all our ordinary judgments and sensibilities having to do with agreement would either measure up, and thereby be shored up, or fail to measure up, and thereby be shown incorrect or confused.

In what's to come, I'll return to my opening theme—that holism about beliefs and concepts tends toward startlingly skeptical conclusions concerning the minds of nonlinguistic animals. You may recall that I drew on passages from Rorty and Davidson when I first sounded this theme. In the present section, I'm going to focus on an argument of Davidson's that purports to show (among other things) that brutes have no propositional attitudes.[12]

* * *

Davidson's argument begins with the identification of a problem:

Some creature is taught, or anyway learns, to respond in a specific way to a stimulus or a class of stimuli. The dog hears a bell and is fed; presently it salivates when it hears the bell. The child babbles, and when it produces a sound like "table" in the evident presence of a table, it is rewarded; the process is repeated and presently the child says "table" in the presence of tables. (Davidson 2001b, 117)

We're inclined to say that the dog is responding to the ringing of the bell and that the child is responding to tables. But are we really justified in so saying?

[T]here is a problem about the stimulus. In the case of the dog, why say the stimulus is the ringing of the bell? Why couldn't it be the vibration of the air close to the ears of the dog—or even the stimulation of its nerve endings. . . . In fact, if we must choose, it seems that the prox-imal cause of the behavior has the best claim to be called the stimulus, since the more distant an event is causally from its perceiver, the more chance there is that the causal chain will be broken. Why not say the same about the child: that its responses are not to tables but to pat-terns of stimulation at its surfaces, since those patterns of stimulation always produce the response, while tables produce it only under favorable conditions? (Ibid., 118)

Although the problem is here introduced in connection with nonlinguistic (or, at least, not fully linguistic) creatures, we might ask something similar about ourselves. Imagine that, on my entering your living room, I say, "I like the new coffee table," whereupon you look over at the table appraisingly and reply, "I loved it when I bought it two weeks ago, but now I can't remember what I thought was so great about it." We might ask: What fixes it that I am (or that you are) responding to a particular distal object rather than, say, the more proximal impact of light on my (or, in your case, your) photoreceptors? After all, my reaction, like that of the dog that Davidson describes, is a link in a long causal chain. Why say that I'm responding to the table rather than to the stimulation of my photoreceptors?

Davidson aims to make intelligible how it is that a behavioral response can be a response to something determinate, and he means to do this by stating a necessary condition on the possibility of such responses.[13] As a step toward bringing this nec-essary condition into view, notice that in the living room scenario just described, there are *two* responders. So there is, on the one hand, a causal chain running through the coffee table and the stimulation of my photoreceptors to my behavioral response and, on the other hand, a different causal chain running through the table and the stim-ulation of your photoreceptors to your behavioral response. The common link in the two chains is the table. Davidson (2001c, 213) writes, "We may think of it as a form of triangulation: each of two people is reacting differentially to sensory stimuli stream-ing in from a certain direction. Projecting the incoming lines outward, the common cause is at their intersection."

Imagine a line of "stimuli streaming" from the direction of the coffee table through the air in the room to my eyes. Now add a second line of stimuli, one that runs through the table via a different route to your eyes. The two lines meet at the table. Finally, add a third line—running between you and me—that represents our awareness of each other as sharing a stimulus in this way, as responding to the same thing. You, the table, and I form a triangle. According to Davidson (ibid., 212–213), if not for the fact that we lead social lives that position us in many such triangles, we could not respond to, talk about, or think about any determinate thing:

[U]ntil the triangle is completed connecting two creatures and each creature with common features, there can be no answer to the question whether a creature, in discriminating between stimuli, is discriminating between stimuli at the sensory surfaces or somewhere further out, or further in. Without this sharing of reactions to common stimuli, thought and speech would have no particular content—that is no content at all.[14]

Now what about nonlinguistic creatures? Are they capable of triangulating and so responding to determinate objects? Prima facie, it doesn't seem as if anything I've said thus far rules out the possibility of, say, two dogs triangulating a chew toy. And Davidson (1999, 41) speaks, in connection with wild chimps, of the possibility of a "primitive triangle of two creatures reacting to a common stimulus and to each other's reactions to that stimulus"—indeed of "repeated reactions to shared situations found similar by two or more creatures each simultaneously observing the other's reactions, these reactions in turn being found similar by each creature to reactions previously observed in the other in the shared situations found similar" (ibid., 41). He goes on, in the next paragraph, as follows:

With a single creature, it is hard to decide what it is reacting to when a stimulus hits. When the frog sticks out its tongue, is the stimulus a fly or the firing of a certain pattern of receptors in the eye? We incline to say the latter. But even if the frog were wiser than it is, and learned to save its fire when the target is a large and distant bird or an airplane, we would be in no position to choose one source of the cause of the reaction over another; the frog would just be habituated to a different, though more complex, pattern of proximal stimuli. The slightly complex social situation I have been postulating eases this problem. The stimulus that matters is the nearest mutual cause of the joint reaction. When the triangle is working normally, the mutual reactions of the two (or, of course, more) creatures *triangulate* the relevant stimulus, locating it in a public space. . . . (Ibid., 41)

Here, Davidson seems to be marking a significant distinction between a "single creature," for example, a frog (even an unnaturally "wise" one) and a social, nonlinguistic creature positioned at one apex of a primitive triangle. When a solitary creature exhibits a bit of behavior—although we might "incline to" pick out this or that stimulus as the one to which the thing is responding—we are really in "no position to choose one source of the cause of the reaction over another." In the case of a social brute, however, "[t]he stimulus that matters is the nearest mutual cause of the joint reaction." Thus, it looks as if Davidson holds that primitive triangulation makes responsiveness to determinate stimuli possible. In the same paper, however, he has this to say about Alex, a famous parrot that seems able to discriminate between presented objects' sharing a color and their sharing a shape:

What is it that tells us that the stimulus (cause) of Alex's "answer" to the question "What's the same?" isn't the activation of certain rods and cones in his eyes, or the firing of certain optic nerves, or the photons bouncing off surfaces we see as the same color? All of these causes, and endless more, are common to the cases where Alex emitted the sound "Color." We have no grounds for choosing one of these causes over the others. (Ibid., 34)

This passage suggests that without language, there just cannot be any fact of the matter concerning what it is that a creature is responding to.

We might try to reconcile these passages in either of two ways. One option is to say that while Davidson thinks some brutes (e.g., chimps) are capable of primitive triangulation and so of responses to determinate objects, he doesn't think Alex is up to either. A second option is to read Davidson as holding that unless a creature is capable of full, linguistic triangulation, there is no fact of the matter about what it is responding to or, anyway, no fact of the matter that is independent of us. How can this second reading be squared with the first passage above? Focus on the word "decide" as it figures in the opening sentence of that passage. The difficulty about the "single creature" is that "it is hard to decide what it is reacting to"—that is, hard for us to decide—where this is not a matter of our discerning that things are a certain way, independently of us. Later in the passage, when Davidson writes, "The slightly complex social situation I have been postulating eases this problem," he means to say that the presence of a primitive triangle eases our problem of deciding for the creature what it is responding to. There's still no independent fact of the matter about what the thing is responding to, as there is when a person responds to a stimulus.[15]

I won't try to settle this exegetical dilemma. For my purposes, it suffices to point out that Davidson does not believe that a primitive triangle—or a long history with such triangles—gives a creature what it needs in order to *think* about a determinate object, state, or event. So, whatever we say about Davidson on the possibility of a dog's *responding to* a determinate thing, it's clear that he does not think that a dog can have, say, a *belief about* a determinate thing. And (at least, for Davidson) this means that a dog cannot have beliefs at all: "Before triangulation can generate thought, the base line between creatures that observe that they share stimuli must . . . be strengthened to include linguistic communication" (Davidson 1999, 42). In order for two creatures, A and B, to participate jointly in the sort of triangle that makes thought possible, A must recognize that B is responding to the same thing that he, A, is responding to. And B must likewise recognize that she and A are responding to the same object. According to Davidson (2001b, 121), this mutual recognition entails that two creatures be capable of rich communication, indeed of *linguistic* communication:

[T]o have the concept of a table or a bell is to recognize the existence of a triangle, one apex of which is oneself, the second apex another creature similar to oneself, and the third an object (table or bell) located in a space thus made common.

The only way of knowing that the second apex of the triangle—the second creature or person—is reacting to the same object as oneself is to know that the other person has the same object in mind. But then the second person must also know that the first person constitutes an apex of the same triangle another apex of which the second person occupies. For two people to know of each other that they are so related, that their thoughts are so related, requires that they be in communication. Each of them must speak to the other and be understood by the other.

Davidson holds that in order to have a concept, a creature must recognize itself and another as reacting to the same stimulus, and this, he thinks, requires linguistic communication. So, as "[t]here is no distinction between having concepts and having propositional attitudes" (Davidson 2004, 137), a nonlinguistic creature can have no propositional attitudes.

*   *   *

At the end of §1, I said that a goal of the present essay is to shed light on the differences between the kind of holism to which Wittgenstein is committed and the kinds that are liable to figure in more contemporary philosophy of mind. I should, therefore, point out that (what we might call) the triangulation theory represents a commitment to a kind of mental holism. According to Davidson, in order for a creature to have a belief about, say, a stick in its path, it must have, as well, beliefs about other creatures and other minds. Davidson (e.g., 1980, 221) has long held that "[t]here is no assigning beliefs to a person one by one," and the triangulation theory commits him to this claim once again. The theory is holistic in another sense as well, for it tells us that in order for a creature to respond to, and have attitudes about, determinate stimuli, *it* must be a part of something larger, a community of at least two coresponders: "If we consider a single creature by itself, its responses, no matter how complex, cannot show that it is reacting to, or thinking about, events a certain distance away rather than, say, on its skin" (Davidson 2001b, 119). This sounds, in some respects, like something Wittgenstein might say.[16]

But this isn't Wittgenstein's holism. To help make the differences apparent, let us consider a mundane story that illustrates how, in a nonphilosophical context, questions might be raised and settled about the responses and attitudes of nonlinguistic animals. Imagine that I'm out walking my dog, Kita. She is on lead, at my left side. A mailman emerges from a building to our left and walks briskly in our direction. As he approaches, Kita lunges past the front of my body, jerking me around clockwise and to the right. I try to calm her down, the mailman walks past, and a neighbor remarks, "Your dog doesn't want to be anywhere *near* that mailman." I reply: "Actually, they get along fine. Her reaction wasn't to him. It was to that squirrel." Here, I point to a squirrel in a nearby tree that's looking down at Kita and chittering loudly. "It ran past us, and she wanted to chase it. Of course, now that she knows there's a squirrel sitting there, I'll have to drag her away from here."

This is how, in a nonphilosophical context, it might look and sound for questions to be settled about a nonlinguistic animal's reactions and attitudes. Davidson, of course, knows this; he knows what ordinary conversations of this sort look and sound like. But he thinks that, viewed from a *philosophical* vantage point, the justification that I offer (or could offer) to my neighbor for the claims that I make about Kita may be seen as taking too much for granted.

What, exactly, do I take for granted that, according to Davidson, ought not to be assumed from a philosophical vantage point? Here's one thing: that Kita, being a dog, is the sort of animal that *hunts*. For hunting involves (or just is) a kind of responsiveness *to* some sorts of things and not others. A question like, "What entitles us to claim that Kita hunts *squirrels* and *rabbits* rather than, say, photons or photoreceptors?" is not, I take it, one that anybody would try to answer seriously. ("Well, as for photons, they're just too *fast* to chase down.") In order for Davidson's problem—we might call it the problem of "stimulus determination"—to get a grip on us, we have to view animals and human beings merely as potential *responders*, not as *hunters* or as *chasers*. We mustn't help ourselves to the concept of hunting or of chasing. And the point extends beyond *hunting* and *chasing* to, for example, such concepts as *fleeing*, *eating*, *mating*, *feeding*, *caring for*, and *playing*. ("Why should we describe that bear as caring for her cub, rather than for her sensory surfaces?" is not a serious question either.) Davidson insists, in effect, on our setting aside all such concepts when we ask ourselves which stimulus, if any, a creature might be responding to. Here, then, is a way to characterize one thing that must not be taken for granted if the problem of stimulus determination—the problem to which triangulation is meant as a solution— is to seem gripping in the first place: that people and animals have *lives*.[17]

In §1, I noted that Wittgenstein's holism expresses itself in his continually urging us to think about mental and semantic phenomena as they figure in what he calls "the weave of our life." He believes that philosophical confusion about meaning and intentionality (as well as about sensations and privacy) typically results from viewing signs and behavior as cut off from life,[18] whereas Davidson's triangulation theory *requires*, in effect, that we consider the behavior of animals and human beings as *lifeless*.

So, that's one significant difference between Davidson's holism and Wittgenstein's. In what follows, I'll try to spell out another.

                                        *   *   *

Davidson's triangulation theory offers, or seems to offer, a philosophical vantage point from which we can judge—as properly justified or not—our ordinary procedures for determining whether this or that creature is responding to, or having thoughts about, this or that object. The theory appears to show that a great deal of what we say about animals, even animals with whom we share our daily lives, is not really true or justified. It seems to give us a kind of *test* of our prephilosophical assessments of, and sensibilities having to do with, ascriptions of responsiveness and intentionality to the animals and human beings around us. We usually pass the test when we speak about adult human beings. We tend to fail in our dealings with brutes and young children.

Here, I want to remind you of an example that was discussed in §3: I draw a line of dots and dashes on a piece of paper and ask a child to extend it, going on in the same way. On observing the child continue the pattern, I wonder whether I'm really justified in judging that he's done what I asked him to do. I imagine that a philosophical account of going on in the same way might underwrite my judgment, that such an account might serve as a standard against which my assessment of the child's behavior would either measure up or fail to measure up. The moral of §3's discussion of this example was that in our search for philosophical accounts or explanations that will serve either to underwrite or to undermine our everyday sensibilities, we are inclined toward a kind of nonsense. By trying to take nothing for granted—by trying to step *way back* from our ordinary procedures for assessing and justifying claims having to do with, for example, whether someone has managed to continue a series or follow an instruction—we leave ourselves without the resources we need in order even to make sense of phrases like "continuing a series," "following an instruction," or "underwriting a judgment to the effect that a child has managed to go on in the same way."[19] And rather than come to grips with this fact (i.e., with the fact that we've lost our grip on our own words), we're liable instead to think that, from the privileged vantage point we have attained by stepping back from our ordinary procedures of assessment and justification, we now see that there is really nothing to the idea of continuing a series or following a rule. We're liable, in this way, to confuse a self-imposed inability to make sense of some semantic or mental phenomenon with grounds for being skeptical about it.

We've seen that Davidson assumes, in effect, that the truth about an animal's state of mind, or lack thereof, comes into view only when we set aside most of what we know about the animal *qua* animal and try to view its movements as though they were not the doings of a living creature. One way to criticize Davidson's position is to point out that he's not entitled to this assumption. But if the Wittgensteinian line of thought sketched in §§3 and 4—and recalled in the preceding paragraph—is sound, then perhaps a further criticism can be made here. Perhaps we can say that the "philosophical vantage point" Davidson would have us attain turns out to be only the illusion of a vantage point. And if *this* is correct, then an important difference between Davidson's holism and Wittgenstein's can be put as follows: the latter is a treatment for the former.

6

In §3, I asked you to imagine a philosopher who says, "I know that there are conventions according to which it's perfectly correct for me sometimes to describe myself or someone else as 'following a rule.' What I'd like to determine is whether we really *do* follow rules—whether what is said in these instances is ever really *true*." A lesson that emerged in the ensuing discussion was that we ought not simply to assume that words like these are *always* significant. We should not take it for granted that this speaker has yet found anything to mean by the word "really" in its occurrences here. Now imagine that someone puts the following question to me: "I understand that, by ordinary standards, you're entitled to say that Kita wanted to chase that squirrel and that she knew it was in that tree. What I'd like to determine is this: Did she *really* want to chase it? And did she *really* know it was in that tree?" It seems to me that the best answer one could give to such an interlocutor would not be "Yes" or "No" but, as a start, something more like this: "I don't think I understand your question."[20]

Appendix

What about the argument for skepticism about animal minds that was (barely) touched on in §1? Perhaps it seemed more modest than the argument from triangulation discussed in §5 and, for this reason, more convincing. In what follows, I'll walk you through Davidson's version of the §1 argument, and I'll say where I think it falls short.

Davidson (2001a, 97) says, "One way of telling that we are attributing a propositional attitude is by noting that the sentences we use to do the attributing may change from true to false if, in the words that pick out the object of the attitudes, we substitute for some referring expression another expression that refers to the same thing." Propositional attitude ascriptions exhibit semantic opacity. But now, Davidson claims, opacity is absent (or, anyway, not clearly enough present) when we try to ascribe beliefs to brutes. Thus, concerning the dog described by Malcolm, Davidson (ibid., 97) writes:

[H]ow about the dog's supposed belief that the cat went up that oak tree? That oak tree, as it happens, is the oldest tree in sight. Does the dog think that the cat went up the oldest tree in sight? Or that the cat went up the same tree it went up the last time the dog chased it? It is hard to make sense of these questions.

The argument here might be schematized as follows:

(1)   A distinguishing feature of propositional attitude attributions is that they exhibit semantic opacity: the truth of such an attribution may be affected by how some object is referred to.

(2)   When we attribute attitudes—beliefs, say—to brutes, the attributions do not exhibit opacity. So we don't find that a belief attribution that picks out a tree *in one way* (as, e.g., "Professor Malcolm's oak tree") is true, while an attribution that differs only in that it picks out the same tree in a different way (as "the oldest tree in sight") is false.

(3)   Brutes don't really have propositional attitudes.

Let's call this the opacity argument.

As I've schematized the argument, the gap between steps (2) and (3) seems rather wide. We might try to narrow it by noting the following: Belief attributions exhibit opacity *because* we think of objects in only some of the ways in which they may be thought of. (This, in turn, reflects our finitude. Belief attributions made to God should not exhibit opacity.) If, when we try to ascribe beliefs to dogs, the ascriptions do not exhibit opacity, this suggests (either that those bumper stickers that read "Dog is my co-pilot" are *really* onto something or) that dogs aren't thinking of the objects to which we're referring *in any way at all*. Now, if a dog isn't thinking of, say, a particular tree in any way at all, then (the thought goes) it can't really be believing anything about the tree; it can't really believe, for example, that some cat went up it.

Perhaps the most obvious objection that might be raised against the opacity argument is this: it *does* seem to matter how we refer to objects when we attribute beliefs to animals; such attributions do seem to exhibit (at least some degree of) opacity. Just compare "The dog thinks the cat went up that tree" with "The dog thinks the cat went up the oldest oak tree in Cook County." We can't take the latter seriously (except as a *de re* ascription). This isn't true of the former. We're inclined to think that while a dog cannot think of some object as the oldest oak tree in Cook County, it can think of something as a tree. Thus, we're inclined to suppose that a belief attribution to Malcolm's dog that referred to some tree as "that tree" might capture, as it were, the dog's *take* on things better than some other attribution that was different only in that it referred to the same tree in another way. If this supposition is correct, then the opacity argument is undermined.

We can think of the following passage, part of which we saw in §1, as representing Davidson's reply to this objection:

In a popular if misleading idiom, the dog must believe, under some description of the tree, that the cat went up the tree. But what kind of description would suit the dog? For example, can the dog believe of an object that it is a tree? This would seem impossible unless we suppose the dog has many general beliefs about trees: that they are growing things, that they have leaves or needles, that they burn. There is no fixed list of things someone with the concept of a tree must believe, but without many general beliefs, there would be no reason to identify a belief as a belief about a tree, much less an oak tree. Similar considerations apply to the dog's supposed thinking about the cat. (Davidson 2001a, 98)

According to Davidson, a dog can no more think of something as a tree than as the oldest tree in sight. Why not? Well, in order for a creature to think of something as a tree, it must have some idea what a tree *is* and so have "many general beliefs about trees."

We should note that Davidson does not assume that a dog couldn't be supposed to have *any* general beliefs about trees. This would be to beg the question. There are, after all, *some* general facts that we might—until we were *convinced* by Davidson's argument—suppose dogs to know about trees: that squirrels climb them, that cats climb them, that squirrels jump from one to another, that there is often dog urine on them, that leashes can get wrapped around them, that they are outside, and so forth. What Davidson claims is that there are, *as well*, many general facts about trees (e.g., "that they are growing things") that we would expect a normal, adult human being to know, but that a dog could not plausibly be supposed to know or to believe. His next move, which is made only implicitly in the quoted passage, is to claim that although, as just noted, we might suppose, prima facie, that dogs have *some* general beliefs or knowledge about trees, even *given* this supposition, they don't have *enough* general beliefs or knowledge to think of an object as a tree.

The trouble with the opacity argument lies in this last move. For how are we to say how many general beliefs about trees a creature must have in order to think of something as a tree? If we rely merely on our intuitions here, we'll probably say that however many general beliefs a dog has is enough. (After all, the skeptical conclusion isn't intuitively appealing.)

At this point, the opacity argument might seem to stand in need of supplementation, that is, it might seem that Davidson does, after all, need to specify precisely *how much* a creature must believe or know concerning trees in order to be capable of thinking of anything as a tree. An alternative argumentative strategy would be for him to claim that some *particular* belief or piece of knowledge is both necessary for thinking of something as a tree *and* impossible for brutes to acquire. In §5, we saw Davidson arguing for just such a claim. According to (what I there called) the triangulation theory, a creature cannot think of an object as a tree (or as anything else) unless it knows something that, according to Davidson, no brute can know, namely, that it is one apex of a triangle (whose second apex is a creature similar to itself and whose third is an object "located in a space thus made common" [Davidson 2001b, 121]). Thus, a consideration of the skeptical argument touched on briefly in §1 leads us back to the argument from triangulation discussed at greater length in §5.

Notes

1. I should emphasize that, in this paragraph, I mean to be describing a position held by Rorty and by *Rorty's* Sellars. I'm bracketing the question of whether the skeptical views concerning animals that Rorty takes himself to find in "Empiricism and the Philosophy of Mind" are actually there. It *is* tempting to read EPM-on-animals more or less as Rorty does. But Sellars's subsequent work suggests a different reading (see Sellars 1975, 303–304 and Sellars 1981).

2. Jerry Fodor and Ernest Lepore (whom I'll be discussing in the next section) complain that this sort of holism makes the acquisition of language look impossible:

> If holism is true, then I can't understand any of your language unless I can understand practically all of it. But then how, save in a single spasm of seamless cognition, could any language ever be learned? (Fodor and Lepore 1992, 9)

Sellars considers (what amounts to) this question in "Empiricism and the Philosophy of Mind." His answer could be put as follows: A child doesn't learn the meanings of words one by one. Instead he masters *"piecemeal* habits of response" (Sellars 1997, 45) until his behavior comes to look enough like that of his elders that it makes sense to credit him with knowledge of a great *many* words (and facts). Learning a language requires—not a spasm of cognition, but—several years during which a child's behavior comes gradually to resemble that of an adult.

3. After noting that "[b]abies and the more attractive sorts of animal are credited with 'having feelings' rather than . . . 'merely responding to stimuli'" (Rorty 1979, 189) suggests that we understand this "as a courtesy extended potential or imagined fellow-speakers of our language (1979, 190)."

4. Understood as an indication of how philosophers use the word "holistic," this is a little misleading. According to Fodor and Lepore's definition, Davidson commits himself to holism about beliefs—or, anyway, to the view that the property of being a belief is holistic—when he says that in order for a creature to have even one belief, it must have many beliefs (when he claims, in other words, that for even one of a creature's states to have the property of being a belief, many of them must). But Davidson *also* thinks this: in order for a creature to have even one belief, it must have many beliefs *and* desires; *moreover*, it must engage in many actions. This view of Davidson's represents a commitment to a different kind of holism about beliefs—one that involves a "whole" that comprises more than just a lot of beliefs. I take it that the meaning of "holism," both in and out of philosophy, involves some idea like this: a single part of something can't be understood, or even what it is, apart from the whole. Thus, a holist about beliefs thinks that a single belief can't be understood apart from *some* larger whole of which it may be understood

to be a part. The larger whole need not be understood as a network of beliefs, however. It might be understood as a network of beliefs, desires, and actions—or, as in Wittgenstein's late writings, something broader still, something more like a life.

5. A surprising number of philosophers—both holists and critics of holism—write as if holism about beliefs does entail that two people cannot share any beliefs unless they share all their beliefs. Thus, having defined "meaning holism" as the view, "roughly, that each representation in a linguistic or mental system depends semantically on every other representation," Eric Lormand (1996, 51) writes: "If meaning holism about a system *S* is true, then a change in meaning of any representation in *S* requires a change in meaning of all representations in *S*." And in the *Routledge Encyclopedia of Philosophy*, Ned Block (1998, 488) says that if "the content of any state depends on all the others, it would be extremely unlikely that any two believers would ever share a state with the same content." Notice that whether or not such statements are true depends entirely on the way in which each element in a system of states or representations is understood to *depend* on the others. There is, after all, more than one kind of dependence. Thus, Henry Jackman (1999, 363) writes:

Holism only requires that the content of any one of one's beliefs *depend upon* or be a *function of* one's other beliefs, and *this* claim need not commit one to the instability thesis [i.e., the thesis that any change in a network of beliefs changes the content of every belief in the network]. After all, one can claim that *A* is a function of *B* without implying that any change in *B* will produce a change in *A*. Consider, for instance, the claim that one's final letter grade in a class is a function of (depends upon) the results of one's exams, quizzes and homeworks. The truth of this claim certainly doesn't entail that no two people could have the same final grade unless they had precisely the same score on all of their homeworks, exams and quizzes.

The point seems hard to miss, and we might wonder why so many philosophers—both holists and critics of holism—appear to take seriously the worry that mental holism entails that two people cannot really agree about anything unless they agree about everything. Block, who is himself a mental holist, recommends that we give up the very idea of agreement and replace it with a graded notion, viz., similarity of content. I would suggest that what's moving Block and others is, ultimately, a metaphilosophical commitment that they share with Fodor and Lepore. I'll say a bit more about this in n. 8.

6. There is a difficulty with the question thus formulated: many philosophers (Fodor and Lepore, among them) would say that someone's believing *either* that Mars is red *or* that tomatoes are red counts *decisively* in favor of ascribing the concept *red* to him. Thus neither of the beliefs mentioned would count either more or less "for having the concept *red*." Fodor and Lepore might, however, have avoided this difficulty by posing a slightly different question, viz., Which counts more *against* the ascription of the concept *red* to someone, that he does *not* believe that Mars is red, or that he does *not* believe that tomatoes are?

7. It may be helpful, as we think about what the objection presupposes, to consider another version of it (one directed at holism about another property): Fodor and Lepore (1992, 12) define R* as the property an expression has "iff it refers to something or other that currently accepted astronomical theories refer to." Now suppose that R* is holistic; suppose, that is, that if one expression in the language of a particular theory refers to something or other that our current

astronomical theories refer to, then many expressions in the language of that theory must also refer to things that our current astronomical theories refer to:

Then it might turn out that no theory could refer to (for example) stars unless it could refer to (as it might be) planets, nebulas, black holes, the center of the galaxy, the speed of propagation of light, and the location of the nearest quasar. It would follow that Greek astronomy (hence, Greek astronom*ers*) couldn't ever have referred to stars. And it would follow from *that* that (what one had naively supposed to be) the Greek view that stars are very nearby and that they ride around the heavens on glass spheres is actually *not contested* by our view that the stars are very far away and don't ride around the heavens at all. In fact, strictly speaking, it would follow that the Greeks didn't *have* any views about *stars*. (Ibid., 12)

Fodor and Lepore think it undeniable that Greek astronomers did, in fact, refer to stars. Still, this argument isn't a reductio ad absurdum. We should reject holism here not because it entails that the Greeks had no views about stars, but because it leaves this open as a possibility. Hence, the passage begins with the words "Then it might turn out . . ." rather than "Then it turns out . . .".

8. Ned Block would reject claim (2). As I indicated in n. 5, he accepts the idea (even though he admits it is "weird-sounding" [Block 1998, 491]) that you and I cannot rightly be said to agree about anything. By his lights, we preserve enough of common sense if we allow that you and I have many beliefs that are *similar* in content. Still, while Block would reject (2), he would, I think, accept a weaker version of it (and this is the metaphilosophical commitment that I mentioned at the end of n. 5):

(2′)   A satisfactory philosophical account of belief content would yield an account of shared belief. Thus a satisfactory mental holism would put us in a position to *evaluate* as true or false both the claim that people often agree in their beliefs and that we are, by and large, correct in our assessments of when we agree.

As should become apparent in what follows, I think we ought to reject (2′) along with (2).

9. The move here from speaking about what I want to what I *think* I want doesn't, after all, accomplish very much. If I don't manage to mean anything by, e.g., "an account of going on in the same way," then it doesn't make sense for me to describe myself *either* as wanting an "account of going on in the same way" *or* as thinking that I do. In writing *about* philosophical nonsense, one sometimes finds that one's own sentences turn out to be nonsense. If one is doing things right, they are ladders that, eventually, could be thrown away.

10. This is a reference to *Investigations* §52:

If I am inclined to suppose that a mouse has come into being by spontaneous generation out of grey rags and dust, I shall do well to examine those rags very closely to see how a mouse may have hidden in them, how it may have got there and so on. But if I am convinced that a mouse cannot come into being from these things, then this investigation will perhaps be superfluous.

  But first we must learn to understand what it is that opposes such an examination of details in philosophy.

11. A reader of *Philosophical Investigations* who does not get into focus the therapeutic aim of Wittgenstein's holism is liable to be struck by some such thought as the following: "While Wittgenstein does point us in the direction of an account of fear (or rule-following or intentionality), he doesn't seem particularly interested in working out the details and actually providing the account. Indeed, he seems oddly, perhaps even perversely, opposed to *anyone's*

providing the account—like a Moses who, having finally led the Jews to a place from which they can see the Promised Land, says, 'I hope none of you people are planning to actually go in there.'" Wittgenstein's commentators too often, I think, leave one with this sort of impression of him. Consider, e.g., Robert Brandom. Early on in his *Making It Explicit*, Brandom (1994, 29) claims that (1) if "anything is to be made of the Kantian insight that there is a fundamental normative dimension to the application of concepts," then a (certain sort of) "theory of practices" must be spelled out, and (2) even though Wittgenstein's arguments establish the "criteria of adequacy" (ibid., 30) that such a theory would have to meet, he (Wittgenstein) would urge *against* the pursuit of a theory of practices: "Wittgenstein, the principled theoretical quietist, does not attempt to provide a theory of practices, nor would he endorse the project of doing so. The last thing he thinks we need is more philosophical theories". (ibid., 29). Although Brandom here calls Wittgenstein's quietism "principled," he doesn't explain what (presumably misguided) principle underlies it. (Surely, it can't be, merely, that the last thing we need is more theories. Moses: "The last thing we need is more walking.") A bit later in his book, Brandom articulates a twofold explanatory task that he aims to meet in order to entitle himself to the concept of intentional content. The task is, first, "to say what it is to *express* a *propositional* content in general, and then to say what more is required specifically for the content expressed to *represent* something *objective*, in the way that matters for empirical science" (ibid., 75). Brandom goes on:

> This is a request that can sensibly be addressed to Wittgenstein, as well. Even his sustained, penetrating discussions do not offer an account of what distinguishes language games within which states and performances acquire specifically *propositional* significances . . . , nor of what distinguishes those within which states and performances acquire specifically *representational* significances. (Ibid., 75)

Here, Brandom doesn't suggest that Wittgenstein's unwillingness to pursue such accounts is principled.

12. By my count, Davidson sets out three arguments that lead to this conclusion: two in "Rational Animals" (Davidson 2001a; originally published in 1982) and one more—the one that I'm about to describe—in a number of his later papers (several of which I'll cite in what follows). Of the three arguments, he seems most satisfied with this last one. (In the appendix, I'll discuss one of the two earlier arguments.)

13. Obviously, it won't do to state just *any* necessary condition, e.g., that in order for a creature to respond to determinate objects, it must be capable of *movement*. This would be, by Davidson's lights, true, but it wouldn't help to make the possibility of such responses intelligible.

14. Remarks such as this one might suggest that when I am by myself, I'm unable to think about determinate objects. Of course, this isn't Davidson's view. Rather: my rich history of triangulating with others enables me to think about particular things even when no one else is around. The point can be put in terms of what interpretation requires. If, alone in my own living room, I say to myself, "That table needs to be fixed," I'm best interpreted as responding to, and thinking about, my table—rather than, say, events in my own eyes—thanks to my history of triangulating with others. If not for this history, however, there wouldn't be sufficient constraint on how best to interpret me for me to be rightly viewed as thinking *about* anything.

15. Bridges (forthcoming) reads Davidson's remarks about Alex as expressing this sort of anti-realism about the responses of (even social) brutes. He writes:

[T]here is really nothing about the behavior, considered in and of itself, that licenses viewing it as specially linked to certain of its causes. What explains our favoritism toward these causes is not something that we discover in the behavior, but something we bring to it, namely our 'natural' dispositions to attend to certain kinds of events and ignore others.

16. To make it sound *more* like something Wittgenstein might say, let this imagined creature be supposed to exist for only an instant.

17. In this paragraph, I've been more or less paraphrasing one of the main points in Bridges (forthcoming). He writes:

To refrain from conceiving an animal as responding to distal events and objects is to refrain from conceiving it as fleeing from anything. Or, by the same token, as playing with, watching over, hiding from, searching for, returning to, threatening, fighting with, attacking, defending territory from, following, stalking, herding, foraging, burying, stealing, greeting, communicating with, grooming, etc.

18. Here are three (of many) passages from the *Investigations* that might be considered in connection with this point:

How does it come about this arrow ≫——> *points*? Doesn't it seem to carry in it something besides itself?— "No, not the dead line on paper; only the psychical thing, the meaning, can do that."—That is both true and false. The arrow points only in the application that a living being makes of it. (§454)

It is possible to say "I read timidity in this face" but at all events the timidity does not seem to be merely associated, outwardly connected, with the face; but fear is there, alive, in the features. (§537)

Look at a stone and imagine it having sensations.—One says to oneself: How could one so much as get the idea of ascribing a *sensation* to a *thing*? One might as well ascribe it to a number!—And now look at a wriggling fly and at once these difficulties vanish and pain seems able to get a foothold here, where before everything was, so to speak, too smooth for it. (§284)

19. This moral should not be overstated. A lesson I would not want to draw from Wittgenstein (or anyone) is that whenever someone who calls herself a philosopher offers a theory or an account of something suggesting that our everyday sensibilities are, to a certain extent, mistaken—i.e., that our ordinary procedures of assessment and justification ought to be revised— she lapses into nonsense or falls into error. I am confident that Diamond agrees with me about this, and *because* I am, I take a passage like the following to be somewhat misleading:

The sense in which philosophy leaves everything as is this: philosophy does not put us in a position to justify or criticize what we do by showing that it meets or fails to meet requirements that we lay down in our philosophizing. (Diamond 1991b, 22)

We could, I suppose, stipulate that the word "philosophy" be used such that when we *are* "in a position to justify or criticize what we do by showing that it meets or fails to meet requirements," we don't count as doing philosophy. But I can't see that this is a good idea.

20. I'm grateful to Jason Bridges, James Conant, Cora Diamond, Jay Elliott, Aidan Gray, Erica Holberg, and Thomas Lockhart for helpful comments on drafts of this essay.

Works Cited

Block, N. 1998. "Holism: Mental and Semantic." In E. Craig, ed., *Routledge Encyclopedia of Philosophy*, 488–493. London: Routledge.

Brandom, R. 1994. *Making It Explicit*. Cambridge, Mass.: Harvard University Press.

Bridges, J. "Davidson's Transcendental Externalism." Forthcoming in *Philosophy and Phenomenological Research*.

Davidson, D. 1980. "Mental Events." In *Essays on Actions and Events*. Oxford: Oxford University Press.

Davidson, D. 1999. "Interpretation: Hard in Theory, Easy in Practice." In M. De Caro, ed., *Interpretations and Causes: New Perspectives on Donald Davidson's Philosophy*, 31–44. Dordrecht: Kluwer Academic Publishers.

Davidson, D. 2001a. "Rational Animals." In *Subjective, Intersubjective, Objective*, 95–105. Oxford: Oxford University Press.

Davidson, D. 2001b. "The Second Person." In *Subjective, Intersubjective, Objective*, 107–121. Oxford: Oxford University Press.

Davidson, D. 2001c. "Three Varieties of Knowledge." In *Subjective, Intersubjective, Objective*, 205–220. Oxford: Oxford University Press.

Davidson, D. 2004. "What Thought Requires." In *Problems of Rationality*, 135–149. Oxford: Oxford University Press.

Diamond, C. 1991a. "Realism and the Realistic Spirit." In *The Realistic Spirit*. Cambridge, Mass.: MIT Press.

Diamond, C. 1991b. "Introduction II: Wittgenstein and Metaphysics." In *The Realistic Spirit*, 39–72. Cambridge, Mass.: MIT Press.

Fodor, J., and E. Lepore. 1992. *Holism: A Shopper's Guide*. Oxford: Basil Blackwell.

Jackman, H. 1999. "Moderate Holism." *American Philosophical Quarterly* 36:361–369.

Lormand, E. 1996. "How to Be a Meaning Holist." *Journal of Philosophy* 93:51–73.

Malcolm, N. 1977. "Thoughtless Brutes." In *Thought and Knowledge*, 40–57. Ithaca: Cornell University Press.

McDowell, J. 1998. "Wittgenstein on Following a Rule." In *Mind, Value, and Reality*. Cambridge, Mass.: Harvard University Press.

Rorty, R. 1979. *Philosophy and the Mirror of Nature*. Princeton: Princeton University Press.

Sellars, W. 1975. "The Structure of Knowledge." In H. Castañada, ed., *Action, Knowledge, and Reality: Critical Studies in Honor of Wilfrid Sellars*, 295–347. Indianapolis: Bobbs-Merrill.

Sellars, W. 1981. "Mental Events." *Philosophical Studies* 39:325–345.

Sellars, W. 1997. *Empiricism and the Philosophy of Mind*. Cambridge, Mass.: Harvard University Press.

Wittgenstein, L. 1953. *Philosophical Investigations*. Trans. G. E. M. Anscombe. Oxford: Basil Blackwell.

Wittgenstein, L. 1978. *Remarks on the Foundations of Mathematics*. Ed. G. H. von Wright, R. Rhees, and G. E. M. Anscombe. Oxford: Basil Blackwell.

Wittgenstein, L. 1992. *Last Writings on the Philosophy of Psychology*, vol. 2. Trans. C. G. Luckhardt and M. A. E. Aue. Ed. G. H. von Wright and H. Nyman. Oxford: Blackwell.

II   The Moral Life

6 Companionable Thinking

Stanley Cavell

It was while I was thinking about preparing a text in which I would attempt to take further some earlier thoughts of mine concerning Wittgenstein's reflections on the concept of "seeing something as something," what he calls seeing aspects, which dominate part 2 of *Philosophical Investigations*, that I reread the paper (I first encountered it as a lecture) that Cora Diamond entitles "The Difficulty of Reality and the Difficulty of Philosophy," a piece in which at a certain point she deploys an idea of mine in a way I found heartening and distinctly instructive. Beyond this, rereading her paper made so strong an impression upon me that I came to feel compelled to articulate a response to it, however unsure I felt my philosophical ground might prove to be. Diamond's paper takes up certain extremities of conflict associated with phenomena of what she calls "the difficulty of reality," cases in which our human capacities to respond—she in effect says the bases or limits of our human nature—are, for some, put to the test, threatening to freeze or to overwhelm understanding and imagination, while at the same time, for others, the phenomenon, or fact, fails to raise, or perhaps it succeeds only in raising, an eyebrow. The principal matter she treats in that paper is the fact, and the understanding of the fact, of our entwinement with the nonhuman world of animals, specifically and most extendedly, our relation or relations to the mass preparation of animals as food for humans. It is a matter to whose implications I have hitherto not devoted consecutive thought—a matter I now feel I have avoided.

I say at once that while relations to animals have come up variously, if intermittently, in my writing over the years, I am neither practiced in the theory of animal rights nor committed in my daily life to vegetarianism. But an idea that is said to test or threaten the limits of human nature reminds me that in my early reflections on Wittgenstein's study of seeing something as something, I raised the issue whether it makes sense to speak of seeing others or ourselves *as* human. If it does, then it makes sense to suppose that we may *fail* to see ourselves and others so—a purported condition I went on to call "soul-blindness." A subtext of my reflections to follow here is the question whether there is a comparable blindness we may suffer with respect to nonhuman animals.

The obvious bearing of Wittgenstein's study of seeing something as something on Diamond's wish to have us ponder the human and the intellectual challenges of the mass production of animals for food lies in its suggestion that the extreme variation in human responses to this fact of civilized existence is not a function of any difference in our access to information; no one knows, or can literally see, anything here that the others fail to know or see. But then if one concludes that the variation is a function of a response to, or of an attitude toward, information that is shared, one may suppose the issue is of some familiar form of moral disagreement. Diamond's discussion specifically questions this supposition. One peculiarity of the case of breeding animals for the manufacturing of food, beyond the extremity of responses ranging from horror to indifference, unlike difficulties over the death penalty, or the legitimacy of a war, or the torture of prisoners, or euthanasia, or abortion, is that the issue is one that touches the immediate and perhaps invisible choices of most of the members of a society every day. Further, those who are indifferent to, or tolerant of, the mass killing of animals for food may well regard the purpose of the institution as producing an enhancement of modes of human life's greatest pleasures, from the common pleasures of sharing nourishment to the rare pleasures of consuming exquisite delicacies. It seems safe to say that no one of balanced mind thinks it an enhancement of human pleasures to perform executions or abortions or to torture. (Nietzsche may have exceptionally divined pleasure taken in such activities, and Himmler may have shared his view in warning the minions under his command that their deeds of extermination must be carried out soberly and dutifully.) The variation of attitudes that Diamond's discussion stresses between the horror of individuals and the indifference of most of society considers moments in which the variation of response seems one between visions of the world, between how its practices are regarded, or seen, or taken to heart, or not.

Wittgenstein's reflections on seeing aspects (most memorably using the Gestalt figure of a duck-rabbit to demonstrate incompatible ways of reading or seeing a situation) was brought into more general intellectual circulation when Thomas Kuhn used the idea of a "Gestalt switch" in understanding certain crises in intellectual history, specifically in the history of science. But in Wittgenstein's elaboration of his reflections he emphasizes that "hugely many interrelated phenomena and possible concepts" (*Philosophical Investigations*, 199) are brought into play, among them the concept of merely knowing (ibid., 202), and of reading a poem or narrative with feeling and merely skimming the lines for information (ibid., 214), and of being struck by, or blind to, a likeness, and of a picture as helping one to read with the correct expression (ibid.). I might characterize Diamond as raising the question of what I will call inordinate knowledge, knowledge whose importunateness can seem excessive in its expression, in contrast to mere or unobtrusive or intellectualized or indifferent or stored knowledge, as though for some the concept of eating animals has no particular *interest* (arguably another direction of questionable—here defective—expression). I think of a remark of Freud's in rehearsing the progress of coming into one's own through the talking cure: "There is knowing, and there is knowing." And I suppose, in another register, this variability of condition is what Paul, in his first letter to the Corinthians, cites in the phrase "now I know in part."

I think too of my efforts to understand the appeal to the ordinary in the philosophical practices of the later Wittgenstein and of J. L. Austin, hence of the tendency they counter in traditional philosophy, since at least Plato's Cave, of seeking systematically to transcend or to impugn the ordinary in human existence. The vivid extremes in responding to the worldwide existence of food factories is a cautionary, even lurid, example warning against supposing that the ordinary is a *given*, as it were a *place*. I would say rather that it is a task, as the self is.

I will not arrive here at some conclusion about how far the concept of seeing aspects may bear on either inordinate or insipid expression. Such a suggestion comes up inconclusively a couple of times in what follows. Its point is to specify moments at which we know we need a convincing account of the extreme differences of response to the eating, and other questionable uses, of nonhuman animals since in lacking it we betray a register of our ignorance of ourselves.

In the paper of Diamond's that I begin from here her reflections are principally cast as a commentary on moments from the presentation depicted in a pair of stories by J. M. Coetzee with the title "The Lives of Animals." The pair appear under this title as two of the seven chapters that make up Coetzee's novel *Elizabeth Costello*. The pair also appear in a separate volume also entitled *The Lives of Animals*, this time accompanied by responses from five writers from various disciplines. It is this latter volume that Diamond considers. She stresses her finding herself, in one decisively consequential respect, in a different, isolated, position from all of these five respondents, despite the fact that she and they all express unhappiness with the state, and the understanding of the state, of the human relation to the nonhuman animal world. We shall come to Diamond's isolating difference in due course.

The first of this pair of Coetzee's stories features a lecture to a college audience in the United States given by a fictional Australian writer named Elizabeth Costello as part of the two- or three-day celebration in which she is being honored by the college. In the opening moments of her lecture, Costello reports herself unable to put aside her perception, or vision, in all its offensiveness, that in the treatment of animals in what she calls our food factories we are, to "say it openly . . . surrounded by an enterprise of degradation, cruelty and killing which rivals anything that the Third Reich was capable of, indeed dwarfs it, in that ours is an enterprise without end" (*Lives of Animals*, 65). (What is our enterprise, and when did theirs end?)

In the second of the stories Diamond is responding to, Coetzee includes near its beginning a letter from someone that Elizabeth Costello's son, who teaches at the college, describes as a poet who has been around the college forever. I quote most of the words of the letter, anticipating my wanting to return to various of them:

Dear Mrs. Costello, Excuse me for not attending last night's dinner. I have read your books and know you are a serious person, so I do you the credit of taking what you said in your lecture seriously. At the kernel of your lecture, it seemed to me, was the question of breaking bread. If we refuse to break bread with the executioners of Auschwitz, can we continue to break bread with the slaughterers of animals? You took over for your own purposes the familiar comparison between the murdered Jews of Europe and slaughtered cattle. You misunderstand the nature of likenesses . . . to the point of blasphemy. Man is made in the likeness of God but God does not have the likeness of man. If Jews were treated like cattle, it does not follow that cattle are treated like Jews. The inversion insults the memory of the dead. It also trades on the horrors of the camps in a cheap way. . . . Forgive me if I am forthright. You said you were old enough not to have time to waste on niceties, and I am an old man too. Yours sincerely, Abraham Stern. (*Lives of Animals*, 49–50)

Costello's daughter-in-law, with whom she does not get along, refers to the letter as a "protest," and the letter does seem to collect, as if to preempt, a number of attacks a reader might want to launch against Costello's speech. But, especially in light of the daughter-in-law's general dismissal of Costello's sensibility (and without speculating about what may be causing it), we can be sure that this is not enough to say about the letter's anguish. In particular the letter avoids considering the specific understanding Stern expresses to account for his absence at last night's dinner. Along with other omissions among the appeals Stern addresses to logic in his distress—to matters of what follows from what—while Stern opens with the coup of raising the question of breaking bread in this context of an invitation to dinner, he omits to say why he had refused precisely to break bread last night with Mrs. Costello. Was this because her words have reached to the point of blasphemy, to dishonoring the work of God? (It is an issue for certain thinking about the Holocaust whether it should be represented at all.) Or was it because she insults the memory of the dead? Or because she invokes horror cheaply? Oddly, or ironically, these are causes Costello could well find pertinent to her own sense of horror, or as she sometimes puts it, disorientation. But this is not how Stern introduced the idea of breaking bread. He was granting (I assume) the truth of the idea that we (are right to) refuse to break bread with the executioners at Auschwitz. That black meal would, let us say, curse communion, incorporating—symbolically, it goes without saying, surely—the human ingestion of bread as the body and wine as the blood of divinity.

Stern's refusal of communion with the executioners at Auschwitz forms a sort of major premise, as it were, of the syllogism he attributes to Costello. Her minor premise is that the slaughterers of animals are in a moral or spiritual class with the executioners at Auschwitz. From which the conclusion follows that we (are right to) refuse to break bread with these further slaughterers. But are we to take it that Stern finds Costello's offensive fault of argumentative assimilation to warrant assimilating her to (receiving a treatment of shunning precisely marking the treatment warranted by) the executioners of Auschwitz, beyond the pale of shared bread? This reaction would seem to make his perception of Costello's fault quite as inordinate as he takes her perception of the slaughterers of animals to be. And/or should this count as Stern's doing what he promised at the outset of his letter to do, namely taking what Elizabeth said in her lecture seriously?

Taking expressions seriously, or a sense of difficulty with realizing this project, is a way I might characterize what Diamond names "the difficulty of philosophy," something she understands to inhabit, or to be inhabited by, "the difficulty of reality." I associate this mutual existence with what I have sometimes discussed as a chronic difficulty in expressing oneself, especially in its manifestation as finding a difficulty or disappointment with meaning, or, say, with language, or with human expression, as such. It is a disappointment I find fundamental to my reading of Wittgenstein's *Philosophical Investigations*.

In an essay from 1978, which she entitles "Eating Meat and Eating People," Cora Diamond identifies herself as a vegetarian and specifies her motive in writing about the question "How might I go about showing someone that he had reason not to eat animals?" as that of attacking the arguments and not the perceptions of philosophers who express the sense of "the awful and unshakable callousness and unrelentingness with which we most often confront the nonhuman world" (334). The arguments, familiarly in terms of animal rights, she finds not just too weak, but the impulse to argument at this level to be itself morally suspicious. I have, I think, felt this way when, in response to my expressing doubt that there are moral truths for whose certainty moral theory should undertake to provide proofs, philosophers more than once have proposed "It is wrong to torture children" as a certain truth to which moral theory has the responsibility of providing an argument, and at least one philosopher added: an argument strong enough to convince Hitler. In *The Claim of Reason*, I reply to this train of thought by saying that morality is not meant to check the conduct of monsters.

I have not, I believe, anywhere considered in detail the dangers of allowing oneself to judge another to exhibit monstrousness. Perhaps this has been because I felt sure that I would be told that the danger of such a judgment is that others might take it into their heads to judge me to be a monster, without argument. It does not, I have to say, make me feel safer to suppose that my defense against a judgment of my monstrousness must be to discover an argument to combat it. The danger I still feel worth pursuing is that, or how, I might discover monstrousness in myself. What is Thoreau seeing when he declares, "I never knew a worse man than myself"?

I do not imagine that it has been a sense of poor argumentation on behalf of vegetarianism that has helped prevent me from becoming vegetarian. A clear inkling of the pertinence of the choice of that form of life for me was likely, I have thought, to present itself in consequence of my discovery of my love of Thoreau's multiple intelligence. I recall the strong effect upon me of his saying that he has no objection to young boys learning to hunt and to fish—taking him to mean that in the age of innocence (the period Emerson calls the "neutrality" of boys), the young should feel in themselves that they are part of, equal to, the wildness of nature, that they sense and relish, not fear, or distrust, their own, let's say, animal aliveness—and his going on to cite the day on which, as Thoreau reports it, he discovered that in fishing he felt a certain lowering of respect for himself. It is from about then, backed by further of his observations, that I have sometimes half expected an analogous feeling to come my way. (Despite the fact that there was no one in my early life from whom to learn how to hunt and to fish.)

In Diamond's earlier essay, she isolates a line from a poem of Walter de la Mare's— "If you would happy company win" (namely the companionship of "a nimble titmouse")—and says of it (in contrast to the idea shared by the five commentators accompanying Coetzee's stories) that it presents "a different notion [of a nonhuman animal, namely], that of a living creature, or fellow creature which is *not* a biological concept"(*Realism and the Realistic Spirit*, 328). What she explains she means by her different notion is one that is not the concept of an animal possessing this or that interest or capacity in common or at variance with our human interests or capacities, but one that "means a being . . . which may be sought as *company*" (ibid., 329; Diamond's emphasis). It is the experience of company, say, of proving to us that we are not alone in the world, and not an argument about the animal's biological powers that on Diamond's view places consuming the animal out of reasonable bounds.

I recall passages in various texts of mine in which I have over the years been prompted to record, coming, it could seem, from nowhere, encounters with animals, real and imaginary. Thinking of Emerson at the moment (perhaps it was Thoreau) observing a squirrel arching across a field and being prompted to note that squirrels were not made to live unseen, I am moved to record, from a time within the childhood of my two sons, my watching almost every day during the early weeks of winter the following scene play itself out beyond the kitchen window looking into the back garden of our house. We had strung a thin rope diagonally across a corner angle of the garden fence in order to suspend from the middle of the rope a bird feeder. This was designed to keep the two or three most familiar neighborhood squirrels away from the seeds before the birds had a chance at them. When initially the squirrels tried to maneuver themselves along the rope, something about it (its thinness, or its slack) foiled them. Then the next day one of the squirrels negotiated the rope all the way to the feeder and tipped it so that some of its seeds fell to the ground, thus providing a repast for his (or her) companions and, eventually, himself. I was surprised at how quickly it became obvious to me that on successive mornings it was invariably the same genius performing this mission on behalf of this little group. Before our family devised a further way to protect the birds' interests, I inwardly looked forward each day to encountering and saluting this gesture of virtuosity and careless sociability. Since it was in part my seeds that this benefactor distributed and ate, it expresses my sense of the situation to say that, as I observed him while having my morning coffee and roll, I was breaking bread with him, in common if not reciprocally.

What would follow? This sense is, I agree, perfectly incompatible with the idea of eating the fellow. But I have in any case never had such an idea with respect to squirrels. The idea has in the past been proposed to me with respect to rabbit and to horse and to snails. In each case I, as it were for the sake of philosophy, tried each just once. But my inward cringe at the idea of repetition in these cases did not transfer to my other carnivorous habits.

Nor am I tempted here to a conclusion about inconsistency. I am impressed, as Diamond is, by Costello's insisting, along with her inordinate knowledge of the use of animals for food, on her relative complaisance, anyway willingness, in wearing leather shoes and carrying a leather purse. (I suppose the insistence is to ward off the attribution to herself of an unknowable purity of spirit.) Diamond speaks in this connection of inescapable but "bitter compromise." This greatly interests me and I mean to return to it.

Diamond's emphasis on "company"—earning the companionship of the titmouse— is a fairly exact precursor, etymologically, of Coetzee's Abraham Stern's sense in his letter of "breaking bread," an idea that Stern charges Costello with pressing into cheap service but that Diamond takes from Costello with utmost seriousness. This means that she takes seriously the inordinateness in Costello's response, I mean she brings into question just what is disproportionate about it. (One could say she respects Costello's brush with madness.) And perhaps she therewith brings into question whether proportionateness is the question. Here is a place we might ask whether it would be helpful to think of Costello to be seeing animals *as* company. But rather than intensifying insipid knowledge, this appeal to seeing something as something seems here to etiolate inordinate knowledge, or rather to make the company of animals something less than a fact, namely the fact that they *are* (not serve as) company (for some, sometimes). Diamond emphasizes Costello's state of raw nerves or, as Costello sometimes describes it, her insecurity with her own humanity.

Diamond gets quickly in her Coetzee essay to that moment she takes most signally to differentiate her perception of his tale, hence to isolate herself, from the position of those who had been invited to respond to it. She focuses on the moment—one she discovers essentially to be passed by in their responses—in which Costello declares herself to be, analogously with Kafka's great ape in "Address to an Academy," "not a philosopher of mind but an animal exhibiting, yet not exhibiting, to a gathering of scholars, a wound, which I cover up under my clothes but touch on in every word I speak" (*The Lives of Animals*, 71). In thus taking her own existence to be one among the lives of animals in the story, it becomes the chief subject, or object, of the story, the singular life depicted in it that counts as multiple, the human as the animal of multiple lives, say drawn between wild and tame, or this way with one person that way with another, open and hidden, old without being sure how to be old, capable of indecorousness in her work, suffering in, and suffering from, what she says, from her own indictment by it. Since Diamond rejects, congenially to my way of seeing things, the idea of *a* way, or a *set* of ways, for all to see, in which nonhuman animals differ from human animals, a way that explains why we might not wish, or allow ourselves, to eat them, I take the suggestion to be that the realms differ, and hence are akin, endlessly, as in the case of the separation, or differences, between the human and the divine. (The appearance of the religious in Coetzee's tale repeatedly becomes pressing. This must be mostly for another time.) For example, an animal's way of eating—and so the diet integral to an animal species' life form—differs from human eating as significantly as an animal's mating or parenting or building or foraging or bonding or mortality or attention or expectation or locomotion differs from, and is analogous to, one might sometimes say is an allegory of, their forms in human life.

Coetzee's book *Elizabeth Costello* opens this way: "There is first of all the problem of the opening, namely, how to get us from where we are, which is, as yet, nowhere, to the far bank. It is a simple bridging problem, a problem of knocking together a bridge. People solve such problems every day. They solve them, and having solved them push on."

(In my piece on the aesthetics, or writing, of the *Investigations* in Mulhall's volume, I am surprised to recall that I speak of a near and a far shore and of "the river of philosophy that runs between" [382]. The near shore is the perspective of philosophical "problems," listed by Wittgenstein in his preface as "the concepts of meaning, of understanding, of a proposition, of logic, . . . and other things." The far shore is the further perspective I describe, or standpoint, "from which to see the methods of the *Investigations*, their leading words home, undoing the charms of metaphysics, a perspective apart from which there is no pressing issue of spiritual fervor, whether felt as religious, moral, or aesthetic." And I go on to say: "One [shore] without the other loses the pivot of the ordinary, the pressure of everyday life; one without the other thus loses, to my way of thinking, the signature of the *Investigations*. There remains a question of priority. From each shore, the other is almost ignorable, and each imagines itself to own the *seriousness* of the *Investigations*' work" [*The Cavell Reader*, 382–383]. I should confess that I like to understand Cora Diamond's title for her already classic collection *The Realistic Spirit* as encoding these banks or shores, indicating that philosophy is perpetually a matter of tracing the loss and recovery [revised, reviewed] of the ordinary, of subjecting to criticism what we would like in philosophy to insist upon as necessarily real—specifically to criticism out of the spirit of realism, of how the human animal actually, let us say, negotiates its life and its understanding of its life.)

I take Coetzee's repetition, in his book's opening that I just now quoted, of "solve" or "solving," three times in two adjacent sentences, ironically but tenderly to picture "people," in attempting to make human life a series of problems, as attempting to construe their existence as itself a problem, an intellectual puzzle to solve and from which to push on. Nietzsche enters a similar complaint of intellectualization against our species, in its regarding life "as a riddle, a problem of knowledge," in *The Genealogy of Morals*. (I cannot but think that Cora Diamond was as intrigued as I to see Coetzee's opening chapter given the title "Realism.") *Philosophical Investigations* is in effect a portrait of the unsatisfiability of the human species with its solutions, a portrait—hardly the first—detailing human life as one of restlessness, exposure, insecurity; and more specifically, of what in an essay of mine on its aesthetics I identify as

its articulation of the modern subject, namely its expected reader, as one characterized by, among other traits, perversity, sickness, self-destructiveness, suffocation, lost-
ness, strangeness, and so on.

This may helpfully return us to the question of taking seriously Elizabeth Costello's
notation of herself as an animal wounded, but with a wound (unlike other suffering
animals) that she exhibits and does not exhibit. That she specifies her concealing it
under her clothes immediately alerts us to the most obvious, or banal, unlikeness
between her condition and that of other animals, namely, just that her species wears
clothes. And since what is concealed, and not concealed, under her clothes, we are
allowed to assume—are we not?—is an aging but otherwise unharmed woman's body,
the torment she expresses is somehow to be identified with the very possession of a
human body, which is to say, with being human. (I say "otherwise unharmed." I am
assuming that there is no visible remnant of harm from the event she describes in a
later chapter when, half a century ago, she allowed herself to be picked up by a tough
who beat her up when he found she wanted to repel his advances. She suffered a
broken jaw, and she describes its treatment and its healing. What counts as a wound
persisting from that incident is her perception that the tough took evident pleasure
in beating her; this produced in her what she describes as her first knowledge of evil,
something not hidden by clothes. I do not know Coetzee's attitude toward the work
of Freud, but I cannot put aside a suggestion that there is something specifically
wounded in the normal female body.)

I emphasize two peculiarities about this revelation of the woundedness that marks
being human. First, since the stigmata of the suffering are coincident with the possession of the human body, the right to enter such a claim universally to other such
possessors has roughly the logic of a voice in the wilderness, crying out news that may
be known (inordinately) to virtually none, but to all virtually. It is a voice invoking a
religious, not alone a philosophical, register: it is uninvited, it goes beyond an appeal
to experiences we can assume all humans share, or recognize, and it is meant to instill
belief and a commentary and community based on belief, yielding a very particular
form of passionate utterance, call it prophecy. We could say that the object of the revelation is not simply to touch but to announce the wound that has elicited its expression and that gives it authority: Costello had said, in matching our behavior with that
in the Third Reich: "*Ours* [our mass-manufacturing of corpses] is an enterprise without
end" (*The Lives of Animals*, 21). It is an inherently indecorous comparison, not to say
offensive, and perhaps deliberately a little mad; fervent news from nowhere. The right
to voice it is not alone an arrogation of a claim every human is in a position to make,
a claim philosophy requires of itself, in speaking for all; it is also a judgment that dis-

tances itself from the human as it stands, that finds human company itself touched with noxiousness.

Here is a place at least to mention the apparent congruence between Costello's comparison of food factories and concentration camps with a pair of sentences attributed to Heidegger by Philippe Lacoue-Labarthe and quoted by Maurice Blanchot, printed in an issue of *Critical Inquiry* a few years ago devoted to Heidegger and Nazism. Heidegger is reported to have said: "Agriculture is now a mechanized food industry. [This much is said essentially word for word in Heidegger's well-studied text "The Question Concerning Technology" from 1955. The attributed pair of Heidegger's sentences continues:] As for its essence [that is, technology's essence] it is the same thing as the manufacture of corpses in the gas chambers and the death camps, the same thing as the blockades and the reduction of countries to famine, the same thing as the manufacture of hydrogen bombs." I rather imagine (but this is not essential to my reflections) that Coetzee knew this citation linking the food industry with, among other things, the death camps and that he meant to be putting Heidegger's words to the test in his novel, in effect to ask whether such a view is credible coming anywhere but from an old artist, tired of, and sickened almost to death by, the responses she receives late in her life of words, crazed by her words' reality to her together with their loss of interest to others and jarred or compelled by her imagination into welcoming the offense she may cause. One of the moments in Heidegger's *What Is Called Thinking?* that I am most impressed by is his description of Nietzsche, in trying to reach his contemporaries with the event of their murder of God. Heidegger writes: "most quiet and shiest of men, . . . [Nietzsche] endured the agony of having to scream." I find it illuminating to think of Elizabeth Costello, in her exhausted way, as screaming.

A further detail suggesting the presence of Heidegger's *What Is Called Thinking?* in Coetzee's text lies in that opening picture of a reader's journey, or a life's journey, as from a near to a far bank, posing a problem from which "people" are able to "push on"; he calls it, speaking for these problem-solvers, a "bridging problem" (48). Heidegger says early in this book of his, with respect to the passage from our scientific or intellectualized mentality to authentic philosophical thinking, that "There is no bridge here . . . only the leap" (8). It follows that the opening paragraph of Coetzee's novel describes us, human beings pushing on, getting on, going along, solving problems (in terms, I take it, dictated by others) as not in a position, or a place, for thinking, or for what is to be called thinking.

One in whose imagination Heidegger survives as a serious thinker is apt to have had to find a way beyond the sense that his thought comes to direct itself as an apology for the practices of Nazism (despite certain of his "reservations" concerning its theories). And, since it is Elizabeth Costello's comparison of food factories with death camps that invoked Heidegger's linking of the camps with the agricultural industry, I mark her difference from Heidegger at the point at which Cora Diamond (in contrast to the initial silence on the point by the five commentators published with Coetzee's pair of stories), unveils (as it were) her now inescapable knowledge of her hidden yet unconcealable wound. Heidegger acknowledges no such wound for him to confess (for *him*), or to scream, and it is perhaps in this continence, or absence, that he is cursed.

I said that there are two peculiarities in Elizabeth Costello's invocation of human existence as wounded. The first is what I described as her identification of woundedness—judging from her own—with the condition of human embodiment, the very possession of the human body, as stigma. The second peculiarity is her claim that the evidence for her invisible/visible wound, or expression of it, is present, or, as she puts the matter, is "touched on," in every word she speaks. In my experience, a precedent for such a thought, or vision, is Emerson's way of speaking, epitomized in his declaration in "Self-Reliance," that "Every word they say chagrins us" (adding that "we know not where to set them right"). But what differentiates "them" from "us"? Every word he hears chagrins him, and all the words he speaks are in essence, to begin with, the words of others, common bread. What other words are there? This means that every word he speaks is touched with, is fated to express, chagrin. To speak—the signature expression of the human life form—is to be victimized by what there is to say, or to fail to say.

A topic that brings Emerson's chagrin to fever pitch is slavery. From "Emancipation of the British West Indies": "Language must be raked, the secrets of the slaughterhouses and infamous holes that cannot front the day, must be ransacked, to tell what negro-slavery has been." Earlier in that essay Emerson had said: "You have just dined, and however scrupulously the slaughter-house is concealed in the graceful distance of miles, there is complicity, expensive races." This somewhat extends his having spoken earlier in the essay of "expensive races,—race living at the expense of race." I will not reargue here my sense that the repeated presence of the slaughterhouse, together with the ambiguity of "race living at the expense of race"—meaning the human race living at the expense of animals but in this context unmistakenly meaning at the same time the white race living at the expense of the black—yields the perception, or vision, that slavery is a form of cannibalism. Essential to his "argument" is that the idea of language as having to be raked compresses a suggestion that in moments high and low the house of language is overrun, overcome, words must be searched for through wreckage and then with force and craft aligned into parallel, justified ranks on a page to work together. Such matters—recalling what Diamond speaks of as the difficulty of reality and of philosophy—will have to be taken seriously if we consider whether it expresses the perception at issue to say that Emerson here sees slavery *as* cannibalism. This would make the concept of seeing-as a kind of explication of allegory, as when at the opening of *Walden*, Thoreau reports his vision of his townspeople of Concord as observing practices meant to torment themselves, as though they are choosing, and not choosing, to make life a set of strange forms of penance, a vision that flares and fades; whereas I wanted to speak of the impression of cannibalism as perhaps irreversible.

I report also in this connection, as I have before, Thoreau's treating human feeding as such as a matter for anxious satire. In the account of his expenses, the literal listing of dollars and cents expended, for surviving his first year at Walden, Thoreau separately itemizes the cost of food, and he comments: "I thus unblushingly publish my guilt." Thoreau here perceives his very existence, the assertion of the will to live in the world by feeding himself, as without certain justification—there are debts in living, conditions of existence, uses to which he puts, or fails to put, the peaceable space cleared for him before he cleared it, that are uncountable. What makes them insupportable is the degree to which they are unnecessary. Then the quest in which an adventurous life may well be spent in search, or experiment, is to replace false by true necessaries, or means, to what one truly finds good (a philosophical quest as ancient as Plato's *Republic*), perhaps promising to allow the cloaking of the wound of existing to become superfluous.

Of course one may wish to ask whether Thoreau would not have more relevance to the way the world is if he were a little more realistic, say more open to compromise. (Albert Schweitzer in Africa, once a more formidable guide to existence than I suppose he is now, instead of [or in addition to] protecting his hoard from the ants, left little piles of sugar for them by his bed in his tent when he retired for the night. Is such a practice, from our contemporary perspective, anything more than precious or quaint? But perhaps it was not meant as more than one man's solace.) Yet Thoreau's key term "Economy," the title of the opening, longest chapter of *Walden*, precisely projects an unfolding register of terms in which compromise at its best—keeping accounts in a fallen world of one's interests and means and losses and wastes and returns and borrowings and dreams and terms (accounts of *all* of one's terms)—can best be articulated systematically and lived. Its moral could even be taken to be that of realism.

I predicted that I would want to return to the idea of compromise. Here more fully is Cora Diamond's response (in her Coetzee essay) when she takes up, in connection with my discussion in part 4 of *The Claim of Reason* of what I call our exposure to the other, Costello's reply to the suggestion that her vegetarianism comes out of moral conviction. Costello hesitantly deflects the suggestion, saying instead, "It comes out of a desire to save my soul." Diamond glosses this as follows: "[We are not] *given* the presence or absence of moral community . . . with animals. But we are exposed—that is, we are thrown into finding something we can live with, and it may at best be a kind of bitter-tasting compromise. There is here only what we make of our exposure" ("The Difficulty of Reality," 111).

Can we specify more closely the cause and strength of the bitter taste of compromise, in a region in which taste may be thought to be everything? Taste—or some discrimination beyond what we readily think of as taste—seems at play in Costello's cautioning, or rebuking, her questioner (who had assured her that he has a great respect for vegetarianism as a way of life, thus in effect discounting her declaration of the threatened state of her soul beyond the matter of moral conviction) by saying: "I'm wearing leather shoes and carrying a leather purse. I wouldn't have overmuch respect if I were you" (*The Lives of Animals*, 43). That is, there is still disproportion between what I know and how I feel and ways I behave, if less than there might be. Costello's questioner (he is identified as the president of the college honoring her) "murmurs": "Consistency is the hobgoblin of small minds. Surely one can draw a distinction between eating meat and wearing leather." " 'Degrees of obscenity,' she replies." Replies to *him*. (I merely take notice of this placement of Emerson's famous, and famously mocked, crack about the hobgoblin of consistency, casually misquoted in the mouth of a decorous college president, used casuistically to take the sting from a declaration of one's soul being threatened. Here is a welcome occasion to show Emerson's uncompromising words compromised; yesterday's radical words picked up by today's stuffed shirt.) But then what are we to make of Costello's use of "degrees"? She is implying that her state participates in obscenity, but the fact is that wearing leather, or the vision of preparation of it for human comfort and vanity, does not seem to cause her body dangerously to signal itself of its woundedness. Is it then in her case not the necessity of compromise that causes bitterness, but rather the discovery that she is, that her body is, capable of compromise? (This may suggest not a fastidiousness but a vanity of spirit.) But how does this reach to the sense of having to conceal, without concealing, a wounded body?

Is it a function of some perception of disproportion between saving one's soul and finding alternatives to wearing leather? This is in fact no easy matter to determine, especially if it begins to lead to questioning more globally the conditions under which our comforts generally are sustained, and we undertake to examine work houses as closely as slaughterhouses. As Emerson phrased the matter: however graceful the distance kept, "there is complicity, expensive races." I cannot doubt that Emerson is here (not for the only time) invoking Rousseau's perception of our stake in the social contract as that of conspirators, even recognizing that the perpetual failure of justice invites the threat of madness, of taking my participation in the difficult reality of my society's injustice or indifference or brutality as it were personally, a sense that seems to measure Elizabeth Costello's sense of isolation in her woundedness. The sense *happens*, happens even beyond sensibilities such as Hamlet's or Antigone's or Phédre's or Melisande's, unrelieved bearers of inordinate knowledge, of human exposure.

The direction out of Costello's condition (as it were against Kafka's report of a passage, or, say, bridge, to a higher species), barring withdrawal from the human race—that is, deciding to stay alive—is to sink within the race, or disguise herself as a voting member of it, at one with Hamlet in the perception that "Mankind pleases not me—nor woman neither." Not prepared to resign from humanity, nor to display rage against others for failing to do so, which would uselessly increase the human being's suffering from itself ("horror of itself," Montaigne says, commending a more amiable wisdom), she insists upon her adorning and comforting herself with things of leather. I do not propose a competition between our degree of compromise with the subjection of animals to human demand and that of our compromise with the degree of injustice in our society. I remain too impressed with Freud's vision of the human animal's compromise with existence—the defense or the deflection of our ego in our knowledge of ourselves from what there is to know about ourselves—to suppose that a human life can get itself without residue into the clear. It is true that I have sometimes felt vegetarianism to be a way of declaring a questionable distance from the human animal, but that can hardly be a reason for my not taking that path when it has beckoned.

I am in any case in accord with Cora Diamond's caution about what should count as a "reason" for or against eating meat. And I think I may have, in the course of working through the present material to this point, learned something about the wish to declare distance from the identification with one's fellow human animals. I have in the past found that in moral confrontation I can never say in my defense (here disagreeing with a moment in the work of John Rawls), "I am above reproach," or rather that to say so is to suggest that the other is morally less competent than I am. Now I find that, in response to reminders of the company we may keep with nonhuman animals, I cannot so much as say, "I am *not* above reproach." If the former defense falsifies my position by claiming an insupportable difference from others, the latter etiolates my position by claiming nothing in particular (declaring a generalized guilt in a guilty world), absolving myself from the task of responding to a reason for abstinence either by denying that I share the vision from which the reason derives its force (I do not see or treat all animals as companions), with or without urging a different vision (eating animals affirms my evolutionary stage as a carnivorous, or rather omnivorous, animal), or by marking a difference in my taste that shields it from the vision (I do not eat species that I perceive as companions). What I would like to say is simply, "I am human"—but to whom can this plea be directed?

Some concluding questions, as of notes to myself. Speaking of saving one's soul, how does one understand the characteristic of religions to impose dietary restrictions? Here are vast regions in which universal commands, unlike moral considerations, serve effectively and consistently to define a separate community, and do not depend upon changing one's individual sensibility with respect to other of God's creatures. It puzzled me, in some way offended me, when, during my preparation for my Bar Mitzvah, the rabbi cautioned a small group of us, in discussing the prohibition against eating pork, that we were not to claim that eating pork was in itself a bad practice, merely that it was not *our* practice, and followed this announcement with a little shudder of disgust and an enigmatic smile, which got a laugh from the small group. Both the smile and the laugh had a bad effect on me. Is absolute obedience to a mark of difference, merely *as* difference, a serious business or is it not? Embarrassed by, and not yet ready to repair, my ignorance of the general state of philosophical argument concerning vegetarianism, for example concerning whether religious dietary restrictions are expected to come into consideration, I took an occasion to ask a young friend studying theology whether the matter is current there. Without answering that, she pointed me back to the astonishing opening book of Daniel, in which Daniel, who "purposed in his heart that he would not defile himself with the portion of the king's meat," contrives to refuse Nebuchadnezzar's lavish hospitality, or say dictation, and instead substitutes for himself and his little group of young captives a meatless regime, and after ten days "their countenances appeared fairer and fatter in flesh than all the children which did eat the portion of the king's meat." However, this story of God's favor, or this part of it, feeds my suspicion of vegetarianism as asserting a moral superiority to the rest of humanity, and now based not on an entire way of life but on the sheer fact of abstinence from meat. (I assume it is internal to the motivation for constructing a moral theory of animal rights to neutralize this danger.) But surely it is justified to declare a difference from such as Nebuchadnezzar? No doubt, but in our world this may require assigning to others the role of Nebuchadnezzar.

Is the threat of inconsistency in relation to other animals a cause of comparable anxiety, or "bitterness," with our inconsistency in our moral relations with other humans—thinking, as examples, of the long and terrible list of treacheries for which one asks forgiveness, or forbearance, every year on the Day of Atonement: asking pardon for sins, for wrongdoings, for transgressions committed under duress or by choice, consciously or unconsciously, openly or secretly, in our thoughts or with our words or by the abuse of power, or by hardening our hearts or by speaking slander or by dishonesty in our work, and so on? Take, as I like to, Emerson's remark about the foolish consistency of minds (little or large) as meant to have us consider what we are made of that we may be, and need not be, foolish (an affliction nonhumans are free from). What is human flesh that its appetites, even needs, express, and threaten, the human soul? If there is a threat of madness (persistent and silent outrage or despair are perhaps enough) in reaction to horrors that others seem indifferent to, is there not an equal threat in finding that one is oneself inconsistent in responding to these horrors? What is a proper response to learning, and maintaining the knowledge, of the existence of concentration camps, or of mass starvation? I confess my persistent feeling that a sense of shame at being human (at being stigmatized for having a human body) is more maddeningly directed to the human treatment of human animals than to its treatment of its nonhuman neighbors. I do not, I think, overlook the point that in relation to nonhumans we can take meaningful personal measures whereas in the human case, if we are conscious of it, we readily sense helplessness. What then? Shall we unblushingly publish our guilt in remaining sane in a mad world? I assume philosophy is meant to help us here, say help us to be philosophical. But it is up to us to ask, to go first, to wonder.

Works Cited

Blanchot, Maurice, and Paula Wissing, eds. Special issue of *Critical Inquiry* 15, no. 2 (1989) on Heidegger and Nazism.

Cavell, Stanley. *The Claim of Reason: Wittgenstein, Skepticism, and Tragedy*. Oxford: Oxford University Press, 1979.

Coetzee, J. M. *Elizabeth Costello*. New York: Viking, 2003.

Coetzee, J. M. *The Lives of Animals*. Ed. Amy Gutmann. Princeton: Princeton University Press, 1999.

Diamond, Cora. "Eating Meat and Eating People" (1978). In her *Realism and the Realistic Spirit: Wittgenstein, Philosophy, and the Mind*.

Diamond, Cora. *Realism and the Realistic Spirit: Wittgenstein, Philosophy, and the Mind*. Cambridge, Mass.: MIT Press, 1991.

Diamond, Cora. "The Difficulty of Reality and the Difficulty of Philosophy." In *Reading Cavell*, ed. Alice Crary and Sanford Shieh, 98–118. London: Routledge, 2006.

Heidegger, Martin. *The Question Concerning Technology and Other Essays.* Trans. William Lovitt. New York: Harper and Row, 1977.

Heidegger, Martin. *What Is Called Thinking?* Trans. J. Glenn Gray. New York: Harper and Row, 1968.

Mulhall, Stephen. *The Cavell Reader.* Oxford: Blackwell, 1996.

Wittgenstein, Ludwig. *Philosophical Investigations*, 3rd ed. Trans. G. E. M. Anscombe. New York: Macmillan, 1958.

7   Comment on Stanley Cavell's "Companionable Thinking"

John McDowell

Early in his essay in this volume, Cavell asks himself whether Cora Diamond's purpose in considering J. M. Coetzee's character Elizabeth Costello might be helpfully framed in terms of Wittgenstein's discussion of seeing aspects. What makes this plausible, he says, "lies in [the] suggestion that the extreme variation in human responses to this fact of civilized existence is not a function of any difference in our access to information; no one knows, or can literally see, anything herre that the others fail to know or see" (this vol., p. 282). Later he answers the question in the negative; he concludes that the idea of seeing something *as* something is not helpful here, on the ground that if we frame Diamond's thinking in terms of aspect seeing, we do not give proper weight to the fact that for her other animals just *are* our fellows, not things we can see as our fellows if we can achieve an aspect-switch. Diamond does not say something analogous to "It can also be seen as a duck." But Cavell does not revoke the thought he expressed at the beginning, that all relevant knowledge is universally shared.

If Diamond's topic were how we should respond to the treatment of nonhuman animals in the production of food, Cavell's apparently offhand remark that no one knows anything others fail to know would surely be wrong in an obvious way. I think this is actually irrelevant to Diamond's point. (On a less obvious interpretation the remark might still seem open to question about Diamond, more relevantly but less straightforwardly. I shall come to that.) But by letting it seem that his remark might be open to objection in the straightforward way I have in mind now, Cavell begins to obscure Diamond's purpose in invoking Coetzee's character. There is a twist to this because the paper Cavell is responding to is a graceful approach to a central strand in Cavell's own thinking. Cavell's response does not do justice to the wonderful way Diamond has found to cast light on Cavellian themes.

If it were right to think Diamond is raising an issue that turns on how nonhuman animals are treated in the food industry, knowledge about that would surely be relevant. And it seems obvious that, contrary to what Cavell seems to say, such knowledge is unevenly distributed. Many people know nothing, or next to nothing, about how food (in general, not just meat) is produced. And even if we restrict attention to those who are open to concern about whether all is well in meat production, so that they try not to be ignorant about it, there is surely always room to learn more detail. It seems obvious that some know more than others. But as I said, I think this is irrelevant to Diamond's point.

Let me give a brief, and necessarily oversimplified, sketch of Diamond's attitude toward eating meat. First consider eating human beings. Imagine a world in which dead human beings are rendered into unrecognizable foodstuffs and fed to the living with a lie about the source, as in Edward G. Robinson's last film, *Soylent Green*. If someone thought there was a topic for debate here, about whether this might be all right (I mean independently of the obvious problem about the lie), that would merely show that her use of the phrase "human being" does not express everything many of us mean by it. (What we mean by it now, that is. Nothing ensures that we keep our concepts.) In a similar way, for Diamond it is not a matter for debate whether it might be all right to eat our fellow creatures. (Which ones? How should they be treated before being killed? And so on.) Those who make meat eating into a philosophical topic of the usual kind just reveal that they do not mean what Diamond means by "fellow creature." And it would be missing her point if one relocated the demand for argument as a request for a justification—at any rate a justification of the sort philosophers typically want—for the claim that nonhuman animals are our fellow creatures in a sense that has that power to exclude debate.

Cavell's remark that no one knows anything, concerning meat eating, that others do not know might now seem questionable in a deeper way. It is tempting to say that Diamond thinks she knows something many others do not know: that nonhuman animals are our fellow creatures in that sense. But perhaps after all Cavell's remark is not so offhand, and perhaps it is closer to correct at this deeper level. It is not that Diamond thinks she has a piece of *information* others lack. That would make Diamond's thinking merely a special case of the kind of philosophical approach she rejects. How could one reject a challenge to justify the claim that the supposed information is indeed that? And how could one avoid casting the supposed information as the basis for an argument that meat eating is wrong?

For Diamond, as I said, it is not a topic for philosophical argument, at least of the usual sort, whether meat eating might be all right. It should not seem to change the situation if we imagine animal husbandry being as it is depicted in a certain genre of children's stories, in which the relations between farmers and their animals are like the relations between people and domestic pets. Such stories necessarily leave unmentioned how the animals' lives end, and if one views animals as Diamond does, one would have to see sending them to be turned into food, however friendly one's previous relations with them were, as a betrayal. Factory farming is not like farming in the children's stories, and this amplifies the evil of meat eating, but it is not the essential thing. Whereas if one does not share Diamond's vision of nonhuman animals, the cruelty of factory farming easily becomes the essential thing. It enters into arguments of an ordinarily philosophical kind, addressing the question *which* meat one should not eat, and leaving it possibly all right to eat meat produced from animals that are treated well, as in the children's stories.

For a sort of parallel, consider this. (The sense in which it is a parallel needs care, and it is noteworthy that Coetzee's Costello does not give such questions the care they need.) Suppose someone said the project of eliminating Europe's Jews would have been a lesser evil if its victims had been treated with the utmost consideration and kindness in all respects apart from being deprived of life, which would of course have been done, in this fantasy, as humanely as possible. Such a judgment could be seriously advanced only in the somewhat crazy environment of academic philosophy. It distorts the way in which how things actually were matters. How things actually were amplifies the horror, somewhat as the cruelty of factory farming amplifies the evil of meat eating as Diamond sees things. But if we suppose ethical argument might warrant judgments to the effect that it would have been better if the Final Solution had been put into practice in such-and-such a different way, we bring that horror into the domain of debate, where it does not belong.

For another case of what I mean by talking of amplification, let me mention another of Diamond's examples of the difficulty of reality. In Ted Hughes's poem "Six Young Men" the poet-speaker contemplates, in the fifties, a photograph taken in 1914, in which six young men are vividly present to the viewer. They were all dead soon after the photograph was taken. The poem is about a kind of impossibility the poet finds in trying to combine that fact, in a single mental embrace, with the vibrant aliveness with which they are present in the photograph. Diamond does not remark on this, but the sense of dislocation the poet expresses, from his ordinary means of taking in reality, surely comes more easily because of the specific facts about the photograph. His frame of mind is colored by the thought that the deaths of *these* young men were pointless in a way that goes beyond the pointlessness of just any death. But this is another kind of amplifier. It would have been a harder poem to write, but the sense of dislocation could still have been voiced if the young men had died peacefully after long and fulfilling lives.

I have brought in the Hughes poem partly because I want to stress that Coetzee's Costello is only one of Diamond's examples. Another is a kind of experience of beauty, in which one seems to confront something beyond the reach of one's ordinary equipment for taking in what one finds in the world. And there are others too. Cavell notes, of course, that Diamond's topic is something with multiple instances, not just the difficulty Costello finds in the reality she takes to be constituted by human treatment of nonhuman animals. But he talks as if Diamond's purpose in discussing Coetzee's work—which certainly occupies much of her attention in the paper he considers— were something on the lines of inducing meat eaters to reflect on their practice, or on the spirit in which they engage in it. I think that obscures the point of Diamond's paper. Costello figures, for Diamond, only as exemplifying, in a richly elaborated way, something that is also exemplified in Hughes's poem, and the specifics of what obsesses Costello are in a way irrelevant.

As I said at the beginning, it is Cavell's own thinking that is getting short-changed here. Let me try to explain.

Hughes's poem ends like this:

To regard this photograph might well dement,
Such contradictory permanent horrors here
Smile from the single exposure and shoulder out
One's own body from its instant and heat.

Here we have in germ the structure Diamond finds in Costello's response to human treatment of nonhuman animals.

The poet acknowledges that contemplating the reality his poem is about might well dement. The putative reality Costello contemplates does something close to dementing her. Her response is over the top, notably in the unqualified way she equates our treatment of nonhuman animals with the Holocaust.

The kind of difficulty both cases exemplify arises when something we encounter defeats our ordinary capacity to get our minds around reality, that is, our capacity to capture reality in language. That dislodges us from comfortably inhabiting our nature as speaking animals, animals who can make sense of things in the way the capacity to speak enables us to. The special kind of animal life we lead comes into question. It is as if a beaver found dam building beyond its powers. In the poem the contradictory horrors shoulder out one's own body from its instant and heat. For Costello, it becomes a problem to live her particular case of the lives of animals: a life in which words are not just a distinguishing mark, as they are for human animals in general, but the central element. Her being as the animal she is, which is her bodily being, becomes a wound.

What Diamond aims to display by invoking Costello does not depend on whether what Costello responds to is the reality she takes it to be. Diamond too takes it to be a reality (though she manages not to be unhinged by it), but that is not the point. What Diamond reads Coetzee's depiction of Costello as conveying is something that, explicitly bypassing that question, I can put like this: if it is indeed a reality that most of us casually make a practice of eating our fellow creatures, with "fellow creatures" in that formulation of the putative reality bearing the sense it bears for Diamond and, presumably, Costello, then it is a reality such that to contemplate it head-on can shoulder out one's own body from its instant and heat, can dislodge one from comfortably living one's life as a speaking animal. One can appreciate that even if one does not suppose it is a reality; that is, even if one does not share that vision of nonhuman animals as fellow creatures.

Diamond's interest in Elizabeth Costello is as much in the commentators on Coetzee's Tanner Lectures as in the fiction itself. (Her topic is the Tanner Lectures, not the novel.) To varying extents, the commentators treat the fiction as a frame for presenting arguments, from which as storyteller Coetzee can distance himself, about the ethical standing of our treatment of nonhuman animals. This is an instance of what Diamond calls—following Cavell—"deflection." Coetzee's Costello responds, in a way that is not quite sane but is, in its way, appropriate, to a putative reality that dislodges her from being at home in her life as a speaking animal. The commentators substitute an issue that has only the different difficulty of academic philosophy. How convincing is such-and-such an argument? Does such-and-such a counterargument work? And so on.

Costello's vision of our dealings with other animals unhinges her. For Diamond, this is an analogue to a certain unhinged, though again in its way appropriate, response to another perception (or putative perception: here too, the point does not turn on its being, at least in any straightforward way, correct). The content of this other putative perception is that one is in a certain sense alone, profoundly unknowable by others. When one tries to get one's mind around this putative perception, one's ordinary linguistic repertoire fails one. That is what leads people to come out with forms of words like this: "Surely someone else cannot know it is *this* that I am feeling." Such wordings are a desperate attempt to force language to express a perception that is unhinging one in the way Diamond is interested in, threatening to dislodge one from one's life as a speaking animal.

In academic philosophy, this instance of the sense that one is losing one's ability to live the life that is natural for one gets deflected into an issue that has only the difficulty of ordinary philosophy: do others have sufficient evidence for their judgments about one's inner life, or, symmetrically, does one have sufficient evidence for one's judgments about the inner lives of others?

Wittgenstein gives an extensive treatment of the wish expressed by saying "Someone else cannot know it is *this* that I am feeling," the wish to credit oneself with a language intelligible only to oneself. In standard readings, he is seen as addressing those academic questions about the strength of our grounds for judgments about one another. He is seen as uncovering, in the sense that skepticism is inescapable here, a merely intellectual error. Such readings are cases of deflection, like the commentators' responses to Coetzee's Tanner Lectures. They leave out what is really the whole point: the fact that the impulse Wittgenstein treats originates in a case of being understandably unhinged by the sense that one's words are failing one, that one is losing the capacity to instantiate one's allotted life form as a speaking animal.

Academic treatments of skepticism about empirical knowledge in general can be seen in a similar light. They are a deflection from a response that is unhinged, though again in its way appropriate, to the perception, or putative perception, that in such supposed knowledge we are pervasively at the mercy of the world—a perception, say, of our finitude and dependence as empirical knowers.

That is a drastically abbreviated sketch of how Cavell explains the significance of philosophical skepticism. The role of Coetzee's Costello in Diamond's paper is not to raise the question whether Costello's unhinging perception is a perception of how things indeed are—that is, whether meat eating is what she thinks she sees it to be, which would certainly have implications about whether we meat eaters should continue with the practice. The role of Coetzee's Costello for Diamond is rather to provide an analogue for the unhinging perceptions of separation and finitude that according to Cavell himself constitute the real point of philosophical skepticism. And—just as importantly—the role of Coetzee's commentators for Diamond is to provide an analogue for how philosophy in the academic mode, in Cavell's own reading, avoids what is really at issue in its engagements with skepticism.

8 "In Spite of the Misery of the World": Ethics, Contemplation, and the Source of Value

Sabina Lovibond

I

This essay is concerned with a question belonging to what might be called "non-practical ethics," namely that of what makes a human life a good one or confers value upon it. Although I cannot expect my positive conclusions to find favor with Professor Diamond (see especially §VI below), I hope that in a more generic way the discussion will not be out of place in a collection in her honor; for one of the most important lessons of Diamond's work in ethics concerns a tendency in contemporary Anglo-American philosophy to overemphasize the "moral agent" at the expense of the theme of *receptivity* to evaluative significance. Practical problem-solving, decision-making, legislative rationality with its emphasis on the business of applying defensible universal rules to particular cases—these things do not exhaust the proper subject matter of moral reflection, nor do they encompass the "heartbreaking specialness" of human existence or the awareness of death that attends it.[1] For her consistent sponsorship of the solitary and non-forensic aspect of moral sensibility, as well as for her success in showing how certain practical matters (such as the treatment of other animals) can be illuminated if we allow that sensibility to operate, Cora Diamond deserves our homage and gratitude.

The question of "what makes a human life a good one or confers value upon it" may appear hopelessly confused. It seems to invite the retort: "What kind of goodness or value do you mean? A life that is morally deplorable may bring a great deal of happiness, and hence may be of great value, to the person concerned." I begin, however (in §II), with some considerations from the early philosophy of Wittgenstein which hint at the possibility of circumventing this protest; and I proceed (in §III) to set these considerations against the background of an ancient philosophical tradition which places at the heart of ethics the idea of a certain kind of *looking* or *witnessing*. To grant such centrality to this looking or witnessing is not to claim that it has any necessary connection with what we normally think of as meritorious conduct: with acts of courage, honesty, fidelity, kindness and the like. Instead, it is to suggest a certain conception of what makes life valuable—that is, what makes it *worthy* of being valued—from the point of view of the living subject. In §§IV and V I try to bring out the attractiveness of this conception, commending it for its innocence of the dubious notion that the best thing life has to offer us is the opportunity to do well morally, while at the same time resisting any suggestion that it licenses us to make light of moral demands. Finally, in §§VI and VII I revisit, but pronounce against, the view that there is ultimately no need to choose between the morality-centered answer to our original question, and another style of answer which privileges the standpoint of the subject—conceived now (not primarily as an agent, but) as one to whom the world *presents itself* in experience. That is: assuming the question makes sense, I think we do have to choose, and that the other style of answer—the one that is not morality-centered—is superior.

In addition to Wittgenstein, the main philosophical sources I draw upon in the course of the discussion are Aristotle and G. E. Moore.

II

It is clear that ethics cannot be put into words.
Ethics is transcendental.
(Ethics and aesthetics are one and the same.)[2]

In Wittgenstein's *Tractatus* there seems to be little room for elaboration on the thesis of the unity of aesthetics with ethics, beyond the familiar negative points that can be made about the character of absolute or unconditional value as conceived in that work: the idea that such value is outside the world, that nothing can (intelligibly) be said about it, and that the attitude it calls into play belongs not to empirical but to transcendental psychology. We do not hear anything about the phenomenological grounds for this treatment of the aesthetic—that is, about the way it might connect with anyone's lived aesthetic experience, or with anyone's sense of the bearing of that experience on the worth of his or her life.

The picture is rather different in Wittgenstein's *Notebooks*,[3] where some remarks from the later months of 1916 show him considering the "one and the same" thesis (the "unity thesis") from the side of aesthetics as well as from that of ethics. Although the relevant passages already show a commitment to the view that good and evil, happiness and unhappiness, "enter only through the *subject*" and cannot be "part of the world" (2.8.16), they contain some pointers to the genesis of the unity thesis in attitudes or states of mind which are communicable, at any rate, to the extent that they evoke themes from elsewhere in the European philosophical tradition. Of these, some of the most important occur at:

(i) 24.7.16 (which introduces the *Tractatus* claim that "Ethics and aesthetics are one");

(ii) 29.7.16 and 30.7.16:

"To love one's neighbour" would mean to will! . . . And yet in a certain sense it seems that not wanting is the only good. . . . It is generally assumed that it is evil to want someone else to be unfortunate. Can this be correct? Can it be worse than to want him to be fortunate?

Here everything seems to turn, so to speak, on *how* one wants.

It seems one can't say anything more than: Live happily! . . .

I keep on coming back to this! simply the happy life is good, the unhappy bad. And if I *now* ask myself: But why should I live *happily*, then this of itself seems to me to be a tautological question; the happy life seems to be justified, of itself, it seems that it *is* the only right life.

(iii) 13.8.16:

Suppose that man could not exercise his will, but had to suffer all the misery of this world, then what could make him happy?

How can man be happy at all, since he cannot ward off the misery of this world?

Through the life of knowledge.

The good conscience is the happiness that the life of knowledge preserves.

The life of knowledge is the life that is happy in spite of the misery of the world.

The only life that is happy is the life that can renounce the amenities of the world.

To it the amenities of the world are so many graces of fate.

(iv) 7.10.16:

The work of art is the object seen *sub specie aeternitatis*; and the good life is the world seen *sub specie aeternitatis*. This is the connexion between art and ethics.

The usual way of looking at things sees objects as it were from the midst of them, the view *sub specie aeternitatis* from outside.

In such a way that they have the whole world as background.

(v) 20.10.16 and 21.10.16:

Aesthetically, the miracle is that the world exists. That there is what there is.

Is it the essence of the artistic way of looking at things, that it looks at the world with a happy eye?

Life is grave, art is gay [the editors point out that this is a quotation from Schiller].

For there is certainly something in the conception that the end of art is the beautiful.

And the beautiful *is* what makes happy.

Bracketing for the moment the *Tractatus* doctrine as to what can and cannot be said, we find in these remarks a conception of the good life with a certain internal coherence. The leading ideas are of an ascetic and contemplative character. Happiness, we might begin (pre-philosophically) by assuming, depends on the successful exercise of the will—on getting what we want in life. But this ambition is doomed, since we "cannot ward off the misery of this world," i.e. defend ourselves effectively against (natural or social) misfortune. Accordingly, it might seem that we should forget about happiness altogether, at any rate as an object of personal desire or striving. But this suggestion is not even entertained: to accede to it would represent, perhaps, a confession of ethical breakdown, a capitulation to the possibility of suicide, which is after all "the elementary sin" (10.1.17). There must, under any conceivable empirical conditions, be a way of living well—and the injunction to do this, the ethical injunction, is one that Wittgenstein is inclined to *equate* with "Live happily!"

The way to live well irrespective of empirical circumstances is "through the life of knowledge." Pursuing the Schopenhauerian ideal of the silencing or supersession of the will, Wittgenstein locates the good life in a distinctive vision, a view of the world *sub specie aeternitatis*. Whereas we normally look at things from a position in their midst, permeated by practical concerns and anxieties, the vision of the good (and hence, in the only way that matters, of the happy) human being limits itself to understanding how things are, and this impersonal understanding yields the reward of a "good conscience." Despite the strangeness of an ethics so austere as to exclude even the commandment to love one's neighbour, it seems ("in a certain sense") that "not wanting is the only good"; the only happy life is one that accepts the world as something offered to it as an object of contemplation, like a work of art in that it is not *for* anything, but simply lies open to our (disinterested) attention.[4] To experience the existence of the world—of anything at all—as a miracle is to receive from it the happiness that an artist hopes to give in placing before us something beautiful; but the ability to receive this kind of happiness from simply *being in the world* is, again, a matter of attitude, of looking at the world *as if* it were a felicitous composition, and in that sense "with a happy eye": an eye ready to be *made* happy in the way cultivated or replicated by art.

Ethics and aesthetics are one in respect of showing us that this is enough—enough, for example, to make happiness possible despite the "misery of the world," or to reveal the amenities of the world as dispensable, as "so many graces of fate." They converge or coincide in this respect with the "life of [pure] knowledge," which likewise discloses itself to us through the experience of not needing or wanting anything of a practical nature, but being content simply to see and appreciate.

III

Wittgenstein's topic in these passages from the *Notebooks* is one with a long history: adopting a phrase from Christine Korsgaard,[5] we can call it the question of the *source of value* in human life. A story told by Aristotle brings out what is at stake here: somebody once asked Anaxagoras what it is that makes life itself valuable, or "for what object one would choose to be born rather than not"—to which the older philosopher replied: "For the sake of contemplating the heavens and the whole order of the universe."[6] The story is illuminating for Aristotle's purposes since he too searches, in Korsgaard's words, for "an activity that would make life worth living even if life had no defects or limitations to overcome"; for "something that human beings can do that gives a point to being human," an activity "unprovoked by needs and therefore done for [its] own sake unconditionally."[7]

The Aristotelian enquiry is not meant to be a merely descriptive one; that is, we are not asking simply what human beings are *capable* of finding satisfying. Rather, we want to know what it is that could be regarded as being unconditionally desirable by a person with a *correct* appreciation of the *telos* or purpose of life. Aristotle's own answer, in Book X of the *Nicomachean Ethics*, seems in effect to amount to an endorsement of the view attributed to Anaxagoras. He argues in that book that the ultimate point of human existence is to "approximate as closely as possible to the condition of God (or immortality)" through the practice of *theoria* (contemplation);[8] or in other words that what has value not merely negatively, as a remedy for life's "defects and limitations," but positively—as something capable in its own right of making life desirable—is the activity of exercising understanding or of keeping our attention fixed on some worthy object.

Ethics, aesthetics, and the life of knowledge—does Aristotle, then, somehow anticipate the view that these are "one and the same"? Dominated as we are by our perception of him as the originator of "virtue ethics," and hence as a theorist of the qualities needed to acquit oneself well in social and civic relationships, such a suggestion may strike us as bizarre. A natural response to it would be to say that, on the contrary, the task cut out for friendly readers of Aristotle is to explain on his behalf how the claims of ethics (in the familiar, interpersonal sense) and those of the life of knowledge are supposed to fit together. For example, one can argue that we are not obliged to read Aristotle as a heartless intellectualist, telling us to disregard all other claims in favor of an uninterrupted pursuit of *theoria*. Some commentators, at any rate, have taken the constraints implicit in the idea of *getting as close as possible* to the condition of God to include those arising from our membership of society and from the obligations this brings with it—obligations that may, in unfavorable circumstances, leave us with little or no leisure to devote to the thing "for the sake of which one would choose to be born rather than not." (That is: sometimes it is more important to perform the functions of a good family member, or a good citizen, than those of a good philosopher, and Aristotle's championship of *theoria* admits of a gloss that would make it consistent with this thought.)[9] If, on the other hand, we can bring ourselves to enlarge our understanding of "ethics" and to take seriously the Aristotelian conception of it as an enquiry into the nature of happiness—an enquiry, moreover, intended to result in our actually living a happy life, "since the goal is not knowledge but action"[10]—then the vision contained in *NE* X should not seem so archaic. The Wittgenstein of the *Notebooks* still means by "Live happily" something like: "Approximate as closely as possible to the condition of God"—that is, the being whom we imagine as seeing the world *sub specie aeternitatis*.

Were any of Wittgenstein's contemporaries drawn to the contemplative ideal? Yes: G. E. Moore makes a move in the same direction in the final chapter of his *Principia Ethica* (1903). Though influential in Moore's own circle, this chapter (entitled "The Ideal") has been largely ignored in the subsequent reception of his book—consigned, perhaps, to the "silence of embarrassment"[11] that is apt to greet a burst of passionate self-disclosure. (While Wittgenstein's *Notebooks* reveal a mind in transition towards full acceptance of the doctrine that value-discourse must be either nonsensical or philosophically uninteresting, Moore can be seen persevering with it as befits one of nature's naive realists.)[12] Despite Moore's low opinion of the ethics of Aristotle,[13] the chapter offers a more or less recognizable successor to the Aristotelian view that our life must ultimately derive its value from some activity whose possibility depends upon the removal of any manifest want. Moore's variation on this theme is to be found in the striking claim that "by far the most valuable things, which we know or can imagine, are certain states of consciousness, which may be roughly described as the pleasures of human intercourse and the enjoyment of beautiful objects"; or that "Unmixed goods may all be said to consist in the love of beautiful things or of good persons."[14] These statements locate the source of value in a condition in which our consciousness plays upon, or is directed toward, something that is itself valuable. It is true that while Aristotle pictures this condition in intellectualist terms, as one of contemplation, Moore conceives of it as a state of love.[15] But this difference between the two philosophers is less striking than their general like-mindedness on the question of what it is that could make life desirable to us in the event of a "sabbath of practicality":[16] a release, however temporary, from the familiar condition of having to run in order to stand still. In particular, Moore seems to accept as self-evident the Aristotelian view[17] that it cannot be mere play or amusement that gives our life such value as it has, but that this value must derive from the ability to fix our minds upon something "serious"—even if, in practice, we lack the stamina to be "serious" all the time.

IV

"The love of beautiful things or of good persons": in the first part of this formula, Moore expresses a thought which we also find Wittgenstein trying out in the *Notebooks* when he says that "the beautiful is what makes happy"—a remark which, as we know, has to be placed in the context of his wish to infuse an ethical coloring into the idea of happiness.

Is there something more than a merely verbal point of contact here? One reason for thinking so may emerge from Wittgenstein's confrontation with the "misery of the world." The life of knowledge, he reflects, is the life that is happy in spite of this misery. So he invokes *theoria*, in the classic Aristotelian manner (though of course without the original qualifications),[18] as a way of safeguarding human happiness against natural and social misadventure. Likewise, the importance of the beautiful within Moore's scheme may be due to the fact that the "love of good persons" is insufficiently dependable to stand alone as the source of value in any given individual life. If this love is supposed not just to consist in the objective appreciation of merit at a distance (as in reading a history book), but to have its place among the "pleasures of human intercourse," then it will be to some extent a matter of luck how much of it I can experience, since I may find myself in an environment where good persons are a rarity; or the ones I know may die or absent themselves. This element of contingency is a relatively constant element in human experience. It may be, then, that Moore's pairing—"beautiful things and good persons"—expresses an insight into our means of defense against such contingency: we need the "things" to fill out our inventory of worthy objects of love and attention, and hence to promote the existence of those complex phenomena ("organic unities," as Moore calls them) which consist in the proper appreciation of such objects by individuals.

But then why doesn't Moore extend his ideal to embrace the "life of knowledge"?[19] Someone who wanted to persuade him to do so might have argued as follows. Admittedly, beautiful objects exist all around us in the natural world (quite apart from the perhaps elusive ability to experience the very existence of the world as an aesthetic miracle). Yet any recognizably human way of life also seems to include the activity of *making things simply in order to be objects of attention*. Artistic creation is one species of this activity, but another is the "making" of objects—such as texts or bodies of theory—

which share the abstract character of "allographic" works of art,[20] yet resemble the sciences in so far as their primary purpose is to advance understanding or disclose truth. Of course, much of "science" aims at the practical improvement of life; but there is no great mystery about our motivation for engaging in that part of it which does not. "Pure" theory, whether in philosophy or in (say) mathematics or physics or history, is produced in the hope of offering to (some appropriate group of) other people a fit object on which to exercise their own understanding, simply for the sake of that exercise and in order to sustain the relevant community of intellectual experience, which is a shared experience of attending to certain questions or problems. (We may see it as a defect in Aristotle that he can think of play only as "mere" play—in effect, as a remedy for weariness—and not as a more differentiated category of free activity, the "expression of superabundant life and movement," which could be extended metaphorically to include the various forms of expression just mentioned.[21] This limitation no doubt informs the whole tradition of "spectator-oriented aesthetics,"[22] not excluding Moore's celebration of the *enjoyment* or *love* of beautiful things in preference to the creative vitality to which many of these things owe their existence.)

Moore, then, could enrich the thought that "the beautiful is what makes happy" by bringing it into connection with his own definition of beauty as "that of which the admiring contemplation is good in itself";[23] and by noting explicitly that this description can apply not just to pictures, novels, music and the like, but also to theoretical works (such as, for instance, *Principia Ethica*—since Moore presumably hoped, in common with other non-cynical writers, to produce something that would be worthy of admiring contemplation).

Even with this amendment to his view, however, we are a long way from the idea of the *world* (as a whole) as something that can be seen "with a happy eye." Moore's beautiful objects, even now, comprise just some of the objects in the world; the discipline of attending to them and appreciating them belongs, not to transcendental psychology, but to general artistic and literary culture and to the life of introspection and memory. It thus demands a conception of the aesthetic under which ethics and aesthetics would no longer be "one and the same," but would give rise to distinct kinds of value and to different possible accounts of the source of value. Consider for example the following words by the Hungarian expatriate philosopher Aurel Kolnai, published in 1971:

If certain churches or certain regions or street-corners in certain cities I peculiarly admire and love did not exist, it "wouldn't make much difference." Yet it is in their contemplation and tangible nearness, undoubtedly an *aesthetic* experience, that I seem somehow to become aware of the ineffable goodness of existence more deeply and vividly than in any experience of benefit or thriving, or even of moral virtue.[24]

Ethics presents itself here through a phenomenon within the world of experience—the "moral virtue" possessed in varying degrees by different persons. Aesthetics presents itself through another such phenomenon—the "tangible nearness" of certain buildings or scenes. Kolnai's observation is that one of these phenomena, the aesthetic, is more effective than the other as a symbol or reminder of the value of life.

Do such remarks convict their author of a heartless "aestheticism," a disposition to let aesthetic considerations take precedence over moral ones? The question recalls one that arose in connection with the putative "intellectualism" of Aristotle, and again the answer is: not necessarily. As Kolnai's discussion brings out, the values whose presence discloses to us most clearly the *goodness of existence* are not usually those that *matter* most, in the sense of making the strongest practical claim upon us. Injustice, wherever it exists, "imperiously demand[s] remedy" or compensation,[25] and human suffering in general, even when it is not due to wrongdoing, is similarly "imperious" in demanding help (so that failure to help *introduces* a moral wrong into the world); whereas, even if the ravages of "development" since Kolnai's time (at least in the Old World) have brought a new intensity to our feelings about street-corners, we can still recognize that there is a natural order of priority to human needs and that, for example, issues of "conservation of the built environment" must take on a different complexion when one's own home is about to be forcibly demolished. Evidently, there are some circumstances in which the loss of an opportunity for one of Moore's favored forms of enjoyment will be among the least of one's problems. (No doubt this is why his candidates for the status of "most valuable things" can sound self-indulgent or comical.) Yet there is nothing here to cast doubt on the distinction to which Moore alludes in the closing pages of *Principia Ethica*, where he says that *unmixed* goods all consist in the love of beautiful things or of good persons. The thought is that much of what we value most in life—courage, self-sacrifice, the refusal to acquiesce in wrong-doing—depends for its value on the existence of (either natural or moral) evil, and in that sense constitutes only a "mixed" good.[26] Of course, since evil (of both kinds) is real enough, this mixed character does nothing to diminish our actual need for such qualities or dispositions. But it does detract from their *self-sufficiency* as grounds for believing in the "goodness of existence." That is, it returns us to the question: what would make life worth living if the evil actually present in it were absent? And this is the question with which Moore is concerned.

V

The idea of a way to happiness through the life of knowledge or contemplation seems to offer a promising, if pessimistic, answer to the question of the source of value. This answer is pessimistic in that it tries to minimize our investment in the "amenities of the world," which can be withdrawn at a moment's notice by an ungracious fate. But that feature merely locates it within a familiar genre of moral philosophy which undertakes to show how we can persist in finding life desirable in the absence of such "amenities." And the idea has a certain merit attributable to its Aristotelian origins:[27] namely, it remains faithful to the intuition that any mode of activity or consciousness *for the sake of which one would choose to be born rather than not* must be, not only one that is appropriate to our capacities as a species, but also one in which we are capable of taking pleasure.

Faced with a declaration like the one I have quoted from Kolnai, it is natural to feel that we have reached a parting of the ways; that we must now choose between radically divergent views about the source of value, and that the Aristotelian principle just mentioned, once accepted, will determine that we take one course rather than the other. This principle does not automatically commit us to a doctrine of hedonism, for as commentators standardly (and rightly) point out, Aristotle does not hold that pleasure in the abstract—or regardless of source—is the best thing in life. But it does, surely, involve a concession that however thoroughly socialized or moralized we may be, the credentials of any putative "source of value" must turn upon its ability to make us want more of life, to issue a promise of happiness, and in particular (since we *are* human) to "seduce us to existence" at those moments when mere animal determination falters.[28]

In order to appreciate what is at issue here, let us see what prospects open up if we take the other path. Both Aristotle and Kant, as Christine Korsgaard reminds us in the essay cited earlier, treat the question of the source of value as dependent on a teleological view of nature as a whole. For Aristotle, all life strives towards the condition of pure activity realized in God, and the human activity of contemplation represents our best effort to emulate this. For Kant on the other hand, nature considered in itself, and likewise the intelligent contemplation of nature, could afford us nothing but "a representation of things without any final purpose,"[29] and such a purpose has to be supplied by "that worth which [man] alone can give to himself and which consists in what he does, how and according to what principles he acts":[30] in other words, it is rational nature—as manifested in the good will—that "confers value on the objects of its choices and is itself the source of all value,"[31] including the value of the whole natural creation. Kant's modernity is reflected in the ("Copernican") move whereby he grounds even the organizing principles of reason, and the merit of an activity such as contemplation, in the requirements of the rational subject. Accordingly, it can be summed up in the humanist conviction that "*[w]e must be the source of value.*"[32]

The fundamental difference between this story and the neo-Aristotelian one lies in the importance that the former gives to *choice*—as if the specific form of response to a thing's value that consists in choosing it were the paradigm case of evaluative experience, and as if the value of life as a whole were dependent on the possibility of *certifying the objects of my choices as legitimate*. This is the feat accomplished, in Kant's picture,[33] by the goodness of the will expressed or exercised in choosing. And this difference seems to yield a reason for preferring the neo-Aristotelian view. For what we may feel is neglected in the Kantian alternative is the indispensable presence of something passive, or *un*chosen, in those moments through which the "goodness of existence" is characteristically disclosed to us. Kolnai can choose to revisit his favorite churches or street-corners (if they have not been destroyed), but the effect they had on him in the first instance, or again after long years of intimacy, was not a matter of choice.

True, it might be argued that the Aristotelian view is exposed to the same objection. Aristotle, after all, holds the source of value to be an *activity*, and moreover regards pleasure in general as identical (in any given instance) with some activity, or anyway as being at most analytically separable from it. Or, to put the objection the other way round: isn't Kolnai's "contemplation" of street-corners also an instance of activity, in the relevant sense—the active fixing of attention upon certain objects? I think the wisest move here would be to concede that Aristotle's account of the contemplative ideal is marked by a certain ideological distortion. The account is shaped not only by a concern to establish what the divine (or perfect) life could consist in, but also by the conviction that such a life could not contain any element of passivity, a condition that for him (as for Greek philosophy generally) bears the mark of subordinate or inferior status. Aristotle could have improved matters by discarding this prejudice and consenting to recognize in *theoria*—or in the business of attending to objects of aesthetic value—an experience that is not one of *pure* activity (whatever that might be), but that also comprises an element of being *captivated* or *absorbed*. Some such ideological shift may be reflected in Moore's use of the word "love," as well as of "pleasure" or "enjoyment" or "admiration,"[34] to specify what he regards as the unmixed goods or "most valuable things."

The suggestion now before us is that some descendant of Anaxagoras's own answer to the original question is correct: that the thing that is capable, above all else, of making life desirable ("in spite of the misery of the world") is *theoria* in our enlarged sense, namely the sense established by treating Moore's remark about beautiful objects as a remark about the whole class of objects worthy of contemplation or attention. Because of this enlargement of our conception of the "beautiful," the amended

Moorean thesis is no longer any more specifically aestheticist than it is intellectualist in content. Yet it does continue to provide a rationale for the idea that Kolnai is, perhaps, expressing in the passage I quoted in §IV: I mean the idea that the "goodness of existence" is something that is revealed to one at those moments when one comes face to face, often in a totally unpremeditated way, with something one can recognize as admirable. In other words, it supports the conviction that a large part of what makes life valuable to us, even in our capacity as creatures of intellect and discernment, consists of experiences that we *undergo*. Without having learned Greek, say, I could not read Homer (in the original); but the point of reading Homer is to *submit to the effect* of the poems, even though this is an effect they can produce in me only to the extent that I understand them. Without some knowledge of the history and culture of Europe and the way it is expressed in buildings, Kolnai might be unable to receive the aesthetic effect of his favorite street-corners; but it is nevertheless something he *receives*. Without some measure of taste and judgment, Moore could have no grounds for confidence that he is not wasting his love on bad people or ugly things; but I take it that like the rest of us, he means by "love" a state of mind that *comes over one*, taste or no taste.

VI

Assuming that we have to choose between an aesthetic/contemplative and a moralistic style of answer to the question of the source of value, the considerations set out above are meant to tell in favor of the former—and to suggest that it is in no way at variance with our existing ontological commitments to the good will, the virtues, or any other item of moral interest. But what if the choice is a spurious one? Can anything be made of the suggestion—still accompanied in Wittgenstein's wartime reflections by a certain (empirically recognizable) emotional atmosphere, but reduced in the *Tractatus* itself to a more controlled gesture in the direction of the transcendental—that there is an attitude to the world, an orientation of the *non*-empirical "will," which is the desideratum of both aesthetics and ethics: a view of the world, and of its contents, *sub specie aeternitatis*? In other words: is it possible to equate the ethically good life with one that is good in the sense of offering us (what can be roughly described as) an aesthetic incentive to live?

The obvious problem here for the *Tractatus* view is that it is debarred from setting up any connection between the ethically good will (as conceived in that work) and a possible good exercise of the will "inside the world," since the standards we apply in evaluating the empirical will can only be instrumental, i.e. relative to an arbitrarily determined standard (which, as such, "has no value" of a properly ethical kind).[35] As Diané Collinson has pointed out, Wittgenstein is united (*mutatis mutandis*) with some of his idealist predecessors in the "difficulty of showing how the disengagement from the empirical world that is the condition of apprehending the Good is the ground of particular good deeds, decisions and judgements";[36] there is a fleeting suggestion (*Notebooks* 29.7.16) that "everything seems to turn . . . on *how* one wants" (sc. empirical objects or states of affairs), but the inside/outside dualism is by now too firmly entrenched to permit elaboration on this "how." ("It seems one can't say anything more than: Live happily!")

Against the tide of current ethical theory and, I believe, of the prevailing philosophical response to Wittgenstein, Cora Diamond urges us to stick with a conception of ethics—or of what is ethically deepest and most important—that would locate it, precisely, on the "outside." She argues that the interpretation of Wittgenstein's later philosophy as licensing, through its criticism of the *Tractatus* account of logic, a move to "put ethics back into the world" is "at best a partial truth,"[37] for it is symptomatic of a "will not to be concerned with the ethical"[38]—that is, "not to make certain distinctions in one's talk and thought and life, and not to have that in oneself, or not to recognize it, that would make those distinctions."[39] The crucial distinction is the one Diamond finds marked in Grimm's Fairy Tales (or some of them: her chosen example is the tale of the Fisherman's Wife, who represents limitless worldly ambition) by "the difference between natural and supernatural evil,"[40] or between common-or-garden moral mediocrity and the "possible terribleness of what may be in our hearts"; something "sinister and dark," "black and unapproachable."[41]

Although Wittgenstein's later philosophy is hostile to any theory-laden talk about what the "world" may or may not contain,[42] Diamond wants to keep the ethical idiom of the *Tractatus* in play by arguing that the relevant use of "outside the world" is "simply one way of marking . . . that mode of thought about human life that Wittgenstein meant by ethics; it is as good as *Rumpelstiltskin* or *The Fisherman and His Wife* at marking it."[43] That is (I take it), we have in this idiom what can now be regarded as a poetic or indirect way of conveying something about Wittgenstein's attitude to the ethical. (Of course, those who follow Peter Hacker[44] in taking at face value the proposition that "[t]here are . . . things that cannot be put into words," but "make themselves manifest"[45] will consider that this is what we have already in the *Tractatus*, but that view seems to be incompatible with the claim that such sentences have no more to do with ethics than do bits of overt nonsense like "piggly wiggle tiggle.")[46] To resist the natural/supernatural distinction, says Diamond, "may represent itself as mere sensibleness, reasonableness, down-to-earthness, matter-of-factness, rational disdain for mystery and mysticism; in other contexts, as being fair, being liberal-minded and sympathetic (or radical-minded and sympathetic) about poor old Rumpelstiltskin, about the unjustly vilified older woman in *Snow-White*, and the poor old witch in *Rapunzel*";[47] but it is really a kind of philistinism, a refusal to acknowledge the existence of those extreme moral phenomena that outrage the imagination[48] or that resist capture within the banal terms of reference supplied by the "spirit of the times."

The continued use of the "inside/outside" metaphor to indicate a distinction between different parts of the subject-matter of ethics might no doubt be accommodated to Wittgenstein's later philosophy of language, if the metaphor is to be seen in the context of that philosophy as "simply one way of marking" the relevant distinction, "as good as" the imagery of Grimm's Fairy Tales for the purpose of marking it. Nor is there anything wrong with the assumption that the ethical sensibility expressed in the *Tractatus* is likely to be present, also, in the later work, which certainly continues to give an important place to things that "cannot be said" but "make themselves manifest": the knowledge possessed, for example, by someone who knows how to continue a series correctly in the absence of reasons why, here and now, one move rather than another is correct; or by someone who understands what it is that "games" have in common, or what is common to a wish and its fulfillment.[49] On the other hand, worrying as it is to have to suspect oneself of complicity with the merely sensible or down-to-earth, the invocation of a category of *supernatural* evil to mark the site once occupied by the bad exercise of the transcendental will seems subjective and uncompelling. While it is true that there is nothing in the later Wittgenstein to encourage "chatter" about what he once called (or purported, nonsensically, to call) by the name of the mystical, there is likewise nothing that favors a deferential attitude toward the *Tractatus* vision of what the "world"—or "nature"—can contain. Thus, to return to the tale of the Fisherman and his Wife: granted (charitably, no doubt, but I think legitimately for present purposes) that there is more at stake here than a stale nostrum about feminine greed being the root of all evil, why should we feel bound to endorse a psychology so impoverished as to banish to a supposedly "supernatural" realm the menacing intimations of moral anarchy present in this story? Why not equally well hear it as an invitation to picture ourselves as inhabitants of a pre-Christian (or post-Freudian) "world," in which "nature" can encompass not just the savagery of seas and winds, but the darker and more terrible contents of the heart? Although we may shy away from that darkness, I do not think a case has been made (nor, perhaps, would Diamond claim to have presented any formal case) for returning to a conception of ethics—or in general of absolute value—in the familiar dualist style: I mean a conception faithful to that philosophical tradition which contrasts the world of experience with something "outside" it that is deeper, better or more important.

But if this is right, we have after all no reason to retreat from the idea I described in §V as a natural one, namely that the question of the source of value admits of (at least) two types of answer—the aesthetic/contemplative and the moralistic. Contrary to the view of the early Wittgenstein, ethics and aesthetics should be allowed to retain their separateness, and should accordingly be understood as responding to our question in different ways. The aesthetic/contemplative response has been commended here for respecting our attachment to those moments of consciousness that reveal to us a value not of our own making (or in which the world takes on the aspect of a gift or "miracle"), in contrast to those in which value is realized through the good exercise of our own will in the face of some natural resistance. Its initially surprising neglect of the merely hedonistic kind of encounter with revealed value, and even of the kind of value-disclosing activity that engages our physical rather than our mental powers, may be explained—for what this is worth—by reference to the philosopher's traditional desire to find a source of value that is immune to contingency.[50] And finally, although it represents an attempt to do justice to our sense that the pursuit of virtue does not qualify as something "for the sake of which one would choose to be born rather than not," this response has been shown to be defensible against the charge of fostering a culpable *indifference* to moral demands.

VII

Yet some doubt may remain: can we really give a satisfactory answer to Anaxagoras's question without mentioning morality? Was Kant wrong to claim that "a good will is that whereby alone [man's] being can have an absolute worth,"[51] and hence that without a good will, any reason we might entertain for attaching value to our existence would be less than genuine?

Rather than confront this question directly, we can observe that in speaking here of "absolute worth," Kant has placed the discussion within a frame of reference that appears to have been foreign to Anaxagoras (and also to Aristotle). Anaxagoras offers a perfectly apposite answer to his interlocutor by attributing to the interlocutor the following thought: "Now that we *are* alive, of course we want to go on living, barring unusually dire circumstances. But what reason could have been given in advance for choosing to live rather than not?" The problem is posed on behalf of "man" in the abstract, since any arbitrary human being might happen to be troubled by it, and might be satisfied or dissatisfied with any putative answer. But "satisfaction" here means only a state of mind in which one can say, "Very well—that would be enough to make me *want* to live." It does not mean being satisfied that one's existence, i.e. the fact of one's being born rather than not, has been shown to be a good thing *sub specie aeternitatis* or from the standpoint of a transcendent God.[52] And although Kolnai at any rate is a theist, and may for all I know hold that without God any talk of the "ineffable goodness of existence" is just sentimental chitchat, the passages I have borrowed from him and from Moore make excellent sense without benefit of any such background: ostensibly, at least, they are contributions to the ancient topic, not the Kantian one.

But doesn't moral goodness stand in some more than merely negative relation to aesthetic value, and to our esteem for it? Isn't there some affinity between them that goes beyond the idea of aesthetic experience (or *theoria*) as that to which we could legitimately devote ourselves once moral demands had been met? Certainly some philosophers have seen such an affinity. The thought can be traced back to Plato, for whom the beautiful is the "most manifest and the loveliest" of all things to be found in the intelligible world, and serves as a channel by which we can transfer our interest from natural to moral value.[53] It recurs in Kant, who says that "[t]he beautiful prepares us to love something, even nature, apart from any interest,"[54] and in more recent times has been revived by Iris Murdoch, who argues that "[t]he appreciation of beauty in art or nature is not only (for all its difficulties) the easiest available spiritual exercise; it is also a completely adequate entry into (and not just analogy of) the good life, since it *is* the checking of selfishness in the interest of seeing the real."[55]

It seems to me that there is something right about this, and that the creative impulse—by which I mean the impulse to make objects worth attending to for their own sake, with no practical end in view—is indeed allied to our interest in the "pleasures of human intercourse," and hence, indirectly, to ethics. It is not just that, as I suggested in connection with Moore, the social pleasures are too fleeting or elusive to provide the whole content of the "promise of happiness." There is the further point that human intercourse itself has to have some content, and if we imagine such intercourse set in a context that is, so far as humanly possible, free from the need to deal with life's "defects and limitations," then the question arises: what will there be to talk about? The creation of works of art and of theory, along with the (partly) collective enterprise of understanding them, removes some of the sting from this question.[56] In the same vein, it may be that theoretical discussion, by virtue of its orientation toward truth, could find its remote evolutionary origins in behavior prompted by the friendly propensity to share information, and to build social bonds on the basis of "that interest in how things are which no agent can lack."[57]

But to make these points is not to find fault with the evolutionary process which has brought about a condition of autonomy between ethical motivation, on one hand, and artistic or theoretical motivation on the other. Philosophy as we know it does not exist to provide social cement; nor should works of art be seen, in themselves, as instruments for the promotion of dinner party conversation, or even of art criticism. What we can say is simply that the exercise of "theoretical" capacities, however useless, should not be dismissed as merely self-indulgent or escapist, since it promotes the vitality of something in us that is "not part of the problem" (i.e. not part of the rapacious or anti-social element in human relations) and that might equip us, subjectively, for a form of *schole* (leisure) devoted to something other than waste and destruction. Of course, this cannot provide an excuse for neglecting those actually existing evils that "imperiously demand remedy." But philosophers who allow their thoughts to stray in the direction of the contemplative ideal should not automatically be presumed to be making that mistake.[58]

Notes

1. Cora Diamond, *The Realistic Spirit: Wittgenstein, Philosophy and the Mind* (Cambridge, Mass.: MIT Press, 1991), pp. 352–353.

2. Ludwig Wittgenstein, *Tractatus Logico-Philosophicus*, trans. D. F. Pears and B. F. McGuiness (London: Routledge and Kegan Paul, 1961), 6.421.

3. Ludwig Wittgenstein, *Notebooks 1914–1916*, 2nd ed., ed. G. H. von Wright and G. E. M. Anscombe, trans. G. E. M. Anscombe (Oxford: Basil Blackwell, 1979).

4. Compare Nietzsche, *The Birth of Tragedy*, trans. Walter Kaufmann (New York: Random House, 1967), §5: "it is only as an *aesthetic phenomenon* that existence and the world are eternally *justified*"; *The Antichrist*, trans. R. J. Hollingdale (Harmondsworth, Middlesex: Penguin, 1968), §57: " *'The world is perfect'*—thus speaks the instinct of the most spiritual, the affirmative instinct." These remarks, however, represent an unstable moment of sympathy on Nietzsche's part with the tradition that surfaces in Wittgenstein's *Notebooks*, since he also attacks Kant's aesthetics as a kind of apologia for sensory impotence (*On the Genealogy of Morals*, Essay III, §6).

5. Christine M. Korsgaard, "Aristotle and Kant on the Source of Value," in her *Creating the Kingdom of Ends* (Cambridge: Cambridge University Press, 1996), pp. 225–248.

6. Aristotle, *Eudemian Ethics* 1216a11–14; translation based on H. Rackham (Loeb Classical Library, Cambridge, Mass.: Harvard University Press, 1967). It is worth noting the possibility that the question put to Anaxagoras was meant to strike a provocatively pessimistic note, i.e. to imply that life is *prima facie un*desirable; the context neither excludes nor positively indicates this.

7. Korsgaard, "Aristotle and Kant . . . ," pp. 235, 243, 245.

8. Aristotle, *Nicomachean Ethics* 1177b 31–34.

9. See Gavin Lawrence, "Aristotle and the Ideal Life,: in *Philosophical Review* 102 (1993), pp. 1–34, §4. However, as David Bostock notes, such interpretations must remain speculative since

Aristotle "never, at any point, tells us how the different demands of the different virtues should be accommodated to one another," and this applies *inter alia* to the potential conflict between practical and theoretical virtue (*Aristotle's Ethics*, Oxford University Press [2000], p. 208).

10. Aristotle, *Nicomachean Ethics* 1095a 5–6.

11. See Mary Warnock, *Ethics Since 1900*, 3rd ed. (Oxford: Oxford University Press, 1978), p. 27.

12. The economist J. M. Keynes wrote that "Moore had a nightmare once in which he could not distinguish propositions from tables. But even when he was awake, he could not distinguish love and beauty and truth from the furniture. They took on the same definition of outline, the same stable, solid, objective qualities and common-sense reality" (quoted in Paul Levy, *Moore: G. E. Moore and the Cambridge Apostles* [Oxford University Press, 1981], p. 246). (Levy also reports that one of the topics of Wittgenstein's first letter to Bertrand Russell, in June 1912, was "how much he disliked *Principia Ethica*": ibid., p. 273.)

13. See G. E. Moore, *Principia Ethica*, ed. Thomas Baldwin (Cambridge: Cambridge University Press, 1993), p. 225 and context. Moore accuses Aristotle (i) of wrongly regarding as good in itself a "virtue" consisting in the merely habitual performance of dutiful actions, (ii) of basing his ethics on the "naturalistic fallacy." Both points are contentious, but this is not the place to pursue them.

14. Ibid., pp. 237; 272.

15. Compare Brentano's statement that "the good is . . . that which can be loved with a love that is correct": Franz Brentano, *The Origin of Our Knowledge of Right and Wrong*, trans. Roderick M. Chisholm and Elizabeth H. Schneewind (London: Routledge and Kegan Paul, 1969), p. 18.

16. As in Schopenhauer's "Sabbath of the penal servitude of willing" (*The World as Will and Representation*, trans. E. F. J. Payne [New York: Dover, 1969], vol. I, p. 196).

17. Aristotle, *Nicomachean Ethics* 1176b 27–1177a 3.

18. I am thinking of Aristotle's concession that even the philosopher will need to possess the practical virtues *pros to anthropeuesthai* or "in order to be human" (*Nicomachean Ethics* 1178b7).

19. Moore maintains that knowledge has "little or no value by itself," but figures as a "constituent in the highest goods" in that the states of consciousness which constitute these goods would not be realized if we did not know that the object of the relevant consciousness was real (*Principia Ethica*, pp. 247–248). Knowledge in general he considers to be valuable mainly as a means (ibid., p. 244). (He takes the same view about virtue: ibid., p. 223; but see note 26 and accompanying text below.)

20. The "allographic" arts are those involving a notation, e.g. literature and (some forms of) music. See Nelson Goodman, *Languages of Art* (Indianapolis: Hackett, 1976), p. 113.

21. See Hans-Georg Gadamer, "The Play of Art" in his *The Relevance of the Beautiful and Other Essays*, ed. Robert Bernasconi, trans. Nicholas Walker (Cambridge: Cambridge University Press, 1986), pp. 123–130, at p. 124. The incentive to make this metaphorical extension will derive,

once again, from an ambition to limit our exposure to the "misery of the world." "Superabundant life and movement" suggests, in the first instance, images of physical activity, but the philosopher characteristically seeks an interpretation of this idea that will be hospitable to "rational nature as such" (circumventing as far as possible the problems of bodily incapacity).

22. See Richard Wollheim, *Art and Its Objects*, 2nd ed. (Cambridge: Cambridge University Press, 1980), p. 228.

23. Moore, *Principia Ethica*, p. 249.

24. Aurel Kolnai, "Aesthetic and Moral Experience," in his *Ethics, Value, and Reality*, ed. Francis Dunlop and Brian Klug (London: Athlone Press, 1977), pp. 187–210, at p. 210.

25. Ibid. For some readers this reassurance may no longer be a matter of urgency, given the efforts of Philippa Foot and Bernard Williams to purge moral philosophy of a contrasting tendency to *moralism*—that is, to the assumption that moral claims, by right, necessarily override all other practical considerations. On the last point, see further Susan Wolf, "Meaning and Morality," in PAS 97 (1996–97), pp. 299–315.

26. *Principia Ethica*, p. 265: "[T]he typical and characteristic virtuous dispositions, so far as they are not mere means, seem rather to be examples of mixed goods."

27. I do not mean to suggest that the contemplative ideal appears *ex nihilo* in Aristotle, but the (still more fundamental) contribution of Plato cannot be discussed here.

28. David Wiggins has written of the desire for one's own mental, or conscious, life to continue: "There is something instinctive here and as irreducible as the rational commitment to make prudent provision for the future. These are things that we need reasons to opt out of rather than things that we have to look for deep reasons to opt into.... The content [of the instinct for survival] is surely that this animal that is *identical with me* should not cease to be, but should survive and flourish" ("The Concern to Survive" in Wiggins, *Needs, Values, Truth: Essays in the Philosophy of Value* (Oxford: Clarendon Press, 1998), pp. 303–311, at pp. 307–308). I do not wish to dispute this, but I take the question of the source of value (as put, for example, to Anaxagoras) to be designed to elicit an "account of the object of a further or post-instinctual rational concern" such as Wiggins goes on to envisage (ibid., p. 308). See also note 6 above.

29. Kant, *Critique of Judgement*, quoted by Korsgaard, *Creating the Kingdom of Ends*, p. 242.

30. Kant, quoted by Korsgaard, ibid., p. 243.

31. Korsgaard, ibid., p. 241.

32. Ibid., p. 246, emph. added.

33. I mean, for present purposes, Kant's picture as mediated by Korsgaard—but I have no quarrel with her account. (Alternatively, the feat of legitimation mentioned in the text might be attributed to the goodness of the general principles which I accept *qua* "moral agent" in the sense outlined—and deplored—by Diamond in *The Realistic Spirit*, p. 350. See also her illuminating criticism of the principle-based conception of morality as it appears in the work of R. M. Hare:

" 'We Are Perpetually Moralists': Iris Murdoch, Fact, and Value," in Maria Antonaccio and William Schweiker (eds.), *Iris Murdoch and the Search for Human Goodness* (Chicago: University of Chicago Press, 1996), pp. 79–109, esp. §§III–IV.)

34. The conceptual connection between aesthetic value and admiration has been worked out in greater detail (though without reference to Moore) by Kendall L. Walton: see his "How Marvelous! Toward a Theory of Aesthetic Value," in *Journal of Aesthetics and Art Criticism* 51 (1993), pp. 499–510.

35. See *Tractatus* 6.41; and compare "Lecture on Ethics" in James Klagge and Alfred Nordmann (eds.), *Ludwig Wittgenstein: Philosophical Occasions 1912–1951* (Indianapolis: Hackett, 1993), esp. at pp. 39–40.

36. Diané Collinson, "Ethics and Aesthetics Are One," *British Journal of Aesthetics*, 25 (1985), pp. 266–272, at p. 270.

37. Cora Diamond, "Ethics, Imagination, and the Method of Wittgenstein's *Tractatus*" in Alice Crary and Rupert Read (eds.), *The New Wittgenstein* (London: Routledge, 2000), pp. 149–173, at p. 171.

38. Ibid., p. 170.

39. Ibid., p. 171.

40. Ibid.

41. Ibid., p. 170.

42. See Ludwig Wittgenstein, *Philosophical Investigations*, 3rd ed., trans. G. E. M. Anscombe (Oxford: Basil Blackwell, 1967), §97: "if the words 'language,' 'experience,' 'world,' have a use, it must be as humble a one as that of the words 'table,' 'lamp,' 'door.' "

43. "Ethics, imagination . . . ," p. 171.

44. P. M. S. Hacker, "Was He Trying to Whistle It?" in Crary and Read, *The New Wittgenstein*, pp. 353–388.

45. *Tractatus* 6.522.

46. "Ethics, imagination . . . ," p. 164.

47. Ibid., p. 171. One half expects to come across "political correctness" somewhere in this catalog, but the brakes are applied in time.

48. Compare Kant, *Critique of Judgement*, §23 (with reference to the "feeling of the sublime").

49. For the last example see *Philosophical Investigations* §§437–438.

50. See note 21 and accompanying text above.

51. Kant, quoted by Korsgaard, *Creating the Kingdom of Ends*, p. 243.

52. I imagine many secular thinkers today will find it quite hard to recapture the sense of personal importance that could provoke a need for satisfaction on this latter point. "Who gives a damn? Certainly not God," as Nietzsche puts it (*On the Genealogy of Morals*, trans. Walter Kaufmann and R. J. Hollingdale [New York: Vintage Books, 1969], Essay III, §22).

53. Plato, *Phaedrus* 250d; *Symposium* 210c.

54. Kant, *Critique of Judgement*, trans. James Creed Meredith (Oxford: Clarendon Press, 1952), §29.

55. Iris Murdoch, *The Sovereignty of Good* (London: Routledge and Kegan Paul, 1970), pp. 64–65.

56. Kant also says in the *Critique of Judgement* (§41) that taste, or the concern with beauty, is a natural expression of human sociability and that "[e]ventually, when civilization has reached its height it makes this work of communication almost the main business of refined inclination." The same theme is developed by Roland Barthes when he posits as an aspect of literary "classicism" a conception of poetic expression as involving "rules *more artistic, therefore more sociable,* than those of conversation" (quoted in Richard Sheppard, "The Crisis of Language," in Malcolm Bradbury and James McFarlane [eds.], *Modernism: A Guide to European Literature 1890–1930* [Harmondsworth: Penguin, 1991], pp. 323–336, at p. 328 [emph. added]).

57. John McDowell, "Meaning, Communication, and Knowledge," in his *Meaning, Knowledge, and Reality* (Cambridge, Mass.: Harvard University Press, 1998), pp. 29–50, at p. 39: "Communication, of its very nature, confers potential benefits, whose usefulness is grounded in that interest in how things are that no agent can lack."

58. I am very grateful for comments on ancestors or earlier versions of this paper to Alice Crary, Brad Hooker, Arnd Kerkhecker, Thomas Nørgaard, Jeffrey Seidman, David Wiggins, and Stephen Williams, and to participants in discussion at the British Society of Aesthetics Annual Conference at St. Edmund Hall, Oxford in September 2001; the University of Oxford Moral Philosophy Seminar; Birkbeck College, London; the University of Reading; Harvard University (Department of Government); SUNY Stony Brook; and the New School University, New York.

9   A Novel in Which Nothing Happens: Fontane's *Der Stechlin* and Literary Friendship

Martha Nussbaum

"Our dear Baroness finds our life tedious and stories like that interesting. I, by contrast, find stories like that tedious and our daily life interesting. . . ."

Melusine stood up and gave Armgard a kiss. "You really are your sister's sister, the product of my education."

I   No "Tensions and Surprises"

The experience of reading Theodor Fontane's last novel, *Der Stechlin* (serialized in 1896–1897, published in 1899, after the author's death in 1898), is very strange indeed.[1,2] Things begin unsurprisingly. As with many nineteenth-century novels of manners, we are introduced to the dwelling-place of an aristocratic family (called Schloss Stechlin, although really, rebuilt after a fire, it is nothing more than a bourgeois house). We hear a great deal about the family's history and traditions. We learn about Lake Stechlin and the odd local superstitions surrounding it: when any major event takes place anywhere in the world, the waterspout in the middle of the lake will shoot up, and if the event is really great, a red rooster will crow! We are introduced in particular to the master of the house, Dubslav von Stechlin, widowed many years ago, father of a single son. As the first chapter ends, Dubslav receives a telegram from his son Woldemar, now in the military, announcing that he is arriving for a visit with two officer friends. The plot seems to be under way.

The plot begins to thicken, or so we think, when, in the second chapter, we encounter Woldemar's two friends, Rex and Czako, and follow the journey of the three young men to Schloss Stechlin, their initial meeting with Dubslav, and their choice of guestrooms. Their lively conversations touch on many themes of general interest: religion, politics, architecture, superstition. The third and fourth chapters continue the narration of the visit, adding new personae, neighbors from the surrounding region, including the progressive social-democratic Pastor Lorenzen and the aristocrat

Katzler. The extended conversations over meals, intrinsically interesting, begin to reveal the characters of all the participants, at the same time weaving a complex tapestry of the intellectual and political milieu of this region of Germany at a time of rapid social change.

Nonetheless, the reader begins to grow impatient. When, after all, is something going to start happening? Chapter 5, the next to last in part 1, brings relief: for father and son discuss the topic of Woldemar's marriage—after all, he is already thirty-two. Tension appears to be in the air. Woldemar may be hiding something from his father: we suspect an unsuitable relationship. Nonetheless, the topic recedes, and more general social conversation follows—on many topics, but including some intriguing exchanges beween Lorenzen and the three young men on the topic of passion and social form. We connect these observations to our suspicion of what the plot will be, although we can't help noticing that these bits about marriage and romance have taken up a very small proportion of the text (we are already on page 86). Still, we are again reassured: something is happening, albeit very slowly.

Our ideas about the plot are strengthened by the ensuing visit of the three young men to Woldemar's Aunt Adelaid, a puritanical and deeply antimodern woman who deals with change by denouncing it and the people who appear to be its bearers. Aunt Adelaid is very eager to get Woldemar married. Woldemar suggests that he is not averse to the idea, but has plans of his own. As Rex and Czako ride off, leaving their friend to dine with his aunt, they talk about Woldemar's frequent visits to the two daughters of the old Count Barby: the young Countess Armgard and her fascinating older sister Melusine, divorced former wife of the Italian Count Ghiberti.[3] There are more signs of tension in the air as the young men speculate: which one will Woldemar choose, and how will his choice go down with his family? The names of the two women themselves serve as signs of dramatic tension: the steady Armgard, so suitable (we imagine) as a wife, is pitted against the seductive and fascinating Melusine, whose name suggests fairy tale magic, the slippery seductiveness of a beauteous but dangerous water sprite.

Soon, however, our expectation concerning a plot of family conflict is somewhat undone, as we meet the women in question and discover that both are of good family, both are rich, and both are very nice people. The sisters are not adversaries, but loving allies; Melusine, seventeen years older, plays the role of mother to the shy young Armgard. Moreover, Woldemar is not in love with either of them: he writes rather coolly in his journal about which one he should begin to court. Even more clearly, the women are not in love with him. Melusine seems to be interested in courting him for her younger sister; Armgard in her silent stolid way does show some slight partiality, but there is nothing that rises to the level of romance. So what, after all, is the plot to be? Our attention focuses increasingly on the beautiful and witty Melusine, around whom the fantasies of many of the characters also cluster. What is her plan? Whom will she seduce and lead to destruction? Or, more to the point given her eligible condition, who will take her away with him and cause her oddly solitary state to end happily in marriage? Will she marry Woldemar? Czako? The lonely Dubslav? The kind and sympathetic Pastor Lorenzen?

What happens, however, is that they all (the sisters, Woldemar, and a baroness who is a close friend of the sisters) take an excursion on the river and talk a lot about life, Portuguese poetry, the singing of Jenny Lind, and much more. Romance is far off; at least if it is there it is lurking very far beneath the surface.

By now we are on page 181, and we have gradually realized that things are not as we expected when we began. This is not a novel like other nineteenth-century novels we know, held together by suspense, tension, and conflict, by romantic adversity and its resolution in marriage. There may still be a marriage, and in the end, indeed, there is one, as Woldemar eventually proposes to and marries the almost silent Armgard. There may still even be sadness and death, and in the end, indeed, there is, as Dubslav dies of heart failure after a long illness. But somehow these events do not form a literary plot. They happen, but they are not woven together into a dramatic story of the usual sort, with tension and resolution. They are not very much connected to one another, and they are not very prominent. They don't take up the whole space of the novel; indeed, very little space at all. Things like that, deaths, marriages, do happen in life, and they happen in *Der Stechlin*. But the world of *Der Stechlin* is no more neat and plotful than most people's daily life is. Is that interesting, or isn't it? (The Baroness likes scandal, tension, and stories of romantic intrigue; Armgard and Melusine find daily life more interesting.)

As we observe the reversal of our usual readerly expectations, a new pleasure has been coming into existence: the pleasure of conversation. Once we start getting used to the idea that this novel is not going to have what we thought it would have, we find that we don't actually miss it all that much. By now (if we are still reading—but this is a beloved novel, with a very large readership) we are simply enjoying being with this group of people and listening to them talk. They became our friends while we still believed that they were going to do something, I mean something of the sort characters in nineteenth-century novels do, behaving like figures in (and of) a plot. But by the time we have spent a good deal of time in their company, they are our friends whatever they do or don't do, and we simply enjoy them. Indeed, there is something oddly relaxing about the fact that nothing (or nothing of the usual sort) is going to happen: for then we don't race through the conversations on the way to the big events. We can afford really to listen to what they have to say about the Prussian state, or religion, or misogyny. We sit back and savor the conversations and the very interesting people whom they unfold. (Or, rather, people some of whom are interesting and witty and some of whom are boring, some of whom are impressive and some of whom are a bit ridiculous. This is a very funny novel.) Large themes are treated as people treat them in life: they talk about them, go off them, come back to them. A soothing feeling comes over the reader, somewhere between page 100 and 200: the feeling that we can enjoy watching these people be who they are and enjoy the surprise of having that relationship to them. (I first read *Der Stechlin* while giving the Tanner Lectures in Australia, an occasion of high tension and anxiety for me, and there was something deeply reassuring about going back to my room and sitting down with Melusine and Armgard, or Rex and Czako; when I took them to the breakfast table in the morning, German dictionary always in tow, it gave the day a lovely calm start, as jam fell upon the pages.) The fact that (in Germany at least) this odd novel is widely loved and regarded as Fontane's masterpiece, rather than being utterly neglected, testifies to the remarkable interest of the characters and the affection they, and their conversations, inspire.

As we might expect, the strangeness of the novel is no accident. Fontane[4] drew attention to it, taking apparent delight in the way he had subverted the conventions of the novel of manners, a genre to which, during the previous twenty years, he had been one of the most influential contributors. In a letter to a friend, he wrote: "At the end an old man dies and two young people get married. That is apparently all that happens in five hundred pages. As for complications and resolutions, as for romantic conflicts and conflicts in general, as for tensions and surprises—one finds nothing like that."[5] Fontane here lists the usual staples of literary plotting ever since Aristotle—complication and resolution, tension and surprise—and adds to them the un-Aristotelian but still very old (at least since New Comedy) theme of romantic conflict, an indispensable ingredient of the nineteenth-century novel of manners. There is nothing of that sort to be found in *Der Stechlin*, and so it *seems* that nothing has happened. But the word "apparently" (*ziemlich*) suggests that this initial judgment may not be altogether correct. Maybe, once we stop looking for the things that are not there, we might find some "happenings" that are there. The letter continues: "Various different people talk at length about God and the world. Everything is conversation, dialogue, in which the characters reveal themselves, and history with them." The novel, then, has a plan, albeit a different plan from the traditional one. It may be without plot, but it is not without movement, as one perceptive critic has written.[6] This movement is, nonetheless, very difficult to relate to, as criticism of the novel testifies: in the academic literature one keeps encountering words like *"bemerkenswert ereignisarm"* (remarkably lacking in incident) and *"Handlungsarmut"* (poverty of plot)—as if the plan had been to write the usual sort of novel and Fontane had failed in its execution.

Thinking about *Der Stechlin* seems to me a good way to honor Cora Diamond. So often, like Fontane, she has asked us all to question assumptions about structure, "plot," and sequence that hobble philosophy as surely as they hobble the novel, asking ourselves what revolutions in style and structure, as well as content, a due attention to life's complexities might require of us. Perhaps, too, Fontane's praise of conversation is an appropriate way of indicating how deeply I value our years of conversation about these and other topics.

II   "For the Sake of Their Actions": Characters Subordinate to Plot

As we think about Fontane's novel and the difficulties readers have coming to grips with it on its own terms, we are led to reflect about the (roughly) Aristotelian structures that Fontane said he would do without, traditional structures of plot that have lain at the heart of literary interest in more than one genre over very many centuries. Aristotle is giving an accurate account of the most common sources of interest in a tragic audience (whatever else he may be doing), when he observes:

> The most important of these elements is the structure of the events, because tragedy is a representation not of people as such but of actions and life. . . . The goal is a certain activity, not a qualitative state; and while men do have certain qualities by virtue of their character, it is in their actions that they achieve, or fail to achieve, happiness. It is not, therefore, the function of the agents' actions to allow the portrayal of their characters; it is, rather, for the sake of their actions that characterization is included. So, the events and the plot-structure are the goal of tragedy, and the goal is what matters most of all. (*Poetics*, ch. 6, 1450a15–22, Stephen Halliwell translation)

Plot is the mainspring of tragedy because it is through plot that we see how people attempt to achieve happiness, and either succeed or fail. (In a subsequent chapter Aristotle plausibly argues that our interest in tragedy is an interest in the possibilities of human life, things "such as might happen.") Thus, he continues, one might have a tragedy with plot but no detailed characterization, but one could not have a tragedy with characterization but no plot. (After all, it is of the essence of tragedy to depict reversals, and there is no reversal without plot.)

Aristotle is describing ancient Greek tragedy; but his description also holds for readers' relation to the nineteenth-century novel. The common English and German practice of publishing novels first in serial form is but one sign of the primacy of plot: for the whole effort was then to break off at a maximally suspenseful point, leaving the reader hanging, eager for the next installment. Readerly suspense was a key factor in the successes of writers as otherwise different as Charles Dickens and Wilkie Collins. In the novel of manners, characterization matters a great deal, as does the depiction of the social milieu. There is more room for all of this, given the length of these novels, than there is in tragic drama, of whatever period. Nonetheless, it remains true that we attend to the characters as people to whom something exciting is going to happen, and who by their actions will create as well as sustain excitement. As Fontane's letter suggests, the reader will expect, not just complication, tension, and surprise, but, in particular, romantic conflict: thus men and women (especially young men and beautiful women) are put into a novel as ingredients of that delicious sort of conflict.

This does not exactly mean that readers aren't interested in a novel's characters. They may be very intensely interested. They may identify with some and hate others; they may befriend some and feel distant from others. Nonetheless, there's a sense in which the characters are subordinate to the story line, vehicles for dramatic tension. I'll spend time with you as long as you're going to do something interesting: that is certainly the novel-reader's attitude to characters in at least most standard novels. There are novels in which interest in plot is more intense and interest in the characters correspondingly attenuated: the novels of Wilkie Collins, for example. And there are novels in which interest in the characters becomes very central and interest in plot is somewhat weakened: the novels of Jane Austen, George Eliot, and Tolstoy, for example. But even in Austen, Eliot, and Tolstoy the plot is very important, and we really cannot imagine loving the whole experience of reading without it. The story of a happily married Anna Karenina, without her tragic plot; the story of an Elizabeth Bennett who lived Jane Austen's own quiet hardworking nonmarried life and never met Mr. Darcy; the story of a Dorothea who marries the right man the first time and spends her life working in politics with him—these stories, even given the same characters, would simply be failed novels. Nobody would read them.

If this is so, then when we read we are in a very significant sense treating the characters as means to the "goal" mentioned by Aristotle, a plot that excites us and inspires our emotions. Our concern for them may not be entirely instrumental, but it is surely conditional: do something interesting, or I'll drop you. Fontane's novel, by contrast, forces us to attend to people in a new way, removing the structure within which we are accustomed to place them. What else can we do? If we continue reading, we have to listen to them, spend time in their presence.

Nor do we have another source of secret drama that the late nineteenth-century novel was beginning to mine: for we do not have access to these characters inside their heads, so to speak. Fontane's austere experiment denies us this voyeuristic sort of drama, as surely as it denies us plot. The characters tell us exactly what they tell one another, and no more. The few apparent exceptions confirm the practice: for they show the inner world only to the extent that it becomes, itself, a kind of conversation. Thus we see a page of Woldemar's journal, the way we read quite a few telegrams and letters. We twice overhear Dubslav talking to himself, an internal monologue that is really conversation, quite possibly spoken aloud, only there happens to be nobody listening except the reader. These few and striking exceptions (really, I think, nonexceptions) aside, we share a public world with the characters and know only as much about them as they choose to tell us. Some are interesting and some boring. Some inspire mirth and some inspire love ("*liebenswürdig*" is a key word in the characters' conversations about one another); some have secrets and some live, like Dubslav von Stechlin, in an entirely open way. We are forced to have a new type of attention to them because the kind that we expected is missing—and because we discover soon enough that the new kind has its own profound pleasures.

This new experience leads us to look back on our more ordinary literary experiences with a critical eye: what way is *that* to treat a person?

III   Plot in Life

If we have that thought, we are likely to have another. The sort of attention that we have been finding problematic is not only a feature of our relations with characters in literary works. It is also a feature of our relations with people in "real life." So often our relationships involve the very expectations that we brought to *Der Stechlin*; we ask them to be part of an interesting drama, we view them as figures in a narrative that excites us. Indeed, we often demand that they play a part in a narrative that excites us, as a condition of our continued interest in them. We want drama in our lives, and we want drama of a particular sort. (What sort that is will vary with social norms and personal history.) But if the people we have cast in that drama won't play their roles, that's that, we don't like them any more. We're bored, we go off looking elsewhere for something, someone more exciting.

These expectations, these scripts, are of many kinds. A parent expects a child to achieve a high success, besting all other children in competition. That same parent expects a child to get married to someone suitable after a suitable period of searching. Romantic partners expect one another to fit an erotic script that must continue to sustain dramatic interest; or to replace someone that they have lost; or to fill a void in their lives; the list goes on and on. Friends often gravitate to "friends" because they find the person dramatic, or, even more often, because that person allows *them* to play a dramatic role that they long to play (the intimate confidant of the famous politician, the rescuer of the troubled soul).

This is not an ideal way to relate to people, to put it mildly. Often it means that we don't see them clearly and don't love them for their own sake. Interest in dramatic narrative is not altogether incompatible with an interest in people for their own sake. But the minute the person is seen as interesting because of his or her role in a grand narrative, misunderstanding and even exploitation are big dangers.

This problem looms especially large in relations between the sexes. Here perhaps more than elsewhere, certain narratives, some conveyed in an individual's process of development and some powerfully conveyed by the culture (and of course the two levels interact in manifold ways) impose their grip on human relations, shaping desires and choices. Often these narratives prevent people from seeing one another as individuals, or listening to the particularity of one another's conversation.

Proust puts this point in its most extreme form: for every person there is a "general form" of erotic love, based on childhood scenarios, that gets reenacted with each new person. The particularity of the person hardly matters at all: she is but an occasion for the playing out of the erotic script. Albertine could have been virtually anyone, and her individuating characteristics fluctuate throughout the narrative, as Marcel attends far less to her than to the drama in him concerning her.

Proust focuses on deep human needs that (as the novel sees it) arise in any close human relationship. Society, he suggests, is superficial and can do little to shape or alter love. But here Proust is wrong: society is far from superficial. Images of what a good man is, what a good woman is, profoundly shape the erotic scripts in which people cast one another. These messages are conveyed early in life; even as parents interact with their children with some degree of individual variation, they transmit shared cultural scripts. These scripts powerfully shape emotion and desire. In many times and places, the dominant social scripts have included the idea that a good man is dominant, the ruler of the household, one who allows no threats to his control. A good woman, by contrast, is dependent, obedient, and pure. But because women's desires are wild and dangerous, they will not behave like this without constant oversight. Thus the good narrative for a man is to marry a chaste young woman and then watch over her.[7] The good narrative for a woman is to marry early, before her chastity is suspect, and marry someone who will use his control benignly—Prince Charming, sweeping Cinderella off to a life not of scandalous independence but of morally acceptable and allegedly happy dependence, Sleeping Beauty awakened from her chaste slumber by the right prince's masterful kiss. Every society rings different changes on these scenarios, but they are as recognizable in Wilhelmine Germany as in twentieth-century Texas (where it was not a criminal offense until 1967 for a man to kill an adulterous wife or her lover). How often such narratives of marriage impede particular love, preventing people from seeing one another as individuals and treating one another as fully human.

The deformation of marital relations by social narratives is a deep and constant preoccupation in Fontane's work. He is particularly obsessed with the way in which narratives of female purity (sometimes further colored by class prejudice) pervert what might have been love, leaving everyone miserable. In *Cecile* (1886[8]) a beautiful woman is on her way to forming a humanly deep and satisfactory relationship with an intelligent man. Then he finds out that some years ago she was the mistress of a prince. Of course he can no longer think of marrying her, and he drops her, making himself miserable and plunging her into a lethal depression. In *Irrungen Wirrungen* (1888), Lena, from a lower middle-class family, and the aristocratic but poor Botho are deeply in love. They respond deeply and precisely to one another's particularity. But they both know that their affair must be short lived since society has decreed that Botho must marry a wealthy woman of his own class—and of course not someone who would have sex with him without marriage. Botho contrasts the love he and Lena shared with what he thinks of as reality: "For one summer we had the happiest days. . . . And then came life, with its seriousness and its expectations" (*Der Stechlin*, 150). The second half of the novel is excruciating, like hearing fingers scrape across a blackboard for two hours. Botho indeed marries an attractive, pure, rich aristocrat, who is also high-spirited, good-looking, and kind. But her shallow humor and vapid good nature drive him to bitter, unhappy isolation, as she insists on finding everything comical and refuses to carry on a serious conversation about anything. She is miserable, he is miserable. (There is no finer account I know of marital irritation, both the effect of an unsuitable companion on her spouse and the reciprocal effect of being found irritating on a person who is perfectly all right and has done nothing except to be the wrong type of person.)

Perhaps the central exhibit in this gallery of deformed marriages is that of Effi Briest and the Baron von Instetten in *Effi Briest* (1894), Fontane's most famous novel. Begin with the fact that it is taken as perfectly all right by all members of this social world that Instetten, a mature man of around forty, marries a seventeen-year-old girl with no experience of life—largely because he used to be in love with her mother. Next, far from trying to figure out what this high-spirited seventeen-year-old is like and what might make her happy, he takes her off to a desolate spot on the Baltic and makes her live (alone for most of the day, while he works as a high-ranking civil servant) in a haunted house. He finds nothing lacking in a daily life in which, for the most part, he plays the role of teacher and she the role of pupil—with no play, no jokes, no conversational intimacy. Instetten simply expects that because he is a good controlling male, and a kind and decent man to boot, Effi will play the role of the properly docile and subservient female. As readers know, Effi eventually is so miserable that she has a brief affair with Major Crampas (who brings her his own seductive narrative of freedom and choice, and is far further from real love of Effi than is her husband). Nonetheless, the passage of years, the birth of a child, and the fact that both people are in the end decent people who try hard to understand one another, learning to see one another more and more accurately, produces what has become a pretty good marriage, with love on both sides.

Then Instetten discovers, hidden in a drawer, letters from Crampas to Effi that reveal the affair that ended six years before. Now a dramatic script, written by society, takes over. A real man who has been insulted in this way must fight a duel and repudiate his wife. In the ensuing dialogue with his friend Wuellersdorf, Instetten admits that he feels no hatred of Crampas. In fact, he says, he loves his wife; his strong personal inclination is to forgive her. But he feels the grip of public expectation—that "social something that tyrannizes over us," as he puts it. It is not just obedience to external norms that makes him yield, it is the knowledge that his own emotions are deeply implicated in this social narrative of male honor. If he didn't challenge Crampas and send away Effi, he tells his friend, he would not be able to hold his head up in society, and he would in the end have to shoot himself. And although he recognizes that he has created this problem for himself by telling Wuellersdorf, when he might have kept the secret, he simply treats his own behavior as part of the necessary workings of a larger social force.

In this case as in the other two I have mentioned, nobody ends up happy. Instetten is miserable, losing his wife, killing his former friend, and raising his daughter in lonely isolation. Effi, separated from her daughter and all her old connections, dies of misery, guilt, and shame. Effi's parents are miserable; Effi and Instetten's child is miserable.[9] Nonetheless, they all somehow feel that it had to be this way. They don't really protest, and it is not until the end of Effi's life that even her parents are willing to take her into their home. At the novel's end, the parents do begin to have doubts about the whole thing. Effi's father talks about Rollo, the faithful Newfoundland dog who loved Effi steadily and who now lies inconsolably by her grave, his head on his paws: maybe he knew something that we didn't, Briest says. The dog is the only one who cannot feel the social tyranny. In consequence, he may well be the only one who was capable of genuine love. As the mother begins to raise her own anxious questions—was Effi perhaps too young to get married?—her husband tells her not to dwell on it, with a phrase that he has used throughout the novel to deflect thought, and that has become so well known that Günter Grass could borrow it for the title of his latest novel: *"Ach, Luise, lass,"* he says. *"Das ist ein zu weites Feld."* ("Let it go, Luise. It is too big a subject," literally "too wide a field.") With this image Fontane underlines the narrow, constricted nature of social thinking about marriage, the way it imprisons both men and women.

What all these tyrannies have in common is a failure to attend respectfully to the individual person and the complex circumstances within which real people make erotic and ethical choices. Fontane connects that sort of genuine attention with both forgiveness and mercy. In an 1882 letter to Eduard Engel, apropos of the happy ending of *L'adultera*, he writes that the sixth commandment is, of course, a commandment like any other. It is bad to break it. But still, sometimes people do break it, and sometimes, depending on the circumstances, other people are able to forgive them. He then says that what he himself really feels is that "'Adultery is a sin, certainly, but in some circumstances (and for that we must examine every particular) a venial sin.' That sentence I accept *de tout mon coeur*. . . . Respect for the law, but not for rigorism." He suggests that mercy in these matters is beginning to be a social norm—but rigorism still typically carries the day.

There are subtle insights in Fontane's depictions of these social tyrannies. He knows, for example, that the fact that scripts are imposed by a dominant social class does not mean that the marginalized are more free. Women's guilt when they violate the rules can kill them, as it kills both Cecile and Effi. And when Lena meets up with a group of courtesans who are having affairs with Botho's bachelor friends, they see her in terms of their own script, a self-defensive reaction to dominant social norms. They expect that she is doing what they are doing, making money out of an affair, and they gleefully talk about all the pleasant things they will do with their money (after marrying some elderly widower who does not object to their past). When they find out that Lena has gone with Botho out of love, they don't know what to say. It is so odd, and so sad. "'My lord, child,'" says the kindest one. "'You're blushing. You're tied to him *here*,' and she pointed to her heart, 'and you're doing all this out of love? Well, child, *that* is bad, that's a real stinking mess.'"[10] What this young woman finds scandalous and a real mess is love because she knows that love doesn't fit into the social rules; it frightens her, it casts a dubious light on her own compromises.

Fontane also knows that people who are willing to flout the social narratives are not necessarily heroic or lovable, though that possibility is not ruled out. (The friendship of Dubslav von Stechlin and the illegitimate child Agnes is a rare such case, two lovable people befriending one another outside the social rules, and it depends on Dubslav's essentially childlike personality.) For such people might simply be weird, or so unattractive that society can think no worse of them than it already does. The elderly civil servant who marries Cecile after the Prince drops her is just a boring man whom nobody would want to marry. She can see his kindness, but it doesn't make her any happier to be trapped for life in his company. And Gideon Franke, who marries Lena after Botho drops her, is an alarming evangelical preacher without a trace of humor or grace. Lena has perhaps done somewhat better than Botho, since Franke is not irritating exactly, and he values truth, which is on the whole a good thing; but we don't expect much happiness in that marriage. (Does he really value Lena for the person she is, or just as an example of his unconventional theories about sin and virtue?)[11]

IV   "'Stockings Aren't Held Aloft'"

In *Der Stechlin* Fontane moves his characteristic preoccupation to the meta-level, fashioning a novel that first elicits the reader's baneful tendencies to see people in terms of social scripts and conventional romantic expectations, and then, by frustrating those tendencies in such a pleasing and interesting way, showing them different sources of pleasure and relationship. If you can't relate to the characters in one way, you can try relating to them in this other way. Isn't it promising? Doesn't it have something to be said for it, this way of attending that respects their freedom and individuality rather than dragooning them into something that comes out of you (and probably, before that, out of the culture)?

Such themes are discussed inside the novel as well, making it easy to connect one's experience as reader to aspects of the characters' conversations. Consider the exchange between the two sisters and their friend the Baroness that forms my epigraph (267). The Baroness loves social gossip—people with guilty secrets, sensational sins. Gossip makes life interesting, she says: for after all, if there were no scandals, how boring everything would be. Armgard responds with sweet simplicity: she finds "our daily life" interesting and such stories uninteresting. Melusine kisses her and exclaims with pleasure that Armgard is indeed her own sister and the product of her sister's education (267). Both sisters "lack an organ" for the scandalous, as Armgard puts it, and Melusine takes credit for having taught Armgard to be unusual in that way. (We shall see later how these commitments are related to Melusine's more general attitudes to sex and marriage, her determination to live, so to speak, in a wide rather than a narrow field.)

Two opposite poles with respect to our issue are exemplified by the antagonistic sib-
lings, Dubslav and Adelaid. Adelaid cannot see people in any way but as examples of
social propriety or impropriety. They simply do not exist for her as people. Woldemar
is a nephew-token who will either make a morally and socially suitable marriage or
not. Melusine is a bad woman because she is divorced. All her interesting individual
characteristics are just seductions that make her all the more problematic. The child
Agnes is not a particular child, but, because of her illegitimacy, a symbol of social
decay. When Agnes shows the long red stockings she is knitting, "Dubslav laughed.
Adelaid also. But there was a difference in her laughter" (411). Dubslav laughs in kindness and friendship, thinking it funny to see such a young child so seriously knitting
a long pair of stockings. Adelaid laughs as someone who triumphs in her discovery of
decay. The ensuing dialogue clarifies their diametrically opposed approaches plainly:

"Why," asks Dubslav, "are you so against the red stockings?"
  "Because they are a sign."
  "That doesn't mean a thing, Adelaid. A sign can be anything. What are they a sign of? That
is the important question."
  "They are a sign of disobedience and perversion. And whether you laugh or not, . . . they are
a sign of the fact that reason has entirely gone out of the world and all social demarcations have
ceased to exist for ever. That is what you are supporting . . . And because you are the way you
are, you are happy that this dainty little doll . . . wears red stockings and is knitting herself new
ones. But I will say to you once again: these red stockings, they are a sign, a banner held aloft."
"Stockings aren't held aloft." (412–413)

Adelaid wants the illegitimate child to cower, to cover herself in ashes, to be a
walking sign of the badness of nonmarital sex. She can't stand the red stockings
because they express a child's delight in color, showing Agnes to be a happy child,
and also because red, for her, is not just a nice color but a sign of the fallen woman
and her illicit pleasure. For Dubslav the child is a child (and she happens to be a very
kindly and attentive child who, more than anyone else, cheers him up during his long
illness). Her red stockings are something nice that she is making for herself. To
Adelaid's claim that the stockings are a flag (the flag of shame and sex run wild), he
responds in the most literal way: stockings aren't held aloft, "Strümpfe werden nicht
hochgehalten." In Adelaid's determination to see things as figures in a social narrative, she has stopped seeing reality.

Dubslav, as this scene suggests, is Adelaid's opposite number, a man who lives in
the individual and the real, a man who can't even state a general proposition about
the world without putting it into ironic quotation marks, to indicate that it doesn't
quite capture the complexities of life. He sees each person with particularity and

accuracy: Woldemar's prosaic decency and lack of poetry, Agnes's kindness, Engelke's devotion, Armgard's serenity (407), the fact that Melusine is both a lady and a sexually fascinating woman, both Frau and Frauenzimmer (294). His inability to subsume people under convenient social categories is not always a source of happiness: for it is presumably what has made it impossible for him to marry again, after the death, many years ago, of his beloved wife. Here his tendency to focus on the particular seems excessive and leads to sadness. But he can see even his own faults and excesses without melodramatizing them. As Lorenzen says in his funeral speech for Dubslav (which we may also hear at the meta-level): "He was genuinely free. He knew it too, although he often denied it. The Golden Calf was not his thing. . . . He had no enemies, because he himself was no man's enemy. He was . . . the embodiment of the old saying, 'What you don't want someone else to do to you . . .' . . . Because he had love. Nothing human was alien to him, because he experienced himself as human and was aware at every moment of his own human weaknesses. . . . He was the best that we can be: a man and a child" (442–443). It would be too simple to say that we hear the author's voice in this speech: for there are many obvious Christian clichés in the speech as a whole, and it emerges from the character of the oddly isolated if genuinely generous and loving Lorenzen. But it does convey the connection we see in Dubslav between a direct or childlike perception and freedom. Because he is able to see people without either greed or malice, "in the open" as Lorenzen says, because he is aware of his own weakness and therefore does not demand perfection of any human being, because he is a child who sees things naively rather than symbolically, for all these reasons he is genuinely free in his relationships with them, free in just the way, for example, that Botho, Instetten, Effi, and Cecile are not free. He lives in the open, in a wide rather than a narrow field.

Let us now move this to the meta-level. The novel fosters habits of Dubslavian perception. In reading it we are led not to generalize hastily or without saving self-irony, to see both with the eyes of an adult, knowledgeable about the world and the variety of people in it, and, at the same time, with the eyes of a child, who doesn't quite know what to expect, who looks to see what is there, who hasn't yet reduced people to social formulae.

If, for example, we expected Dubslav to be the foolish *senex* in a drama of generational conflict, or the tragic protagonist in a tale of lost social influence, our expectations are disappointed. He does have differences of a sort with his son—he is somewhat more poetic, Woldemar more prosaic; he clearly finds Melusine fascinating and Armgard boring, whereas Woldemar is terrified of Melusine and comforted by the stolid but sweet Armgard. But these differences are not plotful; they do not create tensions and complications. The two behave decently and lovingly toward one another, and they do not have conflict, much less romantic conflict. As for lost social status, the theme of political and social change runs throughout the novel's conversations, and one of its most amusing episodes is the election campaign in which Dubslav, running as the conservative candidate, is defeated by a social democrat, representative of the new era. But this is not a plot: it is not tragic, and, though very funny, it is not the stuff of comic plot either. It is just something that happens. Even Dubslav's death, which Fontane acknowledges as one of the two things that actually happens in his novel, is not a death *scene*. The actual (quiet painless) death passes almost without note, and the final days of Dubslav are not so much a literary plot as the element of plot that we can't get rid of in our lives, which do after all have a beginning, a middle (though we don't know ahead of time where it is), and an end.

As we spend time with Dubslav, however, these disappointments turn into pleasures, as we learn to enjoy his company, loving him for himself and not for what a plot might do with him. So too with the other characters: we gradually relax our demand that they prove themselves worthy of our attention by engaging in dramatic action of the traditional sort. We listen to them, and either like them or dislike them, find them either interesting or boring. In the case of Dubslav, however, this relaxation of our demand for conflict is particularly important, because goodness of his sort (being both child and man) lacks narrative structure of the usual literary-dramatic type, and is thus particularly likely to be neglected or distorted if we approach it with the demand that it satisfy a dramatic norm.

Wayne Booth perceptively argued[12] that our relationship with a literary work can be understood as a type of friendship. We spend time with the characters and the implied author of a work, and rather intimate time at that. We allow the text to arouse in us desires that are far from casual. During the time of reading we become a certain type of person, with certain thoughts and desires active, others inactive. Just as the time spent with friends reveals, but also further shapes, character, so too the time spent with the text and its characters shapes desire and choice. Whether this shaping will affect behavior in other parts of one's life is a large question that Booth wisely does not attempt to answer: there are simply too many influences, and all we can say is that the experience of reading is among them. Nonetheless, he argues, we can legitimately evaluate a literary work from a moral viewpoint by evaluating the relationships that it urges us to form, the desires that it renders active.

Booth's analysis invites us to do what I think Fontane has already suggested: to evaluate the friendships we form with his characters and compare them to the friendships we form in "real life," asking normative questions about both. Real life does not come off well in this comparison, unless we are much better than Fontane thinks we are. And yet, he also thinks we have some good tendencies, since he expects people to be able to read his novel and to take pleasure in the relationships it offers.

V   *The Fair Melusine*

At the heart of *Der Stechlin* is a fascinating and seductive woman. She has the name of a fairy-tale mermaid who lured a knight into the water. The name, which apparently first appears in a medieval drama of 1456 by Thüring von Ringoltingen, became famous in the nineteenth century as the title of a drama (*The Fair Melusine*) written by Austrian playwright Franz Grillparzer in 1833 and turned into an opera by Conradin Kreutzer the next year. We know it best, perhaps, as the name of an independent overture written by Felix Mendelssohn in 1834, inspired by the Grillparzer drama. In all these versions, Melusine is a symbol of the forbidden and seductive dangers of a female sexuality that refuses to contain itself within social bounds, posing fatal dangers to men. Somebody in the Barby household thought that this was a good name to give an infant girl; perhaps it was out of a sense of balance that the other infant girl was given the eminently solid and respectable name of Armgard. The fate of the two women is bound up with their naming, since people react to the names as essential descriptions before they make the slightest effort to engage the women themselves in conversation. If by the time of the novel Armgard has become Armgard and Melusine is a Melusine, it is because (as Melusine tells Woldemar) people always treat her in accordance with their fantasies about the name.

Melusine is evidently a beautiful woman, as we see in people's reactions to her. We can see for ourselves that she is a witty, intelligent, and highly complicated woman. So, as readers, we rather expect that she will be a true Melusine, and that the plot of the story will be one of female seduction and male danger. And because she is seductive and dangerous, the right thing to do with her is surely to marry her off to some suitable person, thereby restoring the social order. Single, and especially divorced, independently wealthy, and going by her given name only, she is a threat to the social narrative. The traditional marriage plot is appealing because it will remove the danger that she constitutes in her single condition and also because it will save her, restore her to "happiness" by attaching her to a dominant male, taking her off the shelf and out of a state that is on the borderline of disgrace. As she is, she is somewhere between Cinderella and the fallen woman (for what woman simply abandons her husband after the honeymoon?). Marriage is the cure.

So the reader wants Melusine to marry someone, and we can't believe that this won't happen, so powerful are the expectations with which readers come to such novels of social life. At first, one expects that Woldemar will be swept away by her and marry her. This expectation proves very long lived—despite the fact that from the beginning Woldemar is depicted as a man without imagination or passion, a conventional albeit decent man who could not possibly make someone like Melusine happy; despite the fact that she never shows the least interest in him, but, from the beginning, has her eye on a match between Woldemar and Armgard; despite the fact that she makes a concerted effort to show the all-too-interested Woldemar that he could not be happy with her, belittling him for his lack of imagination (255) and setting up situations in which Armgard's sweet consoling and moral nature can reveal itself.

And: we form these expectations and wishes despite the fact that, if we look things in the eye, Melusine does not like men and does not want to live with a man. From the beginning, she shows interest in the topic of male misogyny (154), and also in the topic of the woman of independent career (Jenny Lind, for example, 173).[13] When Armgard asks her whether she feels any jealousy about her engagement, she says, "'Oh my dear Armgard, if you only knew! I have only the happiness, you have the burden as well'" (286).

The burden she has in mind is the brutality and unresponsiveness of male sexuality. We know that Melusine was briefly married to an Italian count, Ghiberti, whom she left shortly after their marriage. Late in the novel, in a famous scene known to critics as "the tunnel scene," she explains things to her friend the Baroness. The Baroness expresses regret that Woldemar didn't arrange for a private rail compartment for his and Armgard's honeymoon trip to Italy. "'Now she has her Woldemar, and in another sense she doesn't have him,'" she comments.

"A good thing for her."

"But Countess . . ."

"You are amazed, my dear Baroness, to hear me say that. And yet it has its correctness. Only too much, indeed: the burned child shrinks from fire."

"But Countess . . ."

"I got married in Florence, as you know, and traveled the same evening all the way to Venice. Venice is in one respect exactly like Dresden: namely, it is the first stop for married couples. Ghiberti too—I always prefer to say 'Ghiberti' rather than 'my husband'; 'my husband' is always such a horrible expression—Ghiberti too opted for Venice. And so, we had to go through the great Alpine tunnel."

"I know, I know, it's endless."

"Yes. Endless. Oh, my dear Baroness, if only there had been someone with us, a Saxon, yes, even a Rumanian. We were, however, alone. And when I came out of the tunnel, I knew what abject misery I had encountered."

"Dearest Melusine, how sorry I am. Truly, dearest friend, and most sincerely. But a tunnel like that. It is just like a destiny." (346)[14]

Melusine is not the first woman to experience forced sex in marriage as abject misery. (John Stuart Mill wrote that the absence of a consent requirement for sex within marriage makes the lot of women worse than that of slaves.) She is, however, one of the few in her time who is willing, and able, to extricate herself from such a situation. She has expectations for herself that are incompatible with a life of "abject misery." It is not surprising that after such an experience she shies away from sex. What is surprising is that she is happy to live as a single woman, despite the social anomaly she constitutes. She insists on going by her first name alone, which astonishes the other characters (121). Rich, good to her family and friends, active, witty, and happy, she simply has no inclination to seek another husband, and she enjoys confounding the expectations of those who seek to define her in terms of a male. Misery rarely yields autonomy, but Melusine appears to be that rarest of things in the world of fiction, or in the world generally: an autonomous woman, a woman who is there in the world in relation to her family and friends, but, by choice, not in relation to a man.

The other characters have a very hard time understanding this. Woldemar asks himself (very early on) whether he ought to marry Melusine or Armgard, and he simply assumes that both will regard him as a prize catch. Rex and Czako ask similar questions (Czako contemplates a proposal to Melusine)—without asking anything at all about what Melusine wants. Aunt Adelaide thinks of Melusine as the dangerous temptress.

What I want to focus on, however, is the reader. Right up until the novel's end, the reader insists on marrying off Melusine. If not to Woldemar (and why might we ever have entertained this most unsuitable thought?), then surely to someone. We consider Czako; we even think about Dubslav, because Melusine makes a joke about marrying him (339). We think most about Pastor Lorenzen, because Melusine seems genuinely curious about him, and because the novel ends with a letter from her to him. But of course it is not a letter that suggests any erotic interest. Indeed, what clearly fascinates Melusine about Lorenzen is the fact that he is a non-sex-driven man. " 'And he is unmarried? That alone is already a good sign. Ordinary men think they have to immortalize themselves as quickly as possible, so that their splendor will not die. Your Lorenzen looks to me like an exceptional man in all respects' " (176).

In fact, we just can't stand to leave Melusine on the shelf. We think that this is an unsatisfactory ending for her, a form of abject misery, if you will. Even after we understand her history, we want her to be redeemed, consoled by happy love. In short, we are like the (less perceptive) characters: we won't let her be who she is. Melusine is well aware of the fantasies people impose on beautiful women; she takes pleasure in playing with them, she uses her name to create a space of freedom, all the time maintaining that " 'names have no significance' " (160). But she never allows these fantasies to define her in her own eyes. And her rejection of her own marital experience has led to a more general rejection—of the entire tyranny of social conformity. Her father notes the anxiety that she causes to all narrow and puritanical people (336). The one tone that she can never assume in conversation is the tone of moral superiority (447). In short, as we are told, Melusine is the polar opposite of Adelaid, and one is life and the other death (295). She is the too-broad field that scares people who can't live except by the rules.

Out of her pain and her creativity, Melusine, then, has made herself a world of freedom, in which things are not what society says they are, but what a clear eye can see in them. " 'I respect the given,' " she tells Lorenzen. " 'And next to that, what is in process of becoming. For after all this becoming will sooner or later be a given. . . . And above all, as Lake Stechlin teaches us, we should never forget the large connections among things. To cut oneself off is to erect a wall around oneself, and to wall oneself off is death' " (314–315).[15] Society walls people off, giving them dead narratives instead of living conversations.

Melusine is not represented as a perfect person, an ideal spokeswoman for the author's philosophy of life. She is a child who has been burned. Concerning some things, such as the possibility of sexual happiness in marriage, she herself accepts a fixed story and refuses at times to look at particulars. When Armgard and Woldemar are off on their honeymoon, she conjectures that Armgard must already be missing Berlin and her sister (360). But her projection, based on her own history, yields to evidence about someone else: when she reads Armgard's letter, she sees between the lines evidence of delight, and pride in her own delight.[16] So she is a good friend and a good sister, but not an ideal. To view her as an ideal icon would, in any case, be yet one more way of debasing her, turning her from a complex person into a symbol of something else. Nobody who is fond of her should want to do that.

So in the end, although we can't really let Melusine be, we keep weaving fantasies around her, at least we see that letting her be would be the friendly and the just thing to do.

VI   Too Idealistic? Too Austere?

Up to this point, I have presented Fontane's project in a positive light, suggesting that the modes of attention cultivated in *Der Stechlin* are of considerable ethical value. We might, however, have some anxieties about the extent to which he has pushed his assault on dramatic tension. First, we might focus on the connection between narrative and erotic life. Isn't the story of human desire fundamentally a story of dramatic conflict, as adult eroticism grows out of a child's conflict with, and forbidden desire for, parental figures and her struggle with those same figures for access to longed-for objects? One need not accept any particular type of psychoanalytic picture (Freudian, Kleinian, etc.) in order to pose this question. Indeed, one needn't even accept a psychoanalytic approach to development. One need only be convinced that a child's early longings for objects and its intense involvement with parental figures matter greatly for the subsequent erotic life. (Proust is convinced of this, though he knows nothing of psychoanalysis.) In asking people to attend to one another in an utterly undramatic fashion, isn't Fontane asking them to disregard the very roots of the erotic? Isn't he delivering a life that is too Kantian to be happy? Or: If we attend to others only for their own sake, how can we ever fall in love? (A worry that troubles Kant, and to which he can find no fully satisfactory answer.)[17]

This worry is important. Ultimately, however, I believe that Fontane can answer it. His adversary is not human love and the roots of the erotic, it is society. His people are rejecting, not the general idea that human beings strive for love and happiness, but, instead, the particular narrow form their society has given to that search, with its restrictive gendered notions of happiness and purity. Admittedly, Fontane seems to have no interest in the aspects of early life that interest Proust and the psychoanalysts. That is an absence in his work, as in the work of most of the great novelists until Proust—although Goethe certainly has deep insights along these lines. Because this dimension of human life is simply absent, we should not say that the literary experiment of *Der Stechlin* takes a stand against that sort of dramatic tension, or that sort of narrative. It takes no stand concerning it one way or the other—although it does suggest a set of questions that we might valuably pose about the ways in which adult relationships can be deformed (as Proust so clearly shows) by the sort of childhood drama that Proust depicts. At any rate, the novel suggests that whatever else erotic love contains, if it is to be productive of mutual happiness, it will have to contain the element of friendly attention that Fontane's novel constructs.

What Fontane worries about, however, as I said, is not the influence of early object-relations and the drama they contain. It is the hold of familiar *social* narratives over the erotic and even the friendly imagination: especially, as we have seen, his society's social narratives of gender and marriage, involving ideas of male control and female purity. These social narratives get mixed into the developmental process in ways to which psychoanalytic thought has not always done justice, but they are in principle separable from a development that focuses on a child's relationship to beloved objects. So telling people not to look at other people in terms of *those* plots, while a radical enough demand, and a demand that cuts deeply into most cultures' views of human relations, does not amount to the demand to renounce all erotic interest in dramatic/narrative structure. If only we could get beyond *those* narratives (the ones that led to Melusine's trauma) and the harm they do to both the powerful and the powerless, we might be able to imagine other kinds of erotic relations with one another: for example, the happy relationship that Botho and Lena briefly shared, unclouded by the need to yield to "reality." These relationships would have their own narrative structure, as human life imposes changes, illness, loss, aging, and so forth. They would contain the roots of Aristotelian tragedy: the general longing for happiness and various "reversals" that beset it—although their way of presenting these materials would be less tidy than Greek drama's, less single-minded. They would simply reject some of the key materials of the novel of society as that genre has developed.

I believe, then, that this first worry might ultimately be answered, although it is not at all easy to imagine what the answer would look like, so deeply are we all still in the grip of the bad narratives. (Ask yourself, for example, in what novel is there a sexually passionate relationship between a man and a woman that does not end in punishment and death. Jane Austen's *Persuasion* is the only case I can think of,[18] and even that is not free of the problems Fontane worries about, since it is a version of the woman-on-the-shelf-gets-rescued fantasy that he rejected for Melusine.)[19] Proust is right to suggest that our erotic investment in the past brings with it certain dangers when we try to love someone as an individual and real person; but I think he is wrong to suggest that these dangers must always defeat the project of loving someone for that person's own sake.

The second worry is therefore the one on which I want to focus. It is the worry raised inside the novel by the Baroness, when she says that Armgard and Melusine are too idealistic in their rejection of gossip and scandal: "You Barbys are all so terribly discreet and idealistic, but for my part I am different. I take the world as it is. A beer and a vulgar joke, and sometimes putting someone in the pillory, that's how you get ahead."[20] We might elaborate her criticism as follows: "You say that you are interested in daily life, not in gossip. But you have an impossibly idealized view of daily life. You are talking about daily life as it might be, not daily life as it is. In real daily life people drink, gossip, make fun of others, sometimes punish others. That's the reality we are in. I accept it and even take pleasure in it. You do not."

This is a serious criticism of Fontane's project. For, as I have reconstructed it, it gets a lot of mileage out of an idea of seeing people as they are and out of a related contrast between what they are and our narrative/dramatic fantasies about them. The Baroness says that it is Melusine who does not see people as they are: for as they are, they love gossip and the sort of socially shared narratives that enable them to make vulgar jokes and to put other people in the pillory when they violate a social norm. That's life. (Instetten, in *Effi Briest*, says much the same thing when he contrasts his desire to forgive with the exigent reality of social life; so does Botho, when he contrasts his happy days with Lena with the "expectations" of "life." ("Und dann kam das Leben . . .") In Melusine's determination to see people "as they are" lies concealed a refusal to accept humanity as it is. Similarly, in Fontane's insistence that we look at people without the distorting lens of social narrative lies concealed a disdain for social reality, an austere and idealistic refusal to live in the world.

To this the reply should be, yes, this is a normative project, not a straightforward description of people as they currently are. Indeed, the distance between the form of attention cultivated by the novel and forms of attention averagely cultivated in daily life is amply in evidence in the novel itself, as the characters weave fantasies about Melusine, as Aunt Adelaid looks at everyone in terms of a social script, and so on. The desired form of attention is real and possible: indeed, that fact is demonstrated for the reader by the fact that he or she has reached the twenty-fourth chapter of Fontane's novel, and with pleasure, despite the fact that it includes neither the mean joke nor the pillory. If we come to love the novel, as many people have, part of our love may be a sense that it is *not* like the gossipy world the Baroness describes, it offers an escape from that world.

The ability to see people as ends is among our real moral capacities, but these capacities are not well developed in the world in which we live. A work that cultivates them is idealistic, perhaps, austere, perhaps, but nonetheless not unrealistic or out of touch with life. It would be an odd criticism of Ralph Ellison that his novels ask us to see African-Americans as human, whereas in real life we do not typically do that. For Ellison's novel announces at the start that its aim is to work on the reader's "inner eyes," cultivating possibilities of vision that are not fully available in white America in the 1950s. Similarly, it would be an odd criticism of the late novels of Henry James, though one often made, that people in "real life" don't imagine one another with such exacting particularity and nuance. To such a critic, James, in fact, responded that his aim was "to *create* the record, in default of any other enjoyment of it: to imagine, in a word, the honourable, the producible case. What better example than this of the high and the helpful public and, as it were, civic use of the imagination?"[21]

When, then, Fontane asks that people see their friends without certain sorts of socially transmitted narrative fantasies, and, in particular, that men see women, and women see both men and themselves, without the specific fantasies that doomed Cecile, Lena, and Effi, he is asking for something radical, but not unimaginable, as the popularity of his feminist novels for years prior to *Der Stechlin* attests. People are evidently ready to think these thoughts, if not to act on them consistently in their daily life. So the Baroness is too pessimistic. "Life" contains many things, and Melusine and Dubslav are also part of it. Moreover, the situation is not fixed: Fontane's novels are one part of reality that may possibly play a role in shaping the way people see.

VII   Fontane's Modernism

Critics frequently describe *Der Stechlin* as an early "modernist" work and comment on the novelist's evolution from realist to modernist. They usually do not say anything much about what they mean by this. I suggest that what they are reacting to is the deflection of attention from traditional plot to something else, and I believe that we can gain more insight into Fontane's experiment by comparing him to other early modernist writers who also have sought to turn readers' attention away from the grand drama of traditional conflicts, tensions, and reversals to something smaller and different about human beings and their daily life.

I have already mentioned James and Proust, and Fontane obviously shares important commitments with both, and with Virginia Woolf, who can here be associated with them both. James, Woolf, and Proust all repudiate the conventional drama of plot and seek to turn readers' attention to the small movements of thought and feeling that constitute much of our real experience. They share with Fontane the idea that there is something profoundly intriguing about daily life and the idea that traditional literature has failed to capture that something. These three, however, focus on consciousness and the movements of the inner world. Their novels thus depend upon a surgical attitude to the person: the mind of the author simply cuts them open and brings the hidden contents into the light. All three in various ways insist that what is not hidden is not deep. Fontane is like James and Woolf in deflecting readerly interest and desire from the grand narrative to the small and the daily. But they focus on consciousness; their novels thus make people interesting insofar as we see their insides. James and Woolf sometimes depict conversations and public actions, but they continually deflect attention from these to the all-engrossing inner world. Proust represents social interaction at great length, but the force of his contrast between society and psychology is to show the superficiality of the former. The surface is mere surface, and what is truly interesting is love.

Fontane, as I have said, refuses himself access into his characters' thoughts (a technique he used prominently in earlier novels). He shows only what they show to others. He lets them be self-revealing when they want to be, dark and mysterious when they want to be. We know about what happened in the tunnel, to the extent that we do, because Melusine tells the Baroness, and we, like the Baroness, are good at extrapolating from the understated. Our interest in the characters does not spring from the author's authoritative invasion into their privacy.[22] Instead, it springs from what they choose to manifest. They are thus more genuinely free than the characters of James and Woolf, more like friends whom we might encounter in our lives.

These comparisons let us see the crucial importance for Fontane of conversation. Because there is no other device of connection in the novel (such as a mind made transparent to our view), we see clearly that conversation is the way in which people connect if they do, the way in which they manifest, if they do, what is important to them. In James, Woolf, and Proust, conversation is shown to be merely superficial by contrast to the depths within. But for Fontane conversation is not superficial. It is the real mode of human connection, insofar as there is connection, and it is sometimes superficial and sometimes deep, as it is in life. People talk about what matters most to them: God, politics, social change, misogyny, their lives. In most novels people don't talk much about general issues: but in life of course they do, and they do here. They can't live without exchanging thoughts and responses in this way: Dubslav longs for conversation near the end of his life, saying that he prefers even unpleasant conversation with Adelaid to no conversation at all (421). *Lebhaftes Gespräch* is what conversation is several times called (e.g., 163): lively, or life-containing conversation, conversation that is the substance of life.

Sometimes, too, conversation is nonverbal, especially when the subject of their communication is too deep and complex for the words that convention offers on momentous occasions. Thus, the betrothal of Woldemar and Armgard takes place without words alluding directly to it. "Armgard escorted him to the corridor. There was an embarrassment between the two, and Woldemar felt that he ought to say something. 'What a lovable [*liebenswürdige*] sister you have.' Armgard blushed. 'You'll make me jealous.' 'Really, Countess?' 'Maybe . . . Good night.'" Armgard goes inside, moved, and tells her sister that she has the feeling that she has just become engaged (285–286). We have to imagine that they are communicating with one another in a sort of silent conversation of looks and tone of voice. The prospects for their future seem to be better because they have not relied on the hackneyed formulae of the formal wedding proposal. We are given to understand that they are really communicating in a personal way, rather than relying on the social formalities, and that, in turn, gives us the sense that there is a real attraction between them.[23]

Of all the novelists of antiplot modernism, the one to whom Fontane seems closest, oddly enough, is Beckett. (Perhaps the *Molloy* trilogy is the other five-hundred-page novel in which nothing happens.) Beckett's characters set out in a world that, like Fontane's world, contains powerful social plots that shape the characters' expectations of what life will offer. In Beckett's case, these are religious narratives of sin, longing, and transcendence, prominently including a horror of female impurity.[24] So his world, though in many ways so different, shares some of the preoccupations of Fontane's. Setting out in that world, Beckett's characters encounter the disorder and plotlessness of life. Molloy never gets to where is he going; his bicycle, like his body, begins to fall apart. All the characters have to fill the time is talk because the grand design that was supposed to sustain them proves illusory. And much of the talk of the characters involves undoing the grand-symbolic meanings of words, returning them to their ordinary meanings: this aspect too has a close connection to Fontane's enterprise as I have described it.[25]

For Beckett, however, the failure to find a grand narrative in life is not just a social failure, it is a cosmic failure, the failure of human life to be a part of a teleologically ordered universe—the failure of the Unnameable to be "Pupil Mahood," living out God's destiny for the human race. This failure is so deep that it leaves nothing to be hopeful about. Thus the removal of the grand plot leaves characters who are disorderly, pathetic, ridiculous, grotesque. Beckett's stripping away of plot fills the reader (and the implied author) with despair, albeit a despair conveyed through humor. The implied author seems so enamored of the grand religious narrative that he can't envisage anything good without it. Thus there are conversations of a certain sort in Beckett's plays, and lots of talk in the novels, but everything is absurd, grotesque, involving no or little real communication between people. The idea seems to be that if we aren't God's children, then we can't be human either, nothing can be conveyed, and we are talking in a void.

For Fontane, by contrast, the failure is the failure of a particular unjust and corrupt society, a society that is not the only one that one might imagine (although its errors are widespread), a society that is not even the whole of itself, so to speak, in that there exist within it many pockets of resistance, fairness, and perception, Dubslav's life as well as Adelaid's, the Barby sisters as well as the pillory that awaits them. Therefore when we take away society's grand narrative of human beings—and, in particular, its scripts for male-female relationships—we are not left with despair.

We are left with—people. And we can love them, and listen to them, insofar as we want to, insofar as we are able.

Notes

1. I am grateful to the participants in a conference on Literature and Ethics at the University of Helsinki for their valuable suggestions on an earlier draft, and especially to Gabriel Richardson Lear; I would also like to thank Alice Crary for her extremely helpful comments.

2. Throughout I refer to the page numbers of the following German edition: Theodor Fontane, *Der Stechlin* (Frankfurt: S. Fischer Verlag, 1999). All translations are my own, and I apologize for their stylistic inadequacy. There is an English version by William L. Zwiebel, *The Stechlin* (Columbia, S.C.: Camden House, 1995); I was able to get hold of it only after finishing the essay. I therefore refer to it only in connection with the problematic passage discussed in n. 19.

3. The German makes a distinction hard to capture in English: Armgard is referred to by the French "*Comtesse,*" whereas Melusine is referred to with the German word "*Gräfin;*" this distinction is essential to following the many long conversations in which both sisters are participants.

4. Fontane was seventy-seven when he began writing the novel, seventy-nine at the time of his death; his first novel was published when he was fifty-nine. Before that he worked as an apothecary, then as a journalist. He had already published several collections of journalism and travel writings, as well as a collection of poems.

5. Fontane, letter of 1897, in *Der Stechlin.*

6. "Ein Roman fast ohne Handlung also, dennoch nicht bewegungslos," Carolina Romahn, Nachwort to *Der Stechlin,* 460.

7. Rousseau's *Emile* is one of the most insightful accounts of these social scripts and the constraints they impose on female education.

8. I give the book publication dates; each novel was serialized earlier.

9. I gave the Instetten-Wuellersdorf chapter on an exam in a Decision-Making class, asking students to analyze it using the views of Bentham, Kant, and Aristotle. What came out most dramatically was the unequivocal verdict of the Utilitarians that his choice was impossibly and obviously bad. That version of the calculus leaves out the malicious pleasure of society in seeing the fallen woman punished, and in enforcing its rules; so it is probably too good to be true, as a vindication of Utilitarianism.

10. I have not even tried to reproduce the speaker's Berlin dialect. "Stinking mess" translates a colloquialism that means a chaos, an unholy mess, a scandal.

11. His theory is that some commandments are more unbreakable than others: there is forgiveness for adultery, but not for lying.

12. Wayne C. Booth, *The Company We Keep: An Ethics of Fiction.*

13. In this scene Woldemar shows his colors once again, making fun of the name of Lind's husband, the composer Otto Goldschmidt, who very likely was of Jewish origin although the two had a Protestant wedding. Anti-semitism is otherwise not mentioned in the novel, but it is one more of the social prejudices that Woldemar has not thought to question.

14. Note the Baroness's characteristic determination to turn life into low drama: her friend's life is *wie ein Schicksal,* even though, of course, there is no destiny here, there is a group of conventions governing marital age and male behavior.

15. There are interesting comparisons to be made between Melusine and Margaret Schlegel in E. M. Forster's *Howards End* with its famous maxim, "Only connect."

16. Armgard's sexuality remains somewhat unclear: Dubslav says of her, "'She has something so untouched. . . . A person who is once chaste is always chaste'" (407). And Armgard herself, asked whether she'd choose to be Elizabeth of England or Mary Queen of Scots, says, passionately, that she would choose neither, she'd rather be Elisabeth of Thüringen, who spent her whole life in good works for the poor. "'I would like to be able to attain that. But one doesn't attain such things. Everything is grace (285).'" It is right after this that Woldemar "proposes"—perhaps moved by her pious emotion, perhaps also reassured to find an absence of the sister's (as he perceives it) rapacious sexuality. On balance, however, we are given to understand that she is genuinely attracted to Woldemar and happy with her marital life.

17. See Barbara Herman, "Can It Be Worth Thinking with Kant about Sex and Marriage?" Kant's view seems to be that in sex people inevitably treat one another as means to their own pleasure; marriage cannot really solve that problem, but it can contain it, forcing people to have sexual pleasure only in the context of a relationship in which mutual regard is encouraged by the legal framework of the relationship itself.

18. Even *Persuasion* may be erotic only within the bounds of social propriety. As for other nineteenth-century cases, Kitty and Levin do not seem to me to be particularly passionate; and Dorothea's happiness at the end of *Middlemarch*, though a genuine example, is not very convincing or thoroughly realized. A possible counterexample from Fontane's own oeuvre is *L'Adultera* (1882), in which the young woman who leaves her husband, gets a divorce, and remarries, ends up happy and fulfilled. This novella, however, is not, in my view, one of his most fully realized and convincing pieces, much though it embodies themes that are dear to his heart.

19. Drama does better, perhaps: Congreve's *The Way of the World* represents a sort of passionate happiness of which Fontane would have approved, and the divorce scene in Farquhar's *The Beaux Stratagem* contains, at least, the negative side of his vision, as Mrs. Sullen declares a happy independence—with some prospect of later sexual fulfillment since her hatred of her husband has not caused her (like Melusine) to hate the idea of sex.

20. This important sentence is virtually untranslatable into English, on account of the Baroness von Berchtesgaden's use of obscure Bavarian terms that are difficult even to locate in any dictionary and that have no ready English equivalent because they refer to local customs. *Schnaderhüpfl*, which I have translated "a vulgar joke," is a variant of *Schnadahüpfl*, a type of mocking song sung in the Bavarian Alps. I think the institution is like the American custom of having a "roast" of someone and would have used that word were it not clear that it would be misread as the food kind of roast. (Zwiebel writes "a suggestive little ditty," which is arch and bad English, not earthy as is the Baroness's style.) "Putting someone in the pillory" translates "*Haberfeldtreiben*" as a variant for "*Ziegenfelltreiben*," a type of mob justice in which the offender against social rules is made to wear a goatskin. The Zwiebel translation has "a little lynching party," which is, I would say, a bit more violent than the original.

21. James, *The Art of the Novel*, 211–212.

22. See Dorrit Cohn, *Transparent Minds*.

23. Because good conversation is both particular and topical, the novel of conversation may be difficult to export to another culture. *Der Stechlin*, beloved in Germany, has not been nearly as popular outside it, because its characters' preoccupation with German politics and with nuances of region and class have not been easy to export. (Similarly, the parts of Proust dealing with love and jealousy receive much more attention, outside France, than do the parts that focus on social mores, or the vicissitudes of the Dreyfus case.) The novel's non-German reader has to be willing, not only to attend, but also to learn.

24. See my "Narrative Emotions: Beckett's Genealogy of Love."

25. See Stanley Cavell's "Ending the Waiting Game: a Reading of Beckett's *Endgame*."

Works Cited

Aristotle. *Poetics*. Trans. Stephen Halliwell. Chicago: University of Chicago Press, 1998.

Booth, Wayne C. *The Company We Keep: An Ethics of Fiction*. Berkeley: University of California Press, 1988.

Cavell, Stanley. "Ending the Waiting Game: A Reading of Beckett's *Endgame*." In *Must We Mean What We Say?* updated edition, 115–162. Cambridge: Cambridge University Press, 2002.

Cohn, Dorrit. *Transparent Minds*. Princeton: Princeton University Press, 1978.

Fontane, Theodor. *Der Stechlin*. Frankfurt: S. Fischer Verlag, 1999.

Fontane, Theodor. *L'Adultera*. Zurich: Diogenes Verlag, 1998.

Fontane, Theodor. *The Stechlin*. Trans. William L. Zwiebel. Columbia, S.C.: Camden House, 1995.

Forster, E. M. *Howards End*. New York: Penguin, 2000.

Herman, Barbara. "Can It Be Worth Thinking with Kant about Sex and Marriage?" In Louise Antony and Charlotte Witt, eds., *A Mind of One's Own: Feminist Essays on Reason and Objectivity*, revised ed., 53–72. Boulder, Colo.: Westview, 2002.

James, Henry. *The Art of the Novel*. New York: Macmillan, 1934.

Nussbaum, Martha. "Narrative Emotions: Beckett's Genealogy of Love." In *Love's Knowledge*. New York: Oxford University Press, 1990.

Romahn, Carolina. Nachwort to *Der Stechlin*, by Theodor Fontane. Frankfurt: S. Fischer Verlag, 1999.

10   The Mortality of the Soul: Bernard Williams's Character(s)

Stephen Mulhall

My title echoes Bernard Williams's characterization of the topic of his own, early paper, "The Makropulos Case: Reflections on the Tedium of Immortality."[1] However, the same striking phrase—invoking a demythologization of the self, the recovery or reconstruction of what one might call a naturalized spiritual subject from philosophical and religious supernaturalisms of the human being—also characterizes the central concern of Williams's philosophical work as a whole, just as its economical, wittily Nietzschean subversion of a philosophical formulation so familiar as to risk neutralizing genuine reflection exemplifies the distinctive style of the writing through which he pursued it.

This early paper is further characteristic of Williams's philosophizing in that it aims to get a purchase on its subject-matter by invoking a specific fictional character. In this instance, his source is a play by Karel Capek, later made into an opera by Leos Janácek; other pivotal examples would include—at the very least—those involving George and Jim (in his "Utilitarianism: A Critique"),[2] Gauguin and Anna Karenina (in "Moral Luck"),[3] Agamemnon and Oedipus (in *Shame and Necessity*),[4] and Rameau's nephew (in *Truth and Truthfulness*).[5] Williams's eye for a telling tale has been absolutely fundamental in maximizing the impact of his work on the philosophical profession; it is now hard to imagine critical discussions of consequentialism and Kantianism that are not, however indirectly, shaped by the still-ramifying debates surrounding George, Jim, and Gauguin.

I propose to argue that there is a close connection between Williams's basic conception of the self and his use of fictional examples as a medium for philosophical discussion; for what most deeply interests him about the self is its possession of a character, and his attempts to clarify the content of, the conditions for, and the threats faced by individual human character are primarily facilitated by a study of fictional characters. Indeed, changes in the way Williams regards fictional characters—in his sense of their availability for, and resistance to, philosophical appropriation, of their depth and texture, of the extent to which their independent reality outruns the authority of author and reader alike—reflect changes in his conception of the status of human character as such. Accordingly, tracking the development of Williams's treatment of his fictional characters directly reveals the developing character of his philosophical work as a whole.

Since many of Williams's characters started their lives in literary texts, the relations between ethics, philosophy, and literature have always been in the background of his work; and it moves further into the foreground with every book since *Ethics and the Limits of Philosophy*—perhaps his most professionally idiosyncratic publication.[6] Williams's conception of these relations is as considered, angular, and individual as any other element of his thinking. It is also the point at which his work most clearly invites comparison with that of Cora Diamond, whose own interest in how philosophy does and can conceive of ethics and literature is pursued through an eclectic, individually powerful range of fictional and nonfictional examples. My own thinking in this area has been pervasively shaped by her writing; and it is not obvious to me why her influence on the subject has not been at least as deep and wide ranging as that of Bernard Williams, whose preoccupations and procedures seem so signally to overlap with her own. I hope that a detailed exploration of the character of Williams's, work, in the light of issues and emphases derived from Cora Diamond's writing, might help illuminate this puzzle, and so clarify the prospects for a humanly serious moral philosophy.

1   Elina Makropulos

[A] play by Karel Capek which was made into an opera by Janacek . . . tells of a woman called Elina Makropulos, *alias* Emilia Marty, *alias* Ellian Macgregor, alias a number of other things with the initials 'EM,' on whom her father, the Court physician to a sixteenth century Emperor, tried out an elixir of life. At the time of the action she is aged 342. Her unending life has come to a state of boredom, indifference and coldness. Everything is joyless: 'in the end it is the same,' she says, 'singing and silence.' She refuses to take the elixir again; she dies; and the formula is deliberately destroyed by a young woman among the protests of some older men.[7]

For Williams, EM's situation suggests that death is not necessarily an evil—further, that it can be a good thing for anyone not to live too long; for the root of EM's frozen and hence death-embracing state lies not so much in her particular character, but in the fact that she has a human character at all. Her boredom is an all-but-inevitable response to the fact that everything that could happen and make sense to one particular human being had already happened to her. Her character is of course a particular one, largely constituted by the set of desires, concerns, and projects to which she was committed by the time of her first draught of the elixir; and Williams happily allows that, like anyone else, EM's particular character will include "categorical desires"—desires that are not conditional upon her being alive, but rather provide her with reasons for choosing to stay alive, to propel herself into the future, or more typically whose existence ensures that the very question of whether or not to commit suicide simply does not arise. Since that is the usual condition of most human beings, Williams takes it that we typically have a sufficiency of such desires.

Nevertheless, after three hundred years of existence with her character as established at the age of forty-two, EM chooses to die; her version of that characteristically human hope for more life that is grounded in categorical desire has withered. This is because her possession of a definite character necessarily limits the sorts of things that could make sense to her, and hence the kinds of experience she could find sufficiently meaningful to pursue (through her singing, her personal relationships, her children); and over a sufficiently elongated lifespan, those experiences will inescapably form endlessly repeating patterns in which she could take only a steeply diminishing interest. If we try imagining the pattern of her experiences as not repetitious but varied, the problem would simply shift to the intelligibility of her retaining anything like a fixed character in relation to them, and hence the intelligibility of continuing to think of her as a particular person at all. Such experiences must surely happen to her without really affecting her, Williams claims; she must be as EM is portrayed as being— detached and withdrawn. Her boredom and distance from life thus kill desire, including categorical desire, and consist in its death; they are themselves unavoidable, and they make EM's choice of death over life unavoidable in its turn.

If too much more of our familiar mortal life will necessarily tend toward the death of our souls, Williams feels licensed to conclude that immortality in the form of life after death would be equally lethal. For what imaginable arrangements of an unending afterlife could negate the risk to which EM succumbs—that of bone-deep boredom? "[B]oredom . . . would be not just a tiresome effect, but a reaction almost perceptual in character to the poverty of one's relation to the environment. Nothing less will do for eternity than something that makes boredom *unthinkable*. What could that be? Something that could be guaranteed to be at every moment utterly absorbing? But if a man has and retains a character, there is no reason to suppose that there is anything that could be that."[8]

Since the Christian conception of God is precisely that of a being any direct encounter with whom would immediately and endlessly absorb us in worshipful

contemplation, Williams's argument must be that any such relation would demand
the evisceration of any substantial human individuality; it would amount to the death
of the soul rather than its transfiguration or resurrection or reception of eternal life.
But it will be no news to the Christian that the prospect of life after death will seem
like death to anyone whose measure of what can reward attention and define the
self derives from our experience of this mortal life. Take the protagonist of William
Golding's novel *Pincher Martin*;[9] after falling overboard, he constructs and inhabits a
fantasy of a rock in the Atlantic Ocean to defer his own death, and is last seen having
reduced himself to a pair of lobster claws gripping each other around the bare center
of his ego, while the black lightning of God's love seeks to absorb him: "The lightning came forward. Some of the lines pointed to the centre, waiting for the moment
when they could pierce it. Others lay against the claws, playing over them, prying
for a weakness, wearing them away in a compassion that was timeless and without
mercy."[10]

One aspect of Golding's words here expresses Pincher's perspective, with its conflation of life after death with death, love with merciless penetration, and the acceptance of love with soul-destroying weakness; but they have another aspect, according
to which what Pincher sees as merciless is God's mode of compassion, and what he
sees as pitch-black is God's lightning, hence God's light. For Golding, then, to see
death in the light of God is necessarily to turn our understanding of ourselves and
our world upside-down; but to invert words and the understanding they embody is
not to empty them of sense—it is to sense, and to seek out, another way of making
sense. Williams, by contrast, uses Capek's EM to exemplify a familiar way of understanding the self, its interests, and its finitude, and to imply that moving away from
familiar routes of significance means moving away from the realm of significance altogether.

This not only instantiates a common conflation of philosophical authority with
ethical advocacy, as if sheer clarity about the concept of character entailed atheism.
It also exemplifies a familiar way of finding philosophical significance in literature:
the literary text gives Williams a handy illustration of a philosophical point (about
the centrality of character to selfhood) that might as easily have come from another
literary text, or real life, or indeed a purely imaginary scenario. Hardly anything of
the specific texture of the source—whether its content or its form—survives into, or
orients, the reflections in the essay that borrows its title: Williams's EM is as distantly
related to Capek's EM as his "The Makropolus Case" is related to Capek's "The Makropulos Case." In fact, Williams seems unconcerned (even unwilling) to be precise about
which work is the true source of his own reflections—Capek's play or the Janáček opera

made from it. His one-paragraph summary of his "case" is phrased so as to imply that the play is his primary reference point; but certain details within it suggest that it is in fact the opera from which he is deriving his version of EM (her age in Capek's play is 337, not 342; and she remains alive at the play's end).[11]

Does this misleadingly compressed acknowledgement of one's sources really matter? It may matter—it may seem perversely self-denying—if those sources, and the relation between them, embody reflections on the character and situation to which Williams wishes to help himself, and which might lead him (and us) to deepen or otherwise modify his conclusions. For example, Capek's EM primarily desires to recover the formula for her own use, at least until the climax of the action; indeed, she explains the intensity of her search by saying "I'm getting old . . . I'm at the end of my tether. I want to have another try" (177). Capek's EM is thus at least ambivalent about her mortal immortality; it may be obvious to Williams (and to Janácek, insofar as Williams's EM follows his) that her frozen, withdrawn state makes her death a good thing, but it is not to her. Furthermore, Capek's plot links the formula's accessibility with the accessibility of a will that will ensure that a descendant of EM will secure a disputed inheritance; thus, the play connects the desire for immortality and its achievement through one's offspring. On the one hand, procreation is suggested as our best mortal mode of immortality (as another character puts it: "If we were to think of birth . . . rather than of death. . . . Life is not short. As long as we can be the cause of life," 210); on the other, mortal immortality answers to a desire always to protect the new life we create.

And what of the fact that Capek's EM is a singer of preternatural perfection? Janácek's opera constitutes a massive acknowledgement of that fact about her, by displacing EM's vicissitudes into an artistic form that not only foregrounds that aspect of her individuality, but also focuses on the relation between the human voice—understood as expressive of human individuality as such—and the human body. Stanley Cavell has suggested[12] that opera embodies an understanding of that relation in which "not this character and this actor are embodied in each other but in which this voice is located in—one might say disembodied within—this figure, this double, this person, this persona, this singer, whose voice is essentially unaffected by the role. A Cartesian intuition of the absolute metaphysical difference between mind and body, together with the twin Cartesian intuition of an undefined intimacy between just this body and only this spirit, appears to describe conditions of the possibility of opera."[13]

These intuitions are not embodied in the relation between actor and character in theater, where the character takes priority over the actor—the actor yields to the character, working herself into the role, and hence the constancy of the character, our sense of its independent life, is foregrounded (unlike cinema, where something like the reverse is the case). Capek's play can be seen as thematizing this aspect of its own form by crystallizing EM's predicament in terms of her resort to a series of aliases—as if she can make sense of mortal immortality only by constructing personas whose individual constancy of character might compensate for the thinning out of her own. The form of opera, by contrast, focuses on something that cuts across such entanglements of actor and character: for the singer's voice is at once her clearest expression of herself and the mode of her embodiment of her role, understood as defined by song; it is "the grandest realization of having a signature . . . hence of your mortal immortality."[14] One might say, then, that opera allows for a certain kind of study of individuality that is inaccessible to theater, for Janácek's EM is thereby shown as well as said to give the purest possible expression of herself in her singing—as if the full significance of Capek's assignment of EM to singing, and of her view that "I sing as if it froze me," so that "singing and silence are the same to me," can find acknowledgement only outside theater.

Williams's bare plot summary actually quotes the last of these lines of EM, but he makes nothing of them. Hence, he can make nothing of the expansion and displacement of their significance in Janácek's opera, and of the connection that this switch of artistic forms allows him to forge, or to emphasize, with other aspects of Capek's theatrical original—the fact that EM is a woman, that the elixir is invented by and for men and initially forced upon her by them, and that the destruction of its formula is effected by another young woman in the face of opposition from older men (a point that Williams also notes, but leaves unexplored). For one of opera's central subjects is the singing of women, and how this singing might be suffocated or otherwise stopped by the world of men—ultimately, as with Janácek's EM, by killing them; in other words, it aligns the theme of individuality, its expression and its suppression, with gender difference, whether we see this as finding expression only between men and women, or also within every individual.

Beyond the specificities of EM's particular art, one might also take her singing to exemplify artistic achievement as such. In Capek's play, the immortality conferred by one's family is implicitly considered alongside the immortality conferred by artistic creation. But, despite the fact that her audiences respond to her voice as if she were already among the immortals of song, Capek's EM rejects this out of hand: she claims that the great singers of the past were far less perfect than their reputation suggests, and that the actual perfection of her art is not only deathly cold in itself, but also drains its (re)creation of any meaning: "Art . . . has point only as long as you haven't mastered it . . . then it becomes useless" (203). Capek's EM thereby undermines the thought that mortal immortality might be desirable as a way to achieve aesthetic goods otherwise unattainable; and by transposing this claim into a medium that requires the actual display of the perfection it describes, Janácek's EM places her creator in the position of his creation. To succeed in creating the frozen perfection of her song would be to create something inhuman, essentially meaningless—it would mean (impossibly) creating an opera around a role in which the distinction between singing and silence was of no significance. Hence, Janácek's lyric dramatization of her story can only exemplify the truth of her claim that the significance of art for mortals is that of aspiring to perfection without ever being able to attain it; failing to attain perfection is the mode of perfection it aims to attain—the way in which it seeks its own, and hence its composer's, immortality.

To take such lines of thought seriously would mean considering how forms of theater and forms of opera might be capable of reflecting on the issues arising from their narratives without being transposed into philosophical schematizations of their specificity. It would mean attending to their individuality—not just at the level of content (the detailed sequences of events, words, and notes that make them up) but also at the level of form (the logic or grammar of their distinctive modes of representation or expression, and the ways in which that grammar can interact with its content). It would mean raising the question of whether, and if so how, works of art might not only represent but enact ways of thinking with which philosophical modes of reflection might profitably engage. In this early essay, Williams gives no indication of finding such questions to be of any real philosophical significance.

2 George and Jim

1) George, who has just taken his Ph.D. in chemistry, finds it extremely difficult to get a job. He is not very robust in health, which cuts down the number of jobs he might be able to do satisfactorily. His wife has to go out to work to keep them, which itself causes a great deal of strain, since they have small children and there are severe problems about looking after them. The results of all this, especially on the children, are damaging. An older chemist, who knows about this situation, says that he can get George a decently paid job in a certain laboratory, which pursues research into chemical and biological warfare. George says that he cannot accept this, since he is opposed to chemical and biological warfare. The older man replies that he is not too keen on it himself, come to that, but after all George's refusal is not going to make the job or the laboratory go away; what is more, he happens to know that if George refuses the job, it will certainly go to a contemporary of George's who is not inhibited by any such scruples and is likely if appointed to push along the research with greater zeal than George would. Indeed, it is not merely concern for George and his family, but (to speak frankly and in confidence) some alarm about this other man's excess of zeal, which has led the older man to offer to use his influence

to get George the job. . . . George's wife, to whom he is deeply attached, has views (the details of which need not concern us) from which it follows that at least there is nothing particularly wrong with research into CBW. What should he do?

2) Jim finds himself in the central square of a small South American town. Tied up against the wall are a row of twenty Indians, most terrified, a few defiant, in front of them several armed men in uniform. A heavy man in a sweat-stained khaki shirt turns out to be the captain in charge and, after a good deal of questioning of Jim which establishes that he got there by accident while on a botanical expedition, explains that the Indians are a random group of the inhabitants who, after recent acts of protest against the government, are just about to be killed to remind other possible protestors of the advantages of not protesting. However, since Jim is an honoured visitor from another land, the captain is happy to offer him a guest's privilege of killing one of the Indians himself. If Jim accepts, then as a special mark of the occasion, the other Indians will be let off. Of course, if Jim refuses, then there is no special occasion, and Pedro here will do what he was about to do when Jim arrived, and kill them all. Jim, with some desperate recollection of schoolboy fiction, wonders whether if he got hold of a gun, he could hold the captain, Pedro and the rest of the soldiers to threat, but it is quite clear from the set-up that nothing of that kind is going to work: any attempt at that sort of thing will mean that all the Indians will be killed, and himself. The men against the wall, and the other villagers, understand the situation, and are obviously begging him to accept. What should he do?[15]

Williams's aim in creating these two characters is explicitly antiutilitarian: he takes it that any direct utilitarian would judge it to be obvious that George should accept the job and Jim should shoot the villager. Williams claims that many of us would not think that it could possibly be right for George to accept the job, and that even if we did come to think that Jim should shoot the villager, we would not regard that as obviously the right thing to do. He traces its obviousness to the utilitarian back to the general consequentialist doctrine of negative responsibility: "that if I am ever responsible for anything, then I must be just as much responsible for things that I allow or fail to prevent, as I am for things that I myself, in the more everyday restricted sense, bring about."[16] This doctrine flows from the more basic consequentialist view that value attaches ultimately to states of affairs, and hence its concern with what states of affairs the world contains (and so with what states of affairs result from human action or inaction, not with how they do so).

With George and Jim, this means that utilitarianism occludes from deliberation an aspect of the idea that each of us is specially responsible for what *he* does, rather than for what other people do—something Williams sees as closely connected with the value of integrity. For in both cases, to overlook the causal linkages between action and outcome is to overlook the essential role played by others, with their own intentions and projects, in bringing about those outcomes—in George's case, his more zealous contemporary; in Jim's case, Pedro (and his captain). But of course, George and Jim have their own intentions and projects; like anyone else, they will pursue not only particular tastes and fancies, but what Williams calls commitments—projects through which they identify themselves with objects outside themselves, and hence become thoroughly involved with other persons or institutions or causes. What, then, if the right action for George or Jim according to the utilitarian calculus conflicts with some commitment of theirs? How can a man be required to regard as one dispensable satisfaction among others a project around which he has built his life, just because someone else's projects have so structured the causal scene?

It is absurd to demand of such a man, when the sums come in from the utility network which the projects of others have in part determined, that he should just step aside from his own projects and decision and acknowledge the decision which utilitarianism requires. It is to alienate him in a real sense from his actions and the source of his action in his own convictions. It is to make him into a channel between the input of everyone's projects, including his own, and an output of optimific decision; but this is to neglect the extent to which *his* actions and *his* decisions have to be seen as the actions and decisions which flow from the projects and attitudes with which he is most closely identified. It is thus, in the most literal sense, an attack on his integrity.[17]

Here, then, we see another facet of Williams's conception of the self as essentially possessed of a character, this time providing a ground for rejecting utilitarian conceptions of morality; integrity, with its underlying invocation of commitments, recalls his earlier notion of categorical desires. However, Williams's two characters have generated a critical literature sufficiently extensive and unresolved to suggest that the significance of integrity and character for our concept of the self is by no means obvious. I don't propose to survey the full range of this literature, or even its main reference points. For my purposes, two closely related responses repay attention, for they are particularly sensitive to Williams's examples.

In "Absolute Ethics, Mathematics, and the Impossibility of Politics,"[18] Roy Holland offers two very striking critical comments on Williams's portrayal of Jim. The first concerns the kind of character he might possess:

There are or there have been in human history people, very few admittedly, of such marvellous goodness that they have been regarded as saints. And you cannot imagine a saint shooting that Indian. Nor is it imaginable that a saint would do nothing either; for the man I am calling a saint would face the consequences and engage in the suffering in a way that is different from the way an ordinary man would, and his presence would not be without its impact on the outcome. . . . [M]aybe he would manage somehow to take the place of the one Indian; or . . . perhaps he would make sure that he was shot along with him or else as the first of the twenty. That is if the Captain had not thus far been given pause, for there is what a saint might say to be thought of as well as what he might do, and being spoken to by a saint would not be like being spoken to by an ordinary person.[19]

Holland's second comment concerns the general tone or style of Williams's recounting of Jim's situation. He calls it "repellently bland," emphasizing particularly Williams's description of the captain as honoring his visitor with the happy idea of a privileged opportunity to kill a villager. For Holland, such language presents the "ethical problem" Jim faces from the standpoint of the person who had presented him with it, and it participates in the way that the captain's terminology neutralizes the fact that his invitation is a particularly abhorrent form of blackmail. In so doing, Holland believes, Williams draws us away from the true source of our sense of outrage at being asked to contemplate examples of this kind. "The sort of make-believe involved is different from that which occurs when a playwright of the stature to do it shows us something from which we can learn. When Shakespeare for example presents characters imaginatively in their entanglements with evil, our sense of the reality of our own relationship to both good and evil is heightened, whereas here we are drawn into an exercise of fancy about just that relationship. It is a kind of temptation: that is what the revulsion is about."[20] In *Good and Evil: An Absolute Conception*,[21] Rai Gaita focuses on Jim's perspective on the villagers—a perspective constructed for him by the captain's invitation, and given further expression in Williams's articulation of Jim's reasons for not trying to grab one of the soldiers' weapons: we are told that any such attempt will only "mean that all the Indians will be killed, and himself," which implies that the attempt is unjustifiable if it will simply enlarge the group of victims. This confirms Jim's tendency to regard the villagers primarily as a group—a group of possible victims, a group he might save. For Gaita, it is as if Williams's Jim is thinking along the following lines: if I kill one of the villagers, it will be for the sake of the other nineteen, taken together; it will be because there are more of them, because they form a larger group. So, when Williams tells us that every one of the men against the wall are "begging" Jim to accept the captain's invitation, are we meant to assume that they do so because they share Jim's (and the captain's) way of understanding his situation? In particular, must each of the nineteen who will survive if Jim chooses to shoot understand their relation to Jim's victim in the terms in which Jim understands that relation—namely, as mediated by their membership in the group?

Gaita brings out another possibility here by imagining how an individual member of such a group (a group of ten) might address someone in Jim's position:

If he dies, then I will live, because he died, and because there are nine others with me. Each of the nine others will be able to say the same. Yet when he is dead, will I be able to console myself by saying that he died only one-tenth for me? Though you think that you must kill him not for me or for any of the others taken individually but for all of us taken together, when he is dead each of us must accept the fact that insofar as he was murdered for our sake, he died for each of us singly and undividedly. Each of us, in his singularity, is implicated in the evil of his murder. . . .

A person can make a gift of his life to another. Suppose someone had received such a gift, and suppose him to be grateful, but suppose also that he discovers that the one who had sacrificed himself did so not only for him, but also for another. Would he become churlish and complain that his gift had diminished in value . . . ? Could he say that, previously, his gratitude had been excessive? As it is with this person's relation to the good of the other's gift, so it is with each of us in relation to the evil of this person's murder: the relation is unaffected by the presence of the others.[22]

This address is not meant to demonstrate that Jim should not shoot one of the villagers, nor that the villagers concerned should not urge him to do so. It is the expression of an anxiety that Williams's depiction of the villagers as essentially members of a group to be saved risks occluding both the fact and the essentially individuating form of their implication in Jim's deed, and hence risks occluding them as individuals whose own moral integrity is also at stake. Gaita's villager thus reveals that Williams's tale may be implicated in a version of the error it aims to reveal in utilitarianism—that of overlooking the claims of integrity. He thereby suggests that Williams's focus on Jim's terrible decision has resulted in what Holland would call a merely fanciful rather than a genuinely imaginative portrayal of the entanglement of the villagers in the evil of this situation.

It is easy to imagine someone defending Williams as follows: All this shows is that Williams is not Shakespeare. Using the captain's terminology—itself a cliché of school-boy fiction—to present Jim's situation to us may suggest a certain embarrassment about facing up to the evil his tale invokes; but his underlying conception of the greater moral weight of the larger group is surely at least arguable, and its (anyway only superficial) kinship with that of utilitarian moral calculi is only to be expected, given the underlying point of his example—which is to construct a situation of choice that, from a specifically utilitarian point of view, will have a clearly calculable answer, and yet can also be shown to omit something of undeniable moral significance. The example may well abstract from other matters of significance in other contexts of moral reflection—although it seems bizarre to criticize Williams for not writing a saint's self-evidently supererogatory responses into his tale; but such abstraction is an entirely legitimate feature of the use of thought-experiments in philosophy.

Cavell's retelling of an old joke is pertinent here.[23] A soldier being instructed in guard duty is asked: "Suppose that while you're on duty in the middle of a desert you see a battleship approaching your post. What would you do?" The soldier replies "I'd take my torpedo and sink it." The instructor is, we are to imagine, perplexed: "Where would you get the torpedo?" He is answered: "The same place you got the battle-ship."[24] Holland's saint and Gaita's villager individuated by his guilt are, it might be thought, like the soldier's torpedo; they might seem to sink Williams's battleship, but only because they violate the constitutive procedures of thought-experimentation. Williams can simply stipulate that Jim is not a saint, and that no character in the story shares the absolute conception of good and evil that finds expression in Gaita's vil-lager; and if the tale's author so stipulates, then that fixes its content. Since the tale is meant to isolate a specific issue, any criticism of its construction that does not demonstrate its inadequacy to that task must itself be inadequate. Ironically enough, those who criticize Williams for distinctively literary failings thereby betray a failure to appreciate the specific conventions of his fictional genre.

Cora Diamond's essay "Thought-Experiments in Ethics"[25] suggests a way of clarify-ing this dispute. She distinguishes two kinds of thought-experiments in ethics—well-posed problems and exploration-problems. A well-posed problem contains enough information for there to be a unique solution to it; what we know is given (that is, stipulated), and to challenge those conditions is to display incompetence. Alterna-tively, a problem may be set in such a way that assumptions underlying our initial understanding of the problem must be questioned if it is to be resolved; it invites us to probe what we think we know. An example of a well-posed problem might be the following: if A switches the points, a runaway train will kill two people; if he doesn't, it will kill ten: what should A do? An example of an exploration-problem might be the following: if a just and an unjust man were each equipped with a ring of Gyges, their behavior would quickly become indistinguishable. One might accept this con-clusion, and take it to show that people who refrain from acting unjustly do so only because of limitations on their powers; or one might reject it, on the grounds that anyone whose behaviour altered when equipped with the ring could not be a genu-inely just man.

Can we, then, say that Holland and Gaita treat the tales of George and Jim as if they were exploration-problems, whereas Williams intends them to be well-formed prob-lems? The matter cannot be quite so simple, for reasons that Diamond makes clear. For the very idea of a well-formed problem presupposes the availability of a problem-solving method whose application gives a unique solution; this is why many appar-ently well-formed problems tend to arise in discussions of utilitarianism, which provides just such a method. But then, there can be no agreement on what consti-tutes a well-posed problem if there is no agreement on what the relevant problem-solving method is, or indeed on whether there is one. Hence, there is no ethically neutral point of view from which to determine whether or not a problem is well posed, or whether it should rather be seen as an exploration-problem. Accordingly, one might say of Holland and Gaita that they do not misunderstand Williams's invitation to treat the Jim story as a well-formed problem; they reject it, because they believe that to accept the invitation is to commit oneself to assumptions—in particular, assumptions about what it is to reflect on or reason about moral problems—that must themselves be questioned if the "problem" is to be more properly understood.

Even this does not accommodate the full complexity of the dispute, however. For the basic purpose of Williams's tales in fact imposes incoherent demands on their construction. On the one hand, his two imaginary situations must raise questions to which a straightforward application of the utilitarian method will give a unique answer—single, clear, and obvious. On the other hand, those same situations must embody something morally significant that the utilitarian is constrained to overlook. But the first demand requires that Williams construct a well-formed problem from the utilitarian point of view; whereas the second requires that he construct an exploration-problem—one that allows us to question the assumptions underlying our initial understanding of the problem. What emerges from an exploration of George and Jim's situation is an ethical value that Williams holds is necessarily excluded from the utilitarian perspective; but then it could not have any place in a tale deliberately constructed so as to form a well-posed problem from that very perspective. In short, integrity is simultaneously absent and present in the two tales, endlessly flickering in and out of our field of vision; and this merely illustrates the impossibility of treating them simultaneously in these two different ways.

This oscillating dual aspect to George and Jim explains why Holland and Gaita accuse Williams of sliding into an endorsement of the kinds of utilitarian assumptions that he claims to be putting in question; for they see him questioning one such assumption, and wonder why he doesn't do likewise with a range of other related (utilitarian and nonutilitarian) assumptions—including those Williams must treat as stipulations if he is to pose what utilitarians will see as a well-formed problem. It further explains the general feeling among utilitarians that Williams's criticisms are particularly unfair and can anyway easily be avoided; for if the initial situation is stipulated in utilitarian terms, how could it conceivably turn out to contain an essentially nonutilitarian dimension? It may also account for the continuing and peculiarly frustrating dissension among commentators on what exactly Williams's tales illustrate: for as well-posed problems, their moral should be self-evident, and yet as exploration-problems, the course of our reflections might reveal an indefinite range of further considerations to be essential to any genuine understanding of their nature. In the end, then, Williams sets himself an imaginative task, a literary exercise, that neither he nor anyone else could conceivably perform—not even Shakespeare.

3   Gauguin and Anna Karenina

Let us first take an outline example of the creative artist who turns away from definite and pressing human claims on him in order to live a life in which, as he supposed, he can pursue his art. Without feeling that we are limited by any historical facts, let us call him *Gauguin*. . . . Let us take a Gauguin who is concerned about these claims and what is involved in their being neglected (we may suppose this to be grim), and that he nevertheless, in the face of that, opts for the other life. . . .

Whether he will succeed cannot, in the nature of the case, be foreseen. We are not dealing here with the removal of an external obstacle to something which, once that is removed, will fairly predictably go through. Gauguin, in our story, is putting a great deal on a possibility which has not unequivocally declared itself. I want to explore and uphold the claim that in such a situation the only thing that will justify his choice will be success itself. If he fails . . . then he did the wrong thing, not just in the sense in which that platitudinously follows, but in the sense that having done the wrong thing in those circumstances he has no basis for the thought that he was justified in acting as he did. If he succeeds, he does have a basis for that thought. . . .

Consider an equally schematized account of another example, that of Anna Karenina. Anna remains conscious in her life with Vronsky of the cost exacted from others, above all from her son. She might have lived with that consciousness, we may suppose, if things had gone better, and relative to her state of understanding when she left Karenin, they could have gone better. As it turns out, the social situation and her own state of mind are such that the relationship with Vronsky has to carry too much weight, and the more obvious that becomes, the more it has to carry; and I take that to be a truth not only about society but about her and Vronsky, a truth which, however inevitable Tolstoy ultimately makes it seem, could, relative to her earlier thoughts, have ben otherwise. It is . . . a matter of intrinsic luck, and a failure in the heart of her project. But its locus is not by any means entirely in her, for it also lies in [Vronsky]. . . .

[H]er thought in killing herself is not just ["there is nothing more for me"], but relates inescapably also to the past and to what she has done. What she did, she now finds insupportable, because she could have been justified only by the life she hoped for, and those hopes were not just negated, but refuted, by what happened.[26]

Williams's famous discussion of moral luck is essentially guided by these two examples, which differ from those of George and Jim in that they are adaptations of an original—one historical, the other literary. They also differ from each other: for Gauguin's project is such that two distinctions coincide—that between luck intrinsic to the project and luck extrinsic to it, and that between what is, and what is not, determined by him alone; in Anna's (more typical) case, Vronsky's intrinsic significance to their joint project keeps those distinctions apart.

The two examples nevertheless coincide in illustrating certain aspects of the role of moral luck in human life. First, there is the essentially retrospective nature of certain kinds of justification: "Gauguin could not do something which is thought to be essential to rationality and to the notion of justification itself, which is that one should be in a position to apply the justifying considerations at the time of the choice and in advance of knowing whether one was right (in the sense of its coming out right)."[27] This is because the relevant outcomes will importantly condition the agent's sense of what is significant in his life, and hence his standpoint of retrospective assessment. "The project in the interests of which the decision is made is one with which the agent is identified in such a way that if it succeeds, his standpoint of assessment will be from a life which derives an important part of its significance for him from that very fact. . . . If he fails, his standpoint will be of one for whom the ground-project of the decision has proved worthless, and this . . . must leave him with the most basic regrets."[28]

Once again, then, Williams's characters highlight another facet of his conception of the self as possessed of character, hence constituted by categorical desires, commitments, or ground projects. However, these examples are not invoked to warn against the excessive dissipation of the self's substance into the broader (at the limit, the global) causal field it inhabits; they rather emphasize the extent to which the self's substance is unavoidably entangled in its world since the intrinsic significance of its ground projects are subject to the impact of forces outside its control. Accordingly, whereas George and Jim make an antiutilitarian point, Gauguin and Anna Karenina contest the Kantian attempt to contract the essence of selfhood into the extensionless point of the will and its orientation, beyond the reach of luck. For the categorical imperative decision-procedure must function prior to the implementation of its results in action (and how might one formulate Gauguin's candidate maxim for action?); and if a life-defining project's significance is at the mercy of the unforeseeable actual, how can the self be essentially self-determined?

In one sense, then, it is irrelevant to Williams's official concerns that Gauguin's and Anna's ground projects are not "moral" ones in the Kantian sense. Since "becoming a great painter" and "finding romantic fulfillment" might nonetheless constitute intelligible parts of an answer to what Williams calls the broader ethical question of "how should one live?" in that they specify recognizable forms of human flourishing, these characters have been interpreted as serving Williams's broader critique of the morality system—by exemplifying kinds of human value not recognized by a Kantian emphasis on duty and obligation, and capable on occasion of trumping the claims of the moral law (here exemplified by the claims of our two protagonists' families). But this is a separate issue; for a protagonist whose ground project was moral in the

Kantian sense—say, that of moving to central Africa to spend one's life working in a refugee camp—could equally well exemplify the role of intrinsic luck and the essentially retrospective nature of some justifications. Anyway, Williams explicitly recognizes that Gauguin and Anna might have a justification for their actions without its being something that they can offer to others, or expect them to accept. Hence, many passionate denunciations of the immorality of Williams's two characters have simply (although understandably) missed his point.[29]

A deeper worry is Williams's impoverished depiction of the moral claims that his characters acknowledge without meeting. Take Gauguin's wife and children; all that Williams says about what is involved in their claims being neglected (not, notice, what is involved in *their* being neglected, the individual people) is a parenthetical remark "(we may suppose this to be grim)." And when stressing the limited nature of Gauguin's possible justification, Williams says that "he may have no way of bringing it about that those who suffer from his decision will have no justified ground of reproach. Even if he succeeds, he will not acquire a right that they accept what he has to say."[30] Are such relationships solely concerned with supplying or removing grounds for censure and blame (a conception Williams later criticizes in Rawls)? Is family life solely a field for the exercise of rights governing how one's relatives should respond to one's words and deeds? These formulations recall Williams's earlier portrayal of George's wife, when he states that her having a job causes serious trouble for their children (despite the fact that unemployed George is available for childcare), and simply stipulates that she sees nothing much wrong with CBW research (a view "the details of which need not concern us here"). These stories barely register the commitments and ground projects of their supporting cast; their individual reality barely registers in the moral reflections they provoke. Williams's sole comment on his Anna's literary origins is equally striking. In saying that her relationship with Vronsky has to carry too much weight, Williams describes this as a "truth which, however inevitable Tolstoy ultimately makes it seem, could, relative to her earlier thoughts, have been otherwise." Can the truth about Tolstoy's Anna ultimately be other than Tolstoy makes it appear? It is almost as if Williams takes himself to be rescuing Anna from her creator's unduly inexorable sense of the fatefulness of character in society, rather than merely constructing another, more amenable character.

This stance toward Anna seems to me to misconceive, while being made possible by, her distinctive mode of existence in the novel: what John Bayley has called her "vivid insubstantiality."[31] Unlike the other characters in this tale, or indeed any others created by Tolstoy, we learn hardly anything of Anna's appearance or physical presence, of her girlhood and family circumstances, even of how she came to marry

Karenin; she stands subtly outside her own familial and social worlds, and her thoughts and deeds are never fully analyzed or explained, or even documented. This might well create a sense that Anna's concrete individuality remains mysterious even to her author, and hence capable of being misunderstood by him. But the reality is that her author gives her no such individuality, and for good reason: as Bayley sees, its absence makes her seem "as if she were the vehicle through which the force of passion declares itself, like a gale of wind or a roaring fire . . . ; the terrible glow of a conflagration on a dark night" (xi).

This suggests something like the contrary of Williams's assumption that her fate could have been otherwise had the social situation and her state of mind been otherwise. As it happens, in earlier drafts of the novel, Tolstoy altered Anna's social situation, so that she and Vronsky are in fact able to marry and are received back among their friends. But the result was always the same: he found that Anna always found her way to the railway station. Her end is thus not the result of her character's inextricable entanglement in the consequential actuality of her world and its characters; it is not even the unavoidable expression of her character; it rather declares that her character was always already consumed—mere kindling for the terrible conflagration of passion. Against that roaring glow, Williams's recasting of Tolstoy's Anna as making a rational choice in favor of a self-defining ground project whose very coherence is subject to luck can seem a mere parody of its original. Characterizing his broader strategy with both examples, Williams says this:

My procedure in general will be to invite reflection about how to think and feel about some rather less usual situations, in the light of an appeal to how we—many people—tend to think and feel about other more usual situations, not in terms of substantive moral opinions or 'intuitions' but in terms of the experience of those kinds of situation. There is no suggestion that it is impossible for human beings to lack these feelings and experiences. In the case of the less usual there is only the claim that the thoughts and experiences I consider are possible, coherent, and intelligible, and that there is no ground for condemning them as irrational. In the case of the more usual, there are suggestions, with the outline of a reason for them, that unless we were to be merely confused or unreflective, life without these experiences would involve a much vaster reconstruction of our sentiments and our view of ourselves than may be supposed—supposed, in particular, by those philosophers who discuss these matters as though our experience of our own agency and the sense of our regrets not only could be tidied up to accord with a very simple image of rationality, but already had been.[32]

For Williams, the more usual kinds of case (such as the agent-regret of the lorry driver who knocks down a child through no fault of his own) reflect the fundamental fact that our concept of a human action yokes together intentions with actual deeds in the world, so that our answerability for our actions necessarily makes us answerable, beyond what we mean to do, for what actually happens (what we actually do, as well as what results from our doing it). Gauguin and Anna are the less usual kinds of case "whose sense is made plainer"[33] by reference to such fundamental features of our self-understanding. But how easily can the plain implication of this last claim (that the less usual cases have a single, clarifiable sense) be reconciled with Williams's earlier, official disclaimer that he is merely considering one possible way of making sense of them?

This central ambivalence finds its clearest expression in Williams's gloss on the "we" in his opening reference to how "we tend to think" as meaning "many people." One might ask: how far does his use of the third person plural really express a rebuttable claim to moral community, and how far the sheer assumption of it? Williams's uncertainty about the distance between his Anna and Tolstoy's Anna—as if unsure whether his character simply differs from Tolstoy's (being the bearer of a distinct, well-formed ethical problem) or rather reclaims the truth about Anna, the true Anna, from the novel's moral falsifications of her (as if that novel were an ethical exploration-problem)—suggests that he remains unclear about how best to answer this question, and indeed about the fundamental philosophical significance of the distinction behind it.

4 Agamemnon and Oedipus; and Rameau's Nephew

In trying to recover Greek ideas, I shall turn to sources other than philosophy. There is nothing unusual about this, but the fact that the practice is standard makes it more, rather than less, necessary for me to say something about the ways in which I see works of literature, particularly tragedy, as contributing to my undertaking. It is not of course peculiar to this sort of inquiry, which aims at historical understanding, that philosophy should be concerned with literature. Even when philosophy is not involved in history, it has to make demands on literature. In seeking a reflective understanding of ethical life, for instance, it quite often takes examples from literature. Why not take examples from life? It is a perfectly good question, and it has a short answer: what philosophers will lay before themselves and their readers as an alternative to literature will not be life, but bad literature.[34]

One reason for reading the concluding sentences of this passage as implicitly referring to its author's earlier work is that they appear at the beginning of the first of the two book-length studies that primarily constitute the final phase of Bernard Williams's philosophical work, and that together embody a significantly altered sense of how to make the study of literature philosophically fruitful.

A key marker of that difference is the fact that Williams's pivotal examples in these two studies are not schematized adaptations of literary characters but the characters themselves; it is now the original literary texts that invite philosophical reflection, rather than any given philosopher's spectral variation upon them. As the passage's reference to the "recovery of Greek ideas" implies, this late work takes up the project first enunciated in *Ethics and the Limits of Philosophy*—that of exposing the distortions of the morality system through a certain return to a Socratically delineated ethical domain. But that book also signals the first point in Williams's work in which his sense of the self as given individual substance by character seems less firm and foundational; indeed, the book's conclusion characterizes the idea of "individuals with dispositions of character and a life of their own to lead"[35] as an optimistic belief, an assumption, even a hope—rather than, say, an elemental fact about what it is to be human. Is it simply accidental that Williams's altered stance toward this persistently thematized concept coincides with the displacement of his own schematically constructed characters in favor of a detailed contemplation of richly textured literary ones?

I propose to conclude this essay by examining two contrasting points at which Williams takes his later bearings from literature. The first (from *Shame and Necessity*) orients his attempt to grasp the ancient conception of supernatural necessity as it interacts with human thoughts and deeds—something he sees as lost to us moderns, and hence as posing a deep problem of understanding. Williams does not see Agamemnon's tragic dilemma (over whether to sacrifice his daughter to allow his fleet to sail) as exemplifying this challenge: for when Aeschylus's Chorus describes him as "putting on the harness of necessity," this expresses an intelligible relation between supernatural necessity and an individual's recognition of what he must do. For here, the will of Artemis presents itself to Agamemnon as having produced the circumstances in which he must act, and he decides what he must do in the light of those circumstances; what must happen in virtue of a long-term design becomes, through Agamemnon's decision, what he must do. And this, for Williams, gives expression in its own way to the centrality of character for the self: "*Ethos anthropoi daimon*, Heracleitus said, 'a man's character is his fate', and . . . an important feature of tragedy can be captured by reading this saying in both directions. The character's motivations are what shape the life he is fated to have: the way his life is shaped by fate is through his motivations."[36] The case of Sophocles' Oedipus, by contrast, confronts us with the opacities attending such interactions: the absence of answers to questions about what might have been.

Think, for example, of the situation of Oedipus's parents upon reception of the prophecy concerning their son's fate. If it was supernaturally necessary for Oedipus to kill his father, should we say that, even if they had kept him at home, there would necessarily have been a route to the killing that started at their hearth; or should we say rather that it was necessary that he not be kept at home since his expulsion was the first step along the path to the killing? As with many other characters confronting such supernatural necessity, there is simply nothing to be said about ways in which things might have gone differently; and this is not how it is with human affairs when an outcome is in familiar ways inevitable; to explain its inevitability involves understanding how things might have gone otherwise. How can we have even the idea of a world in which all this can, on occasion, be suspended? Williams's answer is: a special use of the indeterminacy of fiction.

> The play represents to us an outcome, together with such things as failed attempts to prevent it, with such power and in such a chain of significance as to kill speculation about alternatives. By compelling our attention and directing our fears to what it presents as actual, tragedy may leave us with no thought, and no need of a thought, about anything else. The general condition with fiction is that, beyond a certain point, there are no interesting or realistic questions about alternatives *to* the action; a special art of Sophoclean tragedy . . . is to convert this into the sense that there are, at certain points, no alternatives *within* the action.[37]

For Williams, then, our sense of supernatural necessity is a product of authorial power, although not an apprehension of it. To be conscious of that power would generate a sense of contrivance; and anyway, the Greek conception of supernatural necessity is not one that stands to the world as an author stands to his created world (as with one version of the Christian God), but a special element to be inserted in it. Sophocles makes this insertion compelling by a variety of means (some depend upon the audience's knowing more of the story than the characters, others upon the audience's uncertainties about which version of the story is being dramatized, which brings them closer to the condition of the characters), all of which conceal the fact that there is no particular way in which the insertion comes about.

   Williams's characterization of the condition of fiction may seem hasty: is "the point" beyond which there are no contentful questions about alternatives to the action supposed to be common to every type of fiction, and clearly specifiable in advance of the pursuit of specific questions about specific fictional characters? Williams's own contestation of the fate and freedom of Tolstoy's Anna suggests otherwise. But his nuanced, detailed readings of Greek tragic characters nonetheless suggest a fascinatingly ambivalent picture of the relation between philosophy and literature. For on the one hand, he claims that, at a basic level, these literary texts fail to make sense; by presenting a power whose exercise occurs in no particular way, they eviscerate the concept they deploy, embodying and inducing a kind of modal bewilderment. On the other hand, he plainly regards such authorial effects as informing a truly special art, a powerful—indeed world-historical—aesthetic achievement, to which such philosophers' qualms seem essentially irrelevant as criticisms (even if they provide indispensable ways of coming to understand the peculiar modes of their aesthetic power). It is as if, at this late stage, he comes to see literature's enduring capacity to refine, reject, or rise above philosophical critique as essential to its mysterious glory.

At a vital point in his last book, *Truth and Truthfulness*, Williams takes his bearings from a much later literary text—Diderot's *Rameau's Nephew*. His overall argument follows from the conclusion of *Ethics and the Limits of Philosophy*, where his commitment to the character-based individuality of the self was one of three notions that he described as hopes or optimistic beliefs: the other two were truth and truthfulness. His final work elaborates the interconnections between these three concepts, their deep importance and their fragility.

Having argued that any human society has good reason to value knowledge, and hence to value tendencies to acquire true beliefs and to convey what one actually believes to others, Williams claims that the maintenance of these dispositions to accuracy and sincerity require the cultivation of dispositions to regard accuracy and sincerity as having intrinsic, not merely instrumental, value. Some such conception of their intrinsic value is therefore necessary to human existence; but which particular one comes to dominate, and how it develops or is threatened, will be culturally specific and ultimately determined by historical vicissitudes.

Chapter 8 of Williams's book examines an eighteenth-century cultural innovation in the dimension of truthfulness, one which associates sincerity with personal authenticity, or rather with two different understandings of authenticity, and hence of the self. That exemplified in the work of Rousseau presupposes the idea of a true self, a reality underlying forms of expression and feeling imposed from without; but since it could offer no guarantee that one's deepest self need be ethically sound, or in any sense well-disposed toward others, this conception of authenticity is open to the (in Williams's view, increasingly realized) possibility of breaking its original connection with sincerity, in that truthfulness to others has no more claim than anything else to constrain the demands of self-expression.

Williams contrasts this conception with Diderot's. *Rameau's Nephew* relates a conversation between "Moi" (the narrator) and "Lui" (the nephew of the famous composer). Lui's social roles, dress, and physical appearance vary as wildly as his moods; he has amazing powers of mimicry and a deafening voice; and his conversation with Moi covers a bewildering array of topics (including virtue and vice, sincerity and hypocrisy). In particular, Lui declares that virtue presupposes a particular type of soul that not everyone possesses, and that he himself does not know who or what he is, although he is committed to expressing directly and truthfully whatever thought or attitude presently possesses him—to being consistently inconsistent.

For Williams, Lui is a paradigm of sincerity in its basic form of uninhibited self-expression; what he is *not* is a unity, all of a piece. He is disintegrated; not only does his temperament make him unreceptive to morality, he does not have a character revealable in sincere self-disclosure at all—he lacks a true self in the Rousseauian sense. Lui exemplifies Diderot's Nietzschean conception of the self as constantly shifting, reacting, and altering, like a swarm of bees; and his relationship with Moi implies that "it is a universal truth, not just a special feature of modernity, that human beings have an inconstant mental constitution that needs to be steadied by society and interaction with other people. Different people, and people in different circumstances, are steadied by these forces to a greater or lesser degree; modernity, perhaps, makes it specially hard, or hard in a special way, to steady them."[38] For Williams, if our declarations are to count as expressions of belief of any sort, they need to be patterned in some way; and beyond straightforward cases of information retention (where the external environment plays a governing role), if what I uninhibitedly declare at a given moment can be taken as a declaration of something I believe, that is because there is a social practice that firms up the expression of my immediate state into something with a future. Since others need to rely on our dispositions, and we want them to be able to do so because we need to rely on theirs, we learn to present ourselves to others, and hence to ourselves, as people with moderately steady outlooks.

We do not, then, inherently possess a transparent self-understanding which we then express to others; at a more basic level, we are all together in the social activity of mutually stabilizing our declarations, moods, and impulses into beliefs, desires, and attitudes. Even bringing the self to the point at which it can seem like an assemblage of different and conflicting voices will already be an achievement. Without it, the stability of character so vital to human interaction and a manageable life would not exist; but such steadiness has its generic costs (as Diderot's fiction attests), and two further costs in the modern period. There is the political problem of finding a form of shared life that is neither too oppressively coercive (the demand of freedom) nor dependent on mythical legitimations (the demand of enlightenment). And there is the personal problem of stabilizing the self into a form that fits with such political and social ideas, without blocking the creation of a life that presents itself to a reflective individual as worth living.

In these conditions, sincerity has to create truth, since through the social practice I become what I have sincerely declared myself to be, or rather become my interpretation of others' interpretation of my sincere declarations. My contribution to this process fills out the idea that acknowledgement is more than factual discovery; but discovery is nevertheless involved, given the need to resist fantasy in making sense of my beliefs and allegiances. Because of this, the risks of wishful thinking and self-deception, the dangers that the virtues of truth (of accuracy and sincerity) at their most flexible and resilient will fail one, are evident, at both the social and the personal level. But the model of sincerity and commitment in Diderot's fiction will better serve us here than that of Rousseau's philosophical autobiography.

In effect, then, Williams's reflective understanding of the interaction between form and content in *Rameau's Nephew* induces a radical revision in the ground project of his philosophical work. It undercuts his previous assumption that the substantiality of the self as constituted by character-defining projects might simply be invoked to correct philosophical accounts of human ethical life that run counter to, and might even entirely occlude, that assumption. Individual character, and thus selfhood, is now understood as the result of a mutable social and political project, rather than a brute fact of experience. Nevertheless, it confirms his sense of the importance of character—to the self and its society: both directly, and insofar as the self's substantiality at once makes possible, and is made possible by, social interpretations of the intrinsic significance of truth and truthfulness (since there can be no selves without the constitutive function of the virtues of truth, and no virtues of truth without selves to incorporate and reproduce them). The peculiar difficulty of modernity is that the very values that make self and society possible have mutated in such a way as to pose a threat to its very continuation, and so to the three hopes to which Williams's late work gives increasingly anxious expression; for a legitimate aversion to naivete and deception has created a generalized skepticism about objective truth and a generalized suspicion of claims to authority. Lacking any metaphysical or spiritual sense that the virtues of truth are guaranteed to survive, Williams at the last finds the conceptual resources needed for understanding and maintaining them not in philosophy, but in the peculiarly characterless fictional character of Rameau's nephew. And in so doing, he finally begins to exploit aspects of the autonomous power of literature—its capacity not only to guide but to put in question our prevailing modes of moral, political, and metaphysical thinking—that his earlier philosophical practice implicitly denied, but around which Cora Diamond's work has circled, with sustained fruitfulness, from the beginning.

Notes

1. Bernard Williams, "The Makropulos Case: Reflections on the Tedium of Immortality," in *Problems of the Self*, hereafter *PS*.

2. Bernard Williams, "Utilitarianism: A Critique," hereafter *UC*.

3. Bernard Williams, "Moral Luck," hereafter *ML*.

4. Bernard Williams, *Shame and Necessity*, hereafter *SN*.

5. Bernard Williams, *Truth and Truthfulness*, hereafter *TT*.

6. Bernard Williams, *Ethics and the Limits of Philosophy*, hereafter *ELP*.

7. *PS*, 82.

8. *PS*, 95.

9. William Golding, *Pincher Martin*, hereafter *PM*.

10. *PM*, 201.

11. In what follows, I will be using Paul Selver's authorized translation of Karel Capek, *The Makropulos Case* (London: Holden, 1927); Williams gives no indication of which edition of play (or opera) he is employing.

12. Stanley Cavell, *A Pitch of Philosophy*, hereafter *POP*.

13. *POP*, 137.

14. *POP*, 144.

15. *UC*, 97–99.

16. *UC*, 95.

17. *UC*, 116–117.

18. Roy Holland, "Absolute Ethics, Mathematics, and the Impossibility of Politics," hereafter *AE*.

19. *AE*, 139, 141.

20. *AE*, 140.

21. Rai Gita, *Good and Evil: An Absolute Conception*, hereafter *GE*.

22. *GE*, 68–69.

23. Stanley Cavell, *The Claim of Reason*, hereafter *CR*.

24. *CR*, 151.

25. Cora Diamond, "Thought-Experiments in Ethics."

26. *ML*, 22–23; 26–27.

27. *ML*, 24.

28. *ML*, 35–36.

29. D. Z. Phillips, "How Lucky Can You Get?" is a good example.

30. *ML*, 23–24.

31. John Bayley, introduction to *Anna Karenina*, by Leo Tolstoy, trans. Louise and Aylmer Maude (Oxford: Oxford University Press, 1980).

32. *ML*, 22.

33. *ML*, 27.

34. *SN*, 13.

35. *ELP*, 201.

36. *SN*, 136.

37. *SN*, 146.

38. *TT*, 191.

Works Cited

Bayley, John. Introduction to *Anna Karenina* by Leo Tolstoy. Trans. Louise and Aylmer Maude. Oxford: Oxford University Press, 1980.

Capek, Karel. *The Makropulos Case*. Trans. Paul Selver. London: Holden, 1927.

Cavell, Stanley. *The Claim of Reason*. Oxford: Oxford University Press, 1979.

Cavell, Stanley. *A Pitch of Philosophy*. Cambridge Mass.,: Harvard University Press, 1994.

Diamond Cora. "Thought-Experiments in Ethics." *Philosophical Papers* 31, no. 3 (2002): 227–250.

Gita, Rai. *Good and Evil: An Absolute Conception*, 2nd ed. London: Routledge, 2004.

Golding, William. *Pincher Martin*. London: Faber, 1956.

Holland, Roy. "Absolute Ethics, Mathematics, and the Impossibility of Politics." In *Against Empiricism*, 126–142. Totowa, N.J.: Barnes and Noble, 1980.

Phillips, D. Z. "How Lucky Can You Get?" In *Interventions in Ethics*, 178–202. London: Macmillan, 1992.

Williams, Bernard. "The Makropulos Case: Reflections on the Tedium of Immortality." In *Problems of the Self*, 82–100. Cambridge: Cambridge University Press, 1973.

Williams, Bernard. "Utilitarianism: A Critique." In J. J. C. Smart and Williams, *Utilitarianism: For and Against*, 77–150. Cambridge: Cambridge University Press, 1973.

Williams, Bernard. "Moral Luck," in his *Moral Luck*, 20–39. Cambridge: Cambridge University Press, 1981.

Williams, Bernard. *Ethics and the Limits of Philosophy*. London: Fontana, 1985.

Williams, Bernard. *Shame and Necessity*. Berkeley: University of California Press, 1993.

Williams, Bernard. *Truth and Truthfulness*. Princeton: Princeton University Press, 2002.

11   Humans, Animals, Right and Wrong

Alice Crary

[Animals have] no consciousness that we would recognize as consciousness. No awareness, as far as we can make out, of a self with a history. What I mind is what tends to come next. They have no consciousness *therefore*. Therefore what? Therefore we are free to use them for our own ends? Therefore we are free to kill them? Why? What is so special about the form of consciousness we recognize that makes killing a bearer of it a crime while killing an animal goes unpunished?
—Elizabeth Costello in J. M. Coetzee's *The Lives of Animals*[1]

Do our interactions with animals have a moral dimension? Can things we do to animals merit moral censure or blame? Over the last thirty years, these questions have attracted a steadily increasing amount of attention. Many thinkers, taking an interest in the immense number of ways in which we interact with and make use of animals, have wanted to argue that our practices with animals are open to moral assessment. A significant proportion of those who argue along these lines are motivated by a concern to show that some of our practices with animals are callous and cruel. This charge of callousness and cruelty depends for its force on an assumption that is both intuitively plausible and poorly represented in the modern history of Western ethics: namely, that there are constraints on how animals should be treated that are more than mere functions of ways in which harming them indirectly harms human beings. The thinkers who level the charge often explicitly undertake to defend this assumption, and, since what is at issue is an assumption about how animals are direct sources of moral claims, we might well speak in this connection of the emergence of a set of *direct claim views* of our moral relations with animals.

Although this set of views is heterogeneous, including contributions to conversations about, for instance, "animal welfare," "animal rights," and "environmental ethics," its best-known members resemble each other to such an extent that they are rightly thought of as composing a tight-knit family, and, in this chapter, I am initially concerned to describe some basic shared characteristics of this family. After discussing a number of familiar direct claim views, I present a series of examples with an eye to showing that there is a fundamental respect in which they are vulnerable to critical scrutiny. The specific criticism I develop, far from being calculated to motivate an indifferent or unfeeling attitude toward animals, is intended to make room for a more satisfactory direct claim view—one capable of underwriting just and sound moral assessment of our practices with animals. In describing this view, I am influenced by the work of Cora Diamond—in even more ways than are explicitly acknowledged in the pages that follow.

1.1   The Argument from Common Capacities

Even if it were true that all and only humans have full moral standing, we should be able to say *what it is* about being human that gives us this special status. Simply being human cannot be what does the job.
—James Rachels, "Drawing Lines"[2]

The members of the family of familiar direct claim views that interest me are united by an argument for representing animals as direct sources of moral claims that can be sketched roughly as follows. The argument starts from the thought that an appeal to the species to which a (human or nonhuman) creature belongs cannot in itself be a reason for treating it one way or another,[3] and that any sound reason will need to mention features or capacities of the animal, independent of species membership, that some ethical principle establishes as morally relevant. It is a corollary of this thought that, if we want to figure out whether we are right to treat an animal differently from the way in which we treat human beings, we need to set aside questions of species membership and ask whether, as an individual, the animal possesses any such features or capacities that distinguish it from all human beings. The argument moves from this corollary to the observation that, although most humans have mental capacities that no animal has (e.g., capacities for reflection), we do not take the possession of such capacities to ground our claims to moral consideration. For we take people who do not yet have, cannot acquire or have irretrievably lost such capacities (i.e., infants, retarded people and severely demented people) to merit moral consideration and, further, we think that such people, no less than those who are mentally better endowed, deserve to be treated in ways that exclude, for instance, being the subjects of crippling experiments, being killed for consumption or other use, being displayed or hunted for entertainment, or being imprisoned at will.

This line of argument appears to underwrite two closely connected conclusions. The first is that our own claim to moral consideration is grounded not in higher capacities of mind like reflection, but rather in lower capacities like sentience. The second is that consistency obliges us to treat *all* (human and nonhuman) creatures as imposing equivalent, and equivalently direct, moral claims insofar as they possess the pertinent capacities. Now we appear to have before us a straightforward argument for a direct claim view, an argument that proceeds by depicting mental capacities common to humans and animals as grounding direct claims to moral consideration.[4]

This argument—hereafter, the *argument from common capacities*[5]—is often presented as showing that nothing justifies the divergences in our treatment of animals and mentally limited humans and, further, that many of our practices with animals should be regarded as morally objectionable.[6] The term of criticism most often used in this connection is *speciesism*.[7] What underlies its use is the idea of an analogy to injustices like sexism and racism, where these are understood as involving moral discriminations grounded in morally irrelevant considerations of sex and race (or color). The suggestion is that to talk about "speciesism" is to make an analogous allegation about moral discriminations grounded in morally irrelevant considerations of species membership. Against the backdrop of this idea, it appears that a reasonable way to develop morally sound, "nonspeciesist" practices with animals is to alter them so that they more nearly resemble our practices with mentally limited human beings.

One of the earliest and most influential versions of the line of thought leading from the argument from common capacities to this kind of engagement with a worry about speciesism is developed in the writings of Peter Singer. Singer, a philosopher whose concerns in this area are aptly placed under the heading of "animal welfare," assumes that simply being human cannot play a legitimate role in moral thought, and that our claim to moral consideration must be grounded in features or capacities we possess apart from our humanity.[8] He argues, partly in reference to our intuitions about how mentally very limited humans merit moral consideration,[9] that what makes us objects of moral concern is our capacity for suffering and enjoyment.[10] He accounts for what he sees as the moral salience of this capacity by appealing to classic utilitarian principles (i.e., principles that stipulate that actions are right insofar as they tend to produce pleasure and wrong insofar as they tend to produce pain). Further, he stresses that this capacity is one that we share with many animals. Singer's goal is not, however, thereby to convince us that we should strive to treat animals in exactly the same way that we treat human beings. He describes a creature's capacity to suffer and enjoy as endowing it with *interests*,[11] and he tells us that the interests that this capacity produces will vary with the creature's other abilities and life circumstances.[12] The moral principle that Singer thus ultimately defends—this is his version of the conclusion of the argument from common capacities—is one that calls for equal attention to the equal interests of any (human or nonhuman) creature.[13]

Singer believes that we often violate this principle by placing greater importance on equivalent interests of human beings, and it is on the basis of this belief that he describes us as guilty of speciesism.[14] He sets out to expose and combat our allegedly speciesist tendencies by urging the development of practices respectful of the principle. If we are to understand what Singer counts as appropriately respectful practices, we need to be aware that his interpretation of the principle, like the line of reasoning that leads him to it, has a classic utilitarian cast. By Singer's lights, satisfactory practices are those that aggregately maximize the satisfaction of equivalent human and nonhuman interests. This utilitarian strategy gets criticized by other advocates of the argument from common capacities,[15] but I will not further discuss disputes here about whether or not the argument is best rendered along utilitarian lines. I am primarily interested in certain basic structural features of the argument that inform the thought of all of the argument's (utilitarian and nonutilitarian) advocates, and, for this reason, I want now briefly to examine the work of one thinker who sympathizes with the argument but does not share Singer's utilitarian commitments.

Consider, in this connection, the work of Tom Regan. Like Singer, Regan presents a version of the argument from common capacities with an eye to showing that many of our existing practices with animals are speciesist, and, also like Singer, he starts from the assumption that a creature's humanity cannot by itself qualify as a reason for treating it in certain ways, and that our entitlement to moral consideration must reflect our possession of capacities apart from our humanity.[16] But Regan differs from Singer in that he develops this assumption by appeal to principles that, instead of having a utilitarian cast, place him "in the Kantian tradition."[17] His main contention is not that certain animals possess welfare interests in virtue of being sentient, but rather that certain animals possess *rights* in virtue of having a range of capacities that endow them with an at least primitive form of subjecthood—rights that no appeal to aggregate human interests can override.

Regan lists the capacities that as he sees it endow creatures with rights as:

beliefs and desires; perception, memory, and a sense of the future, including their own future; an emotional life together with feelings of pleasure and pain; preference- and welfare-interests; the ability to initiate action in pursuit of their desires and goals; a psychophysical identity over time; and an individual welfare in the sense that their experiential life fares well or ill for them, logically independently of their utility for others and logically independently of their being the object of anyone else's interests.[18]

Regan argues that there are good reasons to attribute these capacities to mammals and some other animals,[19] and he links the capacities to the possession of rights, arguing that any creature that possesses them is in a significant sense capable of directing its own life and should therefore be treated not as a mere thing or instrument, but rather as a being whose ends demand respect.[20] His suggestion is that animals that thus possess rights have claims to live and to move freely and develop normally, and, when he describes us as culpably speciesist, he is drawing attention to ways in which our existing practices with animals fail to honor these claims.

One thing these remarks reveal is that the charge of speciesism has a somewhat different practical force for Regan than it does for Singer. Thus, for instance, whereas Singer's work has relatively straightforward implications for how we treat even very primitive sentient creatures, the bearing of Regan's work on our treatment of such creatures is not as clear. It would be possible to describe this and other practical divergences between Singer and Regan in detail, but this is not the project that interests me here. I want instead to critically examine certain fundamental argumentative moves that both make—specifically, moves internal to the argument from common capacities.

Before turning to the particular features of the argument that I am going to criticize, let me mention one feature that I do *not* want to question. The argument depends, for the significance that its different advocates attach to it, on certain claims about the mental capacities of animals. In order to demonstrate its applicability in specific cases, advocates are obliged to represent the animals that interest them as possessing sensations and emotions—and perhaps also the ability to initiate action and orient themselves with regard to the future. Now, although I am going to insist that we should reject the argument from common capacities as defective, it is no part of my project to suggest that we should reject this particular feature of it wholesale. Where some detractors are inclined to reject all of the claims that advocates of the argument advance about the mental capacities of animals, my own view is that many of these claims—for instance, claims about how particular mammals or birds can feel pain or fear—are both philosophically innocent and factually accurate.

1.2   A Different Direct Claim View

[M]*erely being human* has a role in moral thought, a role quite different from that of properties like sentience or rationality or the capacity for moral personality.
—Cora Diamond, "The Importance of Being Human"[21]

Animals—these objects we are acting upon—are not given for our thought independently of . . . a mass of ways of thinking about and responding to them.
—Cora Diamond, "Eating Meat and Eating People"[22]

Advocates of the argument from common capacities are happy to admit that an appeal to the species to which a (human or nonhuman) creature belongs guides us in figuring out what capacities it will normally possess. But they claim that it is the creature's possession of certain individual capacities, not its species membership, that determines moral standing. Thus, for instance, there can be no question of establishing the entitlement to moral consideration of severely retarded and demented people by pointing out that they are human beings. Any entitlement that they have must be grounded in mental capacities or other personal qualities that they themselves possess, and, since some animals possess equivalent capacities and qualities, we are compelled to admit that some animals possess equivalent claims to moral consideration.

It is a premise of this argument that ways in which we humans treat one another can never be justified by appeal to our humanity alone, and in this section I want to attack the argument by first contesting this premise. I present examples suggesting that the recognition that someone is human is by itself (i.e., independently of any observations about her individual capacities) a reason to treat her in certain ways. Further, after thus illustrating that, in opposition to what advocates of the argument from common capacities maintain, being human is by itself morally significant, I attempt to illustrate that being an animal is as well. My aim in offering these illustrations is to bring out not only how they challenge the argument from common capacities but also how they position us to describe a direct claim view very different from the one that the argument bequeaths to us.

A good place to start is with a couple of examples that support the idea, foreign to the argument from common capacities, that simply being human is morally important. My first example is one that Elizabeth Anderson adduces in a recent paper in which she is herself taking to task (what I call) the argument from common capacities.[23]

The example concerns an advanced Alzheimer's patient who is "unable anymore to recognize herself or others, or to care about or for herself,"[24] and, in discussing the example, Anderson emphasizes that, despite what the argument from common capacities might encourage us to think, a person with such diminished capacities places substantial demands on us for appropriate care. Anderson claims that "it is an indignity to [this person] if she is not properly toileted and decently dressed in clean clothes, her hair combed, her face and nose wiped, and so forth."[25] She tells us that these demands cannot be explained in terms of Regan-style rights (since the person has, after all, lost the capacities that endow individuals with such rights), and she adds that these demands also cannot be explained entirely in terms of requirements of health. If the demands that the Alzheimer's patient places on others for appropriate care could be fully attributed to requirements of health and comfort, then it would seem as though they could be understood—in a manner congenial to the argument from common capacities—as expressions of what Singer would call the patients' "interests." But it is not difficult to see that in order to make sense of the demands in question we need to appeal to something beyond requirements of health and comfort. If the relatives of the Alzheimer's patient found her "naked, eating from a bowl, like a dog,"[26] they would rightly be outraged, and it would not wholly placate them to learn that her condition in no way compromised her health or comfort. The right lesson to draw from this case is—and this is Anderson's point—that some forms of treatment are degrading to a human being without regard to the level of her capacities, and that in this respect humanity is by itself morally important.[27]

Let me turn to a second example, one that Cora Diamond presents in a 1978 paper that contains one of the earliest critiques of Singer's and Regan's work on animal and ethics.[28] In the paper at issue, Diamond is specifically concerned with these thinkers' attempts to defend vegetarianism, and it will be helpful to say a word about their efforts before turning to Diamond's reservations about them. Where Singer approaches the issue of vegetarianism equipped with the view creatures have interests in virtue of their capacities to suffer, Regan approaches it equipped with the view that creatures have rights in virtue of their sentience as well as their capacities to move and orient themselves with regard to their own futures. Singer argues that we ought to be unsettled by a question about why we are willing to kill animals for food when doing so causes suffering given that we are not willing to kill humans for food when doing so would cause no more suffering;[29] and Regan argues that we ought to be unsettled by a question about why we are willing to violate the rights of animals by killing them for food given that we are not willing to thus violate the rights of human beings.[30] Singer's argument presupposes that the reason we do not kill and eat other human beings is that doing so would cause them to suffer, and Regan's argument presupposes that the reason we do not do this is that it would violate their rights. These presuppositions are Diamond's main critical targets, and she is attempting to dislodge them when she introduces the example that I now want to discuss, one having to do with our attitudes toward the bodies of dead human beings.

At its heart is the observation that we do not, except in quite exceptional circumstances, eat the bodies of people who are already dead—not even, in Diamond's colorful phrase, "when they have died in automobile accidents or been struck by lightening, and their flesh might be first class."[31] Having made this observation, Diamond immediately notes that it shows that here Regan's talk of rights is clearly beside the point. She then adds that we cannot fully explain the observation by noting that the thought that we ourselves might be eaten when dead would cause suffering or distress. She acknowledges that "it *would* cause distress to people to think that they might be eaten when they were dead." But she adds that, since this is "because of what it is to eat a dead person," we cannot account for our unwillingness to eat the dead by appealing to such distress.[32] Diamond thus attempts to impress on us that, in contrast to what Singer would have us believe, it is not out of a desire not to cause distress that we avoid eating the bodies of people who are already dead. Her goal is thereby to persuade us that "what underlies our attitude to dining on ourselves" is not a desire to respect people's "interests" in not suffering (since, as she shows, we are no less opposed to dining on ourselves where there is no longer any question of such "interests"), but rather the simple view that "*a person is not something to eat.*"[33] It is in this way that Diamond here makes the point that interests me: namely, that "*merely being human* has a role in moral thought."[34]

I want now to move from defending the idea of a specifically human dignity to arguing that there is an important respect in which it admits of further elaboration. I want to suggest that once we see that "merely being human has a role in moral thought," we are well positioned to recognize that this role is one that both distinguishes us from and places us above animals. In this connection, it is helpful to return to Anderson's case of the advanced Alzheimer's patient. Anderson observes that the relatives of this patient who find her naked and eating from the floor might naturally express their outrage by saying "they're treating her like an animal!"[35] Anderson thus forcefully illustrates that humans as such merit forms of moral consideration that go beyond what is merited by animals. Nor are additional illustrations difficult to find. Here we might remind ourselves that, while it is degrading for a human qua human to lack a name, the same cannot be said about animals. Or we might remind ourselves that people are generally humiliated by being forced to live in conditions that allow for nothing beyond the exercise of animal functions, conditions nonetheless clearly fit for animals. The omniscient narrator in J. M. Coetzee's *Life and Times of Michael K* in effect makes this point when he exclaims: "What a pity that to live in times like these a man must be ready to live like a beast."[36] Or, again, we might remind ourselves that humans qua humans merit greater consideration than animals even when they are dead. The Anglican priest in Raimond Gaita's memoir of his father makes a similar observation when, in response to a question about whether he will bury a man who has killed himself, he declares: "Of course. He's not a dog. He's a human being."[37] And here we might add that it is appropriate to hold a funeral for a young child but not for a puppy.[38] What these different cases show is that the concept "human," in addition to being by itself morally significant, possesses a kind of significance that, as

Anderson puts it, needs to be understood within "a system of meaning in which humans qua humans have a status—a form of dignity—higher than animals."[39]

A caveat: It is *not* an implication of this conclusion that animals qua animals lack moral status. In saying that animals have a status in moral thought that is lower than that of humans, we leave open the possibility that this status is significant. Reflection confirms that this possibility is indeed a real one, and that we speak of "animals" in reference to creatures that merit certain forms of moral consideration without regard to any capacities or interests they possess. Thus, for instance, if someone comes home to find a roommate tying bits of rubbish to the cat's tail, she would be justified in being outraged, even if the cat does not notice and is not in any way made to suffer, and she might well give vent to her outrage by saying "it's an animal, not a mere thing!" Moreover, a person would be justified in using similar words if a companion who was out walking with her in a wood started to stomp and kill insects out of nothing but caprice—even if the insects were too simple to possess the capacity for pain.[40] We might summarize these different observations by saying that animals are rightly understood as creatures that, while lacking specifically human dignity, possess a certain dignity of their own, and that it is accordingly no more true of animals than of humans that they are, in Diamond's words, "given for our thought indepedently of . . . a mass of ways of thinking about and responding to them."[41]

Notice how far we now are from the argument from common capacities. The argument turns for its interest on the assumption that a creature's humanity, or its membership in some other species, is never by itself a reason to treat it one way or another. The assumption is what seems to justify the argument's linking of moral entitlements to capacities independent of species membership, and this account of moral entitlements is in turn what, within the context of the argument, seems to allow us to represent animals as direct sources of moral claims. It follows that in repudiating the assumption—as I have been claiming we should—we distance ourselves not only from the argument but at the same time from the direct claim view that it seems to bring within reach.

It does not, however, follow that in repudiating this assumption we close off the possibility of a satisfactory direct claim view. This section's critique of the argument from common capacities includes, in addition to the contention that simply being human is important for moral thought, the contention that simply being an animal is as well, and this second contention lays the groundwork for an alternative direct claim view—specifically, one on which animals impose direct moral claims in virtue of being the kinds of creatures they are. This alternative view is the main concern of this chapter, and in the remainder of this chapter I am concerned to develop it and discuss how it can inform critical assessment of our practices with animals. I need to start by considering a philosophical objection that might seem to speak against taking the view seriously in the first place.

1.3   A Philosophical Objection

[Is it] that what we really intend when we urge someone to an appreciation of the meaning of what he has done is to call upon him to *feel* rightly about the facts, or perhaps to see what moral principles the facts fall under, or a combination of both? The assumption here is that the work of understanding, strictly speaking, is exhausted in the discovery of facts and in subsuming those facts under our principles, or in ordering our principles, or perhaps, in discovering our principles.

—Raimond Gaita, *The Philosopher's Dog*[42]

The direct claim view presented in the last section represents the recognition that a creature is human, or the recognition that it is an animal, as by itself a reason to treat it in certain ways. Its distinctive suggestion is that there is no question of recognizing these things about a creature apart from appreciating that it merits certain modes of treatment, and it is not difficult to see that, in making this suggestion, we are not concerned with *biological* classifications. After all, as I discuss further in the next section (1.4), it is characteristic, not only of biological classifications, but of natural-scientific classifications more generally that it is possible to understand what speaks for and against them in the absence of any even tacit beliefs about how the entities they involve ought to be treated. So, given that we should not think of ourselves as doing biology when we think and talk about humans and animals in reference to the direct claim view I am exploring, it is worth pausing, before turning to the objection to this view that is my main concern in this section, to say a word about how we *should* think of what we are doing.

It will be helpful to introduce some terminology. In quite ordinary contexts we often talk about "what something means" in reference to some quality it possesses that by itself has implications for how we ought to respond to it. Consider a simple example. Suppose that a small business owner, *X*, is approached by an employee who tells her that his mother is dying and that he wants a few days off to be with her. Although *X* has no particular—financial or other—reason to deny her employee's request, she sees no reason to grant it, so she refuses. At this point, a friend of *X*—*Y*—approaches her and, assuming that *X* doesn't know why her employee wants time off, explains that it is because his mother is dying. When, however, *Y* learns that *X* already has all of the relevant information and still doesn't think she has any (even prima facie) reason to accede to her employee's request, *Y* exclaims: "Then you simply don't understand what it *means* to have a parent die!" *Y*'s suggestion is that if *X* truly understood what the death of a parent meant she would, by that token, see that she has reason to grant her employee leave, and what I want to point out here is that the direct claim view I just presented is concerned with what it means to be a human or an animal in the same sense in which *Y* is concerned with what it means to have a parent to die. Insofar as as this view is grounded in the thought that the recognition that a creature is a human, or the recognition that it is an animal, by itself gives us reason to treat it in certain ways, it is rightly seen as dealing with meanings in just this sense. Bearing this in mind, I will in what follows say that, when we think and talk about humans and animals in reference to this view, we are taking an interest in *meanings*.

This terminology makes it possible to perspicuously describe a very basic objection to my preferred direct claim view. The objection takes for granted an enormously influential philosophical outlook that is often credited with faithfully registering the significance of the rise of the natural sciences. This outlook represents natural-scientific discourses as monopolizing the task of illuminating genuine features of the world, and, in order to appreciate what gives this representation significance here, we need to note that the natural sciences aim to free themselves from any concern with what I am calling meaning.[43] It follows from this that, in depicting natural-scientific discourses as having a corner on capturing genuine features of the world, the influential philosophical outlook under consideration also depicts the real world as devoid of meaning.

An image of the real world as lacking meaning is sometimes formulated in terms of the notion of *objectivity*, where "an objective feature of the world" is taken to be a feature that is genuine in the sense of being such that anyone who fails to register it is missing something. Described in these terms, the philosophical outlook at issue becomes one we can characterize by saying that meanings have no foothold in the objective world.

If we start from this outlook, it will seem as though there is something philosophically suspicious about a direct claim view that employs "human" and "animal" to pick out meanings. Very roughly, the problem is that, once we adopt an outlook that excludes all meanings from objectivity, it appears that no investigations of meanings that inform talk about humans and animals—that is, no investigations of meanings of the sort central to the direct claim view I am presenting—can have the kind of objective interest that would allow them to fund authoritative critical reflection on our existing practices with animals.

It is possible to refine this criticism by introducing more terminology. If we describe a *concept* as something that determines objectively the same content in different contexts of its use, then we can say that the objection has to do with the fact that the relevant direct claim view invites us to use "human" and "animal" for concepts that determine meanings. Well, what's wrong with doing that? If in accordance with an influential philosophical outlook we assume that objectivity excludes meanings, it will seem to us that a concern with meanings cannot by itself establish something as a genuine concept (i.e., one that determines objectively the same content on different occasions of its use). Admittedly, we need not conclude that a concept that determines a meaning is thereby disqualified from cognitive respectability. For, in addition to determining a meaning, it may also determine an objective content that is lacking in meaning—a content that gives it full cognitive standing. But, if a concept has this kind of dual character, the portion of its content that lacks meaning will be the epistemically decisive thing, and the meaning it determines will be limited to playing a cognitively accidental role. The upshot is that, even if it is right to observe that we use "human" and "animal" for concepts that determine meanings, there can be no question here of representing these meanings as possessing the kind of cognitive interest that would allow them to underwrite responsible critical assessment of existing practices regarding animals.

If the direct claim view I am presenting seems thus philosophically confused, it is bound also to seem morally dangerous. To the extent that this view is taken to be encouraging us to overlook (what is seen here as) the fact that meanings we connect with the concepts "human" and "animal" simply reflect whatever attitudes toward humans and animals happen to prevail, it will at the same time seem to have a tendency to reinforce these attitudes without regard to how morally benign or morally pernicious they happen to be. So, if, for instance, we live in a society that condones the torture of legally innocent people for the purposes of routine information gathering, we will find that it is part of the meaning of "human" that a human can be tortured when convenient. Similarly, if we live in a society that condones the performance of crippling or lethal experiments on animals for the purposes of developing new cosmetics for humans, we will find that it is part of the meaning of "animal" that an animal can be maimed or killed for the sake of new perfumes or lotions. The result is that the direct claim view seems morally dangerous insofar as, in inviting us to represent meanings picked out by "human" and "animal" as objectively authoritative, it asks us to present ourselves as having legitimized the practices into which the concepts are integrated when (as it here appears) we have in fact done nothing more than engage in a gesture of uncritically affirming them. We might summarize this objection by saying that it represents the pertinent view as veering toward a form of *conservatism* that is both philosophically badly motivated and morally irresponsible, and that is incapable of underwriting responsible criticism of our current ways of interacting with animals.

In light of this objection, it appears that if we want to make room for responsible criticism of our current practices with animals we need to return to the basic structure of the argument from common capacities, treating species-membership as in itself devoid of meaning (or moral significance) and trying to identify features and capacities apart from such membership that give the individual creatures who possess them claims to moral consideration (1.1). But this recoil back toward the argument from common capacities only seems to be well motivated in the context of an image of the objective world as bereft of meaning.

1.4   On the Meaning of (Human and Animal) Life

Sweet is the lore which nature brings;
Our meddling intellect
Mis-shapes the beauteous forms of things; —We murder to dissect.
—William Wordsworth, "The Tables Turned"[44]

Let me briefly review the ground covered so far. I began by discussing members of a family of well-known direct claim views that start from versions of the argument from common capacities (1.1), and I then introduced a direct claim view that, unlike these more familiar candidates, represents being human or being an animal as by itself *meaningful* in a sense significant for ethics (1.2). Finally, I described an objection to this view that depends for its force on a conception of objectivity on which the objective realm is taken to exclude meanings (1.3).

Right now I want to challenge this objection by raising questions about the credentials of the conception of objectivity. My engagement with these abstract philosophical issues here is nothing more and nothing less than an expression of interest in the guiding preoccupations of ongoing conversations about animals and ethics. Although it is difficult to find even one explicit defense of the conception of objectivity I am questioning within the familiar direct claim views that dominate these conversations (viz., those that rely on versions of the argument from common capacities), these direct claim views at least tacitly rely on the pertinent conception's logic. I am questioning this conception only because I hope to exchange these views for a more satisfactory alternative, and because insistence on its constraints hampers efforts to arrive at such an alternative.

Traditional arguments for conceiving objectivity as excluding meanings are grounded in the—unexceptionable—observation that there is a sense in which (the qualities I am calling) meanings count as *subjective* qualities. When earlier I introduced talk of "meanings" I was picking up on the fact that we often speak of "what something means" in reference to some quality it possesses that by itself has implications for how we ought to treat it. Thus, for instance, if we say of someone who is indifferent to the strained circumstances of a neighbor that "she doesn't understand what it *means* to have to put one's children to bed hungry," one thing we are implying is that the very recognition that a neighbor lacks the resources to feed her children has implications for how we ought to respond to her. Where this familiar way of talking about meanings is at issue, there is no question of arriving at an adequate understanding of what something means apart from a reference to responses or attitudes that the pertinent thing merits. Given that our dispositions toward particular responses or attitudes are part of our subjective makeup, we might with justice say that meanings stand in a necessary relation to human subjectivity and that there is therefore an entirely straightforward respect in which they count as subjective qualities.

Within classic philosophical discussions of the nature of objectivity, this subjective character of meanings is what is taken to deprive them of objective standing. Classic philosophical discussions of these matters start from a simple and initially apparently promising strategy for distinguishing reality and appearance. The main thought animating the strategy is that subjective (i.e., perceptual and affective) endowments we draw on in thinking and talking about the world have an essential tendency to distort our view of how things really are, and that it is therefore only by stepping back from such endowments that we can assure ourselves of having our minds around more than mere appearance. This thought frequently gets expressed as a requirement to survey the world from a maximally abstract (i.e., dispassionate and dehumanized) vantage point or, to use some familiar bits of philosophical jargon, as a requirement to survey the world from "an Archimedean point" or "a God's-eye view." The idea of such a requirement, which has an undeniable imaginative appeal, is what seems to underwrite a conception of objectivity that excludes meanings. Insofar as we take seriously a requirement to adopt a maximally abstract vantage point, we seem obliged to conceive progress toward an objectively accurate view of the world as involving a process of elimination that leaves ever fewer qualities, like meanings, that have an essential reference to our subjective responses.

This basic argument against crediting meanings with objective authority turns on the idea of a "God's-eye view" of the world, and there is room to ask whether this idea is fully intelligible. The idea is often represented as suggested by reflection on the distinctive character of our natural-scientific discourses. It is, however, not obviously right to regard these discourses as encoding it.

The feature of the natural sciences that gets mentioned in this connection is their commitment to an abstract investigative stance. This methodological commitment is frequently represented not only as partly accounting for the success of the natural sciences in promoting a valuable mode of understanding the world, but also as illuminating conditions for understanding as such. It is often assumed that the natural sciences' commitment to abstraction licenses us to talk about a ("God's-eye") point of view from which it is possible to determine that abstraction is a necessary prerequisite of *every* legitimate mode of thought about the world and that the world in itself is therefore properly depicted, in the distinctive style of the natural sciences, as excluding every quality that needs to be understood in reference to subjectivity. Although it would be difficult to exaggerate the influence of the assumption that thus seems to speak for granting the natural sciences a metaphysically privileged status, there is good reason to reject it as misleading.

Consider what is clearly right about a characterization of the natural sciences as committed to abstract methods of investigation. One thing that speaks for such a characterization is the fact that natural-scientific discourses aspire to rid themselves of reliance on categories or concepts that are only intelligible in terms of particular attitudes or ethical perspectives. Or, in other words, one thing that speaks for such a characterization is the fact that these discourses aspire to rid themselves of reliance on categories or concepts that pick out meanings. Having identified a respect in which natural-scientific discourses are rightly described as favoring abstract modes of investigation, and as thereby distinguishing themselves from discourses that employ categories for meanings, we might mention an additional sense in which the latter discourses might be thought of as nonabstract or perspectival. Discourses concerned with meanings are governed by argumentative standards that are informed by our existing beliefs about meanings and that accordingly bear the imprint of ethical perspectives internal to these beliefs.

Suppose, as we very well might, that the concept "courage" picks out a meaning and that we lack a satisfactory conception of what it is for, say, an action to be courageous if we fail to conceive its courageous character as giving us a (prima facie) reason to adopt a certain attitude of approval toward it. In making these suppositions, we take it for granted that in order to accurately project the concept "courage" we need to—implicitly or explicitly—ask ourselves which things resemble each other in meriting the attitudes that, by our lights, are internal to the concept. Further, in grappling with this question we inevitably draw on other beliefs about meanings (e.g., beliefs about what aspects of our lives are important enough to be worth protecting, about what constitutes a genuine threat to our lives, etc.). Our judgments about a particular meaning are thus governed, in what might well be described as a *circular* manner, by argumentative standards that reflect the larger body of judgments about meanings to which they belong. This form of circularity is what I have in mind in speaking of a second sense in which discourses that deal in meanings are appropriately characterized as nonabstract or perspectival. My thought is that, if we are inclined to insist that cognitively authoritative discourses must (aspire to) proceed from an abstract vantage point, then the fact that discourses about meaning are in this way circular is bound to strike us as an even greater threat to their cognitive status than the fact, touched on in the last paragraph, that they deal in irredeemably nonabstract or perspectival concepts.

This thought is striking because these is good reason to think that natural-scientific discourses are characterized by an analogous form of circularity. Particular natural-scientific claims are governed by argumentative standards that reflect the very body of historically located, natural-scientific opinion to which the claims belong. Admittedly, it is not uncommon for philosophers to advocate accounts of the natural sciences on which they appear to be free from this kind of circularity. The natural sciences are often portrayed, not only as developing concepts that are as far as possible intelligible apart from any attitudes or ethical perspectives, but also as somehow allowing us to apply these concepts directly to the world, independently of the mediation of standards or criteria that are themselves colored by current scientific beliefs. What emerges is a picture of the natural sciences on which criteria that inform the assessment of candidate scientific theories (e.g., accuracy, consistency, scope, simplicity and fruitfulness)[45] are conceived as making up a sort of transhistoric algorithm that equips us to adjudicate competing natural-scientific claims in a quasi-mechanical manner, free from the influence of our current natural-scientific beliefs.

Despite enjoying widespread philosophical acceptance, this basic picture misrepresents the progress of natural-scientific knowledge. Historians and philosophers of science have illustrated in great detail how the applications and relative weights of our criteria for assessing scientific theories vary dramatically with historical period and area of application. Moreover, even if we set the work of these thinkers aside, it is fundamentally unclear what ground we might have for denying that the account of how we learn from the world that our current criteria represent, is part of our—substantive, historically located—view of what the world is like.

It would be wrong to protest that these reflections are antiscientific, or that they represent natural-scientific discourses as incapable of delivering an objective account of how things stand in the world. What may seem to recommend this protest is the assumption that only a discursive practice that is in principle capable of furnishing an ideally abstract, noncircular mode of access to the world is rightly credited with objective authority. But this assumption is traditionally taken to be motivated by reflection on the natural sciences, and we just saw that the natural sciences fail to provide it with support. So it is not clear that we have any reason to interpret reflections about how natural-scientific discourses encode a form of circularity anathema to an ideal of pure abstraction as an antiscientific attack on their cognitive authority. By the same token, it seems clear that we do have reason to interpret such reflections as an attack on *scientism*, if we speak of scientism in reference to the tendency of philosophers to move from irreproachable observations about the value of the natural sciences to unwarranted conclusions about how the natural sciences illuminate the conditions of knowledge as such. Adopting this vocabulary, we might say that the foregoing reflections, while not antiscientific, represent a direct challenge to pervasive, scientistic habits of thought.

The argument I have been discussing against granting meanings objective status credits the natural sciences with bequeathing to us the idea of an ideally abstract vantage point from which to discern that our subjective endowments tend to block our view of how things objectively are and that objectivity therefore excludes all qualities, such as meanings, that have a necessary relation to subjectivity. In combating this argument, I brought out how natural-scientific discourses resemble discourses about meaning in being characterized by a form of circularity that renders them residually nonabstract. The right conclusion to draw is not that natural-scientific discourses are bereft of objective authority but rather that they do not license us to appeal to the idea of an "Archimedean point" in thinking about what objectivity is and, by the same token, that they do not justify the a priori exclusion of the possibility that (candidate) meanings might qualify as objective. Now there appears to be good reason to reject this gesture of exclusion and to allow the task of determining the cognitive status of (candidate) meanings to devolve upon our ordinary ways of finding out how things are. By the same token, there appears to be good reason to leave open the possibility that, while in some cases we may discover that the ascription of a given meaning is grounded in a mere projection of particular subjective propensities, in others we may discover that such an ascription figures in the best, objectively most accurate account of how things are.

These remarks equip me to rebut the objection to my preferred direct claim view that is outlined in the last section. The objection presupposes that meanings are excluded from objectivity, and, drawing on this presupposition, it alleges that the view wrongly asks us to take an objective interest in meanings that (by the objection's lights) are at best accidentally associated with the concepts "human" and "animal," and that it thus wrongly reinforces whatever attitudes toward animals and humans happen to prevail, without regard to how benign or benighted these attitudes happen to be. But this objection loses force in the context of an argument, of the sort presented above, against excluding meanings from objectivity. Insofar as we have been deprived of a priori, metaphysical grounds for thinking that meanings are locked out of the objective realm, it follows that we are also bereft of a priori, metaphysical grands for insisting that if—say, following the lead of section 1.2, above—we base our direct claim view on claims about the meaning of "human" and "animal" we cannot help but make an objectively impotent gesture that veers toward blindly buttressing existing attitudes toward animals.

The centerpiece of this defense of an alternative direct claim view is the claim that meanings picked out by certain ways of talking about humans and animals may be fully objective and that such meanings may accordingly underwrite genuine conceptual practices (i.e., practices constituted by genuine objective regularities). Notice that the conceptual practices here envisioned involve not our biological concepts "human" and "animal" but rather nonbiological concepts "human" and "animal" that determine meanings and that need not be coextensive with their biological cousins.

Thus, for instance, our willingness to use the concept "human" in speaking, in the fashion discussed in 1.2, of a specifically human dignity does not commit us to demanding equivalent treatment for everything that is biologically human. Despite what some advocates of the argument from common capacities may believe, such willingness does not commit us to following in the footsteps of social conservatives who, prating about the "sanctity of life," claim both that human beings have a dignity in virtue of which they deserve forms of treatment inconsistent with simply killing them and, in addition, that, since a two week- (or two day- or two second-) old human embryo is human, it therefore merits forms of treatment inconsistent with abortion.[46] Nor does our talk of a specifically human dignity automatically exclude any creature that is not biologically human.[47] Moreover, we can recognize a specifically animal dignity, in the manner urged in 1.2, without being obliged, out of respect for consistency, to demand equivalent treatment for everything that biologists classify as animals. Our recognition of such dignity does not oblige us to question our willingness to scratch, breathe, or walk nonchalantly just because we are aware that doing so invariably kills many microorganisms. And we can recognize a specifically animal dignity without thereby committing ourselves to excluding from it everything that is not biologically animate. The concepts "human" and "animal" at play in talk of specifically human and animal forms of dignity are not concepts that we project by determining the presence of sets of properties taken to be distinctive of biological humanity and biological animality, and they are also not concepts that we project by determining the presence of alternative sets of neutrally available properties. On the contrary, the question of whether these concepts apply in given cases is a moral question calling for the exercise of moral judgment.

In arguing that the claims the direct claim view I favor advances about "what it means to be a human being" and "what it means to be an animal," are governed by objective standards, I have implied that questions about the merits of these claims can be settled in an objectively authoritative manner. Consider how we might respond to one such question—specifically, a question about the claim, put forth in 1.2, that animals possess a special dignity in virtue of which they merit forms of treatment that distinguish them from mere things.

Suppose that someone were to object to this claim, insisting that we routinely treat at least some animals—say, dangerous animals and pests of different sorts—as mere things to be killed or disposed of at will. How might we engage this person? We might start by reminding her that our practices with wild animals and pests only make sense in the context of the idea that threats to human interests make a difference, as well as in the context of the further idea that such threats justify us in distancing ourselves from what would otherwise count as appropriate forms of treatment. We might then also remind her that some of our most familiar ways of thinking about these animals reveal methods (e.g., thinking of pests as "vermin" and thinking of dangerous animals as "beasts") for repressing the recognition that it is in fact an animal to which we are doing this and that. By issuing such reminders, we might get our interlocutor to acknowledge more respectful modes of response to animals as correct. And we might then credit ourselves with having defended the idea of a specifically animal dignity in a cognitively respectable manner.

This brings to a close my presentation of a direct claim view that breaks with more familiar direct claim views in asserting that the recognition that a creature is a human being, or that it is an animal, is by itself a reason to treat it in certain ways. The view is distinguished by its concern with modes of thought about humans and animals that, unlike biological treatments of humans and animals, deal in meanings, and I have been arguing that these meanings are properly regarded as furnishing an objectively authoritative critical perspective on our practices of working and living with, experimenting on, slaughtering, consuming, hunting, and displaying animals. One of my goals here has been to show that, far from underwriting a conservative attitude toward our interactions with animals, this view is capable of accommodating a radical political posture of the sort adopted by some advocates of the argument from common capacities. A second goal has been to suggest that, insofar as the view acknowledges that our encounters with animals take place in the realm of meaning, and insofar as it thus refuses to mimic the argument from common capacities in first representing our interactions with animals as devoid of meaning and then trying to describe the proprieties of these interactions in independent theoretical terms, it is both better able to locate sources of the conviction that many of our existing practices with animals are deplorable and, at the same time, better able to address and move those of us who take an interest in the plight of animals.[48]

Notes

1. J. M. Coetzee, *The Lives of Animals*, 44, emphasis in the original.

2. In Sunstein and Nussbaum, *Animal Rights*, 162–174, p. 164, emphasis in the original.

3. Part of what motivates this thought is the belief that there is something suspicious about the idea of a special *human* dignity or that, as James Rachels puts it, it would be wrong to take "the bare fact that one is human [to entitle one to] special consideration" (*Created from Animals*, 5). Another part of what motivates this thought is the belief that there is something suspicious about the idea of a special *animal* dignity. I raise questions about both of these beliefs in section 1.2.

4. Any adequate list of the earliest and most influential works that develop versions of this argument would need to include Peter Singer, *Animal Liberation*, Tom Regan, *The Case for Animal Rights*, and Richard Ryder, *Animal Revolution*. Interest in the basic argument has grown rapidly since the publication of these works. For a relatively recent overview of debates concerning these matters, see Daniel Dombrowski, *Babies and Beasts*. For a more recent illustration of the persistence of enthusiasm for different versions of the argument, see the contributions by Steven Wise and James Rachels to Nussbaum and Sunstein, *Animal Rights*.

5. This label is my own. The argument turns on an analogy between animals and mentally limited or (as some philosophers put it) "marginal" human beings, and for this reason it is sometimes described as the *argument from marginal cases*. But this more familiar label is unfortunate. Some fans of the argument reject the label on the quite reasonable ground that it is offensive to describe mentally limited people as "marginal" human beings.

6. Notice that it is open to an advocate of the argument from common capacities to move from the thought that nothing justifies the divergences in our treatment of animals and mentally limited humans to the conclusion, not that our treatment of animals should more closely approximate our treatment of such human beings, but rather that our treatment of such human beings should more closely approximate our treatment of animals. I neglect this possibility here only because it is hard to find even one advocate of the argument from common capacities who straightforwardly explores it. To be sure, some advocates do suggest that the right response to a thought about how divergences in our treatment of animals and mentally limited human beings is unjustified is to change the way that we treat both, so that we now treat the former somewhat better and the latter somewhat worse. Thus, e.g., Peter Singer suggests that it may sometimes be

permissible to euthanize mentally severely limited human beings as we now euthanize some animals. Although I turn to Singer's work below, I do not further discuss this—politically inflammatory—feature of it.

7. This term was originally coined by Richard Ryder. For central discussions of it, see Ryder, *Animal Revolution*, 5–8; Singer, *Animal Liberation*, 6; and Regan, *The Case for Animal Rights*, 211ff.

8. See esp. *Animal Liberation*, 239. Bernard Williams once observed that, given Singer's impatience with the idea that a creature's humanity is by itself morally important, there is something ironic about his appointment in Princeton University's Center for Human Values. Williams's thought was that, since "human values" presumably means not simply "values possessed by humans" but rather, more interestingly, "values that are reflective of our humanity," it follows that to Singer's ears the center's title must sound something like "Center for Aryan Values" (Williams, "The Human Prejudice," in *Philosophy as a Humanistic Discipline*, 135–152, p. 142).

9. See, e.g., *Animal Liberation*, 81–83.

10. Ibid., 6.

11. Ibid., 7.

12. See, e.g., *Animal Liberation*, 5, where Singer discusses differences between the interests of American children and pigs.

13. Ibid., 8.

14. Ibid., 6, 9.

15. See, e.g., the criticism of Singer's utilitarian commitments in Regan, *The Case for Animal Rights*, esp. chapters 4 and 7.

16. *The Case for Animal Rights*, 155, 184.

17. *Defending Animal Rights*, 43.

18. *The Case for Animal Rights*, 243.

19. Ibid., esp. chapters 1 and 2.

20. Ibid., esp. 243, 276; see also *Defending Animal Rights*, esp. 17–19, 43.

21. In Cockburn, *Human Beings*, 35–62, p. 59.

22. Reprinted in *The Realistic Spirit*, 319–335; quote from p. 331.

23. "Animal Rights and the Values of Nonhuman Life," in Nussbaum and Sunstein, eds., *Animal Rights*, 277–298. Anderson refers to the argument using the more common label "the argument from marginal cases." In this connection, see note 5, above.

24. Ibid., 282.

25. Ibid.

26. Ibid.

27. Notice that it would be wrong to dispute the interest of Anderson's example simply on the ground that it is concerned with culturally specific standards of care for old and demented people. Admittedly, it is true that, within different cultures, such people receive different kinds of care. But this observation would only speak against Anderson's point if it could be demonstrated not only that different ways of treating old and demented people are accepted as appropriate, but also that some of these alternative ways fail to reflect any belief in a human dignity independent of individual capacities. And it is not clear that a demonstration to this effect is forthcoming.

28. "Eating Meat and Eating People."

29. See *Animal Liberation*, esp. chapters 1, 3, and 6.

30. *The Case for Animal Rights*, 314–315.

31. "Eating Meat and Eating People," 321.

32. Ibid.

33. Ibid., 322, emphasis in the original.

34. See the first epigraph to this section.

35. "Animal Rights and the Values of Nonhuman Life," 282.

36. Coetzee, *Life and Times of Michael K*, 99.

37. *Romulus, My Father*, 94, 194. See also chapters 6 and 7 of Gaita, *The Philosopher's Dog*.

38. See Diamond, "Eating Meat and Eating People," 323.

39. Anderson, "Animal Rights and the Values of Nonhuman Life," 283. For additional treatments of the point Anderson is making here, see Diamond, "Eating Meat and Eating People," 324–325, 328–329, and Gaita, *The Philosopher's Dog*, 75ff.

40. And, although I am less confident about this additional point, it seems to me that, while the bodies of dead human beings merit forms of respect that go beyond those merited by the bodies of dead animals, the bodies of dead animals nevertheless merit forms of treatment that distinguish them from mere objects.

41. See the second epigraph to this section.

42. Gaita, *The Philosopher's Dog*, 95–96.

43. This is a topic to which I return in section 1.4.

44. In *William Wordsworth: The Major Works*, 131.

45. For this list of criteria, see Thomas Kuhn, "Objectivity, Value Judgment, and Theory Choice," in *The Essential Tension*, 320–339, p. 322.

46. Peter Singer wrongly assumes that this bit of syllogistic reasoning is valid and that, if we are to avoid affirming its conclusion, we need to deny its major premise. (See "Individuals, Humans, and Persons: The Issue of Moral Status," co-authored with Helga Kuhse in his *Unsanctifying Human Life*, 188–198, esp. 193–194.) To be sure, Singer is not wrong to suggest that there are some social conservatives who, agreeing that the syllogism is valid, insist that we ought to affirm its premises. Thus, to mention but one prominent example, the socially conservative British philosopher Elizabeth Anscombe clearly adopts this position in several posthumously published essays. (See esp. "Knowledge and Reverence for Human Life" and "The Dignity of the Human Being" in *Human Life, Action and Ethics: Essays by G. E. M. Anscombe*, 59–66, 67–73.)

47. Here we might think of how Ridley Scott's 1982 movie *Blade Runner* invites us to acknowledge the humanity of its nonhuman androids or "replicants" and to see that the "blade runners" who, like Harrison Ford's Deckard, are asked to "retire" them are effectively called upon to commit murder.

48. I am grateful to Cora Diamond and Edward Minar for helpful comments on an earlier version of this chapter. I have benefitted from the constructive input of members of the Philosophy Department at the University of Bergen, the Philological Society at Johns Hopkins University, Columbia University's Theory of Literature Seminar, and the Philosophy Department at the University of East Anglia. I would especially like to thank Akeel Bilgrami, Harald Johannessen, Ross Posnock, Rupert Read, Bruce Robbins and Michael Williams.

Works Cited

Anscombe, G. E. M. *Human Life, Action, and Ethics: Essays by G. E. M. Anscombe*. Ed. Mary Geach and Luke Gormally. Exeter: Imprint Academiz, 2005.

Cockburn, David, ed. *Human Beings*. (Supplement to *Philosophy*.) Cambridge: Cambridge University Press, 1991.

Coetzee, J. M. *Life and Times of Michael K*. London: Penguin Books, 1983.

Coetzee, J. M. *The Lives of Animals*. Ed. Amy Gutmann. Princeton: Princeton University Press, 1999.

Diamond, Cora. *Realism and the Realistic Spirit: Wittgenstein, Philosophy, and the Mind*. Cambridge, Mass.: MIT Press, 1991.

Dombrowski, Daniel. *Babies and Beasts: The Argument from Marginal Cases*. Urbana and Chicago: The University of Illinois Press, 1997.

Gaita, Raimond. *Romulus, My Father*. London: Headline Book Publishing, 1998.

Gaita, Raimond. *The Philosopher's Dog*. Melbourne: Text Publishing, 2002.

Kuhn, Thomas. *The Essential Tension: Selected Studies in Scientific Tradition and Change*. Chicago: The University of Chicago Press, 1979.

Rachels, James. *Created from Animals: The Moral Implications of Darwinism*. Oxford: Oxford University Press, 1991.

Regan, Tom. *Defending Animal Rights*. Urbana-Champaign: University of Illinois Press, 2000.

Regan, Tom. *The Case for Animal Rights*. Berkeley: University of California Press, 1983.

Ryder, Richard. *Animal Revolution: Changing Attitudes towards Speciesism*. Oxford: Basil Blackwell, 1989.

Singer, Peter. *Animal Liberation*. New York: Avon Books, 1975.

Singer, Peter. *Unsanctifying Human Life: Essays on Ethics*. Ed. Helga Kuhse. Oxford: Blackwell, 2002.

Sunstein, Cass, and Martha Nussbaum, eds. *Animal Rights: Current Debates and New Directions*. Oxford: Oxford University Press, 2004.

Williams, Bernard. Philosophy as a Humanistic Discipline. Ed. A. W. Moore. Princeton: Princeton University Press, 2006.

Wordsworth, William. *William Wordsworth: The Major Works*. Oxford: Oxford University Press, 1984.

Index

DH

170.
92
WIT